EXPECTATION OF THE MILLENNIUM

EXPECTATION OF THE MILLENNIUM

Shi'ism in History

Edited, Annotated, and with
an Introduction by

SEYYED HOSSEIN NASR

HAMID DABASHI

SEYYED VALI REZA NASR

State University of New York Press

Published by
State University of New York Press, Albany

©1989   State University of New York

For information, address State University of New York
Press, State University Plaza, Albany, N.Y., 12246

Library of Congress Cataloging-in-Publication Data

Expectation of the millennium : Shiᶜism in history / edited,
    annotated, and with an introduction by Seyyed Hossein Nasr, Hamid
    Dabashi, Seyyed Vali Reza Nasr.
        p.   cm.
    Includes index.
    ISBN 0-88706-843-X.   ISBN 0-88706-844-8 (pbk.)
    1. Shīᶜah—Political aspects.   2. Shīᶜah—History.   I. Nasr,
    Seyyed Hossein, 1933–   II. Dabashi, Hamid, 1951– . III. Nasr, Seyyed
    Vali Reza, 1960–
    BP194.185.E96 1988
    297 '.82—dc19   87-35326
                                                                  CIP

10   9   8   7   6   5   4   3   2   1

Dedicated to the blessed memory of three
of the great teachers and scholars of this age

Mahdi Ilahi Qumsha'i
Jalal al-Din Homa'i
Mahmud Shahabi

May God's Mercy be upon them

Contents

III. Shi^cism in History

IV. Shi^ci Minorities in the Islamic World

V. Shi^cism in the Modern World: Early Political Ideas

                         MANGOL BAYAT   281
                    AHMAD KAZEMI MOUSSAVI   283

Chapter 19   Early Propagation of *Wilayat-i Faqih*
                    and Mulla Ahmad Naraqi   287

                         HAMID DABASHI   288

Chapter 20   The Tobacco Rebellion and Haji Mirza
                    Hasan Shirazi   301

                         EDWARD G. BROWNE   302
                         NIKKI R. KEDDIE   305

Chapter 21   The Debates Over the Constitutional Revolution   309

                         HAMID ENAYAT   311
              SHAYKH MUHAMMAD HUSAYN NA'INI   314
                         ABDUL-HADI HAIRI   318
                   SHAYKH FADLULLAH NURI   324

VI. Shi^cism in the Modern World: Later Political Ideas

                    Khumayni and *Wilayat-i Faqih*   332

                         HAMID ENAYAT   334
                         MANGOL BAYAT   343
         AYATOLLAH SAYYID RUHULLAH MUSAWI KHUMAYNI   356

Chapter 23   ^cAli Shari^cati   368

                         SHAHROUGH AKHAVI   369
                         HAMID DABASHI   373
                         ^cALI SHARI^cATI   388

Preface

When the Prophet Muhammad died on June 8, 632 A.D., his cousin and son-in-law — and the man believed by many to have been the first to accept Islam after the Prophet's wife (Khadijah) — assumed the responsibility of arranging a proper burial for the last apostle of God. But, at the same time, a group of eminent Muslims, both those who had migrated from Mecca with the Prophet and those who had welcomed them in Medina, gathered in the *Saqifah Bani Saᶜidah*. The purpose of this historic meeting was to decide who was to lead the nascent Islamic community after its founder. Through an intricate interplay of tribal affiliations and personal persuasion, Abu Bakr emerged as the only figure on whom the political exigencies of the moment could converge.

Although the decision was more or less collectively honored by the Muslim community, there remained a small number of devout Muslims who took exception to it. They believed ᶜAli to be the only Muslim uniquely qualified to lead the Islamic community. ᶜAli's designation was stipulated through a specific combination of divine providence and prophetic pronouncement: he was the rightful leader of the Muslim community because both God and his Messenger had so mandated.

It took decades before this dormant idea gradually developed into a comprehensive doctrinal system and before the adherents to this system were fully recognized as the Shiᶜis, or supporters of ᶜAli. Yet, in many respects, the history of Shiᶜism is the progressive unfolding of that very moment when ᶜAli attended to Muhammad's burial rather than bid for his right in the *Saqifah Bani Saᶜidah* — where his right to the leadership of the *ummah* was ignored.

For twelve successive generations after ᶜAli's death, the Shiᶜi Imams, all descendants of ᶜAli and Fatimah, the Prophet's daughter and his only surviving child, provided spiritual leadership to their community. The Twelfth Imam was providentially destined to go into occultation and thus leave the Shiᶜi community in expectations of his return. The occultation of Muhammad ibn Hasan, moreover, confirmed the Shiᶜi proclivity to dissent the usurpation of the right of ᶜAli, and his successors, to the leadership of the

Islamic community. With no living Imam, quiescent dissent and a de facto recognition of the Sunni rule became the hallmarks of Shiᶜi ethos.

Since the commencement of the occultation, the Shiᶜi community has been in a state of perpetual expectation. Thenceforth, no aspect of Shiᶜi history has remained unaffected by the everlasting hope for the return of the Mahdi, or the rightly guided.

These two central themes — the right of the first Imam to the leadership of the Islamic community and the denial of that right and the occultation of the Twelfth Imam — have been the dominant themes of Shiᶜi history. This volume, therefore, is structured around the formative influence of these two themes on Shiᶜi history and ethos. First, the essential doctrinal positions of Shiᶜism will be examined to demonstrate the institutionalization of these motifs. Then, the chapters deal with the extension of these doctrines into law, societal change, and authority. This will be examined from a variety of perspectives, with a particular focus on the way in which the constituent doctrines of a faith become externally objectified.

Shiᶜism in history is the next unifying theme. Here, the vicissitudes of Shiᶜi political organizations, state and otherwise, will be analyzed by a number of leading scholars of the field. What follows is the position of Shiᶜi minorities in the fabric of the Sunni world. This is of particular significance for a thorough understanding of Shiᶜism in both its active and passive dimensions. The fate of Shiᶜism in modern times brings this volume to a close. Throughout this volume, we have sought to bring to the fore aspects of Shiᶜi doctrinal and societal content in addition to the political manifestations of the faith.

S.H.N.

H.D.

S.V.R.N.

Note to the Reader

In this volume we have used the standard rules of transliteration prevalent in academia. Most words are transliterated according to their Arabic pronounciation. However, for those words where the Persian form is more common to Shi'i studies, transliteration follows the Persian pronounciation. For instance, we have used *marja'-i taqlid* rather than *marja' al-taqlid*. Moreover, in the case of words for which there exist widely used standardized forms in English such as Allah, Qur'an, Muhammad, Imam, Ayatollah, Shi'i, or names of dynasties such as Safavid, Qajar and Pahlavi, no transliteration will appear in the text.

So far as titles such as Hadrat, Imam, Ayatollah, or 'Allamah are concerned, they appear in this volume in the exact form in which they were presented in the original texts. In our preface, introduction, and explanatory paragraphs, the titles of various persons reflect the standard form of reference to that person in Western academic works. Hence, we have used Imam Husayn, 'Allamah Tabataba'i, or Ayatollah Taliqani. The usage of title in no way reflects a judgment on behalf of the editors concerning the political, religious, or spiritual status of the person in question.

In preparing this volume, a single transliteration system has been used, and the various transliteration systems that had appeared in the original sources have been changed in order to foster the unity of the entire volume.

Acknowledgments

In preparing this volume, grateful acknowledgement is made to the following for permission to reprint from previously published materials.

American Institute for Islamic Affairs: excerpt from "The Shia Community and the Future of Lebanon," *The Muslim World Today*, Occasional Papers, No. 2, by Helena Cobban, © 1985 by American Institute for Islamic Affairs, Washington, D.C.

Archives Europeenes De Sociologie: excerpt from Said Amir Arjomand, "Religion, Political Action and Legitimate Domination in Shiᶜite Iran: Fourteenth to Eighteenth Centuries A.D.," © 1979 by *Archives Europeenes De Sociologie*, Cambridge, U.K.

Bulletin of the School of Oriental and African Studies, University of London: excerpt from "From Jabal ᶜAmil to Persia," by Albert Hourani, © 1986 by *Bulletin of the School of Oriental and African Studies, University of London*, London.

Cambridge University Press: excerpt from Hamid Enayat, "Iran: Khumayni's Concept of the Guardianship of the Juriconsult," in James Piscatori (ed.), *Islam in the Political Process*, © 1983 by Cambridge University Press, Cambridge, U.K.

Cornell University Press: excerpt from Fouad Ajami, *The Vanished Imam, Musa al-Sadr and the Shia of Lebenon*, © 1986 by Cornell University Press, Ithaca, N.Y.

Crossroads: excerpt from Shahrough Akhavi, "Shiᶜi Social Thought and Praxis in Recent Iranian History," in Cyriac Pullapilly (ed.), © 1980 by Crossroads, Notre Dame, Ind.

E.J. Brill: excerpt from Abdul-Hadi Hairi, *Shiᶜism and Constitutionalism in Iran*, © 1977 by E. J. Brill, Leiden, Netherlands.

FILINC Press: excerpt from Ali Shariati, *Man and Islam*, translated by Fatollah Marjani, © 1981 by FILINC Press, Houston, TX.

Frank Cass and Co.: excerpt from Edward G. Browne, *The Persian Revolution of 1905–1909*, © 1966 by Frank Cass and Co., London; excerpt from Nikki Keddie, *Religion and Rebellion in Iran, the Tobacco Protest of 1891-92*, © 1966; and excerpt from Abdul-Hadi Hairi, "Shaykh Fazl-Allah Nuri's Refutation of the Idea of Constitutionalism," *Middle Eastern Studies*, Vol. 13, No.3 (October 1977), © 1977.

Iranian Studies: excerpt from Seyyed Hossein Nasr, "Religion in Safavid Persia," © 1974 by *Iranian Studies*, New York; Roger Savory, "The Safavid State and Polity" © 1974 by *Iranian Studies*; and Ahmad Kazemi Moussavi, "The Establishment of the Position of Marja^ciyyat-i Taqlid in the Twelver Shi^cite Community," © 1985 by *Iranian Studies*.

Ithaca Press: excerpt from Hossein Modaarressi Tabataba'i, *An Introduction to Shi^ci Law*, © Ithaca Press, London, U.K.

Leske and Budrich Opladen: excerpt from Karl-Heinrich Göbel, *Moderne Schiitische Politik und Staatstsidee*, © 1984 by Leske and Budrich Opladen, Berlin.

Luzacs and Co.: excerpt from John Hollister, *The Shi^ca of India*, © 1953 by Luzacs and Co., London.

Mazda Publishers: excerpt from Seyyed Mahmood Taleqani, *Islam and Ownership*, translated by Ahmad Jabbari and Farhang Rajaee, © 1983 by Mazda Publishers, Lexington, KY.

Mizan Press: excerpt from Imam Khomeini, *Islam and Revolution*, translated by Hamid Algar, © 1981 by Mizan Press, Berkeley, CA.

Muhammadi Trust: excerpt from *Alserat, Selections of Articles (1975-1983)*, © n.d. by Muhammadi Trust, London; excerpt from: *Alserat, Imam Husayn Conference Number*, Vol. XII, No.1, © 1986; excerpt from Sulayman Kattani, *Imam ^cAli, Source of Light, Wisdom and Might*, translated by I. K. A. Howard, © 1983 by Muhammadi Trust; and excerpt from: Jassim M. Husain, *The Occultation of the Twelfth Imam*, © 1982 by Muhammadi Trust.

New York University Press: excerpt from Peter Chelkowski (ed.), *Ta^cziyah, Ritual and Drama in Iran*, © 1979 by New York University Press, New York.

Oxford University Press: excerpt from John J. Donohue and John L. Esposito (eds.), *Islam in Transition: Muslim Perspective* © 1982 by Oxford University Press, New York; and excerpt from Ann K. S. Lambton, *State and Government in Medieval Islam: An Introduction to the Study of Islamic Political Theory: The Jurists,* © 1981 by Oxford University Press, London.

SUNY Press: excerpt from Abdulaziz A. Sachedina, *Islamic Messianism, the Idea of the Mahdi in Twelver Shiᶜism,* © 1981 by SUNY Press, Albany, N.Y.; excerpt from Shahrough Akhavi, *Religion and Politics in Contemporary Iran; Clergy–State Relations in the Pahlavi Period,* © 1980 by SUNY Press; excerpt from William C. Chittick (ed. and trans.), *A Shiᶜite Anthology,* selected by ᶜAllamah Tabataba'i, with an introduction by Seyyed Hossein Nasr, © 1981 by SUNY Press; excerpt from ᶜAllamah Sayyid Muhammad Husayn Tabataba'i, *Shiᶜite Islam,* translated by Seyyed Hossein Nasr, © 1975 by SUNY Press; and excerpt from Said Amir Arjomand (ed.), *From Nationalism to Revolutionary Islam,* © 1984 by SUNY Press.

Syracuse University Press: excerpt from Mangol Bayat, *Mysticism and Dissent; Socio-religious Thought in Qajar Iran,* © 1982 by Syracuse University Press, Syracuse, N.Y.

The Islamic Quarterly: excerpt from Hamid Dabashi, "Ali Shariᶜati's Islam: Revolutionary Uses of Faith in a Post-Traditional Society," © 1983 by *The Islamic Quarterly*, London.

The Middle East Journal: excerpt from Mangol Bayat, "The Iranian Revolution of 1978–79: Fundamentalist or Modern?" © 1983 by *The Middle East Journal*, Washington, D.C.; and excerpt from Hanna Batatu, "Iraq's Underground Shiᶜa Movements: Characteristics, Causes and Prospects," © 1981 by *The Middle East Journal*.

University of California Press: excerpt from Hamid Algar, *Religion and State in Iran; the Role of the Ulama in the Qajar Period,* © 1969 by University of California Press, Berkeley; and excerpt from John Alden Williams (ed.), *Themes of Islamic Civilization,* © 1971 by University of California Press.

University of Chicago Press: excerpt from Said Amir Arjomand, *The Shadow of God and the Hidden Imam: Religion, Political Order, and Societal Change in Shiᶜite Iran from the Beginning to 1890,* © 1984 by University of Chicago Press, Chicago; and excerpt from Marshall Hodgson, *Venture of Islam,* 3 vols., © 1966 by University of Chicago Press.

University of Texas Press: excerpt from Hamid Enayat, *Modern Islamic Political Thought*, © 1982 by University of Texas Press, Austin, TX.

Yale University Press: excerpt from Shahrough Akhavi, "Shariati's Social Thought," in *Religion and Politics in Iran: Shicism from Quietism to Revolution*, Nikki Keddie (ed.), © 1983 by Yale University Press, New Haven, CT.

List of Abbreviations

This list cites, in alphabetical order, the abbreviated reference to the sources used in this volume and provides information regarding the exact title, author, editor, translator, place and date of publication and the name of the publisher.

Alserat   *Alserat, Selection of Articles (1975–1983)*. London: Muhammadi Trust, n.d.

ASIHCN   *Alserat, Imam Husayn Conference Number*, Vol. XII, No. 1 (Spring 1986).

ASIRUF   Hamid Dabashi, "Ali Shari^cati's Islam: Revolutionary Uses of Faith in a Post-Traditional Society," *Islamic Quarterly*, Vol. 27, No. 4 (Fourth Quarter 1983).

ATSL   Hossein Modarressi Tabataba'i, *An Introduction to Shi^ci Law*. London: Ithaca Press, 1984.

EPMTSC   Ahmad Kazemi Moussavi, "The Establishment of the Position of Marja^ciyyat-i Taqlid in the Twelver Shi^cite Community," *Iranian Studies*, Vol. 18, No. 1 (Winter 1985).

FJTP   Albert Hourani, "From Jabal ^cAmil to Persia," *Bulletin of the School of Oriental and African Studies, University of London*, Vol. 49, Part 1, (1986).

IAR   Imam Khomeini, *Islam and Revolution*, Hamid Algar (trans.). Berkeley: Mizan Press, 1981.

IASLWM   Sulayman Kattani, *Imam ᶜAli, Source of Light, Wisdom and Might*, I. K. A. Howard (trans.) London: Muhammadi Trust, 1983.

IKCGJ   Hamid Enayat, "Iran: Khumayni's Concept of the Guardianship of the Juriconsult," in James Piscatori (ed.), *Islam in the Political Process*. London: Cambridge University Press, 1983.

IMIMTS   Abdulaziz A. Sachedina. *Islamic Messianism, the Idea of the Mahdi in Twelver Shiᶜism*. Albany, NY.: SUNY Press, 1981.

IMTC   Murtaza Muhtahhari, *Islamic Movements in the Twentieth Century*, Maktab-i Qu'ran (trans.) Tehran, Iran: Great Islamic Library, 1979.

IO   Seyyed Mahmood Taleqani, *Islam and Ownership*. Ahmad Jabbari and Farhang Rajaee (trans.). Lexington, KY.: Mazda Publishers, 1983.

IRFM   Mangol Bayat, "The Iranian Revolution of 1978–79: Fundamentalist or Modern?" *The Middle East Journal*, Vol. 37, No. 1 (Winter 1983).

ITMP   John J. Donohue and John L. Esposito (eds.), *Islam in Transition; Muslim Perspectives*. New York: Oxford University Press, 1982.

IUSM   Hanna Batatu, "Iraq's Underground Shiᶜa Movements: Characteristic, Causes and Prospects," *The Middle East Journal*, Vol. 35, No. 4 (Autumn 1981).

MDSTQI   Mangol Bayat, *Mysticism and Dissent; Socio-religious Thought in Qajar Iran*. Syracuse, N.Y.: Syracuse University Press, 1982.

MI   Ali Shariati, *Man and Islam*, Fatollah Marjani (trans.). Houston, TX.: FILINC Press, 1981.

MIPT   Hamid Enayat, *Modern Islamic Political Thought*. Austin, TX.: University of Texas Press, 1982.

MSPS   Karl-Heinrich Göbel, *Moderne Schiitische Politik und Staatstsidee*. Berlin: Leske & Budrich Opladen, 1984.

OTI   Jassim M. Hussain, *The Occultation of the Twelfth Imam*. London: Muhammadi Trust, 1982.

PR   Edward G. Browne, *The Persian Revolution of 1905–1909*. London: Frank Cass and Co., 1966.

RMM   Muhammad Baqir Sadr, *The Revealer, the Messenger, and the Message*. Mahmud Ayoub (trans.). World Organization of Islamic Studies, n.p., n.d.

RPALDSI   Said Amir Arjomand, "Religion, Political Action and Legitimate Domination in Shi^cite Iran: Fourteenth to Eighteenth Centuries A.D.," *Archives Europeenes De Sociologie*, Vol. 20, No. 1 (1979).

RPICSRPP   Shahrough Akhavi, *Religion and Politics in Contemporary Iran; Clergy–State Relations in the Pahlavi Period*. Albany, N.Y.: SUNY Press, 1980.

RRITP   Nikki Keddie, *Religion and Rebellion in Iran, The Tobacco Protest of 1891–1892*. London: Frank Cass and Co., 1966.

RSIRUQP   Hamid Algar, *Religion and State in Iran; the Role of the Ulama in the Qajar Period*. Berkeley: University of California Press, 1969.

RSP   Seyyed Hossein Nasr, "Religion in Safavid Persia," *Iranian Studies*, Vol. 7, Nos. 1–2, (Winter–Spring 1974).

SA   William C. Chittick (ed. and trans.), *A Shi^cite Anthology*, selected by ^cAllamah Tabataba'i, Introduction by Seyyed Hossein Nasr. Albany, N.Y.: SUNY Press, 1981.

SCFL — Helena Cobban, "The Shia Community and the Future of Lebanon," *The Muslim World Today*, occasional papers, No. 2, Washington, D.C.: American Institute for Islamic Affairs, The American University, 1985.

SCI — Abdul-Hadi Hairi, *Shiᶜism and Constitutionalism in Iran*. Leiden: E. J. Brill, 1977.

SFNRIC — Abdul-Hadi Hairi, "Shaykh Fazl-Allah Nuri's Refutation of the Idea of Constitutionalism," *Middle Eastern Studies*, Vol. 13, No. 3 (October 1977).

SGHI — Said Amir Arjomand, *The Shadow of God and the Hidden Imam: Religion, Political Order, and Societal Change in Shiᶜite Iran from the Beginning to 1890*. Chicago: University of Chicago Press, 1984.

SGMI — Ann K. S. Lambton, *State and Government in Medieval Islam: An Introduction to the Study of Islamic Political Theory: The Jurists*. London: Oxford University Press, 1981.

SI — ᶜAllamah Sayyid Muhammad Husayn Tabataba'i, *Shiᶜite Islam*, Seyyed Hossein Nasr (trans.). Albany, NY.: SUNY Press, 1975.

SSP — Roger Savory, "The Safavid State and Polity," *Iranian Studies*, Vol. 7, No. 1–2 (Winter–Spring 1974).

SST — Shahrough Akhavi, "Shariati's Social Thought," in Nikki Keddie (ed.), *Religion and Politics in Iran: Shiᶜism from Quietism to Revolution*. New Haven, CT.: Yale University Press, 1983.

SSTPRIH — Shahrough Akhavi, "Shiᶜi Social Thought and Praxis in Recent Iranian History," in Cyriac Pullapilly (ed.), *Islam in the Contemporary World*. Notre Dame, IN.: Crossroads, 1980.

TIC — John Alden Williams (ed.), *Themes of Islamic Civilization*. Berkeley: University of California Press, 1971.

TRDI Peter Chelkowski (ed.), *Ta^cziyah, Ritual and Drama in Iran*. New York: New York University Press, 1979.

TSI John N. Hollister, *The Shi^ca of India*. London: Luzacs and Co., 1953.

TTI Said Amir Arjomand, "Traditionalism in Twentieth-Century Iran," in Said Amir Arjomand (ed.), *From Nationalism to Revolutionary Islam*. Albany, NY: SUNY Press, 1984.

VI Marshall Hodgson, *Venture of Islam*, 3 vols. Chicago: University of Chicago Press, 1966.

VIMSSL Fouad Ajami, *The Vanished Imam, Musa al-Sadr and the Shi^ca of Lebanon*, Ithaca, N.Y.: Cornell University Press, 1986.

Introduction

In an earlier volume of this anthology, devoted to Shiᶜism, (*Shiᶜism: Doctrines, Thought and Spirituality*, SUNY, 1988) our attention was focused upon the intellectual and spiritual teachings of this oft misunderstood branch of the Islamic tradition. But Shiᶜi Islam (which in the context of this work is confined to Twelve-Imam Shiᶜism), like other authentic manifestations of religion, also possesses teachings which deal with man's earthly life and has its own historical unfolding. Like Sunni Islam, it addresses itself to the needs of man in both this world and the next and has its own interpretation of the Divine Law (*Shariᶜah*) with branches extending to the fields of social life, politics and economics in addition to what concerns man's relation with God through prayer and other acts of religious devotion. Shiᶜism also possesses its own vision of history and has had its particular historical development stretching over some fourteen centuries and affecting lands as far apart as North Africa and India.

Recent events in Iran, Lebanon, Pakistan and elsewhere have focused the attention of the larger public in the West upon Shiᶜism which until quite recently was a veritable *terra incognita* even for the vast majority of scholars who specialized in Islamic studies. It is, furthermore, mostly the political manifestations of Shiᶜism which have attracted so much interest recently. As a result there has come into being a veritable scholarly market for the subject with no shortage of commodities to satisfy the immediately felt need of the general public as well as the educated elite who somehow remained ignorant of Shiᶜism until recently. Unfortunately, many works seeking to fulfil this need, even on the level of the most external manifestations of Shiᶜism, have failed to penetrate beyond the surface of events and phenomena while few scholars have sought to concern themselves with the rapport between the socio-political upheavals of recent years related to Shiᶜism and the deeper forces involved.

We hope to have provided some first hand material and important secondary sources dealing with the basic intellectual and spiritual teachings of Shiᶜism in the first volume of his anthology, which serves as background for the present collection dealing with the manifestations of Shiᶜism in history and Shiᶜi socio-political teachings. It is hoped that in this volume selections of writings by leading Shiᶜi authorities as well as scholars in the field will provide the necessary background for a better understanding of current events related to Shiᶜism, and make it easier to relate these events to the intellectual and spiritual teachings of a religious tradition which begins with the foundation of the Islamic religion itself and has had a continuous life for some fourteen hundred years.

Shiᶜism is at once a meta-historical reality and a faith possessing a distinct history related to the ever present expectation (*intizar*) of the appearance of the Twelfth Imam or Mahdi with all the millennial and eschatological significance that this belief entails. Shiᶜism has been quietistic from a political point of view during most of its history and yet has experienced periods of intense socio-political activity. It has been for the most part the faith of a minority of Muslims and yet became the state religion of Safavid Persia where it has remained the school or *mazhab* of the vast majority of the people while it also constitutes a majority in Iraq and Bahrayn without having the corresponding political power.

Most people identify Shiᶜism with Persia and its classical culture, yet Shiᶜism began among the Arabs and remains an important religious reality in several Arab countries to this day. Moreover, there are not only Persian and Arab Shiᶜis but Turkish, Indian and Pakistani ones as well, not to speak of the important Shiᶜi community in East Africa.

The present volume seeks to deal with all these diverse realities beginning with the classical political doctrines which have been challenged during the past two decades by new interpretations and innovations based upon the theory of the direct rule of the jurisprudent (*faqih*), marking a departure from classical theories and signaling a new phase in the political history of Shiᶜism. The classical theory is based upon the doctrine of the Imamate which is what distinguishes the Shiᶜi world view from that of Sunni Islam with which it shares the primary foundations of the Quran and *Hadith*. The work of the Contemporary Shiᶜi Thinker Muhammad Mughniyah on the Imamate as interpreted by Karl Heinrich Göbel and translated from German by Hamid Dabashi constitutes the first chapter in the first section of the anthology dealing with political doctrines and brings out the role of the Imam as not only the source of intellectual and spiritual teachings but also as the ultimate political power in this world and the source of all political legitimacy—past and present. In this exposition the distinction between the Sunni theory of the caliphate which is also sometimes called "imamate" and the Shiᶜi theory becomes clear. It is a distinction which is crucial to the understanding of the two groups within Islam to this day, and their respective positions toward political power as such.

The political significance of the Imam differs greatly from the time when he is present in the world and living the life of an "ordinary" mortal and when he is in occultation (*ghaybah*) as happens to be the case today according to Twelve-Imam Shi^cis. For the past millennium the last Imam, also called the Mahdi, has been in what Twelve-Imam Shi^cism calls the major occultation (*al-ghaybat al-kubrā*) and Shi^cis have lived and died in the expectation of his appearance (*zuhur*), which is nothing short of an event of major eschatological import. In the second chapter 'Allamah Tabataba'i, Jassim Hussain and Abdulaziz Sachedina deal with the figure of the Mahdi, the relation between Mahdiism and messianism as understood in Western religious history and the political significance of belief in the Mahdi for Shi^ci communities living during the period of the occultation of the Imam.

The suicidal acts of Shi^cis in Iran and Lebanon have led the Western mass media to practically identifying Shi^cism with martyrdom while the politization of this important Shi^ci ideal has itself had a profound influence within the Shi^ci world. In two selections dealing with different aspects of the significance of martyrdom, Sachedina and Hamid Enayat clarify both the religious and political significance of the ideal of *shahadat* or martyrdom which plays such a central role in the ethos of Shi^cism.

Even more popular as a theme identified with Islam in the Occident is *jihad*, usually translated as holy war but meaning actually exertion upon the path of God. The political events of the past decade have resuscitated fears of "Muslim holy war" in the West and the term has been used widely both in the Western press and by a number of Muslim groups possessing very diverse political programs and widely differing attitudes toward Islamic orthodoxy as well as Western inspired ideologies. A single selection by the celebrated 7th/13th century Shi^ci scholar, ^cAllamah Hilli, discusses the classical Shi^ci theory of *jihad* in its social and legal sense. It is against this theory that one can judge the nature of current uses of this powerful idea which is shared by Sunnis and Shi^cis alike and which on the highest level means the constant struggle of the soul to remember God and to live according to His Will.

The second section dealing with authority, law and society complements the discussions of the first section on political doctrines and is inextracably tied to it. Shi^cism has its own interpretation of the *Shari^cah* which is often called Ja^cfari after Imam Ja^cfar al-Sadiq, the sixth Shi^ci Imam, who was an outstanding authority on law and the founder of the Shi^ci school of the *Shari^cah*. In fact, several times during the history of Islam attempts have been made to unify Sunnism and Shi^cism by considering the Ja^cfari school along with the four Sunni schools as the five accepted schools (*mazhab*) of the *Shari^cah*. In chapter five Hossein Modarressi Tabataba'i deals with the principles of jurisprudence (*usul al-fiqh*) from the Shiᶜi point of view, elucidating the principles upon which this particular interpretation of the *Shariᶜah* is based.

Chapter six, dealing with the ruler and his relation with society, begins with one of the most famous writings on the subject by the son-in-law and cousin of the Prophet, ᶜAli ibn Abi Talib, who was at once the first Shiᶜi Imam and the fourth of the "rightly guided" caliphs of Sunnism. The words of ᶜAli have been held in great esteem by both groups and have constituted over the centuries the model for how one should rule and how the ruler should act towards the members of the society in which he has become destined to act as the ruler. This classical work is complemented by the study of Sulayman Kattani on the traditional view of the relation between the ruler and society.

Shiᶜi political doctrines have not been always implemented through the centuries of Islamic history during which Shiᶜism has functioned in very differing circumstances and conditions. In chapter seven in two essays based on the historical perspective, Ann Lambton and Said Amir Arjomand deal with the relation between Shiᶜi political theory and actual practice during diverse periods of history.

The second section of this anthology concludes with a discussion of economic theory and practices. During the past three decades much attention has been paid to Islamic economics both on the theoretical level and in the creation of institutions, especially banks, which seek to base their practices upon Islamic principles. This interest for Islamic economics has not been confined to the Sunni world but has engaged the mind of many of the leading Shiᶜi thinkers of this generation. Two selections, one by Sayyid Muhammad Baqir Sadr and the other by Ayatollah Sayyid Mahmud Taliqani make available some of the most influential Shiᶜi writings on economic questions to have appeared in recent years.

The third section of the anthology devoted to Shiᶜism in history commences with the general study of ᶜAllamah Tabataba'i on the historical growth of Shiᶜism, providing a bird's eye view of the history of Shiᶜism whose central arena soon became Persia. In chapter ten Marshall Hodgson discusses Shiᶜism in the Buyid period which played such an important role in the later spread of Shiᶜism in Persia and Iraq and laid the ground for the consolidation of Shiᶜism in the post-Mongol era leading to the establishment of the Safavids.

The Safavid period is of special significance in the history of Shiᶜism, for during this period for the first time Shiᶜi Islam became the official religiᴐn of a major Muslim empire. From that moment to the present day Persia has remained the only country where Shiᶜism has ruled and constituted the vast majority of the population. The studies of S.H. Nasr, Roger Savory, Said

Amir Arjomand and Albert Hourani clarify different facets of this crucial period of the history of Shi^cism.

In chapter twelve Said Amir Arjomand and Hamid Algar study the significance of Shi^cism in Qajar Persia and especially the relation between religion and the state during this period. Until the Iranian Revolution in 1979, there were few indepth studies of Shi^cism during the Qajar period. It is only during the past decade that the significance of the religious history of that period has been fully realized and scholars have come to see in the relation between the religious and political authorities of that period and also the encounter between Shi^cism and modern ideas, which had entered Persia for the first time during that era, the seeds of powerful ideas and trends which were finally to manifest themselves with the Iranian Revolution.

Finally, in chapter thirteen, the last part of the section dealing with the historical development of Shi^cism in Persia, Shahrough Akhavi and Said Amir Arjomand, turn to the history and life of Shi^cism in the Pahlavi period. They seek to analyze the complex relations between the *^culama'* and the state during this period of rapid economic development, social transformation and increasing cultural and religious tensions resulting from the sudden changes which society was undergoing. Much research needs to be carried out to clarify the history of Shi^cism during the Pahlavi period, a time which was witness on the one hand to the flowering of Shi^ci learning especially in the domain of the intellectual sciences and on the other to the religious alienation which provided the background for the revolution of 1979. The studies of this section provide knowledge of ideas and events which must be known in order to understand the happenings of the past decade that have catapulted Shi^cism into the center of the international political arena.

Shi^cism is not confined to Iran, however, but has had and continues to have millions of followers in many other countries. In fact of over a hundred million Shi^cis living today, less than half live in Persia while the majority are scattered in such lands as India, Pakistan, Afghanistan, Iraq, Lebanon, Syria, Turkey, Soviet Azarbayjan and East Africa. The last section of this anthology deals with some of these minorities. In chapter fourteen John Hollister and Annemarie Schimmel provide insights into the vast world of Shi^cism in India and Pakistan.

In chapter fifteen Michel Mazzaoui turns to the study of the popular aspects of Shi^ci practice in Lebanon while Helena Cobban deals with more general aspects of Shi^cism in Lebanon today. Then Hanna Batatu analyzes the present reality and significance of Shi^cism in Iraq to conclude the study of Shi^cism in the Arab world where it now plays a crucial social and political role in several countries.

Not all people are aware of the presence of Shi^cism in Turkey and the fact that it was Turkish speaking Shi^cis who made possible the establishment of the Safavids in Persia. Metin And provides a rare glimpse into the manifestation of Shiᶜism in Turkey today by describing the ceremonies and rituals of Muharram among the Shiᶜis of that land.

To conclude this section, Jan Knappert studies Shiᶜism in East Africa as both a religious and social reality. He studies the manifestations of Shiᶜism through mostly Shiᶜi immigrants from the Indian sub-continent in the world of Black Africa and the significance that Shiᶜism possesses for a better understanding of the role of Islam in general in that region of the world.

Section five turns to Shiᶜi political ideas in the modern world up to the events and ideas of the past decades. With the establishment of a Shiᶜi state by the Safavids followed by later Iranian dynasties which continued to be of Shiᶜi persuasion and to rule over a predominantly Shiᶜi population, the ground was prepared for the appearance of new currents of Shiᶜi political thought beginning with the *usuli-akhbari* debate which lasted for some two centuries and which had a profound influence upon the theological and juridical aspects of Shiᶜi thought as well as on the political power of the ᶜ*ulama'* and their relation with the rulers. Mangol Bayat and Ahmad Kazemi Moussavi discuss this important struggle within Shiᶜism on the interpertation of the Quran and the sayings of the Prophet and the Imams as well as the role and function of those who carried out these interpretations.

With the declaration of the *wilayat-i faqih* by Ayatollah Khumayni interest has turned to possible historical antecedents for this idea. Hamid Dabashi turns to this subject by discussing the teachings of the Qajar jurist and theologian Mulla Ahmad Naraqi whom some have claimed as the historical antecedent of Khumayni and reveals the differences as well as similarities in the understanding of the concept of *wilayat-i faqih* among older jurists and the founder of the Islamic Republic of Iran.

A major episode in the participation of Shiᶜi jurists in political life was the ban on the use of tobacco declared by Hajji Mirza Hasan Shirazi to curtail the power of the British during the Qajar period. Selections by Edward Browne and Nikki Keddie provide an account of this important historical event and bring out its significance for Shiᶜi political thought.

The most important political activity of the Shiᶜi ᶜ*ulama'* during the Qajar period was their role in the Constitutional Revolution of 1905–06 in Iran, the consequence of which was the establishment of the first elected parliament in a Muslim country. Outstanding figures among the ᶜ*ulama'* stood on both sides of the struggle. In the final chapter of this section, Hamid Enayat and Abdul-Hadi Hari analyze the Constitutional Movement as it reflected the religious and political tensions of that period while selections from the writings of two of the most eminent religious authorities of the day, Shaykh Muhammad Husayn Na'ini and Shaykh Fadlullah Nuri provide first-hand

knowledge of Shi^ci religious thought during this important religio-political
movement.

The final section of the anthology completes the discussion of Shi^ci
political ideas in the modern period by turning to some of the most important religio-political figures of the past few decades. First of all Mangol
Bayat and Hamid Enayat discuss the concept of *wilayat-i faqih* so central to
the Iranian Revolution of 1979. Their study is followed by selections from
the writings of Ayatollah Khumayni himself on *wilayat-i faqih*, a concept
which as currently understood owes its inception and birth to him.

After Ayatollah Khumayni, no figure was as influential in the movement
leading to the Iranian Revolution as ^cAli Shari^cati who for the first time
combined Shi^cism with certain Western revolutionary ideas and transformed it into an ideology in the Western sense of the term. Shahrough
Akhavi and Hamid Dabashi study the thought and impact of Shari^cati in
relation to traditional Shi^ci thought and the Iranian society of his day. A
selection of the writings of Shari^cati himself provides first-hand knowledge
of his ideas and mode of thinking.

The next two chapters are devoted to two of the most influential Shi^ci
thinkers of this period, the Iranian philosopher and theologian Ayatollah
Mutahhari, and the Iraqi jurisprudent and philosopher Sayyid Muhammad
Baqir Sadr. The thought of both men, who are considered among the pillars
of the current revolutionary interpretation of Shi^cism, is presented through
selections of their own writings.

In conclusion, Fouad Ajami provides a study of the half Arab-half Iranian
leader of the Shi^cis in Lebanon, Imam Musa Sadr, whose career as well as
mysterious disappearance a decade ago left such a profound impact upon
Lebanon. He shows the significance of the politically motivated forms of
Shi^cism outside of Iran and in a country where until the rise to power of
Imam Musa Sadr, the Shi^cis enjoyed much less political or economic power
as their numbers warranted.

This anthology takes into account both traditional Shi^cism and ideas and
events of the past decade which are in a sense too recent to be analyzed ob-
jectively in a historical cadre. Major events have taken place recently and
are still taking place in the Shi^ci world and even within Shi^cism itself. How
the traditional orthodoxy will react in the long run to the transformation of
religion into ideology, to the intrusion of Western thought in the garb of
Islam into the matrix of Shi^cism, to the politization of the ethos of Shi^cism
in a form which has been unprecedented in Islamic history and to the
change of the meaning of authority in the religious realm remains to be
seen. What is certain is that Shi^cism faces a major challenge and crisis both
within and outside its borders, and that certain forces within the world iden-

tified with Shiᶜism, whether it be Iran, Lebanon, Iraq or the Shiᶜi minorities of Pakistan and India, have created and will most likely continue to create critical situations which require a better indepth understanding of the doctrines and history of Shiᶜism.

We hope that this work along with its earlier companion volume will be a humble step in providing some knowledge of that background which would make contemporary events more comprehensible. But it is also hoped that this anthology will help to create in the West better understanding based upon the objective appraisal of the thought and beliefs of another religious universe rather than on distorted images of that universe so prevalent today. Finally, it is hoped that these volumes will succeed in creating a deeper comprehension of a major branch of the Islamic religion and the ideas and ideals by which millions of men and women have lived and died over the ages and which still provided meaning for millions of human beings, making possible for them to live according to the Will of God and to fulfill their lives according to the purpose and entelechy for which humanity was created. *Wa'Llahu aᶜlam*

Seyyed Hossein Nasr

Notes on Contributors

Fouad Ajami is a Lebanese scholar of Middle East studies, and the Majid Khadduri Professor of Islamic Studies at the School of Advanced International Studies of Johns Hopkins University. He is the author of *The Arab Predicament*.

Shahrough Akhavi is an Iranian professor of political science at the University of South Carolina and the author of *Religion and Politics in Contemporary Iran*.

Hamid Algar is a professor of Iranian studies of British origin at the University of California at Berkeley and the author of *Religion and State in Iran, 1785-1906*.

Said Amir Arjomand is an Iranian professor of sociology at the State University of New York at Stoneybrook and the author of *The Shadow of God and the Hidden Imam*, and *The Turban for the Crown*.

Metin And is a Turkish specialist in the dramatic arts and teaches at the University of Ankara. He is the author of *Turkish Dancing*.

Hanna Batatu is an Iraqi scholar of Middle East studies and the Shaikh Sabah al-Salem professor of Contemporary Arab Studies at Georgetown University. He is the author of *The Old Social Classes and the Revolutionary Movements of Iraq*.

Mangol Bayat is an Iranian historian of the Qajar and Pahlavi periods and the author of *Mysticism and Dissent*.

Edward G. Browne was a British specialist on Persia and its culture and the professor of Arabic at Cambridge University. He is the author of *A Literary History of Persia* and *The Persian Revolution*.

Helena Cobban is a Senior SSRC - MacArthur Fellow in International Peace and Security Studies at the Brookings Institution, Washington, D.C. and the author of *The Palestine Liberation Organizaton: People, Power and Politics.*

Hamid Dabashi is an Iranian sociologist and currently a post doctoral fellow at the Center for Middle East Studies of Harvard University. He is the author of a number of articles on Shiᶜism and Iranian Studies.

Hamid Enayat was a specialist of Islamic studies and Iranian history, and professor of political science at Tehran University and St. Anthony's College, Oxford University. He is the author of *Modern Islamic Political Thought.*

Karl Heinrich Göbel is a German scholar of Shiᶜi studies and the author of *Moderne Schiitische Politik und Staatstsidee.*

Abdul-Hadi Hairi is an Iranian scholar of Shiᶜi history and the author of *Shiᶜism and Constitutionalism in Iran.*

ᶜAllamah Hasan ibn Yusuf ibn Mutahhar al-Hilli is one of the foremost Shiᶜi theologians and jurists of the 7th/13th century and the author of a number of important Shiᶜi canons and commentaries.

Marshall Hodgson was the professor of Islamic history at the University of Chicago and the author of *The Venture of Islam.*

John Hollister was a British scholar of Islamic thought in India and the author of *The Shiᶜa of India.*

Albert Hourani is a British scholar of Arab origin and former professor of modern history of the Middle East at St. Anthony's College, Oxford University. He is the author of *Arabic Thought in the Liberal Age, 1798–1939.*

Jassim M. Hussain is an Iraqi scholar of Shiᶜism and a fellow at Edinburgh University. He is the author of *The Occultation of the Twelfth Imam.*

Sulayman Kattani is a Christian scholar from Lebanon who has devoted several studies to Shiᶜism and is the author of *Imam ᶜAli.*

Ahmad Kazemi Moussavi is an Iranian scholar of Shiᶜi studies and the author of a number of articles on Shiᶜism in the Nineteenth Century.

Nikki R. Keddie is professor of history at the University of California at Los Angeles. She is the author of *Roots of Revolution: An Interpretive History of Modern Iran* and editor of *Religion and Politics in Iran.*

Ayatollah Sayyid Ruhallah Musawi Khumayni is the founder and leader of the Islamic Republic of Iran and the author of numerous juridical tracts including *Wilayat-i faqih.*

Jan Knappert is a Dutch scholar of Islamic studies who specializes in the Islamic culture of East Africa. He is professor at the University of London and is the author of *Swahili Islamic Poetry* and *A Choice of Flowers: An Anthology of Swahili Love Poetry.*

Ann K.S. Lambton is a British scholar of Persian and Islamic studies, who was professor at the University of London. She is the author of *Qajar Persia* and *Theory and Practice in Medieval Persian Government.*

Michel Mazzaoui is an American scholar of Palestinian origin. He is a specialist in the early history of Shiᶜism and the author of *The Origin of the Safavids: Shiᶜism, Sufism and the Ghulat.* He is professor at the University of Utah.

Hossein Madarressi Tabataba'i is an Iranian scholar of Shiᶜism and the author of *An Introduction to Shiᶜi Law.* He is professor at Princeton University.

Muhammad Jawad Mughniyah was an Iraqi theologian and jurist. He is the author of *al-Tafsir al-kashif* and *al-Shiᶜah wa'l-hakimun.*

Ayatollah Murtaza Mutahhari was an Iranian philosopher, jurist and thinker associated with the formation of modern Shiᶜi thought over the course of the past three decades. He was professor of Tehran University and the author of *Khadamat-i mutagabil-i Iran wa Islam* and *Fundamentals of Islamic Thought.*

Shaykh Muhammad Husayn Na'ini was a leading Shiᶜi jurist of the turn of the century who openly endorsed the goals of the Constitutional Revolution of 1905–06 in Iran, and advocated democracy and constitutional monarchy for Iran.

Seyyed Hossein Nasr is a scholar of Iranian origin who is the University Professor of Islamic Studies at George Washington University. He is the author of *Ideals and Realities of Islam* and *Traditional Islam in the Modern World*.

Seyyed Vali Reza Nasr is an Iranian political scientist and currently a doctoral candidate at the Department of Political Science of Massachusetts Institute of Technology. He is the author of a number of articles on Iranian and Pakistani studies.

Shaykh Fadlullah Nuri was a prominent Iranian Shiꞌi jurist of the turn of the century who rose in opposition to the secularist implications of the Constitutional Revolution of 1905–06 in Iran. Nuri's opposition finally led to his execution at the order of the authorities and with the tacit approval of his constitutionalist cohorts.

Abdulaziz A. Sachedina is an East African specialist in Shiꞌi studies. He is professor of religion at the University of Virginia and the author of *Islamic Messianism: The Idea of the Mahdi in Twelver Shiꞌism*.

Sayyid Muhammad Baqir Sadr was an Iraqi Shiꞌi jurist and thinker who led the resurgence of Shiꞌi political sentiments in the 1970s in Iraq. He is the author of *Iqtisaduna* and *Our Philosophy*.

Roger Savory is a Canadian scholar of Iranian history. He is professor at the University of Toronto and the author of *Iran Under the Safavids*.

Annemarie Schimmel is a German scholar of Islamic studies and the art and culture of the Muslim peoples of Turkey, Iran and the Indian subcontinent. She is professor of Indo-Muslim Culture at Harvard University and the author of *And Muhammad is His Messenger* and *Mystical Dimensions of Islam*.

ꞌAli Shariꞌati was an Iranian thinker known for his innovative interpretation of Shiꞌism and influence upon the emergence of politicized forms of Shiꞌism in Iran in the 1970s. He had taught at Firdowsi University of Mashhad and is the author of *What is to be Done* and *The Sociology of Islam*.

ᶜAllamah Sayyid Muhammad Husayn Tabataba'i was one of contemporary Shiᶜism's most famous philosophers, theologians and thinkers. He is the author of the monumental Quranic commentary *al-Mizan* and *Shiᶜite Islam* (translated and edited by S.H. Nasr).

Ayatollah Sayyid Mahmud Taliqani was an Iranian jurist known for his influence on the politicization of Shiᶜism in Iran in the 1970s and his interpretive approach to aspects of Shiᶜism. He is the author of *Partu'i az Qur'an*, and *Islam and Ownership*.

Part I

Shiᶜi Political Doctrines

Chapter One

Imamate

The Shiᶜi faith and its social manifestations crystallized around the doctrine of Imamate. Succinctly put, the doctrine espouses that God has bestowed upon the Holy Community the gift of an infallible guide at all times, a guide who is to govern all affairs in the temporal realm and, therefore, safeguard its welfare. In the Shiᶜi view, these guides, who oversee the historical growth of Shiᶜism are none other than the Imams, *specifically identified with the Household of the Prophet. The lineage of the Imams began with ᶜAli ibn Abi Talib, whom the Shiᶜis view as rightful successor to the Prophet, and continued seriatim, based on primogeniture, until the occultation of Muhammad ibn Hasan, al-Mahdi in 873–74 A.D. Thenceforth, the Shiᶜi doctrine of Imamate has been manifested in the submission of the community to the writ of the occultation and the expectation of the return of the Twelfth Imam.*

Over the centuries, the Shiᶜi adherence to the Imams, as well as the denial of their right to the leadership of ummah by the Muslim majority, has shaped the world-view of the Shiᶜi community. The doctrine of Imamate has molded Shiᶜi theology, philosophy, and mysticism, as well as politics and historical progression. Since this volume is concerned with Shiᶜi history and socio-political institutions, our focus will be on the pertinence of the doctrine of Imamate to Shiᶜi political thought and practice. In Chapter 7, Ann Lambton has discussed the role of the doctrine of Imamate in classical Shiᶜi political thought. Here, Karl-Heinrich Göbel's interpretative treatment of the contemporary Lebanese Shiᶜi ᶜalim, Muhammad Jawad Mughniyah's work on the Imamate, sheds light on the modern interpretation of this doctrine. Of particular significance is Mughniyah's attempt, typical of a generation of modernist Shiᶜis, to assimilate the Shiᶜi sacred discourse into a patently mundane and revolutionary one. The excerpt is from MSPS, pages 109–127, and has been translated from German by Hamid Dabashi.

Karl-Heinrich Göbel

(Translated by Hamid Dabashi)

In 1961, Muhammad Jawad Mughniyah's *al-Shiᶜah wa'l-Hakimun* (Shiᶜism and the Rulers) was published in Beirut. In 1964, a translation of this book into Persian by Mustafa Zamani appeared under the title of *Shiᶜah va Zamamdaran-i Khudsar* (Shiᶜism and Despotic Rulers). In *al-Shiᶜah wa'l-Hakimun*, Mughniyah provides a historical survey of the relationship between Shiᶜism and the state apparatus and other centers of power. The historical period concerned extends from the time of Muhammad to the present. The historical scheme presented in this study is viewed from the perspective of a politically committed modern Shiᶜi.

The book contains a brief theoretical summary of the Shiᶜi understanding of political authority. The main part (pages 32–204) examines the relationship between Shiᶜism and the state as reflected in the mirror of history. The conclusion provides comprehensive views from the diverse historical perspective of the Shiᶜi, the Sunni, and the Western ("colonial") historians of the twentieth century.

Although, formally, this book is structured on the model of modern Arabic historical discourse, nonetheless it contains elements from the classical Islamic historiography and *adab* (letters), pages 228–235. It is written in simple language, that can be understood by a wide circle of readers. For didactic and edifying purposes *qasidahs* (panigerics; pages 173–82; 124–32) are also utilized occasionaly. In their casuistry, the implications of their subject matter to the civil law becomes rather apparent. Mughniyah's primary political concern here is a historically conscious and effective structuring of society on the idealized model of Muhammad and the Imams.

In every respect, the Imamate of ᶜAli, the first Shiᶜi Imam, serves as a model of a progressive state for Mughniyah in his *Imamat-i ᶜAli bayn al-'aql wa'l Qur'an* (The Imamate of ᶜAli Between Reason and the Qur'an) (Beirut, 1970).

Both of these books provide insights into the social system envisioned by Mughniyah. Mughniyah's criterion for his proclaimed socio-political program is the charter (*ahd*) of ᶜAli to Malik al-Ashtar. For Mughniyah, this charter represents a constitution that is universally applicable. In this charter, ᶜAli had ordered his governor, al-Ashtar, to take care of the well-being of both those in power and those who obey them. According to

Mughniyah, this, applied to the present time, is expressed in the control over the means of production (*wasa'il al-intaj*), and the drafting of five-, seven-, or ten-year programs for securing the general welfare.

Man should not solely be evaluated according to his personality (*Shakhsiyyah*); his social behavior is more decisive. A person who has done something malicious to another should be excluded from human society. Any leniency with antisocial, scrupulous behavior is damaging to humanity at large. The role of family in society is not only limited to the relationship among relatives; rather, all human beings constitute one big family, since they are all descendents of Adam. The relationship among human beings in this big family is characterized by faithfulness, belief, and the commandment of brotherhood. In international relations, our author pleads against any form of nationalism, and in favor of cosmopolitanism. Every country is the homeland of everyone. The fatherland, however, is to be preferred to other countries. The best country, however, is always where the highest standard of living, security, freedom and generosity prevails. The best model for such a country is the city-state of Medina during the time of the Prophet (622–632 A.D.), in which emigrants from Mecca and the local inhabitants lived under similar conditions.

According to Shiᶜite doctrines, Muhammad had selected, through designation (*nass*), ᶜAli as his successor, and Caliph (*Imam*); ᶜAli had in turn appointed the next caliph, and so forth. The particular attributes (*sifat*) of the Imams and, most of all, those of ᶜAli are the criteria to which all rulers will have to adhere. The conditions (*shurut*) that a legitimate ruler must meet are *nass* (written statement), *hikmah* (wisdom), and *afdaliyyah* (seniority). The only one who meets all these prerequisites is the Mahdi or *Sahib al-Zaman* (The Master of Time), who has been in occultation ever since 873–874 A.D. The right of the Mahdi to authority in this world can be traced back deductively from Imam to Imam to Muhammad and the Qur'an, and thereby to God.

Mughniyah reiterates this classical doctrine of *Imamat* in its historical context. But what is his opinion about the present political exigencies? In the modern, very democratically oriented society, the question poses itself as whether the Imamate is still relevant today, because, as Mughniyah implicitly admits, the Imamate exhibits monarchial traits.

Mughniyah answers this question by postulating the following hypothesis. There is no Imam other than the truth (*La imam siwa'l-haqq*). However, since the truth can be fathomed only through the agency of reason, Mughniyah explains that the statement *there is no Imam other than through reason* (*La imam siwa'l-ᶜaql*) is accordingly a rule of truth and right. Mughniyah bases his assumption on the prophetic tradition: "the foundation of my religion is reason (*ᶜasl dini al-ᶜaql*)". The reason, however, stands in opposition to the natural disposition of human fallibility, and thus, it is attainable only through God's help. The attainment of truth through intellect has been bestowed upon only a few blessed individuals, among them Muhammad and the Imams. For men the most important proof (*hujjah*) of the exceptional and divine truth or the divine justice (*al-ᶜadalah al-ilahiyah*) are as manifested in the Qur'an, or by Muhammad and the Imams. If these very obvious proofs of God are overlooked or denied, then punishment in hell is inevitable.

Mughniyah then asserts that the institution of caliphate, through both its divine law (*Sharᶜ*) and its tradition (*samᶜ*), is emphatically prescribed for Islam. However, he also poses the question of the extent to which the caliphate seems to be compatible with rationality. The answer is that humanity will always make mistakes, and thus it is in need of divine guidance. God's grace comes to meet this need through the proofs (*hujaj*) of divinity that bring men back to the right path. Caliphate and Imamate are aspects of such proofs that God provides. The caliphate can, however, perform its functions because of the infallibility of the persons occupying the office.

Caliphs who are not infallible, such as Abu Bakr, are usurpers and unworthy of their office. A further evidence of God is the Imam's knowledge of the unseen (*ᶜilm al-ghayb*). Only the Imam is in a position to understand fully the Qur'an and convey it to others. In this way, the Imam is the agency of the divine will. The knowledge of the unseen encompasses more than just the Qur'an and extends into worldly matters. ᶜAli's statement that "in al-Talaqan there are treasures which are neither of gold nor of silver" is interpreted by Mughniyah as a reference to Iranian oil fields. Before his chapter on the Imam's knowledge of the unseen, Mughniyah emphatically points out that every kind of prophecy, fortune-telling, or witchcraft is blasphemy (*kufr*). He supports this with the Qur'anic passage:

> Lo! Allah! With Him is knowledge of the Hour. He sendeth down the rain, and knoweth that which is in the wombs. No soul knoweth what it will earn tomorrow, and no soul knoweth in what land it will die. Lo! Allah is knower, Aware. (XXX:34)

Muhammad is the seal of the prophets, and the Imams do not have the capability to become prophets. But how are the prophecies of the Imams to be reconciled with this statement? The answer is that the Imam does not possess the knowledge of the hidden things, but merely the knowledge he had received from God through Muhammad. According to Mughniyah, there is no shortage of statements by Muhammad and the Imams with reference to modern situations. For instance, Imam Jaᶜfar al-Sadiq has said:

> There will come a time when people shall see and hear whatever is happening in East and West. Every people will hear the voice in its own

language. The Arabs will rid themselves of the non-Arab domination and become their own rulers.

These are references to radio, television, and democracy, the independence of the Arabs from colonialism, etc. The Qur'anic passages

> [He is] the knower of the unseen, and rendereth unto none His secret, save unto every messenger whom he hath chosen, and then He maketh a guard to go before him and a guard behind him. (LXXII: 26–27)

are allusions to the hidden knowledge that Muhammad received from God. The prophetic statement that "The Euphrates is not far from being a treasure" is a reference to the Iraqi oil reserves. With respect to achievements of modern technology, Muhammad has stated that "The time-span shall shorten, and labor shall lessen." The fast dissemination of new products in the world market is prophecied by Muhammad in his saying that, "the market and the times shall converge." Muhammad had foreseen the modern journalism: "a people will appear who will take on deeds as cows eat grass." Muhammad had anticipated the shameful actions of the colonialists who want to rob the Arabs of their oil with the following words: "There will be sources that the millions among the human beings shall exploit." Muhammad had prophecied the sinful conception of our modern, godless time by saying: "the market will converge, there will be exorbitant interest (*riba'*) charged, people will secretly do corrupt business, godless creatures shall spend the money, and there will be many adulteries. "People will secretly do corrupt business" refers to the way modern business is conducted through telex.

The discoveries of the values and phenomena of the twentieth century within the classical Shiᶜi traditions means the adaptation of the doctrines to a changing historical situation. In expounding the Qur'an and the hadith, Mughniyah applies a markedly modern interpretation. He sees the development of science and technology in complete harmony with the doctrines of Twelver Shiᶜism. The actual forerunners and initiators of modernity, according to Mughniyah, are the *ahl al-bayt* (i.e., Muhammad, Fatimah, and the Imams).

The basis of freedom, peace, equality, social justice, and progress is the science (*'ilm*), whose methodological foundations were already established by the *ahl al-bayt*. The religio-political ideology of Twelver Shiᶜism as expounded by Mughniyah does not bear the characteristic of a retroactive religion, but instead, a futuristic, idealistic one. Mughniyah utilizes science and technology, together with religion and political programs, for the benefit of humanity. Through the use of spiritual mandates, negative repercussions are avoided. The final goal is the fulfillment of the human dream (*hulm al-insaniyah*) of a paradise, an ideal state on earth. Through the reign of the *ahl al-bayt* the dream of the paradise on earth will materialize.

Chapter Two

Messianism and the Mahdi

The doctrine of the Imamate ultimately gave rise to that of the last redeemer, al-Mahdi. *The messianic return of* al-Mahdi, *the twelfth Imam, who is in occultation (*ghaybah*) brings this cycle of history to a close. In the following three passages, first ᶜAllamah Tabataba'i provides a theological exposition of the doctrine of* ghaybah, *then Jassim M. Hussain gives a full historical account of its doctrinal developments, and finally Abdulaziz A. Sachedina discusses the messianic dimension of Shiᶜism. The excerpts are taken from* SI, *210–14,* OTI, *pages 13–30, and* IMIMTS, *pages 150–66, 172–79, respectively.*

ᶜAllamah Tabataba'i

The promised Mahdi, who is usually mentioned by his title of *Imam-i ᶜasr* (the Imam of the "Period") and *Sahib al-zaman* (the Lord of the Age), is the son of the eleventh Imam. His name is the same as that of the Holy Prophet. He was born in Samarrah in 256/868 and until 260/872 when his father was martyred, lived under his father's care and tutelage. He was hidden from public view and only a few of the elite among the *shiᶜah* were able to meet him.

After the martyrdom of his father he became Imam and by Divine Command went into occultation (*ghaybah*). Thereafter he appeared only to his deputies (*na'ib*) and even then only in exceptional circumstances.

The Imam chose as a special deputy for a time ᶜUthman ibn Saᶜid ᶜUmari, one of the companions of his father and grandfather who was his confidant and trusted friend. Through his deputy the Imam would answer the demands and questions of the Shiᶜi. After ᶜUthman ibn Saᶜid, his son Muhammad ibn ᶜUthman ᶜUmari was appointed the deputy of the Imam. After the death of Muhammad ibn ᶜUthman, Abu'l-Qasim Husayn ibn Ruh Nawbakhti was the special deputy, and after his death ᶜAli ibn Muhammad Simmari was chosen for this task.

A few days before the death of ᶜAli ibn Muhammad Simmari in 329/939 an order was issued by the Imam stating that in six days ᶜAli ibn Muhammad Simmari would die. Henceforth the special deputation of the Imam would come to an end and the major occultation (*ghaybah-i kubra*) would begin and would continut until the day God grants permission to the Imam to manifest himself.

The occultation of the twelfth Imam is, therefore, divided into two parts: the first, the minor occultation (*ghaybah-i sughra*) which began in 260/872 and ended in 329/939, lasting about seventy years; the second, the major occultation which commenced in 329/939 and will continue as long as God wills it. In a *hadith* upon whose authenticity everyone agrees, the Holy Prophet has said, "If there were to remain in the life of the world but one day, God would prolong that day until He sends in it a man from my community and my household. His name will be the same as my name. He will fill the earth with equity and justice as it was filled with oppression and tyranny."

In the discussion on prophecy and the Imamate it was indicated that as a result of the law of general guidance which governs all of creation, man is of necessity endowed with the power of receiving revelation through prophecy, which directs him toward the perfection of the human norm and the well-being of the human species. Obviously, if this perfection and happiness were not possible for man, whose life possesses a social aspect, the very fact that he is endowed with this power would be meaningless and futile. But there is no futility in creation.

In other words, ever since he has inhabited the earth, man has had the wish to lead a social life filled with happiness in its true sense and has striven toward this end. If such a wish were not to have an objective existence it would never have been imprinted upon man's inner nature, in the same way that if there were not food there would have been no hunger. Or if there were to be no water there would be no thirst and if there were to be no reproduction there would have been no sexual attraction between the sexes.

Therefore, by reason of inner necessity and determination, the future will see a day when human society will be replete with justice and when all will live in peace and tranquillity, when human beings will be fully possessed of virtue and perfection. The establishment of such a condition will occur through human hands but with Divine succor. And the leader of such a society, who will be the savior of man, is called in the language of the *hadith*, the Mahdi.

In the different religions that govern the world such as Hinduism, Buddhism, Judaism, Christianity, Zoroastrianism and Islam there are references to a person who will come as the savior of mankind. These religions have usually given happy tidings of his coming, although there are naturally certain differences in detail that can be discerned when these teachings are compared carefully. The *hadith* of the Holy Prophet upon which all Muslims agree, "The Mahdi is of my progeny," refers to this same truth.

There are numerous hadiths cited in Sunni and Shiʿi sources from the Holy Prophet and the Imams concerning the appearance of the Mahdi, such as that he is of the progeny of the Prophet and that his appearance will enable human society to reach true perfection and the full realization of spiritual life. In addition, there are numerous other traditions concerning the fact that the Mahdi is the son of the eleventh Imam, Hasan al-ʿAskari. They agree that after being born and undergoing a long occultation the Mahdi will appear again, filling with justice the world that has been corrupted by injustice and iniquity.

As an example, ʿAli ibn Musa al-Rida (the eighth Imam) has said, in the course of a *hadith*, "The Imam after me is my son, Muhammad, and after him his son ʿAli, and after ʿAli his son, Hasan, and after Hasan his son Hujjat al-Qa'im, who is awaited during his occultation and obeyed during his manifestation. If there remain from the life of the world but a single day, Allah will extend that day until he becomes manifest, and fill the world with justice in the same way that it had been filled with iniquity. But when? As for news of the 'hour,' verily my father told me, having heard it from his father who heard it from his father who heard it from his ancestors who heard it from ᶜAli, that it was asked of the Holy Prophet, 'Oh Prophet of God, when will the "support" (*qa'im*) who is from thy family appear?' He said, 'His case is like that of the Hour (of the Resurrection). "He alone will manifest it at its proper time. It is heavy in the heavens and the earth. It cometh not to you save unawares" (Qur'an, VII:187).'"

Saqr ibn Abu Dulaf said, "I heard from Abu Jaᶜfar Muhammad ibn ᶜAli al-Rida [the ninth Imam] who said, "The Imam after me is my son, ᶜAli; his command is my command; his word is my word; to obey him is to obey me. The Imam after him is his son, Hasan. His command is the command of his father; his word is the word of his father; to obey him is to obey his father.' After these words the Imam remained silent. I said to him, 'Oh son of the Prophet, who will be the Imam after Hasan?' The Imam cried hard, then said, 'Verily after Hasan his son is the awaited Imam who is "*al-qa'im bi'l-haqq*" (He who is supported by the Truth).'"

Musa ibn Jaᶜfar Baghdadi said, "I heard from the Imam Abu Muhammad al-Hasan ibn ᶜAli [the eleventh Imam] who said, 'I see that after me differences will appear among you concerning the Imam after me. Whoso accepts the Imams after the Prophet of God but denies my son is like the person who accepts all the prophets but denies the prophethood of Muhammad, the Prophet of God, upon whom be peace and blessing. And whoso denies [Muhammad] the Prophet of God is like one who has denied all the prophets of God, for to obey the last of us is like obeying the first and to deny the last of us is like denying the first. But beware! Verily for my son there is an occultation during which all people will fall into doubt except those whom Allah protects."

The opponents of Shiᶜism protest that according to the beliefs of this school the Hidden Imam should by now be nearly twelve centuries old, whereas this is impossible for any human being. In answer it must be said that the protest is based only on the unlikelihood of such an occurance, not its impossibility. Of course such a long lifetime or a life of a longer period is unlikely. But those who study the hadiths of the Holy Prophet and the Imams will see that they refer to this life as one possessing miraculous qualities. Miracles are certainly not impossible nor can they be negated through scientific arguments. It can never be proved that the causes and agents that are functioning in the world are solely those that we see and know and that other causes which we do not know or whose effects and actions we have not seen nor understood do not exist. It is in this way possible that in one or several members of mankind there can be operating certain causes and agents which bestow upon them a very long life of a thousand or several thousand years. Medicine has not even lost hope of discovering a way to achieve very long life spans. In any case such protests from "peoples of the Book" such as Jews, Christians and Muslims are most strange for they accept the miracles of the prophets of God according to their own sacred scriptures.

The opponents of Shi^cism also protest that, although Shi^cism considers the Imam necessary in order to expound the injunctions and verities of religion and to guide the people, the occultation of the Imam is the negation of this very purpose, for an Imam in occultation who cannot be reached by mankind cannot be in any way beneficial or effective. The opponents say that if God wills to bring forth an Imam to reform mankind He is able to create him at the necessary moment and does not need to create him thousands of years earlier. In answer it must be said that such people have not really understood the meaning of the Imam, for in the discussion on the imamate it became clear that the duty of the Imam is not only the formal explanation of the religious sciences and exoteric guidance of the people. In the same way that he has the duty of guiding men outwardly, the Imam also bears the function of *walayah* and the esoteric guidance of men. It is he who directs man's spiritual life and orients the inner aspect of human action toward God. Clearly, his physical presence or absence has no effect in this matter. The Imam watches over men inwardly and is in communion with the soul and spirit of men even if he be hidden from their physical eyes. His existence is always necessary even if the time has not as yet arrived for his outward appearance and the universal reconstruction that he is to bring about.

Jassim M. Hussain

Sorrow for the Mahdi who is buried!
O best of those who walked on Earth, be not far!

The poet Jarir applies this term to Ibrahim, the prophet. The Sunnis often applied it to the four caliphs after the Prophet, who were called *al-Khulafa' al-Rashidun al-Mahdiyyun*, the divinely guided caliphs. Sulayman ibn Surd called al-Husayn, after his martyrdom, *Mahdi ibn al-Mahdi*.

As for the theological usage of this term, according to Rajkowski, Abu Ishaq Ka^cb ibn Mati' ibn Haysu^c al-Himyari (d. 34/654) was the first individual to speak of *al-Mahdi* as the Saviour. But it is worth mentioning that the second caliph, ^cUmar ibn al-Khattab, had spoken of occultation before Ka^cb. When the Prophet died in 11/632, ^cUmar contended that Muhammad had not died but had concealed himself as Moses did and would return from his occultation. ^cUmar's claim, however, was refuted by Abu Bakr, who reminded him of the Qur'anic verse revealing the death of the Prophet which states:

> *Surely you shall die and they [too] shall surely die. Then surely on the Day of Resurrection you will contend with one another before your Lord* (al-Zumar, XXXIX: 30–31).

The follower of Ibn al-Hanafiyyah (d. 81–4/700–3), al-Mukhtar, who was in revolt in Kufah in 66/685, named him as claimant to the Imamate and called him *al-Mahdi* in the messianic context. Later the name of Ibn al-Hanafiyyah became associated with the Kaysaniyyah sect, which denied his death and held that he was the promised Mahdi, who had concealed himself in Mount Radwa, and who would rise in arms to eliminate injustice. The Kaysaniyyah dogma played an important role in Islamic political history during the Umayyad period, since the ^cAbbasid propaganda, which brought about the collapse of the Umayyads, was in fact derived from this sect. The dogma of al-Kaysaniyyah can be seen in the poetry of Kuthayyir (d. 105/723) and al-Sayyid al-Himyari (d. 173/789). The latter had followed this sect, but it is said that he became an Imamite after a discussion with al-Sadiq, who clarified for him that the concealed Imam mentioned by the Prophet was not Ibn al-Hanafiyyah but the twelfth Imam from the progeny of al-Husayn.

The Zaydis also applied the term *al-Mahdi* in its eschatological sense to their leaders who rose in arms against the ^cAbbasids, such as Muhammad al-Nafs al-Zakiyyah (d. 145/762), Muhammad ibn Ja^cfar al-Sadiq (d. 203/818), and Muhammad ibn al-Qasim al-Talqan, who disappeared in the year 219/834. An example of the Zaydi usage of this term is recorded by Ibn Tawus, who states on the authority of Ibrahim ibn ^cAbdullah ibn al-Hasan, the brother of al-Nafs al-Zakiyyah, that the latter had rebelled hoping that Allah might make him the Mahdi promised by the Prophet.

*   *   *

As for the Imamis, a considerable body among them applied the title of *al-Mahdi* in its messianic sense to each Imam after his death. This can be seen in the claim of al-Nawusiyyah, al-Waqifah and the followers of al-^cAskari, the eleventh Imam. After the death of al-Sadiq in the year 148/765 the Nawusiyyah group held that he was *al-Qa'im al-Mahdi* and that he did not die but went into occultation. The Waqifah group applied this title to the seventh Imam Musa al-Kazim (d. 183/799) and denied his death, contending that he was *al-Qa'im al-Mahdi* and that he would rise to fill the earth with justice after it had been filled with tyranny. Other Imamis held that the eleventh Imam al-ᶜAskari was *al-Qa'im al-Mahdi*, whereas the last important usage of this term was given to the twelfth Imam, who became the magnate of the Imamis' hope in their struggle for justice and equity.

It is worth mentioning that all these claims relating to the eschatological usage of the term *al-Mahdi* were based mainly on Prophetic traditions concerning a future restorer of Islam. Hence it is essential to discuss the traditions of the Prophet and the Imams, especially these traditions which concern the twelfth Imam, so as to see their role in the question of his occultation.

* * *

In Shiᶜi exegesis many Qur'anic verses are regarded as references to the role of *al-Qa'im* and his occultation. The most important is the following verse: *O, but I call to witness the planets, the stars which rise and set* (al-Takwir, LXXXI: 15–16). According to Imam al-Baqir, this verse means that an Imam would go into occultation in the year 260/847; then he would reappear suddenly like a bright shooting star in the dark night.

Ibn al-Furat, al-Kafi and al-Sadduq interpret the following Qur'anic verse: *"Say: Have you thought: If (all) your water were to disappear into the earth, who then could bring you gushing water"* (al-Mulk, LXVII: 30). They maintain that this verse is a metaphor for the concealment of the Imam, whose presence among people is like the water they need to drink.

The Ismaᶜili writer Mansur al-Yaman (ca. 4th century A.H.) agrees with al-Kulayni that some Qur'anic verses which apparently deal with the Day of Judgement actually concern the appearance of *al-Qa'im* after his occultation. According to al-Kulayni the verse *"And those who sincerely believe in the day of Judgement"* [al-Maᶜraj, LXX: 26] refers to those who believe in the reappearance of *al-Qa'im*. Mansur al-Yaman gives a similar esoteric interpretation of another verse:

> And of mankind are some who say, we believe in Allah and the Last Day, when they believe not. They think to beguile Allah and those who believe, but they beguile none save themselves; but they perceive not. (al-Baqara, II: 8–9).

Mansur al-Yaman states that the Last Day (*al-yawm al-akhir*) in this verse is the "Commander of the Age" (*Sahib al-zaman*), that is *al-Qa'im al-Mahdi*. Al-Kulyani interprets many Qur'anic verses with the same kind of approach and links them to the future role of *al-Qa'im al-Mahdi*. In his view, when *al-Qa'im* reappears he will establish the political state of the

"People of the House" (*ahl al-bayt*) that is, the Imams, upon the ruins of the state of inequity. This is *al-Kulayni's* esoteric commentary on the verse: *"And say: The truth has come and falsehood has vanished. Surely falsehood is a vanishing thing."* (Banu Isra'il, XVII: 81).

Al-Tusi follows in al-Kulanyi's footsteps in commenting on certain Qur'anic verses. Take, for example, this passage:

> *And We desired to show favour unto those who were oppressed in the earth, and to make them Imams and to make them inheritors. And to establish them in the earth, and to show Pharaoh and Haman and their hosts that which they feared from them.* (al-Qasas, XXVII: 5-6).

Al-Tusi holds that the above verses predict the establishment of the state of Justice by *al-Qa'im al-Mahdi*, who would inherit what had been in the possession of the wrong-doers.

Other Imami scholars maintain that the fifth Imam, al-Baqir, said that Allah's promise of victory to an Imam from the People of the House is mentioned explicitly in the following verse:

> *And verily We have written in the scripture (al-Zabur), after the Reminder My righteous slaves will inherit the earth.* (al-Anbiya', XXI: 105)

Other verses have also been interpreted by the Imamites to be connected with the role of *al-Qa'im*, after his rising from occultation, such as the verse:

> *Allah has promised such of you as believe and do good works that He will surely make them to succeed (the present rulers) in the earth even as He caused those who were before them to succeed (others); and He will surely establish for them in exchange safety after their fear. They serve Me. They ascribe nothing as a partner unto Me. Those who disbelieve henceforth, they are the wrong doers.* (al-Nur, 24: 55)

Al-Qumi and al-Tusi report that the People of the House mentioned that this verse concerns the Mahdi because he would live during his concealment in a state of fear, would appear after the removal of fear, and would certainly become victorious.

* * *

There are many traditions attributed to the Prophet in the books of tradition concerning the identity of al-Mahdi, his family, his epithet (*kunya*) and his character. The conclusion of these numerous traditions is that al-Mahdi is a descendant of the sons of Fatimah, the daughter of the Prophet; and more particularly, that he is of the progeny of her son Husayn. His colour is similar to that of the Arab, and his body is like the Israelite, and his name and *kunya* are similar to the name and *kunya* of the Prophet. Moreover some traditions claim that the Prophet said that *al-Mahdi*'s father's name is like the name of the Prophet's grandson, Hasan. Below are a number of these traditions.

i) We, the family of ^cAbd al-Muttalib, are the Masters of the inhabitants of Paradise: I, Hamzah, Ja^cfar, ^cAli, Hasan, Husayn and *al-Mahdi*.

ii) *Al-Mahdi* is from my progeny. His name is similar to mine and his epithet is similar to mine. In his physique and character he looks exactly like me. He will be in a state of occultation and there will be confusion (*hayrah*) in which peole will wander about. Then he will come forth like a sharp, shooting star to fill the earth with justice and equity as it was filled before with injustice and inequity.

iii) *Al-Mahdi* is from my family (^c*itra*) from the sons of Fatimah. It is worth mentioning that this tradition was reported on the authority of Umm Salama by ^cAli ibn Nufayl, who died in 125/742.

iv) On the authority of Ibn ^cAbbas, the Prophet is reported to have said, "How shall Allah destroy a nation whose beginning is myself, whose end is Jesus and whose very centre is *al-Mahdi*, who will be from my family?

v) The name of *al-Mahdi*'s father is similar to the name of my son Hasan.

The conclusion of ^cUthman concerning these traditions seems to be rather forced. "All these *hadiths* are weak and contradictory (*mutadarib*), therefore their attribution to the Prophet Muhammad is to be very much doubted." For the use of the epithet al-Mahdi by numerous Islamic groups, particularly the Zaydis, in their struggle for power during the Umayyad period shows that these traditions were well-known among the Muslims of that period. Moreover, many traditionists from different Islamic sects transmitted these traditions before the downfall of the Umayyads in 132/749, and later they were collected in the books of tradition (*hadith*). The earliest of these books was *Kitab Sulaym ibn Qays*, attributed to Sulaym ibn Qays al-Hilali, who died between the years 80–90/699–708. He reports many Prophetic traditions concerning al-Mahdi, his occultation and his reappearance. It appears from these two points that ^cUthman's judgement is somewhat hasty, particularly if one takes into account the fact that Prophetic traditions regarding al-Mahdi were narrated by twenty-six companions of the Prophet. On their authority thirty-eight traditionists recorded these traditions in their collections of *hadith*.

The evidence suggests that from the earliest times in Islam there was a belief that the Prophet had given his followers a promise about a man from the progeny of Husayn, who would rise in arms in the future to purify Islam from innovation. But political rivalry amongst the Muslims encouraged some people to exploit this hope and to distort these Prophetic traditions in order to use them in their struggle for power.

These traditions only mention that *al-Qa'im al-Mahdi* will be from the progeny of the Prophet. But there are also other traditions attributed to the Prophet which state that al-Mahdi will, in fact, be the twelfth Imam.

It is true that Montgomery Watt objects that,

> Until al-ᶜAskari died on 1st Jan. 874, there was nothing to make people expect that the number of the Imams would be limited to twelve or that the twelfth would go into occultation. It follows the theory of the twelve Imams was worked out after 874.

Nevertheless, there is ample proof that traditions claiming *al-Qa'im* would be the twelfth descendant of the Prophet were in circulation before 874. It is thus necessary to throw light upon these traditions, which were transmitted by Sunnis and Zaydis as well as Imamis, so that one can see to what extent these traditions were used by the Imami scholars to support the belief that the twelfth Imam had not died but was in a state of occultation.

*   *   *

The Sunnite books of tradition report three Prophetic traditions pertaining to the twelve Imams who would be the successors of the Prophet. These were narrated on the authority of seven companions of the Prophet, namely Jabir ibn Samurah, ᶜAbdullah ibn Masᶜud, Anas ibn Malik, ᶜUmar ibn al-Khattab, Wa'ila ibn Asqa', ᶜAbdullah ibn ᶜUmar and Abu Hurayrah.

i) Jabir ibn Samurah narrates that he heard the Prophet say, "There will be after me twelve Amirs," Then he mentioned something which I did not hear, so I asked my father, who was sitting beside me, who said, "All of whom will be from Quraysh."

ii) ᶜUmar ibn al-Khattab reports that he heard the Prophet say, "The Imams (*al-A'imma*) after me will be twelve, all of whom will be from Quraysh."

iii) ᶜAbdullah ibn Masᶜud was once reciting the Qur'an in the mosque in Iraq, when a young man came and asked him if the Prophet had informed them about the number of his successors. Ibn Masᶜud replied, "The Prophet informed us that his successors will be twelve caliphs, whose number is similar to the number of the leaders (*al-nuqaba'*) of Banu Isra'il."

These traditions have been related by the traditionists and considered authentic. Ibn Hanbal narrates the first with thirty-four chains of transmitters (*sanad*), all of which are on the authority of Jabir ibn Samurah, although there are slight differences in the versions. Some of the narrators used the words *Amir* and *Khalifah* instead of *Imam*. But these traditions, as reported by the Sunnites, indicate only that the Prophet would be succeeded by twelve successors; none reveals that the twelfth would go into occultation, nor that he would be *al-Qa'im al-Mahdi*. But the Zaydi and the Imamite narrators relate the same traditions with phrases which indicate that the twelfth Imam would be *al-Qa'im al-Mahdi*.

The Imami traditionists are distinguished from the Sunnis and the Zaydis by their claim that the twelfth Imam mentioned in the Sunni and the Zaydi traditions is in fact Muhammad the son of the eleventh Imam al-cAskari, and that he is *al-Qa'im al-Mahdi*. Moreover they have written in more detail about his occultation, and his political role, the signs which would precede his reappearance and the social and political conditions which might pave the way for it.

* * *

The Prophetic traditions concerning the twelve Imams related by the Sunnite and the Zaydi traditionists were also narrated by the Imamis. They applied these traditions to their twelve Imams and added traditions of the Imams themselves which indicate explicitly that the successor of the eleventh Imam was *al-Qa'im*. The traditions attributed to the Prophet do not indicate explicitly that *al-Qa'im* would be the successor of al-cAskari, the eleventh Imam, whereas the sayings of the Imams do.

The earliest reference to a Prophetic tradition concerning the twelfth Imam is recorded by the Imamite traditionists on the authority of Sulaym ibn Qays al-Hilali. He was a companion of five Imams, cAli, Hasan, Husayn, cAli ibn al-Husayn and al-Baqir, and died in 90/701. The Imamites regard his work as the first Shici collection of *Hadith*. He reports numerous narrations concerning the twelve Imams and the political role of the last Imam. The first of these narrations is attributed to a Christian monk who met cAli after his return from the Battle of Siffin. He informed him that he had found in the Gospels that the successors of the Prophet Muhammad would be twelve; the last of them would fill the world with justice, and Jesus would perform the prayer behind him.

All the other narrations in Sulaym's work are attributed to the Prophet. The most important of these is quoted on the authority of the companions cAli, cAbdullah ibn Jacfar al-Tayyar, Salman al-Farsi, Abu al-Haytham ibn al-Tayhan, Khuzaymah ibn Thabit, cAmmar ibn Yasir, Abu Zarr, al-Miqdad and Abu Ayyub. They narrated that the Prophet gathered his companions together at Ghadir Khumm and said to them:

> O people, the legal power (*al-wilaya*) is granted only to cAli ibn Abi Talib and the trustees from my progeny, the descendants of my brother cAli. He will be the first, and his two sons, al-Hasan and al-Husayn, will succeed him consecutively. They will not separate themselves from the Qur'an until they return to Allah.

It has already been pointed out that the Imams from cAli ibn al-Husayn onwards adopted publicly a quiescent policy towards the Umayyads and the ᶜAbbasids. Accordingly, they stressed the propagation of their teachings, which they expected, would result in religious and political awareness among the people and would prepare the ground for the task of *al-Qa'im*. Al-Nuᶜmani reports that al-Baqir advised his partisan Abu al-Jarud to keep quiet at home, and not to implicate himself in the militant activitics of some ᶜAlids against the Umayyads, since the Umayyad state had a natural lifespan and the moment of its downfall had not yet come. He added that any ᶜAlid who rebelled against tyranny before the rise of *al-Qa'im* would inevitably fail. Al-Sadiq and the later Imams followed the same policy. They ordered their followers not to allow despair to find a place in their hearts and to wait for the rise of *al-Qa'im* in the near future. This policy enabled the Imamites to spread their doctrine and at the same time to organize themselves—during the period between 132–260/749–874 —into a well-established political and financial organization (*al-Wikala*). It seems probable that this underground organization was preparing for the rise of *al-Qa'im*. For they expected his rising and placed important political and religious duties upon his shoulders.

Several narrations suggest that the quiescent policy of the Imams was established after their followers caused two abortive rebellions. According to al-Kulayni, al-Sadiq once said:

> This matter (*al-Amr*), that is, the endeavour to reach power, was hidden until it reached the hands of the Kaysaniyyah. They revealed it on the roads and circulated it among the villagers of al-Sawad.

According to al-Nuᶜmani the Imamis endeavoured to rise in arms twice, first in the year 70/689 and second in the year 140/758, but their followers spoiled their plans by revealing the name of their leader to their foes, an act which resulted in the arrest or the assassination of the Imams. In this connection a conversation between al-Baqir and his partisan ᶜAbdullah by ᶜAta al-Wasiti is revealing. Al-Wasiti said to the Imam:

> You have many followers in Iraq and there is no one among your family who has the merit for leadership but you. So why do you not rise in arms? Al-Baqir replied: O ᶜAbd Allah, do not listen to the masses, because none of us has his name mentioned by the people nor a hand pointing at him as the Imam, without soon facing inevitable death. So search for him whose birth is concealed from the people, because he will be the one who will manage such an affair.

Moreover al-Sadiq was reported to have said:

> This matter [the rising in arms] was vested in me, but Allah delayed it; He shall do with my progeny whatever He wants.

These sayings indicate that the Imams had suffered the consequences of revealing the fixed dates of their militant endeavours to reach power. Hence the later Imams did not reveal explicitly to their followers which Imam would be *al-Qa'im* with the sword. At the same time they encouraged their followers to follow their instructions, for this would pave the way for one of the Imams to reach power under the title of *al-Qa'im*.

Several traditions reveal that the establishment of *al-Qa'im*'s political state will occur through the "natural" course of events. A Prophetic tradition states that a group of people from the east will start underground activities and pave the way for the installation of Mahdi by military means. The latter will struggle for power without any miraculous aid and will face difficulties and opposition against the propogation of his teachings, similar to the opposition which the Prophet faced with Quraysh. Furthermore he will not take any militant action unless he has at least 10,000 partisans.

According to al-Baqir the main goal of *al-Qa'im* will be to establish an Islamic state and to apply Islamic law as it was revealed to the Prophet. Al-Sadiq asserts that he will follow the Prophet's policy by eliminating and demolishing all the innovations which derive from a sitution of ignorance (*al-Jahiliyyah*) and apply Islam in a new form. Other narrations indicate that he will apply the law of David and Solomon along with the Islamic law and apply the rules of the Torah to the Jews and the rules of the Gospel to the Christians. According to al-Nuᶜmani, his state will include, in addition to the Islamic lands, the territories of Rum, Sind, India and China.

Some functions attributed to *al-Qa'im* indicate the unrest and disappointment felt by the Imamites in the face of the political and economic situation of the time. Al-Fadl ibn Shazan (d. 260/873) and al-Kulayni report that *al-Qa'im* will rise with the sword as God's avenger against those who caused troubles to ᶜAli and his wife Fatimah. He would also take vengeance against those who were responsible for the suffering of the Imams and their followers, particularly against those who assassinated Husayn. Al-Sadiq considered Husayns' assassination the main reason for the rise of *al-Qa'im* as an avenger. Other functions of *al-Qa'im* depict the political annoyance of the Imams towards the clan of Quraysh who had monopolized political authority since the death of the Prophet. Al-Nuᶜmani mentions a tradition attributed to Imam al-Sadiq: "When *al-Qa'im* rises he will deal with the Arabs and Quraysh only by the sword."

The Imamis also vested *al-Qa'im* with another task which reveals their dissatisfaction with the economic system of the ᶜAbbasid state. According to al-Himyari, al-Baqir stated that when *al-Qa'im* rose all the feudal systems would be abolished. Al-Kulayni agrees with al-Himyari and adds that *al-Qa'im*, after carrying out this opereation, may allow his partisans to administer and cultivate the lands with the condition that they pay the legal land-tax.

In the light of these hopes and the repeated failure of the Zaydi uprisings, as had been expected by the Imams, the Imamites concentrated all their hopes on the uprising of *al-Qa'im*, whose state had been awaited since the time of al-Baqir. Al-Nu^cmani reports that when the ^cAbbasid revolution broke out in Khurasan and black banners were raised, Abu Bakr al-Hadrami and Aban went to the Imam al-Sadiq, and asked his opinion about participating in the revolution. He warned them against it saying: "When you see us follow a man, then you must join us with weapons." Although the Imam did not reveal the identity of the man to be followed, he confirmed that he would struggle for power by militant means and eliminate the rule of his opponents. It appears that because of the militant role of *al-Qa'im* the Imams refrained from giving any explicit statement of his identity. However, they did indicate that since the rulers, first the Umayyads and then the ^cAbbasids, had reached power by "natural" means, their fall would also occur by "natural" means.

There is a good deal of evidence to indicate that some of the Imams would have taken militant action if they had had strong and faithful partisans. But they delayed this task indefinitely until the intellectual activities of their followers could bear fruit and be converted into a political awareness which might enable one of the Imams to gain power by militant means. The Imams also wanted their partisans to be more optimistic in gaining immediate success, and not to leave the task of propagation of their teachings to *al-Qa'im*, whose military uprising relied on the outcome of the activities of the Imamites themselves. Finally, it seems most likely that the uprising of the Imam who would be *al-Qa'im*, was later attributed to the twelfth Imam, because the Imamite propaganda reached a developed, political stage during the life-time of the tenth and the eleventh Imams, and this might have enabled the twelfth Imam to reach power.

*   *   *

The early Imami traditionists delineated five signs which would precede the rise of *al-Qa'im al-Mahdi*: first, the rise of al-Yamani, then the rise of al-Sufyani, thirdly the assassination of the Pure Soul (*al-Nafs al-zakiyya*) in Mecca only fifteen days before the rise of *al-Qa'im*, fourthly an outcry in the morning from the sky in the name of *al-Qa'im*, and finally the sinking of an army into the earth (*al-Bayda'*) during its march on Mecca. Despite the fact that al-Nu^cmani, al-Sadduq and al-Tusi differ as to the chronological occurrence of these signs, they all agree that they will occur in the same year.

It seems that the delineation of these signs along with the expectations of the Imamis and al-Jarudiyyah that *al-Qa'im al-Mahdi* would rise in the near future caused the ^cAbbasid authorities to be suspicious, since some of these signs were connected with their regime and indicated that *al-Qa'ims* uprising was directed mainly against them. The fact that the Imams had the ^cAbbasids in mind can be seen in the discussion between al-Rida, the eighth Imam, and his adherent Hasan ibn al-Jahm, who said to him:

> "May Allah make you prosper! The people are saying that al-Sufyani will rise after the fall of the ^cAbbasids." Al-Rida said: "They lie. He will rise while they are still in power."

This statement has been confirmed in other traditions attributed to al-Sadiq. For example his companion Ya^cqub ibn al-Sarraj asked him:

> "When will your Shi^ca gain their release from suffering?" He replied, "When conflict occurs amongst the ^cAbbasids, and their power begins to decline. Then their partisans and their subjects will be encouraged to threaten the authorities. Thereafter al-Sufyani will rise from the West, while the Yamani will advance from the East, until they both reach Kufa, where they will destroy the ^cAbbasids. At the same time the Hasani will start his rebellion. Then the Master of this matter, *al-Qa'im*, shall advance from Medina towards Mecca to rebel."

According to al-Nu^cmani, al-Sadiq added that because of these events, the fall of the ^cAbbasid regime was inevitable. Its fall would be similar to a piece of crockery dropped from the hands of its possessor, which then splits into pieces.

* * *

In the light of these statements attributed to the Imams it is clear that from the time of al-Sadiq onwards, the Imamis awaited the political uprising of one of their Imams, called *al-Qa'im* while the ^cAbbasids were still in power. Indeed the spread of these traditions caused the ^cAbbasids to fear the Imams, who might have been behind some ^cAlid revolts. Perhaps this is why the ^cAbbasid caliphs became suspicious of the Imams. Even the caliph al-Mansur himself related a tradition on the authority of al-Baqir stating that *al-Qa'im* would be from the progeny of ^cAli. He restricted the movements of al-Sadiq and his followers and made it a policy to discriminate against them. Moreover he invested his successor Muhammad with the epithet *"al-mahdi"* (158–169/775–785) in order to turn the attention of his subjects from the ^cAlid family toward the family of ^cAbbas.

Despite the fact that the movements of the seventh Imam, Musa al-Kazim, were also restricted by the authorities, so that he died in prison, the Shi^ci propaganda for the rise of an Imam in the name of *al-Qa'im* and Mahdi spread on a wide scale, particularly after the rebellion of Ibn Tabataba in 199/814. Probably because of this situation the caliph al-Ma'mun devised a new policy towards the eighth Imam, al-Rida. He made overtures to him asking him to be his heir apparent. By this means he hoped to split the ᶜAlids some of whom were in rebellion and to keep al-Rida within the ᶜAbbasid palace under close watch. Al-Ma'mun followed this same policy with the ninth Imam, al-Jawad, marrying him to his daughter Umm al-Fadl, and keeping him under house-arrest. Thereafter house-arrest became the cornerstone of the policy of the caliphs towards the Imams. It obliged the Imams to stress the idea of the occultation as the means the Imam would employ to avoid the ᶜAbbasid restriction, which increased from the time of al-Mutawakkil onwards.

Because his agents discovered connections between the underground activities of the Imami agents in Baghdad, Mada'in and Kufah and the Imam al-Hadi, al-Mutawakkil followed the policy of al-Ma'mun. He wrote to al-Hadi a letter full of kindness and courtesy asking him to come to Samarrah where they could meet. Afterwards al-Hadi was summoned to the capital in 233/848, where he spent the rest of his life under surveillance. As a result he was prevented from meeting most of his adherents. He was only able to meet a few of his associate agents (*wukala'*) in secret. In fact al-Mutawakkil's policy managed to prevent the ᶜAlids from rising in arms against his regime. However it failed to destroy the system of the *wikala* or to end the underground activities of the Zaydis and the Imamis. These spread throughout the empire to the extent that they were capable of causing a revolt.

Between the years 245–260/859–874 the Imami and Zaydi traditionists were relating traditions stating that *al-Qa'im* would be the twelfth Imam and urging people to join his side when he rose. The Zaydi al-ᶜAsfar (d. 250/864) and the Imami Ahmad ibn Khalid al-Barqi (d. 274–80/887–893) both related such traditions. For example, in 250/864 al-Barqi passed on a narration attributed to ᶜAli ibn Abu Talib and the Prophet al-Khidr, which states explicitly that *al-Qa'im al-Mahdi* would be the twelfth Imam. The spread of such narrations encouraged the Imamites to expect the rise of *al-Qa'im* in the near future and to link his rising with ᶜAbbasid rule. Some of them applied these traditions along with otheres concerning the signs of the rise of *al-Qa'im* to the circumstances surrounding the ᶜAlid revolt which broke out in 250/864. ᶜUqbah relates that the leader of the rebellion, Yahya ibn ᶜUmar, was expected to be *al-Qa'im al-Mahdi*, since all the signs concerning the rise of *al-Qa'im al-Mahdi* related by al-Sadiq occurred during the revolt.

Although Yahya ibn ᶜUmar died in 250/864, the ᶜAbbasids' fear increased because of the continuation of this revolt and Hasan ibn Zayd's (250–270 /864–884) success in establishing a Shiᶜi state in Tabaristan. This fear is not surprising if one bears in mind the fact that there was a well-known Prophetic tradition which stated, "A people will appear in the East who will pave the way for the Mahdi's rise to power. This tradition, at that time, might seem to refer to the establishment of the ᶜAlid state in Tabaristan, which would prepare the way for the rise of *al-Qa'im al-Mahdi*. Other factors supported the ᶜAbbasid fears. According to al-Tabari, ᶜAbbasid spies didscovered secret correspondence between the founder of the ᶜAlid state in Tabaristan, Hasan ibn Zayd, and the nephew of Muhammad ibn ᶜAli ibn Khalaf al-ᶜAttar, a follower of the tenth Imam al-Hadi. Moreoever many pure Imamites took part in the ᶜAlid revolt of 250/864, such as Muhammad ibn Maᶜruf, who held the banner of the rebels in Mecca, and ᶜAli ibn Musa ibn Ismaᶜil ibn Musa al-Kazim, who joined the rebels in Ray and was arrested by the caliph al-Muᶜtazz. It seems that the ᶜAbbasid authorities linked these factors within the activities of al-Hadi. Therefore, they imposed tight restrictions upon al-Hadi and his followers, and arrested prominent figures in Baghdad, such as Abu Hashim al-Jaᶜfari, and Muhammad ibn ᶜAli al-ᶜAttar, and sent them to Samarrah. This campaign of arrest also included al-ᶜAskari and Jaᶜfar, al-Hadi's two sons.

Another reason the ᶜAbbasids' feared the position of al-Hadi and his successor, al-ᶜAskari, is the traditions of both the Prophet and the Imams concerning the series of the twelve Imams, the last of whom would be *al-Qa'im al-Mahdi*. This series could only be interpreted as applying to the Imamites' tenth Imam, al-Hadi, and his successor al-ᶜAskari. So it was plausible that the successor of the latter would be the twelfth Imam, about whom so many traditions were being related. Moreover further traditions, attributed to al-Hadi and al-ᶜAskari, themselves appeared around this period emphasizing the important political and religious role of al-ᶜAskari's son. For example, Abu Hashim al-Jaᶜfar (d. 261/875), the associate and follower of al-Hadi, reports the latter as having said,

> "The successor after me is my son al-Hasan but what will you do with the successor of my successor?" Al-Jaᶜfar said, "May Allah make me your sacrifice! Why?" The Imam said, "Because you will not see his physical body and it is not permissible for you to reveal his name." Al-Jaᶜfar said, "How shall we mention him?" Al-Hadi said, "Say 'The proof [*al-Hujja*] is from the family of Muhammad."

It seems from al-Kulayni's report that the Imamis considered it al-Hadi's statement as applying to *al-Qa'im*. Moreover, they felt it explained a statement by the eighth Imam, al-Rida, who had said that the body of *al-Qa'im* would not be seen and his name would not be revealed. Perhaps al-Baqir and al-Jawad's interpretation of a Qur'anic verse, referred to on page 12, may be linked with the above two statements. For as we have seen, he stated that an Imam would go into concealment in 260/874, and would later rise a bright, shooting star in the dark night.

On account of the spread of the Imami traditions and the ᶜAlid underground activities, the eleventh Imam, Hasan al-ᶜAskari, was forced to stay in the capital under house-arrest and had to report to the ᶜAbbasid court twice a week. The authorities hoped that through these measures they would be able to prevent the appearance of any danger from the twelfth Imam.

Abdulaziz A. Sachedina

The return of the Mahdi, the Islamic messiah, after a long *ghaybah*, was a direct corollary of the doctrine of *ghaybah*. The occultation, however prolonged, was still a temporary state for the twelfth Imam chosen by God, in order to consolidate his position before he rose as the restorer of Islamic purity. As a consequence, from the early period discussion on the return of the Madhi was an intergral part of the doctine of the *ghaybah*. The messianic role of the Imam was emphasized in his return, when the true Islamic rule would be established. But the obvious inability of the Shiᶜi leaders to fix the time when the events foretold in apocalyptic traditions would be fulfilled led to much confusion over the explanation of the nature of the Mahdi's return. This inability is well reflected in a widely quoted tradition concerning the prohibition of fixing the time of the rise of the twelfth Imam. The difficulties of the Imami theologians in the matter of elucidating the final revolution to be launched by the eschatological Mahdi are evident in the use of the terms for this process of transformation. The most frequently used terms for the Mahdi's reappearance in the early works are *qiyam* (rise), *zuhur* (appearance, emergence), and *khuruj* (coming forth). Bearing in mind the chiliastic hopes of the Shiᶜis, who had ceased to attempt immediate and direct political action, it was obvious that the messianic Imam *al-Qa'im* was expected to "rise" in order to fill the world with justice and equity. But the accentuation of the eschatological role of the Imam as *al-Qa'im al-Mahdi* apparently gave rise to the consideration of a much wider connotation of his function at the End of Time. How was the resurrection (*qiyamah*) going to be related to the "rise" (*qiyam*) of the Mahdi? What was the relationship between his rise and the rising of the dead? Will the Mahdi rise before or after the general resurrection of the dead? All such questions had inevitably arisen during the time when the Imami were engaged in giving final form to the doctrine of the Imamate of the Hidden Imam. The term *raj^cah*, which signifies "the returning to the present state of existence after death, before the Day of Resurrection," elucidated the universal role of the Mahdi as the leader of the Final Days. Early Shi^ci factions, such as the Kaysanis, the Waqifis, and others, had maintained that their messianic Imam had not died but had departed to "return" at some future time. The Imamis explained the doctrine of *raj^cah* as the return of a group of the loyal followers of the Imam to this world before the final resurrection occurs, during the days of Mahdi's rule, or before or after that period. The main function of the *raj^cah* will be to demonstrate to the adherents of the Imami faith the rule of their infallible Imam and to exact revenge from the enemies of the *ahl al-bayt*.

*The Rise (*qiyam*) of the Mahdi*

The tradition of the rise of the Mahdi grew and developed with the disintegration of the caliphate, both Umayyad and ^cAbbasid, and the flowering and disappointment of successive hopes which the Shi^cis had nurtured for the establishment of the ideal rule. The oppression of the caliphs and their administrators added much to the dark events foretold in apocalyptic traditions. On the other hand, the inability of several Shi^ci leaders to fulfill their claimed role as the Mahdi afforded new details and characteristics to the promised (*al-maw^cud*) Mahdi. The Imamis had worked out their own traditions, in which many ideas and beliefs concerning other messianic figures from other religions passed through various channels into their traditions. The impatience of the Shi^cis in their expectation of the rise of the Mahdi is well attested in all the early sources. The crumbling of the ^cAbbasid caliphate was taken as the sign of the reappearance of the Imam, and many other events taking place at that time were identified with the vague prophecies and traditions handed down by the Imams about the days before the Mahdi will appear. Under these circumstances most Imami authors who wrote on the *ghaybah* of the twelfth Imam also included an apocalyptic chapter or two at the end of their works. The purpose of including the apocalyptic material in works on *ghaybah* was twofold: first, it consoled the followers of the Imam with hopes of a final restoration of the Islamic rule; second, it justified the delay in the appearance of the Imam because the signs foretold, of the imminent triumph of the Mahdi, had yet to be fulfilled. The method of the Imami authors in such chapters of their writings usually follows three stages: first, some apocalyptic traditions are reported from the Sunni collections of *hadith*, dealing with the *fitan* (plural of *fitnah*, meaning "trial"), in which seditions and civil strifes of the Final days are mentioned; second, to these are appended details of the political and social turmoil of their own time, in the form of prophecies; and finally, the

prophecies are further expanded and developed to give details about the
final outcome of the *fitan*, namely the establishment of justice and equity in
the world. The prophecies are, in most cases, attributed either to the Prophet himself or to the fifth and sixth Imams, al-Baqir and al-Sadiq, the latter
being the eminent figures of the Imami *hadith* literature. The Imams, being
heirs to the prophetic knowledge, were supposed to have been endowed with
esoteric knowledge (*al-cilm*) which enabled them to prophesy future events,
especially those connected with the destiny of their followers. The notion of
the divine prophetic knowledge of the Imams also represented the Mahdi,
the last in the lines of these heirs, as the only leader destined to bring true
Islamic justice to the oppressed. The question asked time and again concerned the "hour" when the final restoration would take place.

The rise of the Imam was described in numerous traditions from the early
times in Imami history, and the signs related there, as mentioned above, encompassed the contemporary tumultous situation in the form of prophecy.
Consequently, the adherents of the Imam interpreted the time of the rise as
being in the near future. In some traditions attributed to al-Baqir the
number of the years which had to elapse before the emergence of the Mahdi
was specified. For instance, a close associate of al-Baqir by the name of
Abu Hamzah Thabit ibn Dinar recalled in the presence of this Imam what
cAli had said about the end of the period of trial for the Shicis after seventy
years, which would be followed by a period of ease and comfort. Abu Hamzah complained that the period had elapsed without the prophecy being
fulfilled. Al-Baqir explained: "O Thabit, God, the Exalted, had set a time to
the seventy years. But when al-Husayn was killed God's wrath on the inhabitants of the earth became more severe and that period was postponed
up to a hundred and forty years. We had informed you [our close
associates] about this, but you revealed the secret. Now God has delayed
[the appearance of the Mahdi] for a further period for which He has neither
fixed any time nor has He informed us about it, since [He says in the
Qur'an]: 'God blots out and establishes whoever He will; and with Him is
the essence of the Book.'"

The alteration of an earlier prophecy of seventy years, then of one hundred and forty to an indefinite future time implied a change of the earlier
divine determination. In Imami dogmatics this divine alteration is known as
bada'. The doctrine of *bada'* was propounded by the early Shici leaders,
who, in order to justify their failure to establish a rule of justice in spite of
their self-declared prophecies about their victory in a particular political
venture, sought to explain the change in circumstances which caused God to
alter His determination in their own interest. Al-Mukhtar seems to have
been the first person to have mentioned the divine intervention, when, contrary to what God had revealed to him about his victory, he was defeated in

his fight against the superior forces of Mus^cab ibn al-Zubayr. The failure of various Shi^ci revolts was conveniently explained by accepting the *bada'* – the intervention of new circumstances which had caused God to alter His early determination. *Bada'* also explained the delay in the appearance of the rightful successor of the Prophet to deliver the *ummah*, which the prophecies like the one cited above had predicted and which should have taken place at a certain moment. Furthermore, it served to demonstrate the limitations of the Imam's knowledge, more particularly when the succession to the Imamate was contested by more than one person. This happened in the case of Isma^cil, the son of al-Sadiq, who was previously designated as the Imam by his father and who predeceased him. The change in the decision about the Imamate of Isma^cil, designated by the Imam endowed with infallible knowledge, and which was now vested in al-Sadiq's other son, was explained as *bada'*. It implied God's change of mind because of a new consideration, caused by the death of Isma^cil. However, such connotations in the doctrine of *bada'* raised serious questions about the nature of God's knowledge, and indirectly, about the ability of the Imams to prophesy future occurrences. The Imams themselves appear to have denied any such knowledge, as it is attested in the tradition about a man from Fars who is reported to have asked al-Baqir if he knew *al-ghayb* (the hidden knowledge), and the Imam replied: "We apprehend the knowledge (*al-^cilm*) when it is unfolded to us and we do not apprehend when it is taken away from us," and added, "It is the secret of God, the Exalted, which He confides to Gabriel (peace be on him); and Gabriel confides it to Muhammad (peace be on him and his progeny), and Muhammad may confide it to whomever God wishes [to be informed]."

The Imami theologians, in general, had adopted an essentially Mu^ctazilite theology which included their thesis on *bada'*. The Mu^ctazilites related *bada'* to the principle of *aslah* (the most salutary), which states that God does the best for His creatures, and His planning is based on what is most salutary and in the best interest of His slaves. But the Ash^caris rejected the doctrine because it was interpreted as implying a change of mind on the part of God due to what He earlier did not foresee and hence a denial of divine omniscience. The Imamis had to exercise much ingenuity to reconcile the theological contradictions which the doctrine implies, especially assumptions of the occurrence of new determining moments in God's knowledge. Ibn Babuyah, taking *bada'* in the sense of "creation," which connoted abrogation of previous faiths and commands by the creation of the Prophet and his *Shari^cah*, protested against those who charged the Imamis with such a doctrine, and likened them to the Jews, who apparently leveled similar charges against the Muslims. In vindicating the Imamite position Ibn Babuyah cites a tradition in which the sixth Imam, al-Sadiq, says: "He who asserts that God, the Mighty and Glorious, does something new which He did not know before, — from him I dissociate myself," and he added, "He who asserts that God, after doing something, repents concerning it — then he, in our opinion, is a denier of God, the Almighty." But the question of the change concerning the Imamate from Ismaᶜil to Musa al-Kazim, the sons of al-Sadiq, remained unsettled. Ibn Babuyah quotes the Imam al-Sadiq concerning this matter, saying: "Nothing manifested [itself] from [the will of] God, Glory be to Him, concerning any affair like which appeared regarding my son Ismaᶜil when He cut him off by death before me, so that it may be known that he was not the Imam after me."

But a more subtle argument in defense of *bada'*, as maintained by the Imamites, was given by al-Mufid, the *mutakallim*. According to him, the Muslims, in general, took the word *bada'* to mean *naskh* (abrogation), whereas the attribution of such meaning to *bada'* was unnecessary, because the Qur'an uses the term *naskh* when it intends "abrogation" and not *bada'*. The ᶜAdliyyah (Muᶜtazilites), in particular, says al-Mufid, have understood the term in the sense of "increase" (*ziyadah*) and "decrease" (*nuqsan*) of the life term and subsistence as a result of a person's good or bad actions. The Imamites, contends al-Mufid, have used the term *bada'* relying on the textual source (*al-samᶜ*), as related by the Imams, who are the mediators between God and His slaves. This source reveals that God becomes angered or pleased; He loves or becomes astonished. These states cannot be denied in God by any rational being, and as such there is no conflict between the Imamites and other Muslims in the implication of the above revelation about God. The only difference lies in the usage of the term *bada'*. In other words, according to the commentator of al-Mufid, while *naskh* explains abrogation in the matters pertaining to the Religious Law, *bada'* signifies the "occurrence" of the events which were not anticipated beforehand in the matters pertaining to the creation (*takwin*). Thus, al-Mufid concludes, the difference lies in the usage, but not in the meaning of the term *bada'* as implied therein.

Tusi, in his vindication of the tradition in which the prophecy about the seventy and the hundred and forty years occurrs, elucidates the alteration caused by the change of circumstances and the consideration of "the most salutary" for the creatures on the part of God. He takes *bada'* in the sense of "occurrence" (*zuhur*), in addition to its generally accepted meaning of "abrogation," in the instances where such abrogation is permissible (e.g. religious injunctions), or in the sense of "the alteration of circumstances" if the report that recounts *bada'* deals with the creation. Thus, maintains Tusi, it is possible that we may find in God's actions things that we did not anticipate or were simply contrary to what we had expected without knowing the reason behind such occurrences. In a tradition which he cites to support his elucidation, the Imam al-Rida is reported to have said: "How can we inform about the future when the verse of the Qur'an says: 'God blots out and establishes whatsoever He will; and with Him is the essence of the Book.'" But as for the one, says Tusi, who maintains that God's knowledge appears on the realization of the object, he has indeed become a non-believer and is outside the belief in *tawhid* (unity of God). Thus the fulfillment of the prophecy about the Mahdi, which was announced by cAli in the tradition, was delayed for another seventy years because of the martyrdom of Husayn; further *bada'* postponing the matter for an indefinite period was caused by the revealing of the secret which was entrusted to the disciples of the Imam al-Baqir. The secrecy in the matter of the rise of al-Mahdi was a necessary condition on which depended the fulfillment of the prophecy. This leads one to doubt all the traditions which predict the appearance of the Imam. Nevertheless, Tusi distinguishes two types of reports in this connection. First are those reports in which it is impossible for alteration to occur, such as the traditions which recount the attributes of God, the past events, and the promise of God that He will reward His creatures with *al-thawab*. Second are those traditions in which it is possible that due to expediency and change of circumstances alterations may occur. These traditions recount future events. But even among the latter group there are reports that have been known to be certain, and the events mentioned in them are definitely going to be fulfilled, without alteration. That the Mahdi will appear was among the definite occurrences, but fixing of the time was in the hand of God. In an account in which a disciple of al-Sadiq asked him if the Mahdi would appear in his lifetime, the Imam replied that he would have done so, but since the disciples of the Imam al-Baqir had publicized the event, God had delayed the emergence of the *Qa'im* until a favorable time in the future.

As a result of the postponement that may occur until the conditions change to bring about the fulfillment of the victory of the twelfth Imam, fixing the time of the Mahdi's rise was prohibited and those who did (*al-waqqatun*) were declared as liars. Nevertheless, among these accounts were reports that described the events that were bound to happen at the future time, and these formed the subject matter of the sections that dealt with the universal signs (*al-calamat al-ka'ina*) of the Mahdi's rise. The vast literature on this aspect of the Mahdi doctrine shows the aspirations of the followers of the Imami school. The associates of the Imam who wanted to know the set time of the Mahdi's rise more often than not prefaced their questions with the reason for their inquiry, namely "the knowledge [of the time] will console our grieving hearts in the separation from the Imam and will help us to await his appearance in peace." A disciple of Imam al-Baqir related an occasion when he rose to leave the presence of the Imam, and, leaning on the latter's arm, he wept. The Imam asked him the reason for his weeping. The disciple said, "I had hoped to witness the great event [of *al-Qa'im*'s rise] while I still had strength in me." The Imam answered angrily, "Are you [*shi*c*ah*] not satisfied that your enemies kill one another while you sit peacefully in your homes? For when that event shall come, each man among you will be given the strength of forty men. . . .You will be the foundations of the earth and its treasures." The report on the one hand, discourages fixing of any particular time of the appearance of the Mahdi in the near future; on the other hand, the reference to the conflict among the enemies, which reflected the political turmoil of that period, assured that Shicis that the great event—the *zuhur*—would take place. Thus, the knowledge of the time, even in vague terms, of the appearance was necessary to sustain the Shicis during the difficult days of trials and seditions of the *ghaybah*. Consequently, the signs of the *zuhur* related in the form of apocalyptic vision became a source of solace for the Imamis, and every generation, having known these through the literature available to them, expected the *qiyam* to take place during their lifetime.

In spite of the prohibition regarding the fixing of al-Mahdi's emergence at a particular moment, many reports related the day on which the Mahdi would appear. Apparently fixing the day was theologically less problematic than appointing the year, when the Imamites had to resort to the doctrine of *bada'*. As a consequence, many traditions report various days of the year, according to their significance in the Shici piety, when the *zuhur* will take place. The most often cited day in all our sources is the tenth of Muharram, the day of *cAshura'*, which would fall on a Saturday, in one of the odd numbered years of the *hijrah* calendar. The *cAshura'* occupies a significant position in Shici history as well as in its piety. The martyrdom of al-Husayn on this day, in the year A.D. 680, stands as a climax of Shici suffering and passion. As a result, the day generates more than anything else the belief in the redemption of the *ummah* through the sufferings of the son of cAli and Fatimah. It is the promise of God, says a tradition on the authority of al-Sadiq, that He will raise the cry of *al-Qa'im* for those who killed Husayn, and He will take vengeance against those who wronged him. The year by year commemoration of the *cAshura'* by the Shici community indicates not only their sorrow for the afflictions suffered by the family of the Prophet, but also their yearning for the descendant of this Imam to rise against unbearable social circumstances and establish the rule of justice and equity. This is clearly evident in the condolences that the Shicis offer each other on the occasion of *cAshura'*, saying: "May God grant us great rewards for our bereavement caused by the martyrdom of Husayn (peace be on him), and make us among those who will exact vengeance for his blood with His friend (*wali*) the Imam al-Mahdi, from among the descendants of Muhammad (peace be on him)." The martyrdom of Husayn, thus, embodies for the

Shi^cis not only their vision of suffering and revenge, but also their final hope for justice, through the rise of his descendant.

Before the Mahdi rises on the day of *^cAshura'*, his name will be called out on the twenty-third night of the month of Ramadan. This night, in the Shi^ci liturgy, is considered to be the *laylat al-qadr* (The Night of Power in which the Qur'an was revealed), in which the angels descend with the decrees from God about the events that will take place during that year from God to *al-Qa'im*, His *hujja*. Following this call in Ramadan, the Mahdi will rise in the month of Muharram, on the day of *^cAshura'*.

* * *

The question of "near future" in the emergence of the *Qa'im* was in some ways resolved by the emphasis laid on the events that had to occur preceding the *qiyam*. These formed the apocalyptic signs of the appearance of the messianic Imam, such as the rise of the sun from the west, and the occurrence of the solar and lunar eclipses in the middle and the end of the month of Ramadan, respectively, against the natural order of such phenomena. Accompanying these traditions were reports relating the merits of waiting for the appearance of the Imam in patience. Al-Sadiq is reported to have described the merits of the latter in these terms:

> That which causes the servants of God to get closer to Him at the time when people will search for the *hujja* of God, who will not appear for them nor will they know of his whereabouts, will be their faith [in the fact that] neither His *hujja* nor His promise [about the *faraj* (freedom from grief)] have been annulled. At that time they should expect *faraj* day and night, because the most severe thing to cause the wrath of God on His enemies [is the loss of their faith] when they will be looking for him and he will not appear for them. [God] knows that His friends will not doubt, [and] if He knew that they would, He would not have concealed His *hujja* from them even for a moment. This is so only for those who are the most wicked among mankind.

In another tradition the Prophet is reported to have addressed his companions and informed them about the future generations of believers, of whom each individual will be entitled to the reward equal to that of fifty among them. The reason for such *thawab* will be their ability to bear patiently the difficult circumstances caused by the disappearance of their Imam. Thus endurance was far more rewarding than being impatient about the rise of *al-Qa'im*. In the course of a tradition al-Sadiq asked his disciples:

> Why have you fixed your eyes [on the rise of the Qa'im] and why do you wish to expedite [his appearance]? Do you not feel secure now? Is it not so that a man among you leaves his home and having finished his

tasks returns without being forcibly arrested? I wish those who were before you had had [the same security] as you, because [in those days] a person was seized by force and his hands and legs were cut off and he himself was crucified between the palm trees, and cut into two pieces with a saw. [After all this] he used to consider [this torture] as expiation of his sins." [Then he read his passage from the Qur'an:] "Or do you think you would enter the garden while yet the state of those who have passed away before you have not come upon you; distress and affliction befell them and they were shaken violently so that the Apostle and those who believe with him said, 'When will the help of God come?' Now surely the help of God is nigh. (II:214).

These traditions indicate the frustration of the Shiᶜis at the delay in the appearance of the Mahdi. But the consequences of the *qiyam* were obvious to them, since they were repeatedly reminded that the rise of the Mahdi would be no less than the sword and death under the shadow of the sword of *al-Qa'im*, the Master of the Sword (*sahib al-sayf*). Hence, Abu Basir and other close associates of the Imams al-Baqir and al-Sadiq were often asked by the latter: "Why are you in haste about the rise of *al-Qa'im?*"

Another remarkable theme in these apocalyptic traditions is consideration about the place where the Imam will rise, whenever he does. Most of the traditions that report the rise on the day of ᶜ*Ashura* also mention the place of *zuhur*. Since the significance of the ᶜ*Ashura* is tremendous in the pious literature of the Imamis, one would have expected Karabala, the battlefield of Husayn's martyrdom, to have been designated as the most likely place for the messianic Imam to rise and commence his mission of conquering the evil forces obstructing his ultimate establishment of the kingdom of God. There are traditions which describe the Mahdi's triumphant entry into Kufah, from where he will dispatch troops to the sources about the Imam's residence after his rise, according to a tradition cited by Majlisi, Kufah will be his place of residence, the mosque of Kufah his seat of government, and the mosque of Sahla, in the vicinity of Kufah, his treasury. Furthermore, since most of the traditions are concerned with the details of *al-Qa'im's* revolution in Kufah, it is assumed to be his capital. Historically, this was also ᶜAli's seat of government, whose rule is idealized in the Shiᶜi writings. The importance of Kufah is reflected in the tradition which says: "The Hour will not commence until all the believers have assembled in Kufah." Karbala will be joined with Kufah by digging a canal from behind the shrine of Husayn which will provide water for the people in Kufah. But the *zuhur* proper will take place in Mecca, the birthplace of Islam. That new order will restore the purity of Islam as taught by the Prophet and the Imams. The order will carry within itself the religio-socio-political aspects of the pristine Islam. Thus the commencement of the appearance of the Mahdi in Mecca, more specifically in the Ka^cbah, between the Rukn and Maqam, the two holy spots in the precinct, not only increases the significance of the twelfth Imam's mission, but also preserves the symbolic unity of the *ummah* by launching it in Mecca. This is the import of the pharse *mahdi al-anam* — the Mahdi of the People — the title on which the Imamite scholars placed great emphasis during the early years of the Complete Occultation.

Both Kufah and Karbala hold an extremely elevated position in Imamite history, because of their being the places where ^cAli and Husayn, the two symbols of opposition to the unjust acts committed by the Umayyads, died as martyrs. Numerous traditions describe the rise of the *Qa'im* in the same manner: When *al-Qa'im* rises he will proceed toward Kufah. The absence of any mention of the rise commencing in Mecca, which seems to have been inserted in some traditions, corroborates the argument that those traditions which emphasize Kufah are the early versions of those reports which accentuate Mecca as the starting point of *al-Qa'im's* rise, especially following the prolonged occultation of the twelfth Imam, which also necessitated the accentuation of his eschatological role as the *mahdi al-maw^cud*. While it was impossible to find a more emotionally inspiring and significant day than ^c*Ashura* in the whole history of Islamic religion which would minimize the highly Shi^ci connotation in the rise of the Mahdi, Mecca held symbolic precedence over Kufah and even Karbala, as the place from which the Mahdi would emerge as the messianic leader of the Islamic peoples. Significantly, the people of Mecca (i.e. non-Imamites) are asserted to be the first group on earth who would be called upon by the Mahdi to pay allegiance to him. The ninth Imam, Muhammad al-Jawad, informed his associates of this by saying: "I see [in future] that *al-Qa'im* is standing between Rukn and Maqam, on a Saturday, the day of ^c*Ashura*, and Gabriel is standing in front of him calling out, "Alegiance belongs to God. Indeed, he (*al-Qa'im*) will fill the earth with justice as it is filled with tyranny and wickedness.'"

In a long tradition reported on the authority of al-Mufaddal ibn ^cUmar, one of the most eminent and close associates of the Imams al-Sadiq and al-Kazim, it is related that al-Mufaddal had once asked al-Sadiq to inform him about the *qiyam* of *al-Qa'im al-Mahdi*. The sixth Imam said: "I see him that he has entered the city of Mecca wearing the apparel of the Prophet and a yellow turban on his head. He has put on the patched sandals of the Prophet and the latter's stick in his hands, with which he is directing some goats before him. In this manner he will enter the Ka^cbah, without anyone recognizing him. He will appear as a youth." The Imam then proceeds to give details about the Mahdi's appearance. He will, relates the Imam, emerge alone, and having proceeded toward the Ka^cbah, he will remain there until it is dark at night. When the people fall asleep, Gabriel and Michael will descend on earth in the company of groups of angels. At that time Gabriel will speak to the Mahdi: "O my Master, whatever you say is acceptable and your commands will be carried out." The Imams will stroke Gabriel's face and say: "Praise be to God whose promise concerning us is fulfilled, and who appointed us as heirs to the earth and we will settle in the Paradise wherever we wish to do so. Verily, what a recompense for those who act according to His injunctions!" Then he will stand between the Rukn and Maqam and in a loud, clear voice he will announce: "Oh the chiefs and the people who are close to me! O you were preserved on earth by God in order to help me when I emerge! Come toward me to obey me!" His voice will reach these people, who at that time will assemble close to him between the Rukn and Maqam, having arrived from the east and the west, from their places of worship and sleep, after hearing the call from the Mahdi. After that God will command the light to raise itself in the form of pillars, rising from earth upward to the heavens, so that the inhabitants of the earth will see it. The light will enrapture the believers, who will not know that the *Qa'im* has appeared. But when the morning sets in all these believers, who will reach three hundred and thirteen in number (of which fifty, according to one tradition, will be women) — the number of those who had fought on the Prophet's side in the Battle of Badr — will be assembled in the presence of the *Qa'im*.

At this point al-Mufaddal asks the Imam al-Sadiq if those seventy-two persons who were killed with Husayn in Karbala will rise with those three hundred and thirteen believers. Al-Sadiq says that only Husayn among the martyrs of Karbala will rise, wearing a black turban on his head, with twelve thousand *shi*ᶜ*ah* of ᶜAli. Then al-Mufaddal asks if people will pay allegiance to Husayn before the appearance and the rise of *al-Qa'im* with the latter. The Imam says: "Any allegiance before the rise of *al-Qa'im* is disbelief, hypocrisy and fraud. May God curse anyone who receives or pays allegiance [before the rise of *al-Qa'im*)." Al-Sadiq then proceeds to describe the manner in which the twelfth Imam will receive allegiance. He will lean his back on the wall of Kaᶜbah and stretch out his arm. There will be light emanating from his hand, and he will say: "This is the hand of God; it is from His direction and through His command," and will read this verse of the Qur'an: "Surely, those who swear allegiance to you do but swear allegiance to God; the hand of God is above their hands. Therefore whoever breaks [his faith], he breaks it only to the injury of his own soul" (XLVIII: 10).

The first being to kiss his hand as a sign of paying allegiance will be Gabriel, who will be followed by all other angels and the noble ones among the *jinns*, who will, in turn, be followed by the other beings of high rank. The inhabitants of Mecca will exclaim and ask about this person and those who are with him and will inquire about the sign they will have seen in the previous night, the like of which they will not have witnessed before. Some among them will tell each other that he is the man with the goats. Some others will say: "Look, do you recognize any of these persons accompanying him?" The people will say that besides the four persons from Mecca and the other four from Medina, who are so and so, they do not recognize any others.

All this will take place at the beginning of sunrise on that day. When the sun is up, a caller from the direction of the sunrays (i.e. east) will call out in eloquent Arabic, which will be heard by all the inhabitants of the heavens and earth. The announcement will be: "O inhabitants of the Universe! This is the Mahdi from among the descendants of Muhammad," and the voice will address him by the name and patronym of his forefather, the Prophet, and will relate him through his father Hasan al-ᶜAskari to Husayn. After this introduction the voice will ask the people to pay allegiance to him in order to be saved and will warn them against opposing him, since their opposition will lead them astray. At that all the angels, the *jinns*, and the chiefs of the people, in that order, will kiss his hand, saying: "We heard the call and we are obeying." There will be no soul on earth on that day who will not hear this announcement. Those who are far in distant lands will cross the lands and seas, will arrive in Mecca, and will relate to each other the call they all had heard.

At sunset on that day someone will call out from the west side, saying: "O inhabitants of the world, your lord by the name of ᶜUthman ibn al-ᶜAnbatha, the Umayyad, among the descendants of Yazid, the son of Muᶜawiyah, has appeared in the dry desert of Palestine. Go and pay allegiance to him so that you might be saved." At that all those who will have paid allegiance to the Mahdi will refute his call, declaring it to be false, and will reply to the announcer by saying: "We heard the call and we are disobeying." Those who will have some doubts in their minds about the appearance of the Mahdi, including those who disbelieved him and the hypocrites, will be lead astray with this second call. At that time the *Qa'im*, leaning on the wall of the Kaᶜbah will say:

> Truly, anyone who wishes to see Adam and Seth, should know that I am that Adam and Seth. Anyone who wishes to see Noah and his son Shem, should know that I am that Noah and Shem. Anyone who wishes to see Abraham and Ishmael, should know that I am Abraham and Ishmael. Anyone who wishes to see Moses and Joshua should know that I am that Moses and Joshua. Anyone who wishes to see Jesus and Simon, should know that I am that Jesus and Simon. Anyone wishing to see Muhammad and ᶜAli, the Amir of the Believers, should know that I am that Muhammad and ᶜAli. Anyone who wishes to see al-Hasan and al-

Husayn, should know that I am that al-Hasan and al-Husayn. Anyone
who wishes to see the Imams from the descendants of al-Husayn, should
know that I am those pure Imams. Accept my call and assemble near me
so that I will inform you whatever you wish to know. Anyone who has
read the heavenly scriptures and divine scrolls, will now hear them from me.

Thus he will begin to read that which God had revealed to Adam and Seth.
The followers of Adam and Seth will acknowledge the authenticity of the
Mahdi's recitation and will confirm that he read and taught even those sections which were omitted or distorted. Then the Mahdi will read the books
revealed to Noah and Abraham, and will also read the Torah, the Gospel,
and the Psalms; the followers of all these scriptures will acknowledge the
truthfulness of the Mahdi and will attest that the Mahdi knew the original
scriptures before they were distorted or altered. Then the Mahdi will read
the Qur'an, and the followers of the Qur'an will say: "By God, this is the
true Qur'an that was revealed unto the Apostle of God and nothing has been
omitted from it and no changes or distortions have taken place."

Al-Mufaddal goes on to ask about al-Qa'im's program in Mecca. Al-
Sadiq replies that the twelfth Imam, having invited the Meccans to respond
to his call and they having accepted, will appoint a person from his family
as his deputy in Mecca, and he himself will move towards Medina. Al-
Mufaddal then asks what the Imam will do to the Ka°bah. Al-Sadiq answers
that the Mahdi will demolish the Ka°bah and will rebuild it as it was
originally done during the time of Adam, will raise it as Abraham and
Ishmael had done, in accordance with the will of God. He will destroy
anything built by the oppressive caliphs and their representatives, in Mecca,
Medina, Iraq, and other places, so that no sign of their wicked rule will remain on earth. He will destroy the mosque of Kufah also and will rebuild it
on its original foundation. Al-Mufaddal asks if al-Qa'im will reside in Mecca. The Qa'im, says the Imam, will not remain in Mecca as he will have appointed his deputy for that city. However, when the Meccans see that the
Mahdi has left, they will attack his deputy and will kill him. The Mahdi will
return and the people of Mecca will plead guilty and repent for their act of
transgression. The Qa'im will exhort them with sermons and the fear of
God. Subsequently, he will appoint a Meccan to represent him and will
leave the city once again. The Meccans will treat this person the same way as
they had done before and will kill this person. On learning this the Mahdi
will send a group of his helpers among the jinns to Mecca with instructions
to kill everyone except those who are steadfast in their belief. The Mahdi
will declare to his followers that had it not been for the consideration about
the mercy of God, which encompasses everything and of which he is the
manifestation on earth, he too would have returned to Mecca, whose
residents have cut themselves off from the mercy of God by committing evil

deeds. The troops of the Imam will return to Mecca; and then, al-Sadiq declares solemnly, not a single person among every hundred or even a thousand will escape this punishment.

The Mahdi will then enter Medina, where he will have such status that the believers will be pleased to witness it. On the other hand, the adversaries of the Imam will resent it. At this point al-Sadiq informs al-Mufaddal about a strange occurrence connected with the first two caliphs, Abu Bakr and cUmar, who are buried beside the Prophet. The whole episode, as reported by al-Mufaddal, reveals the Shici polemics against the Sunnis and the ultimate fate of the two caliphs who usurped the right of the *ahl al-bayt*. The Mahdi will then proceed to Kufa, which will be his capital. On that day, all the believers will be assembled in that city and the surrounding areas, which will expand immeasurably to the neighborhood of Karbala, to accommodate all the Shicis. Karbala that day will be the frequenting place of the angels and the believers.

The *hadith* of al-Mufaddal continues to describe the condition of Baghdad at the time and relates the rise of a *sayyid* among the descendants of Hasan in the land of the Daylamites. The *sayyid* will announce in a loud, audible voice the appearance of the one whose prolonged occultation had disappointed the Shicis: "O people, respond to his call which is coming from the direction of the Prophet's grave." The brave and faithful people of Taliqan (in Khurasan) will respond to this call by riding their swift horses and carrying weapons. On their journey toward Kufah, they will fight the enemies of God and wipe them out, until they enter the city and settle there. When the actual news about the appearance of the Mahdi reaches the *sayyid* and his disciples, the latter will ask about the identity of the person who is said to have alighted in Kufah. The *sayyid* will ask them to follow him, and together they will go and meet with the Mahdi. He will ask the Mahdi to show them the symbols of the Prophet in his possession, such as the Prophet's ring, his coat of mail, sword, and so on, including the Qur'an, which was compiled by cAli. The Mahdi will show them three things, and they will all pay allegiance to him, except for the forty thousand Zaydis, who will have their own Qur'an and who will refuse to acknowledge the Mahdi. The latter will try to persuade them for three consecutive days, but they will persist in their rejection of him, so he will order them to be killed.

Following this the troops will be sent to Damascus to arrest al-Sufyani, the Umayyad messiah. The soldiers of the Mahdi will seize him and behead him on a stone. This will be the time for Husayn to "return" with his twelve thousand *shicah*, in addition to the seventy two persons who were killed with him in Karbala. This will be the illuminated *rajcah*, to be distinguished from the *rajcah*, to be discussed below. Following Husayn, cAli will return and take his place in a huge tent, which will stand on four pillars, of which one will be in Najaf, one in the precinct of the *ka^cbah*, one on the hill of Safa near the Ka^cbah, and the other in Medina. The earth and the heavens will be illuminated. The secrets of each person will be revealed. The mothers who will be nursing their infants will abandon them in fear. At that time the Prophet, with his companions, both the *Ansar* and the *Muhajirun*, and those who believed in him and acknowledged his prophecy and sacrificed their lives for him, will return. With the believers, those who falsified his mission and doubted it will also return so that proper vengeance for their disbelief can be exacted from them.

This is perhaps the longest tradition ever recorded in the Imami *hadith* literature. But before we continue to describe the rule of the Mahdi following his *zuhur*, as related in al-Mufaddal's account, we should turn to the consideration of the doctrine of *raj^cah* (return) of the Imams, to which al-Sadiq alludes in al-Mufaddal's *hadith*.

* * *

The Rule of *al-Qa'im al-Mahdi:*

> "Hasten up, hasten up O son of the Virgin (*al-batul*, the title of Fatimah; i.e. the Mahdi from among her descendants through Husayn), Thy Shi^ca are ever in mourning garb, At the lateness of the coming of thy rule."

These are the lines from the famous *ghadiriyyah* epic, in which the twelfth Imam is called upon to bring an end to the mourning of Husayn by establishing his rule. These lines, which also form an integral part of the most repeated Shi^ci payers, "May God hasten release from suffering through his [Mahdi's] rise," reflect the aspiration of the Shi^cis for the rule of "justice and equity," embodied in the promise of the appearance of the Mahdi. Under such a rule the loyal shi^ca of the twelve Imams will find their exalted position, and under the just government of al-Qa'im they will be able to share the blessings of a world free from "oppression and tyranny." The main purpose of the *zuhur* is to humble or destroy the evil forces of this world and establish the fully just Islamic rule. Indeed, the establishment of the rule of the twelfth successor of the Prophet is reckoned as the climax of Imamite history—a history full of struggle and radical social protest; a history of sufferings, afflictions, and the martyrdom of its leaders and loyal adherents, who, in the course of centuries and under unbearable social and political circumstances, persisted in their faith in the *faraj* (freedom from grief) through the emergence of the messianic leader. The *faraj* depicts the function of the Mahdi, namely to establish justice and redeem the whole world from oppression, suffering, and war to introduce a period of spiritual and physical bliss. Hence al-Mahdi's rule personifies the chiliastic vision of the Shiᶜis, who believe that all their dreams will come true "when God will lay his (al-Mahdi's) [blessed] hand on the heads of the people, through which He will bring their intellects together." The Shiᶜis will, as a result of this blessing, be able to use the accumulated experience of mankind to remove imperfections in their society. As a successor of the Prophet, who held both spiritual and temporal power in the early Islam, Mahdi was the only leader who could accomplish the creation of an ideal Islamic society. Thus the foundation of the Shiᶜi piety is the acknowledgement of the Imam who can ensure the *faraj* through his rise, and in whom culminates the peculiarly Shiᶜi vision of Islamic history.

We have seen in al-Muffadal's tradition the overall significance of Kufah as *al-Qa'im's* seat of government and the subjugation of the east and west by the troops of the Imam, in order to establish the kingdom of God. The Mahdi will rule from Kufah assisted by three hundred and thirteen of his close associates. The first thing that will occur under the rule of the Mahdi will be the Islamicizing of the whole world. The followers of all other religions will embrace Islam and profess faith in one God, just as He has said in the Qur'an: ". . . to Him submits (*aslama*) whoever is in the heavens and the earth, willingly and unwillingly, and to Him shall they be returned" (III:82). Consequently, there will be no place on earth where testimony, "I bear witness that there is no god but God" and "I bear witness that Muhammad is the Apostle of God," and will not be heard. The faith that will be presented by the *Qa'im* will be the pure religion of Muhammad, Islam without any omission or innovation. Al-Baqir is reported to have said, "I can see your religion mixed with blood [in the future]. No one will be able to return to its pristine purity except a man among the *ahl al-bayt* who will distribute gifts twice a year. . . .In his time the knowledge of religion will be spread to such an extent that a woman, sitting in her home, will be able to give rulings according to the Book and the teachings of the Prophet." In another tradition, ᶜAbdullah ibn ᶜAta', an associate of the fifth and sixth Imams, asked al-Baqir regarding the manner in which *al-Qa'im* will proceed among the people. He said: "He will raze that which existed before him just as the Prophet did (before him) [when he began his mission], and will revive Islam once again." However, *al-Qa'im* will not follow the Prophet's example of gentleness and flexibility and winning over the people by uniting them; rather, the *Qa'im* will kill, in accordance with the text of the testament (*wasiyyah*), which each Imam, beginning with ᶜAli to the Mahdi, was required to follow. He will also not follow the example of ᶜAli, who adopted the path of forgiveness and benevolence in his dealings with the people, because he knew that there would follow after his death the rule of tyrants who would oppress his *shiᶜah*. The *Qa'im*, on the other hand, is assured that his *shiᶜah* will not ever be dominated by wicked rulers, and consequently he will fight with his enemies and put them into prison. *Al-Qa'im* will rise with a new authority, a new Book, and a new order, which will be severe on the Arabs (his main supporters, according to some traditions, will be severe on the Arabs (his main supporters, according to some traditions, will be the non-Arabs). His state of affairs will be the sword (he is known as the *sahib al-sayf*, Master of the Sword), and he will not accept repentance from anyone, nor will the rebuke of his adversaries deter him from carrying out the command of God. The Islamicizing and restoring of the purity of the faith will be visible throughout the domination of *al-Qa'im*. In the mosque of Kufah there will be tents pitched, and the followers of the Mahdi will learn to recite the Qur'an the way it was revealed unto the Prophet. The *qibla* (direction of the prayer) of the mosque will also be restored—an indication that the previous rulers had distorted even the direction of the prayer, in addition to all other atrocities committed against the *ummah*. The banner of the Prophet, which was spread for the last time in the Battle of the Camel (36/656–657) by ᶜAli, will once again be spread by *al-Qa'im*, as a symbol of the ᶜAlid victory and hegemony.

The above description gives immeasurable importance to the Mahdi's role as the restorer of faith which was sometimes attacked by the Sunnites, as appears in the attempt to reply to such criticisms in the Shiᶜi sources. Al-Tabarsi (d. 549/1154–1155) has mentioned one of these objections in his biography of the twelve Imams. The objection reads: All the Muslims are of the belief that there will be no prophet after Muhammad, the seal of the prophets. But the Shiᶜis believe that when the *Qa'im* rises, he will not accept the *jizyah* (poll tax) from the Peoples of the Book; anyone over twenty years of age who does not know his religious obligations will be put to death. The mosque and other religious edifices will be demolished, and the Mahdi will judge according to the method of David, who did not require witnesses. All such traditions, assert the critics, are recounted in the Shiᶜi books, which are tantamount to the abrogation of the Islamic religion and invalidation of the religious injunctions. In fact, they say, such beliefs require maintaining the continuation of prophethood after Muhammad, although the term "prophet" is not used for the Mahdi.

Al-Tabarasi denies having seen any reports about the non-acceptance of the *jizyah* from the Peoples of the Book, or of the killing of the youths who did not know their religious obligations. As for the demolishing of the mosques and other religious buildings, argues al-Tabarsi, it may be that these buildings will have been constructed against the requirements of piety; the precedent of such an act is provided by the Prophet, who ordered the mosque of al-Dirar in Medina to be demolished because it was constructed by the hypocrites to disunite the community. The administration of justice according to David's method, says al-Tabarsi, is not substantiated in the Shiᶜi writings. If one accepts such traditions, they can be interpreted thus: In those cases when the Imam has the required information personally, he can judge relying on it, because Islamic Law stipulates that whenever the Imam or the ruler ascertains the truth of the matter, it is necessary to give the ruling according to his own information without requiring witnesses. This provision does not abrogate religion. Moreover, the traditions about not accepting the *jizyah* or not requiring witnesses, provided they are proved to be authentic, cannot render religion abrogated, because abrogation can take place only when the reason for abrogation follows the ruling about abrogation, and not simultaneously with it. If both reason and ruling for an abrogation occur simultaneously, then the former cannot be considered as abrogating the latter, however contradictory they might appear in meaning. It must be remembered, says al-Tabarsi, that the information about *al-Qa'im* was given by the Prophet himself, who exhorted the Muslims to follow his commands. As a result, it is incumbent upon the *ummah* to obey him and carry out his orders. When the *ummah* does so, even if *al-Qa'im's* orders might appear to contradict the earlier injunctions, they do not abrogate Islam, as argued above. On the contrary, they are the original, unadulterated rulings of Islam.

There is no consensus in the Imamite sources on the duration of the Mahdi's rule. According to one report, al-Baqir is said to have related that the Mahdi will rule for three hundred and nine years. This is the number of years the Companions of the Cave (*al-kahf*), as mentioned in the *sura* eighteen of the Qur'an, slept in the cave. During these years, adds the Imam, the rule of justice and equity will spread in the world. Another tradition mentions al-Sadiq saying that the Mahdi will rule for seven yeras, "each year of his rule being equivalent to your seventy yeras." In al-Mufaddal's tradition the sixth Imam was asked about the length of the period of the Mahdi's rule. The Imam cited the following passage of the Qur'an: "The day [when] it (the appointed term) arrives, no soul shall speak but by His leave; then [some] of them shall be wretched and [some] blessed. Then as for those who shall be wretched, they shall be in the (Hell) fire, for them therein shall be sighing and groaning. They shall abide therein so long as the heavens and earth endure, except [as] what wills your Lord; verily your Lord is the [Mighty] Doer of whatsoever He wills. And as for those who will be blessed, they shall be in the garden (of Paradise) abiding therein so long as the heavens and earth endure, except [as] what your Lord will: [it will be] a gift incessant" (XI:105–08). The Imam added, "After that there will be the day of resurrection," meaning there was no time limit to the rule of justice as established by al-Mahdi. According to a tradition reported by Ibn Babuyah, Abu

Basir, a close associate and a narrator of numerous Imamite traditions, once asked al-Sadiq: 'O son of the Prophet, I have heard from your father that there will be twelve Mahdis after *al-Qa'im*." The Imam said, "However, my father said 'twelve Mahdis' and not 'twelve Imams.' But they will be a group among our *shi'ah*, who will call people to friendship with us and inform them about our rights." Tusi reports a variant of this tradition on the authority of the Prophet, who informed 'Ali on the night before his death about the twelve Imams who will follow him and the twelve Mahdis who will follow the twelfth Imam.

Al-Mufid affirms that there will be no government subsequent to that of *al-Qa'im*, except that reported in some traditions in which there is an allusion to the government of the descendants of *al-Qa'im*, if God wills so. But even these traditions, cautions al-Mufid, are not established as authentic. Most of the reports, clarifies al-Mufid, confirm that the Mahdi of the *ummah* will die forty days prior to the day of resurrection. In those forty days chaos and general confusion will prevail, which will be followed by the signs of the resurrection of the dead and the Day of Judgment." And of course, God knows best what is going to happen."

In another account al-Baqir told one of his disciples, Jabir ibn Yazid al-Ju'fi, that a man from the *ahl al-bayt* would rule for three hundred and nine years after his death. Jabir asked, "When will this happen?" Al-Baqir said, "After the death of *al-Qa'im*." Jabir went on to ask, "How long will *al-Qa'im* remain in the world?" The Imam replied, "Nineteen years from the time of his rise until his death." Jabir asked if his death would be followed by chaos. The Imam said, "Yes, for fifty years. At that time the Imam al-Muntasir (al-Husayn, as mentioned at the end of the tradition) will return and exact revenge for himself and his followers. . . ."

The above reports indicate the difficulty of determining the length of time for which al-Mahdi will rule. The confusion also appears to have been intensified because of the tradition about the *raj'ah*, which was the rule of the Imams before the day of the resurrection, and because of the eschatological role of the Mahdi before the Day of Judgment. Some later Imamite scholars have attempted to interpret these traditions in two ways.

First, the rule of the twelve Mahdis means the rule of the Prophets and the rest of the Imams, with the exception of *al-Qa'im*, when they "return" to the world and rule in succession. The term Mahdi, according to these scholars, has been used for all the Imams; *al-Qa'im*, according to some reports, will also return to the world after his death. All these variant traditions together afford explanation for different versions of the time periods of al-Mahdi's rule.

Second, these Mahdis might well be the successors of *al-Qa'im*, who, during the period of *raj'ah* when other Imams will be ruling, would call the people to the path of God, so that the world might not remain void of the *hujjah* of God. The successors of the Prophet and the Imams are also considered *hujjah*.

There is no doubt that the doctrine of *raᶜjah* was a subsequent development in the Mahdi doctrine, as indicated in the difficulty of disentangling confusing reports on the two aspects of the doctrine: the *rajᶜah* and the *zuhur*, especially the former. The function of the twelfth Imam as the Mahdi during the *zuhur* was sufficient to save the whole of humanity and the entire creation from degeneration. The rule of the Mahdi alone will establish the era of absolute prosperity which will obtain until the final resurrection takes place and the cycle of creation is completed. Al-Mahdi will thus accomplish the return of creation to its original purity. The Imamite aspirations are best voiced in the following lines composed by the Shiᶜi poet Diᶜbil ibn ᶜAli al-Khuzaᶜi (b. 148/765–66):

> Were it not for him, who I hope will come today or tomorrow, my sighing for them could cut my heart.
> No doubt an Imam will rise—an Imam who will govern according to the name of God and the Blessings.
> He will distinguish the false and the truthful among us; he will requite with favors and punishments.

Chapter Three

Martyrdom

During the past decade, the martyrdom of Husayn and the tragedy of Karbala have found greater political significance in the works of Shi^ci modernists. Moreover, Western scholars and journalists increasingly have interpreted the Shi^ci doctrine of martyrdom in political and military terms. The recent decades have witnessed a major transformation in the popular image of Imam Husayn. He is no longer that idol whose jihad *was once considered a unique cosmic and ahistorical event, divorced from the socio-political realities of the day, like the crucifixion of Jesus. Rather, in the works of the modernists, he has become an active revolutionary role-model, whose uprising against injustice was a historical event, both commencing and setting the example for all battles between good and evil that constitute the dialectics of history.*

Much confusion, however, persists regarding the image of Husayn in popular Shi^ci culture as well as the extent and nature of the changes that his image has undergone. In this section, first Abdulaziz A. Sachedina will elaborate upon the place of martyrdom in Shi^ci ethos, then Hamid Enayat will outline the essence of the transformation in the traditional image of Husayn in Shi^ci modernist thought. Excerpts are taken from ASIHCN, *pages 196–206, and* MIPT, *181–91, respectively.*

Abdulaziz A. Sachedina

The Imam Husayn's struggle to uphold the spiritual and moral values of Islam becomes comprehensive when seen in the light of the entire struggle of Abrahamic traditions to assert the oneness of God (*tawhid*). In other words, the assertion of monotheism which is pre-eminently attributed to Abraham in the Qur'an (XII: 37–40), calls for the act of submitting to God (*islam*), which means accepting a spiritual and moral responsibility to uphold the standards of action held to have God's authority. Hence, accepting Islam and its challenge meant that Muslims opened themselves to vast new considerations of what life might mean when a person 'submits' to God. So construed, their act of 'submission' could be defined as commitment to the Abrahamic faith enunciated by the Prophet, Muhammad, which required to establishing an intensely creative person as committed to the social and juridical consequences of being a Muslim. Consequently, adherence to Islam presented an opportunity to build a new order of social life such as the Islamic vision had more and more obviously demanded. The 'submission' to God demanded, in the first place, a personal devotion to spiritual and moral purity; but, personal piety and purity implied a just social behaviour. Sooner or later, this challenge of Abrahamic faith was bound to require the creation of a just social order as the natural outgrowth and context of the personal piety and purity (*taqwa*) it required, because Islam is never satisfied with mere exposition of its ideals, but constantly seeks the means to implement them. Obviously, when no Muslim could have remained neutral to this challenge of Islam, how could the Imam Husayn have tolerated a movement spearheaded by the Umayyads which attacked the ideals and principles of Islamic social order and suggested an alternative sort of sanction for their behaviour and especially for social leadership.

It is therefore pertinent to understand the Imam Husayn's revolution within the historical context created by the individual's relationship to God and maintained by the aspirations for the creation of just public order prevalent in the Muslim community as a whole and given form in their corporate life. By regarding the events of Karbala as subordinate, some Muslim scholars, and following them, some Westerners, have tried to reduce the exceptional significance of the struggle of the Imam Husayn and its impact upon the course of subsequent Islamic history. Undoubtably, without full reference to the general socio-political milieu which developed following the death of the Prophet in the year 632, and which culminated in the events of Karbala, the day of *cAshura'* appears to be a mere tragedy without any meaning and significance for posterity. The Imam Husayn's revolution cannot be isolated from the general historical context of the Islamic challenge within which the Imam and his followers acted to make the purpose of the revolution explicit. In other words, it is impossible to appreciate the purpose behind the Imam Husayn's and his followers' martyrdoms without first understanding the historical circumstances that called upon him to defend the spiritual and moral heritage of Islam.

This is indeed a difficult task, because it is usually considered an impossible undertaking to separate two consecutive events in the history of human society. The explanation of this difficulty lies in the gradual nature of change of factors that demonstrate one historical period from another. Moreover, it is even more difficult to demonstrate the end of one period of a society and the beginning of another when two consecutive periods are required to be examined in order to determine the subsequent changes. It is this difficulty adumbrated in sensitive consequences to one's cherished notions about a particular period in Islamic history, especially the early days following the death of the Prophet, which has caused Muslim scholars in general to deviate from the responsibility of preserving their scholarly integrity in treating the history of the Imam Husayn. Thus the imperative need to properly demarcate the period when the Muslim community began to witness their leaders' obvious deviation from the fundamental teachings of Islam, in order to fully discuss the Imam Husayn's reponse, has been ignored by many Muslim historians. It is only through objective evaluation of the early period of Islamic history that it becomes possible to understand the stance the Imam Husayn took in the year 60–61/679–680. However, for a number of Muslim historians, who have generally failed to point out the obvious deviations from the Islamic revelation in the period that followed the Prophet's death, the challenge lies in revising their tendentious historical presentation of that early period, which has been slow in coming forth. Nevertheless, a consensus among all historians belonging to various schools of Muslim thought has emerged that makes it possible, at least, to fix the period of these deviations from Islamic norms, if not earlier, then, from the beginning of the second half of the period of cUthman's caliphate (644–656 A.D.).

cUthman's caliphate typifies a period that caused general political and religious patterns to drift away from the standards that were provided by Islam. Indeed, it became apparent that the new currents in the Muslim community around this period which went towards creating new forms in the realm of public order were the result of these currents interacting with the mentality of the group that held power in the society, namely, the Umayyads, who had very little concern for the ideals of Islam. As a result, it is not sufficient merely to discuss these new forms at that time by limiting ourselves to the evaluation of the external forms only; rather, it is necessary to embark upon a serious discussion of the factors that created these forms and the way they affected the society and the personages who molded the history of this period. Such inquiry remains legitimate public concern, which puts the event of *ᶜAshura'* in its proper perspective. The main question, then, that we intend to treat in this paper is: What had happened to Islam during this period that the Imam Husayn felt it necessary to take upon himself to undo the harm the Umayyads were causing to it?

Islam conceives of human nature in terms of both its spiritual and physical needs, and as such it is never content with mere exposition of its ideals, but constantly seeks the means to implement them. The Qur'an gave Muslims every reason to wish for a government and a society which would be based on the 'noble paradigm' set by the political and the ideal sides of the Prophet's mission on earth. However, major political undertakings of the early Muslim leaders inevitably demonstrated a lack of committment to the 'noble paradigm'. Since ᶜUthman's time the ruling class had used Islam more or less as a badge of identity. Whereas Islamic ideals carried a responsible and egalitarian social committment, these rulers were engaged in creating a privileged class of a small elite tied together by common Arab heritage. The implications of such a deviation from the Islamic ideal became discernable to those Muslims who were most serious about the moral and political responsibilities which an acceptance of the Islamic faith entailed. The most obvious implication of reference to the Arabic heritage in ordering public and private life meant that Islam became the envied badge of a favored ruling class of Arabs who happened to be bound together by Islam. As such, that would have made Islam an Ishmaelism (as the Arabs were the descendants of Ishmael, the son of Abraham), analogous to the Israelism of the Jews, in which converts could enter as members of the community only on the basis of their having descended from Abraham. Despite the comprehensiveness of the Islamic ideal and its universalistic direction, the exalting of the Arabs as being of the line of Ishmael and producing an ethnically bound community became part of the political program of the Umayyads from the second half of ᶜUthman's caliphate. The most important consequence of this political mission, which gradually became clearer, was that Muslims were not treated on an equal basis as prescribed by the Qur'anic dictum regarding the 'brotherhood of all believers', and the Prophet's recommendation to the Muslims to renounce all conflict based on geneology. On the contrary, the great families of Medina who descended from the Prophet's close associates were accorded 'social priority' (*tafdil*), and the sense of the inviolability of the Arab tribesmen was reinforced against the Qur'anic requirement that a Muslim, regardless of his ethnic affiliation, had to be accorded that personal liberty and dignity.

Consistent with this anti-egalitarian attitude of the early Muslim leaders was the development of elaborate forms of urban luxury and social distinction. The fruits of conquest, in the form of the booty and the revenue from the conquered lands, had created an unequal distribution of wealth among all Arab Muslims. Consequently, the wealth was concentrated among the conquering families, affording them privileges based on arbitrary distinctions of rank. According to al-Zahabi, during ᶜUthman's reign there was so much wealth in Medina that a horse would sell for one-hundred thousand dirhams, while a garden would fetch four-hundred thousand. The Umayyads, says al-Zahabi, had, during this period, acted indiscriminately in amassing wealth to the extent that they had discredited the caliphate as the guarantor of the equality of all Muslims in sharing the wealth acquired through the spoils and the taxes from the conquered lands. Muᶜawiyah, who symbolizes the prevailing tendencies of the Arab aristocracy in the first century of Islam, clearly formed his policies as the Arab chief, concerned perhaps less with the directives of the Qur'an or the Prophetic 'pattern of moral behavior'—the *sunnah*. It can be maintained with much documentation that the Umayyad rulers did the minimum for the consolidation of Islamic matters. The Umayyad rulers and their governors—who were by and large neither pious committed to Islam—were not the people to promote a religious and social life corresponding to the *sunnah* of the Prophet. As a matter of fact, reference to the *sunnah* was not necessarily a reference to the *sunnah* of the Prophet; rather, Muᶜawiyah made frequent references to the *sunnah* of ᶜUmar in setting the fiscal policies of the state. There was little concern about the religious life of the population. As true Arabs, they paid little attention to religion, either in their own conduct or in that of their subjects. If a man was observant of his religious obligation and was seen to be devoutly worshiping in the mosque, it was assumed that he was not a follower of the Umayyad dynasty, but an ardent supporter of ᶜAli.

Individual examples cited by several authoritative traditionists indicate the state of affairs in regard to the ignorance prevailing among the Umayyads about the ritual performances and religious precepts in the first century. In Syria, where the Umayyads had the staunchest support, it was not generally known that there were only five canonical daily prayers, and in order to make certain of this fact, it was decided that an associate of the Prophet who was still alive should be asked about it. It is impossible to fully comprehend the state of affairs that prevailed under the Umayyads when the rulers of the people who lived under them showed very little concern for the understanding of the laws and rules of Islam. Indeed, such a period was alluded to in the Prophetic tradition which predicted the critical religious future of the Muslim community:

> There will come rulers after me who will destroy the canonical prayers (*salat*) but continue to perform the prayers at the fixed times all the same.

Moreover, the Umayyad hatred of the Hashemites, especially the Prophet's family, which was evident under Mu^cawiyah and his successors, gave rise to controversies among Muslims on issues of Islam, whether political or doctrinal. The Umayyad spirit of fabrication, dissemination, and suppression of Prophetic traditions is evident in the instruction which Mu^cawiyah gave to his governor al-Mughirah on defaming ^cAli and his companions.

> Do not tire of abusing and insulting ^cAli and calling for God's mercifulness for ^cUthman, defaming the companions of ^cAli, removing them, and refusing to listen to them; praising, in contrast, the clan of ^cUthman, drawing them near to you, and listening to them.

This instruction is in the form of official encouragement to fabricate lies directed against ^cAli and to hold back and suppress those reports that favoured him. Evidently the Umayyads and their political followers had no scruples in promoting tendentious lies in the form of Prophetic traditions, and they were prepared to cover such falsifications with their undoubted authority.

One such pious authority was al-Zuhri, who could not resist pressure from the governing authorities, and was willing to promote the interests of the Umayyad dynasty by religious means. Al-Zuhri belonged to the circle of those Muslims who believed that a *modus vivendi* with the Umayyad government was desirable. However, even he could not cover up the report that Anas ibn Malik had related regarding the critical religious situation under the Umayyads. The report is preserved in al-Bukhari in his *Sahih*, in a section entitled: 'Not offering the prayer at its stated time.':

> Al-Zuhri relates that he visited Anas ibn Malik at Damascus and found him weeping, and asked him the reason for his weeping. He replied 'I do not know anything which I used to know during the lifetime of the Messenger of God. [Everything is lost] except this prayer (*salat*) which [too] is being lost [that is, not being offered as it should be].'

That the manner in which this well-established Prophetic practice of prayer had been altered, either out of ignorance or due to the anti-*sunna* and anti-^cAli attitude of the Umayyads, is further demonstrated by another tradition in al-Bukhari, in the section entitled: 'To end the *takbir* [the saying of 'God is greater'] on prostrating.' The tradition is narrated on the authority of Mutarrif ibn ᶜAbdullah, who said:

> ᶜImran ibn Husayn and I offered the prayer behind ᶜAli ibn Abi Talib [in Basra]. When ᶜAli prostrated, he said the *takbir*; when he raised his head he said the *takbir* and when he stood up for th third unit (*rakᶜa*) he said the *takbir*. On the completion of the prayer ᶜImram took my hand and said: 'He [ᶜAli] made me remember the prayer of Muhammad, peace be upon him.' Or, he said [something to the effect that] 'He led us in a prayer like that of Muhammad, peace be upon him.'

The above facts show sufficiently the prevailing trend in the Umayyad state, where Islam was above all a badge of united Arab aristocracy, the cold and discipline of a conquering elite. As became apparent in subsequent periods, the traditions of Arab aristocracy had relatively little inherent connection with Islam itself. In fact, under the Umayyads a responsible and egalitarian spirit of Islam was ignored in favor of power politics. Under such circumstances, the faithful had to deal with a crucial moral and religious question: To what extent could the Muslims consent to obey the rulers, who were completely opposed to the basic teachings of Islam?

It is possible to surmise from various sources on this period of Islamic history that the Umayyads presented a dilemma for the committed Muslims as to how they were to order their religious life under such rulers. Of course, there were some, like al-Zuhri, who did not consider the deviation from the religious obligations by the Umayyads as sufficient reason to refuse obedience to them and declare them as unjust. These were the Marjaᶜites, who believed that to acknowledge the Umayyads as true believers it was sufficient that they professed Islam outwardly, and that it was not necessary to pry into their un-Islamic behaviour. Accordingly, these people did not raise any objection to the cruel measures adopted by the Umayyads and their governors against those pious individuals like Hujr ibn ᶜAdi and later on, the Imam Husayn, who refused them their allegiance on the basis of their conviction that as an essential consequence of their religious responsibility they could not do so. On the contrary, the Marjaᶜites even defended the massacres which the Umayyads caused among their most pious opponents on the grounds that these individuals were disrupting the unity of the community by challenging the authority that represented the Muslim community as a whole.

There were others among the pious persons, who, although acknowledging the unworthiness of the Umayyads to rule the community on religious grounds, maintained that the *de facto* rule of the Umayyads was in the interest of the state and of Islamic unity. They thereby contributed towards the acceptance of the rulers, and the people, following their lead, tolerated and paid allegiance to the un-Islamic regime. Furthermore, the accommodating outlook of this group laid the groundwork for the acceptance of any claim to legitimacy by a Muslim authority that managed to successfully seize power through upheaval or revolution.

On the other hand, we have persons like the Imam Husayn, who refused to acknowledge these corrupt leaders and their representatives at all, and met them with resistance. As such, the Imam Husayn and his followers provide a clear contrast to accommodation to Umayyad policies. The Imam Husayn's unbending religious attitude stems from his conviction about the political responsibilities which an acceptance of Islamic revelation entailed. In his letter to the people of Kufah, who had urged him to come to Iraq to assume the responsibliities of an *imam*, he reaffirms his penetrating awareness of religio-political responsibilities of the Imam. He says:

> I solemnly declare that a person is not the *imam* if he does not act in accordance with the Book [of God], and does not follow justice [in dealing with the people], and is not subject to the Truth, and does not devote himself entirely to God.

Undoubtedly, one can discern the implication of the above statement in the Imam Husayn's declaration, made in a speech to the army of Hurr, who had come to intercept him on his way to Iraq. This declaration shows the disgust of the pious with the life lived under the ungodly Umayyads:

> Do you not see that truth is not followed anymore, and that falsehood is not being interdicted [by anyone]? Indeed, it is within the right of a believer to desire to meet God. Verily, I do not see death except [in the form of] martyrdom; and I do not see life with the unjust as anything but loathsome.

It is evident that the Imam Husayn was reacting to the general condition of deterioration in the upholding of the Islamic teaching brought about by the anti-religious Umayyads and the prevailing outlook of accommodation among the Muslims encouraged by those theologians who supported the existing order and wanted to prevent civil strife at the expense of the Qur'anic principle of justice. Thus, the events of the year 61/680 become comprehensible when seen in light of the Qur'anic insistence on the establishment of a just social order under the guidance provided by God in the form of the Book and the 'noble paradigm' of the Prophet, and the manner in which the representatives of the Muslim community deviated from this goal following the death of the Prophet. Moreover, it was the commitment to the ideals of Islam that finally decided the course adopted by the Imam Husayn and his followers in Karbala on the day of *cAshura'*—a day which continues and will continue to challenge our conceptions of standards of human respect and recognition for as long as there remains a conscientious being on earth.

It is, I believe, the message of Truth and Justice — the Islamic revelation in its entirety — that makes the study and the commemoration of the Imam Husayn's martyrdom deserving of our wonder and our tears. In Islamic history there is no other occasion which can generate the total responsibility that a Muslim has towards God and his fellow men. Furthermore, there is no other 'paradigm' that equals the paradigm provided by all the members of the Prophet's family in creating an egalitarian social commitment, which Islam obviously demands from its adherents. It is this paradigmatic nature of the Imam Husayn's life that gives it an eternal meaning, promised in the Qur'an, to all those who struggle and sacrifice their lives in the cause of God: *Count not those who are slain in God's way as dead, but rather as living with their Lord, by Him provided.* (III: 169).

Hamid Enayat

In Shi⊂i history, the drama of the martyrdom of Husayn, the third Imam, which was fought out on the plains of Karbala in the month of Muharram in 61/680 ranks next only to the Prophet's investiture of ⊂Ali as his successor at the Ghadir of Khumm. From a political standpoint, the drama is significant for two reasons: first, Husayn was the only Shi⊂i Imam in the Twelver school who died in consequence of combining his claim to the Caliphate with an armed uprising. The remaining eleven Imams either attained political positions through regular constitutional procedures (the first and the eighth) or made formal peace with the ruler of the time after hesitant hostilities (the second), or secluded themselves in a quiet life of piety and scholarship; as regards the last Imam, he disappeared before displaying a preference for any of these alternative courses of action. Second, the element of martyrdom in the drama obviously exercises a powerful attraction for all Shi⊂i movements challenging the established order. Husayn is thus the only Imam whose tragedy can serve as a positive ingredient of the mythology of any persecuted but militant Shi⊂i group os the Twelver school.

*   *   *

Ever since the Iranian Shi^{c}i dynasty of the Buyids popularised the Muharram ceremonies in the fourth/tenth century the Karbala drama has been the object of fervent annual lamentations. In the sixteenth century, the introduction of *ta^{c}ziyyah* (passion play) by the Iranian Safavid dynasty strengthened the popular character of the ceremonies, which together with *rawzah-khani* (recitation of the sufferings of holy martyrs), *zanjir-zani* (self-flagellation) and other street processions formed a distinct cult despite the opposition of the religious hierarchy, who disapproved of them on account of their 'crude dogma' and irreligious histrionics.

The main purpose of these ceremonies was to perform the lamentations in a form which would cause the greatest amount of weeping. Numerous prophetic sayings recommend or praise weeping, or its affection, during prayer, or recitation of the Qur'an or recollecting God, or from fear of God. Wensinck has noted more than forty of them. To this catalogue, the Shi^{c}i tradition has added the virtue of weeping in memory of the Imams, particularly Husayn, who is known as the Lord of the Martyrs (*sayyid al-shuhada'*). . . .Husayn's martyrdom makes sense on two levels: first, in terms of a soteriology not dissimilar from the one invoked in the case of Christ's crucifixion: just as Christ sacrificed himself on the altar of the cross to redeem humanity, so did Husayn allow himself to be killed on the plains of Karbala to purify the Muslim community of sins; and second, as an active factor vindicating the Shi^{c}i cause, contributing to its ultimate triumph. When one adds to all this the cathartic effect of weeping as a means of releasing pent-up grief over not only personal misfortunes, but also the agonies of a long-suffering minority, then the reasons for the immense popularity of the Muharram ceremonies become apparent.

With the increasing tendency of the Shi^{c}is to a passive form of *taqiyyah*, and acquiescence in the established order, the concept of the martyrdom of Husayn as vicarious atonement prevailed over its interpretation as a militant assertion of the Shi^{c}i cause. Concomitantly, weeping, and not edification or political indoctrination, came to be recognised as the sole aim of *all* reminiscences of Husayn. This is primarily clear from the very titles of most of the popular histories of the Karbala drama: *miftah al-buka'* ('Key to Weeping'), *tufan-al buka'* ('Tempest of Weeping'), *muhti al-buka'* ('Ocean of Weeping'), *muthir al-ahzan* ('Rouser of Sorrows') and *luhuf* ('Burning Lamentations'). One rarely, if ever, comes across a narrative redolent of combative vengefulness. The dominant trend is an elegiac account of the episodes in the drama, a concern which seems to stem from the conviction that submissive endurance of pain and suffering is the hallmark of all worthy souls. In the *Amah* ('Discourses') of Shaykh Tusi, ^{c}Ali is quoted as having warned his son Hasan that he would always be 'a hostage of death, a target of adversity, and a victim of pain.' 'O brothers!', to quote again from a popularizer of the story, Mahdi Naraqi, 'affliction is bestowed (only) on the Friends of God, oppression befalls the Chosen Men, and pain and suffering are proportionate to the degree of dignity and pre-eminence (while conversely) exemption from calamity and hardship is the trait of ill fate and wretchedness.' One could establish a link between this exaltation of suffering, and the asceticism of Islamic Sufi traditions, which preaches the acceptance of pain as a necessary stage in the spiritual development of Man.

Husayn's passive and pietistic behaviour in the drama of Karbala, as described in orthodox Shi'i sources, is perhaps best exemplified by the epithet *mazlum* which often follows his name in the popular usage. *Mazlum* literally means injured, oppressed or sinned against, but in colloquial Persian its connotation goes beyond those associated with incurring injustice; it means a person who is unwilling to act against others, even when he is oppressed, not out of cowardice or diffidence but because of generosity and forbearance. That is why it is normally synonymous with *najib*, literally meaning noble, but also gentle and modest. Thus being a *mazlum*, rather than signifying a negative attribute or a deprivation, counts as a moral virtue.

Hence the paradox of the drama of Karbala in Shi'i literature, whether popular or scholarly. True, outside impassioned scenes, the drama is treated as something more than a simple agent of emotional catharsis, and Husayn is praised for his sacrifice to vindicate the just cause of the Prophet's family, or to revive the religion of his grandfather Muhammad, and to save it from the Umayyads' deviation. But his predominant image as a saint with an almost masochistic wish for martyrdom defeats any attempt at using the drama as a means of inculcating political activism.

How passive and harmless this image has been, from such a political point of view, can be understood from the fact that the *ta'ziyyah* was promoted by the financial and political oligarchs who used it under both Safavid and Qajar dynasties as a means of consolidating their hold over the populace; and in its golden age, a despot like Nasir al-Din Shah saw no contradiction between his oppressive methods of government and the provision of the most elaborate amenities for the performance of *ta'ziyyah*.

During the last ten years or so, the quiescent character of the drama of Karbala has started to change at the hands of a number of Shi'i modernists who could not forego its obvious potential as a rhetorical instrument of political mobilization. The modernists have tried to develop this potential primarily as part of their general drive for the reformulation of the crucial themes of Islamic hisotry. . . .Of the few works that have appeared so far [on Imam Husayn in recent years] the most daring and the most influential has been *Shahid-i javid* ('The Immortal Martyr') by Ni'matullah Salihi Najafabadi, a religious scholar from the holy city of Qum. Although the book immediately became the object of a heated controversy among religious circles after its publication in 1968, it went largely unnoticed by the secular intelligentsia, a fact which highlights the dichotomy in Iran's cultural life at the time. But it attracted a great deal of publicity during the uproar provoked in Iran in the spring of 1976 by the murder of a religious figure in Isfahan, Shamsabadi, whose alleged murderers were said to be advocates of the author's thesis. The introduction to the book by the Ayatollah Husayn ᶜAli Muntaziri, now designated as Khumayni's successor, vouches for the militant Shiᶜi approval of its contents.

What essentially differentiates 'The Immortal Martyr' from the works we have considered so far, and from other Shiᶜi writings on the subject, is its semi-scholarly methodology. True, like the bulk of the committed literature on Islam, the book has been written in a style more apposite to political polemics. But it works out its arguments through a detailed, critical analysis of the orthodox sources. Indeed, the underlying notion of all the author's arguments is that a proper understanding of the Shiᶜi history is possible only when all its received dogmas are subjected to a thorough reappraisal. He thus challenges and puts to the test many a familiar anecdote in an attempt to prove the utter unreliability of conventional narratives about Husayn, particularly Husayn Kashifi's *Rawdat al-shuhada'*, Majlisi's account in his *Bihar al-anwar*, Ibn Tawus's *Luhuf*, and the Persian translation of *Kitab al-futuh* by the pro-Shiᶜi Ibn Aᶜtham. Conversely, he does not shy away from freely seeking evidence, in confirmation of his ideas, from Sunni authorities such as Tabari, Ibn al-Athir, Ibn Kathir and Ibn Asakir, whose statements are otherwise treated with the utmost caution by the orthodox Shiᶜis.

Najafabadi's untrammelled approach to historical sources stems from his repeatedly avowed intention of verifying every episode in the drama on the touchstone of what he himself calls 'the ordinary causes, and the natural course of events,' which is presumably his chosen term for rational guidelines of research. He follows these guidelines so far as they help him to demystify the drama, to purge it of all the supernatural, romantic and exaggerated versions of events. But he never allows them to impair his vision of Husayn as a hero who combined readiness for self-sacrifice with foresight and political wisdom.

. . . [Najafabadi] says in the preface that ever since his youth he was tormented by a glaring contradiction in the popular narratives of the drama: if Husayn did possess the prescience that all Shiᶜi Imams are believed to possess by virtue of their divinely inspired knowledge, why did he deliberately choose a course of action leading to his and his family's destruction? Such a suicidal

venture becomes all the more incomprehensible when one remembers that
the Muslim community at the time was in dire need of the leadership of the
members of the Prophet's family. Najafabadi's dilemma in his younger
days thus seems superficially to have been the same as that faced by Mazini.
But, being the produce of a Shi𝑐i environment, his method of solving the
dilemma has been different. Contrary to Mazini, and indeed to the entire
Shi𝑐i consensus, he starts off by questioning the very belief in Husayn's
foreknowledge of his fate. He does this not by openly disputing the Shi𝑐i
theological dogma on the Imams' prescience, but through exposing the ab-
surdity of some of the popular stories about Husayn's foreknowledge.

Although Najafabadi thus succeeds in demolishing much of the authority of secondary Shi𝑐i traditions about Husayn's foreknowledge of his martyrdom, his position is plainly vulnerable because of his refusal, perhaps
deliberate, to come face to face with first-hand Shi𝑐i sources on the subject,
namely the great compendia of Kulayni, Tusi and Shaykh Sadduq, which
abound in the *hadiths* confirming the Imams divinely inspired knowledge
'of the past, present and future affairs'. But the author's main intention in
discrediting the secondary traditions is not so much to rebut the dogma on
the Imams' prescience as to pave the way for the presentation of his thesis
on the uprising itself. Here his difference with the Sunni modernists is that
he does not see the uprising in idealistic perspectives at all. He maintains
that Husayn began his movement neither to fulfil his grandfather's fore-
bodings, nor in a reckless mood of defiance, but as a wholly rational and
fairly well-planned attempt at overthrowing Yazid. Political circumstances
at the outset looked promising: Yazid's regime was very unpopular, and the
Kufans had rallied to the 𝑐Alid cause. He himself was sacredly bound, as an
Imam, not to condone an unjust and impious government. Motivated thus
by a combination of political and religious considerations to start his
rebellion, he took all the precautions that a responsible political leader
should take before embarking on a momentous enterprise. The trepidations
he felt are shown not only by his decision to send Muslim to Kufah, but also
by the doubts that invaded his mind after he heard the news of Muslim's
death. From that moment onwards, his actions were purely in self-defense,
and should *a fortifori* be free from any reproach of precipitance. So the collapse of the rebellion was entirely due to objective, rational causes, with no
room left for the vagaries of supernatural powers.

As can be readily seen, the principal aim of the 'Immortal Martyr' is the
politicization of an aspect of the Shi𝑐i Imamology which until recent times
was generally interpreted in mystical, lyrical and emotional terms. The
result has been a cautious, but growing tendency among the Shi𝑐i militants
to treat the drama of Karbala as an essentially human tragedy, and concur-
rently, to avoid regarding Husayn's heroism as a unique and inimitable

event in history, above the capacity of the common run of human beings. This tendency is epitomised by Khumayni, who, perhaps more than any other Shi^ci theologian of comparable stature, has used the memory of Karbala with an acute sense of political urgency. 'It was', he says in his *Wilayat-i faqih* ('The Guardianship of the Jurisconsult'), 'to prevent the establishment of monarchy and hereditary succession that Husayn revolted and became a martyr. It was for refusing to succumb to Yazid's hereditary succession and to recognise his kingship that Husayn revolted, and called all Muslims to rebellion.' Khumayni likewise calls upon Iranian Muslims 'to create an *^cAshura*' in their struggle for launching an Islamic state.'

The orthodox religious hierarchy in Iran, however, received Najafabadi's book, in a different spirit. They took particular exception to two features of his work: first, his over-reliance on non-Shi^ci sources, and his failure to abide by the rule of *tawthiq*, namely verifying the accuracy and reliability of historical accounts in accordance with Shi^ci criteria; second, his denial of the Imam's prescience, with its clear threat to the doctrine of the Imams' divinely inspired knowledge, and indeed to the entire edifice of the Shi^ci theory of the Imamate. This soon led to an acrimonious debate on a host of issues not directly connected with the drama itself, such as the attributes of the Imams, the nature of their knowledge, the scope left for human will by divine predestination, and the rational limits of self-sacrifice in the fulfilment of religious duties. . . .

Chapter Four

Jihad

The Shiʿi notion of jihad *differs from that of Sunni Islam primarily in that it associates the doctrine directly with that of wilayah, or allegiance to the Imam. Historically, the Shiʿi doctrine of* jihad *was elaborated within the context of Imamate. Therefore, during the earliest phase of its history, Shiʿism argued that only the Imam, as the infallible ruler, could correctly discern the circumstance necessitating* jihad. *Consequently, in Shiʿism, as opposed to Sunnism, entry into paradise as recompense for waging* jihad *may be guaranteed only if the undertaking had been complemented with allegiance to the living Imam.*

The association of the doctrine of jihad *and that of the Imamate, which especially typified the views of the Shiʿis concerning Holy War early in their history, is particularly evident in the Zaydi branch of Shiʿism. The Zaydis believe that the chief function of the Imam, the sine* qua non *condition for his leadership and the basis of his legitimacy, is the ability of declaring* jihad.

Yet another area where the Shiʿi and the Sunni notions of jihad *differ is in the conditions that warrant declaration of* jihad, *which the Shiʿis believe is warranted not only when a nonbeliever fails to adhere to Islam but also when a Muslim fails to obey the Imam.*

In both Shiʿi and Sunni Islam, the concept of jihad *has undergone much change since its elaboration during the early centuries of Islam. This change both reflects and responds to the change in the nature of the political institutions that have governed the Islamic state. In Shiʿism, change in the doctrine of* jihad *has been also necessitated by developments in Shiʿi religious and political thought. Hence, the first change in the doctrine of* jihad *followed the occultation of the twelfth Imam in the year 873/874 A.D. Once the Shiʿi community found itself without an Imam, who had personified the political aspirations of the community, among other things, it rendered much of its political doctrines subject to specific historical exigencies. Thus, while the Shiʿi community under the Umayyads developed the doctrine of* taqiyyah *(dissimulation), the*

Buyids (and also the Fatimids) nearly established a complete Shi^{c}i empire.
With the rise to power of the Safavid dynasty in Iran in 1501 A.D. and
the establishment of Shi^{c}ism as the official religion of that country, the
Shi^{c}i notion of jihad *underwent some essential changes. These changes*
resulted from the need that the Safavid monarchy felt for reactivating
the political and military aspects of the doctrine of jihad. *This need was*
in the first instance a reflection of messianic activism among the Safavid
forces, who viewed their conquest of Iran in religious millenarian terms.
However, once Shi^{c}ism became established as the official religion of the
Safavid state, jihad *became the cornerstone of Iran's religiously-based*
foreign policy. Eager to spread Shi^{c}ism among the Christian population
to the north of Iran and to mobilize Iranian and Anatolian Shi^{c}is against
the Sunni Ottomans, the Safavid Shahs sought to revitalize jihad *as the*
justification for their foreign policy, as well as a framework within
which it could be pursued. The threat that the Ottoman state posed to
Shi^{c}ite welfare in Anatolia, and the territorial integrity of Iran at the
time strengthened the argument of the Safavids.

The most noteworthy change that the doctrine of jihad *was subjected*
to in this period was the doctrinal permissibility of the declaration of
jihad, *even in the absence of the Hidden Imam.* Jihad *was, however, to*
be waged in the name of the twelfth Imam, Imam al-zaman *(Lord of the*
Age). The right to declare jihad, *in this period, was primarily vested in*
the Shahs, who not only claimed descent from the seventh Shi^{c}i Imam,
Musa al-Kazim, but also claimed to rule in the name of, and as vice-
*regent (*na'ib*) to, the twelfth Imam.*

Through the decades, beginning with the Safavid defeat at Chaldiran,
as the Shahs began to lose much of their charistmatic authority, the in-
stitution of the Shi^{c}i ^{c}ulama', under the guidance of the likes of Majlisi
II, gained social and political prominence. Consequently, the right to
declare jihad *gradually passed from the Shahs to the ^{c}ulama'. This was*
particularly true of the reign of Shah Sultan Husayn (1694–1722), the
last Safavid sovereign.

It was not, however, until the Qajar period when the ^{c}ulama''s right to
declare jihad, *which had been established* de facto *during the Safavid*
period, became recognized de jure. *The lesser geneological prominence*
of the Qajars, combined with the rising power of the ^{c}ulama', led the
*Shi^{c}i religious authorities to wrest much of the vice-regency (*niyabat*) of*
the Hidden Imam from the Shahs. As a result, by the time of the reign
of Fath-^{c}Ali Shah Qajar in the nineteenth century, the right to declare
jihad *had become the virtual monopoly of the ^{c}ulama'. This right was*
exercised by the ^{c}ulama', at the instigation of the Qajar Shahs and in
their campaigns against Russian "infidels."

By the middle of the nineteenth century, jihad *also became an impor-*
tant feature of the domestic politics of Iran. As the Shi^{c}i ^{c}ulama' became
increasingly involved in statecraft, jihad *acted as an important instru-*
ment in their quest to influence politics. Jihad *became an important*

issue during the Tobacco Rebellion of 1891–1892, when Ayatollah Shirazi confronted Nasir al-Din Shah Qajar on the issue of concessions given to British interests concerning the tobacco industry.

Thus, on the grand historical scale, following the initial suspension of the doctrine of jihad as a consequence of the occultation of the twelfth Imam, the trend of changes has been pointing toward its reintroduction into the conduct of religious and political life in the Shiʿi communities. This development, in the first instance, propagated Shiʿism within Iran and later beyond its borders and also protected Iran from incursions by its Sunni neighbors. During the Qajar period, the external functions of jihad were complemented with new domestic ones. The dual functions of jihad in Shiʿism may be seen in Ayatollah Khumayni's usage of the threat of jihad against Iraq.

In the following passage edited and translated by John Alden Williams, ʿAllamah al-Hilli will elaborate on the place of jihad in Shiʿi law and the legal injunctions by which the waging of jihad is sanctioned. The excerpt is from TIC, pages 268–272.

ᶜAllamah al-Hilli

Jihad is a religious obligation for every legally responsible free adult male who is sound of body. It is not a duty for a child, an insane person, a woman, an infirm or old man, or a slave. It is a *fard ᶜala al-kifayah* (i.e. must be performed for the Community by a number sufficient to see that the job is done), on condition that the Imam, on whom be peace, is present or has delegated someone to lead the *jihad*. . . .

It does not become an individual, personal obligation unless the Imam orders an individual to perform it for the general good . . . or the number of those performing it is too small to repulse the enemy except by a general effort, or if one has taken it upon himself by a vow, or the like.

Fighting in self-defense is obligatory, even if one is among normally inimical people who are attacked so that one assists them by defending oneself, and this is not *jihad* (but self-defense). . . .This also applies to anyone who fears for himself, his family, and his possessions, if it seems possible that he may succeed (by taking up arms).

Four things that are legal impediments to *jihad* are: blindness; crippling such as paralysis; any weakness that prevents one from mounting and galloping; and poverty which prevents one from caring for himself or his family during the campaign, or paying for the necessary equipment (and this of course differs according to the circumstances).

If a man has an unpaid debt, it is not for his creditor to forbid him to go. Parents may forbid one to participate in a campaign, if one has not been ordered to (by the Imam).

If the legal impediment should appear only after the fighting has begun, it is ineffective, unless it is such as to disable one for duties.

If a poor man is given the wherewithal to go on *jihad*, it becomes an obligation for him to go — unless it is given to him as a salary; then he is not obligated to go. One who is unable physically but has the means to go must delegate another. Some say this is merely commendable, not obligatory.

Raiding during the holy months is forbidden, unless the enemy begins the fight or sees no sacredness in the holy months (*i.e.* non-Muslims).

Although it used to be forbidden to fight in the sacred territory, that is abrogated. (IX:15: "Slay the unbelievers wheresoever you find them.")

One is obligated to emigrate from the territory of polytheists, if he is prevented there from openly practising Islam, if he is able to do it. This *hijrah* lasts as long as unbelief prevails there.

Manning the forts for the protection of the frontiers is commendable even in the absence of the Imam, since it does not necessarily involve fighting, but is for protection and for a show of force.

People against whom *jihad* should be carried out are three categories:

1) Those who rebel against the Imam; 2) protected minorities such as Jews, Christians and Zoroastrians, if they violate the conditions of protection; and 3) whoever is hostile, among the various kinds of unbelievers. The Muslims must bring all of these into submission, either by subjecting them or converting them to Islam. If they begin hostilities, it is obligatory to fight them. Otherwise, it is only necessary to fight them according to one's ability to do so, but it should be at least once a year. If the general welfare requires it, it is permissible to make a peace treaty with them, but no one has the power to do this except the Imam or his depty.

It is worthiest to begin by attacking those who are most accessible, unless some less accessible pose the greater threat. If the enemy's numbers are great, and those of the Muslims small, it is necessary to postpone the war until the Muslims' numbers are sufficient to allow them to attack. Then war becomes obligatory. One may not begin it without first inviting them to become Muslims. This invitation is made by the Imam or by his delegate. The obligation to formulate the appeal does not apply, if they already know the principles of Islam.

It is permissible to fight the enemy by any means which will lead to victory, but it is reprehensible to cut down the trees, and throw fire, or cut off the water, unless it is necessary (for victory); and it is forbidden to throw poison. Some however say that this is only reprehensible.

If the enemy hides behind women and children or Muslim prisoners, one should withhold the attack, if fighting has not already broken out. If a prisoner was killed because this was necessary for the *jihad*, the killer does not have to pay the blood-money. It is not permissible to kill the insane, the children, or the women of the enemy, even if they helped him, unless one is compelled to do so.

It is forbidden to make an example of the prisoners, or to use treachery . . . . It is forbidden to attack by night or before noon, unless it is necessary.

(When a battle is being decided by single combat), if the companions of the enemy champion seek to help him, he has lost his claim to safe-conduct. But if they do it of their own accord and he forbids them, he has kept his agreement. If he does not forbid them it becomes lawful to attack both him and them.

The Zimmah

Only the Imam or his delegate gives the protected status of the *zimma* in general and in particular to the enemy. Faithful observance of the *zimma* is necessary, so long as it is not an agreement contrary to the Law. If the agreement was made under compulsion, it need not be kept. As for the formula, one may say "I protect you," or "I take you under protection," or "You are under the *zimmah* of Islam," or any expression that clearly gives that meaning. But if one says, "May no harm befall you," or "Don't be frightened," that does not constitute protection, since there is nothing in it indicating a safe-conduct. If the enemy asks for it after he is already a prisoner, and is given it, it is not valid. If any Muslim declares that he has extended protection to a polytheist in the time when it was legally premissible, however, it is valid.

When an enemy declares that a Muslim extended him protection, and the Muslim denies it, the Muslim's word is accepted. If an enemy receives protection and permission to live under Muslim rule (*fi dar al-Islam*), his possessions enter into protection with him. If a Muslim makes a slave of a prisoner, he becomes possessor of his possessions as well, by virtue of slavery. A Muslim who enters a hostile territory on safe-conduct and steals something must return it, whether the owner is in Islamic or in hostile territory.

Prisoners

Women prisoners become property (i.e. slaves) the moment they are captured, even if the fighting is still going on. This also applies to boys under the age of puberty. Males above the age of puberty must be put to death, if fighting is still going on and they refuse to become Muslims. The Imam may choose whether to cut off their heads, or if he likes he may cut off their hands and feet and let them bleed until they die.

If they were made prisoner after the fighting is over, they are not killed, and the Imam may choose between showing favor, holding them for ransom, or making slaves of them. Even if they become Muslims upon being made prisoner, this law still applies.

If a prisoner is unable to walk, it is not obligatory to put him to death, since one does not know what the Imam has decided to do with him, and if he should become a Muslim, killing him would be pointless. It is necessary to give a prisoner food and water even if one wishes to kill him (later). It is reprehensible to put him to death by torture, or to carry his head away.

It is obligatory to bury the martyred (Muslim dead) but not the enemy. If there is doubt as to which is which, then those who are circumcised should be buried.

* * *

Booty is in three categories: Movables, such as gold, silver, and furnishings; Non-movables, such as land and buildings; and Slave-captives, such as women and children.

It is not permitted to make use of anything in the first category before being assigned it at the division of the spoils, except fodder and food. Those things which a Muslim may not possess, such as wine and pork, must be destroyed. Wine may be converted to vinegar.

All cultivated land becomes the property of all the Muslims and those who conquered it in general. Its disposition is reserved for the Imam. No one may take it as a private domain, but what it produces may be given by the Imam to projects of general benefit for all. Uncultivated land becomes the special property of the Imam, and no one can develop it without his permission, if he is present. If anyone develops it and cultivates it in a period of the Imam's absence, it becomes that man's property.

(After the Imam's fifth is set aside) the remaining four-fifths are divided among the combatants and those present at the fighting, even if they did not fight, including the child born after the pillage but before the division of spoils. A foot soldier is given one share, and the horseman two shares. Some say three, but the first opinion is more apparent. There is no share given for camels, mules, and asses.

Rules for the Peoples of the Zimmah

The *jizyah*, or protection tax may be taken from those who stay in their own religion. These are Jews, Christians, and those who have a kind of scripture, who are Zoroastrians. From any but these, nothing except conversion to Islam is acceptable.

Part II

Authority, Law and Society in Shiʿism

Chapter Five

The Shiʿi Principles
of Jurisprudence

Fiqh, *or jurisprudence, is one of the most distinctive features of all the schools of the Islamic religion including Shiʿism. Not only does jurisprudence lay the foundations of legal thought, ethics, and practices, but it also affects every other dimension of Shiʿi life. Jurisprudence lies at the heart of the Shiʿi educational system, as found in the traditional* madrasahs, *where the jurists (*fuqaha') *play the leading role as both guardians of the system and its main product. In the following section, Modarresi Tabataba'i provides an introduction to this complex and central aspect of Shiʿism. The excerpt is from* ATSL, *pages 2-4, 13-18.*

Hossein Modarressi Tabatabaʾi

As a doctrinal system, Shiʿism represents a particular tendency of Islam shaped by a chain of theologico-historical analyses. The *Hadith al-Thaqalayn*, a tradition which was handed down by both Shiʿis and Sunnis from the Prophet, according to which the Prophet called on Muslims to follow the Qur'an and his own Family after him, was, along with a number of other traditions, the root and original source of this tendency which was later strengthened by further theologico-philosophical and historical reasonings.

In religious matters, Shiʿism has generally based its views on the instructions of prominent members (Imams) of the Prophet's family. The main difference between Sunni and Shiʿi legal schools is the manner in which they received the Prophet's Tradition and in their legal sources. Whereas Sunnis received Tradition as transmitted by the Prophet's companions, Shiʿis received it through his Family. In another respect, whereas Sunni legal schools follow the juridical opinions of some jurisconsults of Medina and Iraq, Shiʿis follow the opinions of their Imams, who were descendants of the Prophet. The Twelver Shiʿis which is now the prevalent Shiʿi school, follow the opinions of their twelve Imams, especially the sixth, Abu ʿAbdullah Jaʿfar ibn Muhammad al-Sadiq, and for this reason their legal school is known as *Jaʿfari*.

* * *

The Qur'an, Tradition (*sunnah*), the consensus of the Shiʿi jurists (*ijmaʿ*) and reason (ʿ*aql*) form the sources of Shiʿi law.

The Qur'an, in its apparent literal sense, has shaped the spirit and foundation of Shiʿi law.

The Tradition, i.e. the statement, deeds and tacit consent of the Prophet and the Imams, must be handed down by reliable narrators. In respect to this reliability, the doctrinal views of the transmitters are considered irrelevant. A tradition handed down by a reliable non-Shiʿi is viewed as sound and acceptable just as one transmitted by a veracious Shiʿi.

Ijmaʿ, i.e. the unanimity of the views of all Shiʿi jurists on a certain legal question, is not a source on its own, but it can become a means through which the opinions of the Imams may be discovered. This function of *ijmaᶜ* has been explained in various ways, up to twelve. The most popular among these in contemporary Shiᶜi law holds that since *ijmaᶜ* is the unanimity of the views of 'all' Shiᶜi scholars, it naturally includes the views of those scholars who lived in the time of the Imams or the period quite close to it. Many of these were close companions of the Imams and knew their opinions quite thoroughly. The consensus of these very early jurists, most of whom were absolute followers of the Imams, normally demonstrates the view of the Imams.

By 'reason' as a source for Shiᶜi law is meant categorical judgments drawn from both pure and practical reason. A clear instance is the judgment of practical reason that justice is good and injustice is evil. In Shiᶜi *usul al-fiqh* there is a principle which states that whatever is ordered by reason, is also ordered by religion (*kull ma hakam bi al-ᶜaql, hakam bi al-sharᶜ*). In accordance with this principle, which is known as the 'rule of correlation' (*qaᶜidat al-mulazamah*), religious rules may be inferred from the sole verdict of reason. The correlation between the obligatoriness of an act and the obligatoriness of its prerequisite (*muqaddamat al-wajib*), or between prescribing something and prohibiting its opposite (*mas'alat al-didd*), or the impossibility of combining command and prohibition in a single case from a single standpoint (*ijtimaᶜ al-amr wa'l-nahy*), are all rational precepts in the methodology of Shiᶜi law and sources based on pure reason in the juridical efforts to discover legal rules.

* * *

. . . The subjects of Islamic law (*fiqh*) have been classified in different forms. In Sunni law, they are usually divided into two categories: *ᶜibadah* (acts of devotion) and *muᶜamalah* (here meaning worldly affairs). Al-Ghazzali, the Shafiᶜi scholar (d. 505/1111) in his *Ihya' ᶜulum al-din* divided all religious and moral injunctions into four groups, *ᶜibadah, ᶜadah* (ordinary affairs), *munjiyah* (what ensures salvation) and *muhlikah* (what causes perdition). This classification had some influence on later Shafiᶜi legal texts, and inspired another procedure which divided legal subjects into four groups: *ᶜibadah, muᶜamalah, munakahah* (personal status) and *jinayah* or *ᶜuqubah* (penal law). In order to justify this latter division, it is said that the subjects of *fiqh* concern either life in this world or life in the hereafter. The subjects related to the former state of being are divided into three parts: those which regulate human relationships (*muᶜamalah*), those which preserve human kind (*munakahah*) and those which protect both individuals and mankind (*jinayah*). The subjects related to the latter state of being, i.e. the precepts which should bring happiness and welfare in the next life, are *ibadah.

The oldest extant systematic codifications of Shi*i law are found in some works of jurists of the fifth/eleventh century. Abu'l-Salah al-Halabi (d. 447/1055-6) classified, in his *al-Kafi fi 'l-fiqh*, the legal subjects according to the religious precepts. He considered all religious dues to be of three kinds: *ibadah*, by which he meant not only the common acts of devotion but all obligations including part of the category of *mu*amalah*, *muharramah* (prohibitions) and *ahkam* (rules). This latter term refers to all legal precepts which do not impose any religions duty (action or abstention) on Muslims, i.e. which cannot be included in the other two categories.

Qadi *Abd al-*Aziz ibn al-Barraj (d. 481/1088) in his *al-Muhazzab* divided religious precepts into two categories, those which affect *all* the people and those which do not. The former are *ibadah* which are general duties and for this very reason precede the rest of *fiqh*.

Another Shi*i jurist of the same period, Sallar ibn *Abd al-*Aziz al-Daylami (d. 448/1056-7) first classified *fiqh* in two sections: *ibadat* and *mu*amalat*, then he divided the latter into *uqud* (contracts) and *ahkam*, and then divided *ahkam* further into *jinayah* and other types of rules. Al-Muhaqqiq, inspired by this method, classified *fiqh* in his *Shara'i* al-Islam* into four sections: *ibadah, *uqud* (here meaning bilateral obligations), *iqa*ah* (unilateral obligations) and *ahkam*. This method was accepted by jurists who succeeded him. Al-Shahid al-Awwal justified this classification in his *al-Qawa*id* by arguing that religious precepts are concerned either with life on earth or life in the herafter. The former all under *mu*amalah* and the latter under *ibadah*. This first category, the *mu*amalah*, is in turn divided into two parts since these are precepts which either concern the undertakings of individuals themselves or those which are not related to the undertakings of individuals. These latter are known as *ahkam* and include all judicial, penal and inheritance rules, etc. Undertakings too are of two kinds since some are bilateral (*uqud*) and others unilateral (*iqa*at*). Al-Shahid offers the same explanation in his *Zikra* with the exception that in this book, the basic difference between *ibadat* and other categories is that acts of devotion must be practised in order to obey God and move closer to him, whereas other categories do not carry this obligation. Some other scholars considered the basis for separating *ibadah* (from other subjects) to be the intrinsic beauty and superiority of the act of devotion itself.

Nasir al-Din al-Tusi (d. 672/1274) followed a more philosophical approach and proposed a tripartite classification. He argued that the religious laws concern individuals either as individual bearers of responsibility or as members of the family, or as people in society. The first category is the section on *ᶜibadah*, the second is the rules included in the section on *munakahah* and other parts of *muᶜamalah*, and the third is *siyasah* (penal law).

Al-Fadil al-Miqdad (d. 826/1423) proposed two other modes of division in the classification of the legal subjects. Both approaches were inspired by *al-Qawaᶜid* of al-Shahid al-Awwal. One method is based on the belief that in the course of their moral development, human beings must acquire the traits beneficial to human life and character, and reject those which are destructive. Some of these beneficial traits may bring about instant results, others more distant results, depending on the nature of these traits. Acts of devotion belong to the latter category; rules relating to marriage, trans-actions, food and drink (*al-atᶜimah wa 'l-ashribah*) and the like belong to the former. The precepts of penal law aim to combat those destructive traits which inhibit the progress of human beings. This method, thus, divides the subjects of *fiqh* into three categories.

The other mode of classification proposed by Miqdad divides *fiqh* into six sections. This approach is on the basis that religions have been laid down for the protection of the five basic elements of human life, viz: faith, life, property, lineage and reason. Acts of devotion are the pillar of faith; the criminal law which gives the right of retaliation to the offended person is to create a guarantee for life; regulations concerning transactions regulate financial relations and protect property; marriage regulations, related laws and some penal precepts are for the reproduction of the human race; precepts related to the prohibition of alcohol and the punishment of drinkers of alcohol and the like protect human reason. Moreover, legal precepts are laid down in order to protect the totality of the Islamic system and guarantee its correct application.

Muhsin al-Fayd followed a new approach in his works on law and Tradi-tion such as *al-Wafi, Muᶜtasam al-shiᶜah* and *Mafatih al-shara'iᶜ*. He merged some chapters of *fiqh* and changed the locations of some legal headings, mostly for the purpose of ordering it according to the human life-cycle. For instance, he put the chapters on death and the deceased, *ahkam al-amwat* (which in previous texts were in the *al-tahara*, traditionally the first chapter of *fiqh*), at the end, followed by the chapter on inheritance. In this way, he tried to create a new codification for law and Tradition. He divided *fiqh* into two sections: one on acts of devotion and the social duties (*al-ᶜibadat wa'l-siyasah*) and the other on ordinary affairs and transactions (*al-ᶜadat wa'l-muᶜamalah*).

Another method, which is inspired by modern western approaches to the classification of legal subjects, divides topics of *fiqh* into the following categories:

I ᶜ*ibadah*
II Property. This may be of two kinds:
   A. Public property, which does not belong to a person but is allocated for use in the general interests of the community.
   B. Private property. The regulations of this section are discussed in two independent parts:
      1. The lawful means of ownership.
      2. The rules concerning the disposal of property.
III Personal behaviors and practices, i.e. ordinary affairs which do not concern religious devotions or financial matters. These are of two kinds:
   A. Family law.
   B. The rules for social relations and behaviour of individuals in the society.
IV Political subjects in general.

* * *

The chapters of Shiᶜi law, which are called 'books' (*kutub*, sing. *kitab*), are concerned with various legal subjects. Together they provide a catalogue of the personal and social duties of a Shiᶜi Muslim.

The arrangement of these chapters varies in different texts, but generally the chapters on devotions are located at the beginning, those on transactions in the middle and those on inheritance and the penal code, at the end. In some Sunni legal works, the reasons for this arrangment are given at the start of some of the chapters.

Sunni and Shiᶜi authors have stated that the reason why they place some chapters before others is that not only are these intrinsically more important but that religion also endows them with an importance above others.

Qadi ᶜAbd al-ᶜAziz ibn al-Barraj holds that the arrangement of the chapters is related to the generality of the subjects they treat. According to him, acts of devotion which have to be practised by all Muslims at all times and anywhere, have priority over transactions, executive rules, etc., which are restricted by certain conditions. Amongst the acts of devotion, prayer, which is a daily duty for every Muslim and is, in fact, the most regular Islamic duty, together with its requisite ritual purity (*taharah*), come before the other acts of devotion. Ibn Hamzah, another Shiᶜi jurist of the sixth/twelfth century, adopting the same view, evaluated the degree of the applicability of each of these acts to devotion, and included a discussion of this in the preface of his work *al-Wasila*. Abu'l-Fath Muhammad ibn ᶜAli ibn ᶜUthman al-Karajaki (d. 449/1057–58) arranged the chapters of *fiqh* in his legal work called *Bustan* like the branches of a tree. He tried to connect the branches to each other so as to create a natural arrangement of the topics. In his pattern, the first chapter of each section was s smaller branch growing from trunk of the tree itself. Each later chapter in a section was a smaller branch growing from the main one. We do not know any further details of his pattern which was described by one of his contemporaries as a novel plan.

The different approaches adopted by the scholars with regard to the codification of legal subjects resulted in a variety of arrangements of the chapters in their books. There was also much disagreement about the subdivisions of sections. For instance the number of acts of devotion is five according to Shaykh al-Ta'ifah and Ibn Zuhrah, six according to Sallar, ten according to al-Halabi, Ibn Hamzah and al-Muhaqqiq and forty-five according to Yahya ibn Sa{{c}}id.

On the other hand, some authors, especially later ones, merged different chapters and reduced the number of general titles as much as possible. Thus there is considerable variation between legal texts in respect to their arrangement and the number of chapters. For instance, *al-Nihaya* by Shaykh al-Ta'ifah has twenty-two chapters, his *al-Mabsut* seventy one, *Shara'i{{c}} al-islam* by al-Muhaqqiq fifty-two, *Qawa{{c}}id al-ahkam* by {{c}}Allamah thirty-one, his *Tabsirat al-muta{{c}}allimin* eighteen, *al-Lum{{c}}a al-dimashqiyya* by al-Shahid al-Awwal fifty-two, his *al-Durus al-shar{{c}} iyyah* forty-eight, *Mafatih al-shara'i{{c}}* by al-Fayd twelve, and his *al-Wafi* (which is a collection of traditions) ten.

Chapter Six

Ruler and Society

The position of Shi°ism on leadership stems directly from the doctrine of the Imamate. Both leadership (imamah) and the community (ummah) are institutional expressions of Divine Will, and, as such, have their roots in the Islamic revelation. As successors to Muhammad, the Shi°i Imams have comprehensive authority. The first passage selected here is of particular importance. In his famous letter to Malik al-Ashtar al-Nakha°i, °Ali provides one of the earliest records extant, outside the Qur'anic text and the prophetic traditions, on the model of rulership. William Chittick's passage which is a pious reading of °Ali rulership, in theory and practice, is followed by Sulayman Kattani's interpretation of °Ali's position on leadership. The passages are taken from SA, pages 67–77, IASLWM, page 97–108.

Imam ᶜAli

Professing God's unity and accepting Muhammad as His prophet bring in their wake innumerable consequences. If the Qur'an is God's Word and Muhammad His chosen messenger who "speaks out not of caprice" (LIII:3), their instructions concerning all things must be obeyed. Faced with these facts of their faith, the Muslims soon developed a complicated science of the *shariᶜah* or Divine Law, a science which embraces every dimension of human conduct, including the political.

One of the earliest and best expositions of Islam's explicit and implicit instructions concerning government and its role in society is ᶜAli's instructions to Malik ibn al-Harith al-Nakhaᶜi, surnamed al-Ashtar ("the man with inverted eyelashes") because of a wound he received in battle. He was one of the foremost Muslim warriors in the first few years of Islam's spread and one of ᶜAli's staunchest supporters. He advised ᶜAli against making a truce with Muᶜawiyah at the Battle of Siffin and was poisoned on his way to assume his post as governor of Egypt in the year 37/658 or 38/659, shortly after ᶜAli became caliph following the assassination of ᶜUthamn.

*   *   *

ᶜAli wrote these instructions to al-Ashtar al-Nakhaᶜi when he appointed him governor of Egypt and its provinces at the time the rule of Muhammad ibn Abu Bakr was in turmoil. It is the longest set of instructions (in the *Nahj al-balaghah*). Among all his letters it embraces the largest number of good qualities.

*   *   *

In the Name of God, the Merciful, the Compassionate

This is that with which ᶜAli, the servant of God and Commander of the Faithful, charged Malik ibn al-Harith al-Ashtar in his instructions to him when he appointed him governor of Egypt: to collect its land tax, to war against its enemies, to improve the condition of the people, and to engender prosperity in its regions. He charged him to fear God, to prefer obedience to Him (over all else) and to follow what He has directed in His Book—both the acts He has made obligatory and those He recommends—for none attains felicity but he who follows His directions, and none is overcome by wretchedness but he who denies them and lets them slip by. (He charged him) to help God—glory be to Him—with his heart, his hand and his tongue, for He—majestic in His Name—has promised to help him who exalts Him. And he charged him to break the passions of his soul and restrain it in its recalcitrance, for the soul incites to evil, except inasmuch as God has mercy.

* * *

Know, O Malik, that I am sending you to a land where governments, just and unjust, have existed before you. People will look upon your affairs in the same way that you were wont to look upon the affairs of the rulers before you. They will speak about you as you were wont to speak about those rulers. And the righteous are only known by that which God causes to pass concerning them on the tongues of His servants. So let the dearest of your treasuries be the treasury of righteous action. Control your desire and restrain your soul from what is not lawful to you, for restraint of the soul is for it to be equitous in what it likes and dislikes. Infuse your heart with mercy, love and kindness for your subjects. Be not in face of them a voracious animal, counting them as easy prey, for they are of two kinds: either they are your brothers in religion or your equals in creation. Error catches them unaware, deficiencies overcome them, (evil deeds) are committed by them intentionally and by mistake. So grant them your pardon and your forgiveness to the same extent that you hope God will grant you His pardon and His forgiveness. For you are above them, and he who appointed you is above you, and God is above him who appointed you. God has sought from you the fulfillment of their requirements and He is trying you with them.

Set yourself not up to war against God, for you have no power against His vengeance, nor are you able to dispense with His pardon and His mercy. Never be regretful of pardon or rejoice at punishment, and never hasten (to act) upon an impulse if you can find a better course. Never say, "I am invested with authority, I give orders and I am obeyed," for surely that is corruption in the heart, enfeeblement of the religion and an approach to changes (in fortune). If the authority you possess engender in you pride or arrogance, then reflect upon the tremendousness of the dominion of God above you and His power over you in that in which you yourself have no control. This will subdue your recalcitrance, restrain your violence and restore in you what has left you of the power of your reason. Beware of vying with God in His tremendousness and likening yourself to Him in His exclusive power, for God abases every tyrant and humiliates all who are proud.

See that justice is done towards God and justice is done towards the people by yourself, your own family and those whom you favor among your subjects. For if you do not do so, you have worked wrong. And as for him who wrongs the servants of God, God is his adversary, not to speak of His servants. God renders null and void the argument of whosoever contends with Him. Such a one will be God's enemy until he desists or repents. Nothing is more conducive to the removal of God's blessing and the hastening of His vengeance than to continue in wrongdoing, for God harkens to the call of the oppressed and He is ever on the watch against the wrongdoers.

Let the dearest of your affairs be those which are middlemost in rightfulness, most inclusive in justice and most comprehensive in (establishing) the content of the subjects. For the discontent of the common people invalidates the content of favorites, and the discontent of favorites is pardoned at (the achievement of) the content of the masses. Moreover, none of the subjects is more burdensome upon the ruler in ease and less of a help to him in trial than his favorites. (None are) more disgusted by equity, more importunate in demands, less grateful upon bestowal, slower to pardon (the ruler upon his) withholding (favor) and more deficient in patience at the misfortunes of time than the favorites. Whereas the support of religion, the solidarity of Muslims and preparedness in the face of the enemy lie only with the common people of the community, so let your inclination and affection be toward them.

Let the farthest of your subjects from you and the most hateful to you be he who most seeks out the faults of men. For men possess faults, which the ruler more than anyone else should conceal. So do not uncover those of them which are hidden from you, for it is only encumbent upon you to remedy what appears before you. God will judge what is hidden from you. So veil imperfection to the extent you are able; God will veil that of yourself which you would like to have veiled from your subjects. Loose from men the knot of every resentment, sever from yourself the cause of every animosity, and ignore all that which does not become your station. Never hasten to believe the slanderer, for the slanderer is a deceiver, even if he seems to be a sincere advisor.

Bring not into your consultation a miser, who might turn you away from liberality and promise you poverty; nor a coward, who might enfeeble you in your affairs; nor a greedy man, who might in his lust deck out oppression to you as something fair. Miserliness, cowardliness and greed are diverse temperaments which have in common distrust in God.

Truly the worst of your viziers are those who were the viziers of the evil (rulers) before you and shared with them in their sins. Let them not be among your retinue, for they are aides of the sinners and brothers of the wrongdoers. You will find the best of substitutes for them from among those who possess the like of their ideas and effectiveness but are not encumbranced by the like of their sins and crimes; who have not aided a wrongdoer in his wrongs nor a sinner in his sins. These will be a lighter burden upon you, a better aid, more inclined toward you in sympathy and less intimate with people other than you. So choose these men as your special companions in privacy and at assemblies. Then let the most influential among them be he who speaks most to you with the bitterness of the truth and supports you least in activities which God dislikes in His friends, however this strikes your pleasure. Cling to men of piety and veracity. Then accustom them not to lavish praise upon you nor to (try to) gladden you by (attributing to you) a vanity you did not do, for the lavishing of abundant praise causes arrogance and draws (one) close to pride.

Never let the gooddoer and the evildoer possess an equal station before you, for that would cause the gooddoer to abstain from his gooddoing and habituate the evildoer to his evildoing. Impose upon each of them what he has imposed upon himself.

Know that there is nothing more conducive to the ruler's trusting his subjects than that he be kind towards them, lighten their burdens and abandon coercing them in that in which they possess not the ability. So in this respect you should attain a situation in which you can confidently trust your subjects, for trusting (them) will sever from you lasting strain. And surely he who most deserves your trust is he who has done well when you have tested him, and he who most deserves your mistrust is he who has done badly when you have tested him.

Abolish no proper custom (*sunnah*) which has been acted upon by the leaders of this community, through which harmony has been strengthened and because of which the subjects have prospered. Create no new custom which might in any way prejudice the customs of the past, lest their reward belong to him who originated them, and the burden be upon you to the extent that you have abolished them.

Study much with men of knowledge (*culama'*) and converse much with sages (*hukama'*) concerning the consolidation of that which causes the state of your land to prosper and the establishment of that by which the people before you remained strong.

* * *

Know the subjects are of various classes, none of which can be set aright without the others and none of which is independent from the others. Among them are (1.) the soldiers of God, (2.) secretaries for the common people and the people of distinction, executors of justice and administrators of equity and kindness, (3.) payers of *jizyah* and land tax, namely the people of protective covenants and the Muslims (4.) merchants and craftsmen and (5.) the lowest class, the needy and wretched. For each of them God has designated a portion, and commensurate with each portion He has established obligatory acts (*faridah*) in His Book and the Sunnah of His Prophet — may God bless him and his household and give them peace — as a covenant from Him maintained by us.

Now soldiers, by the leave of God, are the fortresses of the subjects, the adornment of rulers, the might of religion and the means to security. The subjects have no support by them, and the soldiers in their turn have no support but the land tax which God has extracted for them, (a tax) by which they are given the power to war against their enemy and upon which they depend for that which puts their situation in order and meets their needs. Then these two classes (soldiers and taxpayers) have no support but the third class, the judges, administrators and secretaries, for they draw up contracts, gather yields, and are entrusted with private and public affairs. And all of these have no support but the merchants and craftsmen, through the goods which they bring together and the markets which they set up. They provide for the needs (of the first three classes) by acquiring with their own hands those (goods) to which the resources of others do not attain. Then there is the lowest class, the needy and wretched, those who have the right to aid and assistance. With God there is plenty for each (of the classes). Each has a claim upon the ruler to the extent that will set it aright. But the ruler will not truly accomplish what God has enjoined upon him in this respect except by resolutely striving, by recourse to God's help, by reconciling himself to what the truth requires and by being patient in the face of it in what is easy for him or burdensome.

*   *   *

Appoint as commander from among your troops that person who is in your sight the most sincere in the way of God and His Prophet and of your Imam, who is purest of heart and most outstanding in intelligence, who is slow to anger, relieved to pardon, gentle to the weak and harsh with the strong and who is not stirred to action by severity nor held back by incapacity. Then hold fast to men of noble descent and those of righteous families and good precedents, then to men of bravery, courage, generosity and magnanimity, for they are encompassed by nobility and embraced by honor.

Then inspect the affairs of the soldiers as parents inspect their own child. Never let anything through which you have strengthened them distress you, and disdain not a kindness you have undertaken for them, even if it be small, for it will invite them to counsel you sincerely and trust you. Do not leave aside the examination of their minor affairs while depending upon (the examination of) the great, for there is a place where they will profit from a trifling kindness, and an occasion in which they cannot do without the great.

Among the chiefs of your army favor most him who assists the soldiers with his aid and bestows upon them what is at his disposal to the extent that suffices both them and the members of their families left behind. Then their concern in battle with the enemy will be a single concern, for your kind inclination toward them will incline their hearts to you. Verily the foremost delight of the eye for rulers is the establishment of justice in the land and the appearance of love for them among the subjects. But surely the subjects' love will not appear with the well-being of their breasts, and their sincerity (toward rulers) will not become free from blemishes unless they watch over their rulers, find their governments of little burden and cease to hope that their period (of rule) will soon come to an end. Therefore let their hopes be expanded, and persist in praising them warmly and taking into account the (good) accomplishments of everyone among them who has accomplished, for frequent mention of their good deeds will encourage the bold and rouse the indolent, God willing.

Then recognize in every man that which he has accomplished, attribute not one man's accomplishment to another and fall not short (of attributing) to him the full extent of his accomplishment. Let not a man's eminence invite you to consider as great an accomplishment which was small, not a man's lowliness to consider as small an accomplishment which was great.

Refer to God and His Messenger any concerns which distress you and any matters which are obscure for you, for God — high be He exalted — has said to a people whom He desired to guide, "O believers, obey God, and obey the Messenger and those in authority among you. If you should quarrel on anything, refer it to God and the Messenger" (IV: 59). To refer to God is to adhere to the clear text of His Book, while to refer to the Prophet is to adhere to his uniting (*al-jamicah*) *sunnah*, not the dividing (*al-mufarriq*).

Then choose to judge (*al-hukm*) among men him who in your sight is the most excellent of subjects, i.e., one who is not beleaguered by (complex) affairs, who is not rendered ill-tempered by the litigants, who does not persist in error, who is not distressed by returning to the truth when he recognizes it, whose soul does not descend to any kind of greed, who is not satisfied with an inferior understanding (of a thing) short of the more thorough, who hesitates most in (acting in the face of) obscurities, who adheres most to arguments, who is the least to become annoyed at the petition of the litigants, who is the most patient (in waiting) for the facts to become clear and who is the firmest when the verdict has become manifest; a man who does not become conceited when praise is lavished upon him and who is not attracted by temptation. But such (men) are rare.

Thereupon investigate frequently his execution of the law (*qada*) and grant generously to him that which will eliminate his lacks and through which his need for men will decrease. Bestow upon him that station near to you to which none of your other favorites may aspire, that by it he may be secure from (character) assassination before you by men of importance. (In sum) study that (i.e., the selections of judges) with thorough consideration, for this religion was prisoner in the hands of the wicked, who acted with it out of caprice and used it to seek (the pleasures of) the present world.

Then look into the affairs of your administrators. Employ them (only after) having tested (them) and appoint them not with favoritism or arbitrariness, for these two (attributes) embrace different kinds of oppression and treachery. Among them look for people of experience and modesty from righteous families foremost in Islam, for they are nobler in moral qualities, more genuine in dignity and less concerned with ambitious designs, and they perceive more penetratingly the consequences of affairs. Then bestow provisions upon them liberally, for that will empower them to set themselves aright and to dispense with consuming what is under their authority; and it is an argument against them if they should disobey your command or sully your trust.

Then investigate their actions. Dispatch truthful and loyal observers (to watch) over them, for your investigation of their affairs in secret will incite them to carry out their trust faithfully and to act kindly toward the subjects. Be heedful of aides. If one of them should extend his hand in a treacherous act, concerning which the intelligence received against him from your observers concurs, and if you are satisfied with that as a witness, subject him to corporeal punishment and seize him for what befell from his action. Then install him in a position of degradation, brand him with treachery and grid him with the shame of accusation.

Investigate the situation of the land tax in a manner that will rectify the state of those who pay for it, for int the correctness of the land tax and the welfare of the taxpayers is the welfare of others. The welfare of others will not be achieved except through them, for the people, all of them, are dependent upon the land tax and those who pay it. Let your care for the prosperity of the earth be deeper than your care for the collecting of land tax, for it will not be gathered except in prosperity. Whoever exacts land tax without prosperity has desolated the land and destroyed the servants (of God). His affairs will remain in order but briefly.

So if your subjects complain of burden, of blight, of the cutting off of irrigation water, lack of rain, or of the transformation of the earth through its being inundated by a flood or ruined by drought, lighten (their burden) to the extent you wish their affairs to be rectified. And let not anything by which you have lightened their burden weigh heavily against you, for it is a store which they will return to you by bringing about prosperity in your land and embellishing your rule. You will gain their fairest praise and pride yourself at the spreading forth of justice among them. You will be able to depend upon the increase in their strength (resulting) from what you stored away with them when you gave them ease; and upon their trust, since you accustomed them to your justice toward them through your kindness to them. Then perhaps matters will arise which afterwards they will undertake gladly if in these you depend upon them, for prosperity will carry that with which you burden. Truly the destruction of the earth only results from the destitution of its inhabitants, and its inhabitants become destitute only when rulers concern themselves with amassing (wealth), when they have misgivings about the endurance (of their own rule) and when they profit little from warning examples.

Then examine the state of your secretaries and put the best of them in charge of your affairs. Assign those of your letters in which you insert your strategems and secrets to him among them most generously endowed with the aspects of righteous moral qualities, a person whom high estate does not make reckless, that because of it he might be so bold as to oppose you in the presence of an assembly. (He should be someone) whom negligence will not hinder from delivering to you the letters of your administrators, nor from issuing their answers properly for you in that which he takes for you and bestows in your stead; a person who will not weaken a contract which he binds for you, nor will he be incapable of dissolving what has been contracted to your loss; a man who is not ignorant of the extent of his own value in affairs, for he who is ignorant of his own value is even more ignorant of the value of others.

Let not your choosing of them be in accordance with your own discernment, confidence and good opinion, for men make themselves known to the discernment of rulers by dissimulating and serving them well, even though beyond this there may be nothing of sincere counsel and loyalty. Rather examine them in that with which they were entrusted by the righteous before you. Depend upon him who has left the fairest impression upon the common people and whose countenance is best known for trustworthiness. This will be proof of your sincerity toward God and toward him whose affair has been entrusted to you.

Appoint to the head of each of your concerns a chief from among these men, (a person) who is neither overpowered when these concerns are great nor disturbed when they are many. Whatever fault of your secretaries you overlook will come to be attached to you.

Then make merchants and craftsmen—those who are permanently fixed, those who move about with their wares and those who profit from (the labor of) their own body—your own concern, and urge others to do so, for they are the bases of benefits and the means of attaining conveniences. They bring (benefits and conveniences) from remote and inaccessible places in the land, sea, plains and mountains, and from places where men neither gather together nor dare to go. (The merchants and craftsmen) are a gentleness from which there is no fear of calamity and a pacifity from which there is no worry of disruption. Examine their affairs in your presence and in every corner of your land.

But know, nevertheless, that in many of them is shameful miserliness, detestable avarice, hoarding of benefits and arbitrariness in sales. This is a source of loss to all and a stain upon rulers. So prohibit hoarding (*ihtikar*), for the Messenger of God—may God bless him and his household and give them peace—prohibited it. Let selling be an openhanded selling, with justly balanced scales and price which do not prejudice either party, buyer or seller. As for him who lets himself be tempted to hoard after you have forbidden him (to do so), make an example of him and punish him, but not excessively.

Then (fear) God, (fear) God regarding the lowest class, the wretched, needy, suffering and disabled who have no means at their disposal, for in this class there is he who begs and he who is needy (but does not beg). Be heedful for God's sake of those rights of theirs which He has entrusted to you. Set aside for them a share of your treasury (*bayt al-mal*) and in every town a share of the produce of the lands of Islam taken as booty (*sawafi al-islam*), for to the farthest away of them belongs the equivalent of what belongs to the nearest. You are bound to observe the right of each of them, so be not distracted from them by arrogance, for you will not be excused if, to attend to the very important affair, you neglect the trifling. So avert not your solicitude from them and turn not your face away from them in contempt.

Investigate the affairs of those (of the lowest class) who are unable to gain access to you, those upon whom eyes disdain to gaze and whom men regard with scorn. Appoint to attend exclusively to them a person whom you trust from among the godfearing and humble, and let him submit to you their affairs. Then act toward them in a manner that will absolve you before God on the day that you meet Him. For among the subjects these are more in need of equity than others. In the case of each of them prepare your excuse with God by accomplishing for him his rightfully due (*al-haqq*). Take upon yourself the upkeep of the orphans and aged from among those who have no means at their disposal and do not exert themselves in begging. (All of) this is a heavy burden upon rulers. The truth (*al-haqq*), all of it, is a heavy burden. But God may lighten it for people who seek the final end, who admonish their souls to be patient and trust in the truth of God's promise to them.

Sulayman Kattani

There is no doubt that the beginning of government was for ᶜAli ibn Abi Talib a crowding in of burdens and the end would never be less than it.

At all events, he did not seek government as a means of pleasure and enjoyment. Rather he sought it for its responsibilities and its burdens.

> The responsibility which has been put on men of knowledge is that they should not show approval of the gluttony of the wrongdoer, nor of starvation of oppressed. They should not follow a path of reconciliation and softness towards that but they should firmly attack it.

Advice came to him from al-Maghirah ibn Shuᶜbah and Ibn ᶜAbbas that he should bargain and be friendly. He refused and said: "I will not cheat my religion. I will not give in to base conduct in my affairs."

How does he do that? Is his path unique and pure? Whom does he fear? What does he fear?

> Whoever ears death will not escape it. Whoever wants to remain here for ever will not be granted it.

Is it from the world that its treasures and bounties and praises are kept away from him? What can a man who has been created for the Next World do with this world? What will a man who will soon be deprived of wealth do with it while his responsibility and his account remain?

He did not wear things of the world except for a shirt of white cotton and respected armour. He did not eat except for a few grains of barley crushed in his hands, a dry morsel for his mouth. He did not live in palaces but rather in the humblest of huts. He did not ride any animals except a good horse in battle. For him poverty was an end, power a means.

> The world is a place in which I will come to end and its inhabitants will emigrate from it. . . . It is pleasant in bloom. It comes quickly to the one who seeks it and it is obscure in the heart of the onlooker. Journey from it with the best of the provisions which are provided for you. Do not ask from it more than what is sufficient to live and do not seek from it more than the means of sustenance.

Once ᶜAsim ibn Ziyad al-Harithi asked him: "Commander of the faithful, why is your dress so rough and your food so coarse?"

"Woe upon you," he answered him, "I am not like you. God has required the Imams of justice to value themselves with the weakest of men so that the poor man is not disturbed by his poverty."

This world, which he dealt with ascetically and piously throughout his life and to which he stretched out his hand in honesty and truth and heroism, was something which he was never able at that time to grasp with the grasp of a beggar who loved it and of a man who was greedy for its apartments. He would never be afraid of it . . . . At that time he only came forward to explain the programme of life which had been drawn up . . . how the world should be looked at; how it was possible to use it as a tool to arrive at the ultimate destination; how it was appropriate for man to act in it as a mature person understanding reason; and how the protection of society could only be carried out on the basis of the consciousness of a rational person who was rightly guided.

Such a clear programme as this was the plan of ᶜAli ibn Abi Talib in all its facets. He laid it on himself and he lived it all his life. He spread it in all his words and actions . . . . He was never able, in any way, in the world to reduce its value and to cut a single thread from the substance of its texture. He became, to the limit of himself, its constant colour and its ultimate support.

From this, bargaining was not a possible way to open its door. Nor did the threat of death have any real role in any part of his plan . . . because death, in his view, when it cut him off from life — and it would certainly do so — would never be able to cut him off from his Lord for Whom he worked and to Whom he would return.

He said: "I patched my cloak until I was ashamed of its patches. Someone asked me: Aren't you going to throw it away. I replied: Get away from me. In the morning the people will praise the generous Lord."

He also said just before his death: "Tomorrow you will look back at my time and my innermost thoughts will be revealed to you. You will recognize me after I have left my position and another has taken my place."

As he looked at ᶜUthman following a plan which had not been drawn up by the Message, it became impossible for him, while he held the reins of government, to abandon the plan as it had been first laid out. Similarly the revolution which blew, rooting out corruption, would not have been born if it had not been for the fact that it drank from his wholesome spring.

Since bargaining was excluded in word and spirit from the speech of ᶜAli, another word to express its meaning had to take its place . . . and it was firmness.

This firmness was not able to convey any frivolity. He had hewn it from that harshness with which the metals of truth and justice are adorned. He had coloured it with that magnamity and honesty and he had given it that bravery and heroism. Indeed it was a true expression of his absolute purity, his great preciousness, his thoughts of genius. He would never be without this firmness because it was sthe support of his unique personality. It was his guide throughout all his life. It is that which accompanied him in all his struggles and it is that which still accompanies him even now in the history of his eternal memory.

He began to carry out the administration at the moment in which he was handed the legal power of administration. He dismissed the governors whom the late Caliph had appointed over the territories, all conquered by the force of the Message. Instead of them he put men tested in virtue and he gave them a new slogan "cleanliness."

This cleanliness would be understood by such words as truth, honesty, sincerity, piety and kindness.

He never entrusted a governor with a task over the people without addressing such words as follows:

> To Ash^cath ibn Qays, Governor of Azarbaijan,
> Your task is not a means of fulfilling your appetite. Rather it is a trust invested in you. You will observe those who are above you. You have no right to offend your subjects. You will only risk trust. In your hands is wealth which is part of the wealth of God, the Mighty and High. You are only its storekeeper until you hand it over to me. Perhaps I may not be the worst of your rulers to you. Greetings.

> To Ziyad, son of his father,
> I swear a true oath before God: If I am informed that you have betrayed any of the Muslims' booty, whether little or large, I will attack you with a violence which will leave you little wealth, a heavy back and meagre affairs. Greetings.

He also said to him:

> Be a moderate man and leave off squandering. Remember tomorrow during today. Take from wealth the amount you need and offer the excess to the time of your need. Do you expect god to give you the reward of the believer while you are one of the proud towards Him? Do you aspire to Him while you wallow in pleasure? The weak and the widow will deny to Him that you should receive the reward of those who give alms. A man will only be rewarded for what he has done before and he will only reach what he set out to reach. Greetings.

In this manner did Imam ^cAli hand over the reins of affairs to men on whom he imposed clean hands from his own hand and an honest programme from his own tongue and resolute actions from his own firmness. He distributed to them a list of the principles which it was necessary to adopt to block errors. . . .

> By God, if you found him whom women marry and by whom maid-servants are owned, you would reject him.
> There is wide scope in justice . . . Whoever justice restricts would be even more restricted by injustice.
> A man who has no manhood has no religion.
> The liar has no honour.
> A branch of anything must grow out of its root.
> The shadow of the lame is crooked.
> The false circulates for an hour while the truth circulates until the Final Hour.

Let not ambition tempt you and then God will make you free.
Be a helper to the oppressed and an opponent to the oppressor.
The poverty of leaders is easier than the leadership of the ignorant.
At the final testing a man will be honored or humiliated.
A man's state is decided by his avoidance of things forbidden and his practice of things which are virtuous.
The wickedest of rulers is the one feared by the innocent.
The administration of justice involves three things: compassion with determination; a thorough examination of justice; and bestowing benefit with a purpose.
Truth is a cutting sword.
A just Imam is better than lands and camels.
The garment of reason is the noblest of clothes.
Be assiduous in doing work whose rewards will not disappear.
The one who rides injustice will be overturned by his mount.

. . . And so the advice and proverbs which this list contains go on . . . and they refer to no other way to behave.

This very firmness is what he gave to his leaders and governors whom he directed to work for the general policy under its inspiration. He restored justice to its true place. The refinement of the man of the Arabian Peninsula was the appropriate refinement for mankind . . . . His opponents seized on it in order by that to meet him with that triviality and futility. They took refuge in the discord which they created. They had a matchstick from the shirt of ᶜUthman.

*   *   *

The crisis which burst forth with the death of ᶜUthamn and began to spread his shirt beyond the Arabian Peninsula, beyond every part of the world which the standard of the new religion had reached, was not a newly originated crisis. It had been the crisis of the Arabian Peninsula since man had been there. It was a crisis which had been with it just like its economic situation had been with it.

The meanness of its land reflected a meanness in its way of life and in all its areas of work and thought. Its affairs had continued to be dealt with from the narrow aspects of customs and traditions in which they were clothed for a long period of time to the extent that to modify them had become something of great difficulty.

It had become known that the new Message had come to proclaim a new man who would be able to take control of his situation and develop it. The first thing which had to be begun was the preparation of reason so that it could become an actual force in the creation of this development and in propelling it to improve the economic situation. This structure, which aimed first as thought, had succeeded to a great extent in creating a man who had begun to use his reason.

In fact, the religious tendency which took possession of the reason of the Arabian Peninsula, really made it a centre for a number of intellectual eruptions, which branched out to East and West and which brought about some victories.

However, the Arabian Peninsula, whose reason the religion had been able to bring into motion, had not yet been able to submit its culture to it because culture is a continuous practice and reflection in the minds of men over a very long period. That culture was like the return of a voice after it had been wandering around all the areas of the cave in which the call had been issued . . . that is, the culture, with which the individual in society was adorned, led him from that society after it had completely embraced him. The new culture of the Arabian Peninsula was of a special kind. It had not reached beyond a position which remembered a time which was not more than four decades away. It was still a culture clearly mixed with what had gone before. It was a culture in a state of transition. Insofar as it was needed to be a basis for an impulse to realise a rational economy by dependence on which it would maintain its motivation and continuation, it did not achieve anything much worth mentioning of this kind. Rather the contrary to that occurred. . . .

The conquests which the Arabian Peninsula achieved sank it inot a superfluity of colonial prosperity insofar as they enabled it to taste luxury without hardship. This permitted wealth was at first distributed among the leaders and the rulers, then gradually to the soldiers . . . until opulent classes were created as innovations. Materialism ruled a tyrant over the spirit. Indeed that materialism became a stumbling-block in the way of a success which would have interwoven souls and minds with the original culture which should have slowly taken its place in society, which in that way would have been supported by a firm generous true economy.

This urge for temporary acquisitions did not include all the individuals among the people . . . Those who were first to take the battlefield were the ones who returned with booty. Out of that was produced a new class consciousness which divided society, awakened in it feelings of mutual envy and spread chaos.

The activists of the conquests came to require much administration in the organization of the army, in the organization of the poll-tax and the booty, in the organization of pay and then also in the organization of ideas and their correct propagation unblemished by errors . . . alongside the organisation of the distribution of booty and wages to the people who had begun to expect an end to their poverty from the new acquisitions to a greater extent than their slender economy could have formerly allowed them to expect. With all that it was not possible for a young state, occupied on every front, to organize itself and produce justice and equity.

Out of that grew deprivation which caused differences to appear in a society which the earnestness of religion had not yet regulated into sound systems of application. Then those leaders and rulers, who sought to enjoy the pleasures of wealth, began to hold on to their positions as a way of acquiring more. They began to protect their positions with a variety of methods. They gathered around themselves supporters and followers.

That was a new tribalism which now an economy of a transitory kind supported so that other groupings of direct opposition arose out of those who were deprived. They could only find this in their old tribalism. They began to gather under the banners of tribalism and to take them with them wherever they went.

In Kufah, for example, they were divided into two groupings. The Eastern division belonged to the Yemenis and the Western division belonged to the tribes of Nizar.

Thus, we see, successively, that the success of the Message which had been brought to build up man in thought and in the economy in the Arabian Peninsula had been brought into conflict with those obstacles which had to be removed before it could continue its advance.

That had escaped it while it was taking its first steps along the road with ᶜUmar ibn al-Khattab, who had only drawn some partial plans which were more concerned with the military aspect than they were concerned with the cultural and spiritual problem and with sound economic direction.

In reality, the Arabian Peninsula was, and still is, in need of a spirituality capable of controlling whims and of preventing the eyes of the inhabitants of the Arabian Peninsula being opened on civilisations which they are not suited to be swallowed up by; and of preventing them from infiltrating into it without spiritual and intellectual preparation to acquire what is good and reject what is bad.

ᶜUmar ibn al-Khattab looked within the society and he saw that the existence of foreign elements in the situation of the Arabian Peninsula was spreading confusion toward the new Message. So he ordered the removal of those elements. The Christians travelled from Najran to Syria. The Jews travelled to Ariha. By way of preparing the Arabian Peninsula to be a basis for a religious republic with pure blood, he prevented marriage with foreigners. He restricted ownership of property outside the Arabian Peninsula and he imposed limitations on this ownership like the payment of tithes, for example. Then he looked at the circumstances of the soldiers and how they had become integrated during the operations of conquest with the conquered peoples in such a way that this integration brought about an evil effect. So he set up special military camps to which the soldiers were to go after the end of every battle.

Al-Jawabi and Hims were the bases for the army in Syria, ᶜAmwas and Tiberias in Jordan, Kufah and Basrah in Iraq. . . . In order to control all these military activities he set up the military registers. This was the first operation to organize the affairs of state, to control its income and to distribute its works.

Similarly the census came as a factor towards the completion of these organizational operations aimed at bringing a distribution of wealth to the Muslims in semi-compensation for their meagre and weak economy. In its planning the economy did not appear to have any direction which could fix it on a sound technical basis. It had been somewhat strengthened in relation to what had come into the state from the widespread conquest which it had achieved with extraordinary speed. However, real concern for it had been abandoned for the time being so that its plans for the develoment of reason were based on borrowing from the surrounding civilizations everything which was beautiful and new.

Those were the aims and plans of ᶜUmar ibn al-Khattab which looked to the future from a scientific point of view. Do you think that he was right in all those techniques? Or do you think that something of this kind would never be able to attain a degree of perfection without proper administrative experience? That had happened at the beginning of the administration in a state which had begun to establish its existence for the first time in its history — and these were only some plans and not all of them, which ought to have been drawn with full understanding and care. Steps toward them ought to have been taken with complete sincerity and impartiality and they should have been studied completely realistically with great restraint. They should then have been adopted fully and applied with every care and consideration.

In the case of ᶜUthman ibn ᶜAffan, he did not look for a plan to build society with the really sincere care or vigilant application which were necessary . . . . The state was allowed to stray away from its true purposes. The great values of the Message began to be dissipated through the temptations of conquest. Conquest itself became an end and a means towards which the people raced insofar as the battle fronts had become a crowded center towards which the majority of the inhabitants of the Arabian Peninsula had journeyed.

As for the rational spiritual structure of society, it had been neglected as a result of the diversion caused by numerous temptations, including property, valuable treasures, prisoners, servants and money . . . and so on down the list of things acquired by plunder and spoil.

The wise people in the Arabian Peninsula became annoyed at this, as did those who were deprived. . . . Even the conquered territories which had been seized by the splendour of the Message began to become annoyed with those who had started to make it lawful for their lands to be expropriated.

The evidence for this is the fact that the support for the revolution against ᶜUthman ibn ᶜAffan came from hundreds of men from Egypt who came to complain against the Caliph's failure to show integrity in government. This was at the beginning of the foundation of the new state. Yet there is no doubt that the firm basis was that which was relied upon in the construction of the vast edifice whose outline the new religion had put forward. The mistakes which had occurred should not only be reckoned against the leadership, since it had failed to show concern for reinforcing the works of the foundation. These mistakes led to results whose gravity began to worry ᶜAli ibn Abi Talib from the moment the helm of government was handed over to him.

We have alluded to such a concern in a previous section of this book, just as we have indicated that ᶜAli ibn Abi Talib was always aware of the situation which had faced the Message in its first stages. . . . Then man could be Now he assumed the reins of government and at his disposal were plans to put matters right, to compensate for what had gone wrong and to resume the operation of building a sound structure.

However, the situation had become much more difficult than the situation which had faced the Message in its first stages. . . .Then man could be gradually brought to awareness and was complaining of the burden of pagan leadership over him because it was the cause of his isolation and poverty. Now man had been awakened, prepared, and had begun to claim leadership as a means of gaining profit and continuing those profits.

Then man had been an innocent child. . . . Now man had become corrupted by sexual temptation. Then a primitive rationality had been easy to acquire. . . . Now rationality had become again a disease which it added to its earlier state. It required treatment for two shared sicknesses. Then the economy was central and customary. . . . Now the economy permitted things which were not fair. Then the culture which had just begun to take on a rapid structure. . . . Now the awareness of civilizations led to the adoption of these civilizations without any proper understanding, and the harm from them was greater than the benefit. Finally, the man who had brought the Message had still been present then to give proper supervision and convey his influence. . . . Now his absence from the scene revealed the weakness of the planning which ought to have been taken at the establishment of the foundation.

All that was something which would never be easy to confront and to work to restore its organization. . . . The conquest had carried it a long way away and it was in need of constant support to preserve its level.

The school of men who ought to have been able to understand these things in order to educate the rulers and leaders to submit to the leadership of these qualities, was not able to acquire the necessary equipment. The army itself, which had become tantamount to the whole community, which had been called upon to undertake these conquests, was not the custodian of any intellectual and cultural value. It was an army which strove for acquisition far more than it strove to spread high ideals truly worthy of the people among the civilizations which had now been provided with a new garb. The leaders did not have effective control over it in view of the weakness of the organization and the weakness of the leadership. Even the Arabian Peninsula did not improve its economy through the new acquisitions. On the contrary these new acquisitions make it enjoy imaginary wealth quickly consumed and leaving a worse effect than the former situation.

Thus the vicious materialistic trend which entered through the conquest clashed with the culture which had gradually began to crystallize in the operation of illuminating reason and the soul. It sent it back to instincts and desires which were a permanent cause of the destruction of flourishing civilizations. How much more did it enter into a civilization which was still shackled by its primitive chains! The extent of the situation existing then brought together the problem in order to throw on the shoulders of cAli ibn Abi Talib the greatest and most extensive responsibility which the history of the Arabian Peninsula had ever known. Thus through that he was the unhappiest ruler to carry the burdens of an entire people from the moment that he became conscious of himself until his death.

Chapter Seven

Political Theory
and Practice

*The concurrent development of Shi*c*i political thought and the historical experience of the Shi*c*i communities have interacted continuously. The initial belief in* c*Ali's right of succession to the Prophet gave rise to the emergence of the first Shi*c*i communities. Subsequently, these communities produced theologians and other religious authorities who gave doctrinal expression to their beliefs. In the following two passages, Ann Lambton gives a description of the main thrust of Shi*c*i political thought, through an examination of some seminal juridical sources. Then Said Amir Arjomand examines the historical complexity of Shi*c*i political thought and ethos when manifested in institutional forms. Taken together, these two passages demonstrate how catagorical statements about Shi*c*i doctrines become difficult when they are taken in their proper historical contexts. The excerpts are from the* SGMI, *pages 220–241, and* RPALDSI, *pages 59–109.*

Ann K. Lambton

The original political basis of the Shiᶜi was reinforced from two sources. The first was mystical speculation deriving from the eastern Hellenistic world and supplemented by metaphysical ideas and the doctrine of predestination. This mystical speculation issued in the philosophy of light, which the Shiᶜi, with the exception of the Zaydiyyah, took over. According to this theory, as it developed among them, it was believed that, from the creation of Adam onwards, a divine light (sometimes called *nur-i muhammadi*) had passed into the substance of one chosen descendant in each generation and was present in ᶜAli and each of the Imams among his descendants. By virtue of this divine light, it was believed that secret knowledge (*hikmah, hikmat*) was granted to the Imam and immunity from sin conferred upon him. He alone possessed the secret source of knowledge and his decisions alone were decisive and final. It was further believed that man could only acquire knowledge of divine mysteries by being joined to this light through the Imams, who, in succession to the prophet, acted as intermediaries between man and God in the search for divine knowledge. Donaldson thinks that the claim that the celestial light substance had been received into the souls of the Imams was most probably first enunciated during the period of the Imamate of the sixth Imam, Jaᶜfar al-Sadiq (d. 148/765).

Belief that the Imams possessed the divine light inevitably gave a special importance to their writings and sayings in the eyes of the Shiᶜi. For the most part, however, these have little bearing on the political organization of the state. There is one notable exception, the *Najh al-balaghah*, a fifth/eleventh century compilation by Sayyid Sharif al-Radi of diplomas, addresses and letters attributed to ᶜAli ibn Abi Talib, who, as the fourth caliph, exercised, in contradistinction to the other Imams, political rule. One in particular of these documents, ᶜAli's charge to Malik Ashtar [see pages 74–82. Eds.] on his appointment to the office of governor of Egypt in 36/658–659, although it probably only dates from the fourth/tenth century, is regarded by the Imami Shiᶜis as a model to be emulated by rulers.

The second source from which the original political basis of the Shiᶜi was reinforced was the Muᶜtazili doctrine that justice (ᶜadl) was an inherent quality of God and that good and evil were rational absolutes. Although the difference between the Sunnis and Shiᶜis had originally turned on the question of political legitimacy, it came later to rest basically on religious doctrine and concerned the assumption of human perfection in the Imam and his claim to absolute rule.

The Shiᶜis, like the Sunnis, sought to establish their particular point of view by a re-interpretation of the history of the community, especially of events during the lifetime of the prophet, including the incident in 10/632 at Ghadir Khumm, where the prophet is alleged to have made a pronouncement in favour of ᶜAli as his successor, and the passing over of ᶜAli in favour of the first three caliphs. It also involved a reappraisal of the work and life of the Companions. Thus, al-Mutahhar al-Hilli (d. 726/1325) criticizes Abu Bakr and rejects the Sunni argument that he was chosen because the first charge on the Imam was to lead the prayers and the holy war, maintaining that if Abu Bakr was designated to lead the prayers it was as the result of an error.

*   *   *

The Shiᶜis believe that the only lawful successor of Muhammad is his son-in-law, ᶜAli, and that the Imamate continues in his house after him. The various splits which subsequently occurred among the Shiᶜis turned on the question of which member of the house of ᶜAli should receive allegiance as Imam. The Zaydiyyah, as stated above, hold that the Imamate can pass to any of ᶜAli's descendants, but the majority of the Shiᶜis believe that the Imamate is inherent in the descendants of ᶜAli by his wife Fatimah, the daughter of the prophet. In later geneartions disputes occurred among them as to which of his descendants through Fatimah was the Imam. The Imamiyyah recognize twelve Imams descended from ᶜAli and Fatimah and are hence also called Ithna ᶜAshariyyah, or 'Twelvers', as opposed to the Ismaᶜiliyyah, who are also called Sabᶜiyyah, or 'Seveners', because they recognize only seven Imams. The Twelfth Imam, the Imam of the Age (*Imam al-Zaman*), or the Hidden Imam, was born in 255 or 256/869–870 and disappeared in 260/873, shortly after the death of his father, Hasan al-ᶜAskari, the eleventh Imam. The Imamiyyah believe that the twelfth Imam had four agents (*nuwwab* or *sufara*), who acted for him as the successive leaders of his community. The period of their agency is known as the 'lesser concealment'. The fourth agent died in 329/940 without naming a successor. With his death the period of the 'greater concealment' began and still continues. Belief in the occultation or concealment (*ghaybah*) of the Imam differentiates the Imamiyyah from both the Zaydiyyah and the Ismaᶜiliyyah. As a religious movement Shiᶜism obtained its inspiration from the death of Husayn ibn ᶜAli at Karbala in 61/680.

Whereas the Sunnis were concerned to hold together 'church' and state and sought to reconcile religious theory and historical precedent, the Shi^cis as an 'opposition' movement were broadly speaking, at liberty to reject historical precedent. They therefore enjoyed a greater freedom of intellectual speculation and it was not infrequently through the medium of Shi^cism, though not primarily through the jurists, that new ideas and new interpretations were introduced into Islam.

During the Umayyad period a large number of Shi^ci or pro-Shi^ci sects or parties flourished in different parts of the empire, but especially in southern Iraq. When the ^cAbbasids came to power and rejected their heterodox origins, seeking a basis for unity and authority in orthodoxy, the hopes of the Shi^cis were frustrated. While their support was for the most part transferred to the Fatimid line of Imams . . . , Shi^cism, in its various forms, continued to be a general umbrella for movements of religious and political dissent which intermittently threatened the stability of the ^cAbbasid caliphate. In the early fourth/tenth century a Shi^ci family, the Buyids, originally from Daylam in northern Persia, established their rule over most of western and southern Persia and in 334/945 Mu^cizz al-Dawlah entered Baghdad and forced the caliph to give him the title of *amir al-umara'*.

It is not clear whether the early Buyid amirs were Zaydis or Imamis. Mu^cizz al-Dawlah (320–356/932–967) and the Buyid rulers after him appear to have been Imamis. In spite of this they kept the ^cAbbasid caliphate in existence. A new freedom was, however, given to the Shi^cis. In 334/945–946 a *naqib* of the ^cAlids was instituted in Baghdad and during the reign of Mu^cizz al-Dawlah the Shi^cis were allowed to celebrate ^c*Ashura'* and Ghadir Khumm in Baghdad. Shi^ci activity and propaganda during the second half of the fourth/tenth century increased; and factional strife between Shi^cis and Sunnis in Baghdad became frequent. From about the beginning of the fifth/eleventh century there was a Sunni reaction. The overthrow of the ^cAbbasid caliphate by the Mongols did not present such a serious problem for the Shi^cis as it did for the Sunnis. They regarded all governments in the absence of the Imam as unjust. Submission to the Ilkhans was thus not very different from submission to a Sunni government and was thus probably easier for them than for the Sunnis. There is, indeed, evidence that the Mongol attack was seen by some Shi^cis as a means of overthrowing the hated Sunni domination; and some distinguished Shi^cis, notably Nasir al-Din Tusi (597–672/1201–1274), entered the service of the Mongol rulers. Uljaytu (703–716/1304–1316), who was the successor of Ghazan Khan (694–703/1295–1304), the second Ilkhan to be converted to Islam, for a brief period accepted Imami Shi^cism. Leaving aside minor dynasties exercising local rule such as the Sarbidarids, who ruled in Sabzawar from 737/1337 until Timur brought them to an end in 783/1381, it was not until the tenth/sixteenth century, with the rise of the Safavids, that the Imamiyyah formed an independent political organisation. By this time Shiᶜi doctrine had largely divested itself of political reality and the jurists had, it seems, largely become captive of their own traditions.

The constitutive dogma of Shiᶜism is belief in the Imamate as the foundation of faith. Whoever died without knowing the true Imam died the death of the infidel and was, by implication, therefore outside the *ummah*. For the Imamiyyah belief in the imamate was inseparable linked with the question of *walayah*, which involved (i) love and devotion to the *ahl al-bayt* (the people of the house of the prophet), i.e. the Imams (ii) following them in religion, (iii) obedience to their commands and abstention from what they prohibited, (iv) imitation of their actions and conduct, and (v) recognition of their rights and belief in their imamate.

The five principles (*usul*) of Imami belief are belief in the unity of God (*tawhid*), prophethood (*nubuwwah*), the Imamate, the day of resurrection (*maᶜad*), and justice (*ᶜadl*). It is, perhaps, because of the importance given to justice as a principle of belief that justice plays an important role in the political thought of the Shiᶜis in medieval times, though their interpretation of justice by then was rather different from that of the Muᶜtazilis. It also perhaps accounts for the tendency among the Shiᶜis to regard tyranny (*zulm*), the opposite of justice, as the great evil.

The three great period of Imami Shiᶜi jurisprudence are the Buyid, the Ilkhanid and the Safavid periods. To the first belong Ibn Babuyah al-Sadduq (d. 381/991–992), Shaykh Muhammad al-Mufid (d. 413/1022), his pupil ᶜAlam al-Huda Sayyid Murtada (d. 436/1044) (the great-grandson of the Imam Musa al-Kazim), and Muhammad ibn al-Hasan al-Tusi Shaykh al-Ta'ifah (d. 460/1067). The *Man la yahduru-hu'l-faqih* of Ibn Babuyah and the *Istibsar* and the *Tahzib al-ahkam* of Muhammad ibn al-Hasan al-Tusi together with the *Usul al-kafi fi ᶜilm al-din* of Abu Jaᶜfar Muhammad ibn Yaᶜqub al-Kulayni (d. 328/939–940 or 329/940–941) are known as 'The Four Books' (*al-kutub al-arbaᶜa*). To the Ilkhanid period belong Najm al-Din Jaᶜfar ibn Yahya, known as al-Muhaqqiq al-Awwal or al-Muhaqqiq al-Hilli (602–676/1205-6–1277), and his nephew Hasan ibn Yusuf ibn ᶜAli commonly called ᶜAllamah-i Hilli or Ibn al-Mutahhar al-Hilli (648–726/1250–1325), both of whom wrote prolifically on jurisprudence and theology. The *Shara'iᶜ al-islam* of al-Muhaqqiq al-Hilli is an important manual of Shiᶜi jurisprudence. *Al-Mukhtasar al-nafiᶜ* is an abridgement of the *Shara'iᶜ* made by al-Muhaqqiq some time before 672/1273–1274. It was translated into Persian by Hasan ibn Muhammad ibn Abu'l-Hasan in 696/1297, twenty years after the death of al-Muhaqqiq and thirty years after its composition. The *Minhaj al-karamah fi maᶜrifat al-imamah* of Ibn al-Mutahhar al-Hilli, which was written for, or at the request of, the Ilkhan Uljaytu, is a statement of the Imami Shi^ci doctrine of the Imamate and a refutation of the Sunni doctrine of the caliphate. It was later refuted by Ibn Taymiyyah in his *Minhaj al-sunnah*. The *Minhaj al-karamah* consists of ten chapters. An eleventh, *al-Babu'l-hadi ^cashar*, was added later by Ibn al-Mutahhar. The commentary, entitled *al-Nafi^c li-yawmi'l-hashr*, on this by Miqdad-i Fazil al-Hilli, who wrote in the latter part of the eighth/fourteenth century, is an important statement of Imami Shi^ci beliefs. The *Tajrid al-^caqa'id* of Nasir al-Din Tusi, another major work on Imami beliefs, which enjoyed much popularity in later centuries, also belongs to the Ilkhanid period.

Muhammad ibn Makki al-^cAmili al-Jazini al-Shahid al-Awwal al-Shami (d. 786/1384–1385), who wrote *al-Lum^cat al-dimashqiyyah*, is perhaps, the most important figure in the period between the Ilkhans and the Safavids. He lived in Syria during the reign of the Mamluk Sultan Barquq. Prominent among those who lived in the time of the Safavids were Shaykh ^cAli ibn Husayn ibn ^cAbd al-^cAli al-Karaki al-^cAmili known as al-Muhaqqiq al-Thani (d. 937/1530–1531 or 940/1533–1534), Zayn al-Din ibn ^cAli al-^cAmili al-Shahid al-Thani (d. 966/1559), who lived in the Ottoman empire and taught for several years at Ba^clbak and wrote a commentary on *al-Lum^cat al-dimashqiyyah*, entitled *Rawzat al-bahiyyah fi sharh al-lum^cat al-dimashqiyyah*, Muhammad Taqi Majlisi (d. 1070/1659), Muhammad Baqir Majlisi (d. 1111/1699), and Baha al-Din Muhammad al-^cAmili (d. 1031/1622), who, in addition to numerous other works, also began, on the command of Shah ^cAbbas, a popular manual of jurisprudence in Persian, the *Jami^c-i ^cabbasi*, but died after completing five chapters. It was finished by Husayn Sawaji, who added fifteen chapters. Muhammad Taqi Majlisi and Muhammad Baqir Majlisi composed a large number of juristic and theological works; the latter wrote in both Arabic and Persian. The *Wasa'il al-shi^cah* of Muhammad ibn Hasan ibn ^cAli al-Hurr al-^cAmili, the *Wafi* of Muhammad ibn al-Murtada (Mulla Muhsin Fayd, d. 1090/1679), and the *Bihar al-anwar* of Muhammad Baqir Majlisi are known as "The Three Books' and these together with 'The Four Books' mentioned above constitute some of the most important works on Shi^ci theology, jurisprudence and traditions.

* * *

The basic doctrine of the Imamiyyah on the Imam was not formulated until the time of the Imam Ja^cfar al-Sadiq and appears to have been largely the work of Hisham ibn al-Hakam. It was primarily and almost entirely a statement of theological beliefs without any clear implications for the political organization of the state. A theory of a spiritual lordship as opposed to an earthly caliphate was developed and was later to be further expand-

ed by Shiᶜi thinkers such as Mulla Sadra Shirazi (d. 1050/1640). Whereas
the Sunnis consider the Imam to be the head of the community, charged
with the execution of the ordinances of the *shariᶜah* in time and place, and
subject to election by consensus or designation by a council or by the
previous Imam, such election or designation to be ratified by the *ahl al-hall
wa'l-ᶜaqd*, the Imamiyyah hold that the Imam is a necessity imposed by God
and that he cannot therefore be subject to election or designation by a group
of persons. They believe that the Imamate is founded on the permanent
need of mankind for a divinely guided infallible leader and an authoritative
teacher in religion. The perpetual existence of the Imamate is thus incumbent upon God and universal. The world can never be devoid of an Imam
whether he is publicly known, surrounded by a few faithful followers or in
occultation. The Imam is the legatee (*wasi*) of the prophet and is infallible
(*maᶜsum*) in all his acts and words. The only difference between the prophet
(*rasul*) and the Imam is that the latter does not transmit a divine scripture.
To ignore or disobey the divinely invested Imam is infidelity equal to ignoring or disobeying the prophet. In contrast to later accepted doctrine Hisham
ibn al-Hakam did not hold that the prophets had to be infallible. Muhammad appointed ᶜAli as his legatee (*wasi*) and successor (*khalifah*) by
designation (*nass*). The community, by turning away from him and accepting Abu Bakr as caliph, apostasized. The imamate is to be transmitted
among the descendants of ᶜAli and Fatimah until the day of resurrection,
each Imam designating his successor.

> Whoever obeyed the imam was a true believer, whoever opposed or re-
> jected him, an infidel (*kafir*). To safeguard the faith and the community
> of believers, the imam and his followers in case of necessity were permit-
> ted or obligated to practise dissimulation (*taqiyya*) concerning their
> religious beliefs. The imam was not expected to revolt against the exist-
> ing illegal government, and rebellion without his authorization was
> unlawful.

Ibn Babuyah in his *Risalat al-iᶜtiqadata'l-imamiyyah* divides creation into
three, first prophets (*anbiya'*), envoys (*rusul*) and Imams, secondly believers
(*mu'minin*) and thirdly unbelievers and beasts. Concerning the prophets he
writes, 'We believe that they brought the truth from Allah, that their word is
the word of Allah, that their command is the command of Allah, that obedience to them is obedience to Allah and that disobedience to them is disobedience to Allah. Each prophet has a *wasi*, who was, by the command of
God, especially instructed and authorized by the prophet (*nabi*) to perform
certain acts. During the lifetime of the prophet the *wasi* held a position next
to him and for particular religious and political functions acted on his
behalf. After the death of the prophet, the *wasi* was his successor (*khalifah*)

and the leader of the community, being the most excellent of men after the prophet. ᶜAli's claim to the leadership of the Islamic community after the death of Muhammad was based on his alleged designation by Muhammad as his *wasi*.

The impeccability and infallibility (ᶜ*ismah*) of the prophets and Imams plays an important part in Imami doctrine. Neither the term nor the concept of ᶜ*ismah* occurs in the Qur'an or in canonical Sunni *hadith*. They were apparently first used by the Imamiyyah, who from the beginning of the second/ eighth century, if not earlier, maintained that the Imam must be immune from sin (*maᶜsum*). The evolution of this doctrine may, as Donaldson suggests, have owed something to the attempt of the Shiᶜis to establish the claims of the Imams against the claims of the Sunni caliphs. The doctrine was in due course expanded and elaborated. Ibn Babuyah states,

> Our belief concerning the prophets (*anbiya'*), apostles (*rusul*), Imams and angels is that they are infallible (*maᶜsum*); purified from all defilement (*danas*), and that they do not commit any sin, whether it be minor (*saghira*) or major (*kabira*). They do not disobey Allah in what He had commanded them; they act in accordance with His behests. He who denies infallibility to them in any matter appertaining to their status is ignorant of them, and such a one is a *kafir* (unbeliever).
>
> Our belief concerning them is that they are infallible and possess the attributes of perfection, completeness and knowledge, from the beginning to the end of their careers. Defects (*naqs*) cannot be attributed to them, nor disobedience (ᶜ*isyan*), nor ignorance (*jahl*), in any of their actions (*ahwal*).

Al-Mufid defines ᶜ*ismah* in his *Tashih al-iᶜtiqad* as follows:

> The impeccability given by God to His *hujjas* is a grace and favour, thanks to which they are secured against faults (*dhunub*) and errors in the religion of God. Impeccability is a grace from God (*tafaddul min Allah*) to those who, He knows, will cling to such impeccability. It does not take away from the one who has it the power to do wrong or force him to do good. But it is something which God knows that when He gives it to one of His servants He will not choose disobedience.

The difference between the Imams and prophets in the exposition of al-Mufid in the *Awaᶜil al-maqalat fi'l-madhahib wa'l-mukhtarat* is largely one of definition. He states that the (existence of the) *sharᶜ* prevented the Imams being called prophets although they had intrinsically the same qualities. Moreover they received revelation (*wahy*) even though they were not prophets. He reserves judgement, however, on the question of the superiority of the Imams over the prophets, which some Imamis asserted.

With regard to the Imams, Ibn Babuyah states,

> Our belief regarding them is that they are in authority (*ulu'l-amr*). It is
> to them that Allah has ordained obedience, they are the witnesses for
> the people, and they are the gates of Allah (*abwab*) and the road (*sabil*)
> to Him and the guides (*dalil*, pl. *adilla*) thereto, and the repositories of
> His knowledge and the interpreters of His revelations and the pillars of
> His unity (*tawhid*). They are immune from sins (*khata'*) and errors
> (*zalal*); they are those from whom "Allah has removed all impurity and
> made them absolutely pure"; they are possessed of (the power of)
> miracles and of (irrefutable) arguments (*dala'il*); and they are for the
> protection of the people of this earth just as the stars are for the inhabit-
> ants of the heavens . . . . And we believe . . . that their command is the
> command of Allah, their prohibition is the prohibition of Allah; obe-
> dience to them is obedience to Allah, and disobedience to them is dis-
> obedience to Allah.

Expressing the Imami belief in the Hidden Imam and his return, Ibn
Babuyah states,

> We believe that the earth cannot be without the Proof (*hujja*) of Allah
> to His creatures—a leader either manifest (*zahir*) and well-known
> (*mashhur*), or hidden (*khafi*) and obscure (*maghmur*).
>
> We believe that the Proof of Allah in His earth and His vicegerent
> (*khalifah*) among his slaves in this age of ours is the Upholder (*al-Qa'im*)
> (of the law of Allah), the Expected One (al-Muntazar), Muhammad ibn
> al-Hasan ibn cAli ibn Muhammad ibn cAli ibn Musa ibn Jacfar ibn
> Muhammad ibn cAli ibn al-Husayn ibn cAli ibn Abi Talib, on them be
> peace. He it is concerning whose name and descent the Prophet was in-
> formed by Allah the Mighty and Glorious, and he it is WHO WILL FILL
> THE EARTH WITH JUSTICE AND EQUITY, JUST AS NOW IT IS FULL OF OPPRES-
> SION AND WRONG. And it is he through whom Allah will make His faith
> manifest "in order to supersede all religion, though the polytheists may
> dislike (it)". He it is whom Allah will make victorious over the whole
> world until from every place the call to prayer will be heard, and all
> religion will belong entirely to Allah, Exalted is He above all. He it is,
> who is the Rightly Guided (*mahdi*), about whom the Prophet gave infor-
> mation that when he appears, Jesus, son of Mary, will descend upon the
> earth and pray behind him, and he who prays behind him is like one
> who prays behind the Prophet of Allah, because he is his vicegerent
> (*khalifah*).
>
> And we believe that there can be no Qa'im other than him; he may live
> in the state of occultation (as long as he likes); and were he to live in the
> state of occultation for the space of the existence of this world, there
> would nevertheless be no Qa'im other than him. For, the Prophet and

the Imams have indicated him by his name and descent; him they appointed as their successor, and of him they gave glad tidings — the Blessings of Allah on all of them.

Al-Mufid in his *Awa'il al-maqalat* draws attention to some of the differences between the Imams and the Mu^ctazilis and mentions some of the
points on which the former differ from other branches of the Shi^cis. The
Imamis, he states, were agreed upon the necessity for the permanent existence of an Imam as proof from God to the *mukallafin*, and through
whose existence all the interests of religion were assured. This was in contradistinction to the Mu^ctazilis, who held that here might be no Imam for a
period, a view which they shared with the Kharijis, Zaydis, Murji^cis, and
those who appealed to the authority of tradition (*al-muntasibun
ila'l-hadith*). Other specific points of difference were the following: the Imamis were agreed that the Imam should be immune (*ma^csum*) from committing opposition to God, learned in all branches of religious knowledge,
perfect in virtue (*fadl*), and singled out from all men by his superiority over
them in such actions as merited heavenly bliss; that the Imamate after the
prophet, in the absence of a miracle, could not be established except by
designation (*nass*) or testament (*tawaqif*); that the Imamate after the
prophet was in the hands of the Banu Hashim, in particular ^cAli, Hasan and
Husayn and the descendants of the last-named to the exclusion of the descendants of al-Hasan; that the prophet during his lifetime had chosen ^cAli as his
successor and designated him as Imam, and had also designated Hasan and
Husayn after ^cAli, and similarly after them ^cAli ibn al-Husayn; and that the
last-named had also been designated by his father and grandfather; and that
there were twelve Imams after the prophet. The Imamis, Zaydis, and Kharijis all agreed that those who had acted wrongfully in Basrah and Syria were
infidels, erring and accursed because of their rebellion against ^cAli and that
they were condemned to eternal fire. Some of the followers of tradition
(*ashab al-hadith*) also agreed that those who left ^cAli had strayed from the
path of (true) religion and were infidels (*kuffar*) condemned to eternal fire.

The function of the Imams, according to al-Mufid, was 'to take the place
of the prophets in executing the decrees (*ahkam*) of the *shari^cah*, applying
the legal penalties, protecting the law (*hifz al-shari^cah*) and punishing men
(*ta'dib al-anam*)'. He is at some pains to justify and defend the occultation
of the twelfth Imam. He states that this did not put an end to the need of the
community for him as the guardian of the law and as God's proof (*hujjah*)
upon earth to his people. But, he maintains, it was not necessary that he
should act personally: just as prophets often acted through vicars and
agents while they were on earth, so, too, the Imam might appoint a vicar.

Further, whereas the earlier Imams did not call their followers to revolt against injustice and were therefore left by the rulers of their day in peace, the twelfth Imam, when he reappeared, would raise the standard of revolt and so must be careful not to expose himself before he had sufficient forces to fight those in power.

For Ibn al-Mutahhar the Imamate is a universal authority (*riyasah*) in the things of religion and the world, which distinguishes it from the dominion of judges and vicegerents. He holds that the Imam must be, like the prophet, impeccable and infallible. The argument he adduces in support of this would appear to go back to the political philosophy of al-Farabi and the Ikhwan-i Safa. Ibn al-Mutahhar's argument runs as follows: man is by nature a social animal; he cannot live alone by reason of the multiplicity of his needs and his inability to satisfy them outside society. But, although he has need of the co-operation of others, pushed by egotism and greed he also covets what others possess and seeks to dominate and enslave them. Conflict would thus be unceasing unless there was an Imam who was immune from all fault and error in his judgements and actions to arbitrate between them. Only thus could the rights of one against the other be effectively defended, the legal penalties of the divine law applied, and peace and order guaranteed to the community. In *al-Alfayn*, a work devoted to a detailed discussion on the reasons for the infallibility of the Imam, he repeatedly emphasizes the need for a leader (*ra'is*) to interpret and preserve the *shari^cah*, to prevent men from committing aggression against each other, to restrain tyrants and to help the oppressed. Without a leader chaos would ensue and the Qur'an and the *sunnah* would not be observed. There had inevitably to be an Imam immune from error and sin appointed by God to make known the decrees (*ahkam*) of the *shari^cah*. An Imam was also necessary to delegate authority to *qadis*, army leaders and governors. Obedience in these matters, upon which the good order of the human race depended, would only be given to someone who was infallible. Similarly an Imam was necessary for enjoining the good and forbidding evil. The Imam was the protector of the *shari^cah*; war and *jihad* were by his command and on his summons; and he applied the legal penalties.

^cAli, the first of the Imams, enjoyed pre-eminence over all the Imams. He was impeccable and infallible, a reformer (*muslih*), designated by providence to correct abuses and to re-establish situations which had been compromised. After the prophet he was the best of the community. The principal virtues which constituted his superiority, which were unequalled and could never be equalled, were, according to Ibn al-Mutahhar, the same states of grace (*ahwal*) also to be found in the Imams who followed him, but never to the same degree of perfection. This pre-eminence ^cAli owed to, among other virtues, an ascetic detachment from the things of this world (*zuhd*), a devotional piety surpassing ordinary human power, an exceptional spirit of charity, and above all to his knowledge, which was divinely inspired.

Ibn al-Mutahhar states that the Imamiyyah believed that the designation of the Imam was an obligatory grace (*luft wajib*) which imposed itself on God in the same way as the sending of prophets. God had in effect created men in their own interest, while making them, however, incapable, as long as they were left to themselves, of raising themselves to happiness and health. Having closed the succession of the prophets with Muhammad, God had therefore to appoint certain holy personages (*awliya'*) destined to guide the world towards the good and to protect it from error, negligence and mistakes. He bases the obligation upon God to provide for the perpetuity of the Imamate upon the same reasons which he uses to establish the need for prophethood, namely the necessity for social cohesion and the revelation of what is good and just. Though he refuses the Imam the special prerogative of prophethood, which was that he should serve as an intermediary (*wasitah*) between God and man, there was no real distinction between the Imam and the prophet: the function which the prophet derived from revelation, the Imam obtained through his infallibility, which made him not only the guardian (*hafiz*) but also the interpreter of the law.

Closely allied to this conception of the prophet as the intermediary between God and man, was the conception of the prophet as mediator before God on behalf of his followers. Belief in the intercession of Muhammad developed after his death and came to be regarded as necessary by both Sunnis and Shi^ci's. Among the latter the idea of mediation and intercession was extended to include the Imams, especially ^cAli. The passion plays are also full of allusions to the redemptive work of Husayn ibn ^cAli and the voluntary sacrifice of his body for the sins of the Muslim world. Muhammad Baqir Majlisi in the *Hayat al-qulub* states explicitly that the true intercessors for mankind are the Imams. They are, he writes, 'the mediators between God and mankind. Except by their intercession it is impossible for men to avoid the punishment of God.

Discussing the necessity of the Imamate from the theological point of view, Muhammad Baqir Majlisi points out that all recognized Shi^ci scholars held that the appointment of the Imams was an actual necessity for God himself and that this was demonstrable by reason and the traditions. He states, 'Whatever advantage lay in the person of the Prophet is also to be attributed to the person of the Imam — all that pertains to warding off evil, to guarding law, to restraining men from violence and oppression and all kinds of disobedience, and even the divine necessity for the appointment of the succeeding Imam'. As the first proof of the necessity of the Imamate he adduces God's kindness (*lutf*), maintaining that 'kindness is responsible for the existence of the Imam, for ordinary intelligence leads people, wherever they are organized as a people, to have someone to restrain them from rebellion and corruption and violence and oppression, to withhold them from various forms of disobedience, and to establish them in faithfulness, in the forms of worship, in practices of justice, and in habits of civility. For it is in this way that the conduct of peoples becomes regular and orderly, and that they approach the best and forsake the base.'

The second proof lay in the necessity of a guardian for the law of the prophet to protect it from change and misinterpretation, and from additions or subtractions. An authoritative interpreter from God was needed to make legal deductions from the Qur'an. Muhammad Baqir Majlisi quotes the Imam Baqir as saying 'that after him [the prophet], in every age, "there is a leader among us who guides mankind towards that which the Apostle of God has revealed; that the leader who followed the Apostle was ᶜAli ibn Abi Talib, with the Imams who came after him, each following the other until the Judgement Day".' He also quotes Ibn Babuyah as stating that the Imam Baqir, when explaining the verse 'To every people a leader', said that the reference was to the Imam, 'for in every time there must be a leader for the people among whom the Imam lives.' Muhammad Baqir also states that Ibn Babuyah recorded that the Imam Zayn al-ᶜAbidin said,

> We (the *Imams*) are those through whose blessings God maintains the heavens, that they should not fall upon the Earth except by His permission at the day of Judgement. It is *by our blessing* that God maintains the heavens, that they do not fall and destroy their inhabitants; and it is *by our blessing* that God sends the rains and shows forth His mercy, and brings forth the bounties of the Earth. For if there were no Imam on Earth to represent us, verily the Earth itself would collapse, with all those who dwell upon it.'

Continuing, Muhammad Baqir states that,

> When the Imam Zain al-ᶜAbidin was asked "How could men profit from a Proof of God that was concealed and hidden from them?" he replied, "They would profit in the same way as they do from the Sun when it is concealed by a cloud. From this it is evident that even in his time of concealment, the grace and blessing of the Imam reaches the Earth. If there should be mistakes among the uninformed, he will guide them in ways they will perceive, and yet they will not know it was he. And there are many times when his concealment works for the blessing of the majority of men. For God knows that if the Imam should come, the majority of mankind would not accept him. And in the personal presence of the Imam the obligations that would fall upon men would be more difficult, such as fighting in the *jihad* (holy war) against those opposing the Faith. There are many times when unseeing eyes and blind hearts have not the

strength to look upon the light of the Imam, just as lots do not have the strength to look upon the light of the Sun. Kings and nobles, also, during the concealment of the Imam, have faith in his coming, but when he shall actually come and reduce the noble and the poor to one level, many will not be able to endure this and will disbelieve. For when ᶜAli, the Amir al-mu'minin, was distributing rewards, he treated Talha and Zubayr in the same way as a slave he had freed but the day before, and it was this that caused them to forsake him."

ᶜAlam al-Huda Sayyid Murtada is then quoted by Muhammad Baqir as refuting the statement that a concealed Imam can be of no profit to mankind. God's part had been to send the Imams and to make them able to discharge the duties of the Imamate. It was necessary for them, for their part, to execute the commands of God: to accept the obligations laid upon them and to carry them out, while the duty of believers was to assist the Imams to fulfil their tasks and to overthrow whatever stood between them and the Imams, that they should obey them, serve them, and carry out their orders.

Muhammad Baqir adduces eight proofs or reasons for the divine appointment of the Imam and the designation by him of his successors. The first three concern the sinlessness of the Imam, the prevention of corruption through him, and God's care for His people in appointing an Imam. The remaining five reasons reveal the authoritarian nature of Shiᶜi doctrine, which the Sunnis had avoided by invoking the (fabricated) tradition, 'My community will not agree upon error'. They also reveal a certain contempt for the common man. They are as follows:

(i) As the Sunnis also believed, it was God's practice from the time of Adam onwards that the prophets did not leave this world until they had appointed their successors. It was moreover Muhammad's custom whenever he left Madina to designate someone to act in his place. He did the same for every town or village when there was a group of believers and when he appointed commanders for the army. He did not leave these matters to the choice of the people, but himself sought the command of the Most High before making such appointments. Could it therefore be conceived that in the matter of his vicegerent he would have been neglected or left it to the choice of the people?

(ii) The office of the Imam was like the office of the prophet in that each had complete authority over all the followers of the faith in matters of religion and government. The people themselves were incapable of judging who was worthy for this responsible office. They would be moved by changing purposes and personal advantage. Their choice might be put into effect by force and might be reconciled with the requirements of an autocratic and oppressive rule, but it would not be a suitable way to determine the imamate or to direct a government based on law. It was as unreasonable to think the people could choose their

Imams as it was to imagine that they were capable of choosing their prophets. Moreover, if a king dismissed the governor of a city and did not appoint anyone in his place or the headman of a village left the village without appointing anyone in his stead, but left everything to the choice of the people, he would be severely censured. How then could conduct of such sort be regarded as acceptable and worthy of God and the prophet?

(iii) Even suppose the people were freed of personal prejudices, their choice might nevertheless be mistaken. In the choice of kings, sultans and prominent men, it often happened that for a time they would be esteemed to be trustworthy, capable and deserving, but it would afterwards turn out that they were the very opposite.

(iv) Even supposing the choice of the people should prove to be correct, it was clear that God knew better who was qualified for each and every work. It was therefore more appropriate for God to exercise the choice. If He did not, this would involve Him in preferring an expedient which would not be the best, a mistake which could not be attributed to Him.

(v) Further, if the Imamate were to be determined by the choice of the people, either their choice might be a mistake and—since God with His foreknowledge would know this—such a procedure could not be attributed to a wise God, or if they chose a good Imam, it would be extremely difficult for the people to secure his recognition, to frustrate opposition and to suppress jealousies, but for God it would be exceedingly easy. It would thus be unworthy of God to force upon His people in their weakness a matter of such difficulty.

While the conception of the Imam as the interpreter and executor of the divine law and the acceptance of the belief that the divine light was present in the house of ᶜAli provided for the possibility of change, which the Sunnis had lost when *ijmaᶜ* was used to declare immutable the codes of the second/ eighth and third/ninth centuries, the apparently greater flexibility of the Shiᶜi position was also lost when the divine light became stationary with the disappearance of the last Imam in 260/873. Since that time political authority is held by the Shiᶜis to be usurped, whether it is exercised by the Sunnis or by Shiᶜis. Two problems in particular faced them. Legal and just government would not, they believed, be re-established until *Imamah* and *walayah* were united in one person, but meanwhile upon whom did the authority of the Imam devolve during the concealment and what was the duty of the believer vis-à-vis political authority which was usurped? So far as general principle were concerned the fact that the Imam was in concealment did not, perhaps, constitute a problem, but for the practical application of certain of these general principles some more tangible authority was required. This was provided by the *fuqaha'*, who were believed to act collectively as the *na'ib ᶜamm* of the Imam in *sharᶜi* affairs. Temporal affairs, which required the coercive power of the government, on the other hand were held to have passed under the control of usurpers. But the separation was not altogether clear-cut; indeed in an Islamic society, whether the majority was constituted by Sunnis or Shiᶜis, it could not be so. The *shariᶜah*, in theory at least, covered all aspects of the believer's life: and even the performance of personal religious duties might have implications for the legality or otherwise of the government.

Said Amir Arjomand

The power and prestige of the Persian religious élite, the *ᶜulama'*, during the Qajar period (1795–1926), and their political importance, in contrast to the relative political feebleness of the *ᶜulama'* of Sunni Islam in modern times, has attracted the attention of students of Persian history and politics.

The power of the *ᶜulama'*, their involvement in politics throughout the nineteenth century, and their leading role in the constitutional revolution of 1905–06 are well-established and salient facts. As to their explanation, there is almost unanimous agreement among Western scholars in attributing the political power of the religious élite *vis-à-vis* the state partly to the Shiᶜi religion. It is argued that a certain characteristic of Twelver Shiᶜism made the legitimacy of the ruler precarious while enhancing the political authority of the *ᶜulama'*. Unlike Sunnism, which emphasizes the primacy of the Muslim community, to whom the *ᶜulama'* are at best learned advisers, Shiᶜism places the ultimate source of legitimacy in the authority of the Imam, who is believed to be in 'concealment' until his reappearance at the end of time, thus making the *mujtahids* (the learned doctors of sacred law) potential rivals to the ruler for the authority of the Hidden Imam which can only be vicariously exercised during the Great Occultation.

The argument rests on the alleged implications of the Shiᶜi doctrines of *Imamah* (religious leadership) and of the Occultation (*ghaybah*) of the twelfth Imam, for the (il)legitimacy of government, and for the political authority of the religious élite. It purports to explain the alleged denial of the legitimacy of political domination as deducible from the doctrinal foundations of clerical (hierocratic) authority. According to this view, the occultation of the twelfth Imam, and the expectation of his *parousia* renders all government illegitimate.

The *culama'* are said to emerge as the representative of the Hidden Imam, and, as such, endowed with legitimate authority and partaking in the charisma of the Imam as the supreme religious and political leader . . . .

Our investigation . . . has shown the prevalent view to be inadequate and misleading. Our objective is therefore a drastic modification of this view through a sociological analysis of the beliefs and attitudes emanating from the Shici religion with regard to their political implications. The framework within which this analysis is undertaken is elicited from Max Weber's sociology of religion, and from the sections of his sociology of domination dealing with the relationship between the hierocracy and the state.

*   *   *

With the organization of the early Shicis into a sect, the divergence of the Shici outlook was reflected in an evolving theory of Imamate which was at marked variance with the Sunni notions of political leadership. For the Shicis, there was no *explicit* recognition of the separation of temporal and religious authority, and *de jure*, the Imam was considered the supreme political and religious leader of the community. However, *de facto*, the conception of Imamate was drastically *depoliticized*. As Hodgson shows, the *de facto* depoliticization of Imamate was concomitant with the sectarian reorientation of the early Shicis which began with the fifth Imam Muhammad al-Baqir, and became firmly established by the sixth Imam, Jacfar al-Sadiq. . . .

Both Muhammad al-Baqir and Jacfar al-Sadiq explicitly rejected the idea of armed rebellion; al-Sadiq preserved the legitimist contention on behalf of the descendants of cAli by insisting upon *nass* (designation) — modelled after the explicit designation of cAli by Muhammad — as the indispensable condition of Imamate. The notion of *nass* implied:

> that the Imamate is located in a given individual, *whether he claims rule or not*; and is transferred from one to another by explicit designation, *nass*.

Against the background of an emerging institution of sacred learning and instruction, the *de facto* disjunction between Imamate and political rule was facilitated by resting the former upon the possession of *cilm* (divine knowledge), and implicitly differentiating the responsibilities of the Imam from those of the political ruler, making him the final authoirty in matters of salvation, conscience, and sacred law. . . .

The elaboration of the conception of Imamate by Hisham ibn al-Hakam and others in accordance with Ja^cfar al-Sadiq's instructions in this formative early stage remained definitive for Twelver Shi^cism. . . .

The death of the eleventh Imam, who apparently had no son, produced serious crisis which was eventually solved by the doctrine of *ghaybah* (Occultation). The twelfth Imam was said to be alive and to fulfill the functions of Imamate in concealment. The doctrine of Occultation, by postulating the necessary absence of the Imam, accentuated the divorce between Imamate and political rule.

Thus, while the early ^cAbbasids, assuming the then-current designation of 'imam', sought to emphasize the Islamic character of their political regime, thereby enhancing the political, theocratic conception of Imamate (the caliphate), their contemporary Ja^cfar al-Sadiq, the author of an influential mystical commentary on the Qur'an, transformed the early political Shi^cism (while disciplining the religious extremism into an introverted and quietistic religious movement). The Imams ceased to be anti-Caliphs (as they were in the Shi^ci revolts of the Umayyad period), and became the spiritual guides of the Imami (Shi^ci) sectarians. With the termination of the line of the apparently living Imams in the third/ninth century, the soteriological and eschatologial transposition of the initially political notion of Imamate was complete. Imamate was destined to become an abstract principle of Shi^ci theology.

Piety and spiritual zeal continued to characterize the Imamiyyah. The sectarian Imami religiosity, whose basic features consolidated in the fourth/tenth century, is best depicted in Kulayni's (d. 328/939) *Usul al-kafi.* In it, *iman* (faith) primarily, and ^c*aql* (reason) and ^c*ilm* (knowledge), emerge as linked with salvation. The observance of the ethic of brotherly love and assistance to the members of the community of faith (*mu'minin*) and devotional piety, are manifestations of faith and the means of attaining salvation.

Consonant with this pietistic religiosity is the de-emphasis on the Islamic 'political ethic'. Of the three principal duties mentioned earlier, the categorical obligationness of *amr bi'l-ma^cruf* (enjoining the good) and *nahy ^can al-munkar* (prohibiting the evil) was relaxed, restricting the circumstances under which they remained obligatory, and making the *intention* to enjoin the good and prohibit the evil suffice in cases of potential danger. As for *jihad* (holy war), the obligation is to undertake it becomes circumscribed in the time of Occultation which was to last until the end of time. The Shi^ci theologian, al-Mufid (d. 413/1022), presented *jihad* as the (nonviolent) struggle to convert the 'Realm of Islam' to the 'Realm of Faith' (*dar al-iman*), postponing the onslaught on the 'Realm of Infidelity' (*dar al-*

kufr). Over two centuries later, al-Muhaqqiq al-Hilli (d. 676/1277–78) ruled that *jihad* was not obligatory unless the believer was summoned by the Imam (it was only *mustahabb* — commendable — on the frontier in the absence of the Imam). Al-Muhaqqiq in effect limited *jihad* to defensive war.

In the fourth/tenth century, the seizure of effective power in Baghdad by the *amirs* of the Buyid dynasty without, however, the deposition of the Caliph, produced a lasting duality in Islamic structure of domination. The first Buyids based the legitimacy of their (purely political) authority largely on the honorific titles (sing. *laqab*) bestowed upon them by the Caliph who, after the loss of political power, came to assume the role of the representative of the Prophet and the guardian of his heritage. They also revived the Persian theories of kingship and assumed the secular title of *malik* (king); and of *Shahanshah* (King of Kings). It is significant that the Imami theologians of Baghdad who had close ties with the Buyids, and were supported and encouraged by them, did not question the latter's temporal authority. Nor did they dispute the legitimacy of the Caliph in the name of the Hidden Imam. In fact, the famous *naqibs* of the Shiᶜis, Sharif al-Radi and Sharif al-Murtada, were both on friendly terms with the Caliph al-Qadir, to whom they addressed many of their *qasidas*.

From the fourth/tenth to the end of the ninth/fifteenth centuries, the Imamiyyah flourished, with many vicissitudes, as a proselytizing sect, producing an impressive corpus of polemical, theological and legal literature. With the works of al-Mufid, al-Murtada, and the Shaykh al-Ta'ifah, al-Tusi, in the eleventh century, the Shiᶜi legal theory and jurisprudence — *fiqh* — developed and was systematized. It is true that Imamate remained the most distinctive and the most salient of Imami tenets. But with the development of this new branch of religious learning, which did not include a systematic theory of authority as temporal rule, the import of Imamate as a topic in *public law* was drastically reduced, while it increasingly appeared as a purely theological topic, its practical implications becoming less and less clear. The ᶜAllamah Ibn al-Mutahhar al-Hilli (d. 726/1325) delineated Imamate as an *asl al-din* (principle of religion) thus firmly integrated it into the Shiᶜi *theological* system and *not* into the Shiᶜi *jurisprudence* (which might have led to the development of a political theory). Like prophecy, Imamate was said to be incumbent upon God because of his grace (*lutf*) to mankind, for whose guidance prophets and Imams are appointed. Like prophecy in the absence of a prophet, Imamate in the absence of an Imam remained devoid of direct implications for political rule. . . .

We have tried to show how the formative sectarian differentiation of Twelver Shiᶜism from the caliphal body politic left its permanent imprint on the delineation of the religiously significant and the profane spheres of life, relegating politial authority to the latter sphere. Doctrinal indifference to political theory amounted to granting *autonomy* to the norms of legitimacy of political rulership. Political rule was thus secularized and viewed pragmatically. . . .

The practice of the Imami Shiᶜis was consistent with the implicit secularization of the political sphere and the consequent pragmatic attitude to political authority. From the time of the formation of the sect, many Imamis entered the service of the rulers and achieved great prominence. The Banu Yaqtiah (the second/eighth century), the Nawbakhtis and some of the members of the Furat family (late third/ninth and early fourth/tenth centuries) are notable examples of Imami Shiᶜis who served the ᶜAbbasid caliphate and attained vizirates and other high governmental positions. During the Saljuq period (eleventh and twelfth centuries), and especially its latter part, again we find many Imamis (*Rafidi*) in government service, including vizirates. So much so that the resentful Sunni historian Ravandi could attribute the decline of the kingdom to 'the tyranny of the *Rafidi* generals and scribes' (*zulm-i sarhangan wa dabiran-i rafidi*). To conclude, let us note that al-Nasir (575–622/1178–1225), the most important ᶜAbbasid Caliph of the post-Saljuq period, had a number of Imami vizirs; and that the Shiᶜi vizier Ibn al-ᶜAlqami played an important role in the events of the reign of the last ᶜAbbasid, al-Mustaᶜsim.

* * *

The Islamic Empire inherited the Sasaniyan political ethos. According to Gibb, 'the nemesis of the over-rapid conquests of the Arabs — and the political tragedy of Islam — was that the Islamic ideology never found its proper and articulated expression in the poltical institutions of the Islamic states'. As early as the second/eighth century, Sasaniyan influences penetrated into Islam through the work of Ibn Muqaffaᶜ, the chancellor of the ᶜAbbasid Caliph al-Mansur, both in administrative handbooks and in mirrors for princes. 'The ᶜAbbasid caliphs themselves at least tolerated the idea that their caliphate was the continuation of Persian royalty'. It remained for the Buyids to revive the Sasaniyan conception of kingship as outlined above. In the fourth/tenth century the Buyid rulers assumed the title of *Shahanshah*, which title continued to be borne by the Saljuq sultans in the following century. Thus, with the eclipse of the ᶜAbbasid caliphate in the fourth/tenth century, political theory came to center around the *de facto* rulers — later to be designated sultan — rather than the Caliph; and by the second half of the fifth/eleventh century, the tradition of acclaiming the sultan as the 'Shadow of God on Earth' became firmly established.

As Lambton points out, in the famous treatise on government, *Siyasat-namah* (written in the last quarter of the fifth/eleventh century), Nizam al-Mulk tacitly regards the theory of divine light (*Farr-i Izadi*) to supersede the classical theory of the caliphate. Although Nizam al-Mulk emphasized the importance of right religion and stability, justice rather than religion — including religious law — became the basis of his theory of kingship: 'The object of temporal rule was to fill the earth with justice'. In al-Ghazzali's *Nasihat al-muluk*, the emphasis on justice is even stronger. The one qualification he makes for a true sultan is the exercise of justice.

This trend continued throughout the Middle Ages. Sasaniyan notions were recast in Islamic and Hellenistic terms (Greek influences had come to color the idiom of philosophical expression in medieval Islam): the theory of the ruler as the Shadow of God on Earth was taken from Sasaniyan sources, and the Hellenistic idea of philosopher-king was assimilated to it. Justice rather than right religion became the foundation of the medieval theory of righteous rule. Furthermore, most 'mirrors for princes' enjoined the care and protection of the subjects (*ra^{c}aya*) and the promotion of their prosperity.

Even prior to the eleventh/fifth century, the Sunni doctrine of Imamate as effective political rule became divorced from the *shari^{c}ah* and moved in the direction of absolutism. With the subsequent substitution of Sultanate for Imamate in medieval Persian political theory after the eleventh/fifth century, this trend was reinforced. The attribution to the sultan, as the Shadow of God on Earth, of extra-religious divine charisma, and the emphasis on the exercise of substantive justice by him — instead of insistence upon the institutionalized formal application of the *shari^{c}ah* — minimized the effects of Islamic tenets on the theories of temporal rule. The notion of justice which came to prevail in these theories was the unformalized substantive justice of Sasaniyan patrimonialism: protection of the weak from the strong, removal of oppression and administration of punishment for wrongdoings, and for contraventions of customary norms of fairness.

The emphasis on justice entailed the abhorrence of injustice and tyranny (*zulm*). Although the overriding fear of anarchy and bloodshed made the Muslim jurist and legal theorists enjoin unconditional obedience to 'those in authority' (*ulu'l-amr*), the latter were held morally accountable. Protection for the subjects and just administration of the kingdom was the responsibility of the sultan, for which he was answerable to God. That the king is also responsible for the action of those to whom he delegates his authority is clearly brought out in a passage in the *Siyasatnama* in which Nizam al-Mulk urges the land assignees and governors to protect the subjects and treat them as the king treats them—i.e., with justice, 'so that the subjects should be content with the justice of the king, and the king be immune from suffering and punishment in the other world'.

The conception and attributes of kingship for the (non-Turkman) majority of the population of Iran remained fundamentally unchanged with the establishment of the Safavid dynasty. It is important to stress this continuity. Iskandar Munshi, the historian of the reign of ᶜAbbas I (early seventeenth century), laid great emphasis on the justice of the king. He stated that the just sultan was the Shadow of God and described his mission as the protection of the creatures of God, and thus an aspect of prophethood and of the divinely ordained sovereignty (*walayah*). According to Chardin (late seventeenth century) the Persians 'say that the Persons of their Kings are Sacred and Sanctified, in a peculiar manner above the rest of the Mankind, and bring along with them wheresoever they come, Happiness and Benediction'. As Lambton admits, 'the theory that the temporal ruler was the Shadow of God upon Earth remained the central theme' in the Safavid period.

However, for reasons which should become clear in our subsequent discussion, little or no attention was paid to the problem of temporal sovereignty in the religious literature of the Safavid period. The persistence of the traditional notions of kingship and justice, alongside the Shiᶜite creed but independently of it, is nevertheless attested both directly and by their restatements in the late eighteenth and early nineteenth centuries.

Early Islam was vehemently opposed to worldly kingship. 'It could not but consider the application of the name king of kings (*Shahanshah*) to any human being as obnoxious and blasphemous'. In a well-authenticated tradition, the Prophet is reported as saying: 'The vilest (*akhnaᶜf*) name in the eyes of God on the day of resurrection is [that of] a man who calls himself king of kings (*malik al-amlak*)' (an early transmitter explains that the expression refers to *Shahanshah*).

As we have seen, Islam did not succeed in eradicating kingship, but the attitude of the Prophet persisted among his 'depositories', the ᶜ*ulama*'. Malik ibn Anas, the founder of one of the four Sunni schools of law is quoted as saying that the ᶜ*ulama*'

> are the depositories of the prophets; yet when they draw near to the rulers and take part in the dealings of this world they betray the prophets. One should beware of such scholars and avoid them.

The problem of the (lack of) propriety of an ᶜ*alim* (sing. of ᶜ*ulama*') being in the *suhbat al-sultan* (association with the sultan) was often discussed in medieval legal and moral texts. Ghazzali devotes a chapter of the *Ihya'* *culum al-din* (Revival of the Religious Sciences) to the permissible and thus forbidden in association with the tyrannical rulers. In it, he quotes the Tradition attributed to the prophet by Abu Zarr: 'Whenever a man accedes to authority, he drifts away from God'. Ghazzali goes on to argue that

> when a religious scholar meets a corrupt ruler in public, he should honor
> him, so as not to incide to rebellion, which Islam strictly forbids. On the
> other hand, when meeting the ruler in private, the scholar must not even
> rise before him — in order to show him the superiority of religion.

In a subsequent chapter on enjoining the good and forbidding the evil upon the *amirs* and the *sultans*, al-Ghazzali cites another Tradition: 'The most excellent of the *jihads* is the utterance of truth in front of the tyrannical ruler'. Therefore, there is no reason to think that the attitude of antipathy to temporal rule is distinctive only of the Shici *culama'*. However . . . the existence of a group of scholars economically independent of the government, and resident abroad, facilitated the *persistence* of this fundamental and deep-rooted Islamic attitude to political power in Shici Iran.

Chapter Eight

Economic Theories and Practices

The rise of interest in Islamic economics has been a pervasive feature of the resurgence of Islam in recent years. Although it is, for the most part, a Sunni concern that addresses Muslim life in general, Islamic economics nevertheless has gained much from modern Shici economic and social thought. For instance, the most important work in Arabic on Islamic economics is Iqtisaduna (Our Economics), written by the Shici faqih of Iraq, Sayyid Muhammad Baqir Sadr. Yet, the Shici conception of Islamic economics differs in some ways from that of Sunni Islam.

In the context of Sunnism, Islamic economics is both a manifestation and the harbinger of the perfect Islamic society, which has its model in the Medinan community. It is a concept that defines the ideal and, at the same time, can be implemented in relation to the ideal. In Shicism, at least in its contemporary interpretations, economics is neither a static definition of the ideal nor is it a reality easily attainable. It is, rather, one component of the cataclysmic process of social and political change that leads history to its eventuality, the reign of justice and the kingdom of the Mahdi. This linear view of history, and the role of economics in it are contemporary formulations based on the apocalyptic and messianic character of the Shici doctrines. Such modern Shici thinkers as Sadr have condensed this general tendency of the Shici philosophy of life into a dialectic outlook onto the modern world. Sadr writes of economics in the context of Shici thought in the following manner:

> *Islamic economics is not a science of political economy. [Rather], it is revolution [i.e., a revolutionary ideology] for changing the corrupt (*fasid) *reality, and turning it into a pure (*salim) *one—it is clearly not an objective analysis of existing reality. (from Homa Katouzian, "Shicite Economics: Sadr and Bani Sadr" in Nikki Keddie (ed.).* Religion and Politics in Iran: Shicism from Quietism to Revolution. *(New Haven: Yale University Press), p. 146.*

With the ideologization of Shiᶜi social thought in recent years, Sadr's successors, such as the former president of the Islamic Republic of Iran, Bani Sadr, abandoned any pretentions at Shiᶜi orthodoxy in discussion of economics and adopted a patently Marxist rubric and Marxian views to a blatant extent.

Although to modern Shiᶜi thinkers, economics is not a quest for an equilibrium in the market but essentially a dynamic force for change, they have contributed immensely to the understanding of the working of economics in the context of Islam and have also elaborated upon the religion's teachings on the material aspects of human life. In this regard, no two Shiᶜi thinkers have played a greater role in formulating the field of Islamic economics or contributed more to the transformation of modern Shiᶜi social and economic thought than Sayyid Muhammad Baqir Sadr of Iraq and Ayatollah Sayyid Mahmud Taliqani of Iran. Excerpts from the seminal works of the two, Sadr's Iqtisaduna *translated by I.K.A. Howard, and Taliqani's* Islam and Ownership *will elucidate the Shiᶜi conception of Islamic economics. The excerpts are from* Alserat, *pages 175–184, and* IO, *pages 88–91, respectively.*

Sayyid Muhammad Baqir Sadr

The Islamic economy is composed of three basic components, according to which its theoretical content is defined. Thus it is distinguished from other economic theories in terms of the broad lines of these components, which are:

1. The principle of multi-faceted ownership;
2. The principle of economic freedom within a defined limit;
3. The principle of social justice.

We will first give a description and explanation of these basic components so that we may form a general view of the Islamic economy. Thus, the scope of the study with regard to its general form will be available to us in examining its theoretical details and characteristics.

*   *   *

Islam differs essentially from capitalism and socialism in the nature of the ownership which it acknowledges.

Capitalist society believes in the private individual form of ownership, i.e. private ownership. It allows individuals private ownership of different kinds of wealth in the country according to their activities and circumstances. It only recognizes public ownership when required by social necessity and when experience demonstrated the need for nationalization of this or that utility. This necessity is an exceptional circumstance, by which a capitalist society is compelled to go outside the principle of private ownership — it is an exception with regard to a utility or form of, whose area is clearly defined.

Socialist society is completely contrary to that. In it common ownership is the general principle which is applied to every kind of wealth in the land. In its view private ownership of any of the wealth is an anomaly and an exception, which it may sometimes admit as a result of a prevailing social need.

In the basis of these two contradictory theories, capitalism and socialism, the term "capitalist society" is applied to every society which believes in private ownership as its exclusive principle and which regards nationalization an exception and as a means of treating a social necessity. Similarly the term "socialist society" is applied to every society which regards common ownership as a principle and which only recognizes private ownership in exceptional circumstances.

However, the basic characteristic of both societies is not applicable to Islamic society because Islamic society does not agree with capitalism in the doctrine that private ownership is the principle, nor with socialism in its view that common ownership is a general principle. Rather it acknowledges different forms of ownership at the same time. Thus it lays down the principle of multi-faceted ownership—i.e. ownership in a variety of forms—instead of the principle of only one kind of ownership, which capitalism and socialism have adopted. It believes in private ownership, public ownership and state ownership. It designates to each of these kinds of ownership a special area in which to operate and it does not regard any of them as anomalous and exceptional, nor as a temporary treatment required by circumstances.

For this reason, it would be a mistake to call Islamic society a capitalist society, even though it allows private ownership of a number of kinds of property and means of production, because in its view private ownership is not the basic rule. In the same way it would be a mistake to use the term "socialist society" for Islamic society, even though it has adopted public ownership and state ownership for some kinds of wealth and property, because in its view the socialist form of ownership is not the general rule. Similarly it would be a mistake to consider it a mixture constructed from this and that, because the variety of the principal forms of ownership in Islamic society does not mean that Islam has blended together the two theories—capitalist and socialist—and adopted a feature from each of them. It only gives expression to that variety in the forms of ownership through a pure theoretical design, which is dependent upon clearly defined intellectual bases and rules, and which is put forward within a special framework of values and concepts. These are in contradistinction to the bases, rules, values and concepts on which liberal capitalism and Marxist socialism depend.

There is no greater evidence for the correctness of the Islamic view of ownership than the reality of the capitalist and socialist experiences. Both these experiments necessitate the recognition of another kind of ownership which is not compatible with the general rule involved in each of them because the reality is proof of the mistake of the ideology which upholds the doctrine of there being only one kind of ownership. A long time ago capitalist society began to adopt the concept of nationalization and to exclude some utilities from the framework of private ownership. This movement towards nationalization is nothing but an implicit recognition by capitalist societies of the unsuitability of the capitlist principle with regard to ownership, and an attempt to treat the weaknesses and contradictions which derive from that principle.

On the other hand socialist society finds itself — despite its recentness — compelled to recognize private ownership, sometimes legally and sometimes in a form that is outside the law. An example of the legal recognition of that is the seventh article of the Soviet constitution which stipulates that every family of a collective farm has the right — in addition to its basic income which comes from the joint provision of the collective farm — to a piece of land exclusively for itself and attached to the place of residence. Thus it has an additional income in the land, a house for habitation, productive livestock, fowl and simple agricultural tools as private ownership. In the same way the ninth article allows individual peasants to own small economic enterprises and for these small kinds of ownership to exist alongside the prevailing socialist system.

*   *   *

The second of the components of the Islamic economy is to allow individuals, at the economic level, a limited freedom, within the bounds of the spiritual and moral values in which Islam believes.

In this component, we also find an outstanding difference between the Islamic economy and the two economies of capitalism and socialism. While individuals practise unrestrained freedom under the protection of the capitalist economy, and while the socialist economy seizes the liberties of all, Islam adopts an attitude which conforms with its general nature. Therefore it permits individuals to practice their freedom within the limit of values and ideals which will train and burnish that freedom and make it into a better tool for the whole of mankind.

The Islamic limitation on social freedom in the economic field has two parts:

1. Personal limitation which springs from the roots of the person and which extends its power and balance from the spiritual and intellectual recesses to the Islamic personality.

2. The objective limitation, which gives expression to an external power, limiting and restraining social behaviour.

3. As for the personal limitation, it is formed naturally under the guidance of the special education, according to which Islam rears the individual in the society over which Islam holds sway in every facet of its life — the Islamic society. The intellectual and spiritual frameworks, within which Islam forms the Islamic personality when it gives the opportunity of direct contact with the reality of life and with the work of history, which is at is basis . . . these frameworks have extraordinary ideational power and great influence in the personal and natural definition of the freedom which has been given to the individual members of Islamic society. They direct them in

a righteous restrained direction without the individuals feeling robbed of any of their liberty. Since the definition springs from their spiritual and intellectual reality, they do not find any limit to their liberties in it. Therefore the personal limitation is not really a limitation of freedom. It is only the process of training the innermost heart of the free man truly spiritually so that under its care freedom performs its true mission.

This personal limitation has had its profound results and its great influence on the formation of the nature of Islamic society and its general disposition. Despite the fact that the complete Islamic experiment was short in duration, it has brought results and thrown light, in the soul of mankind, on their ideal potentialities. It has bestowed on mankind a spiritual stock overflowing with feelings of justice, goodness and charity. If it had been possible for that experiment to continue and to extend into the life of mankind for a longer period than it did extend in short historical phase, it would have been able to prove man's competence to take up custodianship of the earth. It would have made a new world overflowing with feelings of justice and mercy. It would have rooted out from the soul of man most of the elements of evil and tendencies for oppression and corruption, which could be rooted out.

It is sufficient to mention from among the results of personal limitation that it remains the only basic guarantor for works of piety and good in the society of the Muslims, since Islam lost its own actual experiment in life, and was deprived of its political and social leadership. Despite the fact that the Muslims have been set apart from the spirit of that experiment and leadership through a temporal separation which stretches many centuries and a spiritual separation which can be measured by the decrease of their intellectual and psychological standards, and despite the fact that they have become accustomed to different kinds of social and political life, despite all this, personal limitation, whose essence Islam laid down in its complete experiment for life, had a positive and active role in guaranteeing works of piety and good. These are represented in millions of Muslims paying *zakat*, performing other duties to God, and participating in the realization of the concepts of Islam concerning social justice, doing all this with a freedom which was crystalised within the framework of that personal limitation. What do you think would be the result, in the light of this reality, if those Muslims were living the complete Islamic experience and if their society was a complete embodiment of Islam in its ideas, values and policy and their society was a practical expression of its concepts and ideals?

As for the objective limitation of freedom, we mean by it the limitation which is imposed on the individual in Islamic society from outside by the force of revealed law. This objective limitation of freedom in Islam is based on the principle which says that there is no freedom for the person in what the sacred law stipulates concerning the types of activity which contradict the ideals and aims in whose necessity Islam believes.

The execution of this principle in Islam was performed in the following way:

1. The sacred law, in its general sources, provided the textual stipulation to forbid a group of social and economic activities, which hinder, in the view of Islam, the realization of the ideals and values adopted by Islam, such as usury, monopoly and the like.

2. The sacred law laid down in principle the supervision of the ruler over general activities and the intervention of the state to protect and safeguard public interest through the limitation of freedom of individuals in the actions they perform. It was necessary for Islam to lay down this principle in order to guarantee the realizations of its ideals and concepts concerning social justice in the course of time. The requirements of the social justice which Islam propagates, differ according to the economic circumstances of the society and the material situations which surround it. The performance of an action may be harmful to society and its necessary form at a particular time while it is not at another. Thus it is not possible to detail that in fixed constitutional forms. The only way to provide the ruler with the opportunity to carry out his duty as an authority, which controls, directs and limits the freedoms of the individuals with regard to the permissible actions in revealed law which they may do or not do, in accordance with the Islamic ideal for society.

The legal source for the principle of supervision and intervention is the Holy Qur'an where it says: *Obey God and obey the Messenger and those who have authority among you.* This text indicates clearly the necessity of obeying those who have authority. There is no dispute among Muslims that "those who have authority" are those who hold legal authority in Islamic society, even though they disagree about how they are appointed and the definition of their conditions and qualities. Then, the high Islamic authority has the right to be obeyed and the right to intervene to protect the society and to realise the Islamic equilbrium in it. However, this intervention should be within the context of the sacred law. Thus it is possible for the State or the ruler to allow usury, to permit cheating, not to apply the law of inheritance, to annul ownership already established on an Islamic basis in society. Yet the ruler is allowed in Islam to intervene in actions and activities, permitted by the sacred law. He can forbid them or order them to be done according to the Islamic ideal of the society. Thus revival of the land, extraction of minerals and making canals and other such activities, and trading are permittible actions which the sacred law has permitted in a general way. It has laid down for each action the legal consequences which are entailed by it. If the ruler considers that he should forbid or order some kind of activity within the limits of his authority, he has the right to do so according to the previously mentioned principle.

The Messenger of God – may God bless him and his family – applied this principle of intervention when there was a need or situation, which required some kind of intervention and direction. An example of this is reported, in the authentic tradition on the authority of the Prophet, may God bless him and his family: He gave a judgement to the Medinans concerning the irrigation channels between palm trees that *the benefit of good may not be prevented*. He also gave a judgement to the people of the desert that *an excess of water may be prevented* (from flowing) *in order that pasture may be prevented* (from growing). He said: *There should be no harm nor attempt to cause harm*. It is clear according to the jurists that the prevention of the benefit of a thing or the prevention of an excess of water is not forbidden in general in the sacred law. In this light we know that the Prophet did not forbid the people of Medina from preventing the benefit of a thing nor did he forbid the prevention of the excess of water as a Messenger bringing general revealed laws. He only forbade that as a ruler responsible for the organization of the economic life of the society and for directing it in such a way that does not conflict with public interests as he estimates them. It may be for this reason that the narration expresses the prohibition of the Prophet as a judgement and not as an absolute religious prohibition because judgement is a kind of non-revealed legal decision.

We will treat this principle (the principle of supervision and intervention) in a more detailed and elaborate later discussion.

* * *

The third component in the Islamic economy is the principle of social justice. This is embodied in Islam by the elements and guarantees which Islam provided for the system of the distribution of wealth in Islamic society. These enable the distribution to achieve the realization of Islamic justice and to be in harmony with the values with which it is concerned. When Islam put social justice within the basic principles from which its economic theory is composed, it did not adopt social justice in its general abstract conception, nor did it call for a form capable of every kind of explanation, nor did it entrust the matter to human societies which differ in their view of social justice according to their cultural ideas and concepts about life. Rather Islam defined and crystalised this concept within a specific social plan. After that, it was able to embody this determination in a living social reality, all of whose veins and arteries throbbed with the Islamic concept of justice.

It is not sufficient to know only Islam's calls for social justice but we should also know its detailed concepts of justice and the special Islamic evidence for them.

The Islamic image of social justice contains two general principles, each one of them has its own lines and particularities. The first of them is the principle of general mutual responsibility, the other is the principle of social balance. Just social values are realized within the Islamic conception of mutual responsibility and balance and it is in them that the Islamic ideal of social justice is found, as we shall see in the following section. The steps which Islam took in the course of creating the most excellent human society during its glorious historical experiment were plain and clear with regard to its concern for its principal component of its economy.

This concern was clearly reflected in the first speech which the Prophet delivered and the first political action he took in his new state.

The great Messenger inaugurated his guiding statement—as it is reported—with this speech:

> People, make preparation for yourselves. By God, each of you should that he will die and he will leave his sheep without a shepherd. Then his Lord will say to him: Did not my Messenger come to you and tell you? And I gave you wealth and showed preference to you. What have you prepared for yourself. Then each of you will look to the left and the right and he will see nothing. He will look in front of him and he will only see Hell, Whoever is able to protect his face from the Fire—even with half of a date—let him do it. Whoever does not find that, let him use a good word. For one good action will be rewarded ten times to seven hundred times. Peace be on you and the mercy and blessings of God.

His political activity began with the making of a brotherhood between the emigrants from Mecca and the supporters from Medina, and the application of mutual responsibility between them, for the sake of the realisation of the social justice which Islam aimed at.

* * *

These are the basic elements in the Islamic economy:

1. Ownership of varied kinds, in the light of which distribution is determined.
2. A freedom, limited by Islamic values, in the fields of production, exchange and consumption.
3. A social justice, which will guarantee happiness to society, and whose foundation is mutual responsibility and balance.

* * *

The economic theory in Islam has two main qualities, which radiate through its lines and particularities. They are realism and morality. Therefore the Islamic economy is both a realistic and a moral economy in its goals which it set out to realize, and in the method which it adopts for that.

It is a realistic economy in its goals because in its systems and laws it aims at goals which are in harmony with the nature, tendencies and general characteristics of human reality; it always tries not to ask more than is humanly possible in its legal reckoning; and it does not take humanity soaring into high imaginary skies beyond its powers and abilities. It always determines its economic plan on the basis of a real view of man. It sets out real aims which agree with that view. An imaginary economy, like for example communism, may be content to adopt an unreal aim and set forth to attain a new humanity, purified from all tendencies of egotism and capable of distributing works and wealth among men without any need for an instrument of government to direct the distribution, a humanity secure from all kinds of disputes and strike. . . . However, this does not conform with the nature of Islamic legislation, nor with the realism which it is characterized by in its goals and aims.

In addition to this, it is also real in its method. Just as it aims at real goals, which are capable of being realized, similarly it gives a real material guarantee for the realization of these goals. It is not satisfied with the guarantees of advice and guidance, which preachers and teachers give because it means going beyond such aims to the sphere of execution. Therefore it is not content to entrust them to providence of chance and guesses. For example, when it aims at the creation of general mutual responsibility, it does not only seek for this by methods of direction and the arousal of emotion, rather it supports it with a legal guarantee which makes its realization essential in every circumstance.

The second quality of the Islamic economy, the moral quality, means in terms of goal, that Islam does not derive the goals, which it strives to realize in the economic life of society, from material circumstances and natural conditions which are independent of man himself, in the same way that Marxism derives its goals from the position and circumstance of productive forces. Rather it views those goals in terms of them being an expression of practical values which must be realised from the moral angle. For example, when it prescribes the guarantee of life for the worker, it does not believe that this social guarantee, which it has laid down, as something which has arisen out of the material circumstances of production. Rather it considers it as a representative of a practical value which has to be realized. . . . study that in a detailed manner in the course of the discussions in this section.

The moral quality, in terms of method, means that Islam is concernerd with the psychological factor throughout the method which it has laid down to achieve its aims and goals. In the method which it lays down for that, it is not only concerned with the objective aspect—namely that those goals be achieved. Indeed in a special way it attends to the blending of the psychological and personal factor with the method which realizes those goals. For example, money may be taken from the rich to provide sufficient support for the poor and in that it is feasible that the poor may satisfy their needs. Thus, the objective goal, which the Islamic economy aims at in terms of the principle of mutal responsibility, would come into existence. However, in the reckoning of Islam, this is not the problem. Rather there is the method by which general mutual responsibility is reached. For, this method may mean simply the use of force to take tax from the rich in order to support the poor. Even though this would be sufficient to the realization of the objective aspect of the problem — namely providing sufficient support for the poor — Islam would not accept that as long as the method of attaining mutual responsibility was without a moral motive and factor of goodness in the hearts of the rich. For this reason, Islam has intervened and made revealed legally-required acts of religion out of financial duties, by which the creation of mutual responsibility is aimed at. It is necessary that they spring from a shining psychological motive which impels man to participate in the realization of the goals of the Islamic economy in a consciously intended manner out of a desire by that to please God, the Exalted, and to draw close to Him.

No wonder that Islam has this concern for the psychological factor and this care for its spiritual and intellectual formation in accordance with its goals and concepts. The nature of the personal factors, which struggle in the soul of man, have a great influence on the formation of the personality of man and defines his spiritual content. In the same way the personal factor has a great influence on social life together with its problems and solutions. It has become clear to everyone today that the psychological factor plays a major role in the economic field. It has an influence on the occurrence of the periodic crises, from whose misfortunes the European economy clamours. Also, it affects the curve of supply and demand and the productive capacity of the work, in addition to other elements of the economy.

Islam, then, is not limited, in its theory and doctrines, to the organization of the external aspect of society. But it penetrates to its spiritual and intellectual depths to bring about a reconciliation between the internal content and the economic and social plan which it draws. It is not satisfied in its method to adopt any way which guarantees the realization of its aims. Rather, it blends this way with the psychological factor and the personal motive which is in harmony with those aims and conceptions.

Ayatollah Sayyid Mahmud Taliqani

We have seen that Islam expounds upon the general elements, aims, and results of public and private relations of individuals and society. Also, Islam promulgates principles and injunctions based on these ends and elements. The injunctions and the derivatives from them vary, depending on spiritual, material, individual, and social relations and ends. In this chapter are discussed the principles of ownership and economic relations derived from Islam. The following basic principles are deduced from the verses of the Qur'an and sound traditions. Ownership is relative and limited. Ownership means the authority and power of possession. As human power and authority are limited, no person should consider himself the absolute owner and complete possessor. Absolute power and complete possession belong only to God who has created man and all other creatures and has them constantly in his possession. Man's ownership then is limited to whatever God has wisely willed and to the capacity of his intellect, authority, and freedom granted to him. "Say: O Allah! Owner of Sovereignty! Thou givest sovereignty to whom Thou wilt, and Thou withdrawest Sovereignty from whom Thou wilt" (III:26). "And Who hath no partner in the Sovereignty" (XVII:111).

These verses make the believer (the one who confesses the oneness of God) constantly acknowledge that the world, of which he is a part, is always the possession of a victorious power who is just. There are other verses in the munificient Qur'an which explicitly acknowledge that the earth and its resources belong to God. It is He who had made them subservient to man. Man, in this position, is His vicegerent (*khalifah*) on earth: "And the earth hath He appointed for (His) creatures" (LV:10); "Who hath appointed the earth a resting-place for you" (II:22); "Allah hath made all that is on the earth subservient unto you" (XXII:65); "Then We appointed you viceroys on the earth" (X:14); "He it is Who hath made you regents on the earth" (XXXV:39). These and other similar verses explain the vicegerency (*khilafah*) of man on earth in order that the vicegerents may follow the command and the will of the Owner.

"And spend of that whereof He hath made you trustees" (LVII:7)); "And bestow upon them of the wealth of Allah which He hath bestowed upon you" (XXIV:33); "And We help you with wealth and sons" (LXXI:12);

"Think they that in the wealth and sons wherewith We provide them" (XXIII: 55); "And ye have left behind you all that We bestowed upon you" (VII:94). These verses explicitly point out that the absolute owner is God alone. It is He who has, within the capacities of His vicegerent granted (gifted) the right of ownership, helped (power to continue life) and extended the right of transfer (transferring the right of possession). Furthermore, the Qur'an explicitly designates ownership of the earth as that of God. "And Allah's earth is spacious" (XXXIX:10); "So let her feed on Allah's earth" (VII:73 and XI:64).

Based on this principle (relative and limited ownership) which is derived from the Qur'anic text, man is neither the absolute owner nor the total possessor of the earth and its resources. He does not have the right to possess as much as he desires or to obtain material wealth in any way he may choose. Indeed, the earth's wealth belongs to God and man is His vicegerent and servant. Indeed, because vicegerency belongs to all people, each individual is a guardian of the public trust. And his ownership should be limited for the public welfare. Ownership, in this analogy, is limited, borrowed, conditional, and entrusted. (Contrary to this view is absolute, free, complete, and unconditional ownership. Under such a view ownership spreads deep roots in the minds of owners and becomes an idol to the extent that wealth and economic relations are considered the foundations and the bases of all spiritual and social affairs.) From this basic principle of limited and relative private ownership, the following basic injunctions about the desire for ownership are deduced:

1. Land and natural resources are not the particular property of anyone (neither individual nor society). Only the guardian of the Muslims (Imam and *wali-i amr* [the people of authority]) committed to public welfare has supervision over the earth and its resources (reflecting the principle of permissibility and nonpermissibility of private ownership except in special conditions and situations).

2. People have special and limited rights to possession of land and natural resources as long as they put them to fruitful and productive use. They also have special and limited ownership over production and goods.

3. Islamic jurisprudence provides specific definintions and conditions for formalizing ownership and the activities leading to it.

4. Individuals and special groups must not have possession or title over natural resources (*anfal* and *fayᶜ*). Furthermore, no one should be stopped from utilizing them by imposition of special conditions.

5. Money and currencies, which are means of exchange and a standard of value, must not be accumulated by a selected few individuals. When such a thing happens these individuals become powerful, and the necessary

resources and means of life are concentrated in their hands; the normal and just conditions of work and distribution become disrupted.

6. In accordance with Islamic principles and injunctions, when a person's liquid assets and wealth reach a certain level or increase within a certain time they are subject to direct and fixed taxes (*zakat* and *khums*).

7. Based on the principle of public welfare, the Islamic guardian (Imam, men of authority or deputies) has the right to possess wealth and levy tax (*kharaj*) on the lands and natural resources.

8. Profits and wealth earned by illegal means (usury, gambling, and lottery) or wealth obtained from the transaction of harmful goods do not constitute ownership.

9. Children and insane persons have no right to possess their wealth.

10. Islam forbids expenditures which are useless and harmful to individuals and to society; this serves to stop the amassing of unlimited and illegal wealth.

These are the general injunctions and basic principles of Islam on ownership and economic relations. They are explained in detail and properly documented. The sources and the standard of these injunctions, in addition to the aforementioned sources, are found in the Qur'an, the *sunnah*, reason (*caql*) and custom (*curf*). Some examples are "And consume not wastefully your property among yourselves (*binakum*) in vanity" (II:188); "That is become not a commodity between the rich among you" (LVIX:7); "Give not unto the foolish (what is in) your (keeping of their) wealth which Allah had given you to maintain" (IV:5); "fulfill your undertakings." (V:1); "There is neither damage nor compulsion (*la zarar*) in Islam" (the Prophetic tradition); "Necessity removes the objective observance of caution" (either a tradition or a rational or customary principle); "Ignoring the small and particular harm in order to avoid a major and a general one" (rational or customary principles); and "The believers honor their contracts unless they follow what is forbidden (*haram*) and forbid what is allowed (*halal*)" (tradition).

The collection of the principal injunctions, legal and intellectual principles, and their derivatives will become the actual economic and financial contracts based on faith and executive powers.

This summarizes the foundations of the injunctions and the principal injunctions in Islam about ownership and economic relations. Based on these foundations, injunctions, and general and particular rules which conform to the intrinsic nature of man and of reality, men are free and independent. They are not limited to, and their rights are not suspended with respect to, expression of talents and of physical and spiritual gifts which are stimulated by material needs and desires. However, this freedom in particular for gaining and using wealth, is limited by special injunctions and principles of public welfare, so that neither centralization of wealth nor subjugation occurs nor a ruling class emerges.

The ideas of absolute, free ownership (capitalism) and its rival, the absolute negation of private ownership (collectivism and socialism), are the special products of the century of abrupt industrial development and the areas in which they occurred. Whenever one of these two types of uncompromising and different economic systems dominates, the other one is rejected. One has to submit to all the provisions and effects of the accepted system. Free ownership causes subjugation, tyranny, centralization of wealth, emergence of privileged capitalists, and the deprivation of workers. The negation of private ownership limits individual freeedom and, in turn, requires the dictatorship of a special class. Therefore, one has to consent to the provisions of the regime whether they allow private ownership and prescribe its provisions or they accept public or governmental ownership. Because they are products of special and opposite times and places, these two opposing ideas have not materialized anywhere completely. (In the capitalist countries resources and industries have been gradually nationalized and in communist areas private ownership over land and small factories is recognized.) In fact, the theories presented a century ago to solve industrial problems — caused by the means of production, in light of progress and the development of other social principles, rapid developments in technology, a decrease in the number of workers, and an increase in production — have not and could not predict the final solution.

Part III

Shiᶜism in History

Chapter Nine

The Historical Growth of Shiᶜism

The vicissitudes of Shiᶜism in history have been the result of interaction between its doctrines and political developments. From their role as the initial supporters of ᶜAli, the Shiᶜis have grown and experienced drastic changes in their political status: from a persecuted minority to established dynasties and majorities in certain Islamic communities. In the following passage, ᶜAllamah Tabataba'i provides a schematic summary of Shiᶜi history. The excerpt is taken from SI, *pages 39–67.*

ᶜ*Allamah Tabataba'i*

Shiᶜism began with a reference made for the first time to the partisans of ᶜAli (*shiᶜah-i* ᶜ*Ali*), the first leader of the Household of the Prophet, during the lifetime of the Prophet himself. The course of the first manifestation and the later growth of Islam during the twenty-three years of prophecy brought about many conditions which necessitated the appearance of a group such as the Shiᶜis among the companions of the Prophet.

The Holy Prophet during the first days of his prophecy, when according to the text of the Qur'an he was commanded to invite his closer relatives to come to his religion, told them clearly that whoever would be the first to accept his invitation would become his successor and inheritor. ᶜAli was the first to step forth and embrace Islam. The Prophet accepted ᶜAli's submission to the faith and thus fulfilled his promise.

From the Shiᶜi point of view it appears as unlikely that the leader of a movement, during the first days of his activity, should introduce to strangers one of his associates as his successor and deputy but not introduce him to his completely loyal and devout aides and friends. Nor does it appear likely that such a leader should accept someone as his deputy and successor and introduce him to others as such, but then throughout his life and religious call deprive his deputy of his duties as deputy, disregard the respect due to his position as successor, and refuse to make any distinctions between him and others.

The Prophet, according to many unquestioned and completely authenticated *hadiths*, both Sunni and Shiᶜi, clearly asserted that ᶜAli was preserved from error and sin in his actions and sayings. Whatever he said and did was in perfect conformity with the teachings of religion and he was the most knowledgeable of men in matters pertaining to the Islamic sciences and injunctions.

During the period of prophecy ᶜAli performed valuable services and made remarkable sacrifices. When the infidels of Mecca decided to kill the Prophet and surrounded his house, the Holy Prophet decided to emigrate to Medina. He said to ᶜAli, "Will you sleep in my bed at night so that they will think that I am asleep and I will be secure from being pursued by them?" ᶜAli accepted this dangerous assignment with open arms. This has been recounted in different histories and collections of *hadith*. (The emigration from Mecca to Medina marks the date of origin of the Islamic calendar, known as the *hijrah*.) cAli also served by fighting in the battles of Badr, Uhud, Khaybar, Khandaq, and Hunayn in which the victories achieved with his aid were such that if cAli had not been present the enemy would most likely have uprooted Islam and the Muslims, as is recounted in the usual histories, lives of the Prophet, and collections of *hadith*.

For Shi*c*is, the central evidence of cAli's legitimacy as successor to the Prophet is the event of Ghadir Khumm when the Prophet chose cAli to the "general guardianship" (*walayat-i cammah*) of the people and made cAli, like himself, their "guardian" (*wali*).

It is obvious that because of such distinctive services and recognition, because of cAli's special virtues which were acclaimed by all, and because of the great love the Prophet showed for him, some of the companions of the Prophet who knew cAli well, and who were champions of virtue and truth, came to love him. They assembled around cAli and followed him to such an extent that many others began to consider their love for him excessive and a few perhaps also became jealous of him. Besides all these elements, we see in many sayings of the Prophet reference to the "*shicah* of cAli" and the "*shicah* of the Household of the Prophet."

*   *   *

The friends and followers of cAli believed that after the death of the Prophet the caliphate and religious authority (*marjaciyat-i cilmi*) belonged to cAli. This belief came from their consideration of cAli's position and station in relation to the Prophet, his relation to the chosen among the companions, as well as his relation to Muslims in general. It was only the events that occurred during the few days of the Prophet's final illness that indicated that there was opposition to their view. Contrary to their expectation, at the very moment when the Prophet died and his body lay still unburied, while his household and few companions were occupied with providing for his burial and funeral service, the friends and followers of cAli received news of the activity of another group who had gone to the mosque where the community was gathered faced with this sudden loss of its leader. This group, which was later to form the majority, set forth in great haste to select a caliph for the Muslims with the aim of ensuring the welfare of the community and solving its immediate problems. They did this without consulting the Household of the Prophet, his relatives or many of his friends, who were busy with the funeral, and without providing them with the least information. Thus cAli and his friends—such as cAbbas, Zubayr, Salman, Abu Zarr, Miqdad and cAmmar—after finishing with the burial of the body of the Prophet became aware of the proceedings by which the caliph had been selected. They protested against the act of choosing the caliph by consultation or election, and also against those who were responsible for carrying it out. They even presented their own proofs and arguments, but the answer they received was that the welfare of the Muslims was at stake and the solution lay in what had been done.

It was this protest and criticism which separated from the majority the minority that were following ᶜAli and made his followers known to society as the "partisans" or "*shiᶜah*" of ᶜAli. The caliphate of the time was anxious to guard against this appellation being given to the Shiᶜi minority and thus to have Muslim society divided into sections comprised of a majority and a minority. The supporters of the caliph considered the caliphate to be a matter of the consensus of the community (*ijmaᶜ*) and called those who objected the "opponents of allegiance." They claimed that the Shiᶜis stood, therefore, opposed to Muslim society. Sometimes the Shiᶜis were given other pejorative and degrading names.

Shiᶜism was condemned from the first moment because of the political situation of the time and thus it could not accomplish anything through mere political protest. ᶜAli, in order to safeguard the well-being of Islam and of the Muslims, and also because of lack of sufficient political and military power, did not endeavor to begin an uprising against the existing political order, which would have been of a bloody nature. Yet those who protested against the established caliphate refused to surrender to the majority in certain questions of faith and continued to hold that the succession to the Prophet and religious authority belonged by right to ᶜAli. They believed that all spiritual and religious matters should be referred to him and invited people to become his followers.

* * *

In accordance with the Islamic teachings which form its basis, Shiᶜism believed that the most important question facing Islamic society was the elucidation and clarification of Islamic teachings and the tenets of the religious sciences. Only after such clarifications were made could the application of these teachings to the social order be considered. In other words, Shiᶜism believed that, before all else, members of society should be able to gain a true vision of the world and of men based on the real nature of things. Only then could they know and perform their duties as human beings — in which lay their real welfare — even if the performance of these religious duties were to be against their desires. After carrying out this first step a religious government should preserve and execute real Islamic order in society in such a way that man would worship none other than God, would possess personal and social freedom to the extent possible, and would benefit from true personal and social justice.

These two ends could be accomplished only by a person who was inerrant and protected by God from having faults. Otherwise people could become rulers or religious authorities who would not be free from the possibility of distortion of thought or the committing of treachery in the duties placed upon their shoulders. Were this to happen, the just and freedom-giving rule of Islam could gradually be converted to dictatorial rule and a completely autocratic government. Moreover, the pure religious teachings could become, as can be seen in the case of certain other religions, the victims of change and distortion in the hands of selfish scholars given to the satisfaction of their carnal desires. As confirmed by the Holy Prophet, ᶜAli followed perfectly and completely the Book of God and the tradition of the Prophet in both words and deeds. As Shiᶜism sees it, if, as the majority say, only the Quraysh opposed the rightful caliphate of ᶜAli, then that majority should have answered the Quraysh by asserting what was right. They should have quelled all opposition to the right cause in the same way that they fought against the group who refused to pay the religious tax (*zakat*). The majority should not have remained indifferent to what was right for fear of the opposition of the Quraysh.

What prevented the Shiᶜis from accepting the elective method of choosing the caliphate by the people was the fear of the unwholesome consequences that might result from it: fear of possible corruption in Islamic government and of the destruction of the solid basis for the sublime religious sciences. As it happened, later events in Islamic history confirmed this fear (or prediction), with the result that the Shiᶜis became ever firmer in their belief. During the earliest years, however, because of the small number of its followers, Shiᶜism appeared outwardly to have been absorbed into the majority, although privately it continued to insist on acquiring the Islamic sciences from the Household of the Prophet and to invite people to its cause. At the same time, in order to preserve the power of Islam and safeguard its progress, Shiᶜism did not display any open opposition to the rest of Islamic society. Members of the Shiᶜite community even fought hand in hand with the Sunni majority in holy wars (*jihad*) and participated in public affairs. ᶜAli himself guided the Sunni majority in the interest of the whole of Islam whenever such action was necessary.

* * *

Shiᶜism believes that the Divine Law of Islam (*shariᶜah*), whose substance is found in the Book of God and in the tradition (*sunnah*) of the Holy Prophet, will remain valid to the Day of Judgment and can never, nor will ever, be altered. A government which is really Islamic cannot under any pretext refuse completely to carry out the *shariᶜah's* injunctions. The only duty of an Islamic government is to make decisions by consultation within the limits set by the *shariᶜah* and in accordance with the demands of the movement.

The vow of allegiance to Abu Bakr at Saqifah, which was motivated at least in part by political considerations, and the incident described in the hadith of "ink and paper," which occurred during the last days of the illness of the Holy Prophet, reveal the fact that those who directed and backed the movement to choose the caliph through the process of election believed that the Book of God should be preserved in the form of a constitution. They emphasized the Holy Book and paid much less attention to the words of the Holy Prophet as an immutable source of the teachings of Islam. They seem to have accepted the modifcation of certain aspects of Islamic teachings concerning government to suit the conditions of the moment and for the sake of the general welfare.

This tendency to emphasize only certain principles of the Divine Law is confirmed by many sayings that were later transmitted concerning the companions of the Holy Prophet. For example, the companions were considered to be independent authorities in matters of the Divine Law (*mujtahid*), being able to exercise independent judgment (*ijtihad*) in public affairs. It was also believed that if they succeeded in their task they would be rewarded by God and if they failed they would be forgiven by Him since they were among the companions. This view was widely held during the early years following the death of the Holy Prophet. Shiʿism takes a stricter stand and believes that the actions of the companions, as of all other Muslims, should be judged strictly according to the teachings of the *shariʿah*. For example, there was the complicated incident involving the famous general Khalid ibn Walid in the house of one of the prominent Muslims of the day, Malik ibn Nuwayrah, which led to the death of the latter. The fact that Khalid was not at all taken to task for this incident because of his being an outstanding military leader shows in the eyes of Shiʿism an undue lenience toward some of the actions of the companions which were below the norm of perfect piety and righteousness set by the actions of the spiritual elite among the companions.

Another practice of the early years which is criticized by Shiʿism is the cutting off of the *khums* from the members of the Household of the Prophet and from the Holy Prophet's relatives. Likewise, because of the emphasis laid by Shiʿism on the sayings and the *sunnah* of the Holy Prophet it is difficult for it to understand why the writing down of the text of *hadith* was completely banned and why, if a written *hadith* were found, it would be burned. We know that this ban continued through the caliphate, of the *khulafa'-i rashidun* into the Umayyad period and did not cease until the period of ʿUmar ibn ʿAbd al-ʿAziz, who ruled from A.H. 99/A.D. 717 to A.H. 101/A.D. 719.

During the period of the second caliph (13/634-25/644) there was a continuation of the policy of emphasizing certain aspects of the *shariʿah* and of putting aside some of the practices which the Shiʿis believe the Holy Prophet taught and practiced. Some practices were forbidden, some were omitted, and some were added. For instance, the pilgrimage of *tamattu'* (a kind of pilgrimage in which the *cumrah* ceremony is utilized in place of the *hajj* ceremony) was banned by *c*Umar during his caliphate, with the decree that transgressors would be stoned; this in spite of the fact that during his final pilgrimage the Holy Prophet—peace be upon him—instituted in the Qur'an, *surah* II, 196, a special form for the pilgrimage ceremonies that might be performed by pilgrims coming from far away. Also, during the lifetime of the Prophet of God temporary marriage (*mutcah*) was practiced, but *c*Umar forbade it. And even though during the life of the Holy Prophet it was the practice to recite in the call to prayers, "Hurry to the best act" (*hayya cala khayr al-camal*), *c*Umar ordered that it be omitted because he said it would prevent people from participating in holy war, *jihad*. (It is still recited in the Shi*c*i call to prayers, but not in the Sunni call.) There was also additions to the *sharicah*: during the time of the Prophet a divorce was valid only if the three declarations of divorce ("I divorce thee") were made on three different occasions, but *c*Umar allowed the triple divorce declaration to be made at one time. Heavy penalties were imposed on those who broke certain of these new regulations, such as stoning in the case of *mutcah* marriage.

It was also during the period of the rule of the second caliph that new social and economic forces led to the uneven distribution of the public treasury (*bayt al-mal*) among the people, an act which was later the cause of bewildering class differences and frightful and bloody struggle among Muslims. At this time Mu*c*awiyah was ruling in Damascus in the style of the Persian and Byzantine kings and was even given the title of the "Khusraw of the Arabs" (a Persian title of the highest imperial power), but not serious protest was made against him for his worldly type of rule.

The second caliph was killed by a Persian slave in 25/644. In accordance with the majority vote of a six-man council which had assembled by order of the second caliph before his death, the third caliph was chosen. The third caliph did not prevent his Umayyad relatives from becoming dominant over the people during his caliphate and appointed some of them as rulers in the Hijaz, Iraq, Egypt, and other Muslim lands. These relatives began to be lax in applying moral principles in government. Some of them openly committed injustice and tyranny, sin and iniquity, and broke certain of the tenets of firmly established Islamic laws.

Before long, streams of protest began to flow toward the capital. But the caliph, who was under the influence of his relatives—particularly Marwan ibn Hakam—did not act promptly or decisively to remove th causes against which the people were protesting. Sometimes it even happened that those who protested were punished and driven away.

An incident that happened in Egypt illustrates the nature of the rule of the third caliph. A group of Muslims in Egypt rebelled against ʿUthman. ʿUthman sensed the danger and asked ʿAli for help, expressing his feeling of contrition. ʿAli told the Egyptians, "You have revolted in order to bring justice and truth to life. ʿUthman has repented saying, 'I shall change my ways and in three days will fulfill your wishes. I shall expel the oppressive rulers from their posts." ʿAli then wrote an agreement with them on behalf of ʿUthman and they started home. On the way they saw the slave of ʿUthman riding on his camel in the direction of Egypt. They became suspicious of him and searched him. On him they found a letter for the governor of Egypt containing the following words: "In the name of God. When ʿAbd al-Rahman ibn ʿAddis comes to you beat him with a hundred lashes, shave his head and beard and condemn him to long imprisonment. Do the same in the case of ʿAmr ibn al-Himiq, Suda ibn Hamran, and ʿUrwah ibn Nibaʿ." The Egyptians took the letter and returned with anger to ʿUthman, saying, "You have betrayed us!" ʿUthman denied the letter. They said, "Your slave was the carrier of the letter." He answered, "He has committed this act without my permission." They said, "He rode upon your camel." He answered, "They have stolen my camel." They said, "The letter is in the handwriting of your secretary." He replied, "This has been done without my permission and knowledge." They said, "In any case you are not competent to be caliph and must resign, for if this has been done with your permission you are a traitor and if such important matters take place without your permission and knowledge then your incapability and incompetence is proven. In any case, either resign or dismiss the oppressive agents from office immediately." ʿUthman answered, "If I wish to act according to your will, then it is you who are the rulers. Then, what is my function?" They stood up and left the gathering in anger.

During his caliphate ʿUthman allowed the government of Damascus, at the head of which stood Muʿawiyah, to be strengthened more than ever before. In reality, the center of gravity of the caliphate as far as political power was concerned was shifting to Damascus and the organization in Medina, the capital of the Islamic world, was politically no more than a form without the necessary power and substance to support it. Finally, in the year 35/656, the people rebelled and after a few days of siege and fighting the third caliph was killed.

The first caliph was selected through the vote of the majority of the companions, the second caliph by the will and testament of the first, and the third by a six-man council whose members and rules of procedure were organized and determined by the second caliph. Altogether, the policy of these three caliphs, who were in power for twenty-five years, was to execute and apply Islamic laws and principles in society in accordance with *ijtihad* and what appeared as most wise at the time to the caliphs themselves. As for the Islamic sciences, the policy of these caliphs was to have the Holy Qur'an read and understood without being concerned with commentaries upon it or allowing it to become the subject of discussion. The *hadith* of the Prophet was recited and was transmitted orally without being written down. Writing was limited to the text of the Holy Qur'an and was forbidden in the case of hadith.

After the Battle of Yamanah, which ended in 12/633, many of those who had been reciters of the Holy Qur'an and who knew it by heart were killed. As a result ᶜUmar ibn al-Khattab proposed to the first caliph to have the verses of the Holy Qu'ran collected in written form, saying that if another war were to occur and the rest of those who knew the Qu'ran by heart were to be killed, the knowledge of the text of the Holy Book would disappear among men. Therefore, it was necessary to assemble the Qu'ranic verses in written form.

From the Shiᶜi point of view it appears strange that this decision was made concerning the Qur'an and yet despite the fact that the prophetic *hadith*, which is the complement of the Qur'an, was faced with the same danger and was not free from corruption in transmission, addition, diminution, forgery and forgetfulness, the same attention was not paid to it. On the contrary, as already mentioned, writing it down was forbidden and all of the written versions of it that were found were burned, as if to emphasize that only the text of the Holy Book should exist in written form.

As for the other Islamic sciences, during this period little effort was made to propagate them, the energies of the community being spent mostly in establishing the new sociopolitical order. Despite all the praise and consecration which are found in the Qur'an concerning knowledge (ᶜilm), and the emphasis placed upon its cultivation, the avid cultivation of the religious sciences was postponed to a later period of Islamic history.

Most men were occupied with the remarkable and continuous victories of the Islamic armies, and were carried away by the flood of immeasurable booty which came from all directions toward the Arabian peninsula. With this new wealth and the worldliness which came along with it, few were willing to devote themselves to the cultivation of the sciences of the Household of the Prophet, at whose head stood ᶜAli, whom the Holy Prophet had introduced to the people as the one most versed in the Islamic sciences. At the same time, the inner meaning and purpose of the teachings of the Holy Qur'an were neglected by most of those who were affected by this change. It is strange that, even in the matter of collecting the verses of the Holy Qur'an, ᶜAli was not consulted and his name was not mentioned among those who participated in this task, although it was known by everyone that he had collected the text of the Holy Qur'an after the death of the Prophet.

It has been recounted in many traditions that after receiving allegiance from the community, Abu Bakr sent someone to ʿAli and asked for his allegiance. ʿAli said, "I have promised not to leave my house except for the daily prayers until I compile the Qur'an." And it has been mentioned that ʿAli gave his allegienace to Abu Bakr after six months. This itself is proof that ʿAli had finished compiling the Qur'an. Likewise, it has been recounted that after compiling the Qur'an he placed the pages of the Holy Book on a camel and showed it to the people. It is also recounted that the Battle of Yamanah, after which the Qur'an was compiled, occurred during the second year of the caliphate of Abu Bakr. These facts have been mentioned in most works on history and *hadith* which deal with the account of the compilation of the Holy Qu'ran.

These and similar events made the followers of ʿAli more firm in their belief and more conscious of the course that lay before them. They increased their activity from day to day and ʿAli himself, who was cut off from the possibility of educating and training the people in general, concentrated on privately training an elite.

During this twenty-five year period ʿAli lost through death three of his four dearest friends and associates, who were also among the companions of the Prophet: Salman-i Farsi, Abu Zarr al-Ghifari, and Miqdad. They had been constant in their friendship with him in all circumstances. It was also during this same period that some of the other companions of the Holy Prophet and a large number of their followers in the Hijaz, the Yemen, Iraq, and other lands, joined the followers of ʿAli. As a result, after the death of the third caliph the people turned to ʿAli from all sides, swore allegiance to him and chose him as caliph.

*   *   *

The caliphate of ʿAli began toward the end of the year 35/656 and lasted about four years and nine months. During his period as caliph ʿAli followed the ways of the Holy Prophet and brought conditions back to their original state. He forced the resignation of all the incompetent political elements who had a hand in directing affairs and began in reality a major transformation of a "revolutionary" nature which caused him innumerable difficulties. On his first day as caliph, in an address to the people, ʿAli said:

> O People, be aware that the difficulties which you faced during the apostolic period of the Prophet of God have come upon you once again and seized you. Your ranks must be turned completely around so that the people of virtue who have fallen behind should come forward and those who had come to the fore without being worthy should fall behind. There is both true (*haqq*) and falsehood (*batil*). Each has its followers; but a

person should follow the truth. If falsehood be prevalent it is not something new, and if the truth is rare and hard to come by, sometimes even that which is rare wins the day so that there is hope of advance. Of course it does not occur often that something which has turned away from man should return to him.

ᶜAli continued his radically different type of government based more on righteousness than political efficacy but, as is necessary in the case of every movement of this kind, elements of the opposition whose interests were endangered began to display their displeasure and resisted his rule. Basing their actions on the claim that they wanted to revenge the death of ᶜUthman, they instigated bloody wars which continued throughout almost all the time that ᶜAli was caliph. From the Shiᶜi point of view those who caused these civil wars had no end in mind other than their own personal interest. The wish to revenge the blood of the third caliph was no more than an excuse to fool the crowd. There was no question of a misunderstanding.

After the death of the Holy Prophet, a small minority, following ᶜAli, refused to pay allegiance. At the head of the minority there were Salman, Abu Zarr, Miqdad, and ᶜAmmar. At the beginning of the caliphate of ᶜAli also a sizable minority in disagreement refused to pay allegiance. Among the most persistent opponents were Saᶜd ibn ᶜAss, Walid ibn ᶜUqbah, Marwan ibn Hakam, ᶜAmr ibn ᶜAs, Busr ibn Artat, Samurah ibn Jundab, and Mughirah ibn Shuᶜbah.

The study of the biography of these two groups, and meditation upon the acts they have performed and stories recounted of them in history books, reveal fully their religious personality and aim. The first group were among the elite of the companions of the Holy Prophet and among the ascetics, devout worshipers and selfless devotees of Islam who struggled on the path of Islamic freedom. They were especially loved by the Prophet. The Prophet said, "God has informed me that He loves four men and that I should love them also." They asked about their names. He mentioned ᶜAli and then the names of Abu Zarr, Salman and Miqdad. (*Sunan* of Ibn Majah, Cairo, 1372, vol. I, p. 66.) ᶜA'ishah has recounted that the Prophet of God said, "If two alternatives are placed before ᶜAmmar, he will definitely choose that which is more true and right." (Ibn Majah, vol. I, p. 66.) The Prophet said, "There is no one between heaven and earth more truthful than Abu Zarr." (Ibn Majah, vol. I, p. 68). There is no record of a single forbidden act committed by these men during their lifetime. They never spilled any blood unjustly, did not commit aggression against anyone, did not steal anyone's property, never sought to corrupt and misguide people.

History is, however, full of accounts of unworthy acts committed by some of the second group. The various acts committed by some of these men in opposition to explicit Islamic teachings are beyond reckoning. These acts cannot be excused in any manner except the way that is followed by certain groups among the Sunnis who say that God was satisfied with them and therefore they were free to perform whatever act they wished, and that they would not be punished for violating the injunctions and regulations existing in the Holy Book and the *sunnah*.

The first war in the caliphate of ^cAli, which is called the Battle of the Camel, was caused by the unfortunate class differences created during the period of rule of the second caliph as a result of the new socioeconomic forces which caused an uneven distribution of the public treasury among members of the community. When chosen to the caliphate, ^cAli divided the treasury evenly as had been the method of the Holy Prophet, but this manner of dividing the wealth upset Talhah and Zubayr greatly. They began to show signs of disobedience and left Medina for Mecca with the alleged aim of making the pilgrimage. They persuaded "the mother of the Faithful" (*umm al-mu'minin*), ^cA'ishah, who was not friendly with ^cAli, to join them and in the name of wanting to revenge the death of the third caliph they began the bloody Battle of the Camel. This was done despite the fact that this same Talhah and Zubayr were in Medina when the third caliph was besieged and killed but did nothing to defend him. Furthermore, after his death they were the first to pay allegiance to ^cAli on behalf of the immigrants (*muhajirun*) as well as on their own. Also, the "mother of the Faithful," ^cA'ishah, did not show any opposition to those who had killed the third caliph at the moment when she received the news of his death. It must be remembered that the main instigators of the disturbances that led to the death of the third caliph were those companions who wrote letters from Medina to people near and far inviting them to rebel against the caliph, a fact which is repeated in many early Muslim histories.

As for the second war, called the Battle of Siffin, which lasted for a year and a half, its cause was the covetousness of Mu^cawiyah for the caliphate which for him was a worldly political instrument rather than a religious institution. But as an excuse he made the revenge of the blood of the third caliph the main issue and began a war in which more than a hundred thousand people perished without reason. Naturally, in these wars Mu^cawiyah was the aggressor rather than the defender, for the protest to revenge someone's blood can never occur in the form of defense. The pretext of this war was blood revenge. During the last days of his life, the third caliph, in order to quell the uprising against him, asked Mu^cawiyah for help, but the army of Mu^cawiyah which set out from Damascus to Medina purposely waited on the road until the caliph was killed. Then he returned to Damascus to begin an uprising to revenge the caliph's death. After the death of ^cAli and his gaining the caliphate himself, Mu^cawiyah forgot the question of revenging the blood of the third caliph and did not pursue the matter further.

After Siffin there occurred the Battle of Nahrawan in which a number of people, among whom there could be found some of the companions, rebelled against cAli, possibly at the instigation of Mucawiyah. These people were causing rebellion throughout the lands of Islam, killing the Muslims and especially the followers of cAli. They even attacked pregnant women and killed their babies. cAli put down this uprising as well, but a short while later was himself killed in the mosque of Kufah by one of the members of this group who came to be known as the Khawarij.

The opponents of cAli claim that he was a courageous man but did not possess political acumen. They claim that at the beginning of his caliphate he could have temporarily made peace with his opponents. He could have approached them through peace and friendship, thus courting their satisfaction and approval. In this way he could have strengthened his caliphate and only then turned to their extirpation and destruction. What people who hold this view forget is that the movement of cAli was not based on political opportunism. It was a radical and revolutionary religious movement (in the true sense of revolution as a spiritual movement to reestablish the real order of things and not in its current political and social sense); therefore it could not have been accomplished through compromise or flattery and forgery. A similar situation can be seen during the apostleship of the Holy Prophet. The infidels and polytheists proposed peace to him many times and swore that if he were to abstain from protesting against their gods they would not interfere with his religious mission. But the Prophet did not accept such a proposal, although he could in those days of difficulty have made peace and used flattery to fortify his own position, and then have risen against his enemies. In fact, the Islamic message never allows a right and just cause to be abandoned for the sake of strengthening another good cause, nor a falsehood to be rejected and disproven through another falsehood. There are many Qur'anic verses concerning this matter.

*   *   *

During the four years and nine months of his caliphate, cAli was not able to eliminate the disturbed conditions which were prevailing throughout the Islamic world, but he was successful in three fundamental ways:

1. As a result of his just and upright manner of living he revealed once again the beauty and attractiveness of the way of life of the Holy Prophet, especially to the younger generation. In contrast to the imperial grandeur of Mucawiyah, he lived in simplicity and poverty like the poorest of people. He never favored his friends or relatives and family above others, nor did he ever prefer wealth to poverty or brute force to weakness.

2. Despite the cumbersome and strenuous difficulties which absorbed his time, he left behind among the Islamic community a valuable treasury of

the truly divine sciences and Islamic intellectual disciplines. Nearly eleven thousand of his proverbs and short sayings on different intellectual, religious and social subjects have been recorded. In his talks and speeches he expounded the most sublime Islamic sciences in a most elegant and flowing manner. He established Arabic grammar and laid the basis for Arabic literature.

He was the first in Islam to delve directly into the question of metaphysics (*falsafah-i ilahi*) in a manner combining intellectual rigor and logical demonstration. He discussed problems which had never appeared before in the same way among the metaphysicians of the world. Moreover, he was so devoted to metaphysics and gnosis that even in the heat of battle he would carry out intellectual discourse and discuss metaphysical questions.

3. He trained a large number of religious scholars and Islamic savants, among whom are found a number of ascetics and gnostics who were the forefathers of the Sufis, such men as Uways al-Qarani, Kumayl al-Nakha^ci, Maytham al-Tammar and Rashid al-Hajari. These men have been recognized by the later Sufis as the founders of gnosis in Islam. Others among his disciples became the first teachers of jurisprudence, theology, Quranic commentary and recitation.

* * *

After the death of ^cAli, his son, Hasan ibn ^cAli, who is recognized by the Shi^cis as their second Imam, became caliph. This designation occurred in accordance with ^cAli's last will and testament and also by the allegiance of the community to Hasan. But Mu^cawiyah did not remain quiet before this event. He marched with his army toward Iraq, which was then the capital of the caliphate, and began to wage war against Hasan.

Through different intrigues and the payment of great sums of money, Mu^cawiyah was able gradually to corrupt the aides and generals of Hasan. Finally he was able to force Hasan to hand the caliphate over to him so as to avoid bloodshed and to make peace. Hasan handed the caliphate to Mu^cawiyah on the condition that the caliphate would be returned to him after the death of Mu^cawiyah and that no harm would come to his partisans.

In the year 40/661 Mu^cawiyah finally gained control of the caliphate. He then set out immediately for Iraq and in a speech to the people of that land said: "I did not fight against you for the sake of the prayers or of fasting. These acts you can perform yourself. What I wanted to accomplish was to rule over you and this end I have achieved." He also said, "The agreement I made with Hasan is null and void. It lies trampled under my feet." With this declaration Mu^cawiyah made known to the people the real character of his government and revealed the nature of the program he had in mind.

He indicated in his declaration that he would separate religion from politics and would not give any guarantees concerning religious duties and regulations. He would spend all his force to preserve and to keep alive his own power, whatever might be the cost. Obviously a government of such a nature is more of a sultanate and a monarchy than a caliphate and vice-gerency of the Prophet of God in its traditional Islamic sense. That is why some who were admitted to his court addressed him as "king." He himself in some private gatherings interpreted his government as a monarchy, while in public he always introduced himself as the caliph.

Naturally any monarchy that is based on force carries with it inherently the principle of inheritance. Mu^cawiyah, too, finally realized this fact, and chose his son, Yazid, who was a heedless young man without the least religious personality, as the "crown prince" and his successor. This act was to be the cause of many regrettable events in the future. Mu^cawiyah had previously indicated that he would refuse to permit Hasan ibn ^cAli to succeed as caliph and that he had other thoughts in mind. Therefore he had caused Hasan to be killed by poisoning, thus preparing the way for his son, Yazid.

In breaking his agreements with Hasan, Mu^cawiyah made it clear that he would never permit the Shi^cis of the Household of the Prophet to live in a peaceful and secure environment and continue their activity as before, and he carried into action this very intention. It has been said that he went so far as to declare that whoever would transmit a *hadith* in praise of the virtues of the Household of the Prophet would have no immunity or protection concerning his life, merchandise and property. At the same time he ordered that whoever could recite a *hadith* in praise of the other companions or caliphs would be given sufficient reward. As a result a noticeable number of hadiths were recorded at this time praising the companions, some of which are of doubtful authenticity. He ordered pejorative comments to be made about ^cAli from the pulpits of mosques throughout the lands of Islam, while he himself sought to revile ^cAli. This command continued to be more or less in effect until the caliphate of ^cUmar ibn ^cAbd al-^cAziz, when it was discontinued. With the help of his agents and lieutenants, Mu^cawiyah caused the elite and the most outstanding among the partisans of ^cAli to be put to death and the heads of some of them to be carried on lances throughout different cities. The majority of Shi^cis were forced to disown and even curse ^cAli and to express their disdain for him. If they refused, they were put to death.

* * *

The most difficult period for Shi^cism was the twenty-year rule of Mu^cawiyah, during which the Shi^cis had no protection and most of them were considered as marked characters, under suspicion and hunted down by the state. Two of the leaders of Shi^cism who lived at this time, Imams

Hasan and Husayn, did not possess any means whatsoever to change the negative and oppressive circumstances in which they lived. Husayn, the third Imam of Shiᶜism, had no possibility of freeing the Shiᶜis from persecution in the ten years he was Imam during Muᶜawiyah's caliphate, and when he rebelled during the caliphate of Yazid he was massacred along with all his aides and children.

Certain people in the Sunni world explain as pardonable the arbitrary, unjust and irresponsible actions carried out at this time by Muᶜawiyah and his aides and lieutenants, some of whom were, like Muᶜawiyah himself, among the companions. This group reasons that according to certain hadiths of the Holy Prophet all the companions could practice *ijtihad*, that they were excused by God for the sins they committed, and that God was satisfied with them and forgave them whatever wrong they might have performed. The Shiᶜis, however, do not accept this argument for two reasons:

1. It is not conceivable that a leader of human society like the Prophet should rise in order to revivify truth, justice and freedom and to persuade a group of people to accept his beliefs — a group all of whose members had sacrificed their very existence in order to accomplish this sacred end — and then as soon as this end is accomplished give his aides and companions complete freedom to do with these sacred laws as they will. It is not possible to believe that the Holy Prophet would have forgiven the companions for whatever wrong action they might have performed. Such indifference to the type of action performed by them would have only destroyed the structure which the Holy Prophet had built with the same means that he had used to construct it.

2. Those sayings which depict the companions as inviolable and pardoned in advance for every act they might perform, even one unlawful or inadmissible, are most likely apocryphal; the authenticity of many of them has not been fully established by traditional methods. Moreover, it is known historically that the companions did not deal with one another as if they were inviolable and pardoned for all their sins and wrongdoings. Therefore, even judging by the way the companions acted and dealt with each other, it can be concluded that such sayings cannot be literally true in the way some have understood them. If they do contain an aspect of the truth it is in indicating the legal inviolability of the companions and the sanctification which they enjoyed generally as a group because of their proximity to the Holy Prophet. The expression of God's satisfaction with the companions in the Holy Qur'an, because of the services they had rendered in obeying His Command, refers to their past actions, and to God's satisfaction with them in the past, not to whatever action each one of them might perform in the future.

In the year 60/680 Mu°awiyah died and his son Yazid became caliph, as the result of the allegiance which his father had obtained for him from the powerful political and military leaders of the community. From the testimony of historical documents it can be seen clearly that Yazid had no religious character at all and that even during the lifetime of his father he was oblivious to the principles and regulations of Islam. At that time his only interest was debauchery and frivolity. During his three years of caliphate he was the cause of calamities that had no precedent in the history of Islam, despite all the strife that had occurred before him.

During the first year of Yazid's rule Imam Husayn, the grandson of the Holy Prophet, was massacred in the most atrocious manner along with his children, relatives, and friends. Yazid even had some of the women and children of the Household of the Prophet killed and their heads displayed in different cities. During the second year of his rule, he ordered a general massacre of Medina and for three days gave his soldiers freedom to kill, loot, and take the women of the city. During the third year he had the sacred Ka°bah destroyed and burned.

Following Yazid, the family of Marwan gained possession of the caliphate, according to details that are recorded in the history books. The rule of this eleven-member group, which lasted for nearly seventy years, was successful politically but from the point of view of purely religious values it fell short of Islamic ideals and practices. Islamic society was dominated by the Arab element alone and non-Arabs were subordinated to the Arabs. In fact a strong Arab empire was created which gave itself the name of an Islamic caliphate. During this period some of the caliphs were indifferent to religious sentiments to the extent that one of them — who was the "vice-gerent of the Holy Prophet" and was regarded as the protector of religion — decided without showing any respect for Islamic practices and the feelings of Muslims to construct a room above the Ka°bah so that he could have a place to enjoy and amuse himself during the annual pilgrimage. It is even recounted of one of these caliphs that he made the Holy Qur'an a target for his arrow and in a poem composed to the Qur'an said: "On the Day of Judgment when you appear before the God tell Him 'the caliph tore me.''

Naturally the Shi°is, whose basic differences with the Sunnis were in the two questions of the Islamic caliphate and religious authority, were passing through bitter and difficult days in this dark period. Yet in spite of the unjust and irresponsible ways of the governments of the time the asceticism and purity of the leaders of the Household of the Prophet made the Shi°is each day ever more determined to hold on to their beliefs. Of particular importance was the tragic death of Husayn, the third Imam, which played a major role in the spread of Shi°ism, especially in regions away from the center of the caliphate, such as Iraq, the Yemen, and Persia. This can be seen through the fact that during the period of the fifth Imam, before the end of the first Islamic century, and less than forty years after the death of Husayn, the Shiʿis took advantage of the internal differences and weaknesses in the Umayyad government and began to organize themselves, flocking to the side of the fifth Imam. People came from all Islamic countries like a flood to his door to collect *hadith* and to learn the Islamic sciences. The first century had not yet ended when a few of the leaders who were influential in the government established the city of Qum in Persia and made it a Shiʿi settlement. But even then the Shiʿis continued to live for the most part in hiding and followed their religious life secretly without external manifestations.

Several times the descendants of the Prophet (who are called in Persian *sadat-i ʿalawi*) rebelled against the injustice of the government, but each time they were defeated and usually lost their lives. The severe and unscrupulous government of the time did not overlook any means of crushing them. The body of Zayd, the leader of Zaydi Shiʿism, was dug out of the grave and hanged; then after remaining on the gallows for three years it was brought down and burned, its ashes being thrown to the wind. The Shiʿis believe that the fourth and fifth Imams were poisoned by the Umayyads as the second and third Imams had been killed by them before.

The calamities brought about the the Umayyads were so open and unveiled that the majority of the Sunnis, although they believed generally that it was their duty to obey the caliphs, felt the pangs of their religious conscience and were forced to divide the caliphs into two groups. They came to distinguish between the "rightly guided caliphs" (*khulafa'-i rashidun*) who are the first four caliphs after the death of the Holy Prophet (Abu Bakr, ʿUmar, ʿUthman, ʿAli), and the others who began with Muʿawiyah and who did not possess by any means the religious virtues of the rightly guided caliphs.

The Umayyads caused so much public hatred as a result of their injustice and heedlessness during their rule that after the definitive defeat and death of the last Umayyad caliph his two sons and a number of their family encountered great difficulties in escaping from the capital. No matter where they turned no one would give them shelter. Finally after much wandering in the deserts of Nubia, Abyssinia, and Bajawah (between Nubia and Abyssinia) during which many of them died from hunger and thirst, they came to Bab al-Mandab of the Yemen. There they acquired travel expenses from the people through begging and set out for Mecca dressed as porters. In Mecca they finally succeeded in disappearing among the mass of the people.

* * *

During the latter part of the first third of the second/eighth century, following a series of revolutions and bloody wars throughout the Islamic world which were due to the injustice, repressions, and wrongdoings of the Umayyads, there began an anti-Umayyad movement in the name of the Household of the Prophet in Khurasan in Persia. The leader of this movement was the Persian general, Abu Muslim Marwazi, who rebelled against Umayyad rule and advanced his cause step by step until he was able to overthrow the Umayyad government.

Although this movement originated from a profound Shici background and came into being more or less with the claim of wanting to avenge the blood of the Household of the Prophet, and although people were even asked secretly to give allegiance to a qualified member of the family of the Prophet, it did not rise directly as a result of the instructions of the Imams. This is witnessed by the fact that when Abu Muslim offered the caliphate to the sixth Imam in Medina he rejected it completely saying, "You are not one of my men and the time is not my time."

Finally the cAbbasids gained the caliphate in the name of the family of the Prophet and at the beginning showed some kindness to people in general and to the descendants of the Prophet in particular. In the name of avenging the martyrdom of the family of the Prophet, they massacred the Umayyads, going to the extent of opening their graves and burning whatever they found in them. But soon they began to follow the unjust ways of the Umayyads and did not abstain in any way from injustice and irresponsible action. Abu Hanifah, the founder of one of the four Sunni schools of law, was imprisoned by al-Mansur and tortured. Ibn Hanbal, the founder of another school of law, was whipped. The sixth Imam died from poisoning after much torture and pain. The descendants of the Holy Prophet were sometimes beheaded in groups, buried alive, or even placed within walls of government buildings under construction.

Harun al-Rashid, the cAbbasid caliph, during whose reign the Islamic empire reached the apogee of its expansion and power, occasionally would look at the sun and address it in these words: "Shine wherever thou wilt, thou shalt never be able to leave my kingdom." On the one hand his armies were advancing in the East and West, on the other hand a few steps from the palace of the caliph, and without his knowledge, officials had decided on their own to collect tolls from people who wanted to cross the Baghdad bridge. Even one day when the caliph himself wanted to cross the bridge he was stopped and asked to pay the toll.

A singer, but chanting two lascivious verses, incited the passions of the cAbbasid caliph, Amin, who awarded him three million *dirhams*. The chanter in joy threw himself at the feet of the caliph saying, "Oh, leader of the faithful! You give me all this money?" The caliph answered, "It does not matter. We receive this money from an unknown part of the country."

The bewildering amount of wealth that was pouring every year from all corners of the Islamic world into the public treasury in the capital helped in creating luxury and a mundane atmosphere. Much of it in fact was often spent for the pleasures and iniquities of the caliph of the time. The number of beautiful slave girls in the court of some of the caliphs exceeded thousands. By the dissolution of Umayyad rule and the establishment of the ʿAbbasids, Shiʿism did not benefit in any way. Its repressive and unjust opponents merely changed their name.

* * *

At the beginning of the third/ninth century Shiʿism was able to breathe once again. This more favorable condition was first of all due to the fact that many scientific and philosophical books were translated from Greek, Syriac, and other languages into Arabic, and people eagerly studied the intellectual and rational sciences. Moreover, al-Ma'mun, the ʿAbbasid caliph from 198/813 to 218/833, had Muʿtazilite leanings and since in his religious views he favored intellectual demonstration, he was more inclined to give complete freedom to the discussion and propagation of different religious views. Shiʿi theologians and scholars took full advantage of this freedom and did their utmost to further scholarly activities and propagate Shiʿi teachings. Also, al-Ma'mun, following the demands of the political forces of the time had made the eighth Shiʿi Imam his successor, as is recounted in most standard histories. As a result, the descendants of the Holy Prophet and their friends were to a certain extent free from pressures from the government and enjoyed some degree of liberty. Yet before long the cutting edge of the sword once again turned towards the Shiʿis and the forgotten ways of the past came upon them again. This was particularly true in the case of al-Mutawakkil (233/847–247/861) who held a special enmity towards ʿAli and the Shiʿis. By his order the tomb of the third Imam in Karbala was completely demolished.

* * *

In the fourth/tenth century certain conditions again prevailed which aided greatly the spread and strengthening of Shiʿism. Among them were the weaknesses that appeared in the central ʿAbbasid government and administration and the appearance of the Buyid rulers. The Buyids, who were Shiʿi, had the greatest influence not only in the provinces of Persia but also in the capital of the caliphate in Baghdad, and even upon the caliph himself. This new strength of considerable proportions enabled the Shiʿis to stand up before their opponents who previously had tried to crush them by relying upon the power of the caliphate. It also made it possible for the Shiʿites to propagate their religious views openly.

As recorded by historians, during this century most of the Arabian peninsula was Shiʿi with the exception of some of the big cities. Even some of the major cities like Hajar, Uman, and Saʿdah were Shiʿi. In Basrah, which had always been a Sunni city and competed with Kufah which was considered

a Shi‘i center, there appeared a notable group of Shi‘is. Also in Tripoli,
Nablus, Tiberias, Aleppo, Nayshabur, and Herat there were many Shi‘is,
while Ahwaz and the coast of the Persian Gulf on the Persian side were also
Shi‘i.

At the beginning of this century Nasir Utrush, after many years of propagation of his religious mission in northern Persia, gained power in
Tabaristan and established a kingdom which continued for several generations after him. Before Utrush, Hasan ibn Zayd al-‘Alawi had reigned for
many years in Tabaristan. Also in this period the Fatimids, who were
Isma‘ili, conquered Egypt and organized a caliphate which lasted for over
two centuries (296/908–567/1171). Often disputation and fighting occurred
in major cities like Baghdad, Cairo and Nayshabur between Shi‘is and
Sunnis, in some of which the Shi‘is would gain the upper hand and come
out victorious.

* * *

From the fifth/eleventh to the ninth/fifteenth centuries Shi‘ism continued to expand as it had done in the fourth/tenth century. Many kings
and rulers who were Shi‘i appeared in different parts of the Islamic world
and propagated Shi‘ism. Toward the end of the fifth/eleventh century the
missionary activity of Isma‘ilism took root in the fort of Alamut and for
nearly a century and a half the Isma‘ilis lived in complete independence in
the central regions of Persia. Also the Sadat-i Mar‘ashi, who were descendants of the Holy Prophet, ruled for many years in Mazandaran
(Tabaristan). Shah Muhammad Khudabandah, one of the well-known
Mongol rulers, became Shi‘i and his descendants ruled for many years in
Persia and were instrumental in spreading Shi‘ism. Mention must also be
made of the kings of the Aq Quyunlu and Qara Quyunlu dynasties who ruled
in Tabriz and whose domain extended to Fars and Kerman, as well as of the
Fatimid government which was ruling in Egypt.

Of course religious freedom and the possiblity of exerting religious power
by the populace differed under different rulers. For example, with the termination of Fatimid rule and coming to power of the Ayyubids the scene
changed completely and the Shi‘i population of Egypt and Syria lost its
religious independence. Many of the Shi‘is were killed during this period
merely on the accusation of following Shi‘ism. One of these was Shahid-i
Awwal (the First Martyr) Muhammad ibn Makki, one of the great figures in
Shi‘i jurisprudence, who was killed in Damascus in 786/1384. Also
Shaykh al-Ishraq Shihab al-Din Suhrawardi was killed in Aleppo on the accusation that he was cultivating Batini teachings and philosophy.
Altogether during this period Shi‘ism was growing from the point of view
of numbers, even though its religious power and freedom depended upon

local conditions and the rulers of the time. During this period, however, Shiʿism never became the official religion of any Muslim state.

* * *

In the tenth/sixteenth century Ismaʿil, who was of the household of Shaykh Safi al-Din Ardibili (d. 735/1334), a Sufi master and also a Shiʿi, began a revolt in Ardibil, with three hundred Sufis who were disciples of his forefathers, with the aim of establishing an independent and powerful Shiʿi country. In this way he began the conquest of Persia and overcame the local feudal princes. After a series of bloody wars with local rulers and also the Ottomans who held the title of caliph, he succeeded in forming Persia piece by piece in a country and in making Shiʿism the official religion in his kingdom.

After the death of Shah Ismaʿil other Safavid kings reigned in Persia until the twelfth/eighteenth century and each continued to recognize Shiʿism as the official religion of the country and further to strengthen its hold upon this land. At the height of their power, during the reign of Shah ʿAbbas, the Safavids were able to increase the territorial expansion and the population of Persia to twice its present size. As for other Muslim lands, the Shiʿi population continued the same as before and increased only through the natural growth of population.

* * *

During the past three centuries Shiʿism has followed its natural rate of growth as before. At the present moment, during the latter part of the fourteenth/twentieth century, Shiʿism is recognized as the official religion of Iran, and in the Yemen and Iraq the majority of the population is Shiʿi. In nearly all lands where there are Muslims one can find a certain number of Shiʿis. It has been said that altogether in the world today there are about eighty to ninety million Shiʿis.

Chapter Ten

The Buyid Era

Throughout the centuries, the intellectual, social, and institutional characteristics of the Shiᶜi community have undergone considerable changes. Following the occultation of the Twelfth Imam in 874 A.D., Shiᶜism was deprived of the central leadership of the Imam. Thenceforth, the fate of the community of believers was determined by the ᶜulama', on the one hand, and the princes, on the other.

The first historical development that influenced the source of Shiᶜism during the occultation period was the rise of the Buyids to power in 945 A.D. Of Iranian lineage and followers of Shiᶜism, the Buyids used their temporal power to protect the faith and to promote religious and intellectual activities. The reign of the Buyids in Baghdad ushered in an era of Shiᶜi prominence in the heartlands of the Islamic empire, a process that was completed with the accession of the Ismaᶜili Shiᶜi Fatimids to the throne of Egypt. In the following pasage, Hodgson writes of the rise in the political fortunes of the Shiᶜis and the flourishing of their religious sciences. The excerpt is taken from VI, vol. 2, pages 35–39.

Marshall Hodgson

. . . By 945 the three Buyid brothers, with courts at Shiraz, Isfahan, and Baghdad, shared among themselves the most important of the territories that had remained to the last under the caliphs' government. They left the caliph at Baghdad as a figurehead with little authority outside his own household; much of the same vizieral adminsitration continued, but it was responsible to the Buyids as military lords, and acted separately in their several provinces. The three brothers co-operated effectively so long as they lived, from 932 when they seized power till 977, when the last of them died; then cAdud al-Dawlah, the strongest of the next generation, kept the family in order and united much of the area under his personal rule till 983. The Buyids controlled for a time the cUman coast, whence Persian Gulf trade might be threatened, and even expanded somewhat the effective limits of Islamization in southeast Iran. During this period, prosperity remained high and irrigation works were to some degree restored after the disruptions of the last years of the caliphal state.

The Buyids and their viziers took over likewise the task of cultural patronage from the caliphs, though such patronage was now distributed not only among the three Buyid capitals but, of course, among the other capitals of Islamdom. The Buyids, as Shicis, encouraged public Shici festivals and Shici theological writers, so that under them the Twelver Shicis laid its firmest intellectual foundations; they endowed a special Shici school, evidently the first independent Muslim college in Baghdad. Their attitude benefited especially the Twelvers, but they encouraged every sort of Shici on occasion. They separated the organization of the Talibids (including the cAlids) from that of the cAbbasids for purposes of settling disputes on property and genealogy and gave the first official recognition of their special status. Their policy seems to have been to encourage Shici learning and to allow the caliphs, who still were granted substantial income, to encourage Jamaci-Sunni learning (which the court of the caliphs soon proceeded to do in a dogmatically narrow way). But along with Shicism the Buyids encouraged speculation generally: *kalam*, in Muctazili form, and *falsafah*; though they did not patronize the *hadithi* persecutors of Shicism.

* * *

The age of Fatimid and Buyid pre-eminence in some of the central lands of Islamdom has been called 'the Shiᶜi century' because of the prominence of Shiᶜis then in various capacities. It was not a Shiᶜi century in the sense that Shiᶜism as such dominated either political or social and intellectual life. Yet the designation does point up a reasonably striking phenomenon—especially in its contrast to the immediately following period, when Shiᶜis are much less heard from.

In Shiᶜi history, the century stands out as a time of creative religious writing which laid a foundation for all that followed. In the time of the Twelvers' Lesser *ghaybah* (873–940, the period when the Hidden Imam was still represented by wakils in his community), not only the Twelver but also the Ismaᶜili branch of Jaᶜfari Shiᶜis had taken definitive sectarian form (while the Zaydis crystallized their sectarian pattern by establishing local states). Between the end of the lesser *ghaybah* and the Saljuq, occupation of Baghdad (940–1055) cluster the great early names in doctrine, both Twelver and Ismaᶜili. Of the four canonical books of Twelver *hadith*, for instance, that of al-Kulayni (d. 941) belongs to the Lesser *ghaybah*, but the other three, written by Ibn-Babuyah al-Shaykh al-Sadduq al-Qumi (d. 991) and by Shaykh al-Ta'ifah al-Tusi (d. 1067), belong to the Shiᶜi century'; as does the poet, al-Sharif al-Radi (d. 1016), who assembled and edited the poems and sermons ascribed to ᶜAli into a beloved devotional collection called *Nahj al-balaghah*. His contemporary, Hamid al-Din al-Kirmani, chief *daᶜi* under al-Hakim, was the greatest of the Ismaᶜili philosophers.

Even in Muslim history generally, there is some reason to mark off this period as one of Shiᶜi prominence. A disproportionate number of the scholars and littérateurs of the time were Shiᶜis, even in fields other than the explicitly religious. But this fact had little connection with politics. Of the dynasties of Shiᶜi allegiance that ruled then, only the Fatimid and the little Zaydi powers ruled in the name of the Shiᶜis. And while Fatimid patronage does not help account for the refinement of Ismaᶜili thought of the time, Buyid or Hamdanid patronage was probably only of secondary importance in evoking the Twelver Shiᶜi flowering. The intellectual prominence of Shiᶜis at the time probably resulted from developments of the preceding period. The Iraq still played an influential role in the first generations after the end of caliphal power, and in the Iraq many of the old families inherited the Shiᶜism of Kufah. Perhaps it was especially the upper bourgeoisie, inheriting the sympathies of the non-Arab Mawali of Kufah, who were Shiᶜi, while the more recently converted elements had accepted the dominant Jamaᶜi-Sunnism. As we have noted, the Karkh quarter of Baghdad was at once a centre of trade and of Shiᶜism. At the moment when all the culture of the region was flowing, without any rival, within the Islamic context, but before Islamicate culture began to be dispersed in many centres, the older mercantile classes of the Iraq would be especially likely to figure as its carriers; to the extent that these were Shiᶜis, it is not surprising to find Shiᶜis figuring prominently in the cultural scene, apart from any political patronage.

But since the several points of Shiᶜi prominence which go to make up the impression of a 'Shiᶜi century' were of disparate origins, we need not be surprised that the Shiᶜi prominence disappeared fairly quickly in the following generation or so. Not only were the intellectual and the political prominence of essentially unrelated origins. The convergence of political power in Shiᶜi hands had been itself essentially accidental. One may trace the Hamdanid power to the conversion of the Arabs of the Syrian desert to Shiᶜism after Kharijism lost its appeal—evidently the Bedouin felt a need to be in opposition somehow to the ruling settled powers. Indirectly, the Ismaᶜili movement of the Fatimids had the same origin, but in practice it proved to be not the Qarmatians of the Syrian desert, but the Berbers of the Maghrib, that carried them to power. Buyid Shiᶜism is traceable to the conversion of the Caspian frontier by Shiᶜis. If there is something in common among these cases, it is that in the preceding century there was a tendency for those outside the main power structure to become Shiᶜis rather than Kharijis; and now, with the breakdown of the central power, it was those outsiders who were seizing power. But with the passing of the central power, there was less reason for outsiders to be Shiᶜi and, in fact, the newer outsiders proved not to be so. Like the intellectual prominence of the Shiᶜis, their political prominence had a small popular base; and the Shiᶜis having no success, during their moments of apparent advantage, in converting the masses, their prominence was transitory.

Nevertheless, the Shiᶜi connection of much of the intellectual and imaginative work of the period helped the Shiᶜi movement, or (more generally) ᶜAlid loyalism, to exercise the pervasive influence it had in subsequent centuries within Jamaᶜi-Sunni circles. The chemistry or alchemy of Islamdom was founded on the corpus of Jabir, which can be largely ascribed to this period and is of a markedly Ismaᶜili cast. Indeed, Muslim interpretations of the general history of science reflect a notion of the role of ancient prophets as transmitters of secret lore which was congenial especially to Shiᶜis. But even within the realm of personal piety, the Shiᶜi influence appears not merely in the general exaltation of ᶜAli, but specifically in the very widespread use of the *Nahj al-balaghah*, compiled by al-Sharif al-Radi, almost as a secondary scripture after the Qur'an and *hadith* even among many Jamaᶜi-Sunnis. After the Shiᶜis ceased to be so prominent, their works remained as an enduring heritage.

We may consider, at this point, why the Shiᶜis, unlike several other movements of the time—the Hanbalis or the Karramis, for instance—could not be fully assimilated into Jamaᶜi-Sunni Islam at large. As a general stock of sentiments, ᶜAlid loyalism, indeed, was so assimilated. We must recognize that, unlike some movements, such as the Muᶜtazili (always primarily a school of *kalam*, whose members might accept diverse positions in fiqh or the like), the Hanbalis and Karramis, like the Twelvers and Zaydis, formed many-sided religious movements, potentially complete in themselves: they had their own form of piety, their own *fiqh*, and their own viewpoint on *kalam* disputation. Yet they did not, finally, separate from the community at large, however much they were rivals for the allegiance of its masses. One point only seems to have been too far-reaching to allow compromise. Those Shiᶜis who insisted on allegiance to a special Imam apart from the community at large necessarily did form independent sects, even on the level of the populace; maintaining a complete complement of sectarian religious positions, kept jealously distinct from those of others even when substantively identical with theirs. (Thus the Twelvers adopted, in this period, an essentially Muᶜtazili theological doctrine; but they refused to admit any identification with the Muᶜtazili doctors.) It is only the Kharijis (Ibadis) and the sectarian Shiᶜis (Zaydis, Ismaᶜilis, Twelvers) that are thus to be set off from the Jamaᶜi-Sunnis in the sense that a conflict of allegiance would arise if one tried to participate fully in both traditions.

It is, then, not at any point of metaphysical doctrine or even of law, but at a point of historical and political concern that a difference of viewpoint among Muslims became most irreconcilable; a fact consistent with the emphasis of the Qur'anic message upon the historical responsibility of the community. Efforts were made, it is said, already in Buyid times to have the Twelvers recognized in Baghdad, as '*Jaᶜfaris*', as a school of *fiqh* law parallel to the other schools of fiqh recognized there. But such an effort was surely foredoomed; the significant difference between Shiᶜi and Jamaᶜi did not lie in the *fiqh*. Rather, Shiᶜism, however much individual Shiᶜi writers or doctrines influenced Islam generally, remained the persistent custodian of the latent revolutionary challenge of Islam. Especially at the hands of the wealthier merchants, the oppositional implications of Shiᶜism were withdrawn into a subjective personal stance or a hope for a miraculously juster future (just as the oppositional implications of Jamaᶜi-Sunnism became very limited at the hands of the established classes). For all that, Shiᶜism still was a perennial source of chiliastic hopes, which emerged fatefully in later periods.

Chapter Eleven

The Safavid Era

In 1501, amidst political chaos and turmoil in predominantly Sunni Iran, Isma⁣cil Safavi, the spiritual master of the Safawiyyah Sufi order of Azarbaijan, and a Shi⁣ci who claimed descent from the seventh Imam, Musa al-Kazim, conquered a considerable part of the Iranian plateau and established the Safavid dynasty. In the same year, Isma⁣cil was crowned the Shah of Iran. Within a decade, his Qizilbash warriors and fervent Shi⁣ci followers had conquered all of Iran and set out to establish the first Twelver Shi⁣ci empire-state in Islamic history. The Safavid monarchy, a successful marriage between Persian kingship and Shi⁣cism, ushered in a new era in Shi⁣ci history through the intercession of Sufism. Shi⁣ci political doctrines gradually adjusted to the realities of a Shi⁣ci state with a Shi⁣ci sovereign. The protection and patronage given the Shi⁣cism by the Safavids once again fostered learning, intellectual and artistic activities under the banner of Shi⁣cism.

In this section, Seyyed Hossein Nasr elaborates on the role of religion in Safavid Iran; Roger Savory discusses the relation between Shi⁣cism and statecraft in this period; Said Amir Arjomand analyzes the structure of religious authority in this period; and Albert Hourani traces the social and cultural roots of the Shi⁣ci ᶜulama' of the period and discusses the integration of Arab Shi⁣ci scholars into the society of Safavid Iran. The excerpts are taken from RSP, pages 271–81; SSP, pages 182–94, 208–09; SGHI, pages 123–63, and FJTP, pages 136–40, respectively.

Seyyed Hossein Nasr

The Safavid period marks a definite turning point in the history of Persia and the beginning of a new phase in the history of Islam in that country. Yet, despite its distinct character and the break it seems to display with respect to the centuries preceding it, there is definitely a long religions and intellectual history which prepared the ground for the sudden establishment of a Shiʿi order in Persia and and transformation of the country into a pre-dominantly Shiʿi area. There are several centuries of growth of Shiʿi theology and jurisprudence, the development of Sufi orders with Shiʿi tendencies and the establishment of Shiʿi political power — albeit of a transient character — all preceding the Safavid period.

As far as Shiʿi thought is concerned, the advent of the Mongols and the destruction of the major centers of Sunni political power in Western Asia enabled Shiʿism to flower in Persia more than ever before, culminating in the establishment of Shiʿism as state religion for a brief period under Sultan Muhammad Khudabandah. But the most significant aspect of the post-Mongol period as far as Shiʿism is concerned was the appearance of intellec-tual figures of outstanding merit such as Khwajah Nasir al-Din al-Tusi and his student ʿAllamah al-Hilli, with whom Shiʿi theology became definitely established, the *Tajrid* of Tusi as commented upon by Hilli being the first systematic treatist of Shiʿi *kalam*. Other outstanding Shiʿi theologians followed, such as Ibn Makki al-ʿAmili, known as al-Shahid al-Awwal, author of the well-known *al-Lumʿat al-dimashqiyyah*, followed by Zayn al-Din al-ʿAmili, al-Shahid al-Thani, whose commentary upon this work, *Sharh al-lumʿah*, is famous to this day. The works of these and other figures were the props of Shiʿism at the outset of the Safavid period; in fact they are of such importance that the history of Shiʿism during the Safavid and subsequent periods would be incomprehensible without them.

Parallels to this development in the religious sciences, one can observe a remarkable spread of activity in post-Mongol Persia in the domain of religious philosophy and in that combination of Peripatetic philosophy, il-luminationist doctrines and gnosis which came to be known as *al-hikmat al-ilahiyyah* or theosophy and which gradually moved into the orbit of Shiʿism. Such figures as Ibn Abi Jumhur, Ibn Turkah, Rajah Bursi and especially Sayyid Haydar Amuli, who sought to harmonize and in fact identify the Sufism of Ibn ᶜArabi with esoteric Shiᶜi doctrines, are the direct intellectual ancestors of the remarkable Safavid sages such as Mir Damad and Mulla Sadra.

As for Sufism the period between the Mongols and the Safavids was witness not only to a remarkable flourishing of Sufism, as exemplified by the appearance of such great poles of sanctity as Mawlana Jalal al-Din Rumi, Najm al-Din Kubra, Sadr al-Din al-Qunyawi and the like, but it was also the period during which Sufism became a bridge between Sunnism and Shiᶜism and in many instances prepared the ground for the spread of Shiᶜism. The role of the Kubrawiyyah, the Nurbakhshiyyah and the Niᶜmatullahiyyah orders bears close study in the light of their relation to the later spread of Shiᶜism in Persia through a dynasty of Sufi origin. This leads in turn to the Safavid order itself, to the two and a half centuries which separate Shaykh Safi al-Din of Ardabil from Shah Ismaᶜil, to the transformation of a simple Sufi order organized around a saint and ascetic to a militant movement with extreme Shiᶜi tendencies under Sultan Junayd and Haydar and finally to the establishment of the military basis which made the Safavid conquest of Persia possible.

Finally, as far as political aspects of religion are concerned, the brief rule of Shiᶜi under Muhammad Khudabandah as well as such Shiᶜi dynasties as the Sarbadaran in Khurasan, the Mushaᶜshaᶜah in Iraq as well as the Safavid Shaykhs themselves preceeding Shah Ismaᶜil present historical antecedents of greater importance. They point to political and social transformations of a religious nature which are directly related to the whole question of religion in Safavid Persia.

In reality the discussion of religion in its vastest sense as tradition (*al-din*) in the Safavid period includes every facet of life of Safavid society in as much as we are dealing with a traditional world in which all activity is related to a transcendent norm. Whether it be literature as reflected in the poetry of Saᶜib-i Tabrizi and Muhtashim-i Kashani or architecture and city planning as seen in the central region of the city of Isfahan or even sports as in the case of the *zur-khanah*, we are in fact dealing with something that is directly related to religion. Even the cosmic elements, the water that flowed in geometrically shaped gardens and the earth from which the mud walls of structures were made possess a religious significance if seen from the point of view of the men who lived and breathed in the traditional Islamic world, whether it was ᶜAbbasid, Saljuq or Safavid. In the context of this paper, however, it is only with religion and religious thought in the strict sense of the word that we shall deal . . . .

The most noteworthy aspect of religion in Safavid Persia is first of all the rapid process through which Persia became Shiᶜi. Although the ground for this transformation had been prepared by subtle religious changes during the Ilkhanid period, when Shah Isma^{c}il was crowned probably the majority of Persians were still Sunnis. Certainly the city of Tabriz where the crowning took place was about two-thirds Sunni, although the Shi^{c}i element was at that time strongest among the Turkish speaking segments of the population. It was the policy ardently followed by the Safavids to establish Shi^{c}ism as the state religion that led to the rapid change.

To make the process of transforming Iran into a Shi^{c}i land possible, many outstanding Shi^{c}i scholars were invited to Persia from both Bahrain and the Jabal ^{c}Amil in present day Lebanon, both of which had been for some time seats of Shi^{c}i learning. In fact so many scholars from these two regions came to Persia that two works, the *Lu'lu'at al-bahrayn* and *Amal al-^{c}amil* are entirely devoted to their biographies. These scholars ranged from simple mullas who fulfilled small religious functions to men like Shaykh Baha' al-Din al-^{c}Amili and Sayyid Ni^{c}matullah al-Jaza'iri, both of whom came to Persia at a very young age but soon developed into leading religious authorities.

Few modern scholars have examined the effect of the presence of all of these Arabic speaking scholars on the role of Arabic in Persian intellectual circles at this time. Many present day traditional authorities in Persia, however, believe that because of the great power and prestige of these men, some of whom, like Sultan al-^{c}Ulama', hardly knew Persian, there came into being a new emphasis upon Arabic among the religious authorities, and it even became fashionable to use Arabic in situations where in earlier times Persian had been commonly used. Certainly the dearth of Persian prose writings in the religious field at this time in comparison with either the Saljuq and Mongol or the Qajar periods bears this out. More Persian religious works were written in the Indian sub-continent during this period than in Persia itself. The immigration of this class of Arabic speaking scholars, who became rapidly Persianized and absorbed within the matrix of Persian society, had, therefore, an effect upon both the religious life of the country and the type of religious language employed.

The result of the spread of Shi^{c}ism, which as already mentioned did not completely replace Sunnism but became the most dominant form of Islam in Persia, implied the establishment of such typically Shi^{c}i institutions as the religious sermons depicting mostly the tragedy of Karbala or *rawzih-khani*, held especially during Muharram, the *ta^{c}ziyyah* or passion play, the religious feast or *sufrah*, religious processions, visits to tombs of holy men or *imam-zadihs*, in addition to the daily prayers, the pilgrimmage and the fasting, all of which still comprise the main day-to-day religious activity of Persians. As far as the ritual and practical aspect of religion in the Safavid period is concerned, it is nearly the same as what one observes during the Qajar period and up to the present day with certain external changes which the differing conditions of the modern world have necessitated along with the near disappearance of some of the more elaborate forms of the *ta*ᶜ*ziyyah*.

The role and function of other aspects of religion in Safavid Persia after the early period of transformation can perhaps be best understood by studying such elements as classes of religious scholars, the various religious functions in society, the types of religious thought of the period, and finally the position of Sufism and of the guilds which played a paramount role in the religious life of Persians at this time. As far as the classes of religious scholars are concerned, it is important to note that during the Safavid period as in most other periods of Islamic history and even more so because of the particular politico-religious structure of Shiᶜism, there were two classes of religious scholars or ᶜulama': one the class supported and appointed by the Safavid kings and their representatives, and the other that which remained completely aloof from central political power and gained its authority from the support of the populace.

As far as the first group is concerned, its members were chosen from the class of ᶜulama' and were then appointed to a hierarchy of functions which in a sense paralleled the administrative structure of the Safavid state. There was first of all a learned person of high repute called the *mulla-bashi* whom many Safavid kings chose as a close companion, who would counsel them on religious matters and read various prayers for them on different occasions. Then there was the position of the *sadr*, the highest religious office of the land, whose incumbent was chosen directly by the kind and rivalled the *grand mufti* of the Ottomans. The *sadr* was responsible for all the official religious duties of the country, especially the supervision of the endowments (*awqaf*), which he administered with the help of such officials as *mustawfis*, *mutasaddis* and *vazirs* of *awqaf*. Sometimes the function of the *sadr* was in fact divided into two parts, one that of *sadr-i mamalik*, which concerned the supervision of the general endowments, and the other that of *sadr-i khassah*, which was related to the royal endowments. The *sadr* also appointed judges (*qadis*) and the chief official religious dignitary (*shaikh al-islam*) of the bigger cities with the consent of the king.

As for the class of ᶜulama' who stood aloof from the central political power, at their head were the *mujtahids*, literally those who could practice *ijtihad*, that is give fresh opinion on questions of sacred law, men who were and still are highly revered by society because of both their knowledge and piety and whom the Shiᶜis consider as the representative of the Hidden Imam. From among them was chosen the person who was emulated according to Shiᶜi doctrine (*marja*ᶜ*-i taqlid*) and who at times gained a power rivaling that of the king himself. The *mujtahids* were often a protection for the people against the tyranny of various government officials and fulfilled a major function of both a religious and social nature.

Besides the *mujtahids* there were other religious scholars of lower rank whose authority relied upon the people and who catered to their daily needs. Foremost among these were the leaders of prayers (Imams) of various mosques. Because of the stringent ethical conditions set in Shiᶜism for those who lead the daily prayers in the various mosques, these men behind whom people accepted to pray and who also catered to other religious needs of the populace were never appointed by any government authorities. Rather, they were chosen freely by the members of the religious community itself. To this day in fact the Imams of various mosques in Persia are selected by the faithful of the community which the mosque in question serves. Of course occasionally such functions were fulfilled by men who also held state appointed offices, and this reached occasionally the highest level when a leading *mujtahid* also became an official religious dignitary, but this was an exception which did not destroy the basic separation between the two types of religious authority just mentioned.

From the point of view of religious thought, however, both classes of ᶜ*ulama'* mentioned belong to the single category of specialists in jurisprudence and other Islamic legal sciences. They were *faqihs* first and foremost. But there developed in the Safavid period upon the basis of earlier examples another type of religious scholar who rather than being a specialist in law and jurisprudence was a master of Islamic metaphysics and theosophy. The *hakim-i ilahi* or theosopher who came to the fore during this period was successor to earlier Muslim philosophers from al-Farabi and Ibn Sina, through Suhrawardi and Nasir al-Din al-Tusi to Ibn Turkah and Sayyid Haydar Amuli, who were the immediate predecessors of the Safavid sages. But the change that occurred during the Safavid period is that the attempt begun by Suhrawardi and later Ibn Turkah to harmonize rational philosophy, intellectual intuition and revealed religion reached its apogee, and *hikmat-i ilahi* during the Safavid period became more than ever before a most important if not the central expression of religious thought. Therefore the *hakim-i ilahi* also became a much more central figure in the religious life of the community than before.

The founder of this remarkable period of Islamic philosophy, which is coming to be known as the School of Isfahan, is Mir Damad, himself the son-in-law of one of the most influential of the early Safavid ᶜ*ulama'*, Muhaqqiq-i Karaki. Mir Damad was also an authority in the "transmitted sciences" (*al-ᶜulum al-naqliyyah*), including jurisprudence, but he was before everything else a *hakim* who opened new horizons for Islamic philosophy and who was responsible for the rapid spread of *hikmat-i ilahi* through his numerous writings and the training of many students. Among his disciples Sadr al-Din Shirazi, the greatest metaphysician of the age and perhaps the foremost *hakim* in Islamic history in the domain of metaphysics stands out particularly. Sadr al-Din also studied with Shaykh Baha' al-Din al-ᶜAmili in the field of the "transmitted sciences" and possibly with another of the outstanding *hakims* of the Safavid period, Mir Ab'l-Qasim Findiriski. But as far as *hikmat-i ilahi* is concerned, Mulla Sadra built most of all upon the foundations laid by Mir Damad. He followed the attempt of Mir Damad to synthesize the teachings of the Ibn Sina and Suhrawardi within Shiᶜi esotericism but went further by making a grand synthesis of all the major intellectual perspectives of nearly a thousand years of Islamic intellectual life before him. The teachings of the Qur'an, of the Holy Prophet and the Imams, of the Peripatetic philosophers, of the Iluminationist theosophers and of the Sufis were like so many colors of the rainbow which became unified and harmonized in the transcendent theosophy (*al-hikmat al-mutaᶜaliyah*) of Mulla Sadra. No other figure of the Safavid period characterizes as well as Mulla Sadra the special genius of this age for intellectual synthesis and the expression of unity in multiplicity, which is also so evident in the extremely rich art of the age.

Mulla Sadra himself was an inexhaustible source for the doctrines of *hikmat-i ilahi* and the spread of its teachings and continues to dominate traditional religious thought in Persia to this day. He was at once a prolific writer and a peerless teacher, his foremost students Mulla Muhsin Fayd Kashani and ᶜAbd al-Razzaq Lahiji being themselves among the most outstanding intellectual figures of Persia. Moreover, these masters themselves taught a generation of important *hakims* like Qadi Saᶜid Qumi, and the tradition continued despite much difficulty to the very end of the Safavid period. In fact it was revived by Mulla ᶜAli Nuri and Mulla Ismaᶜil Khaju'i in the thirteenth/eighteenth centuries.

It is characteristic of the religious life of Safavid Persia that a dynasty that began as a Sufi order moved so much in the direction of exotericism that Mulla Muhammad Baqir Majlisi, the most powerful ᶜalim of the late *al-anwar*, repudiated the Sufism of his father Mulla Muhammad Taqi and forced the last great *hakim* of the Safavid period in Isfahan, the saintly Mulla Sadiq Ardistani, into exile. Both Sufism and *hikmat-i ilahi*, which also possesses an esoteric character, were finally forced into a form of marginal existence at the end of the reign of a dynasty of Sufi origin.

As far as Sufism itself is concerned, because of the very fact that the Safavid dynasty was originally a Sufi order, its coming into political power eventually made the life of Sufism in Shiᶜi Persia difficult for several decades. At the beginning of the Safavid period many Sufi orders were fully active in Persia. The Nurbakhshi order founded by Shaykh Muhammad Nurbakhsh was at its height. In fact the student of the founder of the order,

Shaykh Muhammad Lahiji, who is the author of that ocean of gnosis in the Persian language, the *Sharh-i gulshan-i raz*, was a contemporary of Shah Isma^{c}il. The order yielded much influence during the first few decades of Safavid rule but then gradually disappeared from the scene.

The Zahabi order, which is still strong in Persia today, was also active at that time. Some of the great Sufis of this age as Pir-i Palanduz (Muhammad Karandihi), Shaykh Hatam Harawandi and Shaykh Muhammad ^{c}Ali Sabziwari Khurasani, the author of the well-known *al-Tuhfat al-^{c}abbasiyyah*, are considered by later Zahabis as poles of their order. But although the Zahabis survived into the Zand period, they too became less visible toward the end of the Safavid era.

Other orders mentioned by various sources, both Persian and European, as being active during the Safavid period include the Qadiris, Baktashis, Khaksars, Mawlawis and Ni^{c}matullahis. The case of the Khaksar and the Ni^{c}matullahi orders, which are still very much alive today, in contrast to the Baktashis and Mawlawis, which no longer have any following in Persia, is of particular interest. The Khaksars somehow fell out of favor at the time of Shah ^{c}Abbas and some of their leaders retired to far away cities in the south of the country. As for the Ni^{c}matullahis, their leaders such as Nizam al-Din ^{c}Abd al-Baqi and Ghiyath al-Din Mir Miran were closely associated with the court and held positions of great eminence at the beginning of the Safavid period, and the order itself had a wide following. But soon they too fell out of favor and were persecuted so severely that their outward organization in Persia disappeared completely. They retired to the Daccan in India and their very history in Persia was interrupted. It was in fact from the Daccan that the order was re-established in Persia during the early Qajar period.

The reason for this rather violent opposition to Sufism and even *hikmat-i ilahi* in the late Safavid period lies in part in the fact that the Safawiyyah order which had become a ruling dynasty tended because of this fact to lose its spiritual discipline as a Sufi order and to become diluted through the intrusion of worldly elements into its very structure. This fact in turn caused the resentment of other Sufi orders, which were eventually suppressed by the Safavids, as well as of the exoteric religious authorities. In the second case, it was not possible to suppress the exoteric authorities, for the very power of the Safavids lay in the support of Shi^{c}ism. Hence the Safavid kings, if not all the members of the order, tended to become ever more detached from their Sufi background and to support exoteric authorities in their opposition to Sufism. As a result, if before the rise of the Safavids a figure such as Sayyid Haydar Amuli could say that "True Sufism is Shi^{c}ism Sufism," at the end of the Safavid period the opposition between Shi^{c}ism and the organized Sufi orders became so great that even in later periods of Persian history Sufism could return to the centers of the Shi^{c}i learning only under the name of ^c*irfan* or under the guise of *hikmat-i ilahi*. The situation that prevails in such centers as Najaf and Qum to this day is inherited from the complete polarity and opposition between the most powerful Shi^ci ^c*ulama'* and organized Sufism at the end of the Safavid period.

Finally a word must be said about the guilds and forms of craft initiation which were widespread in the Safavid period and which bridged the gap between the most inward principles of the tradition and aspects of everyday life, from selling merchandise in the bazaar to constructing mosques. The tradition of "chivalry" (*futuwwat* or *jawanmardi*) as related to various social and artistic activities was already strong in the pre-Safavid period and continued into this period. Those remarkable architects who designed the various mosques, palaces and caravanserais of this era, the rug weavers who have created some of the most remarkable color harmonies of any school of art, the masters of plaster designs and tiles, were mostly members of guilds with a spiritual discipline related to various Sufi orders, especially the Khaksar. In fact to this day what has remained of the techniques of the traditional arts is of an oral nature preserved within the still existing guilds and transmitted by the way of a master-disciple relationship which can still be observed in some Persian cities and towns and which is a remnant of the fully active guilds of the Safavid period. What remains of the art of this period, even those forms which are not strictly speaking religious according to Western categories, is related in the profoundest way to the religious life of the Safavids. No account of religion in Safavid Persia would be complete without taking the role of the guilds and the deep religious nature of their activity into account.

Roger Savory

Sovereignty

Once the territorial boundaries of a state have been settled, or even before then, the question of sovereignty becomes one of paramount importance. It is essential that however much democracy exists at the local level of city ward or village, ultimate power in the state should reside in some person or persons who have the final authority in the making of decisions. In seventeenth and eighteenth century Europe, sovereignty normally resided in a monarch.

> From the end of the Thirty Years' War to the French Revolution abso-
> lute monarchy reigned amost without a challenge as the standard form
> of political organization . . . ; western Europe, for more than a cen-
> tury, was ruled by a number of clearly determinate sovereigns,
> hereditary monarchs in most cases, who exercised an unlimited right to
> make and enforce laws within their respective states. The obligation of
> the subject to obey the sovereign was the highest form of duty.

The Treaty of Westphalia in 1648 "expressly confirmed the right of secular sovereigns to determine the religious duties of their subjects as well as to de- mand their obediance in secular matters. Shah Ismaᶜil would have found no fault with the conclusion reached by Bodin, the sixteenth century French political theorist already mentioned, "that there ought to be, in every state, a single recognized lawmaker, or sovereign, whose decisions were recogniz- ed as having final authority.

The point I am trying to make, at the risk perhaps of belabouring it, is that there was nothing unusual in the fact that the Safavid shah was an ab- solute monarch or that sovereignty resided in the shah. On the contrary, the Safavid shahs were typical of their age, and one of the reasons why Shah ᶜAbbas, for example, was able to maintain such excellent diplomatic rela- tions with the Netherlands, Portugal, Spain, France and England was that all these countries were ruled by monarchs whose view of sovereignty did not differ markedly from his own. I find both historically inaccurate and morally disingenuous the attitude of some writers who hold up their hands in pious horror at the absolutism of the Safavid shahs, as though this was in some way worse than the absolutism of European monarchs like the Bour- bons and the Hapsburgs. (In passing, one may wonder whether Wittfogel did not perpetuate this view by entitling his book "Oriental despotism.") The absolutism of the Safavid shahs was to some extent different in kind, but it was different in degree only in theory. It was different in kind in the sense that the theory of the divine right of kings, held by both the Safavid shahs and by European monarchs, was reinforced in the case of the Safavid shahs by two other powerful factors, namely, their claim to be the repre- sentatives of the Hidden Imam and their position as the *murshid-i kamil*, or supreme spiritual director, of the Safawiyyah order, demanding unquestion- ing obedience from their *murids* or Sufi disciples. Let us consider, very briefly, what the theory of Safavid absolutism was and how it was modified in practice.

The power of the Safavid shahs had three distinct bases: the first was the ancient theory of the divine right of Persian kings, based on the possession by the monarch of the *hvarnah/khvaranah/farr* or "kingly glory." This ancient, pre-Islamic theory was, so to speak, taken out of the closet, dusted off and reinvested with all its former splendor as the *zill allah fiᶜl-arzi* or "Shadow of God upon earth." The second was the claim of the Safavid shahs to being the representative of the Mahdi. This claim was based on the Safavid family's alleged descent from the seventh Shiᶜi Imam, Musa al-Kazim. As the representative of the Mahdi, the Safavid shah was closer to the source of absolute truth than were other men, and consequently opposition to the shah constituted a sin. By virtue of this position (which, as I have shown elsewhere, rested on shaky foundations), the Safavid shahs were entitled to claim the not unimportant quality of *ᶜismah* or infallibility. Thirdly, as the *murshid-i kamil* of the Safavid order of Sufis (the office of *irshad* had been in the hands of the Safavid family since 700/1301), the Safavid shahs were able to insist on the absolute obedience of their Sufi followers by virtue of the relationship known as *pir-muridi*, and their followers were supposed to adhere to rules of conduct termed *sufigari*; the opposite of this, *nasufigari*, was a serious crime punishable by death. For a *qizilbash* to question the actions of his *murshid* was tantamount to *kufr* ("unbelief").

This was the theory, and these were the bases of the power of the Safavid shahs which led that astute Huguenot observer Chardin to assert that their power was even greater than that of the Ottoman sultans: "Le Gouvernement de Perse est monarchique, despotique et absolu, tant pour le spirituel, que pour le temporel . . . il n'y a assurément aucun souverain au monde si absolu que le roi de Perse." Malcolm, writing a century after the fall of the Safavids, strikes the same note.

> The word of the King of Persia has ever been deemed a law; and he has probably never had any further restraint imposed on the free exercise of his vast authority than what has arisen from his regard for religion, his respect for established usages, his desire of reputation, and his fear of exciting an opposition that might be dangerous to his power or to his life.

How did this apparently overwhelming power affect the men in the street and the peasant in the field? Paradoxically, it was the common people—the peasants in the rural areas, and the artisans, shopkeepers and small merchants in the cities—who were least affected by it. Indeed, the absolute nature of the shah's authority was not a threat to, but rather a guarantee of, the individual freedom and security of the lower classes of society. It was those who themselves held positions of power and influence who were at the mercy of the shah's arbitrary power. It was the officials who stood between the shah and the mass of his people—army officers, military governors, the nobility in general, and the serried ranks of the "men of the pen," both lay and ecclesiastic—who were considered to be the slaves of the shah; their lives, their property, the lives of their children, were at the disposal of the shah, who held the absolute power of loosing and binding. Even then, those who could be classified as *arab-i ᶜilm* were usually exempted from capital punishment. In general, it was those who lived by the sword who had to be prepared to die by the sword. Both Chardin and Malcolm assert that the awe in which the Shah was held by the court and the nobility was the primary reason for the relative security and freedom from oppression enjoyed by the lower classes. Of course, the life of the common man was not all beer and skittles, but I said he enjoyed *relative* freedom from oppression. In a country as large as Persia, in which communication was as slow as it was in Safavid times, officials in the more remote provinces could and no doubt did "get away with murder" — for a time. But a ruler like Shah ᶜAbbas was famed for his justice and his remorselessness in punishing misdemeanors committed by his officials anywhere in the Safavid empire. He had an extremely efficient intelligence service and although there might be a time lag of months or even years between the crime and its punishment, the Shah had a long memory and sooner or later the guilty party would be brought to book. This is why Chardin states that "la condition du Peuple y est beaucoup plus assurée, et plus douce, qu'en divers Etats Chrétiens." This state of affairs, of course, depended on the shah's exercising his absolute power over those to whom he delegated his authority, and so the security of the ordinary people was in direct proportion to the strength of the monarch.

A second important factor in mitigating the effect of the Shah's absolute power on the mass of his subjects was the geographic, ethnic, political and social diversity of Safavid Iran. The communication problems posed by the mountainous and, in the north, densely forested, terrain meant that no matter how much power was apparently concentrated at the center, a considerable degree of decentralization occurred in fact. The Safavid state was certainly not bedevilled by that ethnic nationalism which lies at the root of so many of our problems today (perhaps it is the absence of this factor that has led some to deny that such a thing as a Safavid state existed) because, apart from the basic division between Turk and Circassians in large numbers ensured ethnic diversity as well as political and social diversity. There were many other factors which in practice mitigated the theoretical absolute power of the Shah, but a discussion of these would be somewhat tangential to the central argument of this paper, which seeks to establish that the basic prerequisites of a "state" did exist in Safavid times.

Legitimacy

If, as I take it, there is no argument about the fact that the Safavid state satisfied the requirement of "sovereignty," and that the locus of ultimate power in the state has been satisfactorily identified and established, we may proceed to a consideration of the requirement of "legitimacy." Power, in itself, is neutral and merely denotes "the ability to make and carry out decisions that are binding on the rest of the population"; "legitimacy," on the other hand, offers an excuse for and justifies the existence of the state.

It is hard to imagine a ruling institution more preoccupied with the question of legitimacy than the Safavid. Why was this so? After all, the usurpation of power by the *khalifah/Imam* had long since been justified by the jurists. The consensus of opinion among medieval Muslim jurists was that "obedience to the Imam, whether he was good or bad, was incumbent upon the Muslim because it was God's will that the Imam should hold office." Even if the Imam behaved like a tyrant, tyranny was preferable to anarchy. Some jurists even exerted themselves to justify the "imamate of usurpation by military force," that is, the usurpation of power by sultans, *amirs*, and the like. Could not the Safavid Shahs therefore have justified, or given "legitimacy" to, their exercise of sovereignty by claiming to be the "Shadow of God upon Earth," or simply by the right of their seizure of power by military force? Why was it necessary for them to devote so much time and energy to legitimizing their rule still further?

The answer is that the Safavid state possessed one feature which set it apart from all other Muslim states of the period (with some minor exceptions like the small Shiᶜi states in the Deccan), namely, it was a Shiᶜi state. With the accession of the Safavids, Ithna ᶜAshari Shiᶜi had for the first time since the advent of Islam achieved full political power. Not only therefore was the problem of legitimacy different for the Safavid Shahs than it had been for earlier ruling dynasties in Iran, but it was vitally important for them to be able to demonstrate the legitimacy of their claim to power beyond dispute. To this end, the Safavids produced a highly dubious genealogy which purported to establish their descent from Musa al-Kazim, the seventh Ithan ᶜAshari Imam; fabricated a claim to *siyadat* (which actually had no bearing on the legitimacy of their rule one way or the other, but was presumably thought to add "respectability" to the family); and conveniently ignored the rules govening the all-important Shiᶜi doctrine of *nass*, or the designation by a Shiᶜi Imam of his successor. The dubious nature of the Safavid *isnad* from Musa al-Kazim has, I think, been adequately demonstrated by a number of scholars, and anyone who wishes to follow the arguments which demolish the Safavid claim to *siyadat* may do so in the writings of Kasrawi. In this paper I wish to concentrate on the question of *nass*, the importance of which, in regard to the question of Safavid legitimacy, has not, I think, been sufficiently appreciated.

I mentioned earlier that one of the three bases of the sovereignty of the Safavid Shahs was their claim to being the representatives on earth of the Hidden Imam or Mahdi, known as the "Lord of the Age" (*sahib-i zaman*), the Shi^ci messiah whose return to earth will herald the Day of Judgment and whose second coming will be foreshadowed by various eschatological signs. No Persian kings before the Safavids had made this claim, nor have any since (*pace* Jacobs and others who hold the contrary opinion). Why was it necessary for the Safavids to make it?

As I indicated earlier, the problem of the legitimacy of Sunni rulers had been solved (if not to the satisfaction of all, at least well enough to salve the consciences of many) centuries before the Safavids came to power. No such accommodation had been made in regard to Shi^ci rulers. No Shi^ci jurist had done for them what al-Ghazzali, Ibn Khaldun and Ibn Jama^cah had done for Sunni rulers. On the contrary, there was a strong tendency among Shi^ci jurists to regard all secular governments as illegitimate and as a usurpation of the rights of the *^culama'* as a whole and of the *mujtahids* in particular.

The disappearance from earth of the twelfth Imam in 260/873-74 had been followed by the sixty-nine (lunar) year period of the "Lesser Occultation" (*ghaybat-i sughra*), during which the Mahdi was represented on earth by four *vakils*, or agents, in succession. With one exception, these agents were chosen on the basis of *nass* ("designation") rather than heredity. The fourth *wakil*, Abu'l-Hasan al-Samarri, did not designate a successor but according to Shi^ci tradition, declared that the Matter was now "with God." The death of the fourth *wakil* in 329/940-41 accordingly marked the beginning of the "Greater Occultation" (*ghaybat-i kubra*), which is still in progress. During this period of more than one thousand years, the Mahdi has been represented on earth, according to the consensus of the Shi^ci *^culama'*, by the general agency of the *mujtahids*. On the basis of what precedents there were, then, it appeared that designation was more important than heredity in regard to validating a person's claim to be the representative of the Hidden Imam. Indeed, in the case of the selection of the imams themselves, Shi^ci tradition is quite specific on this point: heredity is insufficient without divine appointment, and divine appointment is obtained by means of designation by the incumbent Imam. The Safavid Shahs could not possibly claim "right by designation," so how could they make any claim at all to being the representatives of the Mahdi, and why was it imperative for them not only to make this claim, but to obtain its acceptance by the subjects over whom they ruled?

The question of legitimacy, in any state, is bound up with the question of sovereignty, and the Safavid state was no exception in this respect. If the Safavid Shahs were to retain sovereignty, that is, to remain the ultimate source of power in the state, they had to demonstrate their legitimacy, and the nub of legitimacy in a Shi^ci state was *^cismah*, the "sinlessness" or "infallibility" of the Imams. The doctrine of *^cismah* had been promulgated by Shi^ci theologians as early as the tenth century A.D., undoubtedly with the object of demonstrating the superiority of the Shiᶜi Imam over the Sunni caliph. By virtue of ᶜ*ismah*, the Shiᶜi imams were the sole repositories of truth, but ᶜ*ismah* depended on a combination of designation and hereditary, and consequently was present in the imams alone, strictly speaking. When, after the termination of the "Lesser Occultation" of the Twelfth Imam, the *mujtahids* exercised a general agency on his behalf, they did so by virtue not of designation but of the consensus of the Shiᶜi community and, in the case of those who could prove their descent from one of imams, of heredity. As long as the *mujtahids* remained the representatives or agents of the Mahdi, they were, by virtue of this function, if not the sole repositories of truth (as we have just seen, the imams alone could be this), at least closer to ultimate truth than other men were.

It follows, therefore, that the Safavid shahs, in order to establish the legitimacy of their authority, had to show that their claim to being the representatives of the Mahdi was at least as good as that of the *mujtahids*. The Safavid shahs could not claim designation (*nass*) any more than could the *mujtahids*. Heredity thus assumed crucial importance, and it became absolutely vital for the Safavids to fabricate a genealogy demonstrating their descent form one of the Imams; as we have seen, they selected the seventh Imam, Musa al-Kazim, as their progenitor. Having done this, however, and having obtained the consensus of the community in favor of their claim to being the representatives of the Mahdi, the Safavid Shahs still had no better claims to this function, in actual fact, than had any ᶜAlawi, Hasani or Husayni *sayyid* who could prove descent from ᶜAli or one of his sons. The *mujtahids* may therefore be forgiven if they considered that they had at least as good a claim to the position of representative of the Hidden Imam as had the shah, and, I must reiterate, in the context of a Shiᶜi state this function was crucial because it assured legitimacy which in turn ensured the possession of sovereignty. Since so much hung on this issue, it is obvious that the *mujtahids* would contest this claim of the Safavid shahs, but their objections tended to be voiced in private because, as Chardin graphically explains:

> Les gens d'Eglise, et tous les Dévots de la Perse, tiennent que la domination des Laiques est un établissement violent et usurpé, et que le Gouvernement Civil apartient de droit au Sedra [*sadr*] et à l'Eglise . . . Mais l'opinion la plus généralement recue est que la Royauté, telle qu'elle est dans la main des Laiques, tire son institution et son autorité de Dieu; que le Roi tient la place de Dieu, et des Prophètes, en la conduite des Peuples: et quant au Sedra, et à tous les gens de Loi, qu'ils ne se doivent point mêler du Gouvernement Politique: que leur Jurisdiction est soumise à l'autorité Royale: même dans les choses de la Religion. Cette dernière opinion prévaut, au lieu que l'autre n'est tenue que des

Ecclesiastiques et de ceux qu'ils obsèdent, auxquels le Roi et les
Ministres ferment la bouche comme il leur plaît, et qu'ils font obéir en
tout. De cette manière, le spirituel est aujourd'hui tout-à-fait soumis au
temporel.

The Safavid rulers were obliged to "shut the mouth" of those *mujtahids* who
were inclined to assert that the Shah had usurped their prerogative to being
the legitimate representative of the Mahdi, precisely because of this question of ^cismah, on which depended legitimacy on which depended sovereignty in the state. If the Shah could not claim ^cismah (or the nearest possible approach to it), but someone else could, then the sovereignty of the shah was
called into question and his position threatened.

If the Safavid Shahs could not claim designation, how did they succeed in
convincing their subjects that their right to being the source of ultimate
power in the state was any better than that of, say, the *mujtahids*, the *sadr*,
or any other person or group of persons in the religious institution who
could claim descent from one of the Imams? The answer, I believe, lies partly in the brilliantly effective propaganda which the Safavid revolutionary
planners had carried on for two hundred years prior to the accession of
Shah Isma^cil I, and partly in the fact that these same planners had put out a
smokescreen of other issues which diverted the attention of the people of
Iran from the central issue of designation. The political genius of those who
brought the Safavid revolutionary movement to its triumphant conclusion
lay in the fact that they came forward on a religio-political platform which
was so wide in scope that it contained something for everyone; it was, in
fact, a series of platforms: the "descent from the seventh Imam platform";
the "*murshid-i kamil* platform"; and the "Shadow of God upon earth platform," if I may so call them.

It is often assumed that the Safavid leader, Isma^cil, was responsible for
bringing the revolution to a successful conclusion, but, when one realizes
that Isma^cil was only seven years old in 1494 when he succeeded his brother
^cAli as leader of the revolutionary movement, it is clear that this could not
have been so. When Isma^cil emerged from Gilan in 1499, to try conclusions
with the dominant political power in Iran at that time, the Aq Quyunlu
state, he was still only twelve, and he was barely fourteen when he was
crowned shah at Tabriz in 1501. Who, then, was responsible for maintaining the impetus of the Safavid revolutionary movement from 1494 onwards—bearing in mind the fact that ^cAli, killed by Aq Quyunlu forces in
that year, was the third successive Safavid leader to lose his life in battle,
and it was vitally necessary at that moment to sustain the morale of the
revolutionaries if the whole movement were not to collapse? Obviously, not
a seven-year-old boy. The people responsible, between 1494 and 1499, for

protecting the person of Isma^cil, were a small band of seven men known as the *ahl-i ikhtisas*. The term *ahl-i ikhtisas* means persons who are singled out for some special duty, and in their case, their special duty, apart from that of protecting the person of their young leader, was to maintain in a high state of readiness the Safavid revolutionary organization in Syria, eastern Anatolia, and elsewhere and to plan the final stages of the revolution.

The Safavid propaganda machine, by hammering away insistently at the alleged fact of the descent of the Safavid family from the seventh Imam, succeeded in making most people (though not the *^culama*) forget that even if this were true, it did not in itself prove anything, so to speak, because the Safavids had not, any more than anyone else, been *designated* as the agents of the infallible Imams. Their propaganda was so successful that they convinced at least some of the *hoi poloi* that the Safavid Shah was not only the "representative" or "agent" of the Hidden Imam, but was the Hidden Imam himself! Mazzaoui has quoted the story of the anger of the celebrated philosopher and political theorist Dawwani who, when he put to his students the question: "Who is the Imam?" got the answer: "Shah Isma'il!"

By insisting on the absolute obedience of their Sufi followers to themselves in their capacity as *murshid-i kamil* or spiritual directors of the Safawiyyah Order, the Safavid leaders succeeded in transforming the ordinary *pir-murid* relationship into something outside the range of usual mystical experience and in arrogating to themselves quasi-divine prerogatives. The Safavid family, it is worth noting in passing, had seized the leadership of the order by a piece of purely political opportunism, outmaneuvering their rivals by taking their stand strictly on the principle of designation (this was a perfectly proper posture to adopt), but at the same time asserting that in the matter of the transmission of *irshad* from one *pir* to another, the father–son kinship relationship was of no importance whatever. After the Safavids became leaders of the order, it was, of course, a very different story, and the *pidar-farzandi* relationship not only assumed paramount importance in deciding who the next leader should be, but was quietly assumed to be the only possible basis for selecting him. Once the Safavids acceded to the throne of Iran, and the *silsilah* (Sufi order) had become the *dudman* (ruling dynasty), there was no problem about the succession remaining in Safavid hands, since the principle of succession in the direct male line was clearly asserted in regard to kingship.

Finally, and this is where the smokescreen comes in, the Safavids tried to give extra respectability to their family by claiming *siyadat*, a claim which was not only spurious but irrelevant as far as the legitimization of their sovereignty was concerned. Once the Safavid state was established, the Shahs, by making the office of *sadr* an organ of the political branch of the administration, were able to suppress any threat to their sovereignty on the religious plane; such threats might come either from those who claimed to be the *murshid-i kamil* or from those who claimed to be the representative of the Mahdi. The *mujtahids*, by and large, were content with their lot up to the time of Shah ᶜAbbas I because, although the shahs had usurped their prerogative to act as the general agency of the Mahdi, they still wielded much more power without this prerogative in the Shiᶜi state set up by the Safavids than they had wielded when they still possessed this prerogative under a Sunni regime. In the latter part of the Safavid period, the ᶜ*ulama'* so whittled away the sovereignty of the shah that they themselves became the dominant power in the state, with disastrous results.

*   *   *

To sum up, then, I would adopt the position that a Safavid state without question existed, in the sense of "a geographically delimited segment of human society united by common obedience to a single sovereign," or, if you prefer Max Weber's definition, "a human community that [successfully] claims the monopoly of legitimate [this begs the question slightly] use of physical force within a given territory." It was emphatically not a nation-state like the Third Reich, in which racial purity was of cardinal importance. It was, however (or so I would maintain), a state with strong national consciousness and a sense of national identity. If the social scientists deny that this is sufficient to constitute a nation-state, I am content to let the matter rest there until they can define the concept of nationalism more satisfactorily than they have done hitherto.

As an historian given to feeding on myths and uttering "impressionistic clichés," and hampered by a strong sense of tradition, I would like cautiously to suggest a possible way out of a situation in which the difficulties seem to me to be largely semantic in nature. As we have seen, the concept of the state is ineluctably bound up with the question of sovereignty. Throughout the seventeenth century and much of the eighteenth, in most countries of Europe with the exception of England, where sovereignty was in the process of being transferred from the king to parliament, the entire power and prestige of the state was concentrated in the person of the monarch. After the French Revolution the concept that sovereignty was vested in the people, not the king, slowly but surely gained ground. Democracy became the order of the day, and the state became indistinguishable from its citizens. As a result, interest has shifted from the state to government and political processes. If the "sovereignty of the people" is what political scientists like Cottam mean by "participation in the political life of the state by a broad section of the population," and if he is unwilling to bestow the term "nation-state" on any polity which fails to meet this criterion, then perhaps what is needed is two sets of terms, one of which can be applied to pre-nineteenth century states when sovereignty vested in the king was the norm and another which may be used in regard to nineteenth and twentieth century states in which the sovereignty of the people is alleged to be the norm. I realize, however, that this is a simplistic and totally unscientific solution, and as such is unlikely to find favor with my social science colleagues.

Said Amir Arjomand

The Safavids inherited from the Timurids and the Aq Quyunlu the typical Islamic cluster of intellectual institutions consisting of the quadiships, the mosques, the *madrasahs* (colleges), and the religious endowments (*awqaf*). The state controlled these institutions through the office of the *sadr*, an office with no exact equivalent in the Ottoman or ᶜAbbasid polities. The Timurid decrees recorded in the *Sharaf-namih* of Murwarid (d. 1516/922) show two important facts about the office of the *sadr*. As regards the social position of its occupants, we can note that the office tended to remain within the same families of notables, a fact indicating a strong hereditary tendency in the appropriation of the office. With regard to the extensive jurisdication of the office, its twofold functions can be seen to consist in (1) the supervision and administration of the religious endowments and distribution of their revenue to the students and clerics and to charitable undertakings; and (2) the supervision of the administration of the sacred law as the chief judiciary authority of the state.

Because of its financial control over most religious endowments and many religious activities, the office of the *sadr* was the most important "religious" office of the realm. In the militarized conquest-oriented state of Ismaᶜil I, the *sadr*, as a rule, simultaneously held the rank of an *amir* (general). Ismaᶜil's defeat by the Ottomans at the battle of Chaldiran in 1514/920 marked the end of his military expansionism. Shortly after Chaldiran, with the appointment of Mir Jamal al-Din Shirangi, who remained in office until his death in 1525/931, the office of the *sadr* became clearly differentiated from Safavid military organization, and exclusively concerned with (financial) religious and judiciary affairs. The Safavid *sadrs* thus assumed the functions of the Timurid *sadrs* as the foremost clerical administrator of the realm, with certain judiciary responsibilities which became more extensive in the seventeenth century. As we shall see presently, the hereditary tendency in the appropriation of the office also set in at the beginning of the seventeenth century, and soon became very pronounced.

Under the Safavids, the administration of the religious endowments became centralized, and conducted under the supervision of one, or on occasion, two *sadrs*, who appointed deputies, with or without the title of *na'ib al-sadarah*; to the regions. It is not clear from the sources whether the *sadr* controlled the appointment of the local qadis in the sixteenth century, but in the seventeenth century their centralized control over the religious institutions included the prerogative of appointment of *qadis*.

However, the centralized control of the *sadr* did not extend over the most richly endowed shrines—notably those in Mashhad and Ardabil—whose administrators (sing. *mutawalli*) were appointed directly by the shah. The administratorship (*tawliyat*) of the independent endowments of these shrines was firmly retained by the clerical notables, who were also often entrusted with other purely administrative functions.

The primacy of this administrative (over the religious) aspect of the office of *sadr* is shown by the fact that both its geographical division under Tahmasp and earlier, and much more clearly, its division into *sadr-i khassih* (*sadr* of the royal domains) and the *sadr-i mamalik* (*sadr* of the [fiscally autonomous] provinces) in the seventeenth century, followed a strictly administrative logic. Furthermore, it is instructive that Hazin's detailed picture of the religious and intellectual circles in the early decades of the eighteenth century makes no references to the *sadr*. It is significant that ᶜAbbas II (1642-66) appointed his *sadr*, Mirza Mahdi, to grand vizirate, presaging the post-Safavid transformation of *sadarah*. Under the Qajars (1785-1925), the term *sadr* lost all religious connotations, and as *Sadr-i Aᶜzam* (Grand Sadr) came to designate the highest *administrative* office of the state: that of the prime minister. But neither in the sixteenth century nor at any other time did the *sadr* act as the authoritative custodian of the Shiᶜi doctrine.

The *shaykh al-Islam* of a city was its chief dignitary, and the *qadi* its religious judge. They were appointed by the state. The *qadis*, and certainly the *shaykh al-Islams*, were scholars, and were likely to have students and hold academic classes in their residence or elsewhere. In addition, there were the *madrasahs* under the direction of their respective professors (sing. *mudarris*). Chardin puts the number of the *madrasahs* of Isfahan in the 1660s at fifty-seven. Each of these had dormitories and maintained a number of students indefinitely on the income drawn from its endowments, and subventions from the *sadr*. Finally, there were the mosques with appointed prayer leaders (sing. *pish-namaz*). We know that in the seventeenth century an administrator (*mutawalli*) with distinctly secular/financial functions was appointed for each endowed mosque, in addition to *pish-namaz* as the director of its religious activities. A *qadi* was usually also a professor, and it was possible for a *qadi* to hold the office of *pish-namaz* simultaneously.

Given the royal appointment of the *shaykh al-Islams* and the important *qadis* and the underlying centralized financial control of the *sadr*, this complex of financial, legal, educational, and religious institutions had the potential of being unified into a "religious institution" incorporated into the Safavid state, as were its counterparts in the Ottoman Empire. But it was not. Why?

The answer must be sought, at least in part, in the resistance of the Persian "clerical estate" to the reception of the incoming Arab doctors and their students, who enjoyed the patronage of the Safavid shahs in exchange for the propagation of Shi^cism. As we shall see presently in detail, the first great immigrant Shi^ci theologian, Shaykh al-Karaki (d. 1534/940), failed to capture the permanent control of the complex of religious-legal-intellectual institutions for the Shi^ci hierocracy. A Shi^ci doctor trained by him did hold the office of the *sadr* for twenty years but exclusive control of the office reverted to the clerical notables. The holders of the office of the *sadr*, over the subsequent 150 years, were drawn without exception from the clerical estate.

The office(s) of the *sadr* remained within the hands of a small number of notable families with marked hereditary tendencies, even before the rein of Shah Safi (1629–42). From then onwards—that is, during the last century of Safavid rule—*sadarah* became confined, with the possible exception of a single *sadr*, to three eminent families who were closely related to the Safavids. Meanwhile, the tenure of the office became very long, usually for life. Shah Sultan-Husayn (1694–1722) had a single *sadr* who was his maternal uncle . . . .

Turning now to the other important offices, we note an important trend that adversely affected the institutional domination of the clerical estate. It consisted of a marked decline in the prominence of the *qadis* in the polity, especially with the establishment of a powerful centralized government by ^cAbbas the Great . . . .

This lowered status honor of the *qadis* indicated by the low figure for reign of ^cAbbas is paralleled by a drastic decline in the importance of the office of *qadi mu^caskar*—the army judge (which, however, continued to exist until the end of the Safavid era). The decline in the importance of the qadis was not reversed in the seventeenth century.

To complete our picture with regard to the seventeenth century, we must add another important category of the clerical estate: the *sayyids*, who, either because of the lack of vacant post or for other reasons, did not engage in any administrative functions, but whose (undefined) functions were religious. Though they must have possessed some religious learning, this learning was secondary to the basis of their status honor, which rested primarily on their *charisma of lineage* as the descendants of the Prophet and the Imams. According to Du Mans, they collected the religious taxes (*zakat*), and, more significantly, *khums*. In addition, they received regular stipends from the *awqaf* through the *sadr*'s department, in exchange for praying for the perpetuity of the dynasty (*du^ca-gu'i*). Chardin tells us that the Husayani *sayyids* of Isfahan, belonging to the ancient nobility of the kingdom, even arrogate *ijtihad* to themselves, and often accept penitence (*tawbih*) as do the *mujtahids.*

The incorporation of the estate of clerical notables into the judiciary and administrative offices of Isma^cil's regime was, as we have seen, accompanied by the violent elimination of those notables who opposed the regime and by the migration of those who were not willing to give up their formal profession of Sunnism. Despite the probable insincerity in their initial outward profession of Shi^cism and the persistence of Sunni proclivities among them, there can be no doubt that the vast majority of the clerical notables did in fact become Twelver Shi^cis by the seventeenth century. However, what is of crucial importance is that this change in doctrinal profession affected their cultural outlook very little, if at all. Comparing the descriptions of the intellectual interests and competence of the members of the clerical estate given in *Habib al-siyar* (1520s) and *Jami^c mufidi* (1670s), one is struck by the constancy in their cultural outlook. Perhaps it can be said that rhetoric figures somewhat more prominently in the former source, and religious sciences, mathematics, and calligraphy in the latter, but in both cases the same broad range and catholicity of intellectual interests and training is evident. Philosophy, the religious sciences, grammar and logic, calligraphy, mathematics, astronomy, rhetoric, composition and literary style, and, less frequently, history and the composition of puzzles (*fann-i mu^cam-ma*), appear as the main subjects of study. Though we may infer from our sources that few did naturally specialize in the religious sciences, there can be no doubt that the broad and eclectic cultural outlook continued to be typically characteristic of the clerical mandarins under the Safavids.

The cultural outlook of the Imami *^culama'* of the Arab lands was markedly different from that of the Persian clerical estate. They had had no comparable ties with any state and therefore lacked a similarly broad legal, administrative, financial, and political base, having for centuries acted as private jurists and religious advisors to the Shi^ci minorities in the Arab Iraq, Syria, or in the isolated Bahrain. Consonantly with their more narrowly professionalized function as advisors to the Shi^ci communities in matters of dogma, ritual, and sacred law, the cultural outlook of the Shi^ci *^culama'* was strictly religious. Though philosophy (usually in conjunction with rational theology [*kalam*]), Arabic grammar, (as a tool of religious jurisprudence), and, to a much lesser extent mathematics were included in the syllabus of learning, the overwhelming preponderance of strictly religious interests is clearly reflected in the publications of the Shi^{c}i ^{c}*ulama'* of the Safavid period as reported in Shi^{c}i biographical encyclopedias, and in the Safavid chronicles.

The geographical factor is of crucial importance in understanding the cultural orientation of the Shi^{c}i hierocracy. To show the importance of the centers of Shi^{c}i learning in the Arab lands, it seems useful to begin with a preliminary consideration of the origins of the prominent Shi^{c}i ^{c}*ulama'*.

The combination of the total number of ^{c}*ulama'* resident abroad, and the number of first-generation immigrant doctors in Iran for each period . . . give us a good index of the degree of preponderance of the influence of the Arab centers of Shi^{c}ism. The figures . . . demonstrate that the marked cultural preponderance of these centers continued despite the emergence of a great center of learning in Isfahan under ^{c}Abbas the Great. This continued cultural dominance is explained by the considerable immigration of Shi^{c}i ^{c}*ulama'* from Jabal ^{c}Amil to Isfahan. But the students of the immigrant doctors representing this influx were predominantly drawn from the Iranian population. They remained active in Iran (sixteen of them rose to prominence during the subsequent period as compared to a total of fourteen scholars who were either residents abroad or Arab immigrants). The vitality of Isfahan continued into the last decades of the seventeenth century and the first quarter of the eighteenth century, while its closer proximity to Bahrain, in addition to the flourishing trade in the Persian Gulf, brought a pool of Shi^{c}i scholars in Bahrain into the network of erudite religious communication. However, it should be emphasized that even in the latter part of the seventeenth and the first quarter of the eighteenth century, a substantial proportion of the community of Shi^{c}i religious scholars resided in the Arab lands. Thus the common cultural outlook of the Shi^{c}i ^{c}*ulama'* did not stem from common bases in the Safavid polity — as did that of the clerical notables — but from the identity of their cultural functions as the teachers of, and advisors in, religious jurisprudence, ritual, and dogma. Unlike the estate of clerical notables, the former constituted a sodality of *religious professionals*.

Most of the immigrant Shi^{c}i ^{c}*ulama'* found an (exalted) institutional niche in Safavid society in the more narrowly religious offices of *shaykh al-Islam* of the important cities, and the *pish-namaz* of the royal household, and of the most important mosques. Instances of an eminent theologian's being appointed qadi (not even of the most important cities) have rarely been noticed. Instead, those religious scholars who chose to accept the royal patronage were invariably appointed *shaykh al-Islam* or (less frequently) *pish-namaz*. The number of immigrant doctors was not large enough to exclude the Persian clerical notables from the majority of such offices. The appointees to *pish-namaz*, through the nature of the office, tended to be strictly religious professionals. It seems probable that under the influence of the eminent Shiᶜi doctors, the appointments to "shaykh al-Islamates" also tended to go increasingly to religious professionals, though contrary instances are not lacking. In short, we can say that the Shiᶜi religious professionals came to absorb the offices of *pish-namazi* and "shaykh al-Islamate", and to assimilate the outlook of their holders, who thus came to constitute a decentralized and heteronomous Shiᶜi hierocracy in Iran. In addition, this hierocracy contained members who held no office. A man of learning who had acquired fame and risen to the exalted rank of *mujtahid* could continue to teach and lead a pious life in total independence from the state, and was revered all the more if he chose to do so.

As *mujtahids*, *shaykh al-Islams*, scholars, and *pish-namaz* of the most important mosques, the members of the Shiᶜi hierocracy became increasingly conspicuous in Safavid society. . . .

As the term *ᶜulama'* (the learned, scholars) indicates, teaching is and always has been a primary function of the Shiᶜi doctors. As has been pointed out, even those appointed to the office of *shaykh al-Islam* would usually continue to hold their classes. Because of its amorphousness and flexibility (the students could take lessons in different subjects from *any* professor within the geographical vicinity and often moved to other cities to join the classes of eminent professors), the educational system proper also absorbed its share of the immigrant *ᶜulama'* as professors (sing. *mudarris*) of the "transmitted sciences" and the Shiᶜi jurisprudence. Given the declaration of the Imami doctrine and jurisprudence as the official and only valid religious tradition, the immigrant Shiᶜi *ᶜulama'* had no difficulty in capturing the teaching of the "transmitted" religious sciences (*manqul*) — as distinct from "rational" theology and philosophy (*maᶜqul*) — and are repeatedly mentioned as the professors of *manqul*. However, even within the intellectual institutions, they could not oust the professors of the rational sciences; and their attempt to take over the judiciary and financial branches of the complex of "religious" institutions met with both the firm resistance of the clerical estate and encountered internal obstacles; consequently it came to naught. It is to this undiscovered struggle that we should now turn.

* * *

Though there is no inherent logic in the pattern of change, . . . a comparison between the two suggests that, roughly speaking, the clerical estate's overall loss of institutional power because of the decline of qadiship corresponds to the Shiᶜi hierocracy's gain in prestige and control over the "shaykh al-Islamates." In other words, the configuration of the complex of religious-legal-educational institutions changed: a fairly well-differentiated hierocracy of religious professionals was structurally accommodated within it while the salience of the legal components of the complex was reduced. What underlay this change was a tangled struggle for domination between the two groups. The nature and course of the struggle are difficult to detect and chart because one of the two parties involved, the party of religious professionals, was itself undergoing a major internal transformation determined by two contrary factors: the trend toward professionalization on the one hand, and, on the other, a major change in composition owing to the recruitment of its younger members from the opposing camp, namely, the clerical estate. The detection and charting of these trends can therefore be done only with historical hindsight, as the actors involved were themselves at times only dimly conscious of the full repercussions of their action and the ultimate goal they were striving toward.

Glassen has noted the hostility with which the prominent members of the Persian clerical estate encountered the eminent doctor Shaykh ᶜAli al-Karaki and his party at the time of his arrival in Iran. This hostility persisted throughout the sixteenth century, thus militating against a smooth mutual assimilation between the slowly immigrating Shiᶜi doctors and the Persian clerical notables. In fact, the clerical notables bitterly resented both the intrusion of the Shiᶜi religious professionals under the protection and patronage of the ruler, and their preemption of the term *ᶜulama'* — the learned. One clerical notable and historian of Tahmasp's reign, Qadi Ahmad Ghaffari (d. 1567-8/975), even dared to state bluntly:

> But in his [Shah Tahmasp's] eyes, they were turning the ignorant — *juhala'* — into the learned — *fudala'* — and were attributing the station of the ignorant to the learned. Therefore most of his domains became devoid of men of excellence and knowledge, and filled with men of ignorance; and only a few men of [true] learning are to be found in the entire realm of Iran.

However, Tahmasp's determined support assured the survival of the Shiᶜi hierocracy and paved the way for its eventual triumph. Soon after the rise of Ismaᶜil the Safavid, al-Karaki moved from his native Jabal ᶜAmil in Syria to the closeby Arab Iraq, and is reported to have visited Ismaᶜil in Isfahan as early as 1504-5/910. He repeated his visits to Ismaᶜil and saw him in his camps in Harat and just before the battle of Chaldiran. He finally moved to central Iran toward the end of Ismaᶜil's reign. But his definitive chance to act as the supreme member of the Shiᶜi hierocracy came after the death of Ismaᶜil I, who after all, was himself the incarnation of God.

Ismaᶜil's son, the young Tahmasp, was a devout Twelver Shiᶜi who, unlike his father and forefathers, had no pretense to divine incarnation. He greatly respected al-Karaki, who is often referred to as the "Propagator of the [Shi^ci] Religion" (*murawwij-i mazhab*). In 1532–33/939, a year before al-Karaki's death, in order to put an end to an acrimonious fight between two major factions of the Shi^ci ^culama', Tahmasp issued a *farman* which can be regarded as the milestone marking both the creation of a Shi^ci hierocracy in Iran and the definitive transition from extremism to Twelver Shi^cism. The *farman* designated al-Karaki the *na'ib* (vicegerent/deputy) of the Imam, thus devolving the supreme religious authority upon him as the most qualified or the "seal of the *mujtahids*" (*khatam al-mujtahidin*) and as the guardian of the heritage of the Seal of the Prophets (Muhammad).

Al-Karaki's self-designation as the deputy of the Imam, however, preceded this explicit royal recognition, having begun with his ambitious political project as the foremost Imami jurist. In 1510/916, in a tract on taxation of agricultural land (*kharaj*), he explicitly put forward his views as the deputy of the Imam during his occultation. The reader should recall the positive world-embracing attitude of al-Murtada, who, under the bright political conditions of the Buyid period, moved away from the inner-worldly withdrawal entailed by the pious posture of the traditionalists, and attempted to enjoin world-embracing political attitudes, and to encourage ethically responsible activity within the existing political framework. With the creation of the first Shi^ci empire in history by Isma^cil, al-Karaki had an even greater incentive than al-Murtada to overcome the ideal of pious antipathy to earthly power. He took up the unprecedented challenge of bringing the Safavid political order within the ambit of the Shi^ci religious norms, and of securing an important institutional base for its custodians. To assure the involvement of the *^culama'* in political organization, he not only emphatically ruled in favor of the permissibility of receiving salaries from "tyrannical rulers," paid out of land taxes, but also envisioned some supervision over the distribution of these taxes by the deputy of the Imam. To enhance the world-embracing social aspects of Shi^cism in the controversial issue of the Friday prayer during the occultation of the Imam, he ruled that it was incumbent, thus assuring the weekly gathering of the believers, and, incidentally, securing for the Shi^ci *^culama'* positions as prayer leaders (sing. *pish-namaz*) of the mosques. Numerous treatises were written on this question, for and against the permissibility of the Friday congregational prayer during the occultation, but al-Karaki's affirmative, world-embracing view eventually prevailed over the negative, world-rejecting view. The social commitment of Shi^cism was considerably enhanced by the institution of congregational prayer to be led by the *^culama'* on behalf of the Hidden Imam.

*   *   *

The suppression of millenarian extremism among the Qizilbash by the Safavid rulers at the political level has its religious counterpart in the efforts of the Shi^ci doctors to contain mahdistic chiliasm at the doctrinal level by means of religious instruction. To assert their authority in the regulation of the religious life of their lay congregations, the Shi^ci *^culama'* had to deal with the mahdistic tenet included in their doctrinal heritage.

As we have seen, in the tenth/fourth century two separate concepts of Imamate and mahdihood were welded together, and the Hidden Imam emerged as a bipartite figure: as the Imam of the Age (*Imami-i zaman*) he was said to fulfill the function of imamate, while as the Mahdi and the *Qa'im* (redresser) he assumed the role of the paraclete. In the late tenth or early eleventh century, al-Mufid put the return of the dead (*raj^ca*) and the rising (*qiyam*) of the Mahdi together as the prelude to Resurrection (*Qiyamah*). The notion of the Mahdi was accepted on basis of the tradition attributed to the Prophet, which predicts the appearance of one of his descendants who "will fill the earth with equity and justice as it is filled with oppression and tyranny." Al-Tusi's account of the return of the Mahdi is nevertheless completely apocalyptic, and sets the apocalyptic tone for the subsequent Shi^ci works on the topic, including those of the Safavid period. They tell us of the reign of total chaos and tyranny, the appearance of the *Dajjal* (Antichrist) and Sufyani, the return of Imam Husayn and of Jesus, and the armed rising of the entire believing community under the Mahdi's banner.

Furthermore, from the European sources of the late Safavid period, we hear of an astonishing practice which must be presumed to have perpetuated some kind of apocalyptic mood. Though not as zealously expectant as the Sarbidars, who sent the caparisoned horse to the gate of their city to accommodate the expected Mahdi every day, the Safavid monarchs kept a bevy of well-groomed horses in the richly endowed "stable of the Lord of the Age" (*tawilih-yi sahib al-zaman*) which were strictly reserved for his use upon *parousia*, but which were marched through the streets of the cities on ceremonial occasions. Two of the horses are reported to have been harnessed all the time, one for the Lord of the Age himself, the second for Jesus, who would also appear in his comapny. Chardin mentions the existence of the stable of the Lord of the Age not only in Isfahan, but also in Bandar ^cAbbas, which allows us to infer that horses must have been maintained for his possible use in the major cities.

Despite the retention of apocalyptic tenets and the institution of such practices, how can Safavid Shi^cism be said to have contained the impulse to chiliasm? The statement of the Shi^ci doctrine tended to do so, to some extent, through the obviation of the plausibility of the occurrences of the millennium in the present or foreseeable future. Already in the eleventh century, al-Tusi had prohibited the fixing of a date for the reappearance of the Mahdi. In the twelfth century, the author of *Kitab al-naqd* again ruled out the possibility of cabalistic determination of the time of *parousia*. Furthermore, the juxtaposition of the *parousia* to otherworldly physical resurrection relegated it into as distant a future as possible. Thus Majlisi gave significance to the reign of the Mahdi at the end of time primarily as the earthly prelude to Resurrection and the Day of Judgment. Du Mans's account of popular religious beliefs confirms that this association was as close in the mind of the Shiꞓi as in their religious writings.

Nevertheless, the tenet of the return of the Mahdi itself remains potentially chiliastic. What was decisive for the containment of the chiliastic impulse was not so much the dogma as the attitude of its interpreters: the ascendancy of the Shiꞓi hierocracy assured the continued suppression of the chiliastic impulse, which, under their hierocratic control over the interpretation of dogma, ritual conduct, and prayer, was sublimated into pietistic passive expectancy. Al-Tusi cites a tradition from the sixth Imam to establish that the reward for believing in the reappearance of the rule of the house of Muhammad is tantamount to martyrdom in the company of the Mahdi. Consonantly with this attitude, subsequent Twelver Shiꞓi ethical manuals came to enjoin the virtue of *intizar* (patient expectation) of the Mahdi, which is interpreted as a sign of faith (*Iman*), and becomes a stabilized element in the devotional piety of believing Shiꞓis.

The mahdihood of the Hidden Imam was only one aspect of the doctrine of occultation. In the heyday of chiliasm and before the consolidation of the Shiꞓi hierocracy—i.e., the early Safavid period—this aspect predominated, rendering the doctrine highly chiliastic. Qadi Nurullah Shushtari, in his section on holy places, mentions an island—the Jazirah-yi Akhdar—fifteen days away from Andalusia, on which the Hidden Imam and "his sons and disciples" live, and tells us that the deputy of that holy region has ships brought to the island twice a year, and distributes their loads among the inhabitants. He appears to have based this retrospectively bizarre view on a treatise written by the order of Shah Ismaꞓil I, on the "philosophy and expediency" of occultation. In it, the Imam and his sons and disciples are said to be engaged in the teaching and learning of the religious lore on the island, while armies stand in preparation outside the island, awaiting the Imam's word for the rising.

With the ascendancy of the Shiꞓi hierocracy in the late Safavid period, other elements of the doctrine of occultation, aiming at containing the potential to chililastic action under a claimant to mahdihood, tended to come to the foreground. Following al-Tusi closely, Majlisi insists that the Hidden Imam was alive and lives on earth, and tries to establish that his longevity had precedence among biblical figures, and that it is biologically possible. He alleges that the Imam has been seen from time to time and dreamt of frequently, has performed many miracles, and that he watches over the affairs of his people and takes part, unrecognized, in the *hajj* ceremony at Mecca. Above all, the Shiꞓi community is said to benefit from his presence in spite of concealment: in the first section of his treatise on imam-ate, Majlisi enumerates these benefits. Nor does Majlisi omit to reiterate the message purportedly handed down by the Hidden Imam to disqualify the potential claimants to authority delegated from the Lord of the Age: "If they claim that they have seen and recognized [him] at that time, they are ly-ing, and if, through claims to seeing [him] they claim vicegerency [*niyabah*], they are lying."

Thus, though the Shici tenet on the return of the Mahdi remains in-curably millenarian, the doctrine of occultation, as interpreted by the ascendant hierocracy, removes all plausible justifications for the expecta-tions of imminent *parousia*.

With the establishment of Twelver Shicism under the Safavids, the Shici hierocracy, while allowing for the intermittent appearance of the Imam and especially for visits and favors he vouchsafes upon the prominent *culama'*, and attempting to reserve attenuated forms of contact with the Hidden Imam through dreams and visions as their own prerogative, staunchly op-posed any attempt to translate the eschatology into this-worldly millenarianism on the basis of mahdistic and epiphanic claims. Any such at-tempt would involve a radical break with the Shici orthodoxy of the *culama'*, and was bound to be considered by them a reversion to extremism and, as such, cardinal heresy.

Albert Hourani

If Shicism was to be the religion of the empire, preached in the mosques, taught in the schools and administered in the courts, there was a need for teachers to propagate it and jurists to define and apply the law. Such teachers and jurists scarcely existed in Persia. There were pockets of Shicism in Khurasan, *Iraq-i cAjam* and elsewhere, but the notables of the great cities who were drawn into the Safavid service were for the most part not Shici by *mazhab*, although 'forms of interior piety of Shici type' were widespread. The process by which Shicism spread was a slow one, and in the first stages Shah Ismacil and then his successor Tahmasp brought *culama'* from the Arabic-speaking countries — from Iraq, Bahrain and Jabal cAmil — to rein-force those from Persia.

The first important scholar to come from Jabal ᶜAmil, and in some ways the most influential of all, was Nur al-Din ᶜAli ibn Husayn al-Karaki (?870/1465-66-940/1534). Born into a family of scholars, he studied at Karak Nuh with Zayn al-Din ᶜAli ibn Hilal al-Jaza'iri and other scholars who stood in the line of intellectual descent from the First Martyr; he therefore inherited the central tradition of the Usuli movement. From Karak Nuh he went to Egypt, and then to the holy cities of Iraq, where his fame as a scholar became great enough for Shah Ismaᶜil to invite him to his court; he paid a visit there, and went for a longer period in the reign of Tahmasp, who gave him official functions and endowments.

It was perhaps not only the paucity of Shiᶜi scholars in Iran which made the employment of al-Karaki and others like him valuable to the new dynasty. A scholar from abroad, with no roots in Persian urban society, might be of greater use to a dynasty still unsure of its position than would be one who had links of interest with the dominant classes of the cities. What may have been even more important, al-Karaki had taken from his teachers a tradition which laid emphasis upon the role of the ᶜalim as guardian of the shariᶜah and successor of the Imam, and gave scope to competent scholars to practise *ijtihad* and to draw appropriate conclusions from the sources by the exercise of valid methods of reasoning. Al-Karaki claimed that the *mujtahid* was the deputy (*na'ib*) of the hidden Imam as far as the giving of judicial decisions were concerned, and his writings show examples of decisions which were in harmony with the interests of the dynasty. Muslims, he argued, could collect the canonical land-tax (*kharaj*) for the ruler, and accept their share of it from him, even in the absence of the Imam; they should perform the Friday prayer even if the Imam is not present to lead it. Such teachings went in the direction of accepting the rule of the Safavids and conferring a kind of legitimacy upon it, and in his turn Shah Tahmasp recognized al-Karaki as the Imam's deputy and the seal of the *mujtahids*, with responsibility for maintaining the *shariᶜah*.

The path opened by al-Karaki was followed by others, during the sixteenth and the first half of the seventeenth century. As Said Arjomand has shown, the immigrant scholars, whether from Jabal ᶜAmil or Bahrain, never obtained control of all the high positions in the religious establishment. The office of *sadr*, with its control of religious endowments, and the major judgeships were given mainly to Persians, and, as in the Ottoman empire, there was a tendency for them to be kept in the hands of certain families with a tradition of learning, urban leadership and official service. Immigrant scholars, however, were appointed to the office of *shaykh al-Islam* in major cities, and as preachers in mosques and teachers in schools. They were therefore in a position to play an important part in the spread of moderate and responsible Shiᶜi doctrine and practice among the Persian population.

As with other immigrant groups in other places, a person who succeeded in obtaining a good position would attract and help other members of his family, or of families linked with his. A large proportion of the scholars who went from Jabal ᶜAmil to Persia seem to have belonged to a small number of families linked to each other by ties of blood or intermarriage, or those of teacher and student. Thus the descendants and relations of al-Karaki continued to play an important part in Persian life; his son ᶜAbd al-ᶜAli was also given recognition by the Shah as the chief *mujtahid* of his age. The family of the Second Martyr too came to Persia, but much later. His son Hasan continued to live at Jubaᶜ, and there wrote an important text-book of jurisprudence, *Maᶜalim al-din*. Hasan's son Muhammad studied with his father, then with Sunni scholars in Damascus and later went to Mecca and from there to Karbala. Muhammad's son ᶜAli remained at Jubaᶜ when his father went to Mecca, studied there and at Karak Nuh, and then went to Persia and lived in Isfahan.

Two other families from Jubaᶜ also became important in Persia. ᶜIzz al-Din Husayn ibn ᶜAbd al-Samad al-Harithi al-Hamdani (918/1512–984/1576) was a student of the Second Martyr and went with him on his first journey to Istanbul. In the year of his teacher's death he went to Persia, and for a time was *shaykh al-Islam* in Qazvin when it was Shah Tahmasp's place of residence. He was sent from there to Khurasan after the Safavids conquered it, and became *shaykh al-Islam* at Harat; after a time he asked permission to make the pilgrimage and did not return from it to Persia, but settled in Bahrain where he died. His more famous son, Baha' al-Din Muhammad, known as the Shaykh al-Baha'i (953/1547–1031/1621), was born in Baᶜlbak when his father was teaching there, and taken by his father to Persia when very young. He then acquired a Persian as well as an Arabic education. He wrote in both languages, and on many subjects: poetry, mathemathics, astronomy, a famous anthology, the *Kashkul*, and a work on *fiqh* in Persian. He held various posts, but like his father gave them up for a life of poverty and of travel for the sake of learning and devotion, and spent years abroad before returning to Persia.

Another line from Jubaᶜ was that of Muhammad ibn ᶜAli al-Musawi (946–1009/1539–40–1600–1601), grandson of the Second Martyr through his mother. He lived at Jubaᶜ and there wrote *Madarik al-ahkam*, a commentary on the *Shara'iᶜ al-Islam* of al-Muhaqqiq. His son Husayn studied with him, and then went to Persia and studied further with the Shaykh al-Baha'i. He lived in Khurasan, became *shaykh al-Islam* of Mashhad, and taught in the place of honour beneath the great eastern dome of the shrine of the Imam al-Rida.

Yet another line goes back to that Nur al-Din ᶜAli al-Maysi who had been the teacher of the Second Martyr. His descendant Lutfullah ibn ᶜAbd al-Karim (d. 1032/1622) was born in Jabal ᶜAmil but taken early to Mashhad and studied there. He held posts at Mashhad and then went to Isfahan, where he taught in the famous mosque built for him by Shah ᶜAbbas I and named after him.

In general, these scholars belonged to the Usuli school, but with another scholar we come across another line of thought. Muhammad ibn Hasan al-Hurr al-ᶜAmili (1033/1623-24–1104/1692-93) born in Mashgharah, came of a family of scholars who claimed descent from a famous figure of early Islamic history: al-Hurr ibn Yazid al-Riyahi, who was sent by the governor of Iraq to confront the force of the Imam Husayn which was moving towards Kufah, but decided to join Husayn at the critical moment, and was killed in the final battle. After studying with his father and other members of his family, Muhammad al-Hurr went on to study with the great-grandson of the Second Martyr and others who transmitted his teaching. Then he went to Persia and taught at Mashhad under the dome of the shrine. Unlike most of the scholars from Jabal ᶜAmil, his inclinations were not towards the Usuli school but towards that of the revived school of the Akhbaris, who insisted on strict adherence to the letter of the *Hadith* and were suspicious of too much reliance on reasoning. His most influential work was *Wasa'il al-shiᶜah ila tahsil masa'il al-shariᶜah*, a collection of *hadiths* concerned with legal subjects.

Like the other immigrant scholars, Muhammad al-Hurr founded a family which carried on the tradition of learning and official service and belonged to the religious élite of Persia. Some sense of difference, some memory of the country from which they had come and pride in its place in Shiᶜi history, seems, however, to have continued to exist. When the Shaykh al-Baha'i gave up his official position and started his life of wandering, there may have been more than one reason for it, but he himself evoked the image of a certain way of life which, in his view, was more worthy than that of a court ᶜalim. He regretted, he said, that his life was not like that of the Second Martyr who looked after his vineyard at night and gave himself to study in the daytime, or like that of the Martyr's teacher, Shaykh ᶜAli al-Maysi, who gathered firewood for himself and his students at night.

The Shaykh al-Baha'i's travels took him to his land of birth, and he was well-enough known there among Sunni scholars to have a long entry in one of the main biographical dictionaries of the eleventh Islamic century, al-Muhibbi's *Khulasat al-athar*. Al-Muhibbi records that he visited Cairo, Jerusalem, Damascus and Aleppo, as well as Jabal ᶜAmil. He was well-received and praised, but had to act with caution. In Jabal ᶜAmil the people came out to meet him in waves, and he was afraid that this would reveal his true situation. Engaging in theological discussion in Aleppo, he told a Sunni shaykh in private: 'I am a Sunni, I love the Companions of the Prophet, but what should I do? Our sultan is a Shiᶜi and kills the Sunni men of learning'.

Muhammad al-Hurr gave more explicit expression to his special feeling for the place of his birth. His biographical dictionary of Shi^ci scholars is divided into two parts: the first, entitled *Amal al-amil fi tarajim ^culama' Jabal ^cAmil*, deals entirely with scholars from Jabal ^cAmil, while the second part includes scholars from all the rest of the Shi^ci world. In the introduction he gives eight reasons why he has accorded this priority to Jabal ^cAmil.

The first reason, quite simply, is the preference which is due to one's place of origin (*watan*); he quotes the famous hadiths, *hubb al-watan min al-iman* and *min iman al-rajul hubbuhi li qawmihi*. In giving the other seven reasons, he tries to provide a rational basis for this natural preference. The Shi^cism of Jabal ^cAmil is the oldest of all: he mentions the story of Abu Zarr. A large number of learned and pious men have come from this community. No country has produced more or better Imami scholars: there is no village which has not given birth to them; an author is quoted to the effect that one-fifth of all the Imami scholars of the later period come from Jabal ^cAmil. Many prophets and ^c*ulama'* have their tombs there.

He also gives three quotations from the Qur'an which can be interpreted as referring to Jabal ^cAmil, or to *Bilad al-Sham* of which it forms part. In *Surat al-ma'ida* there is a reference to 'the holy land': 'O my people enter the Holy Land which God has prescribed for you'. *Hadiths* are quoted to show that this refers to *Bilad al-Sham*. In the first verse of *Surat al-isra'* ('Glory be to Him who carried His servant by night from the Holy Mosque to the Further Mosque the precincts of which we have blessed') the expression 'the Further Mosque' is interpreted in the way which is normal in later commentaries, as referring to the Aqsa Mosque in Jerusalem, and its 'precincts' can be regarded as including Jabal ^cAmil. In *Surat ibrahim*, Abraham is depicted as addressing God: 'I have made some of my seed to dwell in a valley where there is no sown land by Thy Holy House; our Lord, . . . provide them with fruits'. Once more, a common later interpretation of this passage is given: God ordered the Angel Gabriel to cut out a piece of the Jordan valley, circumambulate the Haram seven times with it, and put it in the place where it now is, at al-Ta'if, and from which the produce is taken to Mecca. The Jordan valley is part of *Bilad al-Sham*, and so this too can be taken to include Jabal ^cAmil.

Finally, Muhammad al-Hurr records a saying of the Imam Ja^cfar al-Sadiq, transmitted by Ibn Babuyah and the First Martyr but for which he admits that there is no solid textual basis. Asked what would be the condition of his people in the time of the Occultation of the Imam, the Imam replied that the people of a district in *Bilad al-Sham* — the district of al-Shaqif and that lying on the shores of the sea and the lower slopes of the mountains — would be 'truly our partisans and helpers and brothers . . . their hearts inclined to us and severe upon our enemies, the rudder of the ship in the state of Occultation.

Chapter Twelve

The Qajar Era

In 1722 A.D., following the invasion of Iran by the Sunni Afghans, the last Safavid Shah, Husayn, was deposed from power. What ensued was not only a collapse of the Safavid state, but also a fundamental change in the role of Shiᶜism in the social and political life of Iran. The Sunni predilections of the Afghan conquerers and their Persian successors, especially Nadir Shah Afshar, meant a separation of Shiᶜism from state-craft, if not the outright suppression of the faith. Consequently, post-Safavid Iran witnessed the development of monarchial power independent of Shiᶜi influences. Shiᶜi authorities meanwhile changed their status from the senior partner in governing the state to that of the state's counterbalance often acting as the force of opposition.

Therefore, in the Qajar era, when once again Shiᶜism emerged as the religion of Iran, and an important part in the country's politics, the legacy of the relations between Shiᶜism and monarchy in the post-Safavid period marred the prospects of cooperation between the shahs and the ᶜulama'. As an instituiton with an independent existence, Shiᶜism soon became an important political force, serving as a check on the power of the shahs, the activities of foreigners, and the modernizing tendencies of the elite.

As the power of the monarchy declined from the time of Fath-ᶜAli Shah to that of Ahmad Shah, the Shiᶜi institutions found greater independence and hence commensurate power. By the reign of Nasir al-Din Shah, Shiᶜism had become a powerful political force, one that compelled the Shah to retreat from his position concerning tobacco concessions to Great Britain. The rising power of the ᶜulama' reached its zenith in the Constitutional Revolution of 1905–06, which also marked the culmination of the confrontation between the monarchy and the ᶜulama'. The changing character of the Shiᶜi religious establishment in Iran entailed many adjustments and refinements in Shiᶜi political theory. The last section of this book will provide a review of these intellectual developments. Here, however, we shall concentrate upon the dynamics of the interactions between religion and monarchy in Iran.

In the following two passages, first Said Amir Arjomand gives us a detailed account of the relationship between the religious and the political authorities in this period. His account is distinctly marked by a detailed attention to the nuances and vicissitudes of this relationship. Then Hamid Algar provides a more general statement about the same relationship in the same period.

The excerpts are from SGHI, *pages 22–29, 232–33, 238–39, 245–49; and* RSIRUQP, *pages 257–260, 244–248, respectively.*

Said Amir Arjomand

As [is known, Nadir Shah] sought to effect a definitive break with Safavid rule and its principles of legitimacy of kingship. He sought to obliterate the hierocratic trappings of temporal rule (a vestige of extremism perpetuated by the Safavids), as these would restrict legitimate rule to a member of the Safavid house. To emphasize this break, as we have seen, he went so far as to disown Shiᶜism. Furthermore, in a deliberate attempt to reverse the abandonment of the glorification of Genghis-Khanid descent as a "branch of the tree of unbelief" by Ismaᶜil, Nadir tried to revive the pre-Safavid Turkman tribal principles of legitimacy, which had not been given currency since the fifteenth century. In a letter to the Ottoman grand vizier, Nadir states that the dignitaries of Iran gathered in the plain of Mughan "elected our august Majesty to kingship and sovereignty which are the hereditary prerogatives of the noble Turkman tribe." Mulla ᶜAli Akbar, his *Mulla-bashi*, opens his pan-Islamic sermon in Kufah with the eulogy of Nadir not only as the shadow of God on earth, but also as the scion of the Turkman tree and heir to Genghis Khan.

However, after Nadir's death, Safavid descent, often with a marked emphasis on its religious character, remained the most viable ground of legitimacy for rulership. Karim Khan Zand sought a compromise solution to the problem of legitimacy by maintaining an incarcerated Safavid figurehead as Shah Ismaᶜil III while calling himself *wakil al-raᶜaya* (deputy of the subjects). Meanwhile, a serious attempt was made to revive Safavid caesaropapism, with a strong emphasis being put on the religious character of the rule of the Safavid descendants of the Imams. Mir Muhammad, a grandson of Shah Sulayman, specialized in the study of the religious sciences and became known as Mir Muhammad Mujtahid. In the years of anarchy that followed Nadir's assassination, he was drawn into politics by the Safavid loyalists and ruled in Mashhad for forty days in 1163 (January–February 1750) as Sulayman II. But this last attempt at the rival of the Safavid hierocratic caesaropapism collapsed, and Mir Muhammad, who had already been blinded, also had to suffer the mutilation of his tongue.

Aqa Muhammad Khan, the founder of the Qajar dynasty, affirmed the continued adherence of his state to the Twelver Shiᶜism established in Iran by the Safavids. Especially in view of his lay descent, this fact made it all the more imperative for him to establish his rule and that of his dynasty as *tem-*

poral. This could only be done by the exclusion of hierocratic pretensions resting on charisma of holy lineage, which, if retained, would have made a Safavid pretender appear more qualified to rule.

Aqa Muhammad Khan did not live long enough after his coronation to deal with this problem, but his successor Fath-ᶜAli Shah did. As a new dynasty, the need to legitimate their rule must have been felt acutely by the first Qajar monarchs. As Weber remarks, "if the legitimacy of the ruler is not clearly identifiable through hereditary charisma, another charismatic power is needed; normally this can only be hierocracy." In the need to secure such legitimation, Fath-ᶜAli Shah turned to the Shiᶜi hierocracy, many of whose prominent members responded favorably most notably, Mirza Abu'l-Qasim Qumi, the Muhaqqiq, and Sayyid Jaᶜfar Kashfi. Against this background, the interest of Fath-ᶜAli in securing a firm *du jure* basis for the legitimacy of Qajar rule, and the doctrinal interest of the supportive *ᶜulama'* in the removal of inconsistencies between Shiᶜi doctrine and the priciples of legitimacy of the Safavid era, resulted in the completion of the process of rationalization of the normative order governing political and hierocratic domination in the direction of greater congruence with the logic of Twelver Shiᶜism.

With the destruction of the edifice of the Safavid caesaropapist state and the renunciation of its normative basis, and with the reestablishment of the Shiᶜi hierocracy in the early decades of the nineteenth century, a separation of political and hierocratic domination congruent with the normative logic of Twelver Shiᶜism within the polity had in fact come into existence. Against this background, the compatibility of the patrimonial theories of kingship and justice with Twelver Shiᶜism was explicitly stated and elaborately amplified. What is even more momentous is that in the first decades of the nineteenth century we find the culmination of the efforts of al-Murtada and al-Karaki aiming at the overcoming of pious political indifferentism through the creation of a positive political ethic. Consonantly with the logic of Shiᶜism, the blessing of the Hidden Imam came to be bestowed upon the king as *temporal* ruler. Thus, in the reign of the pious Fath-ᶜAli Shah, we witness the consolidation of a Twelver Shiᶜi polity in Iran in which the Shiᶜi normative pattern bearing on political and hierocratic domination found as close an institutional translation as it was ever likely to have,

*   *   *

There are a number of works written by the literati during Fath ᶜAli's reign that belong to the traditional genre of patrimonial political theory. When, in the early years of Fath-ᶜAli's reign, the eminent *mujtahid* Mirza Abu'l-Qasim Qumi (d. 1817–18/1233) set forth the principles of legitimacy

of temporal rule, he too, by and large, reiterated the patrimonial theories of
kingship. However, there were some important qualifications.

For Mirza Abu'l-Qasim as for all previous political theorists, the fundamental basis of legitimate rulership was justice, and he considered the king
the shadow of God on earth. But he stressed the necessity of the correct *interpretation* of the term "shadow of God on earth," and in explicating its
"three meanings" he took great care not to repeat any of the Safavids'
claims. In fact, his interpretation emphatically divests the ruler of divine
power and divine attributes, and, most importantly, links the term with
justice and equity as the "shadow of divine justice," Mirza Abu'l-Qasim
states that God has made the king His lieutenant (*janishin*) on earth (not the
janishin of the Hidden Imam, as the Safavids claimed to be), but immediately proceeds to emphasize the responsibilities implied by such an appointment. In sharp and, one is tempted to say, deliberate contrast to the
Safavids' claim to infallibility, he writes that the actions of the king are not
necessitated by divine decree. The king's rule is a trial; he is not absolved
from performing his ethical duties by virtue of kingship, and will be punished by God for all evil doing. Finally, Mirza Abu'l-Qasim stresses the inter-
dependence of kingship and religion, noting the differentiation of political
and hierocratic functions: kings were needed for the preservation of order,
the *culama'* for the protection of religion.

Even though these modifications of the patrimonial theory are important
in themselves. Mirza Abu'l-Qasim did not take the step of legitimating the
temporal rule in terms of Shiᶜi doctrine. This momentous step was taken by
a prominent member of the Shiᶜi hierarchy belonging to the subsequent
generation, and became possible when nearly a quarter of a century of
stable Qajar rule, accompanied by economic prosperity, had transformed
the conception of the Safavid era from the Golden Age of the anarchical in-
terregnum to a vague and fast-receding historical memory. In the meantime, the demise of Akhbari traditionalism and the decline of the charisma
of Prophetic lineage fostered by it, had relegated the heritage of extremism
to oblivion. Against this background, the legitimation of temporal rule
could once again be related to the theories of Imamate and occultation, but
this time in terms not of extremism but of Twelver Shiᶜism.

An interesting testimony from the period of transition to the full
autonomy of the hierocracy is supplied by the grandson of Bihbihani,
Ahmad ᶜAli, in 1809/1224. In his autobiography, having profusely praised
Aqa Muhammad Khan and Fath-ᶜAli Shah as shadow of God, he comments
on Fath ᶜAli's confirmation of his brother in positions held by his deceased
father, Aqa Muhammad ᶜAli Bihbihani (d. 1801–2/1216):

> From the threshold of the august king, protector of the world, Shadow
> of God, letters containing condolences and orders for holding of

> mourning services arrived; and the affairs in charge of the deceased [in the region of Kirmanshah] . . . *in addition to [being a] divine commission*, were entrusted to him [the author's brother] by the king, the Protector of religion.

Bihbihani thus claims direct divine commission in addition to delegation of authority by the shadow of God.

The final resolution of the normative problem of the legitimacy of political and hierocratic domination was facilitated by an instance of cooperation between the state and the hierocracy as the two organs of the reconstituted Shi^ci polity. The occasion came during the first Perso-Russian War (1810–13) with the initiative taken by ^cIsa Qa'im Maqam, the minister of the reforming regent and crown prince, ^cAbbas Mirza, who tried to enlist the support of the Shi^ci hierocracy in the declaration of *jihad* against the infidel Russians. He dispatched envoys to Arab Iraq and Isfahan to solicit the Shi^ci hierocracy for injunctions and tracts on holy war. Many such *fatwas* and treatises were obtained and assembled in a volume entitled *Risalah-i jihadiyyah*. A crucially important byproduct of this venture was the clarification of the foundations of hierocratic authority de jure.

The most eminent *mujtahid* of the time and the doyen of the hierocracy, Shaykh Ja^cfar, the *Kashif al-Ghita'* (d. 1812–13/1127–28) responded by a long declaration (in Arabic) making the waging of war against the Russians incumbent; and authorizing Fath ^cAli Shah to conduct the *jihad* against the Russians on behalf of the Imam of the Age. He explained that his power to authorize the king rested on the *mujtahids'* collective office of *niyabat-i ^camma* (general viceregency). Shaykh Ja^cfar did explain that the defense of Islam through *jihad*, a duty of the Imam according to the sacred law, falls upon the *mujtahids* by virtue of their general vicegerency during the occultation. He also explained that it was this duty, and his recognition as a *na'ib ^camm*, that empowered him to authorize the sultan. Nevertheless, Shaykh Ja^cfar's use of the phrase "I give permission" (*faqad azintu*), though logically unobjectionable, could be viewed as arrogant. Lambton is therefore correct in supposing that Shaykh Ja^cfar's declaration, like those of some of the other *mujtahids* "carried with it the important corollary that they could give by this authorization validity, or at least temporary validity, to the rule of a Shah whom they appointed to engage in *jihad*." However, it should also be noted that the ministers of the Qajar state who initiated and pursued the *jihad* policy, Qa'im Maqam the Elder and his son Mirza Abu'l-Qasim, Qa'im Maqam the Younger, were quite mindful of this hierocratic pretention and took prompt steps to rectify it. Qa'im Maqam the Elder's name appears as the author of a slim volume in Persian summarizing the views of the Shi^ci hierocracy on *jihad*. After being carefully read and approved by Fath-^cAli Shah, it was printed in Tabriz in 1818 as *Kitab al-*

jihadiyyah and can be safely assumed to have been fairly widely read as one
of the earliest printed books. Qa'im Maqam of course states that the late
Shaykh Ja^cfar authorized Fath-^cAli Shah on behalf of the Imam to engage
in *jihad*. However, in a later passage he takes care, in referring to a treatise
by the shaykh, to quote him as saying "if I be a man of *ijtihad* and worthy
of the vicegerency of the Imam, peace be upon Him, I give permission to the
ruler etc." Similarly, Qa'im Maqam the Younger, in his well-known preface
to the longer *Jihadiyyah*, is as clear as he can be without compromising his
consummately ornate literary style, about the basis of the hierocratic
authority of the *mujtahids*, and about the appropriateness of its exercise in
authorizing the king to engage in *jihad*: When the sun of Imamate passed
beneath the veil of occultation, the star of vicegerency was still left visible
for the guidance of the world. Ethical duties remained just as binding, the
commandments of the sacred law being those given in the "Book" (of God)
and by the "Household" (of the Prophet). The function of the *mujtahids*
embodying the "star of vicegerency" is the protection of the sacred law and
the observance of its provisions. In fulfillment of this function of guidance
of the believers, they have explained the commandments of the sacred law
regarding holy war, and authorized the "*Shahanshah* of the world and of
religion" to unsheath his sword at the service of religion to become the
reviver of the tradition of *jihad*.

Thus the important consequences of the *jihad* episode was that it gave the
Shi^ci hierocracy the opportunity to publicize the concept of general vicegerency (of the Hidden Imam) as the basis of *hierocratic* authority, de jure,
and to secure its respectful acknowledgment by the spokesmen for the Qajar
state. What remained to be done was the legitimation of *political* authority
in a manner consistent with Shi^ci doctrine. This was done by a prominent
member of the Shi^ci hierocracy, Aqa Sayyid Ja^cfar ibn Abu Ishaq Kashfi (d.
1850–51/1267). In *Tuhfat al-muluk*, written in 1817–18/1233, Kashfi at last
put forward a systematic treatment of political and hierocratic domination
within a unified Shi^ci normative perspective. Kashfi could go beyond
Qumi's reiteration of the patrimonial ethos and produce a consistently
Shi^ci political theory incorporating the authority of the Imam of the Age
with reference to the doctrines of Imamate and occultation.

With the conclusion of historical Imamate in the form of occultation of
the Imam of the Age, the twin functions of imamate—supreme political and
religious leadership of the community—devolved upon two groups entitled
to his deputyship or viceregency (*niyabah*), the rulers and the *^culama*':

> Thus it becomes clear that the *mujtahids* and the rulers both hold the
> same office, which office is the office of imamate, transferred to them
> from the Imam through vicegerency, and consisting of two pillars
> [*rukn*]: knowledge of the prophetic matters, which is called religion; and

the implementation of the same in the course of imposing order upon the world, which is termed kingship or sovereignty. These two pillars are also referred to as "the sword" and "the pen" or "the sword" and "knowledge." Both these pillars were found in combination in the imam . . . and they should similarly coexist in the person who is his deputy. But the *culama* and the *mujtahids*, because of the contention of the rulers with them leading to sedition and anarchy, have abandoned sovereignty and the organ of the sword. Similarly the rulers, because of their inclination from the beginning of sovereignty toward the baser world—that is, mere worldly sovereignty consisting solely in the imposition of order in the world—have foregone the acquisition of the knowledge of religion and understanding of the prophetic matters, and have made do with the science of politics only. *Thus, the function of vicegerency inevitably became divided between the* culama' *and the rulers.*

Doubtless to stress the importance of maintaining the concord established between the hierocracy and the state in the contemporary reconstituted Shici polity, Kashfi continues his disquisition:

> In some ages, [the rulers and the *culama'*] cooperated with mutual consensus and ruled and directed the subjects through partnership and cooperation. . . . At other times, they became mutually antagonistic and parted from each other. Consequently religion and sovereignty, which must be conjoint, became separated from each other. The knowledge of the *culama'* and the endeavor of *muhtahids* became stagnant because of disorder. Similarly, the sovereignty of the rulers, because of its divorce from the upholding of religion and the traditions of the sacred law, became sheer sovereignty. The matter of politics and vicegerency . . . became disturbed, and both groups fell short of [discharging] the office of vicegerency.

After thus deriving his theory of the two powers from the doctrine of imamate (*pace* the Shici commentators on the Qur'an), Sayyid Jacfar is able to adduce the "authority verse" of the Qur'an as enjoining obedience to the just ruler.

Kashfi, a rationalist (*usuli*) jurist, had stated at the outset of the chapter that, as men left to themselves are *lupus lupendi*, they need a ruler. Obedience to this ruler is necessary to prevent anarchy, and therefore incumbent upon men according to the dictates of reason. He returns to the employment of "reason" (formally admitted by the Usuli school as a fourth basis for the validity of legal norms) in an original instance of *ijtihad* (deduction of legal norms) with the aim of deriving the legitimacy of political and hierocratic domination as differentiated instances of vicegerency of the Imam from the "sources" of sacred law.

Aqa Sayyid Jaᶜfar cites the tradition related by Ibn Hanzalah: "Look to him who is among you and has explored our 'lawful' and 'unlawful' and knows our commandments," as the basis of the *niyabat-i* ᶜ*amma* of the *mujtahids*, and proceeds with a consideration of ᶜAli's instructions to Malik al-Ashtar — the famous covenant (ᶜ*ahdnamih*) we have already mentioned — to derive a second category of *niyabah*. Malik is said to be the *na'ib khass* (specific deputy) and ᶜAli's delegation of authority to him sets the precedent for the *niyabat-i khassih*. It follows that

> in these times when "knowledge" and the "sword" have become separated from each other, and knowledge is lodged with the ᶜ*ulama'* and the *mujtahids* and the sword with the [political] leaders and the rulers, the instructions of the covenant which relate to the organ of knowledge and the conditions of the ᶜ*ulama'* regard the *mujtahids* and men of knowledge; and those which relate to the organ of the sword and the affair of sovereignty and politics and order regard the kings and rulers. As we have mentioned, the rulers who act according to those clauses [of the covenant] which relate to and regard them is of course the "specified deputy" [*na'ib-i khass*] of the Imam. Similarly, the *mujtahids* who act according to those clauses which relate to and regard them, of course they too are the "specified deputy" of the Imam. And this covenant is the proof of the "specified viceregency" [*niyabat-i khassa*] of these two groups of men.

Kashfi then reproduces the covenant (which, as words of the first Imam constitues a "source" of law in Twelver Shiᶜism) together with its Persian translation.

An important feature of Kashfi's political tract is the consistent and successful integration of the patrimonial theories of kingship, with a cursory mention of the phrase "shadow of God on earth" and copious emphasis on justice, "paternalism" (*abawiyyah*), and finally on charity. In fact, both explicitly and by clear implication, justice is made the condition of legitimacy of temporal rule and the qualification of the ruler for the "specified vicegerency" of the Imam.

Kashfi's theory does not invest the ruler with any hierocratic authority. He does put forward a novel and broad interpretation of the notion of "specified vicegerency," but only to provide religious legitimation for kingly rule as (differentiated) secular political domination. Differential hierocratic authority is said to devolve on the *mujtahids* through their collective office of "general vicegerency." Kashfi legitimizes just rulership as tantamount to the vicegerency of the Imam only in temporal matters. Thus, while Fathᶜali Shah's contemporary Nasir al-Din Haydar, the Shiᶜi king of Oudh, struck coins in 1830 bearing the inscription, "The Na'ib of Mahdi, Nasir al-Din, Haydar, the King . . ." the clear separation of the political and the religious spheres and the renunciation of the Safavid heritage in Qajar Iran precluded any such designation of the ruler. It should be pointed out, however, that, in practice the king did retain some of the Safavids' "caesaropapist" prerogatives regarding a number of important clerical appointments.

The importance of Kashfi's political theory cannot be exaggerated. It is a consistent synthesis of the traditional Persian theories of kingship and the Shi^ci doctrines of imamates and occultation. As such, it represents not only the removal of the anomalies of Safavid legitimacy but also the definitive reconciliation of the secular and the religious cultures of premodern Iran.

Temporal power, in turn, acknowledged the uncontested religious authority as the general viceregents of the Imam *and* their prerogative to legitimate temporal authority in that capacity. At the very outset of his reign, Fath-^cAli Shah sent money to the *^culama'* so that they would absolve the oppressive wrongdoings of the wielders of temporal authority (*radd-i mazalim*), and asserted that he was ruling on behalf of the *mujtahids* of the age.

We find Kashfi's dualistic theory of legitimate authority restated in the second half of the nineteenth century. For instance, the theory is set forth in an important letter to Nasir al-Din Shah (1848–96) written in 1873, by the influential *mujtahid* of Tehran, Mulla ^cAli Kani, who, upon his death in 1888/1306, was ceremoniously mourned by the population of the capital as the deceased "vicegerent [*na'ib*] of the Prophet." Denying all intention of stepping beyond the limits set to hierocratic authority by the prevalent consensus on the division of labor in the polity, Kani expressly upheld the theory of the two powers. Having asserted the unity of the offices or functions of "sovereignty" (*saltanah*) and "knowledge" (*^cilm*), i.e., of political and religious authority under the Prophet and the Imams, Kani turned to their separation during the "times of occultation." During the occultation, God has appointed a "vicegerent" (*na'ib*) for each of the Imam's functions or offices: the *^culama'*, as the embodiments of knowledge, as the vicegerents for the office of sovereignty, for the maintenance of law and order and for the protection of the subjects.

The theory of dual power during the occultation of the Imam is upheld by the foremost religious authority of the closing decade of the nineteenth century, Mirza Muhammad Hasan Shirazi. In response to the request to intervene in politics concerning the question of imported sugar, the Mirza restated this theory with an interesting nuance, using the terms *dawlah* (government) and *millah* (community) as the respective repositories of executive and religious authority:

> In the ages when government [*dawlat*] and community [*millat*] were established in one place, as at the time of the Seal of the Prophets, political duties regarding this kind of general affairs [*umur ^camma*] were

entrusted to that same person. Now that according to the requirements
of divine wisdom each is found in a separate place, it is upon both these
[powers] to aid each other in protecting the religion and worldly interests [*din va dunya*] of the servants of God and the safeguarding of the
citadel of Islam [*bayda-i Islam*] during the occultation of the Lord of
Time.

However, the theory of the two powers was not legally binding for the
members of the hierocracy. The Shi^{c}i sacred law was a "jurists' law" to be
interpreted in each and every case by the independent *mujtahid*: Especially
in view of the tremendous enhancement of hierocratic domination, there
was nothing other than pious indifference to political power to prevent the
individual doctors from putting forward a variety of more or less preten-
tious or more or less realistic claims. In interpreting the extent of the
authority of their collective office of vicegerency, the doctors arrogated to
themselves the power of making clean the goods and property wrongfully
acquired by the ruler and his officials as well as private individuals in exchange for receiving the booty tax (*khums*), rent (on inadvertently usurped
property), and alms. Nevertheless, because it successfully reconciles the
ethos of patrimonial kingship and the political ethic of Twelver Shi^{c}ism and
because it adequately reflects the institutional division of authority between
the state and the hierocracy, Kashfi's political theory can be taken to represent the unified normative order that governed the relations of authority of
the Qajar body politic.

To conclude our survey of Shi^{c}i political theory [in this period], the king remained, as he had always been, the shadow of God on earth or his shadow on
the temporal world, while the designation "vicegerent of the Imam" and the uncontested religious authority of the most eminent of the *mujtahids* was fully
acknowledged by the official spokesman for the royal court in the latter
part of the century. There was little change in the notion of the king as the
shadow of God on earth, but with Kashfi we do find a more thoroughly
consistent legitimation of kingship as secular rule on the part of the
hierocracy. The posture of the hierocracy toward the legitimated temporal
ruler continued to be what had been affirmed by Majlisi two centuries
earlier. Throughout the nineteenth century, *du^{c}a-gu'i* or praying for the
preservation of the king, who, against the background of European imperialist encroachments, came more emphatically to be referred to as the
padishah-i Islam (king of Islam) or the "*padishah* [king] of the Shi^{c}i
nation," remained the self-defined function of politically active members of
the hierocracy, including those who led the nationalist opposition movement in the closing decade of the nineteenth century. Both sides thus recog-

nized and reaffirmed the prevailing division of political and hierocratic authority in Iran's definitively reconstituted Shiᶜi polity.

* * *

Once the objections to *ijtihad* had been overruled and the practice of *ijtihad* taken for granted, the *mujtahids* could then proceed, as they in fact did, to claim the *niyabat-i ᶜammah* (general vicegerency) of the Imam on its basis. Furthermore, the obligation of the believer to observe the sacred law was of course given. As Scarcia has remarked, in the Shiᶜi legal system the layman cannot understand the code, and needs the help of a jurist to determine the binding legal norm. The incumbency of the observance of the sacred law in fact necessitated recourse to its authoritative interpreters. Thus, in his *Awa'id al-ayyam*, Mulla Ahmad Naraqi (d. 1828–29) would rule on the "incumbency of following upon the common man [ᶜammi]". In the same work he adduces a number of traditions to establish the general vicegerency of the jurists, using the term *wilayah* to denote the latter's delegated authority on behalf of the Hidden Imam during the occultation [see Chapter Nineteen in this book—Eds.]. But perhaps the most influential and concise discussion of the concept is found in the *Jawahir al-kalam* of Shaykh Muhammad Hasan Najafi (d. 1850/1266). Shaykh Muhammad Hasan adduces the traditions of Ibn Hanzalah and of Abu Khadijah and the ordinance handed down by the Hidden Imam to affirm and establish the general or collective authority (*wilayah ᶜamma*) of the Shiᶜi jurists on behalf of the Hidden Imam by virtue of their knowledge of the commandments of the sacred law and the methods of deriving them. The authority of the hierocracy is said to extend to every field except where the Imams knew of its inability to exercise authority, such as in a *jihad* for the propagation of faith, which would require a commander and armies, and like matters that would necessitate the appearance of the rightful reign (of the Imam; *dawlat al-haqq*).

The world-embracing aspect of the rationalism of the early phase of the Usuli movement in the first decades of the nineteenth century was reflected in the formal elevation of reason into a "proof" of validity of legal norms, and the formal qualification of such proofs as the "four proofs" (*adilla*). Reason was exercised more freely in the creation of norms in the early than in the later phase. The category *hukm ᶜaqli mustaqil* (independent rational norm) recognized as valid by the Usuli jurists was referred to by Kashfi in his aforementioned political treatise. Another case of exercise of *ijtihad* which was intended to increase the impingement of the Shiᶜi religion upon "the world" and had momentous consequences was Sayyid Muhammad Baqir Shafti's (d. 1844/1260) treatise on "the incumbency of the implementa-

tion of the *hudud* upon the *mujtahids* during the occultation of the Imam."
Shafti thus diverged from the *Jamiᶜ ᶜAbbasi's* cautious justification of the
implementation of the *hudud* in general, and, even more sharply, from its
prohibition of their implementation in cases requiring capital punishment.
Furthermore, to set an example, he himself proceeded to implement the
hudud vigorously, and is said to have executed some seventy persons. Thus
the abeyance of *hudud* according to the sacred law, bemoaned by our
sixteenth-century polemicists, ceased to be the case, in Isfahan at any rate.
Though the other *mujtahids* did not follow Shafti in this particular respect,
his legal writings, as well as those of Shaykh Muhammad Hasan Najafi a
generation later, were indicative of a much more positive attitude of the *mujtahids* toward the administration of law.

In fact, in this phase, the Usuli movement made not only theoretical jurisprudence but its application a very important component of the activity of
religious professionals. The courts of the *mujtahids* and other prominent
members of the hierocracy such as the *shaykh al-Islam* and the *imam-jumᶜah*
enjoyed an unprecedented level of activity, eclipsing totally the courts of the
qadis, whose offices, in the course of the century, turned into sinecures or
went out of existence. The virtual disappearance of state-appointed *qadis*
represented yet another change away from the Safavid "caesaropapist" constitution in the direction of a sharper bifurcation between the state and the
hierocracy. This trend was encouraged by Fath-ᶜAli Shah, who personally
referred cases to the courts of the eminent *mujtahids*. Though the ᶜurf
jurisdiction, with its typical patrimonial features (such as the lack of clear
differentiation between administration and adjudication and the king's
prerogative of passing death sentences) remained very widespread, the
religious courts reached the peak of their importance in Iran's judiciary
organization.

Thus, in the reconstituted Shiᶜi polity of Fath-ᶜAli Shah, the hierocracy
found an enlarged role in the administration of justice much more congruent with the legal authority they were entitled to according to Twelver
Shiᶜism than had been the case under the Safavids. In this respect, too, the
institutional translation of the Shiᶜi religious system reached its furthest point.

*   *   *

The creation of a unified normative order regulating political and hierocratic domination of course did not eliminate conflicts between the
hierocracy and the state but rather established the framework within which
these conflicts would be played out, along with much cooperation.

As we have seen in Max Weber's discussion of institutionalization of
charisma, one finds two basic types of charisma whose antagonism he con-

siders primeval: the political and the religious, as prototypically embodied in the warlord and the divinely inspired. Weber's juxtaposed and analogous definitions of ruling organization/hierocratic organization and state/church replicate this dichotomy at the organizational level. After the fall of the Safavid dynasty, whose rulers enjoyed a caesaropapist admixture of political and religious authority, religious charisma came to reside exclusively with the men of religion. With the separation of political and hierocratic domination under the Qajars, political and religious charisma in institutionalized form could, and in the instance to be described did, face each other in stark mutual antithesis.

Sayyid Muhammad Baqir Shafti (d. 1844/1260), whose insistence on the administration of the Sacred Law during the occultation of the Imam has already been noted, was undoubtedly the most powerful — and the wealthiest — of the Shiᶜi ᶜulama' residing in Iran after the death of Mirza Abu'l-Qasim Qumi. He is probably the first religious dignitary to be given the title of *hujjat al-Islam* (proof of Islam). He never visited any of the governors of Isfahan, and would receive them with utmost disdain. He would pay visits to the king whenever he was in Isfahan, but even then with much arrogance. When he was taken to visit Fath-ᶜAli Shah for the first time, the king granted him the usual favor of making a request. The "proof of Islam" saw this as an opportunity to remind the earthly ruler of the antithesis of divine and worldly charisma which they respectively represented. He asked that the royal *naqarih-khanih* (music house), indispensable for ceremonial regal pomp, be banned. The king remained silent, and the point was not lost on him. When the Sayyid left, he marveled at how he could have dared to ask for the banning of the "royal *naqarih-khanih* which is the insignia of kingship."

The stark opposition between the two forms of charisma was brought out much more clearly in Shafti's encounters with Muhammad Shah. When riding on a mule on his way to visit the king, Shafti, the "proof of Islam," had a cantor walk in front of him reciting the Qur'an. As they approached the royal residence, surrounded by a crowd kissing Shafti's hands, his mule, and the mule's hooves, he ordered the cantor to recite the verse, "We sent a Prophet to the Pharoah [the symbol of worldly despotism] and the Pharoah rebelled against the Prophet." When returning his call, Muhammad Shah made the *naqarih* precede him with ceremonious pomp. Shafti was coming to the gates of his house to welcome the king, but, "upon hearing the sound of the *naqarih*, he raised his hands toward the sky and implored: 'Oh God, do not wish the humiliation of the descendants of Fatimah the Radiant (the daughter of the Prophet) any more!' and returned to his house."

Needless to say, there was no need for constant expression of this potential antagonism between political and religious charisma, which in fact remained completely latent, allowing much cooperation between the hierocracy and the state. It is important to note that this cooperation was even extended to the political sphere proper: one can cite numerous instances of the ᶜulama's intercession in internal political disputes and in its diplomatic relations with the Ottoman Empire. The Shiᶜi religious dignitaries residing in the holy cities of Iraq often mediated between the Qajars and the Ottoman governors of Arab Iraq in order to settle important disputes.

The tension between the hierocracy and the state reached its highest point under Muhammad Shah. The tension was provoked by Muhammad Shah's Sufism and his anticlerical attitude. Owing to the fact that the hierocracy, though formally acephalous, was dominated by Shafti and a handful of other *mujtahids*, hierocratic opposition to the state became polarized. However, the tension between the hierocracy and the state abated during the long reign of the subsequent monarch, Nasir al-Din (1848–96), until it suddenly flared up in the last decade of the nineteenth century.

* * *

Kashfi had stressed that the king needed the ᶜulama' and the ᶜulama' needed the king. In the second half of the nineteenth century, the dependence of the ᶜulama' on the king became considerably greater.

A crucially important fact that has not been noted in the literature is the massive increase in the number of *mujtahids* in the second half of the nineteenth century. In the second half of the seventeenth century, Chardin had remarked that the *mujtahids* were very few. Writing during the second decade of the nineteenth century, Malcolm stated: "There are seldom more than three or four mooshtaheds." The total number of *mujtahids* in the first four decades of the nineteenth century was certainly less than a dozen. Let us compare this period with the first forty years of Nasir al-Din Shah's reign (1848–88). Nearly one-half of the 359 noteworthy ᶜulama' of the period mentioned by Iᶜtimad al-Saltanah in *al-Ma'athir wa'l-athar*, or some 175 persons, are, either explicitly or by inference, classifiable as *mujtahid*. At the end of the nineteenth century, the inflation of the rank of *mujtahids* got worse. A single scholar, the famous Akhund Khurasani is said by a careful author to have trained at least 120 "definitive" (*musallam*) *mujtahids*. The title of *hujjat al-Islam*, "proof of Islam," too, having been conferred upon an eminent *mujtahid* of Kashan after Shafti, depreciated very sharply thereafter.

Its rapid growth during the second half of the century gave the hierarchy of deference a very large undifferentiated sector. To this upper sector of the hierocracy was appended a group of non-*mujtahids*, who owed their prestige to their offices. This latter group consisted of *shaykh al-Islam*s and *imam jum^cah*s, appointed by the government, directors and professors of the seminaries, and finally prayer leaders of the mosques. There were no organizational links between the holders of these offices and the *mujtahids*, their overlapping relationship being determined by their respective position in the hierarchy of deference.

The absence of any hierarchical organization had a number of important consequences. The clearly defined and sharply stratified hierarchy of deference was incapable of generating action, or of controlling the individual members and disciplining them as a unified organization and in consistent pursuit of doctrinal and institutional interests. The incipient modernization of the state in the second half of the nineteenth century entailed actual and planned encroachments upon the judiciary prerogatives of the ^culama' and upon their control over the *awqaf*, and thus threatened their institutional vested interests. Yet the Shi^ci hierocracy did not react as an institution, and many of its members continued to display accommodating docility toward the government. As an organization, the hierocracy was poorly isolated from its sociopolitical environment and was therefore permeable by environmental forces. The forces of its political environment, extraneous factors emanating from the interests of the state or of social groups, could easily impinge upon the action of the hierocracy or prevent such action from being initiated. Let us illustrate the point with an important example. Until the 1880s, Nasir al-Din Shah's public behavior was decorous from the religious point of view. The new year (*nowruz*) royal audience in 1881, for instance, was marked by the presence of the most respected *mujtahids* of the capital. From 1885 onwards, the aging monarch's rampant pedarastic proclivities filled the new year royal audiences with young children donning the mantles of the highest officials of the state. Nasir al-Din's love for his favorite, Malijak II, became increasingly engrossing and scandalous. We hear of the people grumbling profusely, but not the hierocracy. On the contrary, some of the most eminent *mujtahids* of Tehran unmistakably condoned the immorality of the shah and his debauched prime minister, Amin al-Sultan, who was the object of their constant flattery. It was only with the advent of a countervailing extraneous factor in the form of the agitation of the reformers and the merchants opposed to autocracy in general and to injurious concessions to foreign entrepreneus, and at the direct instigation of the famous advocate of reform, Afghani, that the hierocracy received the decisive impetus to speak out against the ruler as the custodian of religion and morality. It was only then that the king's pederasty and the journey of the harem favorite, a Muslim woman, to Europe for an eye operation would be publicly denounced, and the cries of "Woe to religion, woes to the sacred law" be raised from the pulpits of the important mosques.

In contrast to the inability of the Shi^ci hierocracy to initiate institutionalized action in pursuit of its institutional and doctrinal interests, the absence of an authoritative hierarchy and of disciplinary procedures meant that the *^culama'* could engage in politics in pursuit of personal gain with complete immunity. Paradoxically, their engagement in politics, institutionalized as their crucial role of mediation and intercession in political conflict, was premised on their material disinterestedness. However, against the background of a "push" factor consisting of the immense growth in the number of *^culama'* and intensified competition for the control of *awqaf*, professorships and directorships of schools, as well as the offices of *imam jum^cah* and *shaykh al-Islam*, and the "pull" factor of the spoils to be gained in the highly factionalized late Qajar period, the involvement of the *^culama'* in pursuit of personal interests and material gain became extremely common. For instance, they frequently acted as political brokers to secure appointments of local governors and state officials and often engaged in the hoarding of grain in collusion with the latter.

Consequently, the age-old rift between the worldly *^culama'* and those who upheld the ideal of pious aloofness to all political involvement was sharpened. The former group as a rule showed little hesitation in using their hierocratic domination over the masses as an asset to enter the political arena in pursuit of material gain with the help of the state, in exchange for which they were on occasion ready to act as the legitimators of Qajar rule by praying for its glory (*du^ca-gu'i*) and cooperating with the ruler. Those who did not tended to uphold the attitude of pious distrust of politics, and withdrew from all entanglements with the earthly powers into religious scholarship in the holy centers of Arab Iraq.

Alongside the organizational amorphousness of the hierocracy and the massive growth of its upper section, a contrary trend toward stratification at the apex of the hierocracy—and only at the apex—had set in. Already in the first half of the century, Fath-^cAli Shah had been greatly displeased to see a loaded elephant carrying the "share of the Imam" from his Shi^ci followers in India to Shafti, the "proof of Islam." Shaykh Murtada Ansari, emerging as the vicegerent of the Imam in the subsequent period, is said to have received some 200,000 *tumans* annually on behalf of the Imam. In this manner, especially with the improved channels of communication in the second half of the nineteenth century, what amounted to the designation of the vicegerents of the Imam by the Shi^ci community through payment of their religious taxes, worked indirectly to stratify the Shi^ci hierarchy at the very highest level. The acephaly of the Shi^ci hierocracy, which was a feature of the first half of the nineteenth century, came to an end. Mirza Muhammad Hasan Shirazi (d. 1895/1312) in due course succeeded Ansari as the vicegerent of the Imam. This development enhanced the capacity of the head of the hierocracy to mobilize mass action in situaitons of national crisis, even though the plethora of independent *mujtahids* precluded unified routine action by the religious institution.

* * *

The confrontation between Muhammad Shah and Shafti belongs to the period in which the tension between the hierocracy and the state reached its highest point. Owing to the fact that the hierocracy, though formally acephalous, was dominated by Shafti and a handful of other *mujtahids* in this period, hierocratic opposition to the state became polarized and led to serious disturbances in Isfahan and Shiraz in 1839–40. However, the state was victorious. Muhammad Shah himself put down these disturbances in 1840, and humbled Shafti and the *mujtahid* of Shiraz.

The tension between the hierocracy and the state remained high during the first years of the reign of Nasir al-Din Shah (1848–96), whose first prime minister, Amir Kabir, immediately embarked on a policy of strengthening the central government. But the tension abated in the 1850s as a result of judicious gestures by the young monarch. The hierocracy–state relationship remained reasonable for some four decades until a critical conflict between the two suddenly flared up in the last decade of the nineteenth century. Throughout this period the state was very much the dominant partner in the dual polity. The hierocracy remained cooperative, and many of its members established close ties with the Qajar political elite.

Nevertheless, at least in one respect the rift under Muhammad Shah was never repaired: the Shiʿi hierocracy lost its role as the legitimator of the monarchy. By some curious coincidence, the reign of Muhammad Shah, which marked the sharp rift between the Qajar state and the Shiʿi hierocracy, also marked the beginning of a keener interest in the pre-Islamic imperial past, an interest that was to reach its culmination under the Pahlavis. It was to Muhammad Shah that Sir Henry Rawlinson presented the first Persian translation of the inscriptions on Bisutun, and it was one of Muhammad Shah's sons who wrote a history of ancient Iran after centuries of relative neglect. Whether for this or for other reasons, the state no longer sought any formal legitimatory action from the hierocracy. Beyond the cessation of this legitimacy function, the rift between the hierocracy and the state would not become critical so long as the attempts at centralization and modernization of the state remained feeble and largely ineffective, as they did in the nineteenth century. (The rift was to become critical and irreparable only in the twentieth century with the effective measures toward centralization and modernization of the state under the Pahlavis.)

Toward the end of his reign, alarmed by the spread of Western political ideas, especially by what he referred to as "nihilism," Nasir al-Din Shah did seek religious legitimation for monarchical rule, and a number of treatises were produced. One such treatise by Hajj Muhammad Na'ini emphasized the "incumbency of monarchy" and the incumbency of working for government along the lines of al-Murtada's political ethic. One clerical author went too far, claiming that the "authority verse" of the Qur'an referred to the king, and consequently incurred excommunication from other members of the hierocracy.

Another legacy of Muhammad Shah's period is worth mentioning in this connection: the persistence of Sufism in the courtly circles, among the literate strata in the capital, and in one or two other cities, notably Shiraz. Considering the capital a safer refuge "for a group like us," especially under Nasir al-Din Shah, Safi-ᶜAli Shah of Isfahan (d. 1899/1316), the guide of the Niᶜmatullahi order, moved to Tehran and spent over two decades in the gradual cultivation of "high" Sufism and gnosis among a select circle of literati. It is therefore not surprising to find a Sufi amongst the latter-day legitimators of monarchy. Mirza Muhammad Zu'l-Riyasatayn (d. ca. 1894–95/1312), in a treatise on the "incumbency of praying for the king," written to allay criticisms of Nasir al-Din's wasteful trips to Europe and the extravagant favors he bestowed upon the male harem favorite, ᶜAziz al-Sultan, takes on the ᶜulama''s traditional function of *duᶜa-gu'i* (praying for the king). He is cautious in saying that "according to one interpretation" the "authority verse" refers to the king, but categorical in stating that the king is appointed by the Imam, peace be upon him, the Lord of Time. Praying for the king is an incumbent duty, especially upon the ᶜulama', who can propagate religion and learning in the peace and security provided by him, and especially in the light of the king's respect for the sacred law and its interpreters, those in the clerical garb.

To conclude, despite the cooperation of individual clerics, Nasir al-Din's solicitaiton of legitimation met with a somewhat lukewarm response from the Shiᶜi hierocracy, which was no longer accustomed to performing the legitimatory function, and was increasingly alienated from the state and increasingly reliant on the people, by now massively opposed to it.

Hamid Algar

The Constitutional Revolution appears as the culmination of a long period of conflict between the state and the *culama'*. This conflict was perhaps inevitable, given the functions assigned by Shici Islam to the *culama'* and its refusal to provide that state with any theoretical justification, to allot it a place in the system of belief. The resultant tension between clerical and secular authority received growing expression throughout the century. Whether this constituted an irreversible process or not, events almost continually reinforced the basic alienation and turned theoretical contradiction into open conflict.

The rise of Qajar rule had coincided with a reassertion of Shici theological technique, and this reassertion placed heavy emphasis on the functions and duties of the *culama'*. The condition of Iran under the first Qajar monarch, Agha Muhammad Khan Qajar, was still too unsettled to permit any widespread manifestation of clerical influence, but the relative order and security provided by Qajar administration established the environment in which the *culama'* were to fulfill their role.

By the end of the reign of Fath-cAli Shah, many of the themes repeated in relations between the state and the *culama'* later in the Qajar period had already found express. The monarch, motivated both by personal piety and considerations of policy, sought an accommodation with clerical power. The tyranny of the state he ruled, however, was ultimately irreconcilable with his protestations of devotion to the *culama'*, and on many occasions the contradiction became apparent. Fath-cAli Shah's concern to restrict its scope was able to achieve no more than a temporary truce. Russian aggression against Iran, taking place during his reign, evoked a powerful response from the *culama'*, and their function as national leaders — possibly self-appointed, but also popularly approved in the face of both internal tyranny and foreign encroachment became established.

Muhammad Shah, with his attachment to Sufism, made no attempt to secure any kind of a working relationship with the *culama'*, and as a result their hostility to the state, partially restrained by the policies of his predecessor, became more explicit.

It was in the long reign of Nasir al-Din Shah that this hostility, with all its ramifications, began to cast a constant shadow over the affairs of Iran. The piety of the monarch was effusive, but not of a kind likely to impress the *culama'*. Moreover, tentative attempts at reform which would strengthen the state, undertaken by Amir Kabir, Mirza Husayn Khan Sipahsalar, and others, threatened the *culama'* with a reduction of their powers and prerogatives. The question of reform was also linked with that of foreign influence, and the predominant hostility of the *culama'*s reaction inevitable.

As Nasir al-Din Shah abandoned all serious attempts at reform, the growing corruption and extravagance of the court led to the necessity for foreign loans, and thus invited the establishment of foreign economic influence in Iran. This was bound to be resisted by the *culama'* as much as Russian expansionism in the Caucasus earlier in the century. At the same time, thoughts of reform were taken up by other elements in opposition to the state, with these the *culama'* found themselves in uneasy and temporary alliance.

The outcome of this alliance was the movement of 1905–06 culminating in the establishment of a consultative assembly. In these events, the *culama'* not only gave the greatest display of their political power, but also effectively ended their previous role as principal leaders and organizers of resistance to the state.

The role fulfilled by the *culama'* throughout the period from 1785 to 1905 was fairly constant, both in inspiration and mode of expression. In conclusion, a qualitative judgment on the nature of that role and its effectiveness may be hazarded. In the attainment of immediate political aims, the *culama'* were frequently successful. Yet while specific causes might give rise to much determination and courage, ability to foresee consequences and even concern for secondary results were all too often lacking. This is seen clearly in the agitation leading to the Perso-Russian War of 1826–28, which ended disastrously for Iran with military humiliation and territorial losses. Similarly, the campaign led by the *culama'* in 1891 against the tobacco monopoly resulted in the repeal of the obnoxious concession, but also ended in Iran's taking up the burden of foreign debt in order to pay compensation. We have spoken of the *culama'* as leaders of political opposition, and this indeed they were. Throughout the period of our concern (and still more later) they allied themselves, however, with various groups and interests, and when their alliance was with "liberal" reformers in the early stages of the constitutional movement, they failed to perceive the nature of what was being demanded and its implications for Iran and themselves.

Above all, they failed to provide any real answer to the manifold problems — political, social, economic — facing Iran in the second half of the nineteenth century, as a result of its own stagnation and the impact of the West. *Ijtihad* was on the whole used narrowly, in a strictly legalistic sense; its genuine potentialities, much vaunted by a few reformers, were seldom activated with honesty or perceptiveness. The Prophet is reputed to have said: "The ᶜulama' of my community are as the Prophets of the Children of Israel." The ᶜulama' of Qajar Iran failed to exert the comprehensive and assured leadership thus demanding of them.

Yet perhaps it would be altogether wrong to expect so high an achievement from the ᶜulama'. Their traditional preoccupations and the scholastic nature of the learning that was the basis of their entire function hardly permitted accurate comprehension of problems deriving from the Western impact. In addition, their essential lack of hierarchic organization would have been an obstacle to any active reshaping of the political structure. Most important, while the Qajar dynasty possessed no legitimizing authority, the ᶜulama' enjoyed only that conferred by the process of *taqlid*, one for which no adequate machinery was ever established. Intervention in political affairs to gain permanent control thereof never appears to have been even a distant aim of the ᶜulama'. The continued occultation of the Imam meant, inescapably, the absence of all legitimizing authority from worldly affairs, so that the political attitudes of the ᶜulama' could, in the final analysis, be only quietism or opposition. Any wish to reshape definitively the norms of political life and the bases of the state was foreign to the ᶜulama' in Qajar Iran. Thus it was that the forces of renewal passed them by.*

---

*Algar also provides an illuminating example of the confrontations between the ᶜulama' and Qajar Statemen. Here, two well-known clergymen, Bihbahani and Tabataba'i express their grievances against the Qajar prime minister ᶜAyn al-Dawlah.

Although in all these incidents, an element of planning, and of cooperation, both among the ᶜulama' themselves, and between the ᶜulama' and the merchants is discernible, conscious preparation for the overthrow of ᶜAyn al-Dawlah and for the achievement of more far-reaching aims appears to have begun only with the alliance between Sayyid ᶜAbdullah Bihbihani and Sayyid Muhammad Tabataba'i founded on Ramadan 25, 1323/November 23, 1905. The motives of the two men, and the nature of the plans they agreed upon, will be discussed below; here it is enough to note the importance of the event. The historian Kasravi considers it to mark the beginning of the Constitutional Revolution. The leadership of the movement, at least outwardly, was to be provided by these two men, in particular the latter, and the large popular following their prestige commanded was a force considerable enough to arouse fear in the government and readiness to submit to the ᶜulama' demands. Around them centered the later agitation during the emigrations to Shah ᶜAbdul-ᶜAzim and Qum, and also the attempts of ᶜAyn al-Dawlah to suppress the constitutional movement.

The first visible product of their alliance was the destruction of the new building of the Russian Bank in Tehran. A plot of land, occupied by the ruins of a *madrasah* (Madrasah-i Chal) which had been turned into a coal depot, and by a disused graveyard, had been selected by the officials of the Russian Bank for the erection of a new headquarters. The land being *waqf* the agreement of the *ᶜulama'* was necessary for its disposal. Certain parts had already been sold (as conducive to the improvement of the *waqf*: *tabdil ba ahsan*), but Tabataba'i refused to give his consent to the plans of the Russian Bank. Shaykh Fadlullah Nuri, on the other hand, agreed to the sale of the land in question for a sum of 750 *tumans*. The opposition to ᶜAyn al-Dawlah, centered on Bihbihani and Tabataba'i, saw in the affair a means of striking a blow both against him and against his principal clerical supporter. Their plans were put into execution by Mirza Mustafa Ashtiyani, who had under his control the Madrasah-i Khazin al-Mulk, situated opposite the disputed site. Toward the end of Ramadan, a suitable pretext offered itself for an attack on the half-finished structure of the Russian Bank. In the course of the building, a number of corpses that secretly been buried in the disused graveyard during the cholera epidemic of the previous year, were discovered by the workers, and disposed of down a well. Arousing anger at this lighthearted treatment of the dead, Mirza Mustafa was able to persuade a mob (among them his own *tullab*) to attack and destroy the half-completed buildling. Here again, we observe the use of a well-chosen, expressive pretext to arouse agitation against the government: religious feelings were shown to be affronted, and the government to be associated with the foreigners who behaved thus insultingly.

If the *ᶜulama'* were thus diligent in their search for pretexts, ᶜAyn al-Dawlah for his part seems to have been almost eager to supply them. The beating given to some of the merchants of Tehran on *Shawwal* 14, 1323/ December 12, 1905, started the chain of events that culminated in the issue of the decree granting the constitution. Various circumstances, notably the disruption of the Russian economy by wars with Japan, had caused a rise in the price of sugar, and using this as pretext, ᶜAyn al-Dawlah decided to punish the merchants of Tehran for their protests against his policies, and at the same time to intimidate the *ᶜulama'* allied to them. A number of merchants, not all concerned with the sale of sugar, were summoned by ᶜAla al-Dawlah, governor of Tehran, and bastinadoed in his presence. Far from intimidating the *ᶜulama'*, however, ᶜAyn al-Dawlah provided them with the final pretext for conducting open agitation. As the news of the bastinadoing became known, the people of Tehran, led by the *ᶜulama'*, gathered in the Masjid-i Shah to protest. Mirza Abu'l-Qasim Imam Jumᶜah attended the meeting, but only in order to carry out the wishes of ᶜAyn al-Dawlah. He insisted on Sayyid Jamal al-Din Waᶜiz mountain the *minbar* to address the crowd. Then, interrupting the Sayyid's speech at a certain point, the Imam Jumᶜah gave a signal to his followers scattered among the crowd, who began to create panic, and finally the meeting dissolved in chaos. This use of force by ᶜAyn al-Dawlah against the *ᶜulama'* was to characterize his policy throughout the agitation. His attempted use of bribery to bring about dissension among the *ᶜulama'* largely failed, and no way remained to oppose the *ᶜulama'* demands except that of force. By thus provoking the mass emigration of the *ᶜulama'* from Tehran, he succeeded only in giving the movement greater momentum. Their withdrawal from the capital was a symbolic demonstration of the illegitimacy of the government, clear enough to be acted upon and understood by the people of Tehran.

After the dispersal of the first meeting in the Masjid-i Shah, the *ᶜulama'* decided, at the suggestion of Sayyid Tabataba'i, to leave Tehran for the security offered by Shah ᶜAbdul-ᶜAzim. Here they formulated their demands to be submitted to Muzaffar al-Din Shah. The precise nature of these demands is crucial for the whole question of the participation of the *ᶜulama'* in the constitutional movement, yet cannot be determined with certainty. Up to now, we have seen little more than a clerical movement against the government, comparable with many earlier ones; no demand for a representative form of government had been voiced. Among the demands presented to the Shah, in the name of the *ᶜulama'*, was, however, one for the foundation of a "house of justice" (*ᶜadalatkhana*). It is not clear that this demand emanated in fact from the *ᶜulama'*. The secret societies working for the establishment of a constitutional regime had decided to establish contact with the *ᶜulama'* in Shah ᶜAbdul-ᶜAzim, and the brother of Yahya Dawlatabadi was dispatched to receive from them the list of their demands. According to Dawlatabadi, the list did not contain any mention of the *ᶜadalatkhanah*, and he took it upon himself to add this item before forwarding it to Shams al-Din Biy, the Ottoman ambassador, for presentation to Muzaffar al-Din Shah. The account given by Nazim al-Islam Kirmani, himself active in the secret societies, confirms Dawlatabadi's claim, adding that the *ᶜulama'* had intended to include the demand for an *ᶜadalatkhanah* in their petition, but forgot to do so. Such forgetfulness appears highly improbable. It is on the other hand possible than the *ᶜulama'*, or their leaders, while intending to demand a constitution, did not yet think the time ripe, and that the secret societies wished to force them to move more quickly than they thought wise . . . .

Doubts about the real nature of the *ᶜulama'*s intentions were evidently widespread and resulted in pressure being exerted on them from various directions. ᶜAyn al-Dawlah sent emissaries to Shah ᶜAbdul-ᶜAzim to attempt to divide the leadership of the ^c*ulama'*. On Zu'l-Qa^cdah 14, 1323/ January 12, 1906, four of their number were delegated to discuss their demands with ^cAyn al-Dawlah in Tehran; whether their prolonged stay in his residence was voluntary or compulsory is not clear. At the same time, many of the tullab at Shah ^cAbdul-^cAzim attempted to dissuade Bihibihani and Tabataba'i from returning to Tehran. After Muzaffar al-Din Shah had accepted in principle the demand for an ^c*adalatkhanah*, on Zu'l-Qa^cdah 16/January 14, they decided, however, to return and were met in the capital with popular rejoicing.

Chapter Thirteen

The Pahlavi Era

The half century of Pahlavi rule in Iran was probably one of the most dynamic periods of Shiᶜi history, both intellectually and politically. A plethora of works on philosophy and theology came out of Qum, Mashhad, and Tehran. Shiᶜi political thought was transformed by a number of ᶜulama' from its spirit of quiescent dissent to an active contention for power. At the end of this period, the works of Ayatollah Khumayni chartered a new course for Shiᶜism in politics, while the writings of ᶜAli Shariᶜati made Shiᶜism a major force for social change in Iran.

Modern Shiᶜi political thought will be examined later in the final section of this volume under Shiᶜism in the modern world. Here, we shall concentrate only on the interactions between the ᶜulama' and the Pahlavi state, which lay at the root of the political developments of Shiᶜism in recent years. Shahrough Akhavi and Said Amir Arjomand explain the pattern as well as the outcome of interactions between the Shiᶜi clerical establishment of Iran and the two Pahlavi Shahs. The excerpts are from RPICSRPP, pages 28–31, 58-59; SSTPRIH, pages 172-81; and TTI, pages 221-31, respectively.

Shahrough Akhavi

After becoming Prime Minister but before his coronation as Shah (i.e., between October 1923 and December 1925), Rida Khan pursued a policy of alliance with the *culama'* which bore fruit for his own career. By 1920 the British were prepared to impose a League of Nations mandate over Iraq. However, upon reconsideration produced by the widespread internal rebellion in that year, it was decided that the establishment of a monarchy, a limited form of constitutional government and an alliance with the United Kingdom would better serve the purpose. The preparations for elections to the parliament precipitated a crisis with the Iranian *culama'* in the *catabat*. Led by Isfahani and Na'ini the religious leadership condemned the elections, and the two *marajic* issued *fatwas* forbidding participation in them by the masses. This created a direct confrontation between the *culama'* and the British, who thereupon ordered the departure of the former. As mentioned Isfahani and Na'ini made their way to Qum, where they arrived in August 1923.

Their residence in Iran engendered competition between the ruling monarch, Ahmad Shah, and Rida Khan. Each, on different occasions, visited Qum and paid his respects to the *marajic*. They, for their part, tried to persuade the Shah and the Prime Minister to conduct *jihad* against Britain. While holy war stood in first order of priority for the *culama'*, keeping the exiled *mujtahids* in Iran until after the elections in Iraq represented the chief British objective. Between these two demands, Ahmad Shah and Rida Khan jockied to gain the confidence of both the clergy and the British. Both political figures needed the *culama'* as allies. Yet, neither could afford to antagonize the British. It was in this context that ideas of republicanism began to take shape, as the Iranian language press outside the country (notably, *al-Habl al-Matin* from Calcutta and *Iranshahr* from Berlin) and some internal publications began to agitate for a secular state.

Now, the *culama'*'s position seemed to be that the monarchy should be preserved on grounds that it was the most suitable form of government for Iran. It was impossible to overlook the connection between republicanism and Western political development; this undoubtedly comprised an important factor in the calculation of the Iranian religious leadership. True, Islam does not demand monarchy; indeed, the tragedies that befell the early *Shici* have been explained by its leaders in terms of the corruptive effects of the Umayyad dynasty. Yet, the seeds of doubt as to what republicanism held out for the future of religion in Iran were too firmly embedded in the clerical consciousness to permit a cool-headed appraisal of its merits.

Since Rida Khan was strongly suspected of harboring republican views and intent on leading the country along the path of Kemalist Turkey, Ahmad Shah tried to capitalize on the ᶜulama's fears of Kemalism. He promised them a speedy end to the humiliation inflicted on the Shiᶜi *mujtahids*. If Rida Khan had, for his part, been at all interested in republicanism, he now gave to believe the opposite and took action to imprint this orientation in the public consciousness. Thus, he journeyed to Qum and met with Ayatollahs Ha'iri, Na'ini and Isfahani. These individuals thereupon sent a telegram to the ᶜulama' of Tehran stating the collapse of the republican idea:

> There have been expressed certain ideas concerning a republican form of government which are not to the satisfaction of the masses and inappropriate to the needs of the country. Thus, when His Excellency, the Prime Minister . . . came to Qum . . . to say goodbye [to the exiled *mujtahids*], we requested the elimination of this rubric [of republicanism], the abolition of the above-mentioned expressed ideas and the proclamation of this to the whole country. He has accepted this. May God grant that all people appreciate the extent of this act and give full thanks for this concern.

For his part, Rida Khan issued the following proclamation in response to the wishes of the three leaders of Shiᶜism:

> It has become clear from experience that the leaders of the government must never oppose or contradict the ideas of the public, and it is in keeping with this very principle that the present government has avoided impeding the sentiments of the people, no matter whence they may derive. On the other hand, since my one personal aim and method from the beginning has been and is to preserve and guard the majesty of Islam and the independence of Iran, and fully to watch over the interests of this country and nation, assuming anyone who opposes this method to be an enemy of the country, and striving mightily to repel him; and determined to continue, henceforth in this method; and inasmuch as at the present the thoughts of the masses have become divergent and the minds poisoned, and since this confusion of thought can produce results contrary to what lies at the bottom of my heart: i.e., to preserve order and security and to stabilize the foundations of the state; and insofar as I and all the people in the army have, from the very beginning, regarded the preservation and protection of the dignity of Islam to be one of the greatest duties and kept before us the idea that Islam is always progress

and be exalted and that respect for the standing of the religious institutions be fully observed and preserved: thus, when I went to Qum to bid farewell to the [exiled *mujtahids*], I exchanged views with their excellencies regarding the present circumstances. And we ultimately saw it necessary to advise the public to halt the [use of] the term, republic. Rather, everyone should spend his efforts to eliminate the impediments to the reforms and progress of the country, and to help me in the sacred aim of consolidating the foundations of the religion, the independence of the country and of the national government. It is for this reason that I advise all patriots of this sacred aim to avoid calls for a republic and to unite efforts with me to achieve the supreme objective upon which we are agreed.

Having thereby placated the *culama'*, it remained for Rida Khan to forge more positive links with them by gaining their support for his government. This support came not from Qum but from Najaf, whence Isfahani and Na'ini had returned in late April 1924. Rida Khan had played a significant role in facilitating their return, although it is true that the British and Iraqi government authorities were predisposed to their resumption of residence in the holy cities. Shaykh Na'ini had sent a letter to the Prime Minister of Iran thanking him for the military escort he had provided the exiled *culama'* for their return journey. Further, as demonstrations of his appreciation, Na'ini sent along with his letter a revered picture of Imam *cAli*, together with the sword reputedly used by the third Imam's brother, Hadrat *cAbbas* on the battlefield of Karbala in 680 A.D.

Despite this strong manifestation of support by Na'ini for Rida Khan, the *culama'* of Tehran seemed to have been offended by the entire episode and regarded the dispatch of the portrait and the sword as a British trick. They accordingly boycotted the ceremonies at the Shrine of Shah *cAbd al-cAzim*, a shrine some eight miles to the south of Tehran. Undaunted, Rida Khan moved to follow up his advantage in his relationship with Na'ini by paying a visit to Najaf in January 1925. There, it appears he made a concerted effort to win the support of Isfahani and Na'ini in an attempt to block the return from Europe to Iran of Ahmad Shah. The trip to Najaf became all the more attractive an idea after the publication by *al-Habl al-Matin* of a manifesto attributed to Isfahani and Na'ini and dated a couple of months earlier for October 1924. The two *marajic* never repudiated authorship of this manifesto, which unmistakably endorses the government of the Prime Minister, Rida Khan:

> It should be specified for all the Muslims that those who revolt against the Islamic government of Iran are like those who fought against the prophet during the battles of Badr and Hunayn. Such people are those to whom the Qur'anic verse [about polytheists] is applicable. The

punishment for polytheism is death [in this world] and torture in the hereafter; therefore, it is obligatory for us to inform the people not to deviate from this Muhammadan circle [the government of Rida Khan] which gives currency to Islam. Those who oppose this command will be considered infidels willing to destroy this religion, and consequently it is necessary to anathemize them according to the rules and proofs of the Qur'an.

Out of this complex series of developments the following points emerge: monarchy was important to the *ʿulama'*, although not in its Qajar form; Rida Khan was keenly aware of the power of the *ʿulama'*, and actively solicited its use on his behalf; the Iranian clergy in Iraq backed the Tehran government with a view to the latter's help against British plans to expand its colonial influence in that country; Shaykh ʿAbd al-Karim Ha'iri Yazdi stood aloof from these developments as a hedge against political repression against his efforts in Qum; the Tehran *ʿulama'* seems to have been suspicious of Rida Khan as a possible instrument of British policy. Although the reason for their suspicion was misplaced, in retrospect they were correct in their assessment of his purely tactical orientation to Islam. It may be that Rida Khan sensed this opposition, as manifested not only in their avoiding the ceremonies at Shah ʿAbdul-ʿAzim in June 1924, but also the campaign led by some of them—especially Sayyid Hasan Mudarris— against his mounting the throne.

* * *

[Throughout his reign as monarch,] Rida Shah had often insisted that the intellectuals of the age could no longer be, as had been the case in Iranian history, the *ʿulama'*. Their art and their craft was incapable of answering the difficult social and economic issues of the times, he believed. Yet, even Rida Shah had needed the clergy in the beginning of his rise to power. There is also evidence of his capitulating to the *ʿulama'* on rare occasions. Apparently, for example, the Military Conscription Law of 1925 originally contained no provision for exemption of the clergy. However, a delegation of religious leaders from Qum met with him and petitioned for the insertion of the exemption. The Shah's concession included the further promise "to preserve the greatness of Islam and the *ʿulama'* leadership" so that "in carrying out their convictions and intentions, as well as in distributing the sacred religious texts, they would not meet with any obstacles."

A more typical reflection of the regime's relationship with the *ʿulama'*, nonetheless, is the disturbance in 1935 at the shrine of the Imam Rida in Mashhad. The Shah apparently had been impressed by the Turkish law forbidding the wearing of the brimless hat. He thereby decreed that males must wear brimmed hats, which were disliked by Muslims because they prevented them from touching their heads to the ground in prayer. Attempts by local police to apply the law in the sanctuary of the shrine in Mashhad led to an ugly incident in which officials fired on a crowd that had developed and had staged a sit-in. Many hundreds either lost their lives or were wounded, both in the mosque precincts and even within the sanctuary itself. The government undertook an inquiry and convicted and then executed *na'ib al-tawliyah* (administrator) of the shrine. Such measures failed to erase the impression held by the clergy and their supporters among the masses that the government's real intention amounted to the shutting down of the religious centers. On the whole, the Shah's legacy in the matter of clergy–state relations was that of a ruler who sought to prohibit the public enactment of passion plays, narratives or even mourning for the death of contemporary *maraji*-i taqlid*, rather than a ruler who received petitions of redress from the clergy, solicited their support in establishing order and stability, and sought their spiritual guidance, as mandated by the Constitution.

The *ulama*'s capacity for *active* protests againt Rida Shah's efforts was confined to the behavior of Ayatollah Hasan Mudarris in the Majlis. But even he was silenced when he was arrested in the fall of 1928 and exiled to eastern Iran. Indicative of the entropy of the religious institution in its relationship to the state was the devastating decline in Majlis deputies with clergy background.

> Whereas the *ulama*' constituted forty percent of the deputies in the Sixth Majlis [1926-1928], and around thirty percent in the Seventh [1930-1932], the Eleventh Majlis which met in 1937 did not include even a single well-known and important figure from the *ulama*'.

Shahrough Akhavi

The clergy's resurgence after WW II was led by Ayatollah Sayyid Muhammad Husayn Burujirdi, the leader of Qum between 1946 and 1961 (when he died). Qum was—and continues to be— the center of the Iranian religious institution and Burujirdi sought to raise it to the eminence enjoyed in the Sunni Islamic world by al-Azhar in Egypt.

Now, Burujirdi's efforts to invigorate Shiᶜism in Iran did not consist of the modernization of the curriculum of the theological seminaries (*madrasahs*); nor did it amount to bold innovations in administration and organizational matters. Instead, his tenure can be characterized as one during which the state acknowledged the clergy's continuing interest in public morality; worship (especially the construction, upkeep and refurbishing of mosques); anti-leftist propaganda (*tabligh*); dialogue with Sunni Islamic leaders; increasing enrollments in the *madrasahs*; anti-Baha'ism; admonitions against the clergy's trafficking in politics; and redoubling efforts to enshrine *fiqh* as the cornerstone of Islamic education.

Burujirdi enjoyed deference of such magnitude among his colleagues and the Iranian masses in general that he was endowed with the title of *marjaᶜ-i mutlaq-i taqlid*. This title meant that (theoretically at least) he was considered the sole source of emulation on the part of Shiᶜi adepts, each of whom is required by the faith to follow a living *mujtahid* in matters of religious belief and practice.

The enrollment of religious studies students in the *madrasahs* increased dramatically during the 1950's, a pattern that stood in marked contrast to the Rida Shah and WW II periods. The resurgence of Shiᶜism had a great deal to do with the government's willingness to make concessions to the clergy on questions of: (1) alcoholism, gambling and easy living; (2) greater stress upon sermons and homiletics in public broadcasting and television; (3) pressure upon the press to delete "anti-Shiᶜi" articles; (4) women's rights; (5) vigilance in observing Shiᶜi days of mourning, fasting and similar commemorations; (6) more intensive and frequent consultation on the part of the government leaders with the clergy.

Left almost untouched were social organization, finance, curriculum reform, social theory, ideology, political authority and its exercise, and constitutionalism. In the 1950's any rare instance of clergy assertiveness in these areas either had no wider impact or else redounded adversely against innovators. The classic example of an innovator who came under the regime's censure and opprobrium was Ayatollah Sayyid Mahmud Taliqani (d. 1979), co-founder (with Muhandis Mihdi Bazargan) of the Freedom Movement. Imprisoned by the regime, Taliqani's new edition, in 1954, of the classic constitutionalist treatise of 1909 written by Ayatollah Aqa Shaykh Muhammad Husayn al-Na'ini (d. 1936) and entitled *Tanbih al-ummah wa tanzih al-millah* symbolized his liberal position on political rule.

As against the Burujirdi "mainstream" faction of the ᶜulama' one must mention the political activism of Ayatollah Sayyid Abu al-Qasim al-Kashani (d. 1962). This individual, supported by such popular preachers as Hujjat al-Islam Muhammad Taqi Falsafi, represented the archtype of the politically "engagé" clergyman. Ranged against him, on the left and in the camp of the nationalist Prime Minister Muhammad Musaddiq were individuals such as Ayatollah Sayyid Abu'l-Fadl al-Musawi al-Zanjani. Finally, outside the ranks of the clergy proper, but sometimes receiving at least the tactical support of individuals in the *culama'* stratum such as Kashani and Falsafi, was the militant fundamentalist movement known as the Fada'iyan-i Islam. This organization, utilizing assassination tactics to realize its aim of returning to a "pure Islam", was established in 1945. In particular, its ties to the *mujtahids* (most of whom disapproved of it) was through Kashani, who nevertheless obstructed their wishes to share in political power and thereby caused them to break with him in March 1951.

The complex relationships involving Burujirdi, Kashani, Zanjani, and the Fida'iyan highlight for us the fact that the clergy was not a monolithic social force. In the denouement between the Shah and Dr. Musaddiq in August 1953, Zanjani and his supporters lost out and were imprisoned; Kashani was thoroughly discredited and promptly sank into obscurity; and what had remained of the Fida'iyan was systematically crushed. This permitted Burujirdi, with his solid ties to the important Tehran-based *mujtahid*, Ayatollah Sayyid Muhammad al-Musawi al-Bihbihani (d. 1965?), to establish a dominant role in the next eight years. He entered into an alignment with the Court that was to last for about five of these eight years. In this period, he and his supporters attacked the left and maintained a studied silence on issues which had historically excited the clergy — namely, foreign influence in the country. Such influence was represented in the mid-fifties by Iran's adherence to the Western sponsored defense alliance (Baghdad Pact) and Iran's dealing with the Consortium of oil companies after the overthrow of the Musaddiq movement.

* * *

Between 1959–1963 serious problems began to arise between the government and the clergy. More and more in the previous year the *culama'* came to feel that the Shah and his government were reneging on their tacit agreement to maintain close communications and consultations with the clergy on various matters of public policy. Dr. Musaddiq's National Front (a coalition of political parties and personalities that survived his downfall) increased its agitation against some of the same issues that had come to excite the clergy, without, nevertheless, having significant contact with the *culama'* apart from Ayatollah Taliqani. The regime sought to depict clerical opposition to the Shah's "White Revolution" as rooted in opportunistic and reactionary motives. Yet, such charges were recognized both in the religious institution and among many secularists for what they truly were, that is, polemics for the sake of discrediting one's opponents.

Ayatollah Burujirdi's death in March of 1961 disconcerted the clergy and emboldened the Shah's government to push forward with its programs and policies. About this time, though, a group of modernist *culama'* and lay supporters of a stronger clergy role in social affairs came together under the leadership of Ayatollah Shaykh Murtada Mutahhari (d. 1979) [See Chapter Twenty-Four in this book—Eds.]. In many significant respects, the activities of this group comprised the first truly meaningful reform effort in the twentieth century among Iranian clergymen. That the movement was overdue, may be gathered from Mutahhari's ironic comment in 1961 that things had reached such a pass in Iranian Shicism that soon people would be saying that its latest reformer (Shaykh Murtada Ansari "*al-Mujaddid*" [d. 1864]) lived a hundred years ago!

Now, the clergy as a whole challenged various facets of the Shah's behavior and principles. These included arbitrary rule by decree and disregard for constitutionalism. The *culama'* demonstrated against the government for its land reform law because it disregarded the sanctity of private property as underwritten by the Qur'an and it was feared that its provisions would be used against the clergy to declass its members. The enfranchisement of women was anathematized by the clergy, who saw in it the potential corruption of Iranian womanhood, the disruption of traditional family life and the buying off of women through the extension to them of meaningless suffrage. The clergy attacked the Literacy Corps as an instrument designed to replace the rural preachers and therefore eliminate at one blow whatever exemplars of Islamic piety were considered to exist in the villages of Iran.

But Mutahhari's group was primarily interested in matters that were intrinsic to the religious institution. While its members were also involved in the general protest movement of the early sixties, their concentration was the reform of Iranian Shici thought and organization.

* * *

[The activities of Mutahhari's group, the Monthly Religious Society,] consisted in monthly lectures and roundtables and lasted from 1960 to early 1963. The participants in the movement argued in favor of a socially active clergy and a Shicism to which believers had responsibilities surpassing mere private worship. Revitalization of Iranian Shicism involved for them a broad range of innovations. Among these may be listed the following:

1. Curriculum reform in *madrasahs*. This in particular meant more frequent and more challenging courses in *tafsir* (commentaries on the Qur'an); *ma'rifat al-rijal* (biography); *tarikh* (history); *caqa'id* (ideologies).

2. A dynamic interpretation of such principles as *taqwa* (piety). Accordingly, the faithful were invited to insist upon righteous behavior from their leaders, including political rulers.

3. A view that religion and politics had common goals—a line of thinking that was inevitable, given the three principles of the faith that these

reformers felt lent themselves to "political" matters; *al-amr bi'l-ma^cruf wa'l-nahy ^can al-munkar* (commanding the good and forbidding evil); *jihad* (holy war); *khums* (a 20 percent tax on annual income).

4. Rationalization of the financial administration and organization of the religious institution.

5. Dividing *marja^ciyyat* (the principle of emulating a *mujtahid*) so as to obviate pressures for the emergence of a sole *marja^c-i taqlid*, in light of the complexities of law in the modern period; and given the improbability of one individual mastering the knowledge necessary for providing model solutions to any and every problem.

6. Constituting a collective body of *mujtahids* with the authority to issue *fatwas* (authoritative opinions in matters of Islamic law) on any issue of public policy or interest. This seemed an attempt to activate the provisions of Article Two of the Constitution of 1906, entailing the creation of a five-member council of high-ranking clergymen with the power of judicial review.

7. Urging that the clerical leadership provide exemplary guidance for youth — not only on the level of ethical conduct but also in terms of committing itself to the need for public and social mobilization, interest articulation, recruitment of cadres, inculcation of political consciousness, etc.

8. The delegation of the Imam's authority being a *sine qua non* of any Shi^ci society, it was argued that only those who have shown outstanding achievement as to piety, justice and administration were the rightful legatees of such authority. Secular rulers, including those of the twentieth century, had sinned and shown their inability to imitate the traditions of the prophet as befits the task of him to whom the Imams' authority is delegated. Therefore, doctrinal grounds are established implicitly for rule by the clergy (*ula al-amr minkum*—those in authority among you) as the only social stratum with the potential to avoid sinful behavior.

The government's suppression of this reform movement occurred simultaneously with its violent reactions against the clergy's participation in the 1962–63 demonstrations. It is clear that, given the range of demands set forth by the movement, the regime greatly feared its success. It was determined not to permit a social and political role to the *^culama'* because of their own views. The bottom line of these reform demands, as the government saw them, was independent organizational capability. It therefore came as no surprise that the regime, in crushing the political opposition, also stifled the religious reform efforts.

This does not mean that religion was uprooted; not at all. Many of the Westernized intellectuals, for whom religion continued to provide symbolic significance, turned toward *^cirfan* and *tasawwuf* (gnosis and sufism respectively). The leading example of an individual who was attracted toward mysticism was Seyyed Hossein Nasr.

Now, Sufism has always been suspect in Qum, although *ᶜirfan* has been tolerated. Rarely at least, *mujtahids* (including Ayatollah Khumayni at one point) have instructed in this subject. Non-*mujtahids* of the stature of ᶜAllamah Muhammad Husayn Tabataba'i, have also been able to hold forth in the bastion of Iranian Shiᶜism itself, the holy city of Qum.

The principal difference between the *ᶜulama'* and those Westernized intellectuals who nevertheless decried the West's "materialism" and opted for mysticism is the latter's insistence upon intuition and anti-rational symbolism. The variant of mysticism followed by individuals such as Nasr represents a self-consciously elitist and highly cosmopolitan reflective orientation. For the clergy, it seems to be a sort of intellectual escapism from the social reality of the daily deprivations faced by the masses. The willingness of the Court to underwrite Sufism and parade it as the genuine spiritual heritage of Iran also offended the *ᶜulama'* who regarded it as an effort to distort what they held was true Shiᶜism.

* * *

[Another group of Shiᶜi intellectuals opted for a left-leaning revival of Shiᶜism. Aside from Ayatollah Taliqani from the ranks of the *ᶜulama',*] Engineer Mihdi Bazargan and Dr. ᶜAli Shariᶜati (d. 1977) have probably been the two most outstanding examples of laymen with non-Sufi affinities of a revitalized Shiᶜism.

* * *

Shariᶜati encountered problems with the *ᶜulama'* almost from the begining of the activities of the Husayniyyih Irshad in 1965 [See Chapter Twenty-Three in this book — Eds.]. His father's background and library brought Shariᶜati into contact with the religious sciences at an early age; moreover, the young Shariᶜati had attended lessons in his father's *madrasah* up to the intermediate cycle. He was therefore familiar with the discourse of the *ᶜulama'*. Yet, the latter wished to dispute with this person who was urging a new approach to Shiᶜism. And, in this process of disputation some technical "errors" on his part were alleged. Among the most commonly cited of his miscues, in the view of the clergy, were:

1. In a 1968 volume on the prophet, Shariᶜati is alleged to have suggested that *shura'* (a collegial decision-making body) was the appropriate way of selecting the leader of the *ummah* (Islamic community); whereas the Shiᶜi have always held that the *wasayah* (bequeathal); and *walayah* (delegated

authority) of the prophet flow to Imam ᶜAli and his issue (i.e., the twelve Imams).

2. He used Sunni sources (the history of Tabari and the biography of Ibn Hisham) in discussing the life of the prophet; whereas sound Shiᶜi sources exist and should be utilized to avoid error.

3. He declared that the forbidden fruit in the Garden of Eden was symbolic of knowledge; whereas Shiᶜis have long held this to be a Christian view with no foundation in the Islamic tradition.

4. He used the word *ijmaᶜ*, to mean majority opinion; whereas Shiᶜi ᶜ*ulama'* understand it to be a technical concept describing agreement by the learned men of the religious law on the basis of which they can issue a *fatwa*.

5. He claimed that the Prophet was so happy to see his followers praying at the time of his illness that, upon getting up from bed and joining them, he placed himself beside Abu Bakr, rather than taking over the duties of leading the prayer.

6. He regarded Buddha, Confucius and other great historical personalities as prophets; whereas no Muslim could call an individual a prophet who lacked a divine religion.

* * *

Shariᶜati's plans for religious education in Iran were radical. They involved a major shift of attention away from the staple of the *madrasahs: fiqh* and *usul* (principles of jurisprudence); and a redirection of emphasis to sociology, history, and biography. The names of Western scientists such as Einstein, Jung, Planck, Marx studded his model curriculum for the Husayniyyih Irshad. Now, the references, in themselves, to such thinkers were not new, since the more recent generation of *madrasah* professors (including Ayatollah Nasir Makarim Shirazi) have illustrated their lectures by using their names. What made Shariᶜati's approach unique was the thorough analysis of people such as Marx or Sartre as progenitors of schools of thought.

* * *

[In conclusion,] there is no question that the efforts of the clergy for nearly three decades (1950–1980) to reinvigorate the religious institution had much to do with the revolution and its outcome. Although the various religious leaders and the religiously-oriented lay intellectuals differed in their approaches and emphases, it is clear that Iranian Shiᶜism was the rallying point for all of them; furthermore, those active in Shiᶜi movements during this time, seemed to have as their common foe the secularization of society under the aegis of the state.

The sociologist Max Weber considered social action to consist of an event, together with the meaning attributed by individuals to that event. And for Weber such social action derives from the *ideal and material* interests of the actors as they perceive them. The Iranian revolution may be seen in these terms. The clergy and their supporters alone did not make the revolution. But, the symbolic discouse and praxis of the *culama'* and their lay supporters were absolutely crucial for its success.

Shi^cism, it has often been suggested, provides a sharper cutting edge than Sunnism for social protest and political activism. This has to do with such doctrinal principles as the imamate, *walayah* and *ijtihad* (mental exercise by legal specialists to render interpretations on points of law). It also has to do with the financial autonomy of the religious institution from the state; and finally, it stems to a large degree from the vocabulary and dramaturgical elements familiar to practitioners of the faith. Sunni Islam differs in these respects.

Said Amir Arjomand

Two chief factors can be singled out to account for the politicization of the Shi^ci traditionalist movement in the 1970s: the repressive policies of the Pahlavi state, and the determination of Ayatollah Ruhullah Khumayni.

Once he felt securely in control, Muhammad Rida Shah put an end to the *rapprochement* with the Shi^ci clergy who had helped restore him to the throne in 1953, and initiated a ruthless attack on the religious institution. This attack produced a series of crucially significant events which punctuate the progressive revolutionary politicization of the Shi^ci traditionalism.

It is true that, after the death of the apolitical Burujirdi (1961), Khumayni, the 'decisive experience' of whose generation was Rida Shah's repression and the betrayal of the westernised intellectuals and who saw the reassertion of royal power and initiation of a new reform programme as replete with *motifs* encountered during the dreadful reign of the first Pahlavi, had begun to make a bid to take the place of Kashani in the political arena. Furthermore, the Shah's suddenly increasing popularity after the successful Peasants' Congress of January 1963 must have alarmed Khumayni and roused his apprehension. Nevertheless, he was not propos-

ing any revolutionary programme at that time. In March 1963, he was ac-
cusing the Shah of violating his oath to defend Islam and the Constitution,
opposing the enfranchisement of women, and attacking the Shah for maintaining relations with Israel. Like Kashani a decade earlier, he was upholding the legitimacy of the Constitution. The critical event which changed the
situation drastically was the violent sack of the main theological college of
Qum, Faydiyyih, in March 1963, an event which, according to the testimony
of one of his most important aids and students, made a deep impression on
Khumayni. As is made clear by the Preamble of the Constitution of the
Islamic Republic of Iran, in reaction to these events, Khumayni set out to
create, in contradistinction to the nationalist and the socialist political parties, a traditionalist political movement which was to be led by the clergy as
the guardians of the Shiᶜi tradition. The following statement is made in the
Preamble of the Constitution of the Islamic Republic:

> Although the Islamic way of thinking and militant clerical leadership
> played a major and fundamental role in [the constitutional and the
> nationalist/anti-imperialist] movements, these movements rapidly disin-
> tegrated because they became increasingly distant from the true Islamic
> position.
>   At this point, the alert conscience of the nation, led by . . . the Grand
> Ayatollah Imam Khumayni, realised the necessity of adhering to the
> true ideological and Islamic path of struggle.

A bold innovation by Khumayni consolidated the traditionalist movement and gave it a definite direction. Around the year 1970, Khumayni took
the unprecedented step of assuming the title of Imam, and put forward a
political theory which advocated direct hierocratic rule on behalf of the
Hidden Imam. (Here, one should mention the influence of the activities of
the Shiᶜi leaders in the Arab land. The Lebanese leader, Musa Sadr, was
also assuming the title of Imam which, however, is a good deal less elevated
in Arabic than in Persian.) At the same time, Khumayni elaborated a blueprint for the ideal of Shiᶜi government, an Islamic theocracy, to be realized
by the movement he had launched. Thus, as the Preamble declares:

> The plan for an Islamic Government based upon the concept of the
> Mandate of the Clergy, which was introduced by Imam Khumayni . . .
> gave a fresh, stong incentive to the Muslim people and opened the
> way for a genuine ideological Islamic struggle. This plan consolidated
> the efforts of those dedicated Muslims who were fighting both at home
> and abroad.

Khumayni's theory of the *Wilayat-i faqih* (Mandate of the Clergy, or the
Sovereignty of the Jurist), published in 1971, is a major innovation in the
history of Shiᶜism. He converts a highly technical and specific legal discus-

sion of the rights of the gerent into a theocratic political theory. Although Khumayni cites Mulla Ahmad Naraqi (d. 1828-29) as a forerunner, the latters' ᶜ*A wayid al-avyam*, the only legal work to which Khumayni refers in support of his theory of the Mandate of the Clergy, pointed only to an implicit invidious contrast between religious and political authority [See Chapter Nineteen in this book—Eds.]. The primary objective of Naraqi's discussion of the 'mandate of the jurist' was to strengthen the *juristic* authority of the Shiᶜi doctors on behalf of the Hidden Imam. The bulk of the discussion was devoted to the 'delimitation' of the scope of the authority of the jurists as the vicegerents of the Imam, and their authority was delimited to the exclusion of temporal rule.

Khumayni extends the early Usuli arguments such as Naraqi's, which were designed to establish the legal authority of the Shiᶜi doctors, to eliminate the duality of hierocratic and temporal authority altogether. For him, Islamic government will differ from representative and/or constitutional monarchies in its elimination of the separation of powers. Khumayni categorically states that 'the Mandate [of the clergy] means governing and administering the country and implementing the provisions of the Sacred Law'. Thus, having firmly rejected the separation of religion and politics, he argues that in the absence of the divinely inspired supreme leader of the community of believers, the infallible Imam—that is, from AD 874 to the end of time— sovereignty devolves upon the qualified jurists or the Shiᶜi religious leaders. It is therefore the religious leaders as the authoritative interpreters of the Sacred Law of Islam who are entitled to sovereignty. Furthermore by assuming the title of Imam, he paves the way for the eventual restriction of the Mandate of the Clergy to that of *one* jurist as its presumed *supreme leader*.

Not only did the Islamic traditionalist movement of the 1970s consider itself to have superseded the imperfect and misconceived nationalist movements of the earlier periods, but it was also fully on guard against any possible tapping of the energy of the movement by nationalist and other intellectuals. Writing in the summer of 1978, Mutahhari, a chief architect of the movement sardonically states:

> I regret to say that these respected intellectuals have woken up a bit too late because the old custodians of this immense source of movement and energy have demonstrated that they themselves know very well how to utilise this immense source, and will give no one the opportunity for a take-over (*khalᶜ-i yadd*).

He went on to add that the Shiᶜi clergy must write books themselves so that others 'could not fish in murky waters.'

The assumption of the title Aryamihr (Sun of the Aryans) by the Shah and the celebration of the 2500th anniversary of the founding of the Persian

Empire provoked Khumayni into a vehement denunciation of the institution of monarchy. In a speech in anticipation of the celebration made on 22
June 1971, Khumayni, having adduced the tradition 'king of Kings is the
vilest of words' cites the recurrent Qur'anic verse *'Lahu'l-mulk'* as meaning
that sovereignty belongs to God alone. He proceeds to tell his audience that
rising against the Pahlavi monarchy is incumbent upon them by Sacred
Law. Meanwhile Khumayni had taken up the anti-foreign and anti-Zionist
traditionalist themes. He vigorously protested against the granting of extre-
territorial judiciary rights to American Advisers in 1964, and had issued
constant invectives against the agents of the foreign powers and of Zionism.

The critically significant events of the 1970s consisted of a series of
repressive measures against the religious institution. Already in 1964, Khumayni had reacted violently against a proposal by the regime to set up an
Islamic university which was taken to signal the state's intention to encroach
upon the religious sphere proper. Such direct encroachments materialized in
the 1970s. Totally disregarding its political costs, the Shah embarked on an
attempt to invade the religious sphere proper by creating a 'Religion Corps'
(modelled after the 'Literacy Corps'), and a group of 'Propagators of
Religion.' Despite their inefficiency and lack of vigour, the religious leaders
perceived these measures as a bid to liquidate the religious institution and
annihilate Shi^cism altogether. In 1975 under the pretext of the creation of
green space around the shrine of the eighth Imam, the government demolished most of the theological seminaries of the holy city of Mashhad, a
measure which caused a good deal of apprehension in Qum. In the same
year, the Faydiyyih Seminary was attacked by the troops during a prolonged
commemoration, by pro-Khomeini students, of the sack of 1963. Furthermore, the Shah replaced the Islamic calendar with a fictitious imperial one.
With their backs to the wall, the clergy within Iran increasingly heeded Khumayni's incessant appeals, and the latter's position among the Grand
Ayatollahs was strengthened. Clerical reaction to the Shah's aggressive encroachments was to prove decisive. In an interview conducted in 1975, a
prominent cleric spoke of 'the awakening of Iran's religious community
after the frontal attack of His Majesty'. (He went on to boast about the
clergy's new political maturity: in the 1960s the eligibility of women for elections was a major preoccupation of the religious leaders, now they would
not lose any popularity by incautiously opposing women's electoral rights.)

Throughout the 1970s, Khumayni's sense of alarm at the destruction of
the Shi^ci culture and mores was augmenting. In March 1975, he would refer
to the Shah's 'White Revolution' as 'the revolution intended to spread the
colonial culture to the remotest towns and villages and pollute the youth of
the country.' Reacting to the public performance of explicit sexual acts by
an *avant-garde* theatre group in the Shiraz Festival, he would be moved to

say, in a speech made in September 1977 in Najaf, that the function of this government

> is tyranny and oppression and the spread of prostitution. You do not know what prostitution has begun in Iran. You are not informed: the prostitution which has begun in Iran, and was implemented in Shiraz — and they say it is to be implemented in Tehran, too — cannot be retold. Is this the ultimate — or can they go even further — to perform sexual acts among a crowd and under the eyes of the people? (the speech of 14 Shawwal 1397A.H.).

One final significant event, or rather the anticipation thereof, should be mentioned as of utmost importance in turning political traditionalism into an intransigently revolutionary movement: the imminent beginning of the fifteenth century of Islam. The Shi^ci scholars' long-established tradition of the designation of a great *mujaddid* (Renovator) for each century, against the background of the sudden explosion of popular rage and the crumbling of the Pahlavi monarchical edifice, can safely be assumed to have changed the clerical estate's conception of time (and certainly Khumayni's) from a chronological to a kairotic one; the moment when time was to be pervaded by eternity seemed at hand, empirically and numerologically.

Like Nuri in the first decade of the century, Khumayni was primarily addressing the clerical estate:

> I know what dangerous dreams the tyrannical establishment has for Islam and the Moslems. You, the ^culama' and the clergy (*ruhaniyyun*) are the culprits in their eyes . . . You must be conscripted into compulsory military service, spend your time in jails, under torture and oppression and humiliation, and in exile, so that the way would be open for the agents of the foreigners and of Israel.

However, he also instructed a large number of preachers and clerical publicists to spread his message in Iran, and among the Iranians pilgrims abroad (for example, in Mecca). Furthermore, Khumayni put much emphasis on preaching, an activity confined, as he himself had stressed in 1943 to the lower ranks of the Shi^ci clergy. Not only did he urge preachers to spread the traditionalist propaganda, but also, unlike some other Grand Ayatollah, he personally delivered a large number of sermons.

The separation of political and religious authority, *de jure* and *de facto*, had become the distinctive feature of Shi^ci Islam by the early decades of the nineteenth century. The Shi^ci clergy's separation from the state, and especially their championship of the Shi^ci nation against a state subservient to the foreign imperial powers in the period 1890–1906, disposed them towards some measure of populism. However, the measure of paternalistic populism, which made them differentiate the community of believers from the ruling élite, sold to the foreign infidels, went hand-in-hand with a pronounced élitist attitude as regards the stratification of the community of believers into the élite (*khawas*) and the common masses (*cawam*). Nuri's phrase, 'the masses more benighted than cattle' is indeed a recurrent one in the writings of the Shi^ci *culama'* of the period. Elitism pervades the manifesto of the Fada'iyan: 'We are capable of sending these traitors [the ruling élite] to hell and of avenging Islam. But we delayed action to prevent probable dangers, and prevented forcefully the revolt of foolish ignoramuses.' Furthermore, by 1950, a marked status consciousness, typical of declining social strata, finds expression in certain recommendations of Nawwab Safawi which were subsequently to be faithfully implemented in the Islamic regime's recruitment policies. Proposing schools of political science for the training of the Islamic ruling élite, Nawwab Safawi writes:

> The students in this field must be selected from among pious families that are well-known for honesty, and unknown applicants from low-classes or dishonest families should not be allowed to register for it. . . . Yes, only the children from honest and pious Muslim families who will not betray their country can be trusted with the political missions and management of the country's political affairs . . . Yes. Every applicant's family background must be studied before his acceptance, and only the children of honest and pious families will be admitted.

The situation changed drastically in the period 1963–78 when the Shi^ci clergy came under relentless attack and had to appeal to the masses more assiduously in order to mobilize them against the Pahlavi state. It is crucially important to note that this period was witnessing the rapid and enormous growth, through migration from the rural areas, in the size of the urban masses who came to constitute a new clientele and a new audience for the Shi^ci clergy. Meanwhile, the land reform of the 1960s was completing the process of disengagement of the Shi^ci clergy from the Pahlavi state which had already gone very far as a result of Rida Shah's reforms of the 1930s. It has already been pointed out that this disengagement, and the consequent separation of religious and political powers, put the Shi^ci clergy in a very similar position to the Indian *culama'* in the nineteenth century, and similarly disposed them to leading nationwide Islamic traditionalist movements. It should now be added that the same disengagement from the Pahlavi regime not only dispossessed the Shi^ci clergy but also oriented it towards the growing urban masses; its populism became markedly more pronounced owing to its acute sense of dispossession.

In his study of social movements, Heberle makes an important distinction between the constitutive ideas of a movement, which form the foundation of group cohesion, and those ideas which are of merely accidental or pragmatic significance. To the persistent constitutive ideas of the traditionalist movement expressed in the writing of Nawwab Safawi were now added an emphasis on social justice, and a host of secondary and demagogical ideas and rhetoric. The preachers and clerical publicists readily borrowed from Shariᶜati, and from the translation of such works as the Muslim Brotherhood leaders Sayyid Qutb's *Social Justice in Islam*. Above all, Shariᶜati's apt term, the Disinherited, with its enormous appeal to the uprooted masses, came to occupy a prominent place in the revolutionary rhetoric of the traditionalist party, and to enhance the paternalistic populism of its leaders.

Early in January 1978, in reaction to a slanderous government-instigated personal attack in a leading newspaper's editorial, following the somewhat mysterious death of his son, Khumayni decided the time was at hand and inaugurated a thriteen-month period of nationwide revolutionary agitation whose outcome is well-known. After the revolution of February 1979, Khumayni and the other leaders of the movement set out to implement the blueprints contained in the writings of Khumayni and Nawwab Safawi with unswerving determination and consummate Machiavellian skill. A 'Council of Constitutional Experts', along the lines foreseen in *Kashf-i asrar* was set up, and incorporated Khumayni's theory of the Mandate of Clergy into the Constitution of the Islamic Republic, taking the step which Khumayni had not dared to make explicit in 1971: the restriction of the collective office of the Shiᶜi jurists, the General Viceregency (*Niyabat-i ᶜammah*), to *the* jurist as the supreme leader of the community of believers. The state was put under the firmest possible domination of the clergy, as Nuri would have wished, and the preparations were made for the dismantling of the unIslamic laws, as Nawwab Safawi had recommended. Music was banned, sexual desegregation and virtual re-veiling were reimposed, adulterers and sodomites were executed or stoned in anticipation of triple repetition of the crimes, and a host of Qur'anic and pseudo-Qur'anic atavistic punishment reintroduced. Above all, the westernised intelligentsia was gradually but decisively liquidated.

With the clerical coup d'état of November 1979, the desecularization of the judiciary, the closure of universities and the suspension of secular higher education, the 'Islamicizing' purges of summer 1980 and the installing of the lay traditionalist activists in the highest executive offices of the state, the Shiᶜi traditional movement spent itself in creating Khumayni's chaotic theoochlocracy, with the turbanned juristochlocrats fulfilling both functions of rousing the club-wielding mobs—suitably designed as the Party of God (*Hizbullah*)—and representing God by leading the Friday congregational prayers and by presiding over the administration of the Sacred Law through the all-powerful religious tribunals. . . .

Traditionalism is viewed as a broad cultural movement, a 'revitalization' movement in Wallace's terminology. In the preceding pages, I have sketched (i) the factors which transformed its bearers, the *ᶜulama'*, from one of the two organs of pre-modern government into publicists, ideologues, and finally revolutionaries; (ii) the socio-demographic and organizational factors which facilitated its widening appeal and consequent growth; and (iii) the political factors and critical events which caused its irrevocable politicization by the 1970s. Other collateral economic and social factors were excluded from consideration because of their insufficient analytical pertinence. As the above procedure highlights the overriding salience of the cultural factor, it seems appropriate to conclude with a typological characterization of contemporary Shiᶜi traditionalism as a cultural movement, a movement for revitalization.

A meaningful typological characterization of Shiᶜi traditionalism can proceed along two mutually complementary lines, the one approach locating it within the cultural and historical context of Islam, the other, in the contemporary global perspective. A highly selective contrast with comparable movements at the broadest possible level of generality suggests the following ideal types as significant points of reference: from the first perspective, revivalist traditionalism or puritanical revivalism, especially though not exclusively notable in the Hanbali tradition, and Islamic radicalism of the variety espoused by the Muslim Brotherhood; from the second, commodity millenialism of contemporary Melanesia, and revolutionary reaction in the form of Western fascism.

One need not be an Hegelian to appreciate Mannheim's remark that 'no antithesis escapes conditioning by the thesis it sets out to oppose'. Of course the common reference to the sources of the Islamic tradition gives all revitalization movements within Islam a strong family resemblance. Indeed, the Islamic activists, whether they are partisans of Ayatollah Khumayni or Sayyid Qutb or Mawlana Mawdudi, regard themselves as participants in *the* Islamic movement of our time. Nevertheless, one would expect significant differences among the Islamic movements corresponding to differences in their respective antithetical conditioning. Such antithetical conditioning can vary fundamentally depending on whether the revitalization of tradition takes place under the threat of erosion from popular Sufism or from Western culture. Islamic traditionalism oriented towards popular Sufism and unorthodox religious practices of the masses may conveniently be designated 'revivalism'. The distinctive feature of revivalism as an ideal type is its puritanical reaction to popular laxity and supernaturalism which takes the form of insistence on orthopraxis and the purification of 'associationist' practices (*shirk*), and on the reiteration of the pristine Abrahamic message of monotheism. As instances of revivalism, we may mention the Almohad movement in twelfth century north-western Africa and the reivivalism of the Wahhabi *Muwahhidun* in the eighteenth and twentieth century Arabia. In contrast to revivalism, the *ideological* quality of Shi^ci traditionalism — its presentation of an authentic, consistent and 'total way of life' in opposition to 'Western materialism' — emerges as distinctive.

On the other hand, the ideological quality of Shi^ci traditionalism, stemming from the threat of erosion posed by Western influences, is shared by the Muslim Brotherhood and its currently active offshoots whose movement may be characterised as 'Islamic fundamentalism' or . . . 'Islamic radicalism'. The key contrast between the two types of Islamic movements is that the former is dominated and led by the clergy, the latter, by laymen. Islamic fundamentalism represents the revitalizing synthesis not of the *^culama'* but of Muslim laymen. Consequently, it does not share the pronounced clericalism of Shi^ci traditionalism and in fact is usually critically oriented towards the *^culama'*. The latter synthesis involves a somewhat greater dissociation from the immediately transmitted pattern of the Islamic tradition, and gives greater attention to its sources, especially the Qur'an.

Shi^ci traditionalism is a contemporary movement generated from within a world-religion. As such, it is instructive to contrast it with ideal types of contemporary movements which are *either* nurtured by a primitive religion (a pre-world-religion belief system) *or* which attempt to transcend a world-religion. From this perspective, let us consider the marginal individuals who have emerged as the charismatic leaders of the Melanesian cargo cults, of 'commodity millennialism'. They have done so in the context of Melanesian materialistic cosmogonies tinged with the ideas of Christian missionaries. Their Golden Age was in the future; and it contained venerated elements of Western culture as shown by the cults of cargo. Commodity millenialism can thus be seen as an extreme case of maximal receptivity and absorption of Western cultural elements. By contrast, the dispossessed estate which created and directed Shi^ci traditionalism, did so with emphatic reference to the heritage of the past. They were the custodians of a world religion with a dogmatically-formulated belief system and a consolidated ethos. This means that we are dealing with the opposite extreme case of minimal absorption and maximal rejection. The revitalizing synthesis, therefore, did not entail the meaningful absorption of any Western beliefs and ideas through the reinterpretation of the sources of the Shi^ci tradition, but rather the mere adoption of the *ideological* frame of thought, a frame of thought which tends to present itself whenever a tradition becomes self-conscious. A systematizing tendency thus set in and Shi^ci Islam was presented as 'a total way of life', with a set of blueprints and of vaguer outlines of Islamic economic, administrative social, educational and governmental 'systems'.

'Revolutionary reaction' writes Ernst Nolte, 'this is the underlying characteristic of fascism.' Western European fascism was, according to Nolte's interpretation, a reaction from within a tradition against its latest stage of development—that is, a reaction from within the Western tradition in the form of 'the denial of transcendence'. It is hard to see how the level of symbolic differentiation, and consequently the theoretical accommodation of transcendence, could be increased beyond that attained by the world-religions of salvation. As a teacher of philosophy and *cirfan*, Khumayni recognizes and endorses the kind of theoretical transcendence Maurras and Hitler sought to repudiate and overcome. Despite the similarity of the techniques of mobilization and other features, therefore, the overworked term 'fascism' seems typologically inappropriate (in part owing to the fact that we have no satisfactory typology of fascism, one which would contrast the intensely Christian fascism of Romania and Hungary with the anti-religious Western fascism which Nolte's characterization is based). What Nolte terms 'resistance to practical transcendence', on the other hand, does not distinguish the Islamic movement in Iran from the other conservative movements, and therefore does not need to be built into our ideal-typical characterization of it.

To conclude, therefore, I propose 'revolutionary traditionalism' as a contrasting typological characterization of the Islamic movement in Iran. The term conceives of Shici traditionalism as a reaction to an external cultural tradition, which reaction entails the repudiation of any change consequent upon its imposition by a Western-oriented ruling élite. This repudiation is tantamount to a revolutionary change in political institutions and the social structure. Such revolutionary changes have been and will continue to be insisted upon as a result of the transformation of ingrained traditional sentiments and dormant attitudes into an explicit and adequately systematized traditionalist ideology.

Part IV

Shi^ci Minorities in the Islamic World

Chapter Fourteen

Shiʿism in the Indian Subcontinent

In the West, Shiʿism has often been associated with Iran. More recently the Iran–Iraq War, and the conflicts in Lebanon have also brought the world's attention to the sizable Shiʿi populations of Iraq and Lebanon. However, beyond the cluster of Shiʿi communities in these countries there are important and often large communities of Shiʿis living throughout the Muslim world. Since these communities have often been politically inactive, they have escaped the attention of academicians and journalists. Their importance to any study of Shiʿi history, theology, or religious life is paramount, however. Indonesia, Kuwait, Afghanistan, the Soviet Union, Bahrain, Saudi Arabia, the Emirates of the Persian Gulf, Pakistan, India, Turkey, and East Africa all have Shiʿi minorities of varying magnitude. In this section some aspects of the life of Shiʿism in these countries will be presented.

The Shiʿis of India constitute one of the largest and oldest Shiʿi communities. Shiʿism spread to India as a result of the gradual migration of persecuted Shiʿis from the heartland of the Islamic world during early centuries of Islamic history.

The earliest signs of Shiʿi political presence in India can be seen in the Bahmani Kingdom of Delhi (1347–1526 A.D.) The migration of Shiʿis to India, which had increased during the period, reached its zenith during the Mughal Empire, when Shiʿism became an established religious community with substantial influence in the Mughal court. Hollister writes on this episode of Shiʿism.

In addition to working within the Mughal Empire, the Shiʿis also found greater influence in the principalities of northern India, such as Kashmir or Lucknow. They even formed governments in the Deccan Kingdoms. Their most noteworthy kingdom was, however, Oudh, where the state was built upon the Safavid model.

Shiᶜism continues to play an important role in Indian Islam. In the following passage Hollister writes on the active presence of Shiᶜism in today's India. The excerpts are from TSI, *pages 139–40, 182–83, 187–90.*

Then, Annemarie Schimmel will discuss the significance of the Shiᶜi marthiyyah *in Sindhi literature of the subcontinent. The excerpt is from* ASIHCN, *pages 33–39.*

John Hollister

There can be no doubt but that the *sayyids* were in politics for what they could get out of it, rather than to promote Shiᶜism. But Shiᶜis and Shiᶜism gained from their influence. Awrangzib was a fanatical Sunni, and although a majority of his officials were Shiᶜis they did not vaunt their Shiᶜism because of his known fanaticism. Bahadur Shah I, a Shiᶜi, led by the *sayyids*, abolished the *jizyah* or poll tax, and issued an order for the use of the Shiᶜi formula in the *azan* and the *khutbah* throughout the empire. Strong opposition to the term *wasi* (executor) developed in Lahore, Agra and other centres. Some leaders of the opposition were sentenced to life-imprisonment in the fort at Gwalior. In Ahmadabad the *khatib* was warned the first time not to read this form the next week. But in obedience to his superiors he read the same form the next Friday.

> The moment the word *wasi* fell from his tongue, a Punjabi rose, seized him by his shirt, dragged him from the top of the pulpit, and treated him with harsh scorn. A Turani Mughal jumped up, drew his knife, stuck it into the stomach of the *khatib* and threw him down under the pulpit.

He was later dragged into the forecourt "and there he received so many stabs from daggers and blows from slippers that he died ignominiously." So widespread was the opposition to the king's order, that he reconsidered. After days of debate,

> at the end of Shawwal, the Sadr presented a petition on the subject of the *khutbah* and on this His Majesty wrote with his own hand that the *khutbah* should be read in the form used during the reign of Aurungzeb.

During the short and troubled reign of Faruksir, there was a violent affray between the Shiᶜis and the Sunnis at Delhi. The nephew of Saᶜadat Khan, Safdar Jang, became the *vizier* under Ahmad Shah, during whose reign there was another very bitter clash between Shiᶜis and Sunnis in Delhi. Nadir Shah invaded India in 1738 and after sacking Delhi returned to Persia. A second invasion from Persia was made in the reign of ᶜAlamgir II (1754–1760). The Mahrattas captured Delhi in the battle of Panipat in 1760, which marked the virtual close of the Mughal Empire with the breakdown of its extensive territory into separate states. The influence of Shiᶜism continued among 'the Mughals' even until 1853, when Bahadur Shah II secretly declared his allegiance to Persia and declared himself as a Shiᶜi.

Outside of these eddies that swirled around the court circles and royal decisions, there were many other incidents illustrating Shiᶜi penetration during this period. Only two examples are chosen. First, not all the influx of the Shiᶜis reached the court. There were numerous families that settled down in quiet life. Such, for instance, was the family of Sayyid ᶜAli al-Ha'iri Mujtahid Shiyan of Lahore. He belongs to an ancient family of *sayyids*, tracing its descent to Imam Musa, one of whose descendants left Qum and moved to Kashmir. Their descendants have scattered in the Punjab and United Provinces. Sayyid ᶜAli al-Ha'iri's ancestors settled in Lahore about the time that a Qizilbash family arrived in India from Afghanistan, which also settled in the Punjab. Through the spiritual relations which sprang up between the two families, the Qizilbash family of the Nawwabs, and many others have received religious profit and spiritual gain to the mutual advantage of all concerned.

A second illustration is that of Sayyid Nurullah ibn Sharif al-Husayn al-Marᶜashi Shushtari, who had been born in the year 1549 and had lived at Shushtar in Persia, from where he migrated to India about 1587. He was a Shiᶜi, with a reputation as a devout, pious, just and learned man. He held the office of *qadi al-qudat* in Lahore by appointment of Akbar. He accepted on condition that he could render his decisions according to any of the four recognized legal systems of the Sunnis. With this freedom, he continued to give his fatwas in accordance with Imamiyyah teaching. He was the author of many works, among them the *Majalis-al-mu'minin* in 1604. Sunni ᶜulama', who had suspected his orthodoxy, used this work as evidence of heterodoxy and he was condemned and flogged to death by order of Jahangir. He is known to Shiᶜis as al-Shahid al-Thalith, The Third Martyr. His tomb is in Agra and is a place of pilgrimage for Shiᶜis from all parts of India.

*   *   *

Shiᶜis are scattered throughout India. According to the 1921 census they are least numerous in Assam, most numerous in the Punjab and Delhi, and in Baroda find their highest proportion in the total Muslim community. Where in the past Shiᶜi courts existed there is the probability of a noticeable, even if small, residue of Shiᶜi population. Friends in the Deccan told me that while the Shiᶜis were not numerous in the Hyderabad State, yet a large number, perhaps half of the jagirdars in the Hyderabad-Vikarabad section, were Shiᶜis. Similarly, many of the *taᶜalluqdars* in Oudh are Shiᶜi. Faydabad, as an old capital, has a large and influential Shiᶜi community in the District. A considerable community of Shi^cis at Amroha in the United Provinces, may be traced to the fact that one of the emperors gave a grant of land to an officer under whose shelter ancestors of these Shi^cis gathered. This could be duplicated in many places.

As many Persians were attached to the Shi^ci kingdoms of the Decca, so "mercenaries still come as recruits to the Persian regiments of the Nawwab of Cambay."

The Hazaras are a sturdy race of mountaineers in Afghanistan, dominantly of Mongolian blood and speaking a Persian dialect. They are Shi^ci. For long they were practically independent, but about 1895 were subjugated by the Amir. Many are found throughout the Punjab, sometimes in seasonal employment, but many as permanent residents. In 1904 the enlistment of a battalion in the British India Army was sanctioned.

Our reference to costly *Imambaras* at Hugli and Murshidabad, bespeaks the presence of those places of Shi^ci communities albeit they have dwindled. Murshidabad, formerly known as Makhsudabad, was in fact the last Muslim capital of Bengal before Calcutta attained that position under the East India Company. Several of the Nawwabs who ruled there have been professing Shi^cis. Notwithstanding the great decrease in the Muslim population of the city, including also the Shi^cis, Shi^ci practices continue at Muharram and other times.

* * *

Acting under the conviction that it is necessary for any community to organize both to achieve its own advancement and to pull its weight in society, the Shi^cis have their All-India Shi^ci Conference; organized in 1907 and meeting annually. It is non-political. It devotes its attention chiefly to organizations, to schools, hostels, orphanages and to other institutions or causes that might be called community-building. It also expresses its opinion concerning legislation. For instance, it has expressed its view against the Sarda Act which seeks to restrict marriages of girls under the age of fourteen, and it has favoured joint electorates in all elections with reserved seats for Muslims. It watches legislation regarding *waqfs*, or trusts.

There is also an All-India Shi^ci Political Conference to which Shi^cis may belong. This has usually been a pro-Congress body. Some Shi^cis are members of the Muslim League in purely political matters. In some Provinces, as in Bihar, United Provinces, and Punjab, there are Provincial Shi^ci Conferences, and in some cases district organizations also, but few of the latter function efficiently.

As the demand of the Muslim League for the recognition of Pakistan has increased, the Shi^cis' demands for protection as a minority Muslim community have grown stronger. The community appears unwilling to trust itself to a Sunni regime without very definite safeguards for its religious freedom, and a guarantee that it will receive due representations in ministries, legislative bodies and local boards. Replying to a representation of the working committee of the Shiᶜi Political Conference, Mr. Jinnah, President of the Muslim League, assured the Shiᶜis that the League stood for fair-play and being confident that "the majority of the members are with the League" he refused to discuss any safeguards. The natural consequences of such an attitude has been to make the Shiᶜis more community-conscious with increasing insistence on their rights to representation now through their own representatives, either nominated or elected, in all places where their numbers can at all justify it.

The Shiᶜis have an Intermediate College in Lucknow, a few high schools elsewhere, and hostels and orphanages. They also have in Lucknow a school for training preachers known as the Madrasat al-Waᶜizin. The Maharajah of Mahmudabad, a leader among the *taᶜalluqdars* of Oudh, has long been a patron of this institution. Connected with it is the Muᶜayyad al-ᶜUlum Association which publishes books and tracts setting forth Shiᶜi doctrines.

In Lucknow the Shiᶜi have a committee known as the Tanzim al-Mu'minin which directs efforts for the more effective organization of the Shiᶜis when any communal issue is at stake. It was this organization that provided leadership in the Shiᶜi-Sunni conflicts a few years ago.

* * *

To see the whole picture of the Shiᶜi community today, it is necessary to make a brief statement concerning recent events in Lucknow which show how sensitive both the Shiᶜis and Sunnis still are concerning matters that are really very old. It has been a time-honoured custom for Sunnis to recite praises of the rightly-guided *khulafa'* in private, in mosques, and at times in public procession. This is known as *madh sahabah*. It has likewise been the custom for Shiᶜis to recite comminations called *tabarruᶜ* against the first three *khulafa'*, whom they consider usurpers of ᶜAli's rights. So long as both communities followed these practices in private, or in mosques where the communities do not mix, there was no grievance. But in public, either practice stirred emotions and opposition from the other side, especially if it was done on certain holidays. Between 1904 and 1908 conflicts became so frequent that the Government of the United Provinces appointed a committee to study the situation. In 1909 Government forbade both *madh sahabah* and *tabarruᶜ* in public on three days: ᶜ*Ashura*, the tenth of Muharram; *chihilum*, the fortieth day of mourning; and the twenty-first day of Ramadan, which was the day of ᶜAli's death. The order did not forbid the public practice of either custom on other days, but required that permission for such practice should first be obtained, as it would be an innovation; and permission might be refused if the magistrate feared breach of the peace.

Things went quietly until in 1935, when two Sunnis publicly recited *madh sahabah* and were arrested. On ᶜ*Ashura* in 1936, again two men deliberately violated the order and at *chihilum* of the same year some fourteen were arrested for a like offence. The Sunnis then asked permission for a procession on *Bara wafat* which is celebrated as the Prophet's birthday. This fell on the third of June. Permission was refused. Then the Sunnis conceived weekly processions, every Friday, a procedure requiring permission for which they made no request. These came under a weekly interdict. In November and December the Governor met with deputations of both parties. Every effort was made for a friendly settlement of the dispute. When these failed the Government appointed a committee headed by Judge Allsopp of the High Court of Allahabad to study the whole situation. They recommended a continuance of the practice commenced in 1909, and the Government issued orders accordingly. This did not satisfy either group, but agitation subsided.

In the spring of 1939 the Government of the United Provinces gave permission for *madh sahabah* to be recited on *Bara Wafat*, the second of May. This led many Shi^{c}is to court arrest by reciting *tabarru^c*. Thirty thousand Sunnis are said to have gathered at their ^{c}*Idgah*. The only speaker on the occasion "congratulated the Sunnis for having won their rights after thirty-two years of struggle." Complete military and police preparations had been made, but Shi^{c}is, following their leaders' advice, stayed inside and there was no disturbance. But — agitation greatly increased. Clashes of both sides became common. Some were killed, many injured. The Ahrars, a party of nationalist-minded Muslims, supported the Sunnis. The Khaksars, another Muslim party ready for action, threatened to decide the dispute if others could not. They were stopped at the borders of the Province by police.

During the period of these communal clashes Shi^{c}is from Bengal, Bihar, Bombay, Central Provinces, North-West Frontier Province and the Punjab came to the help of their co-religionists and courted arrest. As many as ten thousand are said to have come from the Punjab. During the whole period about seventeen thousand Shi^{c}is courted arrest, and many thousands of Sunnis. As late as March 1945 "thirty-two Muslims were arrested for contravening the ban on the recitation of *madh sahabah* on the occasion of *Bara Wafat*."

The hope for the future is in those leaders of both communities who have consistently urged forbearance and tolerance, always looking to the welfare of the larger whole rather than the victory of a part. In that spirit alone will the finest progress of still larger units be achieved.

Annemarie Schimmel

. . . As in many other fields of Sindhi poetry, Shah ᶜAbd al-Latif of Bhit (1689–1752) is the first to express ideas which were later taken up by other poets. He devoted *Sur Kidaru* in his Hindi *Risalu* to the martyrdom of the Prophet, and saw the event of Karbala as embedded in the whole mystical tradition of Islam. As is his custom, he begins in *media res*, bringing his listeners to the moment when no news was heard from the heroes:

> The moon of Muharram was seen, anxiety about the princes occurred.

What has happened?

> Muharram has come back, but the Imams have not come.
> O princess of Medina, may the Lord bring us together

He meditates about the reason for their silence and senses the tragedy:

> The Mirs have gone out from Medina, they have come back.

But then he realizes that there is basically no reason for sadness or mourning, for

> The hardship of martyrdom, listen, is the day of joy.
> Yazid has not got an atom of this love.
> Death is rain for the children of ᶜAli.

For rain is seen by the Oriental poets in general, and by Shah ᶜAbd al-Latif in particular, as the sign of divine mercy, of *rahmah*, and in a country that is so much dependent on rain, this imagery acquires its full meaning.

> The hardship of martyrdom is all joyful rainy season.
> Yazid has not got the traces of this love.
> The decision to be killed was with the Imams from the very beginning.

This means that, already in pre-eternity, Hasan and Husayn had decided to sacrifice their lives for their ideals: when answering the divine address *Am I not you Lord?* (VII:171), they answered *'Balah* (= Yes)', and took upon themselves all the affliction (*balah*) which was to come upon them. Their intention to become a model for those who gain eternal life by suffering and sacrifice was made, as Shah ᶜAbd al-Latif reminds his listeners, at the very

day of the primordial covenant. Then, in the following chapter, our Sindhi
poet goes into more concrete details.

> The perfect ones, the lion-like *sayyids*, have come to Karbala;
> Having cut with Egyptian swords, they made heaps of carcasses;
> Heroes became confused, seeing Mir Husayn's attack.

But he soon turns to the eternal meaning of this battle and continues in
good Sufi spirit:

> The hardship of martyrdom is all coquetry (*naz*).
> The intoxicated understand the secret of the case of Karbala.

In having his beloved suffer, the divine Beloved seems to show his coquetry,
trying and examining their faith and love, and thus even the most cruel
manifestations of the battle in which the 'youthful heroes', as Shah Latif
calls them, are enmeshed, are signs of divine love.

> The earth trembles, shakes; the skies are in uproar;
> This is not a war, this is the manifestation of Love.

The poet knows that affliction is a special gift for the friends of God —
'Those who are afflicted most are the prophets, then the saints, then the
others in degrees' — and so he continues:

> The Friend kills the darlings, the lovers are slain,
> For the elect friends He prepares difficulties.
> God, the Eternal, without need — what He wants, He does.

Shah ᶜAbd al-Latif devotes two chapters to the actual battle, and to Hurr's
joining the fighters 'like a moth joins a candle', e.g., ready to imolate himself in the battle. But towards the end of the poem, the mystical aspect
becomes once more prominent; those who 'fight in the way of God' reach
Paradise, and the *huris* bind rose chains for them, as befits true bride-
grooms. But even more:

> Paradise is their place, overpowering they have gone to Paradise,
> They have become annihilated in God, with Him they have
>   become He. . .

The heroes, who have never thought of themselves, but only of love of God
which makes them face all difficulties, have finally reached the goal: the
fana' fi-Allah, annihilation in God and remaining in Him. Shah ᶜAbd al-
Latif has transformed the life of the Imams, and of the Imam Husayn in
particular, into a model for all those Sufis who strive, either in the *jihad-i
asghar* or in the *jihad-i akbar*, to reach the final annihilation in God, the

union which the Sufis so often express in the imagery of love and loving union. And it is certainly no accident that our Sindhi poet has applied the tune *Husayni*, which was originally meant for the dirges for Husayn, to the story of his favourite heroine, Sassui, who annihilated herself in her constant, brave search for her beloved, and is finally transformed into him.

Shah ^cAbd al-Latif's interpretation of the fate of the Imam Husayn as a model of suffering love, and thus as a model of the mystical path, is a deeply impressive piece of literature. It was never surpassed, although in his succession a number of poets among the Shi^ci of Sindh composed elegies on Karbala. The most famous of them is Thabit ^cAli Shah (1740–1810), whose specialty was the genre of *suwari*, the poem addressed to the rider Husayn, who once had ridden on the Prophet's back, and then was riding bravely into the battlefield. This genre, as well as the more common forms, persists in Sindhi throughout the whole of the eighteenth and nineteenth centuries, and even into our own times (Sachal Sarmast, Bidil Ruhriwaru, Mir Hasan, Shah Nasir, Mirza Baddhal Big, Mirza Qalich Big, to mention only a few, some of whom were Sunni Sufis). The *suwari* theme was lovingly elaborated by Sangi, that is the Talpur prince ^cAbd al-Husayn, to whom Sindhi owes some very fine and touching songs in honour of the prince of martyrs, and who strongly emphasizes the mystical aspects of the event of Karbala: Husayn is here put in relation with the Prophet.

> The Prince has made his *mi^craj* on the ground of Karbala.
> The Shah's horse has gained the rank of Buraq.

Death brings the Imam Husayn, who was riding his Zhu'l-janali, into the divine presence as much as the winged Buraq brought the Prophet into the immediate divine presence during his night journey and ascent into heaven.

Sangi knows also, as ever so many Shi^ci authors before him, that weeping for the sake of the Imam Husayn will be recompensed by laughing in the next world, and that the true meditation of the secret of sacrifice in love can lead the seeker to the divine presence, where, finally, as he says

> Duality becomes distant, and then one reaches unity

The theme of Husayn as the mystical model for all those who want to pursue the path of love looms large in the poetry of the Indus Valley and in the popular poetry of the Indian Muslims, whose thought was permeated by the teaching of the Sufis, and for whom, as for the Turkish Sufis, and for ^cAttar (and innumerable others), the suffering of the Imam Husayn, and that of Hasan ibn Mansur, formed a paradigm of the mystic's life. But there was also another way to understand the role of Husayn in the history of the

Islamic people, and importantly, the way was shown by Muhammad Iqbal, who was certainly a Sunni poet and philosopher. We mentioned at the beginning that it was he who saw the history of the Ka°bah defined by the two sacrifices — that of Isma°il at the beginning, and that of Husayn ibn °Ali in the end (*Bal-i jibril*). But almost two decades before he wrote those lines, he had devoted a long chapter to Husayn in his *Rumuz-i bikhudi*. Here, Husayn is praised — again in the mystical vocabulary — as the Imam of the lovers, the son of the virgin, the cypress of freedom in the Prophet's garden. While his father, Hadrat °Ali, was, in mystical interpretation, the *b* of the *bismi °illah*, the son became identified with the 'mighty slaughtering', a beautiful mixture of the mystical and Qur'anic interpretations. But Iqbal, like his predecessors, would also allude to the fact that Husayn, the prince of the best nation, used the back of the last prophet as his riding camel, and most beautiful is Iqbal's description of the jealous love that became honoured through his blood, which, through its imagery, again goes back to the account of the martyrdom of Husayn ibn Mansur al-Hallaj, who rubbed the bleeding stumps of his hands over his blackened face in order to remain *surkh-ru*, red-faced and honoured, in spite of his suffering.

For Iqbal, the position of Husayn in the Muslim community is as central as the position of the *Surat al-ikhlas* in the Holy Book.

Then he turns to his favourite topic, the constant tension between the positive and negative forces, between the prophet and saint on the one hand, and the oppressor and unbeliever on the other. Husayn and Yazid stand in the same line as Moses and Pharaoh. Iqbal then goes on to show how the *khilafah* was separated from the Qur'anic injunctions and became a worldly kingdom with the appearance of the Umayyads, and it was here that Husayn appeared like a raincloud — again the image of the blessing rain which always contrasts so impressively with the thirst and dryness of the actual scene of Karbala. It was Husayn's blood that rained upon the desert of Karbala and left the red tulips there.

The connection between the tulips in their red garments and the bloodstained garments of the martyrs had been a favourite image of Persian poetry since at least the fifteenth century, and when one thinks of the central place which the tulip occupies in Iqbal's thought and poetry as the flower of the manifestation of the divine fire, as the symbol of the Burning Bush on Mount Sinai, and as the flower that symbolizes the independent growth of man's *khudi* (= self) under the most difficult circumstances, when one takes all these aspects of the tulip together, one understands why the poet has the Imam Husayn 'plant tulips in the desert of Karbala'. Perhaps the similarity of the sound of *la ilah* and *lalah* (= tulip), as well as the fact that *lalah* has the numerical value as the word *Allah*, e.g., 66, may have enhanced Iqbal's use of the image in connection with the Imam Husayn, whose blood 'created the meadow', and who constructed a building of 'there is no deity but God.'

But whereas earlier mystical poets used to emphasize the person of Husayn as model for the mystic who, through self-sacrifice, finally reaches union with God, Iqbal, understandable, stresses another point: 'To lift the sword is the work of those who fight for the glory of religion, and to preserve the God-given order.' 'Husayn's blood, as it were, wrote the commentary on these words, and thus awakened a sleeping nation.'

Again, the parallel with Husayn ibn Mansur is evident (at least with Husayn ibn Mansur in the way Iqbal interprets him: he too claims, in the *Falak-i mushtari* in the *Javidnamah*, that he had come to bring resurrection to the spiritually dead, and had therefore to suffer. But when Husayn ibn ᶜAli drew the sword—the sword of Allah—he shed the blood of those who are occupied with, and interested in, things other than God; graphically, the word *la*, the beginning of the *shahadah*, resembles the form of a sword (preferably a two-edged sword, like Zu'l-faqar), and this sword does away with everything that is an object of worship besides God. It is the prophetic 'No' to anything that might be seen beside the Lord. By using the sword of 'No', Husayn, by his martyrdom, wrote the letters 'but God (*illa Allah*)' in the desert, and thus wrote the title of the script by which the Muslims find salvation.

It is from Husayn, says Iqbal, that we have learned the mysteries of the Qur'an, and when the glory of Syria and Baghdad and the marvels of Granada may be forgotten, yet, the strings of the instrument of the Muslims still resound with Husayn's melody, and faith remains fresh thanks to his call to prayer.

Husayn thus incorporates all the ideals which a true Muslim should possess, as Iqbal draws his picture: bravery and manliness, and, more than anything else, the dedication to the acknowledgement of God's absolute Unity; not in the sense of becoming united with Him in *fana'* as the Sufi poets had sung, but, rather, as the herald who by his *shahadah*, by his martyrdom, is not only a *shahid*, a martyr, but at the same time a witness, a *shahid*, for the unity of God, and thus the model for all generations of Muslims.

It is true, as Iqbal states, that the strings of the Muslims' instruments still resound with his name, and we may close with the last verse of the chapter devoted to him in the *Rumuz-i bikhudi:*

> O zephir, O messenger of those who are far away—
> Bring our tears to his pure dust.

Chapter Fifteen

Shi^cism in the Arab World

Shi^cism was originally born among the Arabs of Hijaz and Mesopotamia. It was only after the rise of the Safavids to power in 1501 that Iran became the center of Shi^cism, and Iranians came to constitute the majority of the followers. Despite the dominant role that Iranians have played in the history of Shi^cism, the contribution of the Arabs to Shi^cism before the Safavid era and ever since has been quite substantial. The Shi^ci communities in the Arab world, the most important of which are those of Iraq, Kuwait, Jabal ^cAmil and Biqa' Valley in Lebanon, the Qatif region and the al-Hasa' area of the Persian Gulf, and the eastern Hijaz region of Saudi Arabia remain centers of Shi^ci learning and religious life.

Although, doctrinally, there is no distinction between Arab Shi^cism and the Shi^ci faith as practiced in Iran or India, at the popular level there are cultural differences. For instance, while Shi^cism in Iran and India is closer to Sufism, Arab Shi^cism emphasizes the exoteric to a greater extent. Michel Mazzaoui elaborates on the doctrinal unity of Shi^cism as well as some of these parochial differences in his observation of Muharram rituals in southern Lebanon. Helena Cobban will explicate the political life and activities of the Lebanese Shi^cis, while Hanna Batatu will outline the workings of Shi^ci resurgent movements in the political life of Iraq since 1979. The excerpts are from TRDI, 230, 234–35; SCFL, 2–4, 8; and IUSM, 580–90, respectively.

Michel Mazzaoui

In short, the so-called "Three early Muhammads" (Kulayni, Ibn Babuyah, and Tusi "Shaykh al-Ta'ifah") who flourished before and partly during the great era of the Buyid dynasty, may have been responsible for the early efflorescence of Shiᶜi Imami thought during the classical Islamic period, but the "Three later Muhammads" (al-Hurr al-ᶜAmili, Mulla Muhsin-i Fayd, and the great Muhammad Baqir Majlisi) who flourished during the high Safavid period are not possible to understand and explain without reference to the ᶜAmilis, Qatifis, Bahrainis, and Ahsa'is who in many ways laid the foundations for what may be referred to as "Iranian Safavid Shiᶜism." The influence of these latter-day Shiᶜi scholars on the *ishraqi* philosophy of Mulla Sadra and Mir Damad — not to mention Mulla Hadi Sabzawari — has yet to be fully investigated.

This is the high-Islam Shiᶜi orthodox picture as it has been preserved by the great Shiᶜi *ᶜulama'* throughout many centuries: scribal, argumentative, elaborate, dogmatic, but balanced. It was made to start with Hadrat-i ᶜAli, through Muhammad, from the beginning of time, and concealed the Twelfth Imam, the Mahdi, till the end of time in inexorable religious-eschatological continuity.

On the other hand, the great Shiᶜi dimension of the Islamic tradition has with time developed a more human, folk-Islamic, popular aspect preserved in the Husayn-Karbala-ᶜAshura-taᶜziyyah complex. Away from the formalism of the scholars, this aspect of Shiᶜi Islam has survived over the centuries and has kept Shiᶜis of all countries united in their search for a more meaningful expression of their everyday life. Many Muslim peoples have shared in this tremendously vital experience: but the Shiᶜi Arabs who brought forth the family that held this tradition around its members (Muhammad, Fatimah, ᶜAli, Hasan, and Husayn), and the Iranians who established Shiᶜism as the official religion in Iran with the advent of the Safavids in 1501 — these two Muslim peoples have among themselves kept the popular, folk-Islamic aspect of this tradition alive in their countries for a very long time. There is every reason to believe that this self-expression of the religious image will develop, artistically and otherwise, forever — or at least until such time as religion ceases to be a meaningful dimension to the everyday life of Muslim communities.

However, it appears that there has always been a difference between the Arab and the Iranian approach to the problem. The former is harsher, social, down-to-earth realistic; the latter idealistic, more mythical, more sympathetic.

* * *

On the basis of Ibn Khaldun's theory of *ʿasabiyyah*, therefore, Husayn's movement was a mistake. For the pre-Islamic *ʿasabiyyah* of the Arabs, according to Ibn Khaldun's succinctly expressed argument, lies ultimately in the House of Umayyah as recognized by all. During the prophetic and miraculous days of Muhammad this traditional *ʿasabiyyah* was laid aside (in favor of Banu Hashim), but as soon as the new religion was firmly established the situation reverted to its previous state and Umayyads recovered their supremacy. Thus Ibn Khaldun is sternly correct, and there is no room in his rigorously balanced argument for Husayn or his cause.

This rather harsh position of the Sunni-Arab Muslim attitude toward the Husayn tradition made life very difficult for the Shiʿi communities of Jabal ʿAmil in south Lebanon (who, incidentally, claim a history that dates back to the Prophet's companion Abu Zarr al-Ghifari who is said to have been banished to that region by the Caliph ʿUmar). Their difficulties were further exacerbated during the Mamluk period when Syria (including Lebanon) was controlled from Cairo. This was the period that witnessed the martyrdom of Ibn Makki, "al-Shahid al-Awwal" (the first martyr). The activities of Ibn Taymiyyah in the next generation made things even worse.

As regards *taʿziyyah* proper, the practice in south Lebanon with its center in the hilly town of Nabatiyah is said to have been a recent nineteenth-century import from Iran. It is difficult to document this, but perhaps it can be explained on the basis of the ostracized position of Jabal ʿAmil during the long Ottoman period of three centuries. The ʿAmilis, after losing another *shahid*, naturally looked to Iraq and Iran for guidance. The old Lebanese-Safavid experience is now a reversed Iranian-Lebanese process. To a considerable degree this is still so today.

And aside from the religious fervor which is common to *taʿziyyah* both in Lebanon and in Iran, the situation in Jabal ʿAmil has certain peculiarities most of which arise from the different political and geographical milieu. Some of these may be briefly noted as follows, bearing in mind that they are very closely interrelated:

1. The deprived status of the area which has led quite recently to the rise of the socio-political movement of the so-called *mahrumin* (i.e., those "deprived" of social justice, etc.).

2. The physical nearness of the region to the newly created state of Israel which borders it immediately to the south, and the presence in the area of a large community of Palestinians. Over the past three decades the assimilation between the ʿAmilis and the Palestinians has reached a degree whereby, as a modern Lebanese sociologist puts it (in French, of course!): "Husayn, c'est la Palestine: Yazid n'est qu'une prefiguration du Zionisme!" It is a total identification of Husayn, the martyr of Karbala, with the tragic fate of the Palestinians; and of the arch-enemy Yazid with the alien Zionist movement responsible for the tragedy.

3. The struggle, feudal or otherwise, between traditional families in the region (Asʿads, Usayrans, Zayns, Khalils, etc.) and the helpless fate of the small farmers and peasants who seem to be totally lost in the middle.

4. The commanding position and stature of the Lebanese-Iraqi-Iranian political-religious leader, Imam Musa Sadr. His charisma touches everything that happens in Jabal ʿAmil and throughout the whole Shiʿi community in all Lebanon. His "gray eminence" and powerful personality are felt in all political, social, and religious circles in the country.

These conditions, peculiar to the Shiʿi community in Jabal ʿAmil, should be seen within the framework of a highly confused but essentially "free society" in Lebanon, as compared with say, the more centrally stable and somewhat more uniform political and social conditions in Iraq and Iran.

If one is permitted to make a final judgement in this context, one would like to say that in Iran *taʿziyyah* will safely develop (as indeed it has during the past several years) within the relative safety of art forms. This is politically neutral ground. In Lebanon, on the other hand, I would venture to guess that *taʿziyyah* will remain for a long time to come an expression of "opposition, martyrdom, and revolt."

Helena Cobban

Sizeable groups of Shiʿis have been living in what is now Lebanon since as long ago as the seventh century A.D. In the eleventh century, three local Shiʿi dynasties each enjoyed a brief moment of glory. From the twelfth century onwards, the Shiʿi of Lebanon were reduced to the status of dissenters, from a surrounding orthodoxy which was not their own.

The Shi^ci dissenters congregated in two areas of present-day Lebanon. The first was Jabal ^cAmil ("Mount ^cAmil"), which is that part of the Mount Lebanon range which lies in South Lebanon, between the Shouf and northern Galilee. The second was in the northern reaches of the Biqa', around the towns of Ba^clbak and Hirmil. . . .

Each of these two groups of Shi^ci followed a distinctive path of development. In the Jabal ^cAmil region rain-fed agriculture predominated. Shi^ci society there was dominated by a handful of large landlords, who exercised strong feudal power over their cultivators. The political power of these landowning families was balanced only slightly by that of the local Shi^ci learned men, or *^culama'* (singular, *^calim*). The *^culama'*, however, played an important social role in the life of the Jabal throughout the centuries. They retained and transmitted the people's beliefs, and they kept their small group of Shi^cis in touch with the much larger Shi^ci communities in southern Iraq and, later, in Iran. The *^culama'* network of Jabal ^cAmil produced many religious teachers whose fame spread throughout the Shi^ci world.

In the northern Biqa', by contrast, intensive agriculture was seldom feasible. The driest part of Lebanon, this region could only support a relatively sparse population. The Shi^ci there were clanspeople, living under honor codes similar to those which regulated the lives of nomads in the deserts of the Syrian interior.

These two groups of Shi^ci, politically weak and economically backward, took little part in the events which led to the establishment of an inter-sectarian system in the central parts of Mount Lebanon from 1585 on. The Ottoman Empire, which ruled the entire region, did so in the name of Sunni Muslim orthodoxy. The Ottomans were willing to recognize a degree of "separateness" for the Maronite Christians and Druze who dominated the population of central Mount Lebanon, but they treated the Shi^cis as they did other Muslims.

During the latter years of Ottoman rule, the Shi^cis constituted only about 5 percent of the population of the emerging inter-sectarian regime in central Mount Lebanon. However, in 1920 the French incorporated Jabal ^cAmil and the Biqa', together with Mount Lebanon and the Sunni-dominated coastal cities to the west, into the new "State of Greater Lebanon." The proportion of Shi^cis in the new entity was now around 17 percent.

Until World War II, the French continued to control Greater Lebanon under a mandate from the League of Nations. The Maronite Christians, who had been the strongest group in the previous regime in Mount Lebanon, remained the strongest in Greater Lebanon. The major threat as seen by the French-backed regime was from the Sunnis of the coast, who agitated to resume their previous links with the Syrian interior. The Shi^cis, who had no sizeable group of co-religionists in the immediate hinterland, were not regarded as constituting any such threat.

Furthermore, the French and their Maronite collaborators were able to co-opt the handful of land-owning families from Jabal ᶜAmil and the key clan leaders from the Biqa'. They gave them honorary positions in the state administration, good salaries, and access to Beirut's commercial riches. In return, these community leaders dealt with opposition movements inside their villages and clans. They were usually able to deliver their part of the bargain because they retained near-total control over their community's internal affairs.

During World War II the British replaced the French as the major power in the Eastern Mediterranean. In 1943, under British auspices, Sunni and Maronite leaders from Beirut reached an unwritten agreement called the "National Pact", which became the political basis for the country's independence.

The Pact divided the most important positions in the Lebanese administration between the country's major religious groups. First and second places were allotted to the Maronites and Sunnis, respectively. The Maronites were given the Presidency and the powerful post of Army Commander. The Sunnis were allotted the Premiership, which in theory could make or break any President's regime.

The Shiᶜis came in a poor third. They were given only the Speakership of the Parliament, a position that formally ranked second to the President, but in practice offered only occasional opportunities to affect the course of events.

* * *

When Lebanon became independent at the end of World War II, the new republic adopted *laissez-faire* economic policies, and during the next few years the merchant leaders of Beirut achieved unparalleled prosperity. Change came more slowly to the Shiᶜi communities of Jabal ᶜAmil and the Biqa'. By the end of the 1905's, however, the impact of modernization was being felt there as elsewhere, especially in infrastructural projects such as the national road and school systems. The number of school children in Jabal ᶜAmil and the Biqa' rocketed from 62,000 in 1959 to 225,000 in 1973; during that period all but half a dozen of the country's remotest villages were tied into the national road network.

The effects on Shiᶜi society were profound. Previously, enterprising Shiᶜi youths had usually found their ambition stifled by the conservatism of their traditional leaders. One means of escape had been emigration, to West Africa and elsewhere. By the mid-1960s, however, Shiᶜi youths could attend local schools, and then pursue heavily-subsidized courses at the new national university in Beirut, before returning to their villages as teachers or lawyers.

Many of the newly-mobilized Shiᶜi migrated permanently to Beirut, whose glittering business complex still dominated the country's economy. By the early 1980s, fully one-third of the Shiᶜi population of Lebanon was living in the capital and the teeming new suburbs which grew around it. In Beirut, Shiᶜis from South Lebanon and the Biqa' started mingling on a large scale, weaving the interests of what were now three geographically distinct Shiᶜi communities into a single national constituency.

The community experienced extremely rapid social mobilization during this period. A variety of radical movements found support, particularly among the younger generation. These movements were inspired by opposition to the continuing ascendancy of the Maronites, and by antipathy toward traditional Shiᶜi leaders, who were seen as collaborating in Maronite rule.

* * *

Amal had been founded as a broad-based military-political movement in 1975 by the charismatic religious leader Musa Sadr . . . . [see Chapter Twenty-Six in this book — Eds.] Despite early claims that it was non-sectarian, Amal always enjoyed close links with the Shiᶜi clerical hierarchy, also led by Sadr. During the 1975–76 civil war Amal played a marginal role, and during the 18 months which followed it seemed to have lost its direction. Some Shiᶜi analysts consider that the movement might have faded from the scene if it had not been spurred into new activity by three events in 1978 and early 1979.

- The first was Israel's invasion of South Lebanon in March 1978, which encouraged the Shiᶜis of that region to define their own interests, as opposed to those of the PLO and its leftist allies.
- The second was the disappearance of Musa Sadr while he was on an official visit to Libya in August 1978. Increasingly, evidence pointed to the responsibility of Libyan leader Muᶜammar Qazzafi. Sadr's quasi-martyrdom turned many Shiᶜis away from the pan-Arab leftism which Qazzafi represented, and toward increased support for Sadr's survivors in the Amal leadership.
- The third event was the meteoric rise of Khumayni's Shiᶜi movement in Iran, and the collapse of the Shah's regime in January 1979. The success scored by the Iranian clergy prompted many previously secular Lebanese Shiᶜis to look again at the potential of a religiously-based movement — without, however, necessarily accepting Iran as a model.

Amal's new prominence was supported and stimulated by the developments of the previous two decades. By the late 1970s, the community boasted hundreds of fully-trained professionals, now well-established, within their chosen fields. In 1977, for example, the first Shiᶜi-owned bank opened its doors in Beirut, to be followed by half a dozen others.

Amal was uniquely placed to utilize the full energies of these new Shiᶜi business and professional classes in a community-building effort which was free of the divisive influence of imported leftist ideology. Amal had no need to import any ideologies, because the *ᶜulama'* tradition in which it was rooted already contained important strands of indigenous social radicalism which stressed the good of the community as a whole.

On the basis of Amal's specifically Shiᶜi appeal, Shiᶜi doctors moved out of successful practices in Beirut to perform volunteer work in Amal's rural clinics. Shiᶜi bank-owners secured loans for Amal's rehabilitation and development projects. And many of Amal's expenses were met by the Shiᶜi emigrants of an earlier generation who had their own grudges against their sect's old-style leaders and who had prospered in West Africa and the Gulf.

By the early 1980s, therefore, the Shiᶜi of Lebanon were experiencing a social, political and economic renaissance. Taken in conjunction with the sect's new demographic strength, . . . this rebirth brought the Shiᶜi community close to the point where it could challenge the Maronite ascendancy. But before this challenge could be articulated, the Shiᶜi had to live through further painful days, in South Lebanon and in the suburbs of West Beirut.

* * *

The first major clash between Amal fighters and the Lebanese army took place in West Beirut in July 1983. Larger clashes occurred in late August, ending in an uneasy cease-fire, but the army's problems were just beginning. Following Israel's withdrawal from the Shouf mountains south-east of Beirut, the army found itself in pitched battle with Druze units there, and did not fare well. Further fighting erupted with Amal militias in West Beirut. On September 23, the threat of a total army breakdown, and the presence of a reinforced U.S. naval presence offshore, persuaded all parties, including the Syrians, to agree to a cease-fire and to political negotiations in Geneva.

A month later, extremists believed to be linked to one of the radical Shiᶜi groups drove a truck laden with explosives into the U.S. Marines' main compound near Beirut airport, 241 Marines were killed in that attack, and 57 French soldiers died in a simultaneous explosion in a French barracks.

During the following months, tensions remained high. It became increasingly clear that the Geneva talks were stalemated over the American-sponsored agreement Gemayyel had concluded the previous March with the Israelis. At the beginning of February 1984, a new clash erupted between Amal and the Lebanese army in Beirut. This time, the army started firing its tank guns directly into some of the heavily-populated Shiᶜi neighborhoods along the Green Line. On February 4, Amal leader Nabih Berri asked Muslim troops in the army not to take part in the shelling of civilian areas.

Berri was still *not* calling on the Muslim troops in the army to desert. However, in the tension of the hours which followed his appeal, a majority of the Shiᶜi soldiers did just that. Their flight from the army was so massive that by the morning of February 6, its authority had collapsed throughout West Beirut.

Amin Gemayyel was faced with the imminent disintegration of his regime, and the Americans with the possibility of their Marines being caught in the midst of a major new Lebanese maelstrom. Within hours, President Reagan announced his intention to withdraw the Marines. And Amin Gemayyel, in an abrupt about-face, went to Damascus to ask the Syrians to help save his regime.

The Syrians helped to negotiate the formation of a new Lebanese government, headed by the veteran ex-Premier Rashid Karami. One of the most powerful personalities named to this new government was Nabih Berri, who had headed Amal since 1980. . . . At first reluctant to accept a ministerial post, Berri agreed after being promised a major responsibility for the sensitive issue of South Lebanon.

Nabih Berri, and by implication the rest of Amal's reformist leadership, was asked to help the government resolve the country's many continuing disputes. But Berri's first months in office saw virtually no progress in the two fields which most concerned the Shiᶜis—the withdrawal of foreign forces, and curbs on the Maronites' ability to dominate the system. As of late 1984, Berri's failure to achieve results had strengthened the hand of Shiᶜi extremists, some of whom reportedly received substantial financial backing from Iran.

It is presumably one or more of these extremist groups which masks itself behind the shadowy appellation of "Islamic Jihad". That so-called organization has claimed responsiblity for all the major truck bomb explosions against American, French and Israeli targets in Lebanon in 1983 and 1984. The September 1984 attack against the relocated American Embassy underlined once again the seriousness of the threat posed by radical elements of the Shiᶜi community, both to Lebanon's prospects for peaceful reconstruction and to U.S. interests in Lebanon and the region.

Hanna Batatu

The conditions that dispose Shi'is of humble background favorably towards the Da'wah or the Mujahidin are quite different than the conditions that actuate their leaders and organizers.

In Greater Baghdad the two parties draw much of their support from al-Thawrah, a township which accounts for more than a quarter of the entire population of the capital and in which are to be found Baghdad's worst slums. In militant Shi'i literature, al-Thawrah is identified as "the stronghold of heroes."

The inhabitants of al-Thawrah are clearly disgruntled with their living conditions. At first glance this seems to be disputed by pertinent statistics. Thus, the minimum daily wage for unskilled laborers—a class to which most of the people of al-Thawrah belong—rose from 450–550 *fils* in 1973 to 1100 *fils* in 1977, that is, by 200–244 percent, and to 1300 *fils* in 1980, that is, by 236–289 percent. Moreover, a pick-and-shovel workman could earn in 1980 as high as two or three *dinars* a day. At the same time, thanks to control or subsidies by the state, prices have increased from 1973 to 1978, according to official figures, by only 53.4 percent for foodstuffs, 54.7 percent for housing, 55.9 percent for clothes, and 108.1 percent for shoes.

* * *

The Iraq-Iran war may also have had a negative impact on the daily life of the laboring people. It is true that there is at present an important boom, that trade in the cities is still buoyant, and that the government has gone out of its way to shield consumers from the effects of the war. But the shortage of oil and electricity has slowed down industrial activity. Over and above this, the escalating cost of the long drawn-out conflict and the need to finance the replacement or the repair of badly damaged oil and other economic installations are bound eventually to pinch the government's ability to spend for social welfare.

Finally, the people of al-Thawrah have an additional reason to be aggrieved: the government has not been providing their district with such services as sewers and asphalted streets because of its belief that the town lies over a rich oil field.

In brief, it is clear that the living conditions of the Shi'is of al-Thawrah have much to do with their susceptibility to the influence of the Da'wah and the Mujahidin. By way of further evidence, one could underline that it is from this same township or its old component districts that the Communist Party derived much of its strength in the 1940s, 1950s, and 1960s. In fact, the deep wound inflicted upon its cadre in 1963, the course of compromise with the Ba^cth regime that its leadership steered from 1973 to 1978, and the going into exile in 1979 of no fewer than 3,000 of its hardened members left the disadvantaged of the capital with no organized means of protest and produced a void in the underground which the Da^cwah and Mujahidin hastened to fill.

But what role does the Shi^cism of the sympathizers of the Da^cwah and the Mujahidin play in their affection for these militant movements? Of course it would be foolish even to attempt to infer what is in their hearts, and the analysis must confine itself to the objective and observable phenomena of Shi^cism. In this connection, it is necessary to bear in mind that the inhabitants of al-Thawrah are all of recent rural origins and hail from districts in which, . . . religion was very feebly organized.

Does the scarcity of rural religious institutions argue a lack of religious vigor on the part of rural Shi^cis?

Of course, there is here no intrinsic correlation of cause and effect. Moreover, at least in the past, in certain villages resident tribal *sayyids* or claimants of descent from the Prophet used their *mudif* or guest-house as a sort of mosque or *husayniyyih*. To other villages itinerant preachers—the *mu'mins* —came from neighboring towns. However, although some of these preachers were trainees of religious schools and bonafide representatives of Shi^ci religious leaders, others specialized in superstition or even quackery and lived off the peasant-tribesmen. Certain of the *sayyids* were also of this latter type.

At the same time it is necessary to remember that many of the rural Shi^cis were of relatively recent bedouin origin and the bedouin have not been known for the vigor of their religion. . . .

It is also significant that the agricultural, sheep-tending, or marsh-dwelling tribesmen are not strict in their Shi^cism or well versed in their faith. It is true that on the whole they conform to certain traditional rites and participate in great religious events. For example, most of them—but not the Shi^cis of the marshes—will not eat meat of an animal slaughtered by Muslims as yet uncircumcized. Many will also not miss participating in the lamentation for the martyred Husayn or visiting in their lifetime the sacred places at Najaf and Karbala if they can afford it, and the followers of the Usuli sect—as contradistinguished from the Akhbaris [see Chapter Eighteen in this book—Eds.]—nurse the hope their bodies will be taken after death for burial in Wadi al-Salam (the Valley of Peace) between the resting place of the Commander of the Faithful ^cAli ibn Abi Talib and Husayn, "the Lord of Martyrs."

On the other hand, except for those who live on the Euphrates in the neighborhood of the Shi^ci holy cities, the tribesmen are by and large lax about their prayers or in keeping the fast. They are also much prone to perjury, having for so long been harassed by usurers and tax-collectors and by the importunities of arbitrary *shaykhs*.

Moreover, at some unknown point in the past, they developed a heterodox cult around ʿAbbas, Husayn's half-brother, who stood out for his bravery and tenacity in the historic battle of Karbala in 680 A.D. They would indeed swear falsely by God, the Prophet, his cousin ʿAli and his grandson Husayn, who were all, in their view, compassionate and forgiving, but not by ʿAbbas, who was stern and quick to anger when roused. A violation of an oath by him, they believe, is bound to be visited by a swift and apposite punishment.

More than that, down to the 1958 Revolution, and even afterwards, they continued on the whole to be governed more by their ancient tribal customs than by the *shariʿah* or Islamic law as developed and interpreted by the Twelve Shiʿi Imams and the great Shiʿi *marajiʿ*.

When peasant-tribesmen moved to Baghdad (and Basrah) from the countryside in the 1930s and succeeding decades in great waves, sometimes emptying whole villages, and hundreds of thousands became fixed in what eventually came to be known as al-Thawrah township, little concern was at first shown, except by the Communists, for their ideological development. Shiʿi men of religion were not conspicuous in their districts until after the mid-1960s and the rise of the Daʿwah movement, when the migrants became the object of sustained attention.

* * *

It was not a riviving Islam or an ascendant Shiʿism that prompted elements within the *hawzah al-ʿilmiyyah* (the circle of *ʿulama'*) at Najaf to organize ranks in the late 1960s and set on foot the Daʿwah party.

On the contrary, they were moved by a growing sense that the old faith was receding, that skepticism and even disdain for traditional rites were rife among the educated Shiʿis, that the belief of even the urban Shiʿi masses was not as firm, and their conformism to ancient usages not as punctual or as reverent as in times past, and that the *ʿulama'* were losing ground and declining in prestige and material influence.

There were many signs of the weakening of the religious sense of the people. For one thing, the students of religion had been palpably decreasing. In 1918, no fewer than 6,000 students attended the theological *madrasahs* or schools of Najaf. By 1957 the number of students had declined to 1,954, of whom only 326 were Iraqis. Because of the lack of any time limit on the learning process, which went on for very many years and could be continued for life, the ages of the students ranged from 20 to 60, and the turnover of graduates was not large. Moreover, some Iraqis enrolled in the *madrasahs* only in name in order to secure exemption from military service, a privilege accorded to all students of religion.

For another thing, the monopoly of the Shi^{c}i ^{c}*ulama'* over the molding of the world-view of their followers, which they enjoyed down to the 1920s, had been broken by reason of the entry of Shi^{c}is into modern schools and the penetration of European influences. As early as 1929 they found themselves defied in their own citadel when the government took the decision to open a girls' school at Najaf itself. The governor of the place dismissed their vehement protests against this step as dictated by "selfish motives." "With the advance of education and knowledge," observed another high official, "the influence the ^{c}*ulama'* at present exercise over the more ignoant people is bound to be weakened with a consequent falling off in their income."

Indeed, their material position depended on the strength of the old pieties, inasmuch as they could expect little financial backing from the government and did not have control over rich *awqaf* as did their Sunni counterparts. "The Shi^{c}i ^{c}*ulama'*," wrote King Faysal I confidentially in1933, "have no connection with the government and are at present estranged from it, particularly inasmuch as they see the Sunni ^{c}*ulama'* in possession of funds and properties of which they are deprived, and envy, notably among the religious classes, is something well-known."

Formerly, however, the distinguished Shi^{c}i ^{c}*ulama'* received large contributions from their co-religionists in the form of *zakat, khums, radd mazalim,* and *sawm wa salat.* The *zakat* was the tithe for the poor. The *khums* or fifth part of the income formed the prerequisite of the claimants of descent from the Prophet. *Radd mazalim* was the special forgiveness purchased from the ^{c}*ulama'* for earning state salaries derived from taxes which to a strict Shi^{c}i were forbidden. *Sawm wa salat* were fees for the observing of prayers and fastings on behalf of certain persons for periods varying in accordance with the amount paid. In 1918 these contributions were so ample that the chief Shi^{c}i *marja^c* at Najaf, Sayyid Muhammad Kazim al-Tabataba'i al-Yazdi, alone distributed upwards of 100,000 pounds sterling in charity. But in 1953 the Najafi Imam Ayatollah Muhammad al-Husayn Kashif al-Ghita' complained:

> In bygone days the people and the chiefs of tribes were virtuous and openhanded. They showed deference to the ^{c}*ulama'* and came to their aid. The religious schools lived on their gifts and charities . . . But since the change in conditions, the shrinking of benevolence, and the corruption of the wealthy . . . the religious schools have fallen on bad days . . . The Ministry of Education sends us every year only a small grant-in-aid . . . and the contribution of the *Awqaf* Department is even less substantial . . .

A visitor to Najaf in the 1960s could not help noticing the straits to which many of the Shiᶜi legists and students of religion were reduced.

The deep penetration of Communism in the 1940s and 1950s into Najaf itself also alarmed the conservative instincts of many of the *ᶜulama'*. Ayatollah Kashif al-Ghita' noted in 1953 with a sense of peril not untinged by wonder how "wide nests" comprising "spirited and ardent young men" throve in its name in the holiest of Shiᶜi cities, even though it was "without logic or proof and unassisted by funds or patronage or dignity of rank." Even more disconcerting must have been the conversion to communism of descendants of *ᶜulama'* and provincial town *sayyids*.

The pronounced Sunnism of the regime of ᶜAbdul-Salam ᶜArif (1963–66) and the secularly-oriented policies of the Baᶜth government which came to power in 1968 were other important factors in galvanizing the Shiᶜi *ᶜulama'* into action.

The earliest sign of restlessness on the part of the *ᶜulama'* was the emergence in 1964 of the Fatimiyyah group, which never took on a regularized expression and was soon penetrated by the political police and effectively dispersed. It aroused enough apprehension, however, to cause the government to create a special branch within the Directorate of Public Security—the Second Branch—devoted exclusively to the combating of underground Shiᶜi activities.

The exile from Iran to Najaf in 1964 of Ruhullah Khumayni marked an event in the life of the Shiᶜi *ᶜulama'*. The power he exercised, and continues to exercise, over others lies in his stern and unswerving idealism. He was one of the few of Iran's religious dignitaries who did not kiss the hand of the Shah or fawn at his feet. "I am a Husayni not a Hasani," he often reminds his followers, referring to the claim that Husayn held fast to his principles and won martyrdom, wheras Hasan compromised with the Umayyads only to die by poison at their instigation. Consistently, Khumayni had no hand in the rise of the Daᶜwah party, which is known to have had in the earliest phase of its history links, probably of an indirect nature, with the Shah, whose objective at the time was the overthrow of the Baᶜth regime.

Many Shiᶜis identify the founding of the Daᶜwah in 1968 or 1969 with no less a figure than the highest Shiᶜi *marjaᶜ* of the day, Sayyid Muhsin al-Hakim al-Tabataba'i of Najaf. What can be said with certainty is that he was under harassment or surveillance by the authorities in 1969 and that his sons, Sayyid Mahdi al-Hakim, who was accused by the government in the same year of "spying on behalf of the CIA" and "conspiring to overthrow the existing regime," was associated with the Daᶜwah from the very beginning. These appear to be the only grounds for the presumption that the Shiᶜi world's highest personage gave the movement his blessings.

At the outset the Da^cwah penetrated among the men of religion in Najaf, Karbala, and Kazimiyyah and tended to attract in particular elements from their lower and younger ranks. In this connection it should be pointed out *muquddasins* or pious men who are addressed as *Thiqqat al-Islam* ("the Trust of Islam") and are qualified to receive charity and settle minor *shari^cah* cases. Of more significance are the lesser *mujtahids* or *hujjat al-Islam wa al-muslimin* ("the Proof of Islam and of the Muslims") and the greater *mujtahids* or *hujjat al-Islam wa al-muslimin, ayatallah fi al-^calamin* ("the Proof of Islam and of Muslims, the Sign of God in the World"). Both the lesser and the greater *mujtahids* are capable of giving a *fatwa* or binding opinion, but the *fatwas* of the latter are given more consideration in view of their greater influence and the larger number of their followers. The most important *mujtahids* are the *maraji^c* ("authorities") who are addressed as *ayatollah al-^cuzma* ("the Great Sign of God"). Their *fatwas* are, as a rule, final unless revoked by the highest *marja^c*, which is unusual. It should be added that after the death in 1970 of the chief *marji^c*, Muhsin al-Hakim, there were only three *marja^cs* in Iraq, all at Najaf: his successor Abu'l-Qasim al-Khu'i, Ruhullah al-Khumayni, and Muhammad Baqir al-Sadr. None became associated with the Da^cwah party.

It is also worth emphasizing that the Shi^ci men of religion in Iraq are not as numerous per capita as they are in Iran. A recent French book affirmed that in 1979 there were in Iran 180,000 *mullas*. An informed Shi^ci source gave a more conservative estimate of 120,000. This, if true, would mean that there was in that year one *mulla* for every 308 Iranians, assuming a total population of 37 million. There are no up-to-date statistics on the size of the religious class in Iraq, but in 1947, when the population was about 4.5 million (at present it is 14 million), the number of persons employed in the "religious services" of all denominations did not exceed 7763, and this figure included persons who were not men of religion, such as servants in mosques or churches. As could be expected, more than one-sixth of the total were concentrated in the Shi^ci holy cities: 601 at Karbala, 474 at Najaf, and 232 at Kazimiyyah.

It is in the mosques of these cities that the Da^cwah began spreading its ideas. It also gave considerable attention to the vast crowds that take part there annually in the ceremonial processions commemorating the martyrdom of Husayn on 20 Safar [Martyrdom of Imam Husayn is on the 10 Moharram; the fortieth day of his martyrdom is commemorated on the 20 Safar. Eds.], and hoped to attach the people's feelings to its ideological conclusions.

In its efforts the Da^cwah was greatly assisted by the drought that struck the Najaf-Karbala region and other Shi^ci areas in the middle 1970s in the wake of the reduction of the flow of the Euphrates River because of Syria's newly-built dam at Tabqah. The drought ruined fruit orchards and the rice crop, affecting hundreds of thousands of peasants.

The Daᶜwah's first test of strength with the government came in 1974 when the Husayni processions broke up into angry political protests. But this was as nothing compared to the fury that greeted the forces of the police in 1977 when they attempted to interfere with the processions half-way between Najar and Karbala. Outraged, the crowds stormed a police-station at nearby al-Haydariyyah chanting rhythmically:

"Saddam, shil idak! Shaᶜb al-ᶜIraq ma yiridak!"

(Saddam, remove your hand! The people of Iraq do not want you!)

The Iranian Revolution of 1978–79 radicalized the Daᶜwah and prompted the appearance of the Mujahidin. This signalled before long a shift in the method of struggle, the two movements now resorting to sporadic guerilla attacks on the posts of the police, the Baᶜth party and the People's Army.

The Iranian Revolution also turned the gaze of the Shiᶜis increasingly towards Sayyid Muhammad Baqir al-Sadr [see Chapter Twenty-Five in this book — Eds.], who had no political or organizational connection with either the Daᶜwah or the Mujahidin. But he was Iraq's most distinguished and most enlightened Shiᶜi legist and inspired much devotion among the common people. Moreover, without any encouragement from him, more and more Shiᶜis began to look up to him for political leadership and Iran's Arabic radio broadcasts repeatedly referred to him as "the Khumayni of Iraq." In the eyes of the government he loomed as a rival pole of attraction and a symbol of approaching danger.

Chapter Sixteen

Shi^cism in Turkey

*The spread of Shi^cism in Anatolia is inseparable from the Islamization
of that area, but it became particularly strong during the initial years of
the Safavid state, when Shah Isma^cil dispatched Shi^ci missionaries into
the Ottoman territories. The Safavid Shah's patronage of Shi^cism in
Anatolia, whether out of religious or political considerations, planted
the seeds of the faith in that land. The confrontations between the
Safavids and the Ottomans and the final defeat of Shah Isma^cil at the
Battle of Chaldiran led the Ottoman sultans to desecrate the Shi^ci community of Anatolia. Despite the conscious efforts of the Ottoman
sultans to root out Shi^cism from their territories, the faith has survived
in that land up to modern times. This has partly been due to the influence of the Azari and Caucassian Turks, whose culture resembles
that of the Anatolians but who are predominantly Shi^ci. In the following passage, Metin And writes on the Shi^ci communities of Turkey and
their religious life. The excerpt is from* TRDI, *pp. 238–254.*

Metin And

Ta^cziyyah performances and elaborate Muharram processions are to be found among the Turks, especially among the Azarbaijan Turks of Caucasia, and there are some extant manuscripts of *ta^cziyyah* plays in Turkish. For instance, out of 1054 *ta^cziyyah* manuscripts in the Vatican Collection, 35 are in Turkish, only 4 are in Arabic, and the rest are in Persian. Yet in Anatolia there is no tradition of *ta^cziyyah* performances, since the Sunni element is predominant there. Also in the traditional Anatolian Turkish theatre, tragedy does not exist, comedy being considered the only acceptable form of dramatic art. However, both at the urban and rural levels there is a great variety of dramatic forms. In the larger towns the most usual dramatic performances are *Urtauyunu*, popular improvised comedies which very much resemble the *ta^cziyyah* performances in the style in which they are presented and in their form and staging. In the villages mummery farces and pantomimes are performed by the thousands, most of them survivals of seasonal fertility rites. They also are very much like the *ta^cziyyah* performances in dramatic structure. Another dramatic form is story-telling by a *middah*, or *kissahan*, whose repertoire contains episodes of the Karbala passion cycle. Similarly there are also *marthiyyah*, *nifis* (elegy) and other literary forms depicting the Karbala Passion, narrated or recited in the Muharram assemblies in dramatic fashion with the narrator gesticulating, shouting, singing and crying. Here the audience participates by weeping for the martyrs or cursing the slayers of Husayn.

In countries like Iran, where Turks are in the minority, their participation in the Muharram rites differs according to whether they are Shi^cis or Sunnis. For instance, a seventeenth-century Italian traveler who gives a detailed account of the Muharram mysteries he witnessed in Persia in 1694 mentions that "until the very end of the doleful festival, which the Persians call *Asciur* or mourning, no Turk can appear in public without great danger to his life." Another seventeenth-century traveler who gives a detailed account of Persian Muharram mysteries in 1666 mentions that ". . . After them enter'd three hundred Turks, which were fled from the Borders of Turkey. . . ." Yet some European writers erroneously associate the *ta^cziyyah* tradition with Anatolian Turkey. For instance, an article, entitled "Turkish Theatre," giving short definitions of various dramatic forms, devotes most of its space to explaining *ta^cziyyah*, identifying it with Turkey. On the other hand, an Englishman who spent many years in rural Anatolia, in his article on Shi^ci Turks, briefly describing Muharram observances in an ^cAlawi village, clearly states that there is no *ta^cziyyah* tradition among them.

*   *   *

All over Anatolia, especially among the adherents of the Biktashi order, and the village ^cAlawis—who are mostly heterodox tribes, seminomadic, having summer pasturage as well as a fixed winter domiciles under various names—such as Tahtaci (woodcutter), Yuruk, Turkomen, Qizilbash (Red Head) and others—various rites and beliefs are practiced. In their mourning there is no excess. For instance, the Biktashi mourn only with tears, never with dirges and wailing. The most widespread acts of mourning are fasting and other forms of abstinence. All food and drink are avoided between dawn and sunset. The Biktashis mourn the passion of Karbala with fasting during the first ten days of the month. Fasting has come to be regarded by many as the most important act. In some other tribes twelve days' fast is observed, one day for each of the twelve Imams, the first being for ^cAli, the tenth for Husayn, and the last for Mahdi, since the history of the Imams comprises a continuous martyrdom. The last is a short one of three hours since Mahdi is believed to be alive in a cave hidden from his enemies and friends, from which he will return one day. . . .

*   *   *

There are other abstinences which are acts of mourning (I shall discuss abstinence from water later). They do not wash or change their underclothing; they do not use soap; they do not shave; they do not look in the mirror because doing so would be considered making up one's face—but another reason is that a mirror has an important part in the cults of the dead which are very prevalent in many societies. They also abstain from smelling anything; they do not sing, play a musical instrument, dance, laugh or amuse themselves. They do not drink alcoholic beverages, do not kill bugs such as lice and fleas, do not have sexual intercourse, and abstain from inhaling tobacco. They also cautiously abstain from all other indulgences. Only on the eleventh day is underclothing washed or changed, and in the evening they drink three draughts of water while cursing Yazid.

As a meritorious act some people do not drink a drop of water even after the fasting period. For most people who keep the fast for ten or twelve days, abstention from water is practiced only from the evening of the ninth till the afternoon of the tenth. However, abstention from water is carried on at times other than for the Karbala passion; to practice it only once a year would be separating the Muharram fast completely from whatever connection with natural phenomena its origins may have had. The agony of the thirst of the Martyrs is almost the only feature not imitated by the Azarbaijan Turks. Their ceremonies afford manifold occasions to show and to make ceremonial use of the blessing of water. Yet in Anatolia they do recall the Karbala calamity with a ceremonial thirst. Some who are not so rigid during the fast do drink water, but this must not be pure water. As a substitute they drink tea, coffee, fruit syrup, buttermilk, or a drink made from yogurt and water called *ayran*. From the evening of the ninth day until the afternoon of the tenth the Biktashis especially commemorate Husayn's suffering by drinking no water. Then they sometimes break their fast by drinking water mixed with dust. To make this drink, which is also used for its prophylactic effects, they scrape dust from tablets of dried earth brought by pilgrims from near Husayn's tomb at Karbala and Najaf, and called *Sicdi Tasi* by the Biktashi, who keep these relics of the Martyrs to press against their foreheads when at prayers, or to use as charms and amulets.

In Istanbul a mosque called Haji Mustafa Chami has been believed, since Sultan Mahmud's time, to hold the apocryphal graves of Fatimah and Zaynab, the daughters of Husayn. Tradition holds that these daughters, having been captured by the Greeks, and brought to Istanbul, killed themselves in prison rather than marry unbelievers. Another popular belief was that St. Andrew of Crete, the miracle-working Christian Saint, was buried there also.

There are many popular beliefs like that connected with the Karbala passion. For instance, one of the explanations as to why the hare is taboo is that the soul of Yazid passed into that animal. In Qizilbash mythology there are several variations concerning the fate of Husayn's head. The best established version runs as follows: After Husayn had been decapitated, the head was stolen by an Armenian priest, Aq Murtada Kisis, who substituted for it the head of his eldest son. When the Turks discovered the fraud, the priest cut off the heads of all of his seven sons and offered each in turn as the head of Husayn. He received a divine warning to smear the head of his youngest son with Husayn's blood, and thus deceived the Turks. He then kept for himself the holy relic which he placed in a special apartment, adorning it with gold and silver and silk. His only daughter, on entering that apartment did not see the head of Husayn but instead, a plate of gold filled with honey. She tasted the honey and became with child. One day the girl complained of a cold and when she sneezed her father suddenly saw issue from her nose a bright flame, which changed at the same instant into the form of a child. Thus did Imam Baqir, son of Husayn, come into the world. That a descendant of °Ali had been born immediately became known to the Turks, who thereupon sent people to search for the child and slay it. They came to the priest's house while the young mother was washing the household linen. On being told the reason for their visit she hastily put the child into a copper cauldron which was on the fire and covered him with linen. By magic the Turks knew that the child was in a house of copper, but as they were unable to find any such house in the proximity of the priest's dwelling, they were baffled, and the child's life was saved. Because of this incident the child received the name of Baqir, which in Turkish means copper.

As was stated at the beginning of this chapter, Anatolian Turks do not have *ta͑ziyyah* plays to be enacted, but instead a great number of literary texts, both *marthiyyah* (elegies) to be recited and *maqatils* to be narrated dramatically in the Muharram assemblies. A great many of them are written by established poets and some are collective, anonymous folk poetry transmitted either by written texts or by oral tradition.

Chapter Seventeen

Shi^cism in East Africa

Finally, mention should be made of the sizeable Shi^ci communities of East Africa. Shi^cism in East Africa exists mainly among the Asian settlers in Tanzania, Somalia, Kenya, and up until recently, Uganda. East African Shi^cis are predominantly either of Iranian or Indian origin. Their lineage can be traced to Iranian merchant families who settled in Zanzibar or north Indian and occasionally south Indian (such as Gujrati) Shi^cis who arrived in East Africa during British rule. Some Shi^cis are also of Arab origin, from the Hijaz or the Persian Gulf.

The Africanization campaigns promoted by the East African states in recent years has caused major socio-economic setbacks for all Asian communities in the region. Consequently, the cultural life and activities of East African Shi^cis has been disrupted to a great extent. Yet, as Knappert's account of the epic of Imam Husayn in Swahili litearture portrays, Shi^cism continues to be a pervasive aspect of Muslim life of the region. The excerpt is from Alserat, *pp. 69–74.*

Jan Knappert

The Swahili people live on the East African Coast from Barawa in Somalia southwards well into Mozambique, now called by its Swahili name Msumbiji. The Swahili have been influenced by Islam ever since the first Muslims arrived from Arabia, according to their own traditions in the reign of the Caliph ᶜAbd al-Malik ibn Marwan. This would be before 85 A.H./705 A.D. However, there is a tradition that the first Muslims were the *Ummah zaydiyyah*, the community of Zayd, presumably Zayd ibn ᶜAli Zayn al-ᶜAbidin. The followers of the latter were driven southwards into Yemen by the Umayyads after Zayd's abortive attempt to dislodge them. This would be close to the East African coast for such a migration. However, it would make the date somewhat later than the earlier date suggested. Nothing remains of this group in modern Swahili society, but we know that Indian influence was present on the East African Coast in the late Middle Ages; this may have been a source for the propagation of the Shiᶜi on both sides of the Arabian Sea. It is true to say, however, that the great influx of Indians into East Africa began only early in the nineteenth century. We do not know that some of these first settlers were Indian families of the Shiᶜi communities: Ismaᶜili, Buhuri and Ithna ᶜAshari.

The poet of the Swahili epic about Husayn's tragic death was called Himidi (the Swahili form of Ahmad) ibn ᶜAbdullah Buhry whose family settled in Tanga in the 1820s. The name Buhry seems to suggest that they were of the Buhura persuasion but this is uncertain. There is an Arabic word *buhri* meaning "asthmatic", and *buhuri* 'brilliant". Himidi ibn ᶜAbdullah ibn Saᶜid ibn ᶜAbdullah ibn Masᶜud died in Tanga c. 1922. He wrote several works, mostly long epics, drawing his material from ancient stories about the Prophet Muhammad. Some of these epics were in fact actually composed by his grandfather, Saᶜid ibn ᶜAbdullah who died c. 1875. The al-Buhry family is known throughout Tanzania for their scholarship and saintly lives. The poet's son was a well-known law expert and *qadi* of Tanga.

*   *   *

The Swahili epic begins by stating somewhat incredibly that Muᶜawiyah loved Husayn, thus seeming to present the view that Muᶜawiyah as a Companion of the Prophet must have been a righteous person. It is only with his son, Yazid, that corruption begins. When Muʿawiyah died in 680, his son, Yazid, demanded the oath of allegiance from Husayn, but the latter refused and went to Mecca. The epic emphasizes that on his deathbed, Muʿawiyah delivers a long warning to Yazid, urging him to respect Husayn and his children because "we are the servants and they, the grandchildren of the Holy Prophet, are the masters." This is the view accepted by the majority of Muslims: that the servant reigns, while the master, i.e. the legitimate heir to the caliphate, succession of the Prophet, spends his time in devotion and study. However, when the servant becomes a tyrant and neglects the laws of Islam, it becomes the duty of the incorruptible scholar to assume the rule of leadership and bring the community back to pure Islam. This is the crucial point in the epic about Husayn.

Yazid immediately began life of dissolute extravagances at the expense of the people. There is a long description of the luxury in which Yazid indulged which the poet regards as wasteful. The ideal ruler of Islam lives in austerity, spending his money on alms for the poor and wars against the infidel. Yazid, according to the poem, had a throne made for himself inlaid with pearls, rubies and emeralds. Then he called the chiefs of all the tribes in his empire to come and pay homage to him. In the Swahili text, he says: *mji kwanga musujudi* "Come ye and prostrate yourselves before me." This indicates Yazid's sacreligious character, since prostration may only be peformed before God.

One day, Husayn went to visit Yazid. To his horror he saw the latter drinking wine and eating pork. He hurried home and wept after seeing the sacred laws of his grandfather flouted by the man who was in authority over the Islamic community. His sister, Sakinah, said to him: "My prince you must not weep, for your crying makes the jinn and the angels in Heaven shed tears and the sea will freeze with sorrow".

Husayn decided to move to Medina, and the family all set out on their camels towards Medina. The people of Medina, all faithful followers of the Prophet, greeted Husayn with joy and reverence. Husayn visited the grave of his grandfather and the spirit showed its joy by emitting a brilliant light from the tomb. In Medina, Husayn settled down to a quiet life of study and prayer. Often his friends suggested that he should set himself up as Caliph, but Husayn made it clear that he preferred the prayer mat to the throne of empire.

Yazid appointed ʿAbdullah (the Arabic name is ʿUbaydullah) as his governor in the important Iraqi city of Kufah. ʿAbdullah was a ruthless and cruel exploiter of the people. They decided that their only hope was to invite Husayn to come and expel this tyrant and make himself ruler of Kufah. They sent two letters to Husayn to tell him of the atrocities that were being committed against them. Husayn paid no attention to the letters. The moral of this is that he did not seek personal power or personal aggrandizement, but lived exclusively in the fear of God. It was to that fear that the Kufans appealed in a third letter. They wrote: "If you do not come here and put an end to this oppression of faithful Muslims, we will accuse you before the Almighty on the Day of Judgement of neglecting your duty as the grandson of Muhammad, on whom be peace". When he read this Husayn was disturbed and wrote: "To the citizens of Kufah, your letter cut my heart. Soon I will come if the loving God wills. For now I send you Msilimu and Nuᶜman. Msilimu will lead the prayers."

Msilimu was a historical person; his proper name is Muslim ibn ᶜAqil, the cousin of Husayn. The idea of leading the prayers indicated that he was Husayn's religious and political representative, though Nuᶜman was to undertake the everyday political duties.

The poet describes how Ibn Ziyad went from bad to worse. He was like the kite in the story of the peaceful farm.

> He that has a wife — not his wife —
> he that has a daughter — not his daughter —
> it is like the chicken and the kite.

This is a perfect example of classical Swahili style: compact and expressive. The poet means that anyone in the city who has a beautiful wife and daughter is in danger of seeing her raped by the tyrant, who will behave just as the kite behaves with the chicken. The kite is a common image in Swahili for the adulterer, the rapist; the chicken is the metaphor for a virtuous woman, full of fear of being attacked.

Eventually Husayn decided to go and restore order in Kufah. Many friends tried to dissuade him, offering to make him king in Mecca. He declined, since his purpose was not to become king, but to restore justice and re-establish the law of the Prophet in Iraq. So he set out with a small group (77 according to the sage). As soon as they were in the desert, he had a vision. Visions are part of the desert world, and there are *hatifu* (Arabic *hawatif*) voices that whisper from nowhere. It is indeed appropriate, within the context of the poem, that the grandson of the Prophet should have visions when he has embarked on his divine mission.

> When he arrived in the wilderness,
> angels descended
> with swords and holding
> the weapons of the Holy War.

These apparitions from the sky said to Husayn: "O Husayn, we have been sent by the Giver to help you. May we join you? If you wish, we will do anything that is necessary." But Husayn replied that it was unnecessary for them to join his army for: *Amriyi hairudi.* "His command does not return" (i.e. God does not go back on His words. If he wishes Husayn to win there will be no need for other help). The angels disappeared and Husayn continued his journey. . . .

* * *

By that time Husayn had arrived at Karbala, near the river Euphrates, and 62 miles sout-west of Baghdad. Soon Husayn was surrounded by enemies who occupied the river so that he and his part were without water. The saga interprets these tactics as a typical sign of cowardice on the part of Yazid. One by one the Muslim heroes went out to fight their way through the enemy lines. One by one they were killed, after defeating an average of 1,000 men each. Each time Husayn went and retrieved their bodies, after fierce fighting so that they might be given a proper Islamic burial. When his son, ᶜAli, still a suckling infant, was overcome by thirst, he carried him to a nearby house, hoping to find some water. While the child was still in his arms, it was hit by an arrow in the ear. The child cried out and died. Muhammad, another of Husayn's sons was so shocked at the indiscriminate killing of the child that he said to his father: "I am tired of waiting to die. Paradise is prepared for us, why wait before going in? I want to go into battle now."

> Give me permission to go in.
> I am resigned to perish.
> All these things are written,
> predestined by the Giver.
> All that happens to us
> is the command of the Loved One.

The last stanza seems to express the idea in Qur'an (XI: 51) and with this philosophy, he went into battle and was finally killed.

ᶜAbdullah, another son of Husayn, was killed in battle while saying: "I witness God". According to the poet, God called to the nymphs of Paradise: "Ye clear-eyed love-nymphs stand by ready to receive the souls of those fighting men whom I love so much.

> Stand by, stand by.
> Don't let them fall in the sand.

The *huris* hurried to the battlefield and as each Muslim was killed, one of them took his soul, as it left his bleeding body, tenderly into her arms and flew up to Paradise with him. Seventeen young men went to the Garden of Paradise in this way. Husayn remained alone. He looked to right and to left but there was no helper in sight, only enemies surrounded him and weeping women. The women mentioned include many of the names of the women of the house of the Prophet who had long since died, including some of the daughters of the Prophet such as Fatimah. The purpose is deliberate within the context of the myth, for the poet must have been aware of such elementary Islamic history. The presence of these great women of the family of the Prophet at the scene emphasizes the power of the myth. Similar names had occurred earlier at the death of Muhammad ibn al-Husayn. He had cried out: "Come up here, my father Husayn, look! Here are your parents and your grandfather Muhammad, your grandmother Khadijah, and Hasan, and Fatimah, my grandmother, and your father, Shaykh cAli, come quickly." The poet does not say so, but this was a beatific vision, a vision of Paradise as he died upon the battlefield. All his ancestors, all the loved ones, appeared there to welcome him.

Husayn decided to go into battle for the last time. He knew he was going to die, for the month was Muharram, and the white sand in a bag, which the Prophet had given Fatimah for him, had turned red.

> He sat on his horse
> like the lightning that accompanies the South wind
> with a big black cloud,
> dark and cool.

> Husayn stopped
> and said goodbye to the women
> "Adieu, adieu
> I go and shall not return".

Part V

Shiᶜism in the Modern World: Early Political Ideas

Chapter Eighteen

The Usuli–Akhbari Controversy

The position of the ᶜulama' in Shiᶜism is to a large extent a function of their right to ijtihad. *This concept, however, was not a part of the religious doctrines of early Shiᶜism; it developed as a juridical doctrine over the centuries, especially since the advent to power of the Zand dynasty in Iran (1750-95). The evolution of the office of the* mujtahid *was not free of religious debates or controversies. A group of Shiᶜi ᶜulama', known as Akhbaris vehemently opposed the concept of* ijtihad *and its implications for religious and social functions of the ᶜulama'. The advocates of* ijtihad, *the Usulis, meanwhile, argued for the right of the ᶜulama' to decree opinions and to apply Shiᶜism to increasingly diverse aspects of social life. Bayat and Kazemi Moussavi explain the doctrines of the two schools, identify the leading propagators of each, and explain the way in which the usuli–Akhbari controversy has shaped Shiᶜi jurisprudence. The excerpts are taken from MDSTQI, pages 20-23, and EPMTSC, pages 35-38, respectively.*

Mangol Bayat

Though the practice of *ijtihad*, the endeavor to determine the Imam's true opinion, was limited in the tenth and eleventh centuries, with time it gained increasing recognition. The religious dignitary who exercised it, the *mujtahid*, came to acquire the highest ranking position amongst the ^c*ulama'*. The qualities of infallibility and supreme authority, however, were still denied the office. It is worth noting here that, despite the jurists' argument to the contrary, the legal basis of Shi^ci jurisprudence is no different from the Sunni's, at least in practice. For, in the last analysis, the method used to "discover with certainty" the Imam's opinion amounts to following the judgment of individual *mujtahids* who would prove arbitrarily that their opinion was the Imam's.

The position of the *mujtahid*, however, was to be contested from within the ranks of the religious organization itself, by members of the Akhbari school of theology. Founded by Shaykh Muhammad Sharif Astarabadi (d. 1624), it rejected the function of *ijtihad* as incompatible with the authority of the Imam. Like the view of earlier Shi^ci jurists, it conceived the entire community as followers of the Imam's teachings, and declared the position of the *mujtahid* unnecessary. It denounced the practice of *ijma^c*, accused the *mujtahids* of practicing analogical reasoning like the Sunnis, and claimed that the Traditions of the Prophet and the Imams (or *akhbar*, hence the name of their school) provide sufficient guidance to understanding the Shi^ci faith and doctrine.

Contemporary scholars view the Akhbaris' literal acceptance of the holy texts as an indication of a traditionalist, inflexible attitude, "non-systematic and dominated by purely doctrinal considerations," that would not tolerate individual rational judgment. In contrast, the *mujtahid* stand (which came to be known as the Usuli* view) is depicted as ensuring "a living continuous leadership of the believers" and providing "flexibility regarding legal and especially political questions" which would make it possible for them to act as legislators for their followers. Such an analysis needs rectification.

---

*The *usul* are the fundamental principles the jurists relied upon to derive the religious law from the compiled Traditions of the Prophet and the Imams.

The bitter Usuli-Akhbari controversy that dominated Twelver Shiᶜi circles in the seventeenth, eighteenth and early nineteenth centuries must be viewed as a reaction to the power acquired by the *mujtahids*. Some leading Sufi masters and theosophers also strongly resented the *mujtahid's* domi-nance of the Shiᶜi intellectual scene, and objected to the limitations imposed by the official Usuli determination of Shiᶜi doctrines. Some of them echoed the Akhbaris in charging the *mujtahids* with literalism and a narrow-minded interpretation of the holy texts. It is significant that the Akhbari school suffered final defeat at the end of the eighteenth century at the hand of Aqa Muhammad Baqir Bihbahani (d. 1780-91) and his son, Mulla Muhammad ᶜAli Bihbahani (d. 1801-02), who earned himself the title of Sufi-killer. Both religious leaders acquired reputations as the fiercest and most revengeful opponents of those who challenged Shiᶜi orthodoxy, as defined by the Safavid and post-Safavid *mujtahids*. It was not only a matter of doctrinal disputes, but also a struggle to consolidate the *mujtahids'* power that lay behind the ruthless elimination of any form of religious dis-sent. The controversy led to open scenes of violence in the streets of Najaf and Karbala in Iraq, as well as the major cities of Iran. Many leading Akhbaris were killed, and others were declared heretics.

The Usuli *mujtahids* ensured their direct influence upon their followers' conduct, and provided a basis for their power, by making *taqlid* (following the directives of one particular *mujtahid* whom the believer considered most worthy) incumbent upon the believers. Following the ruling of a deceased one was forbidden. A *mujtahid* had to be learned in theology, grammar, Arabic, logic, and jurisprudence. He must have demonstrated his knowledge and established for himself a scholarly reputation through the number of licenses he held from reputable ᶜulama', and through his teaching, lectures, and writings. Such qualifications, in addition to certain personal features (maturity, intelligence, being of the male sex, piety, justice, and legitimate birth), were necessary conditions to attain such a prestigious post. Because scholastic learning was inaccessible to the or-dinary people, who were neither socially nor individually distinguished for such a career, the subordinate rank of *mulla* or *akhund*, was available to them. Their function was to execute the *mujtahid's* orders, teach in the lower schools, and perform religious services. The position of *mujtahid* in-creasingly became either hereditary, and/or kept in the hands of an ex-clusive group of ᶜulama' who appointed their successors from among their favorite disciples.

By the nineteenth century, an official hierarchy of orthodox ᶜulama' had come into being, whose source of power was not to be found in the classical Shiᶜi doctrine as developed by generations of Imami theologians. The entire Shiᶜi community came to be regarded as consisting of two distinct groups:

the small group of *mujtahids* acting as the guides, and the majority of their dutiful followers. Imami Shi^{c}i produced its own class of law-minded ^{c}ulama' who, like their Sunni counterparts, declared themselves the guardians of the law, and the protectors of religion against the deviators. Consequently, the original spirit of speculative radicalism which characterized the early formation of the sect.

"The institution of the *mujtahid*," writes Hamid Algar, "had the practical merit of ensuring a continuous leadership of the community and of providing a source of immediate authority that was neither too great to offend the claims of *wilayah* (belief in the Imam as leader of the community), nor too restricted to be without practical effect." However, such a claim clearly reflects the *mujtahids'* own arbitrary judgment that only they could personify the religious leadership of the community. In fact, they did not hesitate to use coercive means to enforce their views and suppress any other that might contradict, and hence challenge, their position as the sole interpreters of the religious law, and as its protectors against any kind of innovation. Sheer force helped them to establish their power, and force also kept them in power. Algar's assertion that "the ^{c}ulama' were deemed the leaders of the nation, and it was natural for leadership to enforce its directives," is questionable. In the beginning of the nineteenth century the ^{c}ulama"s concern was not the nation. Their religious policy was not a national policy; nor was it meant to be. Similarly, the centralization of the religious hierarchy, which was essentially the result of Usuli religious policy was not aimed at "modernizing the national church." To attribute to the ^{c}ulama"s activities any kind of nationalist, modernist ideology would be entirely misleading and anachronistic, to say the least. Furthermore, a concern with the religious deviators' threat to the ^{c}ulama"s authority, rather than their desire to check temporal power, lies behind the centralization of clerical power in modern Iran. The rise to power of the *mujtahids* occurred at a time when a corresponding center of state power did not exist.

Ahmad Kazemi Moussavi

Usul implies the doctrine of the "principle" of Muslim jurisprudence, and ^{c}ilm al-usul is generally considered to be the science of the proofs which lead to the establishment of the legal standards. The proofs, according to Twelver Shiᶜi are: the Qur'an, the traditions of the Prophet and the Imams, *ijmaᶜ*, and *ᶜaql*. *Ijmaᶜ* is the unanimous consensus of a group of Shiᶜi *mujtahids* which conveys the word of the infallible Imam. *Ijmaᶜ*, because it expresses the Imam's opinion, is considered to be proof. *ᶜAql* may be translated as intellect, but, technically, in the Shiᶜi jurisprudence it applies to the four practical principles (*usul-i ᶜamali*), namely, *bara'at* (immunity), *ihtiyat* (precaution), *takhyir* (selection), and *istishab* (continuity in the previous state). These principles should only be employed by qualified jurists when other religious proofs are not applicable. In fact, these principles are no more than speculative reasoning (*zann*). Placing jurist's speculation on a par with explicit proofs was objected to by the Akhbaris, another branch of the Shiᶜi school.

In contrast to the Usulis, the Akhbaris rely primarily on the traditions (*akhbar*) of the Prophet and the Imams as the source of religious knowledge. Opposing Usuli and Akhbari currents were apparent in Twelver Shiᶜism from its beginning, although they multiplied in the course of time. In the first juridical period (fourth and fifth centuries after *hijrah*) the Twelver jurists of Iraq, including Shaykh al-Mufid (d. 413/1021), Sayyid-al Murtada (d. 436/1044), and Shaykh al-Tusi (d. 460/1067) adopted and introduced the principles of *usul* under the influence of both Shafiᶜi and Muᶜtazili doctrines. Shafiᶜi (d. 204/819) is known as the first Muslim jurist who wrote the principles of Islamic jurisprudence in his *al-Risalah*. Muᶜtazilite logical approach to Islamic thought helped the formation of Shiᶜi scholastic theology (*ᶜIlm al-kalam)*. Under such influences Sayyid Murtada wrote the first Shiᶜi book on *Usul al-fiqh*, namely *al-Zariᶜa*. It was Shaykh al-Tusi, however, who established these principles in his treatise *ᶜUddat al-usul*.

In contrast to the above Iraqi circle of Shiᶜi *ᶜulama'*, the Qum and Ray Twelver jurists such as Kulayni (d. 329/940) and Ibn Babuyah Sadduq (d. 381/991) leaned toward a more traditionalist position. Nevertheless, neither the term "Akhbari" nor its categorical differences with Usuli appeared in the early works of the Twelvers. Shaykh al-Tusi referred to Akhbaris as *ashab al-jumal*, literalists who stopped short of reasoning by basing the fundamentals of religion on the text of reported *hadith*. Akhbaris and Usulis as two antagonistic factions are first mentioned by ᶜAbd al-Jalil Qazwini (d. 565/1170), an Ithana ᶜAshari writer who characterizes Akhbaris as narrow traditionalists.

The second wave of the Usuli trends, which shaped the third juridical stage, occurred in the Mongol period. In this period the principle of *ijtihad* was applied to Shiᶜi jurisprudence. According to Ayatollah Mutahhari, Ibn al-Mutahhar al-Hilli (d. 726/1325) was probably the first jurist among the Shiᶜis who used the term *mujtahid* in a sense of one who deduces a religious ordinance (*hukm-i shar^ci*) on the basis of the authentic arguments of the *shari^cah*.

In the first stage, *ijtihad* as well as *qiyas* (analogy) were not appreciated by the Shi^cis. Shaykh al-Tusi negated both *qiyas* and *ijtihad* in his famous book *^cUddat al-usul*. But Ibn al-Mutahhar employed *ijtihad* as meaning disciplined reasoning based on the *shari^cah*. He also developed the principles of *^cIlm al-usul* in order to introduce more legal and logical norms. This led the meaning of *^cIlm al-usul* to extend beyond the four principal sources of the *shari^cah*. By carefully studying Ibn al-Mutahhar's perception of *ijtihad*, we notice that Ibn al-Mutahhar differentiates between *ijtihad al-mukallafin* and *ijtihad al-mujtahidin*. He does not appreciate the former and evaluates the latter as a striving that leads to speculation (*zann*) not to knowledge (*^cilm*). In fact, Ibn al-Mutahhar is the first Shi^ci jurist who manipulated *ijtihad* as a prerogative of the *^culama'*. The principles of *ijtihad* and *taqlid* are fully formulated by ^cAmili (1011/1602), who devoted an independent chapter to the above-mentioned topics.

The Usuli trend lost momentum in the eleventh century after *hijrah*, largely because of an Akhbari resurgence through the work of Mulla Amin Astarabadi (d. 1033/1623). But time was on the side of the Usulis, thanks to the prolonged concealment of the Imam of the Age and the growing need for the wider interpretation of the *shari^cah*.

The emergence of a pragmatic jurist, Aqa Baqir Bihbihani (1118/1706–1208/1793) in Karbala, not only helped the Usuli school to re-establish itself, but it also gave the school a new momentum. Bihbihani enjoys the titel of founder (*mu'assis*) of a new stage in Twelver-Shi^ci jurisprudence, although he was never considered to be a brilliant scholar like Ibn al-Mutahhar or Shahid al-Thani. His significance lies in the practical method that he used to win popular support, against the Akhbaris and to eliminate them in Iran and Iraq. In pre-Qajar periods, the question of Akhbarism was a matter of orientation and style, but Bihbihani, by refuting the Akhbaris, managed to outlaw them as heretics.

Bihbihani's lifelong argument with his rival Shaykh Yusuf Bahrayni (d. 1172/1758), centered on the problem of the validity of the *mujtahids'* speculative reasoning after the gate of the acquisition of knowledge was closed by the occultation of the Twelfth Imam. Bihbihani set forth the validity of the *mujtahid's* speculation and the validity of his general knowledge (*^cilm-i ijmali*) in a way which had no precedent in Shi^ci jurisprudence.

> It is proverbial among *^culama* that the gate of acquiring knowlege concerning religious ordinances (*ahkam*) is closed (upon the absence of the Imam). How? We see a large number of *ahkam* which become known after effort. This is true despite the fact that effort leads to speculative reason (*zann*) which is neither proof (*hujjah*) nor beneficial; despite the

fact that Akhbaris claim that the gate of acquiring knowledge is not
closed and it is a matter of controversy; and despite the fact that in
many cases we know things without searching, because they are obvious. We say that no speculations are proofs, nor may *ijma*ᶜ (which is
reversible by contradictory *ijma*ᶜ) nor even self-evidency (*bidaha*)
amount to absolute proof. It is only the *mujtahids'* speculation acquired
after endeavour (*ijtihad*) that weigh as proof.

Bihbihani's conviction of the *mujtahids'* ability to establish proof led him to
consider the *mujtahids* as vicegerents of the Prophet (*khalifat al-Rasul*),
but he did not elaborate on this theme, as Naraqi (d. 1245/1830) and Khumayni later did. What Bihbihani gained was not merely the establishment of
the validity of juristic *ijtihad*, but also the necessity to emulate the most
learned *mutjahid* by ordinary *mukallafs*.

Chapter Nineteen

Early Propagation of Wilayat-i Faqih *and* Mulla Ahmad Naraqi

One of the most important doctrinal categories that has characterized modern Shi^ci political thought and action is without doubt Wilayat-i faqih: *the chief ideological apparatus of the Islamic Revolution in Iran. Although this idea is often associated with the works of Ayatollah Khumayni, it found one of its earliest manifestations in the works of Mulla Ahmad Naraqi. The nature of Naraqi's reference to* Wilayat-i faqih *and the extent to which he ascribed political significance to it have been the subject of great debate amongst academicians who are attempting to chart the course of the Shi^ci political thought over the centuries as well as determine the roots of Khumayni's political world view. In the following article, which is published here for the first time, Hamid Dabashi has addressed some of the essential aspects of the debate, particularly through an exposition of Naraqi's pertinent works.*

Hamid Dabashi

Mulla Ahmad Naraqi and the Question of the Guardianship of the Jurisconsult (Wilayat-i Faqih)

Introduction

The Islamic Revolution in Iran, now institutionalized in the state apparatus of the Islamic Republic, was ideologically charged and guided by perhaps the most significant doctrinal development of the Shiᶜi juridical history. The doctrine, *wilayat-i faqih* (the guardianship of the jurisconsult), became the most elaborate political claim of the Islamic movement, which not only mobilized various domestic and external forces to topple the old regime but also successfully superseded the competing ideological constituencies to the point of their nullifying pacification or neutralizing assimilation. The central tension that holds this doctrine together, and makes it of utmost significance for the modern Shiᶜi history, is the metamorphical nature of religion and politics as converged into a credal concept.

Perhaps it would not be an exaggeration to suggest that the development of this political doctrine in its integral juridical context has been in dormant process since the very inception of the Shiᶜi cause in the early Islamic history. As the most successful doctrinal-political movement to perpetuate Muhammad's charismatic legacy, Shiᶜi Islam has endured and surpassed persistent tensions that chiefly characterize its understanding and recognition of political authority. The doctrinal development of *wilayat-i faqih*, long before its institutional crystalization in the Islamic Republic, is the chief nucleus of that characterizing tension of Shiᶜi Islam: 'By what authority?

This question leads to perhaps the most significant aspect of this doctrine: its "personal" as opposed to "institutional," character. *Wilayat-i faqih* is the attempted doctrinal legitimization of an individual, the *faqih*. This conceptual development — to avoid the category of innovation for its strong Islamic connotations — happens, or is happening, fourteen centuries after the initial establishment of Shiᶜi Islam as the most charismatically charged branch of Islam. This remarkable tenacity of Shiᶜism for reenacting its seminal experience on a perpetual basis makes, and has made, institutional Shiᶜism something of a contradiction in terms. *Wilayat-i faqih* is the latest doctrinal representation of the permanently charismatic feature of Shiᶜism. Its logistics within the general credal context of Shiᶜism is of immediate importance.

Wilayat-i Faqih *as a Shiᶜi Doctrine*

As a doctrine, *wilayat-i faqih* is closely related to a number of crucial Shiᶜi tenets that together constitute the theological trajectory of this branch of Islam. This connection, however precarious it may appear occasionally, makes the doctrinal development not altogether inimical to the general theological texture of Shiᶜi Islam. To be sure, *wilayat-i faqih* is much too recent in its theoretical development to be in any significant way articulated in its reciprocal relations with other Shiᶜi dogmas. However, certain credal dimensions of Shiᶜism, in their historical constitution, perhaps are, inevitably and inadvertently, conducive to *wilayat-i faqih*.

The most immediate intrinsic Shiᶜi dogmatic force with which *wilayat-i faqih* is organically related is the doctrine of *Imamah*. The inevitable and divinely ordained continuity of Muhammad's charismatic authority in the physical and metaphysical lines of descent through the Imams has kept the tenacious spontaneity of Shiᶜi political tract much too alert and responsive to be circumscribed by institutional routinization. Perpetually keeping Shiᶜism on the edge of political outburst, the doctrine of *Imamah* has been its single most important surviving and flourishing force. While in the pre-*ghaybah* period, *Imamah* was the legitimating doctrine of the specific Shiᶜi Imams; in the post-*ghaybah* period it has grown gradually into the tacit, yet most emphatic, source of authority for the Shiᶜi jurisconsults (*fuqaha'*). Thus, the very seminal doctrine of *Imamah*, so crucial to the theological foundation of Shiᶜism, has anticipated some mode of authority, the specifics of which is always the subject of legal disputations, for the jurisconsult. To be sure, the constituency and range of this stipulated authority were primarily, if not entirely, within legal and not specifically political domains. But to the degree that these two domains — legal and political — were metamorphical, one had considerable repercussions for the other.

The doctrine of *ghaybah* is equally instrumental in the gradual development of *wilayat-i faqih* as the legitimizing conception of clerical authority. Although *ghaybah* brought the doctrine of *Imamah* to a specific metalogical conclusion, at the same time, it also extended the implications of Imamate authority from the realm of the infallible (*maᶜsum*) Imam to the constituency of the indominable *faqih*.

"The Imam of the Age" (*Imam-i zaman*) was the doctrinal device that extended the atemporal authority of the Household of the Prophet through history. In the post-*ghaybah* period, while the world awaited its apocalyptic end in the "peace of the Mahdi," the political apparatus and its basis of legitimacy always faced the equivocal approval of the religious order. On the religious end of this equilibrium, the political attachment was always problematic, often negational, and occasionally revolutionary. To forge or formulate doctrinal basis of political activity or inactivity became as much a matter of genuine juridical speculation, in the original sense of the word, as directed repercussions of explicitly political forces.

Doctrinaires of Wilayat-i Faqih: For and Against

In recent assessments of its historical development, *wilayat-i faqih* is believed to have "a long jurisprudential ancestry," (Enayat, 160), and as Amir Arjomand's superb study of the dimensions of authority in Shiᶜi Iran has demonstrated, it is intricately connected to the institutional vicissitudes of Shiᶜi doctrines (Amir Arjomand, 1984 *et. passim*.).

The question of *wilayah* has been so central to the Shiᶜi doctrinal developments that from very early on specific messianic movements in Shiᶜi communities had utilized it to justify their cause. For example, Abu Salih al-Hilli (d. 683/1284) argued for his "specific guardianship" (*wilayah al-khassah*), as opposed to the "general guardianship" (*wilayah al-ᶜammah*), as the doctrinal basis of his charismatic movement. (Al-Shaybi, 84, 104). This doctrine, explicitly or implicitly, seems to have been congenial to messianic movements in the Shiᶜi communities.

Occasional references by some of the seminal theoreticians of the Shiᶜi law to jurisprudential postulates may be reconstrued as justifications of some mode of political authority for the jurisconsult. The founding fathers of Shiᶜi jurisprudence, for example, Kulayni and Ibn Babuyah, opposed the idea of "representing the Hidden Imam" on the basis of his being eternally alive and present. Most Shiᶜi scholars never specifically stipulated the possibility of any "deputy" for the Hidden Imam or even, as in the case of al-Tusi, emphatically forbade it. Al-Tusi had specified that "other than the Hidden Imam nobody can occupy the position of the prophet" (Al-Tusi, 249).

Muhaqqiq-i Hilli (d. 672/1273) had stipulated that "it is necessary to confer upon those who have authority because of their right of representing [the Hidden Imam] the expenditure of the Imam's share [a form of religious tax] from the existing commerce, as [other such things] which is due to the Hidden [Imam] is delegated to them too" (Muhaqqiq-i Hilli, 53). There is no specific reference here to the potential political dimension of the Hidden Imam's authority. In fact, the preceeding clause, which is specifically a legal-commercial statute, makes a political reading of the latter part quite problematic.

ᶜAllamah Hilli (d. 726/1325) had referred also to the prerogative right of the religious scholars particularly in judicial matters:

> It is incumbent upon the Shiᶜi *fuqaha'* who are knowledgeable of judicial sources and thus possess the necessary qualifications to pass judgement amongst the people; and this is incumbent upon them in the absence of the Imam, even if they incure hardship, and they should not fear for themselves or for any other Muslim (Hilli, ᶜAllamah, 459).

This passage, too, specifically stipulates the passing of judgement (*al-ᶜifta'*) as the prerogative of the religious authorities. However, the conjunction that "they should not fear for themselves or for any other Muslim" (*wa lam yakhafu ᶜala anfusihim wa la ᶜala ahadin min al-mu'minin*) can be read as an indication of reference to dimensions of authority other than merely legal, for example political. However, although taking issue with the Sunnite position in selecting an Imam by the community, ᶜAllamah Hilli does not specifically stipulate the recognition of any deputy for the Hidden Imam.

Al-Shahid al-Thani (d. 966/1558) had articulated the specifics of the *faqih's* authority in the absence of the Twelfth Imam, but this was mainly in legal domains as well as those cases that a *jihad* pronouncement became inevitable (al-Shahid al-Thani, 255).

Of prominent Shiᶜi scholars after Mulla Ahmad, Shaykh Murtada Ansari (d. 1281/1864) is of particular significance because of his articulate disagreement with a political reading of *wilayat-i faqih*. In his exposition of Ansari's position on *wilayat-i faqih*, Enayat concludes that

> according to Ansari, "absolute authority" over the people in both temporal and spiritual matters falls within the jurisdiction of the Imams. But statutory and discretionary penalties . . . measures depriving people of their rights, and solutions to unforeseen events . . . are specifically delegated to the *faqihs* in the absence of the Imams. Thus what remains for the *faqihs* is residual *wilayah*, in the sense that only certain kinds of power can be exercised and, then, only with regard to those Muslims who, for different reasons, are unable to administer their own affairs, such as the minor, the insane, the ailing, and the beneficiaries of public endowments (Enayat, 162).

Ansari is quite specific about the judicial nature of *wilayah*, and this is supported by clear characterization of any claim to political authority as that of the (Hidden) Imam. "In principle," Ansari believes, "no individual, except the prophet and the Imam, has the authority to exert *wilayah* over others" (ibid.).

Another eminent modern Shiᶜi theologian and jurisconsult who, despite his admiration for the Islamic Revolution in Iran, has taken issue with the conception of *wilayat-i faqih* is Muhammad Jawad Mughniyah (1904–79). His disagreement is principally on the doctrinal basis of the infallibility of the Imam (*ᶜismah*). The jurisconsult simply cannot claim overriding authority as that of the Imam; this would equate his status with the Infallible, which is not permissible (Enayat, 168; Göbel, 131-32). Amplifying the position of Ansari, Mughniyah restricts the *wilayah* of the *fuqaha* to specifically juridical domains and supports his argument by referring to such luminaries of the Shiᶜi jurisprudence as Bahr al-ᶜUlum and Mirza-yi Na'ini (Mughniyah, 33-4).

Despite the diverse currents of opinions in the background of modern debates over the question of *wilayat-i faqih*, it is primarily Mulla Ahmad Naraqi's treatment of the subject that has assumed significance. A closer attention to this nineteenth century activist-jurisconsult should illuminate the reasons of this renewed prominence.

Mulla Ahmad Naraqi

Mulla Ahmad Naraqi (1185/1771-1245/1829) was a prominent jurisconsult (*faqih*) whose introduction of a number of unprecedented legal issues have recently come to the fore. Perhaps one of his most significant contribution to Shiᶜi jurisprudence was the elaboratin of a dialectical logic into the fabric of legal disputations. *Ijtimaᶜ al-amr wa'l-nahi* is a treatise on legal injunctions that expounds the logical feasibility of simultaneously adopting two opposite points of view.

His primary interest in the principles of jurisprudence (*usul al-fiqh*) is evident in his education in Karbala, where he studied with the eminent Shiᶜi legal theorist Aqa Baqir Bihbihani (d. 1208/1793). After the death of Bihbahani, Mulla Ahmad continued his legal studies (1210/1795-1212/1797) with two of the late teacher's most prominent students: Sayyid Mihdi Bahr al-ᶜUlum and Shaykh Jaᶜfar Najafi.

Mulla Ahmad's work on the principles of jurisprudence (*usual al-fiqh*) includes an extensive commentary on *Tajrid al-usul*, written by his fahter, Mulla Mahdi Naraqi (d. 1209/1794). Mulla Ahmad began writing his commentary in 1220/1805; the result is the voluminous *Sharh tajrid al-usul*, an encyclopedic canon of the Shiᶜi principles of jurisprudence. In 1224/1809, Mulla Ahmad prepared a concise summary of this work, *Manahij al-usul wa'l-ahkam*, wherein he further elaborated on the communal binding of legal extrapolations on part of the religious scholar.

Other than these theoretical works on the principles of Shiᶜi jurisprudence, Naraqi also wrote a number of treatises on specific legal injunctions. These include *Mustanad al-shiᶜah, Asas al-ahkam, Asrar al-hajj, Hidayat al-Shiᶜah,* and *al-Rasa'il wa'l-masa'il.*

Mulla Ahmad also has many treatises on ethics. On Fath-ᶜAli Shah's request he translated his father's *Jamiᶜ al-saᶜadah* from Arabic into *Miᶜraj al-saᶜadah* in Persian. He also composed *Wasilah al-nijah* in both Arabic and Persian. His *Sayf al-ummah* is a canonical treatise on the universality of

Islam, directed polemically against an English missionary, Henry Martyn (*"padri"*) (Algar, 99, Tunika-buni, 129; Amir Arjomand, 1988, 306).

Mulla Ahmad Naraqi on Wilayat-i Faqih

In his two most important works on the principles of jurisprudence, *Manahij al-usual wa'l-ahkam* and *ᶜAwa'id al-ayyam*, Mulla Ahmad Naraqi expounded the necessity and legitimacy of "legal speculation" (*al-mazannah*) on part of the jurisconsult in the absence of the Twelfth Imam. *Al-mazannah'* is most probably introduced as an speculative or legal apparatus to expand the rather limited initiative possibilities inherent in the Shiᶜi legal theory. The fact is that, in the absence of the Hidden Imam, as al-Tusi had argued, the *fuqaha'* had a difficult theological position to appropriate for themselves what doctrinally belonged to the "Rightly Guided." They had no claim to infallibility, nor could they have any. As such, they were theoretically as much in danger of error as the political powers. The significance of Naraqi's notion of *"al-mazannah"* lies in its providing the *faqih* with a doctrinal basis to speculate rather more freely in judicial issues, with its political repercussions.

In his opus, Mulla Ahmad's primary concern seems to have been the establishment of a solid judicial foundation for the legal authority of the jurisconsult in the period of the Greater Occultation (*ghaybah al-kubra*).

Before addressing the more political dimensions of the legal authority of a jurisconsult in his *ᶜAwa'id al-ayyam*, Mulla Ahmad had discussed extensively the legal and doctrinal prerogative of the *faqih* and *mujtahid* in exercising their opinion. This discussion, which was first formulated in *Hujjah al-mazannah*, was developed further in *ᶜAwa'id al-ayyam*. The doctrinal legitimizaton of *mazannah* was the necessary conceptual stepping stone for the development of *wilayat-i faqih*.

On the whole, the question of *wilayat-i faqih* does not receive specific or extensive treatment in the early history of Shiᶜi judicial development. This issue assumes priority with Naraqi; and this, of course, has to be understood in the context of Mulla Ahmad's social background. The political exegencies of Mulla Ahmad's career and the essential aspects of *wilayat-i faqih* come in close contact in the context of his *ᶜAwa'id al-Ayyam*.

ᶜAwa'id al-ayyam

ᶜAwa'id al-ayyam is the last book composed by Mulla Ahmad (1245/ 1829). It is divided into eighty-eight topics (*ᶜa'idah*), mostly on judicial regulations (*qawaᶜid al-fiqh*), a relatively new branch of the Shiᶜi religious sciences.

In one of these topics, titled "On the Limitation of the *hakim's* Guardianship," Mulla Ahmad elaborates on the question of *wilayah*. The primary source of *wilayah*, whose authority upon man is permanent (*thabit*), is

Allah (Naraqi, 185). The recipients of this *wilayah* are (1) the Messenger [Muhammad] and (2) his successors (*awssiya'*) (ibid.). These two secondary sources of authority are infallible, and thus *wilayah* is incumbent upon them on a permanent (*thabit*) basis. On qualifying these two sources, Mulla Ahmad considers them "the rulers of the human race" (*salatin al-anam*), "the kings" (*al-muluk*), "the governors" (*al-wullah*), and "judges" (*hukkam*) (ibid.). There are those, however, whose *wilayah* is not on a permanent basis (*ghayr thabit*)—because of their fallibility—and, furthermore, is limited to that to which they have been delegated (ibid.). The latter kind of *wali* includes "the just jurisconsults, fathers, grandfathers, guardians [in the sense of father figures, or foster parents], husbands, masters [of slaves], and the representatives [of such figures]" (ibid.). Naraqi then complements this statement by specifying exactly who falls under the supervision of these figures, on a one-to-one correspondence: "they are guardians upon: the people (*al-ᶜawam*), children, he upon whom guardians have been put (*al-musi lahu*), wives, slaves, and clients" (ibid.). However, the *wilayah* of all these figures, other than the *fuqaha's'*, is circumscribed (*khassah*) by the specific mandate according to which they are entitled to authority. The *fuqaha's'* authority, on the contrary, is general (*ᶜammah*), not limited by any specified mandate (ibid.). As such, the *fugaha'* are the judges (*hukkam*) and deputies (*al-nawwabin*) of the Imams. The word *hukkam'* is very crucial here: by the kinds of examples that Naraqi provides, e.g., the question of 'pure' (*halal*) and 'impure' (*haram*), the distribution of *khums* [a religious tax], and controlling the property of the insane, the reference is clearly to judicial authority; however, Naraqi extends the boundaires of this delegated authority to the *faqih*, in the absence of the Hidden Imam, to the point to assert that "and indeed their [the *fuqaha's*] *wilayah* is general because of its being as permanent [*thabit*] as that of the original Imam" (ibid.).

Then Mulla Ahmad proceeds to enumerate nineteen different *hadiths* in support of the *wilayat-i faqih*: among them, that "the learned men [*ᶜulama'*, a word also used interchangeably with *fuqaha'*] are the successors of the prophets"; and "the *ᶜulama'* of my people are like prophets before me." This emphasis on successorship to Muhammad as the prerogative of the religious authorities is particularly important in reading a political dimension into the doctrine of *wilayat-i faqih*.

The eleventh tradition introduced in support of the doctrine is of immediate significance. According to this tradition, "the kings have authority over [*hukkam ᶜala'*] the people, while *ᶜulama'* have authority over the kings" (*al-muluk hukkam ᶜala'l-nas wa'l ᶜulama' hukkam ᶜala'l-muluk*) (186). Here, by *hukkam*, the reference is clearly to political and not merely judicial authority. In fact, in this formulation, the mode of authority established between the *ᶜulama'* and the kings is precisely that of the king over his subjects.

Mulla Ahmad's explication of these *hadiths*, which follows, is essentially directed through specifically legal domains, with a strong emphasis on the question of "immitation" (*taqlid*) of the *faqih* by the community. The conceptual elaboration of the relationship between *wilayat-i faqih* and *taqlid* is precisely where Mulla Ahmad provides the strongest argument for both quantitative and qualitative expansion of the jurisconsults' authority.

Mulla Ahmad's treatment of the specific direction of this expansion is not altogether clear. Amir Arjomand is correct in observing that, in Naraqi's elaboration of the doctrinal conception of *wilayah*, "the invidious contrast between religious and political authority remains unstated and implicit" (265). However, the following emphatic conclusion of Amir Arjomand (1984) is rather problematic:

> The primary objective of Naraqi's discussion of vicegerency is to strengthen the *juristic* authority of the *mujtahids*. The bulk of the discussion is devoted to the "delimitation" of the scope of the authority of the jurists as the vicegerents of the Imam, and their collective authority is delimited to the exclusion of temporal rule (325: note 3).

What makes this assessment problematic is precisely the direction and nature of this "delimitation." Amir Arjomand is quite right: Naraqi is principly a "jurisconsult" and is engaged in a "judicial" argument. However, once the "collective authority" of the jurists is "delimited" far enough it will, inevitably, include political (temporal) domains.

The following two passages from *ᶜAwa'id*, one already quoted, make it quite clear that this delimitation is *not* to "the exclusion of temporal rule." The first passage is the previously mentioned tradition that Naraqi quotes in support of his argument for the "delimited" authority of the jurisconsult; this is the eleventh tradition quoted from what Mulla Ahmad believes to be authentic and undisputed sources:

> The kings have authority over the people and the religious scholars have authority over kings (*al-muluk hukkam ᶜala'l-nas wa'l ᶜulama' hukkam ᶜala'l-muluk*) (186).

Now, it is obvious that kings have no judicial authority over their subjects; even the most moderate jurisconsults would agree with that. So *hukkam ᶜala* cannot mean having merely judicial authority. The authority of the kings (*muluk*) over their subjects is political, so, the tradition commands, is the authority of the *ᶜulama'* over the kings, and of course by extension their subjects. The symmetry leaves no doubt that Mulla Ahmad's intention is to locate the jurisconsults above, and not even next to, the kings; that is, the supreme political figures of the community.

The second passage is even more emphatic. This section comes after a lengthy discussion of the range of the jurisconsult's authority:

> It is so obvious that any common or learned man understands and admits that if a prophet on the verge of a trip or his death had said of a certain person that: "so and so is my inheriter (*warithi*), and he is exactly like me (*mithli*), and has the same position as I do (*bi-manzilati*), and is my vicegerent (*khalifati*), and is my trusted person (*amini*), and the proof of [my authority upon you] (*hujjati*), and I have bestowed upon him authority upon you (*wa'l-hakim min gibali ᶜalaikum*), and that he is the source of authority for you in all your incidents (*wa'l-marjaᶜ lakum fi jamiᶜ hawadithikum*), and in his hands are the proper mandates of your affairs and obligations *(wa bi yadihi majariᶜ 'umurikum wa ahkamikum)* and that he is the representative of my subjects [i.e., he is the spokesman for the common people] (*al-kafil li-raᶜiyyati*), then undoubtedly to him belongs whatever belonged to the prophet in matters of the common subjects and whatever pertains to his [the prophet's] community [of believers] (Naraqi, Mulla Ahmad, 188).

Then, Mulla Ahmad repeats the same wide range of authority solicited for the *faqih* after Muhammad and the Imams for a representative of an earthly power (*hakim wa sultan*), in which case, too, all dimensions of the absent ruler's authority is claimed for his appointee (ibid.). But before extending his example from a divine figure of authority to an earthly one, Mulla Ahmad supports his proposition by arguing that the *fuqaha'*

> are the best of God's creatures after the Imams, and superior to all men after the prophets, and their superiority over the people is like the superiority of God over everything, and [it is also] like the superiority of the Prophet [Muhammad] over the subordinate subjects (ibid.).

This delimitation of authority is no simple quantitative extension of a jurist's authority into wider benign juridical domains; this is a total mobilization of the most sacred symbolics of the religious culture—Allah, Muhammad, Imams—to bid for a radical qualitative shift in the nature and organization of authority claimed by the *faqih*.

Conclusion

What can be concluded from a general overview of the doctrinaires of *wilayat-i faqih* is that there is no concrete doctrinal exposition or justification of active political authority for the jurisconsult. Principally, the doctrine of *wilayat-i faqih* is a judicial and not, using the word very specifically, political proposition. However, it is immediately obvious, within the Islamic context in general and the Shiᶜi in particular, that legal and political are peculiarly metamorphical. Based on this metamorphic nature of the relationship between the legal and the political, it is not altogether difficult to understand the political use and extension into which the doctrine has been put by certain jurisconsults. As an examination of those *fuqaha'* who have expounded or advocated the doctrine clearly should demonstrate, a revolutionary predisposition on the part of an activist religious authority can transform *wilayat-i faqih* from an innocuous jurisprudential proposition into a powerful doctrine of political action.

In modern Iranian history, three prominent figures have advocated, with varying degrees of elaboration, the prerogative of the *faqih* in assuming political power: al-Karaki, Mulla Ahmad Naraqi, and Ayatollah Khumayni. The active involvement of these three figures in the political affairs of their respective social contexts demonstrates the chief significance of *wilayat-i faqih* as a potential revolutionary doctrine.

Al-Karaki (d. 941/1534), known as al-Muhaqqiq al-Thani, was *shaykh al-Islam*, that is, the most prominent religious authority, of Shah Tahmasp I (ruled 930/1524–984/1576). Al-Karaki's revolutionary reading of *wilayat-i faqih* is coupled with other similar political interpretations of established Shiᶜi doctrines. As Enayat has observed:

His strong conviction on this issue [*wilayat-i faqih*] was in keeping with his other major theses, including his activist's perception of the principle of "enjoining the good and prohibiting the evil" (*al-amr bi'l-maᶜruf wa'l-nahy ᶜan al-munkar*) as an unconditional duty incumbent on every individual Muslim . . . (Enayat, 161).

In opposing the judicial authority of a dead *mujtahid* (Amir Arjomand, 140), al-Karaki demonstrates the same emphasis on preserving the spontaneity of the living Shiᶜi tradition of active political involvement. Furthermore, his articulation of the judicial doctrine of general representativeness (*niyabat-i ᶜammah*) (Amir Arjomand, 142) comes closest to incorporating "political" into the "judicial" domains.

Mulla Ahmad Naraqi, too, was directly involved in the political affairs of his time. On his return from Najaf, he expelled the governor of Kashan, of whose conduct he did not approve (Algar, 57). Summoned by Fath-ᶜAli Shah to answer for his behavior, Mulla Ahmad refused to repent and even accused the king of being unjust (ibid.). Fath-ᶜAli Shah was nevertheless quite close to Naraqi, and repeatedly visited him at his residence or invited him to Bagh-i Fin, the Shah's residence in Kashan (Naraqi, Hasan, 75). The translation of Mulla Ahmad's father's *Jamiᶜ al-suᶜadat* into Persian, *Miᶜraj al-suᶜadah*, was on Fath-ᶜAli Shah's specific request. Naraqi was also instrumental in proclaiming *jihad* against Russia and her aggressive policies against the Russian Muslims. During the first round of the Perso-Russian Wars (1219/180–1228/1813), Mulla Ahmad responded favorably to ᶜAbbas Mirza's request to proclaim *jihad* against the Russians (Lisan al-Mulk

Sepehr, I: 94, and 184; Algar, 79). In 1241/1825, during the second round of the Perso-Russian Wars, "Mulla Ahmad Naraqi and Mulla ᶜAbd al-Wahhab Qazwini arrived at the royal camp clad in shrouds as a sign of their preparation for jihad and martyrdom" (Algar, 89).

Ayatollah Khumayni's revolution against the Shah's regime was of course predicated on his fundamental belief that the duty of the *faqih* is to "administer and rule the state and to implement the laws of the sacred path" (quoted in Enayat, 163). By, among other things, demystifying *wilayah* from an esoteric notion into an ideological lever, Khumayni charged the doctrine with its most explosive political component. Enayat recognized this revolutionary aspect of *wilayat-i faqih* as formulated by Khumayni (ibid.). But he was wrong in believing that this demystification "stands opposed to popular Shiᶜism" (ibid.) Enayat's later recognition that "the requirements of political power since 1978 have fostered a psychological environment which does accord extraordinary status to the *faqihs*" (ibid., 164) was only a clue to the more essential fact that the political simplification of a juridical or mystical doctrine carries within itself the elements of its further, perhaps even more powerful, mystification. As the art of orchestrating cultural symbols for specific alterations in the relations of power, politics sustains and mobilizes its own mythology.

Perhaps the mobilizing power of *wilayat-i faqih* as a potentially revolutionary doctrine should be considered not in its conceptual isolation but in its powerful logarithmic interaction with a charismatic figure. That the trilateral doctrines of *Imamah, ghaybah,* and *the Hidden Imam* are actively conducive to the emergence of charismatic figures in Shiᶜi Islam is a crucial, and as yet not totally explored, question which cannot be examined here. What is certain and historically verifiable, however, is the chronic emergence of such figures in the course of Shiᶜi history. These figures, needless to say, did not require, nor did they necessarily mobilize, the doctrine of the *wilayat-i faqih* to justify their actions. But, once this doctrine was developed, out of a peculiar interaction between genuine jurisprudential speculation and actual political exegencies, it had an alchemical effect on the subsequent Shiᶜi charismatic leaders, enabling them to justify their call for reconstituting the relations of power not only in political but also in juridical semantics.

The interest of such charismatic figures does not lie in complex and exquisite theological or jurisprudential disputations: they are, if anything, theologians of revolt. As Enayat rightly recognized: "In Khumayni's treatment of the basic questions concerning the *wilayah*, all the nuances of Ansari's discussions are reduced to a much simpler classification . . ." (Enayat, 163). A charismatic leader, as Weber identified this "plebiscitarian ruler," (Weber, 79) is no theologian, philosopher, or moralist. He is principally a revolutionary mobilizer of popular pieties. As a common symbolic apparatus shared by the Shiᶜi constituency, *wilayat-i faqih* was there to be employed. There is nothing inherently revolutionary about the doctrinal category, as Ansari's exposition, for example, clearly shows. But charismatic figures of authority can read to a receptive audience mobilizing content to an otherwise opaque semantic. The claim that the responsibility of the *faqih* is "to administer and rule the state and to implement the laws of the sacred path" (Khumayni, quoted in Enayat, 163) is primarily a political manifesto and not a jurisprudential proposition.

To orchestrate the optimum of public pieties that unifies the revolutionary leader and his mobilized audience-followers into a political thunder requires, but is not totally contingent upon, immediate access to active sacred symbols that still strike responsive chords. It is futile, and missing the point entirely, to refute the doctrinal basis of a revolution after its successful accomplishment. The question is so pedantic, it is not even academic.

References

Algar, Hamid. 1969. *Religion and State in Iran: 1785–1906*. Berkeley: University of California Press.

Amir Arjomand, Said. 1984. *The Shadow of God and the Hidden Imam: Religion, Political Order, and Societal Change in Shiᶜite Iran from the Beginning to 1890*. Chicago: The University of Chicago Press.

Amir Arjomand, Said (ed.). 1988. *Authority and Political Culture in Shiᶜism*. New York: SUNY Press.

Shahid Thani, Zayn al-Din ᶜAmili. 1308/1929. *Al-Rawdah al-bahiyyah fi sharh al-lumᶜ ah al-mushfiqiyyah* Tehran: ᶜIlmiyyah Islamiyyah.

Enayat, Hamid. 1983. "Iran: Khumayni's Concept of the 'Guardianship of the Jurisconsult,' in *Islam in the Political Process*, edited by James P. Piscatori, 160–180. Cambridge: Cambridge University Press.

Göbel, Karl-Heinrich. 1984. *Moderne Schiitische Politik und Staatsidee*. Shriften des Deutschen Orient-Institut. Opladen: Leske Verlag & Budrich GmbH.

Hilli, ᶜAllamah, H. Y. M. 1334/1955. *Tazkirah al-fuqaha'*. Tehran: Maktabah Murtadawi.

Hilli, Muhaqqiq, A. N. J. H. 1337/1958. *Sharayiᶜ al-Islam*. Tehran: ᶜIlmiyyah Islamiyyah.

Lisan al-Mulk Sepehr. 1325/1946. *Nasikh al-tawarikh*. Tehran: Islamiyyah.

Mughniyah, Muhammad Jawad. 1979. *Al-Khumayni wa'l-dawlah al-Islamiyyah*. Beirut: Dar al-ᶜIlm.

Naraqi, Hasan. 1348/1969. *Athar-i Tarikhi-yi Kashan*. Tehran: Anjuman-i Athar-i Milli.

Naraqi, Mulla Ahmad. no date. *ᶜAwa'id al-ayyam*. Tehran: Basirati.

Al-Shaybi, Kamil Mustafa. 1359/1980. *Tashayyu* *wa tasawwuf*. Tehran: Amir Kabir.

Tunikabuni, Mirza Muhammad. 1365/1985. *Qisas al-culama'*. Tehran: cIlmiyyah Islamiyyah.

Al-Tusi, Abu Jacfar Muhammad ibn Hasan. 1389/1969. *Al-Mabsut fi fiqh al-imami*. Tehran: Maktabah Murtadawi.

Weber, Max. 1946. *From Max Weber: Essays in Sociology*. Translated, edited, and with an Introduction by H. H. Gerth, and C. Wright Mills. New York: Oxford University Press.

Chapter Twenty

The Tobacco Rebellion and Haji Mirza Hasan Shirazi

> *In the name of God the Merciful, the Forgiving. Today the use of* tanbaku *and tobacco, in whatever fashion, is reckoned as war against the Imam of the Age (may God hasten his glad advent). (Haji Mirza Hasan Shirazi, quoted in Edward G. Browne,* The Persian Revolution of 1905–1909. *London: Frank Cass and Co., 1966, p. 22 n.)*

The words of this fatwa *by Haji Mirza Hasan Shirazi in 1892 set in motion the Tobacco Rebellion, the culmination of almost a century of confrontations between the Qajar shahs and the* ^c*ulama''s active stance against monarchial despotism and foreign imperialism, from 1892 to 1909.*

Shirazi's fatwa *was a reaction by the* ^c*ulama' to Nasir al-Din Shah's grant of the tobacco concession to the Persian Tobacco Monopoly Company of the Great Britain in 1890. The Shah's move created great concern among nationalist as well as religious groups. With the encouragement of the nationalist elements, as well as the active role of Jamal al-Din al-Afghani, the* ^c*ulama' moved to the forefront of the protest movement and assumed its leadership. E. G. Browne and Nikki Keddie describe al-Afghani's efforts to involve Ayatollah Shirazi in the controversy and provide a vivid account of the impact of the* fatwa *and the political power of the* ^c*ulama' in 1891–92. The excerpts are from PR, pp. 22–23, 52–55; and RRITP, pp. 88–91, respectively.*

Edward G. Browne

And in truth Sayyid Jamal al-Din's [al-Afghani] hopes and expectations were not deceived, for it was apparently this letter which induced the great *mujtahid*, Haji Miraz Hasan of Shiraz, to issue his *fatwa* declaring the use of tobacco to be unlawful until the obnoxious concession was withdrawn; it was this *fatwa* which gave to the popular resentment the sanction of Religion, thus enabling it to triumph over the Shah, the Amin al-Sultan and the foreign governments and *concessionaries*; and amongst the ultimate results of all this were the violent deaths of Nasir al-Din Shah and the Amin al-Sultan, the successful demand for a Constitution, rendered possible only by the alliance between the clergy and the people, and the whole momentous struggle which has convulsed Persia during the last four years, and of which the history will be traced in these pages.

The remarks appended by Sayyid Muhammad Rashid to the text of this letter are worth quoting, and run as follows:

> This letter inspired a spirit of heroism and enthusiasm in that great doctor, who possessed so strong a spiritual influence over the Persian people, and he accordingly issued an edict (*fatwa*) forbidding the use and cultivation of tobacco. The ᶜ*ulama'* published his *fatwa* abroad with lightning speed, and the people bowed their necks to it to such a degree that it is related that on the morning of the day succeeding the arrival of the *fatwa* at Tehran the Shah called for a *nargile* (*qalyan*, or water-pipe), and was told that there was no tobacco in the Palace, for it had all been destroyed. He demanded with amazement the reason of this, and was informed of the *fatwa* of the Proof of Islam (*i.e.* Hajji Mirza Hasan-i-Shirazi, the *mujtahid*); and when he asked why they had not asked his permission first, they replied, 'It is a religious question concerning which there was no need to seek such permission!' Thereafter the Shah was compelled to rescind the concession and satisfy the English company by a payment of half a million pounds. Thus did Sayyid Jamalu'd-Din save Persia from an English occupation by abolishing the cause which would have led to this, namely this concession, and the other concessions of which you have read the description in his letter. Such are true men and such are true ᶜ*ulama'!*

* * *

At the beginning of December, 1891, a letter arrived from the *mujtahid* of Samarrah, Haji Mirza Hasan of Shiraz, enjoining on the people the complete abandonment of tobacco until the concession should be repealed. One cannot sufficiently admire either the wisdom of this master-stroke, which, without any act of rebellion, rendered worthless the monopoly of an article now declared unlawful, or the loyalty and self-abnegation with which the people followed the lead of their spiritual guide. "Suddenly, with perfect accord," says Dr. Feuvrier, "all the tobacco-merchants have closed their shops, all the *qalyans* (water-pipes) have been put aside, and no one smokes any longer, either in the city, or in the Shah's *entourage*, or even in the women's apartments. What discipline, what obedience, when it is a question of submission to the counsels—or rather the orders—of an influential *mulla*, or of a *mujtahid* of some celebrity!

"The *mullas*," continues Dr. Feuvrier, "are really the masters of the situation. It is all very well to make the Chief of the Merchants, Haji Muhammad Hasan, responsible for the closure of the shops, and to exile him to Qazwin: everyone knows that one must strike elsewhere if one wishes to cut the root of the evil. None the less is the Tobacco concession sadly compromised, to such a degree that its natural defenders [*i.e.* the British Legation] seem anxious to abandon it to its fate. I have heard the director himself speak of it in terms of despair, while the British Minister on his part is reported to have said that, in face of this new attitude of the Persians, of this resistance of which he had not judged them capable, he considered that it was no longer possible to sustain with advantage the work of his predecessor."

Throughout the month of December, 1891, matters continued to get worse. On December 3, says Dr. Feuvrier, the Shah, "whether unwilling to change his habits, or in order to escape from his nightmare, the Tobacco Question," decided to go for a tour in the country surrounding the capital, leaving the Amin al-Sultan to deal with the situation in Tehran, where "the storm had begun to growl"; nor would he return at the request of the Russian Minister, who "regarded the moment as critical, and considered that there was ground to fear for the lives of the Europeans." In Tabriz also the agitation, which had been temporarily calmed by the promise that the *Régis* should not take immediate effect, broke out again, apparently in sympathy with the general protest of the nation. The *mullas* grew bolder, and in a conference convened by the Amin al-Sultan to discuss the amount of the compensation which would have to be paid to the corporation to rescind the concession, one of them told the Prime Minister that those who had received bribes to obtain the Shah's consent (and he mentioned their names) should first of all be compelled to disgorge their ill-gotten gains. "At Qazwin another *mulla*, seeing a man smoking, requested him to stop, and, on his refusal, broke his *qalyan*. The smoker complained to the governor, who sent to summon the *mulla*; but he had stirred up the populace to such an extent that the governor, threatened in his palace, left the town and escaped to Tehran. It is even said that he owed his safety only to his prisoner, the chief of the merchants, the crowd having allowed the carriage containing the two to pass, believing that it carried the pardoned Haji Muhammad Hasan and one of his friends."

On the night of Christmas Day the walls were placarded with notices threatening foreigners with death unless the tobacco concession was rescinded within forty-eight hours. The anxiety of the European community and especially of the legations increased to an intolerable extent, and all sorts of rumours were current. On December 28 soldiers were posted at different points in the European quarter, and a proclamation announcing the withdrawal of the concession was published by the Shah. The people were somewhat tranquillized, but Haji Mirza Hasan Shirazi, the *mujtahid* of Samarrah, still refused to withdraw the prohibition against the use of tobacco until it was certain that effect had been given to the Shah's promises.

On January 1, 1892, a telegram at length arrived from Haji Mirza Hasan Shirazi, who congratulated the Shah on having withdrawn the tobacco concession, and urged him to withdraw likewise all the other concessions accorded to foreigners; but made no allusion to the prohibition against smoking of which he was the author, and which, as he was well aware, profoundly troubled the habits of the Persians. The shares of the Imperial Bank fell to half their value. On January 3 the Shah sent a message to the *mujtahid* Haji Mirza Hasan Ashtiyani bidding him either set the example of smoking, or leave the country. He chose the latter alternative, but took no steps to carry it out. Great excitement was manifested by the people on learning this, and soon a crowd, headed by a sayyid in his dark blue turban, surrounded the Shah's Palace, uttering loud cries of anger, and throwing stones. The troops fired on the crowd, of whom several fell, including the sayyid. Seven persons were killed and about twenty more wounded, but the crowd was dispersed. Two days later the *mujtahid* Haji Mirza Hasan Ashtiyani, who had neither smoked nor left the town, received from the Shah a diamond ring as a sign of reconciliation; but he would not accept it until he was assured of the withdrawal of the tobacco concession by the issue on the part of the director of a declaration formally stating that the monopoly was at an end, and inviting those who had sold tobacco to the *Régie* to come and reclaim it. But it was not until January 26 that the public crier announced in the streets the definite withdrawal of the *mullas*' interdict on smoking, an announcement received with universal joy. Two days later some forty of the *employés* of the late Imperial Tobacco Corporation, their occupation gone, started for their homes. "Most of them," says Dr. Feuvrier, "will doubtless not forget for many a long day the crises through which they have passed since they arrived in Persia, especially those who were here on the day of the riot. Handsomely compensated, they depart well pleased, to seek their fortune elsewhere, to the equally great satisfaction of the Persians."

The tobacco concession was ended, but not its consequences, and amongst these consequences was undoubtedly a great loss of prestige to England, which had certainly not played the most admirable *rôle* in this deplorable episode, and a corresponding gain of prestige to Russia.

Nikki R. Keddie

Further trouble was to break out almost immediately. Both the inhabitants of Isfahan and the chief *mujtahid* of the Iraq shrine cities, Haji Mirza Hasan Shirazi, now entered the fray. Amin al-Sultan was sure that even during the Tabriz disturbances, the chief *mujtahid* there had been in constant communication with Shirazi as well as with the Russian Consul-General. And on September 22, Feuvrier noted that Shirazi from the shrine cites:

> who holds there all the strings of the insurrection, has written a long letter to the Shah to prove to him, Qur'an in hand, that the concession of any monopoly to foreigners is against the holy book. I do not believe His Majesty is much concerned with the reasoning of the *mujtahid*, but he knows his influence and must take account of it.
>
> The Persian consul at Baghdad has been sent to Karbala with the aim of acting on the *mujtahid*. It does not appear that he has succeeded in modifying the convictions of the holy man.

The telegram referred to condemns the interference of foreign subjects in the internal affairs of the Muslim peoples, and specifically names the English Bank, the tobacco concession, and railroad concessions; and speaks of the killing and wounding of a number of Muslims in Shiraz, and the exile of Sayyid ᶜAli Akbar, as manifestations of the bad results of such policies. It calls for the end of all concessions, showing again that this broader aim was held by some of the leaders throughout the tobacco movement. The text of his telegram was later translated in one of de Balloy's despatches. A translation from the French follows:

> Up to the present I have only addressed myself to His Majesty with wishes of happiness, but because of the various news which has reached me and which is against the rights of Religion and Government I ask permission to say: The entry of foreigners into the interior affairs of the country, their relations and trade with Muslims, the concessions such as the Bank, Tobacco Régie, Railroads, and others are, for many reasons, against the exact sense of the Qur'an and God's orders. These acts weaken the power of the Government and are the cause of the ruin of order in the country, and they oppress the subjects. The proof is in what has just occurred in Shiraz, where there has been disrespect for the tomb of the venerable Imamzadih Ahmad ibn Musa, a great number of Muslims have been killed and wounded, and His Excellency Sayyid cAli Akbar chased in the grossest fashion—all this is the consequence of what I said above.
>
> It is certain that His Majesty has not been informed of it. He who wishes only the prosperity of his subjects would have been very dissatisfied and would not have allowed today these affairs which in the future will provoke troubles and paralyze Religion and Government, which will, God forbid, lose the glorious renown acquired for many years. I have the highest confidence in the generosity of His Majesty who, if the country's Ministers have authorized these affairs, will show the foreigners that the whole population is united to reject them, and so calm will be reestablished. I have also confidence in seeing His Majesty grant once more his favor to the venerable personage expelled from Shiraz with so little respect and who took refuge in the holy places. The *mullas* will pray again for His Majesty and confidence will be restored among the subjects. The decision is in the hands of His Majesty.

Despite the milder tone, as befitting a letter sent to the Shah, the similarity of the grievances to those outlined in Sayyid Jamal al-Din's earlier letter to Shirazi . . . is striking. It thus seems that Sayyid Jamal al-Din's letter, plus what he may have conveyed personally through Sayyid cAli Akbar, did have an immediate effect on Shirazi, who, as his telegram states, had not previously addressed the Shah on political questions.

Taymuri gives details of the Shah's and Amin al-Sultan's efforts, *via* telegram and a personal visit of the Iranian representative at Baghdad to Shirazi, to change the latter's position. In the same period Shirazi was receiving telegrams and letters from all parts of Iran asking him to help cancel the concession, and he did not yield to any of the government's arguments. He also continued pressure for the lifting of Sayyid cAli Akbar's exile, in which he succeeded ultimately.

The continuous telegraphic communication in this period between Shirazi and the leaders of the Iranian ᶜ*ulama'*, between Shirazi and the Shah, and among the leaders of the Iranian ᶜ*ulama'*, helped make the tobacco movement perhaps the first coordinated national movement of Iranians. Partly this coordination was due simply to the introduction of the telegraph, an infidel innovation which the ᶜ*ulama'* did not scorn to use. The coordination also owed something to new ideas and to the simultaneous impact of the growth of foreign influence in Iran. The restrictions on native banking caused by the Imperial Bank were felt quickly in several cities, while the simultaneous arrival of agents of the tobacco corporation who forced growers to sell to them, and in many cases behaved badly, also brought a series of immediate reactions. Russian encouragement of the opposition was also coordinated. Because the leaders of the ᶜ*ulama'* in each city could be the most effective spokesmen, discontented merchants and growers turned to them. Top direction within Iran was confided in the most respected leader of the Tehran ᶜ*ulamla'*, Haji Mirza Hasan Ashtiyani, and he and others turned for support and direction to the even more respected leader of the shrine ᶜ*ulama'*, Shirazi. Few of the leading ᶜ*ulama'* remained aloof—in Tehran only Sayyid ᶜAbdullah Bihbihani, a partisan of the English and of the Amin al-Sultan, and accused of taking bribes from the company, and the Imam Jumᶜah of Tehran, a relative of the Shah's, refused to back the protest.

In September the anti-*Régie* movement spread to Isfahan, where the *mullas*, led by the powerful and unscrupulous Aqa Najafi, began to preach in the mosques against the *Régie*, and the merchants, encouraged by the example of Azarbaijan, presented a petition against it to the Zill al-Sultan. The Zill al-Sultan being an Anglophil, and not a Russophil like his counterpart at Tabriz, gave a threatening answer to the merchants which restated his traditional autocratic-pretentions:

> Your petition through the *Imam Jumᶜah* has reached us. You deserve to be summoned and have the consequences of your impertinence meted out to you, namely, such as bastinaodoing punishments, and truly to have your heads cut off, in order that no one else be able to say "Why?" and "Wherefore?" in Government affairs, but out of respect for the *Imam Jumᶜah* we have let you off this time, conditionally on your desisting from such impertinence and opposition to Government orders.
>
> H.I.M. the Shah is the master of the inhabitants of Persia and their property and knows better what is the "rayots'" advantage. You have no right to make such objections. Mind your own business without impertinence and let such matters alone.

In sending home the Zill al-Sultan's answers to the Imam Jumᶜah of Isfahan, Kennedy reported approvingly, 'His Royal Highness acted with great firmness in checking this movement . . .' Despite the Zill al-Sultan's threats, however, trouble was to break out again in Isfahan in November.

After the September troubles, the French Minister was more skeptical about the *Régie's* prospects than was Kennedy. On September 30, 1891, de Balloy doubted the Shah's determiantion to save the *Régie*, though he says that everyone in the Council except the Amin al-Dawlah favored resistance to the suppression demand... .

Chapter Twenty-One

The Debates Over the Constitutional Revolution

The Constitutional Revolution of 1905–06 was a major watershed in the history of Shiᶜi political and religious thought. The impact of the constitutional movement on the political outlook of Iranian Shiᶜism is more apparent. The Revolution of 1905–06 marked the culmination of the struggle of the ᶜulama', in their capacity as the representatives of popular will and the guardian of national welfare, against Qajar absolutism and foreign imperialism. The revolution took the process set in motion by the Tobacco Rebellion to its natural conclusion, and hence placed the clerical institution at the midst of the constitutionalist movement, and assigned considerable political power to the ᶜulama'.

The increase in the political fortunes of the Shiᶜi establishment, however, coincided with a breakdown in internal concensus and therefore institutional unity. The involvement of the ᶜulama' in the Constitutional Revolution and the need to elaborate political liberalism in religious terms brought to the fore latent theological disputes, which had been brewing for over a century in Shiᶜi clerical circles; this debate is known as the Usuli-Akhbari controversy, as it was, discussed in Chapter Eighteen. The disputes that ensued and the conflicts that it precipitated among the ᶜulama' all but shattered the internal unity of the clerical establishment.

Throughout the constitutional period, the political involvement of the ᶜulama' was characterized by absence of institutional unity. Various ᶜulama' espoused an array of individual opinions, which were reflective of their personal theological and juridical stances. There existed staunch constitutionalists among the ᶜulama', such as Khurasani and Na'ini, and moderate constitutionalists, like Tabataba'i and Bihbahani. There were also anticonstitutionalists, such as Nuri. Just to realize the intensity of the debates, suffice it to say that Nuri was hanged by the government authorities, no doubt upon the insistence of his Constitutionalist opponents and their allies. His execution was undertaken, however, only after his death was sanctioned by the mujtahids of Najaf, Khurasani, Mazandarani, and Khalili Tihrani, who disagreed with Nuri on the latter's reasoning against the Constitution. (See Hamid Algar, "The Oppositional Role of the Ulama in Twentieth-century Iran," in Scholars, Saints, and Sufis; Muslim Religions Institutions Since 1500, *ed. Nikki Keddie. Berkeley: University of California Press, 1972, p. 238. See also, Said Amir Arjomand's "Ideological Revolution in Shiʿism," in Said Amir Arjomand (ed.)* Authority and Political Culture in Shiʿism. *Albany: SUNY Press, 1988, pp. 178–209.)*

The Constitutional Revolution ushered in a new era in Iranian politics and confirmed a central role for the ʿulama' in it. More important, the entire episode concluded the Usuli-Akhbari debate and, in the process, added elaborate new axioms to Shiʿi political thought in the twentieth century. In this section, Hamid Enayat and Abdul-Hadi Hairi will present the framework in which the theological-political debates of the ʿulama' took place. Extracts from the works of Na'ini and Nuri (translated and edited by William Darrow and Abdul-Hadi Hairi respectively) will shed more light on the attitudes of the ʿulama' towards constitutionalism and, more generally, on politics at the turn of the century. The excerpts are from MIPT, pp. 166–69; ITMP, 287–91; SCI, pp. 81–90; and SFNRIC, pp. 330, 334–37, respectively.

Hamid Enayat

The Constitutional Revolution represents the first direct encounter in modern Iran between traditional Islamic culture and the West. All the earlier attempts at modernization, although involving important changes in the legal, governmental and administrative systems, were conducted in areas tangential to underlying traditional values. None of them openly and radically challenged any of these values. The great modernizing minister, Mirza Taqi Khan, known as Amir Kabir, certainly took vital measures for centralizing the judicial system, such as his curbs on the powers of the Imam Jum^{c}ah (leader of the Friday Prayer), or abolition of *bast* (sanctuary from secular oppression offered by mosques, residences of the ^{c}*ulama'*, etc.), in the teeth of the 'clerical' prerogatives, but they did not aim at undermining any specific Islamic institution and principle. Such measures, just as the modernizing campaign of men such as Mirza Malkam Khan, the advocate of the 'total Westernization of Iran', were individual enterprises whose repercussions never went beyond a small élite. By contrast, Constitutional Revolution was a movement of unprecedented dimension in Iran's modern history which embraced vast groups of people from every social quarter, thus generating a heated debate between diverse ideologies, old and new. The implication of many a constitutionalist idea challenged the very foundation of the religio-political consensus as well as the relative cultural harmony of the traditional order, thereby causing a deep rift among the élites. Perhaps the significance of this rift can be better understood if a comparison is drawn with the constitutional history of Ottoman Turkey. When similar controversies broke out in Turkey during the famous Mesrutiét period from 1908 to 1918, that country had long passed through the travails of the Tanzimat period (a half-century of reforms from 1826 onwards), and the Young Ottoman movement (formed in the mid-1860s). By that time both sides in the debate had accumulated considerable eristic ability and sharpened their polemic tools, particularly over the thorny issues of the legal codification and judicial reforms, and modernization of the educational system.

Neither side in the constitutional debate in Iran had such precedents to fall back on. Even the duality of the judicial system (between the religious and non-religious courts) had lasted so long (since the Safavid times) that it had become part of the traditional structure, and lost its potential for initiating ideas of change. So discussions on the uses and abuses of man-made laws inevitably provoked in its train dissensions over the virtues and vices of modernization. The novelty of the controversy and the complexity of the issues involved could hardly be helpful to mutual understanding between the two sides of the debate. But there was one precedent which gave the religious proponents of the constituion an edge over all other groups in terms of argumentative skills. This was the development of the science of *usul-i fiqh*, the 'roots' or theory of jurisprudence, which had achieved great subtlety among the Shiᶜis, but reached new peaks in the nineteenth century. Tension between the Usulis and their opponents, the Akhbaris (Traditionalists) [see Chapter Eighteen in this book — Eds.], had grown sharply since the middle of the eighteenth century. The Akhbaris dominated the centres of religious teachings until the beginning of the Zand period, but with the emergence of Muhammad Baqir Wahid Bihbihani (1704–91) they were decisively routed. The ground was then prepared for men like Mirza-yi Qumi, Shaykh Murtada Ansari, Mulla Muhammad Kazim Khurasani and Muhammad Husayn Na'ini to afford philosophical depth and methodological precision to this most stimulating of traditional Islamic sciences. Now there were of course some distinguished ᶜalims who opposed constitutionalism: Shaykh Fadlullah was a *faqih* of the highest rank. But it is noteworthy that while the opponents resorted to simple canonical strictures on the Constitution (such as the conflict between the superiority of Islam, and the recognition of all Iranian citizens as equals before the law, irrespective of their religion; the dangers of a free press which could open the way to atheistic foreign ideas; and the unacceptability of compulsory education for girls), the proponents countered by using concepts drawn from the science of *usul*. The presence of Khurasani and Na'ini among the foremost champions of constitutionalism, and the fact that Na'ini was the author of the only well-known and fairly coherent treatise in defence of its principles can, of course, be no more than circumstantial evidence of the link between their jurisprudential theory and their political outlook. But when one examines the principles of the Usuli school, one can hardly escape the conclusion that they were more likely to produce a pre-constitutionalist mentality than its opposite.

The chief doctrine of the Usuli school is the competence of reason (after the guidance of the Qur'an, the Tradition and consensus) to discern the rules of the *shariᶜah*. This faith in reason brings forth other essential teachings: the necessity of *ijtihad*, the refusal to accept uncritically the contents of the four principal codices of Shiᶜi traditions (by Kulayni, Shaykh Sadduq and Shaykh Tusi), adoption of more precise criteria for ascertaining the reliability of sayings attributed to the Prophet and Imams, and prohibition of the imitation of deceased authorities to ensure the abiding dynamism of *ijtihad*. The Akhbaris contradict the Usulis on all these points: they reject reason and consensus, and find all individuals to be of the same level of mediocrity, and hence worthy of being only *muqqallid* (imitators). They forbid *ijtihad*, and believe in the imitation of deceased authorities, saying that the truth of a proposition is not affected by the death of its expositor: the rulings of the past ᶜ*ulama'* should be rejected if they are the products of their own arbitrary, probable knowledge or conjecture (*zann*), and accepted if they prove to be based on definite knowledge (ᶜ*ilm-i qat'i*), but this can only be communicated by the Imam. Instead of *ijtihad*, they regard the collection of sayings or narratives of the Imams to be an obligatory duty, and reckon that every Muslim, even the uninitiated and the ordinary (ᶜ*ammi*), is capable of performing this. Meanwhile, the Usulis allow wide scope for juridical innovations through their belief in the validity of 'probable knowledge' to deduce canonical rules, whenever access to 'definite knowledge' proves impossible. They also maintain that any act should be presumed to be permissible (*asalat al-ibahah*), except when explicitly forbidden by the *shariᶜah*. The Akhbaris again disagree with them, saying that all knowledge is untrustworthy, except that conveyed by the Imams, and that whenever an act is not explicitly permitted by the *shariᶜah* one should refrain from performing it by way of precaution (*ihtiyat*) against committing a sin.

The political implications of these principles can hardly be overstated. By upholding the authority of reason and the right of *ijtihad*, the Usuli doctrines could not fail to render the Shiᶜi mind susceptible to social changes, and inspire confidence in the human ability ot regulate social affairs. The reassertion of the status of the *mujtahids* and particularly the emphasis on the necessity of following a living authority certainly could help to mitigate the effects of the sclerosis of legal thought, and remove, at least partially, the stigma attached to intellectual dynamism. Moreover, principles such as those of the validity of probable knowledge and the permissibility of actions not specifically forbidden by the sources, encouraged a more flexible approach to the application of jurisrudence to emerging social and political problems. Before elaborating on the political significance of these conclusions, a word of caution is in order. It would be patently simplistic to portray the Usulis as outright 'progressives', and their traditionalist opponents as 'reactionaries'. As can be gathered from the above summary, there were in fact many features in the Akhbari doctrines too which could have made them equally receptive to certain democratic notions, for instance their stance against the *mujtahids* had strong anti-élitist, and consequently populist, implications, just as their distrust of reason could develop into a Lockian belief that ideas come from the senses. Indeed, some recent Shiᶜi scholars have hinted at a possible impact of the European school of sensationalism on the genesis of the Akhbari ideas. Nevertheless, by proscribing rationalism, and urging imitation (*taqlid*) as the only permissible way of learning the canonical rules, the Akhbaris placed an interdiction on all the mental processes which could be turned to integrating new rules and institutions in the traditional political structure.

Shaykh Muhammad Husayn Na'ini

This work is an introduction describing the essence of tyranny and constitutional government, investigating the fundamental law and the consultative national assembly and describing the meaning of freedom and equality.

Know that nearly all the Muslim nations and all reasonable people throughout the world are agreed that the preservation of world order and the livelihood of humankind depends on rulership and politics. This is so whether rulership is entrusted to one person or to a general council and whether it is acquired by right, by usurpation, by violence, by inheritance or by election. By the same token it is also axiomatic that the preservation of the honor, independence and nationality of every people, both with regard to their religious and national prerogatives, depends on the placing of the actual ruling power with the people according to their will. Otherwise their privileges and laws, the greatness of their religion and religious group, the honor and independence of the fatherland and their nationality would be annihilated, even if they were to reach the highest level of wealth, power and prosperity. Therefore the holy Islamic law holds that the preservation of the core of Islam is the most important of all duties and has proclaimed Islamic rulership as one of the duties of the Imam. . . . It is clear that in all respects the establishment of a system in the world according to the principle of rulership and for the preservation of the honor and nationality of each people is their own affair. It has two principles:

> 1. Preservation of the internal order of the country, the education of the people, the respecting of each other's rights, the prevention of tyranny and the oppression of any portion of the country by another and such other duties as are related to the internal interests of the county and the people.

2. Preventing the interference of foreigners and stopping their typical cunning and preparing defensive forces and other military needs and the like. This principle in the language of the keepers of the holy law is called preserving the core of Islam and in the language of other nations, preserving the fatherland.

The provisions in the holy law for establishing these two duties are known respectively as political and civil laws and the wisdom of prudence. . . .

The characteristic of authority and the possession of a country by a ruler is either by the virtue of having a complete monopoly over it or by having supervision over it. There is no alternative to these two forms.

In the first type (which is tyranny) the one who rules considers the country and its people as his personal property and imagines everything in the country as his own and the people as his slaves, or at least his attendants and retainers, created and compelled to serve his wishes and lusts. Anyone who devotes himself completely to serving the desires of the ruler is rewarded by him. Anyone who is repulsed by this considering of his country as someone's personal possession is exiled or destroyed. . . .

The actual degree of oppression in this sort of rule depends on the actual amount of corrupt characteristics the rulers have, and on the wisdom and insight of the rulers and their assistants. It also depends on the insights and knowledge of the people of a country concerning the duties of rulership and its rights. The highest degree of such rulership is the claim to divinity and the intellectual power of the people of the country must resist this degree and each one leading to it. Of necessity in such a country the interaction of the people will be according to the religion of their kings and they will injure those below them as does the king. The reasons for this wicked system are twofold: 1) the ignorance of the nation concerning the duties of rulership and common and specific rights and the justic they embody and 2) the absence of responsibility on the part of the ones in charge and their not being subject to check and observation.

In the second form of government the basis of rulership should not be ownership subjugation, arbitrary despotism and dictatorship. The basis of rulership is the performance of the duties for the sake of public benefit. The establishment of a rulership and the authority of a ruler are limited to that extent and he is bound and conditioned from transgressing those rights.

These two types of rulership are in actuality different. The conditions and the effects of the two differ. The first is based upon power and subjugation of the country and of keeping the people under the whims of the ruler and using his power, financial and otherwise, to satisfy his own desires and not being responsible for whatever evil deeds are committed. Whatever such a ruler doesn't do one should be thankful for! . . . The second type in reality is based upon supervision of what are set as duties for the organization and protection of the country. It is not based on ownership. It is like a trustee-ship that has been put at the disposal of the country. This power is to be used for the benefit of the people, not for personal desire. In this respect the measure of authority of the ruler accords with the proportion of supervision (*wilayah*) in the above mentioned affairs and is limited, and his occupation of the office, whether by right or by usurpation, will be circumscribed by the conditions and not be oppressive. Every citizen of the nation is a partner with the ruler in financial and other affairs and is equal in this partnership, and those who are government officials are curators for the people. There is not a relation of owner and servant. Like members of a family who are re-sponsible and obliged to each other, they have responsibility for the whole nation and should be reprimanded for the slightest trespass.

All the individuals in the country as a result of this partnership and equality have the right and power to criticize and question and oppose. They have such power and security and are free in the expression of their opposition. They should not yield to derision and power that arise out of the wishes of the ruler and government officials. This sort of rulership is called bound, limited, just, conditioned, responsible and authoritative. . . .

[The establishment of such a government] is based upon two principles. First, there must be the establishment of a constitution limited to what has been mentioned. . . . It must be free from all interference and tampering. It must be perfectly composed and set out clearly the duties and level of authority of the king and the freedom of the nation. It specifies all the rights of the classes of the people according to the requirement of their religion of-ficially and definitely. Not performing these duties of protection and curatorship and going either to the extreme of too little or too much would be considered treason, and would be, like any betrayal of a trust, grounds for removal from office and other punishments as necessary. This is because the constitution sets the form in the political and social realm which must be actualized and followed in all affairs. The basis for the preservation of the limitations it establishes is preventing the trespassing of those limits. It is called a charter and fundamental law. The soundness and completeness of the constitution arises from its dealing with all aspects that are relevant to the limits it sets and its endeavoring to deal with all affairs that are necessary for the society, with the proviso that none of its provisions are in contradiction with the holy law of Islam. . . .

Second, there must be reliance on the elements of perfect guardianship, calculation and responsibility and the entrusting of a group of people gathered (in a consultative assembly) which is composed of those who are wise ones of the country and the good intentional. They must know the details of international law and be acquainted with the general political situation of the times. They should be assigned the oversight and guardianship and the organization and establishment of the duties that are necessary. They should prevent all forms of oppression. Thus the whole intellectual power of the country is put into service within the official setting of national consultative assembly. . . .

[The question arises as to] whether in this age when the Imam is absent and the community falls far short of purity and of being under the supervision of an Imam or his regular deputies and the above-mentioned duties are trampled upon and disregarded, is there any reason to turn from the path of extreme tyranny and oppression on top of oppression towards a second path in which the authority (of the ruler) is limited to what is appropriate? . . .

. . . Three topics should be discussed in answer to this question. First, in the case of the responsibility to forbid what is evil (that is incumbent on all Muslims), it is well known that when a person does a number of things which are prohibited, he bears responsibility for each thing that he does. The person who seeks to forbid what is evil, should seek to stop each one of them to the extent that it is possible.

Second, one of the prerequisites for those of us who are Twelver Shiᶜis is that in the time of the absence of the Imam, . . . our religion has established the essential duty that is indispensable in the area of supervision: that is that there be the deputyship of the jurisprudents in the age of the absence of the Imam. The proof the deputyship of the jurisprudents and his assistants in the period of absence is the most important issue in the period of absence in order to establish the above-mentioned duties as the central features of our religion.

Third, in the area of Islamic law that deals with the supervision of pious foundations, both special and general, in whatever is written about the area of such supervision, the following is clear and agreed upon. If someone seizes something and we are unable to take it back, in any way, then a group should be assigned who would be able to take back what has been illegally seized, for example to be used in the pursuit of lusts. This assigning of a group to take back what has been illegally seized is the prime goal of the Shiᶜi wisemen. What else would be expected by the least intelligent of people?

When these three points are explained, there can be no doubt about the necessity of taking rulership from the hands of the tyrant, which is the first path and entrusting it to the second path. When you know that the first path is a direct insult to the name of God and that a tyrant's taking of the position of supervisor and clothing tyranny in the garb of religion is an insult to the position of the Imam and that doing so is a seizing of the rights of individual, which involves all of mankind, then (it is clear one should prefer the second form of government). . . .

The law of equality is among the most noble of the blessed derived laws of Islamic polity. It is the basis and foundation of justice and the spirit of all the laws. . . . The essence of the holy law consists in this. Every law which is to ap-

ply in all fields and conditions legally in all circumstances is executed equally
with respect to individuals and without discrimination. Personal and special
connections are not considered. Choice in disposition and suppression, deceit
and pardon are closed to everyone. Violation of the law, bribery, and arbitrariness in legal issues is blocked to all. Regarding basic rights, which are common
to all people and should be enforced, such as security of life, honor, possessions, dwelling, the absence of harassment without cause, no unreasonable
search, no imprisonment or exile without cause, no hindering of religious
assembly and the like, these are common to all and are not attached to any one
special group. They should be put into effect for all. In the case of special rights
among individuals who are entitled to them, within that group there is no arbitrariness or differences. For instance, a defendant is called for trial whether
he is lower class or noble, ignorant or learned, unbeliever or Muslim. . . . The
special laws for Muslims, and those which apply to the protected religious
minorities, are applied uniformly among the members of each of these groups.

Abdul-Hadi Hairi

. . . Sayyid Muhammad Tabataba'i . . . was, without doubt, under
the intellectual influence of both Shaykh Hadi and al-Afghani. He was, according to Nazim al-Islam Kirmani, a disciple of Shaykh Hadi and studied
ethics under him. There can be mentioned several factors in his life which
were instrumental in his acquaintance with liberal thought and Western
ideas. His contacts with freemasonry, his travels in Russia, the Arab world,
and Turkey, his personal meetings with leaders and statesmen, and his
association with Persian secret societies, made him informed about modernism. As mentioned above, while studying under Mirza Muhammad Hasan
Shirazi in Samarrah, Tabataba'i had corresponded with Sayyid Jamal al-Din al-
Afghani, obtaining instructions from the Sayyid for rising against misgov-
ernment. Upon his arrival in Tehran in 1894, he began his campaign against
the tyrannical rule of the Qajar Shah.

Tabataba'i himself tells us about his coming to Tehran as follows:

> In 1894, I came to Tehran, from Samarrah. Nasir al-Din Shah had
> thought that Mirza-yi Shirazi, may God's forgiveness be his place of
> return (*ghufran ma'ab*) . . . had sent me to Tehran to change the ex-

isting situation. As soon as Nasir al-Din Shah heard of my arrival in Kirmanshah he said to the government officials that they should make me return at any price. But, I did not pay attention to [the Shah's desires] and moved to Tehran. When I arrived at Hadrat-i ᶜAbdul-ᶜAzim the Nayib al-Saltanah said to the Shah that since I would arrive in Tehran there would be need for a ceremonial reception on the part of government, but the Shah said that there would be no need for that.

Tabataba'i's real challenge to the ruling authorities started effectively when he allied himself with another militant clerical notable, Sayyid ᶜAbdullah Bihbahani. Tabataba'i asked the Shah and his *Sadr-i Aᶜzam* for the establishment of an assembly (*majlis*), in which the affairs of the people might be settled. The conservative Shiᶜi *ᶜulama'* were also engulfed in a long-lived hostility against the Qajar rulers.

*   *   *

In his activities against the government of the ᶜAyn al-Dawlah, Tabataba'i determinedly pursued his demand for the establishment of a house of justice and an assembly to serve the people's needs. The following is a paraphrase of parts of his statements pronounced on different occasions: "Iran is our country where our aspirations come true. We must work toward its progress and make every effort to save it from dangers. Reason does not allow us to pass in silence over these dangers and to wish the extinction of the state. All the corruptions which we presently encounter will be remedied if we establish an assembly of justice and a council (*anjuman*) formed of different groups of people. In this council, justice will be given to all the people, and the king and the poor may be treated equally." "The removal of these corruptions depends on the foundation of an assembly and the union of the government with the people and the *ᶜulama'*. Reform will soon take place, but we want our King and Chief Minister to carry them out, not the Russians, the British, or the Ottomans. With some slight carelessness and delay, we will lose Iran. Iran is my country; whatever reputation I have belongs to this country; my service to Islam is in this place; the respect I enjoy depends on the existence of this state. But unfortunately, I see it falling into the hands of the foreigners. Therefore, as long as I am alive I will make my efforts to protect it and, if necessary, I will sacrifice my life for it." "We have not demanded anything from government but justice. Our aim is to establish an assembly by which we may find out how much our helpless people suffer from the oppressive provincial governments. We want justice, the execution of Islamic law, and an assembly in which the king and the poor may be treated according to the law. We do not talk about constitutionalism and republicanism."

The above paraphrases indicate why Tabataba'i rose against the existing régime. He even clearly mentions that he is not fighting for constitutionalism. He announces that a constitutional régime would not fit the Persian society of that age, because constitutionalism can operate only amongst a people who understand nationalism and are literate and knowledgeable.

The basis of this statement is perhaps what Kasravi suggests. He holds that Tabataba'i, together with his fellow *mujtahid*, Bihbahani, understood well and genuinely aimed at a constitutional form of government. But they hid their real intention in the beginning in order to habituate their unprepared audiences to this Western idea. Kasravi's view, though contradicted by another of his opinions given elsewhere, is acceptable, because first of all, the attitude of hiding the real intention for tactical reasons was suggested to Tabataba'i by al-Afghani in one of his letters.

Secondly, Tabataba'i himself testified that his real intention in his campaign against the Qajar rulers was to support the formation of a constitutional government in Iran. In his diary, in 1911, Tabataba'i wrote that,

> I arrived in Tehran in 1894. Right from my arrival in Tehran I had planned to establish constitutionalism (*mashrutah*) and a national consultative assembly in Iran. From pulpits I used to talk about these two. Nasir al-Din Shah often complained about me and sent me messages saying that Iran was not yet prepared for constitutionalism.

Tabataba'i's awareness of the idea of constitutionalism is also evidenced in passages included in his scattered speeches.

By making a comparison between Tabataba'i's views given above and those of other Shi^c^i ^c^ulama' of his time, it seems that Tabataba'i was the only distinguished *mujtahid* to pronounce statements bearing a nationalistic sense. He frequently mentioned that he was devoted to his country, Iran, and that his service to Islam lay within that country. Moreover, the fact that he deemed literacy necessary for a modern constitutional régime proves that he knew well what constitutionalism was all about. He even knew that the new system he was fighting for would not bring him any worldly profits. He had said once to the ^c^Ayn al-Dawlah that "By the establishment of the Majlis (parliament) and ^c^adalatkhanah (house of justice), we ^c^ulama' would lose our prestige, but we both are old: do establish a good name by establishing a *majlis*."

A British official document shows that,

> On the occasion of the discussion of the Courts of Justice he [Tabataba'i] expressed some doubt, perhaps not without a touch of grim humour, as to whether there would be anything left for the Mollahs to do after the institution of these Courts.

Unlike many of his colleagues, Tabataba'i advocated the idea of modern education. He notes: "It is necessary to study modern sciences. We should study international law, mathematics and foreign languages. Why should not even one of the *ʿulama'* know any foreign language? If we had any connection with modern sciences and if we knew history and the science of law, we would have understood the real meaning of monarchy." On the latter subject he points out: "People should choose a person as the king as long as he gives his service to the people. If the king turns careless and lascivious, the people should remove him from the throne and appoint another one."

By making the latter statement, Tabataba'i strongly rejected the Persian traditional concept of kingship which gave sanction to the king's claim to be God's shadow on earth. In addition, Tabataba'i, unlike the orthodox Shiʿi *ʿulama'*, did not refute the idea of kingship on the grounds that it was a usurpation of the authority of the *ʿulama'*. He sanctioned a sort of secular monarchy by considering the Shah an authority who may be recognized as long as he serves his people.

This attitude toward modernism still does not establish Tabataba'i as a fully fledged secularist. In the same speech in which he attempted to refute traditional systems, he also said, as noted above, that he was fighting for Islamic law side by side with justice and a national assembly. He even protested in a parliamentary session against ". . . a clause having been read relating to charitable bequests [*awqaf*] stating that the Government had the right to supervise the administration of such a bequest, . . ." However, Tabataba'i was very realistic and knew the needs of the time. He found it expedient to give large concessions (very much more than his colleagues) to modernism. His discerning remarks concerning nationalism, constitutionalism, and modern education, plus his associations with a number of international figures in Russia, in Turkey, and in the Arab world, indicate that Tabataba'i, in contrast with what is implied in a view, was not confused about the meaning of the *mashrutah* (constitutionalism); nor does the view, which holds that "the *ʿulama'* saw in the constitution a means of applying the *shariʿah* in its entirety", entirely apply to Tabataba'i.

* * *

Before we discuss the views of the Persian *ʿulama'* of Iraq, we should examine the circumstances under which the leading *ʿulama'*, i.e., Tihrani, Khurasani, and Mazandarani and their assistants and co-thinkers, such as Na'ini and Mahallati, expressed their motives for participation in the Persian Constitutional Revolution. Right from the beginning of the Persian Revolution, the three high ranking *ʿulama'* were on the side of the constitutionalists. When Shaykh Fadlullah rose against the Constitution, these

ᶜulama' continued their support to Tabataba'i, Bihbahani and other consti-
titionalists in Iran, and openly condemned Shaykh Fadlullah.

To this point, not many effective measures had been taken by these
clerical residents of Najaf. But the combined Shah-Russian aggression in
Iran led the *ᶜulama'* to take a series of serious actions. To suppress the
Revolution, Muhammad ᶜAli Shah, with the help of the Russians, bom-
barded the Persian Parliament and executed a great many liberals. Vladimir
Ilich Lenin, on August 5, 1908, thus describes the situation:

> There has been a counter-revolution in Persia—a curious combination
> of the dissolution of the first Duma in Russia and of the revolt at the
> close of 1905. Shamefully defeated by the Japanese, the armies of the
> Russian Tsar are taking revenge by zealously serving the counter-
> revolution. The Cossacks, who took part in the mass shootings, primi-
> tive expeditions, manhandling and robbery in Russia, are performing
> new exploits in Persia where they are suppressing the revolution.

The *ᶜulama'* rose against the Shah and Russians because the latter were
considered enemies of Islam and murderers of the Iranian Muslims. The
violation of democratic principles was not a matter of substantial concern
for the *ᶜulama'*. What concerned them rather was the need to overthrow an
un-Islamic ruler and to expel the infidels from Iran. With this motivation
the *ᶜulama'* intensified their campaign against the tyrannical rule of
Muhammad ᶜAli Shah and their support to the constitutionalists.

As mentioned earlier in this chapter, the *ᶜulama'* of Iraq, i.e., Najaf, Karbala, Kazimayn, and Samarrah, gave a favorable response to the Pan-
Islamic appeal of the Ottomans. The reason for the *ᶜulama's* response seems
to have been twofold. First, the revolutionary government of the Young
Turks (from 1908) became rather friendly with the Iranian constitutionalists
because of the common cause (constitutionalism) agitating the two nations.
Second, since the Pan-Islamic interests of the Ottoman Empire survived the
1908 Revolution, the Young Turks welcomed any support on the part of the
Shiᶜi leaders residing in Iraq. Therefore, when the *ᶜulama'* saw Muhammad
ᶜAli Shah in alliance with the Russians, murdering Iranian Muslims, they
found it expedient to appeal to the Ottoman Sultan and to demand his intervention as the Caliph of Muslims. Needless to say, it was very incongruous
for the Shiᶜi *ᶜulama'* to appeal to a Sunni Caliph—and one who was the
traditional enemy of Iran in addition.

Both for the Ottomans and the Persian *ᶜulama'*, it was found useful to co-
operate in the name of Pan-Islamism. Cooperation appealed to the Ottomans because the *ᶜulama'* were instrumental in the Pan-Islamic propaganda; it attracted the *ᶜulama'* because they wanted, with the help of the Ottomans, to remove the Russian infidels from the Muslim territory of Iran, and
to depose Muhammad ᶜAli Shah. Therefore, Khurasani and Mazandarani

declared that, "Now it is the most important duty of Muslims to remove this blood-shedding man [Muhammad ᶜAli Shah] and not to pay taxes to his government."

To help overthrow the Persian King, the clerical leaders sent a telegram to the Ottoman Sultan explaining that,

> We suppliants of high government and beseechers of the Sultan's compassion, after fulfilling our duties of prayer and expressing the praises due by us to the Amir-el-Muminin, the Shadow of God on the People and the Protector of the Islamic World . . . beg to state that we are companions and servants of the sublime religious law sheltered by the protection of the illustrious Government . . . [The Shah] brought about disburbances between the Government and the subjects, which resulted in fear and dispersion from what the hands of bad people committed and from what the hands of tyrants gained; so much so that the Muslim women and their children were bought by misbelievers . . . The people applied to us asking for our intercession because they supposed that the Sharaa [*Sharicah*] was to be obeyed and the word of its people ought to be listened to. We did our best to preserve the nation and begged for obedience from the Government by sufficient advice and eloquent and ample preachings . . . A few days passed by, and he started this tyranny, withdrawing his firm promises, destroying the kind respect of the subjects, putting behind his back the Book of God, and ill-treating its prescriptions which are not hidden to you. We complain to God of this serious calamity and beg for the compassion of the Sultan of Islam in this desperate misfortune, which has no equal . . . In that we pray for the putting out of the flame, the stamping out of the prevailing discord and the removal of the grievances from this nation, the claim of Moslems' rights, and their safety from the victory of the infidels . . . Among the facts that our belief gathered is the ambition of the compassionate Sultan for conciliation. We beg from the compassion of that sublime spot and the pity of the high Government to exercise kindness before the intervention of foreigners and the lopping off of the nation and the country from every side . . .

The British Consul-General in Baghdad writes that " . . . the Shiahs are indignant at this appeal to the Sunni Sultan, and I hear that objection is particularly taken to the use of the term 'Amir-el-Muminin' . . ." Using this kind of expression for the Sultan on the part of the Shiᶜi *ᶜulama'* is, of course, very strange.

It is perhaps for this reason that Nazim al-Islam Kirmani who reproduced the Arabic version of the telegram expressed doubts on the authenticity of the telegram pointing out that he had not obtained it from reliable sources.

It is difficult to determine the authenticity of the telegram's exact wording. One may assume that the phrase *Amir al-mu'minin* was added by one of the *ᶜulama's* supporters simply to attract a greater sympathy from the

Sultan. This assumption may be supported by other communications which were addressed to the Ottoman Sultan by the Najaf *ᶜulama'* and which lacked the phrase *Amir al-mu'minin*. In an Arabic telegram, most probably sent to Sultan Mehmed V, on the same occasion the *ᶜulama'* called him *khalifatuna* (our Caliph), not *Amir al-mu'minin* (the Commander of the Faithful), a title which exclusively applies, among the Shiᶜi, to ᶜAli ibn Abi Talib. Three years later again the *ᶜulama'* sent a telegram to Sultan Mehmed V concerning the Anglo-Russian invasions of Iran; in this telegram the phrase *khalifah-i Islam* was used.

On the other hand one may assume that the *ᶜulama'* out of expediency did employ the term *Amir al-mu'minin* in their 1908 telegram (to ᶜAbdul-Hamid II) but they ceased to do so in their subsequent communications because of the Shiᶜi objection which the British reporter claims to have arisen over the usage of the term.

On August 4, 1908, Shaykh Ismaᶜil, a son of Mirza Habibullah Rashti went to J. Ramsay, the British Consul-General at Baghdad, and asked him, on behalf of the leading *mujtahids* of Najaf, if the British will continue to support the Persian constitutionalists, and if so, whether or not the Consul-General would give the *mujtahids* his advice as to their best line of conduct. He did not give the envoy of the *mujtahids* any firm answer and commented regarding the envoy's question:

. . . it seems fairly clear that the Mujtaheds of Nedjef have only turned to the British Representative because they find themselves helpless . . .

He also adds that the *ᶜulama'* probably doubt the wisdom of their authorizing the Sultan to interfere in Iranian internal affairs which meant an encouragement of the Turks to occupy Azarbaijan.

Shaykh Fadlullah Nuri

In the Name of God, the Beneficient,
the Merciful

Praise be upon His friend [ᶜAli ibn Abi Talib], and blessing be upon His Prophet and the Prophet's virtuous family, and may God's curse be upon all their enemies, until the Day of Judgment.

This is to bring to the notice of my religious brothers and fellow-believers, may God strengthen their faith and [increase their] success, that first of all I thank the Master of the universe, may His greatness be exalted. Who in this great calamity [which is like that] of the end of the world, and in this gigantic test [which is given to] the Muslim people and to the believers — a calamity which ages the minors and makes the old decrepit — granted this feeble and helpless [writer] such a great grace, and honoured [him] with such a lofty honour, despite the volume of the enemies, to announce the truth of Islam to the people of all cities with a sufficiently loud voice in the meetings, from the pulpits, and by [writing] communiqués. [This duty was done despite the fact that] the corrupt people were in a thoroughly victorious position, and the commotion [which resulted from] this fiery world calamity was stirred by pig-headed people. [This task was performed] by way of obedience to the command of the master [cAli ibn Abi Talib] and by refraining from [personal] interests and desires. When these 'great' men, whose foundations are shaky, [in the words of the Qur'an, had their] 'hearts reach to the threats' [XXXIII:10], I did not fear, and performed my necessary duty; thanks to God, first and last, outwardly and inwardly.

* * *

For instance, the *zimmi* infidels are subject to special provisions in their marital relations with Muslims. It is not allowed for a Muslim to marry an infidel, but Muslim men can have non-Muslim women as concubines and on a temporary basis. Also, apostasy of either partner of the married couple entails the cancellation of the marriage.

Conversion of either partner of a [non-Muslim] couple to Islam also has special different provisions. With regard to the problem of inheritance, unbelief (*kufr*) denies a person inheritance. An infidel may not inherit from a Muslim, but the reverse is permissible. Also, an apostate has special definite provisions; his property will be transferred to his heirs, his wife [automatically] is divorced, his body becomes unclean, and it is obligatory to punish him with death. Also, there are different provisions concerning usurious transactions. The *zimmi's* transactions in lands require the payment of the *khums* [one-fifth of the net income] if the *zimmi* buys the land from a Muslim. About crimes, punishments, and blood money, various provisions have been made.

Oh! [my] religious brother! How can Islam, which thus distinguishes among provisions of different matters, tolerate [the idea of] equality? [One only has to admit that] it is intended to open a business over against the founder of the *sharicah*, and to establish new rules; may God, the exalted, protect us from it.

The principal part of this game—constitutionalism—was played by the erroneous group [i.e., the non-Muslim citizens and most probably the Babis] in order to escape from the four definite provisions which are made for those who renounce Islam. What a wrong idea! What a [set of] vain thoughts! The house [i.e., the territory of Islam] has a lord and the religion has [its] master. Strangely [enough], they ascribe their misrepresentation and their own casting of doubt on the people, to the state law [because, having in mind the proverb] 'the liar has a poor memory', [they want to be safe from any objections regarding their possible contradictory remarks [sic]].

* * *

Oh, heretics! If this state law is in conformity with Islam, it is not possible to include equality in it, and if it is at variance with Islam, it would be against what is written in the previous part [of the constitution], that is: 'whatever is against Islam cannot be lawful'.

Oh, Knavish and [individuals] devoid of zeal! See how the master of the *sharicah* has granted you honors because you have been embellished with Islam. He has granted you privileges, but you deny them by saying that you must be equal brothers with Zoroastrians, Armenians and Jews; God's curse may be upon those who approve this [equality]!

Strangest of all is that they say that the articles of the law can be changed. Is this change from Islam to infidelity, or from infidelity to Islam? Both alternatives are obviously wrong. One may argue that this change [only] consists of a change from Islam to Islam, that is to say, from a permissible [action] to another permissible [action]. Although this [kind of] change can be conceived, it is wrong to make and put into effect a law which regulates a permissible action, the performance and non-performance of which is all the same to the founder of the *sharicah*. [It is wrong especially if] a punishment may be given to those who do not obey such laws. The secondary meanings (*canawin-i thanawiyyah*), which are considered in order to explain the basis of differences among the provisions, such as the obedience [of a child to his] father, or vows, oaths, and the like, are limited in *fiqh*, and are beyond [the authority of] the votes of grocers and drapers.

Oh, irreligious [individuals]! You want to establish a new innovation in religion and change [it] by these guiles and impostures. God forbid! [Your idea would never] enjoy any success, because false [ideas] have a limited period: [as the Qur'an says:] 'Those who do wrong will come to know by what a [great] reverse they will be overturned!' (XXVI:227) Within two astronomical hours (*du sacat-i nujumi*) all the erroneous devices they had made for a long time were ruined. I praise God with all His commendable [attributes], and [thank Him] for all His graces.

Another erroneous article of the constitution concerns freedom of the press. After a series of changes and alterations, the text [of the article finally] went as follows: 'All publications, except erroneous books and matters harmful to the perspicious religion [of Islam], are free and censorship of them is forbidden.' According to this article, many of the unlawful things which should be forbidden have been made lawful because only two matters are excepted, whereas [in fact] one of the imperatively unlawful things is malicious accusation (*iftira'*). Another indisputable unlawful matter is back-biting of a Muslim (*ghaybah*). Also, slander against a Muslim, harm, abusive language, insult, intimidation, threatening, and the like, are forbidden by the *shariᶜah* and are considered unlawful by God. Is freedom in these things not solely declaring lawful what God has made unlawful? And [of course] the status of one who declares lawful what God has made unlawful is obvious, and the provision concerning him is clear.

It is strange that in cases other than those which have been excepted, censorship has been forbidden [in the law], whereas forbidding indecency (*nahy-i az munkar*) [*nahy ᶜan al-munkar*] is one of the basic principles and the writer or opinion-giver [who supports the idea of censorship over evil publications may want] to carry out the Islamic duty of *nahy-i az munkar*. More strange than this is that at the bottom of this article [no. 20] a punishment has been laid down for one who may disobey [the law], and [in this case] reference is made to the press law. This is also wrong and is an innovation because in matters related to the *shariᶜah* we do not have [any provision for] a cash penalty for committing unlawful things: whereas there [in the article] cash penalty has been laid down.

Oh, Muslim brothers! It is an annoying situation (*zaqa al-sadr*); all these nonsensical and extravagant statements are given in order to destroy the foundation of religion and to cause the disappearance of the *shariᶜah* of the master of the messengers. I swear to the One [i.e., God] Who split the seed and exhausted the breath that religious thieves have entered [the scene] and their only concern is to take [our] religion and to destroy its adherents. Otherwise, giving currency to justice does not need these arrangements.

In order to remove any obscurity related to [the ideal of] justice, a term which has been the most important means of attracting most of the people to this incident [i.e., the constitutional revolution], here we give some explanation.

Know that heaven and earth depend on justice, the necessity of which is obvious according to both reason and the *shariᶜah*. The question, however, is to find out its applicability. This famous phrase [which says]: 'equal oppression is justice' seems to be incorrect. Oh Muslims! Islam which is our

religion and the religion of [all] adherents of the Prophet is more complete
than all other religions. It is based on perfect justice, as God, the exalted,
says:

'Lo! Allah enjoineth justice and kindness.' [XVI:90] Thanks to God, the exalted, that in Islam, there is but justice. Prophecy and kingship among preceding prophets were different: sometimes the [two authorities] were
centered [in one person] or were divided. [The two authorities were
centered] in the blessed person of the most honorable Prophet, the last of
the prophets, [God's] blessing may be upon him and his family as long as
the universe lasts. Such was [also] the case with the caliphs of that magnani-
mous [personality, i.e., Muhammad], either lawfully or unlawfully. But
several months after the occurrence of accidents, these two affairs, namely
the assumption of religious affairs and the using of power and glory, and
alertness over the security [of the state], centered in two [separate]
authorities.

In fact, these two authorities are complementary and supplementary to
each other, that is to say, the foundation of Islam is laid upon these two
[sets] of affairs: deputyship in the affairs of prophecy and kingship.
Without these two, Islamic provisions would be inactive. As a matter of
fact, kingship is the executive power of Islamic provisions, and doing justice
depends on executing them. In Islam warnings, promises, and threats, and
carrying out punishments are all used as executive procedures. Even warning is more important [because] it consists of fear of God and believing in
the origin and return [of creation] (*mabda' wa ma^cad*), from which will
result the [state of having] fear and hope. These two things which have to do
with heart, soul, and conscience, are more influential in taking good actions
and in avoiding indecency, [both of which] form the truth of justice. The
stronger [one's] certainty may be about the origin and return [of creation],
and the more fear of God, and hope [one may have of God's mercy], the
more widespread justice will become. [By the same token], the more [the
state of fear and hope] diminishes, the more injustice will be increased.

In early Islam, due to the closeness of the time of the Prophet and
manifestations of God's Agents (*awliya'-i haqq*) [i.e., the Imams], justice
was more widespread. However, after the Occultation of the Imam of the
universe, peace may be upon him, when his Specified and General Agents
were entrusted with the affairs, a gradual weakness appeared in the
[people's] beliefs because of certain accidents. Therefore, injustice increased
[in various ways] depending on the different circumstances and the existence and non-existence of the endeavour [both] of the *^culama'* and the
kings.

According to these preliminary remarks, it has become evident that, if justice is to be spread, it is necessary to strengthen these two groups. That is to say, those who know [Islamic] provisions and those who possess power among Muslims. This is the way for earning the correct and useful justice.

Yes, in our epoch, currency has been given to a subject which [falsely] sounds like justice. Thus, a number of naturalists who deny the origin and return [of creation] and consider [our] life limited only to this world, saw that with anarchy and without setting up a 'law' they would not be able to achieve their benefits of life. Therefore, they made [a mixture of] sacred heavenly laws, as well as [the devices created by their own] defvective minds, and called it 'law'. They accepted this law in order to satisfy their desires. With this arrangement they established order, [but] the commander and prohibitor in this order are the same law, plus the punishment which has been considered in the law. It does not create any commander and prohibitor inside one's heart. It is for this reason that shameful actions are current in keeping with the [established] system, and equal oppression given to all has been increased. As soon as they find themselves in security of the law they commit treason and injustice.

Now, Oh Muslims and children of the Muslims who do not appreciate the divine grace, what a firmly [founded] religion we have; what benefits one can enjoy from it; and what reforms can be made [through it] on [the affairs related to] this world and to the world to come! It is proper to recant this straight path and to follow these defective-minded people whose deficiency is, if you pay attention, testified by the assembly (*hay'at*) itself? [Should] we bear this great oppression that, simply because of its omnipresence, has been called 'justice'? [Are we to] become preoccupied with worldly [affairs], to turn away from the origin and return [of creation], and to seek only worldly improvements and wealth?

So many prophets were appointed by God to persuade the children of Adam to [be concerned with] the world to come and [induce them] to abstain from this ephemeral world (*dunya-i fani*). On the contrary, whatever our [constitutionalist] orators have said to the people during the past two years [consists only of the suggestion that] one should go after these worldly [affairs], and earn wealth and have pleasure. At one time one of these devils, out of 'sympathy', said in private to [some] of our countrymen that the removal of poverty in this country depends on two things: firstly, the decreasing of expenses, and secondly, the increasing of incomes. The most important thing which limits expenses is the lifting of veil from women, [because] the home dress would be sufficient for outside and inside. [They also argued that] one set of servants is enough; needs would be met with one carriage; one party with both women and men would be enough, and other things of this sort. Oh, zealous [people]! [Do] deliberate [and see] what [evil] thoughts they had about you. Many examples of these evil thoughts were found [in the writings of] the newspaper editors and [the speeches of] orators. Thank God that they did not reach their aim, and [let us] hope that by divine favour, they [also] will not reach [their aim] in the future. 'So, of the people who did wrong, the last remnant was cut off. Praise be to Allah. Lord of the Worlds!' (VI:45)

Part VI

Shi^cism in the Modern World: Later Political Ideas

Chapter Twenty-Two

Ayatollah Sayyid Ruhullah Musawi Khumayni and Wilayat-i Faqih

Like most great religions of the world, Shiᶜism entered the modern age under the threats of modernism, syncreticism, and the decapitation of fundamental religious Truth. To this threat, Shiᶜism responded with a call for a mixture of continuity and change. Traditional Shiᶜi religious, political, social, and philosophical ideas have persisted to this day, surfacing in an array of intellectual and communal activities in various parts of the Shiᶜi world. Meanwhile, the fundamental ethos of Shiᶜi political thought and religious practice, in some instances, have undergone considerable change. These changes both reflect and respond to the pressures brought on by alien ideas, on the one hand, and change in the Muslim world, on the other. This section examines the evolution of Shiᶜi political thought, and the continuity evident in modern Shiᶜi philosophy, as well as issues such as women's rights or political dissent, as reflected in the corpus of modern Shiᶜi thought.

The tradition of the Shiᶜi political thought that evolved throughout the Qajar period changed further during the Pahlavi era. The encounter of Shiᶜism with both modernity and crises of modernization in the recent decades radicalized the political doctrines of the faith to produce a direct claim to power and elaborate doctrines of social reform. The dynamics of the interactions between the clergy and the state led to the emergence of the idea of Wilayat-i faqih. *Following its early propagation by Mulla Ahmad Naraqi, and as we saw in Chapter Nineteen, the idea was first resuscitated by Ayatollah Khumayni and gained hold in traditionalist circles after the death of Ayatollah Burujirdi and the weakening of the traditionalist hold over Shiᶜi heirarchy.*

During the same period, such lay Shi^ci thinkers as ^cAli Shari^cati, and a number of ^culama', Ayatollahs Mutahhari and Taliqani in particular, developed novel approaches to social action. Similar social and political trends catapulted Shi^cism into the political arena in Iraq and Lebanon, where the ideas of Sayyid Muhammad Baqir Sadr and Imam Musa Sadr developed political ideas analogous to those in Iran. In this chapter, Enayat and Bayat discuss the various aspects of Wilayat-i faqih, *while sections from Khumayni's writings edited and translated by Hamid Algar illustrate the directions of the changes introduced by this school of Shi^ci thought. The excerpts are from IKCGJ, 160-61, 163–67, 169-75;* IRFM, *30-42, and* IAR, *40-54, respectively.*

Hamid Enayat

. . . [W]hat distinguishes the regime set up by the Islamic revolution from all such antecedents is a notion related not so much to the nature of the political order, but to the person or persons considered to be solely qualified to act as ultimate rulers or arbiters of that political order. This notion has now come to be recognized by the phrase *wilayat-i faqih*, which can be translated as the 'guardianship (or rulership) of the jurisconsult' (and not 'of the theologian', as is sometimes suggested, for the simple reason that the theology and *fiqh*, or Islamic jurisprudence, are two different disciplines which can on occasions be at odds with each other). Although it has a long jurisprudential ancestry, it is a notion which is almost totally identified with the political outlook of Iran's religious leader, Ayatollah Ruhullah Khumayni.

Exponents of the 'guardianship of the jurisconsult' can be found among classical and medieval masters of the Shi^ci *fiqh*, of whom perhaps the most influential was al-Karaki, known as Muhaqqiq al-Thani (d. 1534). This becomes more understandable when one remembers that as the *shaykh al-Islam* (paramount relilgious leader) of Shah Tahmasp, al-Karaki was a powerful figure in the Safavid administration. His strong conviction on this issue was in keeping with his other major theses, including his activist's perception of the principle of 'enjoining the good and prohibiting the evil' *al-amr bi'l-ma^cruf wa'l-nahy ^can al-munkar* as an unconditional duty incumbent on every individual Muslim—which means that no Muslim, even one who lacks proper knowledge of religious principles is exonerated from the obligation to do all he can to secure the adherence of his fellow Muslims to those principles.

But what makes Khumayni unique as a religious writer is his contention that a *faqih* should be not just one high offical among the many who form the top echelon of the state administration, but its supreme overseer, judge, and guardian. And the significance of the Iranian revolution lies partly in the fact that it has—at least for the time being—fulfilled this old ambition of some ardent religionists. What is extraordinary is that this has come about in a moment of Iranian history when—for two main reasons—it was least expected: first, the process of modernization or Westernization, with all its aberrations, setbacks, and imbalances, seemed to have gone too far to allow the return to what many think of as an anachronism — that is, the subordination of politics to religious precepts; second, although religious thinking among Iranian Shiᶜis displayed an unusual vitality during the last decade of the Shah's era, it was far from reaching any consensus over the feasibility or advisability of *faqihs'* governing. . . .

* * *

Although Khumayni's assertion of the right of the *faqih* to act as a full-fledged political ruler cannot be strictly regarded as an innovation in the history of Shiᶜi political theory, it does represent an unexpected revival of an old, dormant theme. His arguments on this issue deserve close study if one is to understand the ruling ideology of present-day Iran. Although other sources have been consulted, my main source for Khumayni's ideas has been a booklet published in his name in Tehran in 1978, entitled *Namih-i az Imam Musawi Kashif al-Ghita, (A Letter from the Imam Musawi, the Dispeller of Obscurity)*, which was used by his followers as the manifesto of the Islamic revolution. In the remainder of this chapter, I will consider its contents in the context of modern ecumenical trends in Islam, since this can explain the enormous appeal of many of his ideas to large groups of Muslims, both Shiᶜi and Sunni, inside and outside Iran.

One point can be disposed of quickly. In Khumayni's treatment of the basic questions concerning the *wilayah*, all the nuances of Ansari's discussions are reduced to a much simpler classification: *wilayah* is either existential (*takwini*) or relative (*iᶜtibari*). The former is a spiritual preeminence exclusive to the prophets and the Imams; the latter is the social and political duty of the *faqihs* to 'administer and rule the state and to implement the laws of the sacred path'. One important consequence of this classification is that while it enhances the political status of the *faqih*, it tries to dispel any impression of his 'supernaturalness'. As such, Khumayni's thesis stands opposed to popular Shiᶜism and comes close to Sunnism. '*Wilayah*', he says, 'consists of government and administration of the state and implementation of the laws of the sacred path. This is a heavy and important duty, [but] not something which would create a supernatural status for its holder, elevating him to a position higher than that of an ordinary human being. in other words, the *wilayah*, of which we are talking, means government and implementation. *Contrary to what many people might think*, it is not a privilege, but a grave responsibility.' This is meant to refute the conception, held by some uninitiated Shiᶜis, as well as by their Western or Sunni critics, that as *ayatullahs* ('Signs of God') the leading *faqihs* are superhuman, as if partaking of a quality almost tantamount to the Imams' infallibility. However, as will be noted later, the requirements of political power since

1978 have fostered a psychological environment which does accord extraordinary status to the *faqihs*.

The doctrine of the *wilayat-i faqih* is predicated on a belief in the Islamic state as the best form of government. This is a belief which has been advocated by many other fundamentalist Muslim thinkers in modern times, of whom the Syrian Rashid Rida, the Egyptian Muhammad al-Ghazzali, and the Pakistani Abu'l-A^cla' Mawdudi have been the most widely known. Although, in contrast to them, Khumayni is a Shi^ci *faqih*, there is nothing specifically Shi^ci or sectarian about his case for the 'obligatoriness' of an Islamic state, based as it is on the same premises as those employed, say, by al-Ghazzali—namely, that the implementation of some of the most important religious injunctions, whether on defending the Muslim territory, collecting the alms-tax, or applying the penal system, is impossible without the creation of a state. In agreement with all these authors, Khumayni maintains that the restoration of Muslim unity, either through recovering Muslim sovereignty from foreigners or removing internal lackeys, depends solely on the establishment of a government having the real interests of Muslims at heart. He shares Mawdudi's conviction that such a government can only be born of a revolution, but, unlike him, Khumayni does not give a systematic descripton of 'Islamic revolution'. However, his scattered remarks and statements make it clear that he does not share Mawdudi's idea of revolution as something purely spiritual, gradual, and peaceful, but that he sees it as political, brusque, and violent, even while its final goal is the spiritual regeneration of man. Although any regime which is corrupt or serves the interests of foreign powers would thus qualify as the target of such a revolution, monarchies in particular are singled out as being intrinsically anti-Islamic because they are considered to be in conflict with the most fundamental article of faith—the belief that sovereignty belongs only to God.

But to the extent that Khumayni elaborates his arguments on all these points within the general framework of the *shari^cah*, his political ideas, with their revolutionary tone, can be addressed to any Muslim audience without offending sectarian susceptibilities; in this respect, his thinking belongs to the mainstream of Islamic political thought. This statement applies particularly to the earlier stages of the Islamic revolution, when his ideas were less specific and when he used the general slogans of Muslim unity and authenticity. As, however, the revolution increasingly turned to violence and was rent with internal dissensions, Sunni criticisms of his ideas proliferated. But these were more political than religious, emphasizing some of the anti-democratic consequences of government by the *faqih*. The few religious criticisms that were published during 1979 concentrated on his intellectual formation as a Shi^ci, and, therefore, as an advocate of the doctrines of the infallibility of the Imams, the occultation of the Twelfth Imam (*ghaybah*), and the denial of the right of Abu Bakr, ᶜUmar, and ᶜUthman to Muhammad's successorship — topics which have no direct bearing on Khumayni's notion of the Islamic state. Such strictures might grow in scope and depth whenever there is a conflict of political interests between Iran and the Sunni Muslim regimes.

As we suggested here, Khumayni's most daring contribution to the modern debate on the Islamic state is his insistence that the essence of such a state is not so much its constitution, or the commitment of its rulers to complying with the *shariᶜah*, but the special quality of its leadership. He thinks that this special quality can be provided only by the *faqihs*. It is true that the position of the *faqih* assumes greater significance in Shiᶜism than in Sunnism as the 'custodian' of the community in the absence of the Imam. It is also true that the canonical references used by Khumayni to prove his point are all taken from Shiᶜi sources. But the idea that only the *faqihs* can provide sound leadership for an Islamic state is not exclusive to the Shiᶜis. Among modern Muslim thinkers, Rashid Rida also has expressed this opinion in his treatise on the caliphate. In his outline of the Islamic state, the highest political position after that of the caliph (who is also himself a *mujtahid*, i.e. someone who exercises independent judgement or *ijtihad*) is allotted to a respected elite, *ahl al-hall wa'l-ᶜaqd* ('the people who loose and bind'), who are the genuine representatives of the Muslims. After enumerating the qualities required of this elite, Rida deplores the decline in the political power of the *ᶜulama'* in Egypt, Tunisia, India, and Turkey, thus revealing his wish to see them regain their paramount place in the administration of Muslim affairs. To drive his point further home, he contrasts the diminishing status of the Sunni *ᶜulama'* with the irrepressible popularity of the Shiᶜi *mujtahids*, and praises the political dynamism of the latter, as demonstrated in their leadership of the Tobacco Rebellion in Iran in 1892 and in the Iraqi revolt of 1920.

Khumayni's vindication of the role of the *faqihs* is much more forceful, and his demands upon them much more explicit and exacting, than anything envisaged by Rida or Mawdudi. He wants to see the *faqihs* not simply as benign dispensers of advice and consent, but as real wielders of power. He knows that such a commanding position cannot be secured for him without making the *shariᶜah* the incontestable and unique law of the land. Thus, whereas Rida and Mawdudi were willing to make room for some secular legislation by permitting *ijtihad* and other accommodating devices, Khumayni unyieldingly holds that the *shariᶜah* must be the *only* law, and that human regulation is allowed only as a practical contrivance for the enforcement of the divine law. This conception deprives all man-made laws,

however wisely conceived and properly enacted, of any inherent binding
force and subordinates them to the *faqih*'s approval.

* * *

None of these provisions clashes with any of the fundamental beliefs of
the average Muslim, of whatever denomination, since no Muslim sect or rite
has in principle prohibited the *culama*'s assumption of political leadership.
Even the homage that Khumayni pays to such Shici symbols as *cAshura*,
commemorating the martyrdom of Husayn, Imam (and Caliph) cAli's son,
at Sunni hands, and the anticipation of the Mahdi do not necessarily disqualify his blueprint in the eyes of Sunni Muslims. This is so because, first,
these symbols and concepts are respected, if not adhered to, by many Sunnis as well, and, second, they do not impinge on the substance of
Khumayni's proposed Islamic state. Ironically, if any canonical objection
has been raised against his concept of the Islamic state, it has come, as we
shall presently see, from some of the Shici *faqihs*, who have disagreed with
his interpretation of the sacred sources. Part of his argument amounts in
fact to a historical criticism of the *culama*'s subservience to rulers, and their
dereliction of duty and responsibility as guardians of the Muslim conscience, with which no fair-minded religionist would disagree. But in addition to this criticism he quotes a number of *hadiths*, or sayings, from the
Prophet Muhammad and the Imams, in which the *culama*' have been
described alternatively as 'the heirs of the prophets', 'the fortress of Islam',
and 'the trustees of the emissaries [of God]'. He also refers to the famous
Qur'anic verse enjoining the Muslims to 'obey God and the Prophet and the
holders of authority' (IV:59), and to two *hadiths* (known as the 'narratives' of
cUmar ibn Hanzalah and Abu Khadijah) attributed to the sixth Shici Imam,
al-Sadiq, prohibiting the Shicis from seeking redress from 'the unjust rulers
of the age'.
      The conclusion he draws from all these and other quotations is that, with
the obvious exception of the privilege of receiving the divine revelation, all
the other responsibilities and powers of the Prophet have been devolved on
the *culama*' after the disappearance of the Twelfth Imam. The two narratives of Ibn Hanzalah and Abu Khadijah have stark anti-Sunni connotations, but his interpretation of them and of other *hadiths* and his conclusion
cannot be offensive to the Sunnis.

* * *

Khumayni has ancitipated . . . objections in his treatises, as well as doubts
concerning the *culama*'s technical expertise and professional acumen in

managing governmental affairs. His answer to all of them, which is couched very much in the style of classical dialectics, is that it would be absurd to acknowledge the *culama'* as the inheritors and successors of the Prophet without recognizing their authority and duty as political leaders as well. He dismisses the argument that they lack technocratic expertise and adminitrative ability by turning it on their detractors and pointing to the mediocrity and incompetence of Muslim rulers both in the present and in the past: 'Which one of them', he asks, 'is more qualified than an ordinary person? Many of them are not educated at all. Where has the ruler of the Hijaz [i.e., Saudi Arabia] received his education? Rida Khan (the founder of the Pahlavi dynasty] was not even literate . . . It has been the same in history. Many autocratic and over-weening rulers were devoid of the competence to administer the society and lead the nation, as well as of knowledge and virtue.' By way of contrast, the *faqih* has learned, through his comprehensive training, what is necessary for the supreme control and administration of the country and for promoting justice among people. Sciences and techniques are required only for executive and administrative affairs, and the *faqihs* can always call for executive and administration of the country and for promoting justice among people. Sciences and techniques are required only for executive and administrative affairs, and the *faqihs* can always call on the services of those who are well-versed in them.

Running through all these arguments is the conviction that no amount of opposition to the thesis of 'government by the *faqih*' can outweigh the compelling need for a vigorous intervention by the *culama'* to save Islam from the dual challenge of Western aggressiveness and the internal dissolution of religious values. 'Protecting Islam is a more imperative duty than uttering the prayers, or fasting,' he says in denigration of the ritual and theological niceties obstructing the politicization of the religious leadership. On one occasion, in condemning the attitude of Shurayh, a judge in Kufah at the time of the 'rightly-guided' caliphs (AD 632–61), he uses the word *akhund* to describe him (a generic Persian term which was formerly used to refer to a Shici *mulla* but now has a derogatory meaning, referring to a hide-bound 'clergyman'). In this way, he denotes his contempt for the traditional type of religious leaders who either are devoted to an aloofness from politics or allow themselves to be used by the rulers.

This predominance of politics in his religious thinking differentiates Khumayni from most Shici religious leaders of the recent past and present. 'It is, of course, essential for you', he says, addressing the Shici *faqihs*, 'to teach ritual matters. But what is important are the political, economic, and legal problems of Islam. This has always been, and still ought to be, the pivot of [our] activity.' He also says: 'Many of the ritual rules of Islam are the source of social and political services. Ritual acts in Islam are as a rule bound up with politics and administration of society. The congregational prayer, for instance, and the Pilgrimage have political, as well as moral and doctrinal, implications. Islam has provided for these gatherings so that . . . its followers may find solutions to their social and political problems.'

These manifestations of activism are striking, not so much because they come from a spiritual figure but because they collide with Khumayni's own background: he was a teacher of Islamic philosophy, a discipline well-known for its sublime detachment from politics. Equally conspicuous has been his penchant for Sufism, and for a highly theosophical understanding of Islam, which surfaces in his attacks on materialism and on those of his critics who worry that preoccupation with religion might hinder Muslims' economic and technological development.

But his activism stands out most sharply against the background of his intellectual formation, which is deeply rooted in solid, traditional scholarship. As a revolutionary, he has been uncompromising in his appeal for the punishment of all those who had cooperated politically, administratively, or culturally with the old regime. But as an authority on Shi^{c}i jurisprudence he offers a different image: keeping well within the bounds set by the great masters of the past, he adheres to a juridical logic which, when fully developed in the realm of Islamic penal law, often protects the individual against unfair accusations. This emerges most clearly in his scholarly discussion of the problem of 'accepting office from unjust rulers' — an old irritant in Shi^{c}i political theory. Although as the 'leader of the Islamic revolution and the founder of the Islamic republic', his name has often been invoked by various revolutionary officials in blanket condemnation of all the associates of the Pahlavi regime, he is often highly meticulous and discriminating in his assessment of what can be regarded as right or wrong by Shi^{c}i jurisconsults. Instead of issuing a single, sweeping rule for all those who 'accept office from unjust rulers', he classifies them according to their motives: (1) those who do this to enhance the honour and save the liberty of the faithful; (2) those who do it both for this reason and to secure their own livelihood; (3) those who do it purely to secure their own livelihood; and (4) those who do it to assist and strengthen the rulers. Whereas the first three types are pardonable, the fourth is guilty of a grave offence, as are all who in any form aid and abet tyrants.

But Khumayni does something more: he shows that even the term 'unjust' (*zalim, ja'ir*) is ambiguous and must be clarified before judgement can be passed on those described as such. Four groups of people, he says, can be regarded as unjust: (*a*) ordinary criminals, such as thieves and bandits; (*b*) kings and rulers violating the norms of justice; (*c*) those claiming the successorship to the Prophet; and (*d*) usurpers of the rulership of the righteous Imam — namely, the Sunni dynasties, the Umayyads and ^{c}Abbasids. He has no doubt about prohibiting people from working for groups (*a*), (*c*), and (*d*). He elaborates on group (*d*) in order to bring out the complexity of the issues involved: in addition to the question of motive, one should take account of the possibility that the rulers are Shiᶜi. Distinction should also be made between low and high officials: obviously petty officials can be excused, but even the conduct of high-ranking administrators should be scrutinized before any judgement is made on them.

While the context of Khumayni's teachings is thus largely traditional, the methods he has employed for propagating his views, both before and after achieving power, are populistic and revolutionary. This is seen in his direct appeal to the masses, his emphasis on the necessity of observing the people's wishes, and his fearless, uncompromising attitude towards those whom he considers to be the enemies of Islam. In so far as his denunciations of American imperialism and of Zionism and his attacks on capitalists and plutocrats can be considered substantive rather than rhetorical, his ideology also should be regarded as revolutionary; as such it has captured the imagination of many Muslims outside Iran. Moreover, his declarations in favour of political activism and against excessive concentration on ritual matters have delighted militants, who regard it was a warrant for subordinating canonical niceties to the demands of high politics. This accounts for the behaviour of many radical but self-avowed Muslims in Iran for whom solidarity with the people of El Salvador is more important than solidarity with the people of Afghanistan, since fighting American imperialism takes precedence over the fear of Soviet expansionism.

* * *

This principle proved extremely difficult to put into practice after the creation of the Islamic republic. It is one thing to disagree with a *faqih*, by virtue of the permissibility of difference of opinion on secondary matters, while he is a mere religious dignitary among his peers; it is quite another to oppose his views when he is acting as head of state. This is a point on which the Persian and the Arabic versions of Khumayni's writing differ. The Arabic version, *Kitab al-bay*ᶜ (*Book of Sale*), which was written about a decade before the revolution, clearly asserts the superiority of the *faqih* who has acquired the status of political ruler (*hakim*) over the others.

According to the devoted interpreters of Khumayni's doctrine, the commands of such a ruler are of two types. The first type purports merely to stare a well-established canonical notion or a religious precept, without requiring Muslims to do something which had not been required of them before; such a command is called *al-hukum al-kashif*, an order which simply indicates a religious rule. The second type is issued on the basis of the ruler's personal discretion and his understanding of what is expedient or beneficial for Muslims, even if there is no religious warrant or precedent for such a command; this command is called *al-hukm al-wilayati*, custodial order. An example of the first type is a ruler's pronouncement on 'the vision of the crescent of the moon' to determine the beginning of the lunar month; an example of the second type is the fixing of commodity prices. Commands of the first type are not binding on other *faqihs*, if these choose to dissent from the ruler; however, he does make exception of the ruler's legal orders for the settlement of disputes, since otherwise disputes would never end. But commands of the second type are binding at all times: here the dissenting *faqihs* must submit to the ruler's will for the sake of preserving Muslim unity and public order.

On the whole, Khumayni's arguments in favour of the subordination of non-ruling or 'apolitical' *faqihs* to the ruling *faqih* are pragmatic rather than purely juristic or derived from traditional texts. Moreover, if there is anything novel or unprecedented in his views on *wilayah*, it is not so much the concept of the government by the *faqih* as this requirement of the superiority of one *faqih* over the others.

Political leadership in the Islamic Republic has been organized along the lines prescribed by Khumayni in *Kitab al-bay^c*. Although the *marja^ciyyat*, or religious authority of the principal *faqihs* of the land, such as Sayyid Kazim Shari^catmadari, Sayyid Muhammad Rida Gulpayigani, and Sayyid Shahab al-Din Najafi Mar^cashi in Qum or Sayyid Hasan Qumi and Sayyid ^cAbdullah Shirazi in Mashhad, has remained intact, in political matters it is the 'custodial commands' of Khumayni that often prevail. The emerging system is thus an autocracy, which cannot possibly be reconciled with republicanism or democracy as understood in the West. But the duality that Khumayni has introduced into the institution of *marja^ciyyat*, dividing it into a religious and a political variety, has enabled the system to accommodate that principle of juristic pluralism which has always been a hallmark of Shi^cism. However, as the legal system of the Islamic Republic becomes gradually Islamized in conformity with Khumayni's, or his disciples', perception of Islam, the strains on this duality are bound to increase: there will be more and more pressure on the independent religious authorities to refrain from dissent in order to safeguard the 'consensus of the *ummah* (community of the faithful)'.

Khumayni's thesis also has certain theological implications that are not entirely free of political significance. One of them is the weakening, if not the outright rejection, of a major tenet of popular (but by no means classical) Shi^cism—the anticipation of the Mahdi (*intizar*). As is well known, not only the critics, but even some of the more enlightened defenders, of Shi^cism regard this tenet as one of the main causes of the notorious political passivity of its adherents during the greater part of their history. *Intizar* is often understood by ordinary Shiᶜis to signify that the fulfilment of real justice, whether in its cosmic or in its socio-juridical sense, is conditional only upon the return of the Hidden Imam, and that such an apocalyptic redress can take place only after the world is 'filled with injustice'. While never relinquishing his faith in the doctrine of Mahdism, Khumayni tries to denude it of its negative political content by summoning the Shiᶜis to set up an Islamic state, and by openly pouring scorn on the popular belief that justice cannot prevail until injustice engulfs the whole universe.

Taken together, Khumayni's main political ideas thus obliterate some of the most important differences between the Sunnis and the Shiᶜis. He minimizes the extent of the rift by stating that the essence of the Shiᶜi case is nothing other than a legitimate objection to the failure of the first three caliphs to fulfil one of the main preconditions of rulership — ᶜilm (religious knowledge). But his appeal to the Shiᶜis to revolt against injustice and to install an Islamic state indicates his denunciation of the practice of expedient concealment of one's convictions (*taqiyyah*), as well as criticism of the popular conception of anticipation; he thus attacks two Shiᶜi practices that have become staple themes of Sunni polemics against Shiᶜism.

Mangol Bayat

Until the turn of the present century intellectuals in the Muslim world were members of a loosely defined class of men who wore the turban as a sign of their learned status. Islam enforces the belief in the Qur'an as the source of all knowledge men need to know. Learned men were by definition men learned in religious sciences. Theology, jurisprudence, political philosophy, metaphysics, mysticism, Arabic language and grammar, history, among other disciplines, were all viewed as components of ᶜilm, or knowledge of the divine. In fact, in Islamic centers of learning no attempt was made to distinguish the sacred from profane knowledge.

When tensions arose as a result of the incompatibility of philosophical mystical or scientific views with basic tenets of the faith, censorship was effectively imposed by the specialists of the Islamic law, who emerged as a

group of self-appointed protectors of the community from "religious deviation." Throughout the centuries, however, scientists, philosophers, mystics,
and speculative thinkers in general, allowed themselves freedom from commonly enforced views and developed their respective disciplines in private.
While outwardly abiding by the directives of the jurists, arguing that
religion is a social necessity since popular morality is tied to religious
beliefs, they safeguarded their knowledge by confining it to a restricted circle of disciples and adepts. A smooth and discreet transmission of ideas
through generations of followers was thus ensured, and intellectual change
was barely perceived by the society at large as Islamic speculative thought
remained exclusive and esoteric. When the views of the established religious
leadership of a particular Muslim community were openly challenged, however, the dissenters were persecuted.

The establishment of Shiᶜi Islam as the official state religion in Iran in the
sixteenth century and the arrival to social prominence of high ranking
religious leaders who were specialists in Shiᶜi law sharpened intellectual differences that divided the ranks of the religious institutions. While the jurists
forcefully imposed their religious policies and required strict adherence to
the law, mystics and philosophers defended their right to expand their
understanding of religion. Shiᶜi intellectuals continually offered alternative
doctrinal views to those of the jurists, despite increasing harassment and
threats.

In the second half of the nineteenth century the battle against official
religion was taken over by a new type of intellectual who began to shift the
premises for understanding man from the religious to the sociopolitical
realm. Sociopolitical development resulting from contact with the West, in
addition to their realization that religious reform was futile, given the power
of the higher Shiᶜi hierarchy, caused some progressive-minded thinkers to
change their intellectual interests and abandon the philosophical-theological
outlook they had defended until then. For many it resulted in a loss of concern with religious issues. Thus, their effort to understand and diagnose the
ills that plagued their society drew their attention away from the private, exclusive domain of theology, philosophy, and mysticism, to a more public
political arena. With them the secularization of religious dissent effectively
took place.

Although they were simultaneously combatting the despotism of the
reigning dynasty and the encroachment of Western powers in internal affairs, the real alienation of the intellectuals was from the traditional
sociocultural order dominated by the guardians of the Islamic law. The controversial issues they raised were not mere doctrinal disputes but underlay
forceful social movements for change, aiming at curbing the jurists' influence and control over educational and juridical systems. Ideas such as con-

stitutionalism, sovereignty of the people, liberal democracy, secularism, threatened the socio-cultural order.

Having failed to meet the challenge of the religious dissidents in the nineteenth century, relentlessly forcing the confinement of innovative thought to small private circles of esotericists, the traditional centers of Islamic culture in Iran rapidly lost influence and prestige among progressive-minded thinkers. The change in intellectual outlook, traditionally initiated from within the ranks of the "turbaned" class of learned men, was undertaken by groups outside the religious institution. The secularization of social thought and institutions in the early twentieth century took place as a result of the failure on the part of the religious leadership to respond to the lay intellectuals and religious dissidents' call for reforms. Contemporary opponents of modernization tend to overlook this historical reality: the first generation of Muslim modernizers had perceived socio-cultural change as a moral necessity to meet the needs of their society and not so much as an attempt to copy the West. In their view the root of the socio-cultural problems was not the West, but prevailing religious and intellectual conditions which they deplored and which they, and their predecessors, were unable to change from within.

In the first decade of the twentieth century, lay intellectuals and politicians, and their clerical allies (the religious dissidents who then broke from their religious rank and file to join the secularists), laid the basis of secular nationalism. The modernizing policies they had initiated however, were fully implemented only with the advent to power of one modern element, the army. Seriously weakened by internal ideological strife, unable to resist the onslaught of conservative forces at home or the increasing encroachment of Western powers in internal affairs, incapable of establishing law and order in a country devastated by tribal raids and invading foreign armies in World War I, the short lived Constitutional government established by the revolutionaries in 1906 proved itself politically powerless. In 1925 the military regime of Rida Khan, who rose to power in 1921, was transformed into an absolute monarchy. The official nationalist culture that emerged then was urban-centered, officially monolingual, anti-clerical, cultivating the pre-Islamic cultural heritage, and Western-oriented. New generations of Iranian intellectuals educated in modern secular schools either at home or in the West became culturally more alienated from the traditional class of "learned men."

By the mid-twentieth century the modern class of lay intellectuals had come of age, taking for granted the social and cultural changes their counterparts in the nineteenth and early twentieth centuries had so vigorously fought for, enjoying the fruit of the seeds planted by the latter, secular nationalism, which was still raw and unpalatable since as yet unfamiliar to the tradition bound–illiterate masses. Often these intellectuals were better versed in modern scientific disciplines and ideas than in traditional Islamic thought. Many were ignorant or poorly informed of the abuse of clerical power and religious intolerance that Iranian thinkers in pre-modern times had to encounter periodically . . . .

*   *   *

The emergence of Islamic revolutionary ideology from among the modern educated lay intellectuals is a social phenomenon that can best be understood when viewed as an important phase in, rather than reaction to, the process of modernization. Secure in their lay profession and secular nationalist identity, Iranian professional middle class men and women were ready for active political life. A responsible role, which some had briefly enjoyed during the short interlude of political freedom that followed the abdication of Rida Shah and his son's accession in 1941, was repeatedly denied to them. The increasingly dictatorial regime which followed the 1953 coup against the nationalist government of Musaddiq led some politically conscious intellectuals and lay professionals to transfer their commitment from the secular nationalist cause (by now closely identified with the Pahlavis), to an Islamic revolution. Shiᶜi Islam provided them with a useful means to two different ends: to assert an independent national ideology in opposition to Western, especially American, involvement in domestic affairs, and to reach the masses in order to mobilize their force for the revolution they wished to undertake.

Whereas at the turn of the century the dissidents were essentially aiming at socio-cultural changes, in 1978–79 middle class lay professionals and intellectuals were aiming at gaining political power. Both were anti-traditionalist and anti-clerical; both were envisioning a progressive, modern society where qualified secular educated professonals would reinterpret and adapt religion to the conditions of modern times. In the nineteenth and early twentieth centuries, the revolutionaries' target was the clerical establishment. Their contemporary counterparts, while combatting Western influence and Pahlavi absolutism, overlooked the fact that secular nationalism and modern socio-cultural reforms, barely three-quarters of a century old, were still precarious and vulnerable to attack by resurgent clerical socio-cultural conservatism. To accomplish the political tasks they set for themselves they sacrificed their predecessors' hard won achievements, and helped the clerics come to power.

In 1978, the Shah's liberalization measures, though meager, opened up possibilities for the old guard of Musaddiq's National Front and the more recently formed Liberation Movement parties. Its members, mostly lay professionals and intellectuals, seized the opportunity to organize at home and establish contact with human rights activists abroad. The modest gains they acquired in the spring and summer of 1978 encouraged them to push for significant political reforms. None of those prominent members of the secular nationalist parties were revolutionary. They were reformers.

The revolution, when it came in the late fall of 1978, was Khumayni's. But he did not make it single-handedly. He inherited and made use of the reformers' groundbreaking tools and ideas, which he supplemented with his own ideologized and politically assertive interpretation of Shi'i doctrines and traditions. It is important to note here that the lay reformers finally joined his ranks because of, and not despite, his rhetoric. In the early phase of the revolution Khumayni spoke their language, though more radically and less willing to compromise.

Khumayni can best be understood when studied as a man of his time, and his movement as a phase in, rather than reaction to, the modernization process, paradoxical as it may sound. With the secularization of the judicial and educational systems at the turn of the century, the *culama'* had emerged as a more narrowly defined ecclesiastical class of spiritual leaders wearing the turban as a sign of their expertise in Islamic law and theology. What the *culama'* lost in prestige and influence was made up in increased cohesiveness and unity as a social group which, given the opportunity and the charismatic leadership of a man like Khumayni, could close ranks and engage in a fierce struggle for power. Their opponents were no longer the traditional religious dissidents, the mystics, philosophers and speculative theologians who challenged their supreme religious authority, but the secular order of the Pahlavis. Religious disputes and doctrinal controversies gave way to a deadly political fight against the tide that had so severely eroded their traditional role and influence in society. Thus in Khumayni's revolutionary works politics displaced theology, and political goals acquired priority over theological concerns.

His message appealed to all types of revolutionaries, and to men and women simply in revolt against the political oppression of the Shah, the abuses of SAVAK, and the disastrous consequences of foreign economic and military presence. He readily spoke of the right of the masses, the destitute, the workers, the oppressed at home and abroad. He incited the populace to rise for freedom and independence in the name of Islam, hailed the universities as the "strongholds of the self-sacrificing student struggles," and repeatedly denounced the attacks on campus as "barbaic and medieval." It was this message that attracted the lay Islamic ideologists and the secular dissidents in general.

In this respect Khumayni's rhetoric was almost identical to Shari'ati's. 'Ali Shari'ati (d. 1977), the Paris-trained sociologist, had denounced the traditional Shi'i political stand of passive acquiescence as contrary to the original revolutionary spirit of the Imams. Both Khumayni and Shari^cati held "conservative" theologians responsible for rendering Shi^ci Islam a religion of apathy, corruption and abuse of power. Both strove to radicalize the concept of the Imamate in order to provide their potential constituency with a viable ideology to fight the Shah's regime and the Western powers' interference in domestic affairs. However, whereas Shari^cati based his arguments on modern sociology, Khumayni used the discursive reasoning of traditional Islamic theology. Moreover, whereas Shari^cati was essentially anticlerical, upholding an Islam that is reformed and reinterpreted to fit the needs of contemporary society, Khumayni aimed at restoring clerical hold over vital social institutions and firmly consolidating clerical power by assuming supreme political authority.

* * *

In its earliest formative phase the idea of the Imamate in Shi^ci Islam came into being as a necessary consequence of, rather than cause for, social discontent and political dissent. Various movements of revolt organized under the Shi^ci banner against the nascent Sunni state were essentially politically oriented, aiming at achieving their respective leaders' political goals. Gradually, the quest for a just social order and the aspiration for a world free from oppression transformed the political opposition into a religious sectarian movement with serious doctrinal implications as to the qualifications and functions of the "rightful" leader of the community of believers. However, repeated defeats and relentless persecution encountered by the Shi^ci dissidents, in addition to rival claims to succession, forced some moderate leaders to give up armed struggle. The *de facto* depoliticization of the Imami or Twelver Shi^ci sect of Islam (to which the majority of the Iranians adhere) occurred as early as the mid-eighth century when the sixth Imam, Ja^cfar al-Sadiq, reportedly renounced, albeit temporarily, political rule, and the political functions of the Imam (declaring holy war against the enemies of religion; delivering sermons during the Friday mosque prayer; requiring allegiance and obedience from followers) were indefinitely postponed. Thus, the Imamate, defined as the exclusive authoritative source of knowledge of the divine, whose task was to teach and perfect the interpretation of the Prophet's Revelation, was divorced from political rule until such time as God would decide otherwise. With al-Sadiq, then, the central emphasis of Twelver Shi^ci Islam was shifted from politics to theology. This trend was reinforced when in 873–74 the Twelfth Imam was declared in Occultation (alive, ever present but hidden from view).

The doctrine of the Imamate in classical Shi^ci theology developed into an eschatological ideal, maintained and upheld in the works of Shi^ci ^culama' throughout the centuries. The temporal state was accommodated, and, in Safavid and post-Safavid times, viewed as an integral part of the Islamic Shiᶜi social order. Both the state and the top hierarchy of the religious institution perceived political opposition and religious non-conformism as inseparable. In fact, through the centuries, serious challenge to the state came from extremists religious movements declared heretical by the Shiᶜi establishment. In the 1960s and 1970s political unrest and social tensions helped Khumayni reverse the official Shiᶜi attitude of acquiescence, and recapture the early Imams' spirit of revolt against the "unrighteous" government.

Central to Khumayni's argument is his strong belief in the necessity for an Islamic government in times of Occultation. Conceiving the Imam as the holder of executive power whose function was to implement divine laws revealed and promulgated by the Prophet, he insists that the latter appointed a successor for the execution of the law and *not* to expound it. Here Khumayni's definition of the Imamate already differs drastically from the classical doctrine. In Sunni Islam the law itself acquired a central role in the formation of government, being a *raison d'être* for the state that protects it and applies it. In contrast, the Shiᶜi, regarding the individual Imam as the source of divine knowledge, viewed him as the interpreter of the Revelation, and not merely an executor of the law. Early Shiᶜi theologicans who were engaged in a polemical battle in defense of their views against the onslaught of the Sunnis insisted that knowledge of the interpretation of the Qur'an should not be based on deductive methods and human reasoning as in Sunni Islam. They claimed the Imam "informs the people about the purpose of God and explains it from God so that his explanation be the proof for the people. In times of Occultation, *ijtihad* (the chief function of the *mujtahid*, the highest ranking Shiᶜi jurist), was defined as the endeavor, or the competence to exert oneself, to reach with certainty the correct opinion of the Imam on religious and legal matters.

Khumayni describes the Imams as "soldiers, commanders, and warriors," although he admits that the "later Imams" did not have the opportunity to go into battle. He leaves unsaid the historical fact that with the exception of ᶜAli, whose reign was marred by civil strife, the Shiᶜi successors to the Prophet never formed a government. Anxious as he is to provide historical legitimacy to his concept of the "Governance of the Jurist," he finds himself forced to accept the Sunni Caliphate as evidence of continued existence of government after the death of the Prophet. Far from following the time-honored Shiᶜi practice of cursing the Sunni Caliphs, he praises the first two Caliphs for preserving the Prophet's personal example, mildly adding "in other matters they committed errors." He denounces the Umayyads and the ᶜAbbasids merely because of their monarchical government, which he declares anti-Islamic and reminiscent of the ancient Persian Kings, Byzantine Emperors and Egyptian Pharaohs. In fact, the early Sunni state provided Khumayni with a more acceptable, or at least less objectionable, historical frame of reference than the Safavid or Qajar states, which he dismisses as un-Islamic since dynastic and part of a Western imperialist plot to undermine Islam. When Khumayni first developed his theory of the "Governance of the Jurist" in the late 1960s and early 1970s, he was already in exile in Iraq waging a relentless campaign against the Pahlavi regime. His earlier hostile denunciation of the "unconstitutionality" of the Shah's political oppression and modernization programs turned into a radical condemnation of the monarchical system of government and of the 1906 Constitution as contrary to Islam, which recognizes the sovereignty of God alone. Thus, Khumayni's repudiation of any claim to succession based on hereditary right leads him to proclaim that the dispute that divided the ranks of the Prophet's companions following his death was over the identity of the person to succeed him and not over qualifications. Khumayni emphatically states that Muhammad appointed ʿAli "not because he was his son-in-law . . . but because he was acting in obedience to God's law." Once more Khumayni's interpretation runs counter to classical Shiʿi views of the hereditary right to succession of the Prophet's descendants through ʿAli and Fatimah. Khumayni goes so far as to claim that Husayn, the second son of ʿAli and the third Imam, "revolted in repudiation of the hereditary succession of Yazid (the Umayyad Caliph), to refuse it his recognition."

Again and again in his famous *Islamic Government* Khumayni stresses the executive role of the "successors of the Prophet," using more widely the Sunni term *khulafa* (caliphs) rather than the preferred Shiʿi term of Imams. Indeed, this argument that the function of government was not a privilege derived from the Imams' spiritual status, and that executive power was entrusted to them only because they were best able to establish a just government, is a Sunni argument. Traditional Shiʿi theologians insist that the Imam alone has the right to succeed the Prophet because of his "special spiritual status," and that his authority to rule is based on his spiritual attributes. When Khumayni admits that "the spiritual status of the Imam is separate from his government function" he does come close to the classical view, but from a reverse stand. Whereas traditional theologians have come to accept in practice the historical necessity of separation of religious authority from temporal power, and have emphasized the spiritual aspects of the Imamate, Khumayni feels the need to reassert its political role and function. Such an emphasis on the executive role of "the successor of the Prophet" is determined by his need to provide a doctrinal basis for his own political views and his desire to demonstrate that in times of Occultation an

Islamic Government is still necessary and that the only legitimate "holder of authority" is the *faqih* (jurist).

From the time the Imam was declared in Occultation in 873–74, one of the most important issues that concerned Shi^ci circles was related to the question of who holds religious authority in his prolonged absence. Traditions (sayings attributed to the Prophet and the Imam) were compiled and commented upon to prove the legitimacy of the claims of the traditionists (those theologians who compiled and tested the authenticity of the traditions). Through the centuries some key traditions were interpreted and, when deemed necessary, altered to substantiate the individual commentator's argument and confirm their respective points. The alteration and varying interpretation of such traditions by themselves constitute important indicators of socio-religious change.

One tradition Khumayni discusses is attributed to the Prophet saying: "O God! have mercy on my successors," and when asked to identify his successors replying: "They are those who come after me, transmit my traditions and practice, and teach them to the people of after me." Early Shi^ci theologians have used this tradition as one evidence of the Imams' legitimate claims to succession. Writing at a time when the Imams' legitimacy is no longer an issue in Shi^ci Iran, Khumayni argues that this tradition has been wrongly interpreted, identifying the Imams alone as the successors who "teach the people." He claims that earlier commentators have erroneously assumed that "Islam must be without any leader to care for it," in times of Occultation, and that the "religious scholars cannot act as successors, rulers, and governors." In a long and elaborate commentary of his own he vehemently denies the fact that the *faqih*'s function is limited to jurisprudence and the application of the law, and emphatically concludes that the jurists are the successors of the Imams. Khumayni pushes his argument further by differentiating the *mujtahid*, the high ranking Shi^ci jurist, from the specialist of the traditions, whom he declares subordinate to the *mujtahid*. The successors, he asserts, are not the transmitters of traditions, "Who are mere scribes." Here then is a traditional distinction in rank based on scholastic merit is transformed into distinction of social functions.

In another interesting and equally significant commentary of a tradition Khumayni deduces the jurist's right to rule by divine command. The tradition in question, which he refers to as "a signed decree of the Hidden Imam," appears in the earliest collections. A Shi^ci follower in the Lesser Occultation period (874–940 when the Hidden Imam was believed to be in direct communication with his "representative") wrote a letter to the Hidden Imam asking guidance for certain issues that had arisen in his absence. The Imam allegedly wrote back a letter in his own hand saying: "As for the events which may occur, refer to the transmitters of our sayings who are my Proof to you and I am the Proof of God to you all." This tradition seems to have played an important role in determining earlier theologians' authority. In the ninth and tenth centuries it was used to identify the "transmitter" as the representative of the Imam for juridical matters. In the seventeenth century it was altered in such a fashion as to make the "transmitters" alone (and not every individual Shiʿi believer) answerable to the Imam, thus establishing the supreme authority of the ʿulama' in religious matters. In the nineteenth century when opposition to the *mujtahid*'s power came from within the religious institution itself, the term "transmitters" was interpreted to mean the *mujtahids* exclusively. Although both the seventeenth and nineteenth century interpretations of the text could imply a potential political power for the *mujtahids*, there is no evidence that the Safavid or Qajar theologians meant to acquire political power in addition to religious authority. In fact prior to Khumayni the *mujtahids* had fought to establish themselves as the custodians of religion alone.

Khumayni, acting at a time when the supreme autority of the high ranking *mujtahids* in religious matters had already been established and consolidated for more than a century, interprets the tradition in a fashion to suit his own political purpose. At stake is not the issue of who represents the Imam or who is answerable to the Imam, as was the case with the Safavid and Qajar theologians, but the implicit sociopolitical meaning of "events which may occur." He attempts to deduce doctrinal justification for the political power he wishes to acquire. He writes:

> What is meant here by new occurrences is not legal cases and ordinances. The writer of the letter did not wish to ask what was to be done in the case of legal issues that were without precedent. For the answer to that question would have been self-evident according to Shiʿi school, and unanimously accepted traditions specify that one should have recourse to the fuqaha in such cases. What is meant by new occurrences is rather the newly arising situations and the problems that affect the people and the Muslims. The question that the follower was implicitly posing was this: "Now that we no longer have access to you, what should we do with respect to social problems? What is our duty?"

With this interpretation, Khumayni tries to refute the traditional conception of the jurists as mere experts of the religious law. He even interprets the term *Proof of God* (*Hujjat-Allah*) to mean the holder of authority in political as well as religious affairs. A Proof of God, he argues, is one whom God has designated to "conduct all affairs." Today the jurists of

Islam are proofs to the people, proofs of the Imam. Total obedience is owed to them, since they are specially appointed by the Prophet to be his successors and to rule. The jurists' authority in government affairs is equal to that of the Prophet and of the Imams, since they all share in common the burden of executive power to apply the divine law. Although Khumayni hastens to admit that the jurists do not possess the Prophet's and the Imams' special spiritual status, his definition of the jurist's position and function in society constitutes a radical departure from traditional Shi°i views.

In traditional Twelver Shi°i theology the Imam's title of *Hujjat-Allah* stresses his religious and spiritual function. Khumayni's interpretation of this title is more reminiscent of the Isma°ili use of the term. The Isma°ilis are the adherents of a Shi°i sect who, following Ja°far al-Sadiq's death in 750, refused to abide by his command to lay down arms, and maintained a militant opposition to the Sunni state. In Isma°ili terminology, the *Hujjah* is the Imam himself and, in the case of his Occultation, his sole deputy, a chosen individual amongst his followers who knows where he is and is in constant contact with him. Such a deputy or *Hujjah*, through whom the faithful could know the Imam, held the highest ranking political office in the Isma°ili state of Alamut (which ruled over small communities of believers clustered all over the Iranian highlands for a century and a half until the Mongol invasion put an end to it.)

Khumayni admires Nasir al-Din Tusi (d. 1273), the Twelver Shi°i theologian, philosopher and scientist who had lived with Alamut court officials for a long time and had written most of his important works of ethics and philosophy while enjoying Isma°ili patronage. Tusi had developed the neo-Platonic concept of the Perfect Man as the Perfect Teacher who, in times of Occultation, acts as the supreme interpreter and guide of the community. Khumayni's conception of the *faqih* (jurist), in the last analysis, is neither the jurist of the Buyid or post-Buyid period, nor the *mujtahid* of the Safavid or even of the Qajar times, but the personified ideal of the neo-Platonic philosopher-king which for centuries had inspired the Muslim philosophers and mystics alike.

However, Nasir al-Din Tusi and other Muslim philosophers who developed their neo-Platonic concept of the Perfect Man as the Perfect Teacher were writing in an age when philosophy and mysticism were separate fields of knowledge not tolerated by law-minded jurists. Their scriptural interpretations allowed them to offer their contemporary Muslim intellectuals a legitimate but more progressive, more challenging and innovative view of knowledge as an alternative to the official teachings of the conservative theologians. Some of them even attempted to renew their understanding of the dogma from within the traditional centers of Shi°i theology. Khumayni is writing in the twentieth century from within a *madrasah* (religious school) system turned seminary where classical Islamic philosophy and mysticism had lost a great deal of its vitality and relevance since abandoned by new generations of modern educated Iranians who sought a more contemporary intellectual basis for their social views in modern disciplines and systems of thought.

Khumayni's challenging and innovative thought is political and is not concerned with intellectual and religious renewal. Nor is he concerned with doctrinal reforms. His perception of the law is indeed fundamentalist; so is his understanding of religious rituals and obligations pertaining to all aspects of the believers' life in this world. Moreover, as a leader of the Islamic struggle against the onslaught of the modernizing reforms of the Pahlavi state, he has to champion an Islam and an Islamic law conceived as universal and immutable, and therefore in no need of reforms. This, despite his interest in and knowledge of Islamic philosophy (and in particular Tusi), despite his borrowing from the philosophers many terms and views which traditional Shiᶜi jurists in pre-Pahlavi times would have rejected as heretical.

Khumayni's "Governance of the Jurist" threatens the very foundation of Twelver Shiᶜi Islam as expounded by the sixth Imam. Jaᶜfar al-Sadiq had provided the doctrinal basis for the depoliticization of the sect with the often quoted tradition: "*Taqiyyah* (concealment of one's true beliefs in times of danger) is my religion and the religion of my forefathers." *Taqiyyah* was widely practiced by the moderate Shiᶜi in pre-Safavid times when they were a minority. It accommodated the "unrighteous" government and ensured the survival of the sect as an important school of theology. It also allowed the Shiᶜi scholars and theologians to enter government services of the ᶜAbbasids. By the time the sect acquired official status when proclaimed the state religion in Iran in the early sixteenth century, the Imamate had become a spiritual ideal divorced from politics, and the *de facto* separation of state and religion remained in effect as a necessary consequence of the doctrine of the Occultation of the Imam.

Khumayni draws a mythical history of the Imams all fighting against unrighteous government and calling for *jihad* against them. He goes so far as to claim that *taqiyyah* was enforced only in matters of religious rituals but not with respect to principles of Islam, overlooking the fact that the Imam's right to rule constitutes the most important principle of the Shiᶜi sect. He emphatically states that the religious leaders cannot practice *taqiyyah*, and must not work for the unrighteous government. By proclaiming *taqiyyah* defunct he is in effect putting an end to Jaᶜfari Shiᶜism, which had accommodated the temporal state, and introduces a new phase in the long history of the sect.

Despite the tensions that traditionally existed as a result of conflicting views, Shiᶜi centers of learning in pre-twentieth century Iran included most groups of thinkers: mystics, theosophers, speculative theologians. All were members in their own right of the broadly defined class of ᶜ*ulama'*. All contributed equally to the development of what is collectively known as Shiᶜi Islam, and which embodies a variety of schools of thought. The current re-politicization of the sect and the centralization of all power, political, social, cultural as well as religious, in the hands of the clerics is instituting in Iran a regime the nation has not experienced before. It combines the rule of a modern political dictatorship, ruthlessly suppressing opposition, with the socio-cultural dominance of a religious leadership which is establishing its hegemony firmly based on religious populism.

Khumayni attempts to break loose the nation's ties to the religio-political culture in which it has been reared, and to replace it with, not an old belief system, but a radically reinterpreted, ideologized conception of the old system. Hence his regime, like any other political regime, has to provide itself doctrinal legitimacy in order to institutionalize its power. To do so effectively, the concept of the "Governance of the Jurist" must gain acceptance among the circle of respected and knowledgeable religious scholars. So far, the official reaction of Khumayni's colleagues has remained true to the Shiᶜi tradition: passive acquiescence or intimidated silence. The promulgation of the new constitution of the Islamic Republic which grants absolute power to the jurist was a political affair, based on a national referendum. Consequently, such acts as the recent demotion and public disgrace of Shariᶜatmadari was accomplished on constitutional, and not doctrinal, ground, no matter how heretical his political dissent might appear to the eyes of the clerical ruling establishment. To confer doctrinal legitimacy to Khumayni's theory of government necessitates a thorough reformulation of the doctrine of the Imamate agreed upon by all the principal leaders of Shiᶜi Islam, and an official definition of the "righteous" government in the absence of the Imam. Will Khumayni succeed where centuries long Shiᶜi juridical tradition has failed? Centuries-long dominance of the socio-cultural scene by the conservative jurists had not succeeded in stifling dissent in pre-modern Iran. Will Khumayni succeed where his predecessors failed?

Ayatollah Sayyid Ruhullah Musawi Khumayni

A body of laws alone is not sufficient for a society to be reformed. In order for law to ensure the reform and happiness of man, there must be an executive power and an executor. For this reason, God Almighty, in addition to revealing a body of law (i.e., the ordinances of the *sharicah*), has laid down a particular form of government together with executive and administrative institutions.

The Most Noble Messenger (peace and blessings be upon him) headed the executive and administrative institutions of Muslim society. In addition to conveying the revelation and expounding and interpreting the articles of faith and the ordinances and institutions of Islam, he undertook the implementation of law and the establishment of the ordinances of Islam, thereby bringing into being the Islamic state. He did not content himself with the promulgation of law; rather, he implemented it at the same time, cutting off hands and administering lashings and stonings. After the Most Noble Messenger, his successor had the same duty and function. When the Prophet appointed a successor, it was not for the purpose of expounding articles of faith and law; it was for the implementation of law and the execution of God's ordinances. It was this function — the execution of law and the establishment of Islamic institutions — that made the appointment of a successor such an important matter that the Prophet would have failed to fulfill his mission if he had neglected it. For after the Prophet, the Muslims still needed someone to execute laws and establish the institutions of Islam in society, so that they might attain happiness in this world and the hereafter.

By their very nature, in fact, law and social institutions require the existence of an executor. It has always and everywhere been the case that legislation alone has little benefit: legislation by itself cannot assure the well-being of man. After the establishment of legislation, an executive power must come into being, a power that implements the laws and the verdicts given by the courts, thus allowing people to benefit from the laws and the just sentences the courts deliver. Islam has therefore established an executive power in the same way that it has brought laws into being. The person who holds this executive power is known as the *wali-i amr*.

The *sunnah* and the path of the Prophet constitute a proof of the necessity for establishing government. First, he himself established a government, as history testifies. He engaged in the implementation of laws, the establishment of ordinances of Islam, and the administration of society. He sent out governors to different regions; both sat in judgment himself and appointed judges; dispatched emissaries to foreign states, tribal chieftains, and kings; concluded treaties and pacts; and took command in battle. In short, he fulfilled all the functions of government. Second, he designated a ruler to succeed him, in accordance with divine command. If God Almighty, through the Prophet, designated a man who was to rule over Muslim society after him, this is in itself an indication that government remains a necessity after the departure of the Prophet from this world. Again, since the Most Noble Messenger promulgated the divine command through his act of appointing a successor, he also implicitly stated the necessity for establishing a government.

It is self-evident that the necessity for enactment of the law, which necessitated the formation of a government by the Prophet (upon whom be peace), was not confined or restricted to his time, but continues after his departure from this world. According to one of the noble verses of the Qur'an, the ordinances of Islam are not limited with respect to time or place; they are permanent and must be enacted until the end of time. They were not revealed merely for the time of the Prophet, only to be abandoned thereafter, with retribution and the penal code of Islam no longer to be enacted, or the taxes prescribed by Islam no longer collected, and the defense of the lands and people of Islam suspended. The claim that the laws of Islam may remain in abeyance or are restricted to a particular time or place is contrary to the essential credal bases of Islam. Since the enactment of laws, then, is necessary after the departure of the Prophet from this world, and indeed, will remain so until the end of time, the formation of a government and the establishment of executive and administrative organs are also necessary. Without the formation of a government and the establishment of such organs to ensure that through enactment of the law, all activities of the individual take place in the framework of a just system, chaos and anarchy will prevail and social, intellectual, and moral corruption will arise. The only way to prevent the emergence of anarchy and disorder and to protect society from corruption is to form a government and thus impart order to all the affairs of the country.

Both reason and divine law, then, demonstrate the necessity in our time for what was necessary during the lifetime of the Prophet and the age of the Commander of the Faithful, ᶜAli ibn Abi Talib (peace be upon him) — namely the formation of a government and the establishment of executive and administrative organs.

In order to clarify the matter further, let us pose the following questions: From the time of the Lesser Occultation down to the present (a period of more than twelve centuries that may continue for hundreds of millenia if it is not appropriate for the Occulted Imam to manifest himself), is it proper that the laws of Islam be cast aside and remain unexecuted, so that everyone acts as he pleases and anarchy prevails? Were the laws that the Prophet of Islam labored so hard for twenty-three years to set forth, promulgate, and execute valid only for a limited period of time? Did God limit the validity of His laws to two hundred years? Was everything pertaining to Islam meant to be abandoned after the Lesser Occultation? Anyone who believes so, or voices such a belief, is worse situated than the person who believes and proclaims that Islam has been superseded or abrogated by another supposed revelation.

No one can say it is no longer necessary to defend the frontiers and the territorial integrity of the Islamic homeland; that taxes such as the *jizyah*, *kharaj*, *khums* and *zakat* should no longer be collected; that the penal code of Islam, with is provisions for the payment of blood money and the exacting of requital, should be suspended. Any person who claims that the formation of an Islamic government is not necessary implicitly denies the necessity for the implementation of Islamic law, the universality and comprehensiveness of that law, and the eternal validity of the faith itself.

After the death of the Most Noble Messenger (peace and blessings be upon him), none of the Muslims doubted the necessity for government. No one said: "We no longer need a government." No one was heard to say anything of the kind. There was unanimous agreement concerning the necessity for government. There was disagreement only as to which person should assume responsibility for government and head the state. Government, therefore, was established after the Prophet (upon whom be peace and blessings), both in the time of the caliphs and in that of the Commander of the Faithful (peace be upon him); an apparatus of government came into existence with administrative and executive organs.

The nature and character of Islamic law and the divine ordinances of the *shari*c*ah* furnish additional proof of the necessity for establishing government, for they indicate that the laws were laid down for the purpose of creating a state and administering the political, economic, and cultural affairs of society.

First, the laws of the *shari*c*ah* embrace a diverse body of laws and regulations, which amounts to a complete social system. In this system of laws, all the needs of man have been met; his dealings with his neighbors, fellow citizens, and clan, as well as children and relatives; the concerns of private and marital life; regulations concerning war and peace and intercourse with other nations; penal and commercial law; and regulations pertaining to trade and agriculture. Islamic law contains provisions relating to the preliminaries of marriage and the form in which it should be contracted, and others relating to the development of the embryo in the womb and what food the parents should eat at the time of conception. It further stipulates the duties that are incumbent upon them while the infant is being suckled, and specifies how the child should be reared, and how the husband and the wife should relate to each other and to their children. Islam provides laws and instructions for all of these matters, aiming, as it does, to produce integrated and virtuous human beings who are walking embodiments of the law, or to put it differently, the law's voluntary and instinctive executors. It is obvious, then, how much care Islam devotes to government and the political and economic relations of society, with the goal of creating conditions conducive to the production of morally upright and virtuous human beings.

The Glorious Qur'an and the *sunnah* contain all the laws and ordinances man needs in order to attain happiness and the perfection of his state. The book *al-Kafi* has a chapter entitled, "All the Needs of Men Are Set Out in the Book and the *Sunnah*," the "Book" meaning the Qur'an, which is, in its own words, "an exposition of all things." According to certain traditions, the Imam also swears that the Book and the *sunnah* contain without a doubt all that men need.

Second, if we examine closely the nature and character of the provisions of the law, we realize that their execution and implementation depend upon the formation of a government, and that it is impossible to fulfill the duty of executing God's commands without there being established properly comprehensive administrative and executive organs. Let us now mention certain types of provision in order to illustrate this point; the others you can examine yourselves.

The taxes Islam levies and the form of budget it has established are not merely for the sake of providing subsistence to the poor or feeding the indigent among the descendants of the Prophet (peace and blessings be upon him); they are also intended to make possible the establishment of a great government and to assure its essential expenditures.

For example, *khums* is a huge source of income that accrues to the treasury and represents one item in the budget. According to our Shi[c]i school of thought, *khums* is to be levied in an equitable manner on all agricultural and commercial profits and all natural resources whether above or below the ground — in short, on all forms of wealth and income. It applies equally to the greengrocer with his stall outside this mosque and to the shipping or mining magnate. They must all pay one-fifth of their surplus income, after customary expenses are deducted, to the Islamic ruler so that it enters the treasury. It is obvious that such a huge income serves the purpose of administering the Islamic state and meeting all its financial needs. If we were to calculate one-fifth of the surplus income of all the Muslim countries (or of the whole world, should it enter the fold of Islam), it would become fully apparent that the purpose for the imposition of such a tax is not merely the upkeep of the *sayyids* or the religious scholars, but on the contrary, something far more significant — namely, meeting the financial needs of the great organs and institutions of government. If an Islamic government is achieved, it will have to be administered on the basis of the taxes that Islam has established — *khums, zakat* (this, of course, would not represent an appreciable sum), *jizyah*, and *kharaj*.

How could the *sayyids* ever need so vast a budget? The *khums* of the bazaar of Baghdad would be enough for the needs of the *sayyids* and the upkeep of the religious teaching institutions, as well as all the poor of the Islamic world, quite apart from the *khums* of the bazaars of Tehran, Istanbul, Cairo, and other cities. The provision of such a huge budget must obviously be for the purpose of forming a government and administering the Islamic lands. It was established with the aim of providing for the needs of the people, for public services relating to health, education, defense, and economic development. Further, in accordance with the procedures laid down by Islam for the collection, preservation, and expenditure of this income, all forms of usurpation and embezzlement of public wealth have been forbidden, so that the head of state and all those entrusted with responsibility for conducting public affairs (i.e., members of the government) have no privileges over the ordinary citizen in benefitting from the public income and wealth; all have an equal share.

Now, should we cast this huge treasury into the ocean, or bury it until the Imam returns, or just spend it on fifty *sayyids* a day until they have all eaten their fill? Let us suppose we give all this money to 500,000 *sayyids*; they would not know what to do with it. We all know that the *sayyids* and the poor have a claim on the public treasury only to the extent required for subsistence. The budget of the Islamic state is constructed in such a way that every source of income is allocated to specific types of expenditures. *Zakat*, voluntary contributions and charitable donations, and *khums* are all levied and spent separately. There is a *hadith* to the effect that at the end of the year, *sayyids* must return any surplus from what they have received to the Islamic ruler, just as the ruler must aid them if they are in need.

The *jizyah*, which is imposed on the *ahl al-zimmah*, and the *kharaj*, which is levied on agricultural land, represents two additional sources of considerable income. The establishment of these taxes also proves that the existence of a ruler and a government is necessary. It is the duty of a ruler or governor to assess the poll-tax to be levied on the *al-zimmah* in accordance with their income and financial capacity, and to fix appropriate taxes on their arable lands and livestock. He must also collect the *kharaj* on those broad lands that are the "property of God" and in the possession of the Islamic state. This task requires the existence of orderly institutions, rules and regulations, and administrative processes and policies; it cannot be fulfilled in the absence of order. It is the responsibility of those in charge of the Islamic state, first, to assess the taxes in due and appropriate measure and in accordance with the public good; then, to collect them; and finally, to spend them in a manner conducive to the welfare of the Muslims.

Thus, you see that the fiscal provisions of Islam also point to the necessity for establishing a government, for they cannot be fulfilled without the establishment of the appropriate Islamic institutions.

The ordinances pertaining to preservation of the Islamic order and defense of the territorial integrity and the independence of the Islamic *ummah* also demanded the formation of a government. An example is the command: "Prepare against them whatever force you can muster and horses tethered" (Qur'an, VIII:60), which enjoins the preparation of as much armed defensive force as possible and orders the Muslims to be always on the alert and at the ready, even in time of peace.

If the Muslims had acted in accordance with this command and, after forming a government, made the necessary extensive preparations to be in a state of full readiness for war, a handful of Jews would never have dared to occupy our lands, and to burn and destroy the Masjid al-Aqsa' without the people's being capable of making an immediate response. All this has resulted from the failure of the Muslims to fulfill their duty of executing God's law and setting up a righteous and respectable government. If the rulers of the Muslim countries truly represented the believers and enacted God's ordinances, they would set aside their petty differences, abandon their subversive and divisive activities, and join together like the fingers of one hand. Then a handful of wretched Jews (the agents of America, Britain, and other foreign powers) would never have been able to accomplish what they have, no matter how much support they enjoyed from America and Britain. All this has happened because of the incompetence of those who rule over the Muslims.

The verse: "Prepare against them whatever force you can muster" commands you to be as strong and well-prepared as possible, so that your enemies will be unable to oppress and transgress against you. It is because we have been lacking in unity, strength, and preparedness that we suffer oppression and are at the mercy of foreign aggressors.

There are numerous provisions of the law that cannot be implemented without the establishment of a governmental apparatus; for example, blood money, which must be exacted and delivered to those deserving it, or the corporeal penalties imposed by the law, which must be carried out under the supervision of the Islamic ruler. All of these laws refer back to the institutions of government, for it is governmental power alone that is capable of fulfilling this function.

After the death of the Most Noble Messenger (peace and blessings be upon him), the obstinate enemies of the faith, the Umayyads (God's curses be upon them) did not permit the Islamic state to attain stability with the rule of ᶜAli ibn Abi Talib (upon whom be peace). They did not allow a form of government to exist that was pleasing to God, Exalted and Almighty, and to his Most Noble Messenger. They transformed the entire basis of government, and their policies were, for the most part, contradictory to Islam. The form of government of the Umayyads and the ᶜAbbasids, and the political and administrative policies they pursued, were anti-Islamic. The form of government was thoroughly perverted by being transformed into a monarchy, like those of the kings of Iran, the emperors of Rome, and the pharoahs of Egypt. For the most part, this non-Islamic form of government has persisted to the present day, as we can see.

Both law and reason require that we not permit governments to retain this non-Islamic or anti-Islamic character. The proofs are clear. First, the existence of a non-Islamic political order necessarily results in the non-implementation of the Islamic political order. Then, all non-Islamic systems of government are the systems of *kufr*, since the ruler in each case is an instance of *taghut*, and it is our duty to remove from the life of Muslim society all traces of *kufr* and destroy them. It is also our duty to create a favorable social environment for the education of believing and virtuous individuals, an environment that is in total contradiction with that produced by the rule of *taghut* and illegitimate power. The social environment created by *taghut* and *shirk* invariably brings about corruption such as you can now observe in Iran, the corruption termed "corruption on earth." This corruption must be swept away, and its instigators punished for their deeds. It is the same corruption that the Pharaoh generated in Egypt with his policies, so that the Qur'an says of him, "Truly he was among the corrupters" (XXVIII:4). A believing, pious, just individual cannot possibly exist in a socio-political environment of this nature and still maintain his faith and righteous conduct. He is faced with two choices: either he commits acts that amount to *kufr* and contradict righteousness, or in order not to commit such acts and not to submit to the orders and commands of the *taghut*, the just individual opposes him and struggles against him in order to destroy the environment of corruption. We have in reality, then, no choice but to destroy those systems of government that are corrupt in themselves and also entail the corruption of others, and to overthrow all treacherous, corrupt, oppressive, and criminal regimes.

This is a duty that all Muslims must fulfill, in every one of the Muslim countries, in order to achieve the triumphant political revolution of Islam.

We see, too, that together, the imperialists and the tyrannical self-seeking rulers have divided the Islamic homeland. They have separated the various segments of the Islamic *ummah* from each other and artificially created separate nations. There once existed the great Ottoman State, and that, too, the imperialists divided. Russia, Britain, Austria, and other imperialist powers united, and through wars against the Ottomans, each came to occupy or absorb into its sphere of influence part of the Ottoman realm. It is true that most of the Ottoman rulers were incompetent, that some of them were corrupt, and that they followed a monarchical system. Nonetheless, the existence of the Ottoman State represented a threat to the imperalists. It was always possible that righteous individuals might rise up among the people and, with their assistance, seize control of the state, thus putting an end to imperialism by mobilizing the unified resources of the nation. Therefore, after numerous prior wars, the imperialists at the end of World War I divided the Ottoman State, creating in its territories about ten or fifteen petty states. Then each of these was entrusted to one of their servants or a group of their servants, although certain countries were later able to escape the grasp of the agents of imperialism.

In order to assure the unity of the Islamic *ummah*; in order to liberate the Islamic homeland from occupation and penetration by the imperialists and their puppet governments, it is imperative that we establish a government. In order to attain the unity and freedom of the Muslim peoples, we must overthrow the oppressive governments installed by the imperialists and bring into existence an Islamic government of justice that will be in the service of the people. The formation of such a government will serve to preserve the disciplined unity of the Muslims; just as Fatimah al-Zahra (upon whom be peace) said in her address: "The Imamate exists for the sake of preserving order among the Muslims and replacing their disunity with unity."

Through the political agents they have placed in power over the people, the imperialists have also imposed on us an unjust economic order, and thereby divided our people into two groups: oppressors and oppressed. Hundreds of millions of Muslims are hungry and deprived of all forms of health care and education, while minorities comprised of the wealthy and powerful live a life of indulgence, licentiousness, and corruption. The hungry and deprived have constantly struggled to free themselves from the oppression of their plundering overlords, and their struggle continues to this day. But their way is blocked by the ruling minorities and the oppressive governmental structures they head. It is our duty to save the oppressed and deprived. It is our duty to be a helper to the oppressed and an enemy to the oppressor. This is nothing other than the duty that the Commander of the Faithful (upon whom be peace) entrusted to his two great offspring in his celebrated testament: "Be an enemy to the oppressor and a helper to the oppressed."

The scholars of Islam have a duty to struggle against all attempts by the oppressors to establish a monopoly over the sources of wealth or to make illicit use of them. They must not allow the masses to remain hungry and deprived while plundering oppressors usurp the sources of wealth and live in opulence. The Commander of the Faithful (upon whom be peace) says: "I have accepted the task of government because God, Exalted and Almighty, has exacted from the scholars of Islam a pledge not to sit silent and idle in the face of the gluttony and plundering of the oppressors, on the one hand, and the hunger and deprivation of the oppressed, on the other." Here is the full text of the passage we refer to:

> I swear by Him Who causes the seed to open and creates the souls of all living things that were it not for the presence of those who have come to swear allegiance to me, were it not for the obligation of rulership now imposed upon me by the availability of aid and support, and were it not for the pledge that God has taken from the scholars of Islam not to remain silent in the face of the gluttony and plundering of the oppressors, on the one hand, and the harrowing hunger and deprivation of the oppressed, on the other hand—were it not for all of this, then I would abandon the reins of government and in no way seek it. You would see that this world of yours, with all of its position and rank, is less in my eyes than the moisture that comes from the sneeze of a goat.

How can we stay silent and idle today when we see that a band of traitors and usurpers, the agents of foreign powers, have appropriated the wealth and the fruits of labor of hundreds of millions of Muslims—thanks to the support of their masters and through the power of the bayonet—granting the Muslims not the least right to prosperity? It is the duty of Islamic scholars and all Muslims to put an end to this system of oppression and, for the sake of the well-being of hundreds of millions of human beings, to overthrow these oppressive governments and form an Islamic government.

Reason, the law of Islam, the practice of the Prophet (upon whom be peace and blessings) and that of the Commander of the Faithful (upon whom be peace), the purport of various Qur'anic verses and Prophetic traditions—all indicate the necessity of forming a government. As an example of the traditions of the Imams, I now quote the following tradition of Imam Rida (upon whom be peace):

> ᶜAbd al-Wahid ibn Muhammad ibn ᶜAbdus an-Nisaburi al-ᶜAttar said, "I was told by Abu'l-Hasan ᶜAli ibn Muhammad ibn Qutayba al-Naysaburi that he was told by Abu Muhammad al-Fadl ibn Shadhan al-Naysaburi this tradition. If someone asks, 'Why has God, the All-Wise, appointed the holders of authority and commanded us to obey them?' then we answer, 'For numerous reasons. One reason is this: Men are commanded to observe certain limits and not to transgress them in order to avoid the corruption that would result. This cannot be attained or established without there being appointed over them a trustee who will ensure that they remain within the limits of the licit and prevent them

from casting themselves into the danger of transgression. Were it not for such a trustee, no one would abandon his own pleasure and benefit because of the corruption it might entail for another. Another reason is that we find no group or nation of men that ever existed without a ruler and leader, since it is required by both religion and worldly interest. It would not be compatible with divine wisdom to leave mankind to its own devices, for He, the All-Wise, knows that men need a ruler for their survival. It is through the leadership he provides that men make war against their enemies, divide among themselves the spoils of war, and preserve their communal solidarity, preventing the oppression of the oppressed by the oppressor.

'A further reason is this: were God not to appoint over men a solicitous, trustworthy, protecting, reliable leader, the community would decline, religion would depart, and the norms and ordinances that have been revealed would undergo change. Innovators would increase and deniers would erode religion, inducing doubt in the Muslims. For we see that men are needy and defective, judging by their differences of opinion and inclination and their diversity of state. Were a trustee, then, not appointed to preserve what has been revealed through the Prophet, corruption would ensue in the manner we have described. Revealed laws, norms, ordinances, and faith would be altogether changed, and therein would lie the corruption of all mankind.'

We have omitted the first part of the *hadith*, which pertains to prophethood, a topic not germane to our present discussion. What interests us at present is the second half, which I will now paraphrase for you.

If someone should ask you, "Why has God, the All-Wise, appointed holders of authority and commanded you to obey them?" you should answer him as follows: "He has done so for various causes and reasons. One is that men have been set upon a certain well-defined path and commanded not to stray from it, nor to transgress against the established limits and norms, for if they were to stray, they would fall prey to corruption. Now men would not be able to keep to their ordained path and to enact God's laws unless a trustworthy and protective individual (or power) were appointed over them with responsibility for this matter, to prevent them from stepping outside the sphere of the licit and transgressing against the rights of others. If no such restraining individual or power were appointed, nobody would voluntarily abandon any pleasure or interest of his own that might result in harm or corruption to others; everybody would engage in oppressing and harming others for the sake of their own pleasures and interests.

"Another reason and cause is this: we do not see a single group, nation, or religious community that has ever been able to exist without an individual entrusted with the maintenance of its laws and institutions — in short, a head or a leader; for such a person is essential for fulfilling the affairs of religion and the world. It is not permissible, therefore, according to divine wisdom, that God should leave men, His creatures, without a leader and guide, for He knows well that they depend upon the existence of such a person for their own survival and perpetuation. It is under his leadership that they fight against their enemies, divide the public income among themselves, perform Friday and congregational prayer, and foreshorten the arms of the transgressors who would encroach on the rights of the oppressed.

"Another proof and cause is this: were God not to appoint an Imam over men to maintain law and order, to serve the people faithfully as a vigilant trustee, religion would fall victim to obsolescence and decay. Its rites and institutions would vanish; the customs and ordinances of Islam would be transformed or even deformed. Heretical innovators would add things to religion and atheists and unbelievers would subtract things from it, presenting it to the Muslims in an inaccurate manner. For we see that men are prey to defects; they are not perfect and must needs strive after perfection. Moreover, they disagree with each other, having varying inclinations and discordant states. If God, therefore, had not appointed over men one who would maintain order and law and protect the revelation brought by the Prophet, in the manner we have described, men would fall prey to corruption; the institutions, laws, customs, and ordinances of Islam would be transformed; and faith and its content would be completely changed, resulting in the corruption of all humanity."

As you can deduce from the words of the Imam (upon whom be peace), there are numerous proofs and causes that necessitate formation of a government and establishment of an authority. These proofs, causes, and arguments are not temporary in their validity or limited to a particular time, and the necessity for the formation of a government, therefore, is perpetual. For example, it will always happen that men overstep the limits laid down by Islam and transgress against the rights of others for the sake of their personal pleasure and benefit. It cannot be asserted that such was the case only in the time of the Commander of the Faithful (upon whom be peace) and that afterwards, men became angels. The wisdom of the Creator has decreed that men should live in accordance with justice and act within the limits set by divine law. This wisdom is eternal and immutable, and constitutes one of the norms of God Almighty. Today and always, therefore, the existence of a holder of authority, a ruler who acts as trustee and maintains the institutions and laws of Islam, is a necessity — a ruler who prevents cruelty, oppression, and violation of the rights of others; who is a trustworthy and vigilant guardian of God's creatures; who guides men to the teachings, doctrines, laws, and institutions of Islam; and who prevents the undesirable changes that atheists and the enemies of religion wish to introduce in the laws and institutions of Islam. Did not the caliphate of the Commander of the Faithful serve this purpose? The same factors of necessity that led him to become the Imam still exist; the only difference is that no single individual has been designated for the task. The principle of the necessity of government has been made a general one, so that it will always remain in effect.

If the ordinances of Islam are to remain in effect, then, if encroachment by oppressive ruling classes on the rights of the weak is to be prevented, if ruling minorities are not to be permitted to plunder and corrupt the people for the sake of pleasure and material interest, if the Islamic order is to be preserved and all individuals are to pursue the just path of Islam without any deviation, if innovation and the approval of anti-Islamic laws by sham parliaments are to be prevented, if the influence of foreign powers in the Islamic lands is to be destroyed—government is necessary. None of these aims can be achieved without government and the organs of the state. It is a righteous government, of course, that is neglected, one presided over by a ruler who will be a trustworthy and righteous trustee. Those who presently govern us are of no use at all for they are tyrannical, corrupt, and highly incompetent.

In the past we did not act in concert and unanimity in order to establish proper government and overthrow treacherous and corrupt rulers. Some people were apathetic and reluctant even to discuss the theory of Islamic government, and some went so far as to praise oppressive rulers. It is for this reason that we find ourselves in the present state. The influence and sovereignty of Islam in society have declined; the nation of Islam has fallen victim to division and weakness; the laws of Islam have remained in abeyance and been subjected to change and modification; and the imperialists have propagated foreign laws and alien culture among the Muslims through their agents for the sake of their evil purposes, causing people to be infatuated with the West. It was our lack of a leader, a guardian, and our lack of institutions of leadership that made all this possible. We need righteous and proper organs of government; that much is self-evident.

Chapter Twenty-Three

cAli Shariᶜati

Modern Shiᶜi political thought is often believed to have emerged in response to the confrontations between the ᶜulama' and the Iranian state since the 1920s. The process of modernization in Iran also produced a politically conscious corpus of social thought in Shiᶜism, mostly associated with cAli Shariᶜati. This body of ideas did much to mobilize many segments of Shiᶜi society and to articulate their political grievances, facilitating the mass popular uprisings directed by the clergy.

Shariᶜati's writings on the various aspects of Islam, from its sociology to its attitude toward women, and his reinterpretation of Shiᶜi political and social world views in active and combative terms aroused the consciousness of many Iranians and galvanized them into a religio-political movement. Although wary of the ᶜulama', Shariᶜati's ideas and the movement inspired by them went a long way in facilitating the revolution led by the clergy. In the following passages, Shahrough Akhavi will examine Shariᶜati's philosophy of history; then Hamid Dabashi will analyze Shariᶜati's work against the background of Islamic thought; and, finally, excerpts from the thinker's views on ideology selected and translated by Fatollah Marjani will present a glimpse into his ideas and system of thought. The excerpts are from SST, pp. 131-135; ASIRUF, pp. 203-20; and MI, pp. 82-101, respectively.

Shahrough Akhavi

Sharicati's philosophy of history is rich with themes and the interplay of ideas. While eclectic in the borrowing from other traditions, notably Marxism, it contains analysis that is original in the context of existing Shici interpretations. According to him, the philosophy of history of Islam is based upon what he terms "scientific determinism" (*jabr-i cilmi*). This signifies that science, especially anthropology, sociology, and political economy, can usefully be applied to gain a true understanding of historical development in Islam.

Influenced again by Marx, he argues that "history unfolds through dialectical contradiction[s]." History has evolved in the context of a struggle between mutually opposing forces. This struggle, he holds, "began with the first man on earth and has always and everywhere been waged."

Sharicati's evident historicism can be detected in his conviction that history "started from somewhere and of necessity must lead to somewhere; it must have a goal and a direction." He thus seems to be advocating a universal history within the framework of which man can then choose, at various stages in his development, to follow the Imams, opt for *laissez-faire* economics, prescribe Marxist views, and so forth.

Moreover, Sharicati additionally argues that historical change occurs not only through contradictions but contradictions involving the mode of production. Couching his analysis in terms of the Cain and Abel legend, he asserts that the brothers in fact provide the archetypes of mode-of-production conflict: in the one case Cain is the agriculturalist; in the other Abel is the pastoralist. Whereas Cain's social rank and "class" position in society were anchored in his ownership of productive means, that of his brother rested on what he was capable of securing by his hands in hunting, fishing, gleaning. Ultimately, Sharicati regards the conflict between Cain and Abel to be an "objective" (*cayni*) one that sets the stages for all future struggles, themselves each also objective in nature.

It will be recalled that Sharicati had already taken a position on the nature of reality in which the basis of the universe is the unity of God, nature, and man. It is to be assumed, in light of what he now says about contradiction's being an abiding element of social change, that the alleged unity exists only in a genuinely Shici community. Other societies face the certainty of conflict. If this be a correct inference from Shari^cati's position, then the question presents itself, What is the mechanism of historical development and social change in a true Shi^ci community? Shari^cati would likely respond that the mechanism of change would be a combination of leadership based on justice and allegiance of the people to the *wilayah* (delegated rule) of ^cAli, the Imams, and the general agency.

Despite the foregoing, Shari^cati's notions of historical change suggest that it is appropriate for us to see Marx's influence upon him. On this level he rebukes the *^culama'* (clergy) for deriving a merely moral lesson from the Cain and Abel legend—that is, an admonition that "thou shalt not kill." Social science argues that this historic dispute between the two brothers must be seen as a class struggle. The methodology of the social sciences requires that we establish the causes of certain effects by eliminating constants in comparing two entities, and the only differentiating factor between the two brothers is their social occupation. They had had the same parents, grew up in the same social environment, had had the same influences brought to bear upon their personalities as infants, children, adolescents. Therefore, an ancient legend spawned by the scriptures of the great religions may now be interpreted in a new light, yielding a more powerful explanation through the use of Marxist-influenced sociology.

A major departure from Marx, nonetheless, is to be seen in his contention regarding the relations between ownership of productive means and power. Shari^cati asserts that it is power which determines ownership and not (as Marx says) that ownership shapes power. This point of difference with Marx suggests a more deeply rooted variance between Shari^cati and Marx concerning free will and historical determinism, to which we shall return shortly.

Meanwhile, it is worth stressing that Shari^cati wishes to differentiate between fundamental change (*harakat-i jawhari*) and small-scale (transitional) change (*harakat-i intiqali*). All societies witness the cumulation of many discrete, small-scale changes affecting different facets of life. Hence, a social institution such as the family undergoes small-scale change if the basis of authority is transferred from age/wisdom to virility/wisdom. We can speak of fundamental social change, however, if we observe the following transformation. Suppose that at an earlier time divorce was forbidden, marriage of near relatives prohibited, polygamy sanctioned, only marriage through ecclesiastical auspices permitted, and the extended family formed the basis of the household economy. If we then perceive that at a later time, in the same society, divorce was permitted, first-cousin marriage allowed, monogamy alone was tolerated, civil ceremony became the legitimating practice, and the nuclear family formed the foundation for the household economy, then one is speaking of major social change. This example is not Shari^cati's, but it is presented here to clarify his meaning.

Shariᶜati is convinved that, at the level of fundamental change, all societies face the problem of the rise and decline of their civilizations. The motor force of historical change being contradiction, is there any escape from decline and disintegration? he queries. Historical determinism suggests not, he holds. But, continuous revitalization of society is possible, according to Shariᶜati, through the doctrine and practice of permanent revolution. Shariᶜati does not mean permanent revolution in Trotsky's sense of periodically intensifying revolutionary ardor and praxis in a society undergoing its travails. Instead, Shariᶜati argues that the three dynamic principles of *ijtihad* (independent judgment), *al-amr bi'l-maᶜruf wa'l-nahy ᶜan al-munkar* (commanding the good and forbidding evil), and *muhajirat* (emigration) will protect the Islamic community from decline for an unspecified long-run period of time.

How can this be so? To begin with, *ijtihad*, correctly applied, renews and rebuilds itself. The problem in Shiᶜi society since the disappearance of the twelfth Imam has been that *ijtihad* has been implemented within a narrow compass. Consequently, its scope has been limited to legal specialists deducing derivative ordinances (*ahkam-i farᶜi*) of law. Yet, *ijtihad* should be applied in its broadest sense of clarifying one's ideology, Shariᶜati remonstrates. And in this sense it becomes "an objective duty [for] every individual to exert himself through *ijtihad* in regard to his own ideology." With respect to the second principle in Islam that will aid in revitalizing Islam, Shariᶜati is just as forceful. Commanding the good and forbidding evil is "the mission and objective duty of all individuals—among the masses, the wretched, the intellectuals, the bazaar merchants—all are responsible for implementing *al-amr bi'l-maᶜruf wa'l-nahy ᶜan al-munkar*. This principle will rescue societies from the rise and fall [doctrine]. No one can be uncommitted or neutral on this issue."

The third principle is not clarified by Shariᶜati, except to say that the emigration he speaks of may be internal to the person or may involve his external relocation. The implication, however, is that emigration prevents routinization and keeps one in touch with newness in existence.

Is Shariᶜati then arguing for free will? Emphatically so. He accepts Sartre's point that man is free to choose; the only limiting factor upon man's will is his own mortality and the requirements of food, shelter, health, and the biological necessities associated with these. In all other respects, man is absolutely free to make his own decisions and consequently absolutely responsible for the choices he does make.

Shariᶜati argues against the materialists, whom he charges with viewing man's will as being determined and therefore not autonomous. He believes in historical determinism, but he prefers the French *déterminisme historique* —to him a more flexible concept—to *jabr-i tarikh*. The latter concept has, at the hands of Iranian intellectuals, led to the caricature of man as an automaton. For Shari^cati, however, historical determinism means that history "is a single, ongoing and uninterrupted phenomenon in time which is influenced by specific [*mu^cayyan*] causes (*mu^cayyan* is not *jabri*)."

Man in history is like a fish in a river. Now, the river courses its way through shallows, rapids, narrows, wide gorges, and over waterfalls in a bed shaped by geological formations over time. Yet, the fish can go in various directions, even upstream. Man, for his part, is influenced by scientific laws of causation; yet, man is free to choose his own course, even to the point of taking his own life.

Sometimes, Shari^cati seems to be saying that history is the motor of change rather than man. For example, he declares, "History is the factor that changes man from a quasi-savage being into contemporary man. The latter has reached a certain degree of perfection up to the present and will be, in the distant future, the ideal person, noblest of all creatures in the material world." At other time, history for him is a "crucible" in which man is transformed. Interestingly, he hearkens to Greek notions of man as a social creature in the process of realizing the best that is in him — "man is a being in the process of becoming." The goal defines the individual, then, and we have here a teleological conception of man's growth toward a certain end. This parallels Shari^cati's teleological view of historical development which has already been identified above as his hitsoricist philosophy of history.

With respect to the question of free will versus determinism, Shari^cati believes that he has established an interpretation of Islam which differs from both idealism and materialism. Whereas both of those philosophies of life denature man (in the case of idealism by making man the object of an abstract and disembodied Absolute Idea; in the case of materialism by making man derivative to matter), Islam ennobles him. Shari^cati's view is expressed in the following passage:

> Islam's doctrine of first principles [ontology] is based upon belief in the hidden. By "hidden" I mean that unknown reality that exists in the base material, natural phenomena which are accessible to our senses and mental, scientific, and experiential comprehension. This unknown reality is reckoned as a higher grade of truth and the fundamental focus of the totality of movements, laws and manifestations of this world.
>
> This "hidden" is in reality the absolute spirit and will of existence. Contrary to idealism, which supposes phenomena of the material world to be the product of the Idea; and in contrast to materialism, which imagines ideas to be the emanation of the material world; Islam counts both matter and idea as different appearances (signs) of that "absolute hidden being." Thus, Islam rejects both idealism and materialism simultaneously; Islam recognizes the existence of the world of nature beyond

our ideas; and it holds that man, as a being having ideas in the face of material nature and the material social environment and material production, is autonomous and genuine.

Yet, we also have a Shariᶜati who, as we have seen, believes in historical determinism. Rejecting happenstance and disjunction in historical progression, Shariᶜati equates historical determinism with God's will. But that, in turn, is integrated into the principle of *intizar*. The exact linkage between causation, God's will, historical determinism and *intizar* are not clarified by Shariᶜati, but we are told that ultimately the Shiᶜi philosophy of history places man in the forefront of change.

Hamid Dabashi

The most serious exponent of that familar and up-to-date Western therapy, the revolutionary uses of faith, in the recent history of the Islamic lands is a Paris-educated Iranian sociologist, who can probably be considered the chief ideologue of some of the major political trends in modern Iran as well as other Islamic societies. He has been recognized as a theorist who "did the most to prepare the Iranian youth for revolutionary upheaval." It has also been suggested that "events made this Muslim sociologist, shortly after his 1977 death, the ideologist of the revolt."

Shariᶜati was born into a religious family. His father, though not one of the religious authorities (*ᶜulama*), was an active preacher. He grew up in Mashhad, the city in which the Eighth Shiᶜi Imam is buried and is next to Qum the spiritual capital of Iran and the center of the most intense religious activities. At the age of nineteen, Shariᶜati already had started writing and translating works on political aspects of Shiᶜi Islam. After his graduation from Mashhad University, and upon his arrival in Paris, he actively participated in many political movements, particularly the Algerian liberation movement. There he was particularly associated with Franz Fanon and Jean-Paul Sartre, who influenced him both intellectually and politically. Shariᶜati translated Fanon's *Wretched of the Earth* into Persian and corresponded with him frequently.

Shari^cati expressed his revolutionary ideas in the context of a fundamentally traditional (in the Weberian typological contradistinction to rational/
legal) society. Despite its hasty adoption of some major secular aspects of
the modern West, Iran essentially remained a traditional society. Yet the
imitation of the West was on such a grand social scale that it inevitably led
to the creation of a deep cultural confusion. The dimensions and attributes
of the traditional foundations of this society, and its bonding elements of
coherence, Shari^cati, as a sociologist, realized and sought to break permanently. As a revolutionary ideologue, his most serious obstacle was the
persistent tradition against which he was to launch his ideological movement.

Particularly evident from the title and content of one of his major lectures on Shi^cism, "Shi^cism, A Complete (Political) Party," ^cAli Shari^cati
considered this branch of Islam a "revolutionary ideology," capable of
mobilizing the masses for political purposes. Signalled by this very title,
Shari^cati sought to transform Shi^cism from a religious tradition into a
political ideology. As a former student of Marxism, actively supporting the
revolutionary causes of Cuba and Algeria, Shari^cati had been convinced of
the necessity of ideological conviction to augment the "material condition"
of the revolution and mobilize the masses. He disagreed with Franz Fanon,
in this particular regard, that Third World countries should abandon their
religion in order to be ideologically equipped to either defeat the imperialis-
tic powers or launch a revolution against their government. Shari^cati, on the
contrary, sought to use an already established "ideology" in the Islamic
world in order to create the necessary political apparatus—party, slogan,
banner, and popular force—to achieve revolutionary ends. As an observer
of the political movements in the Islamic world, he witnessed the failure of
radical Western political ideologies attempting to take root in the political
consciousness of the masses. In his own country, he particularly witnessed
the bloody consequences of the Communist Tudeh Party's endeavor to
transform a deeply religious society into a socialist camp.

* * *

In order to systematize his revolutionary reading of Shi^ci Islam, Shari^cati
developed an ideology which he called "^cAlid Shi^cism," i.e., a Shi^cism identified with the authoritative figure of the first Shi^ci Imam. N. Keddie summarizes the functional importance of this idea:

> By systematizing the concept of ^cAlid Shi^cism, Shari^cati attained a dou-
> ble result; he detached himself from the petrified official Islam rejected
> by idealistic youth, and he brought a new and combative meaning to
> Shi^ci concepts. Even prayer in this renovated Islam took on a political

meaning, tied to action. This insurrectional meaning of common prayer was particularly developed in the 1978–1979 revolution.

To counterbalance, in his political vocabulary, the revolutionary ᶜAlid Shiᶜism Shariᶜati constituted Safavid Shiᶜism, i.e., the Shiᶜism identified with the Safavid dynasty (1501–1722), which for the first time established Shiᶜism as the state religion. He identified Safavid Shiᶜism with the traditional Shiᶜism under the patronage of the Iranian state in particular, or any other state in general. He subsequently proceeded to conceptualize the main Shiᶜi religious terminologies in a new and revolutionary way. Every religious concept, e.g., *Imamah*, ᶜismah, etc., assumed, under the rubric of ᶜAlid Shiᶜism, a revolutionary and combative meaning and significance. In general, as opposed to Safavid Shiᶜism, "ᶜAlid Shiᶜism represents original Islam and is a movement of progress and revolution, with no division between intellectuals and the people—Islam in its progressive and dynamic phase."

In the new terminology of Shiᶜism, Imamate was not "belief in twelve pure, saintly, extraordinary names . . .," but "pure, honest, revolutionary conduct of the people and the correct foundation of society in terms of conscience, the expansion and independence of people's judgement . . ." *Ghaybah* (Shiᶜi belief in the occultation of the Twelfth Imam and the expectation of his return to establish the perfect society) meant "total irresponsibility; the uselessness of all action under the pretext of the Imam's absence . . ." in the official Safavid Shiᶜism; whereas in his ᶜAlid Shiᶜism it means "responsibility of men to decide their destiny, faith, spiritual and social life . . ."

* * *

In order to legitimize his revolutionary reading of Islam, Shariᶜati sought to discredit the traditionally maintained view of this faith in all its diversities. He maintained that:

> The problem which is now at hand is the thirteen-hundred year old complex of the misery of a people, the intellectual hopelessness of an *ummah* [Islamic community], the metamorphosis and going astray of an emancipating and consciousness-giving belief, the going astray, passivity and going-to-sleep of a people with tyranny, ignorance, and poverty; and that with the most sacred, most exalted, and the most progressive belief and eternal divine values that we possess, and that with the dearest personalities and epic-making figures that each one of them is enough for the awakening, self-consciousness, movement and freedom of a nation or a people... ."

In trying to establish legitimacy for his revolutionary version of Islam
among the alienated intelligentsia, Shariᶜati had to distinguish himself from
the traditional figures of authority. Early in his lecture on "Shiᶜism, A Complete [Political] Party," he indicates that he is not a philosopher or a
historian, or a religious scholar [*faqih*], or an artist, a writer, a literary
figure, or a theologian, in a traditional sense. "I am none of these [figures]."
These are, of course, among the traditional figures of authority in any
Islamic society. Yet, since Shariᶜati's Islam is a new Islam, he has to create,
in himself, a new prototype of authority: a Western-educated, politically
conscious and active, and a revolutionary ideologue of grand social causes.
This necessitated a new reading of Islam. For that purpose, traditional
authorities had to be discarded and discredited. A significant proportion of
Shariᶜati's energy was devoted to negating the legitimacy of all figures of
traditional authority in the fabric of any Islamic society.

With a similar perspective, Shariᶜati also thought traditional ways of
learning to be cumbersome, long, scholastic, boring, and totally outmoded.
He imagined an action-Islam, as successor to a knowledge-Islam, and a new
class of teachers in action.

> Others admonish us and [give us] guidance, good advice and wise,
> knowledgeable and rational counsel that "first you should think, study,
> acquire knowledge, do scientific research, read many books, attend
> many religious schools, be student to many learned professors, learn
> philosophy, sufism, jurisprudence, doctrine, theology, logic, language,
> literature, history, theosophy and ethics with "learned masters," until
> you are master of both intellectual and transmitted [knowledge], and
> after passing through this period (which is not ever possible), [then] you
> enter the second phase, the phase of action, phase of correction, but in-
> dividual action, the correction of self.

Shariᶜati consciously believed that his Islam was different from and opposed to the traditional Islam. Attacking two cardinal tenets of traditional
Islam, knowledge and virtuosity, and celebrating the revolutionary attitude,
he proclaimed:

> O how strange! Notice the difference between the two Islams! The other
> one postpones the Persuasion to Good Deeds and Prohibition from Evil
> Deeds . . . —social responsibility—to after the completion of the [two
> attributes of] knowledge and virtuosity; the two stages that in order to
> reach their perfection even the life of Noah is not enough. And this
> [Islam] puts the social responsibility of the Persuasion to Good Deeds
> and Prohibition from Evil Deeds upon the delicate shoulders of a young
> girls or boy, exactly from the moment that invites them to pray and keep

fast! Praying and fasting, simultaneous with the responsiblity of Persuasion and Prohibition of good and evil social deeds, and also the Holy War.

In his active revolutionary Islam, the sacred presence of the divine will and intellect that, according to the traditional view, permeates and directs the human life, was not a necessary doctrine of the true faith.

> Because in life [we] cannot be in the course of understanding and comprehending the truth through intellectual genius, or inner illumination, or scientific thinking and subjective ratiocination. [Because] it is in becoming that [we] can be. Just as one can only 'understand' a fiery bullet when a fiery bullet hits him, so he can understand a concept precisely when he stands in the current course of the application of [i.e., experiencing] that concept. It is in action that truth manifests itself.

Shariᶜati's Islam as a revolutionary ideology was to mobilize the masses, challenge the authorities that be, compete and fight with other ideologies on their own ground and with their own armament. His Islam was not that of individual man standing vis-à-vis their God, striving for salvation, or seeking that through the established modes of religious authorities. His is collective "salvation" through collective political expression. His politicizing Islam is far from Islam's sanctifying politics. Politics is the conduct of human social affairs; as such Islam sanctifies and brings it into its universality. As such, man's political life is always situated within the larger frame of his religious and spiritual life. Shariᶜati's vision of Islam, however, is to reduce it to a political formula best suited for particular revolutionary objectives. In doing so, what ramifications may endanger the very universal claim of Islam as a revealed faith is of no concern to Shariᶜati.

He equally attacked the secular intellectuals' preoccupation with contemplative examination of different schools of political ideology before embarking on any course of action. He considered that "idle intellectuality." "You see," he complained, "that they both [religious scholars and secular intellectuals] say: first 'thinking' then 'action', [the former] says in the name of religion . . . and [the latter] says in the name of ideology . . . " Consequently, he sought to transform Islam into a "religious ideology" of action prior to thinking, maintaining that it is in becoming (constantly acting politically) that one is. "It is in 'becoming' that we can 'be.'"

Shariᶜati's opposition to the traditional Islam was manifested in a number of directions: first, against its intellectual, spiritual, and theological aspects; second, against the operative Islam, particularly its submission to divine will as a religious doctrine; and consequently he sought to revitalize Islam in a way best suited for revolutionary temperament. For this purpose, he concentrated on the household of cAli and Fatimah (the Prophet's daughter). This household has provided the Shici world with two of its most revered martyrs, cAli and Husayn. These two figured particularly important in Sharicati's scheme of "Islamology."

> But when someone [such as I], with all of his being and life and belief deeply loves this household [of cAli's], both faithfully and humanistically, and believes that the only way for the freedom of this people [i.e., Muslims in general, Iranians in particular] is in genuine return to cAli's school and Fatima's house[hold], then, how can he . . . remain 'indif-' ferent'?

As the strategical means to his political ends, Sharicati attacked some of the most fundamental doctrinal positions of Shicism, whenever they appeared to pose an obstacle to his revolutionary uses of faith. While cAli and Hussayn constantly appear in Sharicati's portrayal of a revolutionary way of life, in which one sacrifices one's life for a common cause, he severly attacked *taqiyyah*. *Taqiyyah* is one of the most important characteristics of Shici Islam, whose meaning and significance have been interwoven with the entire history of this faith. In doctrinal terms, it means the religious obligation on the part of the Shici believer to conceal his true identity in face of the danger of persecution and other adversities. It developed particularly under the Umayyads (661–750) who persecuted Shicis severely. As a doctrinal position of Shici Muslims, *taqiyyah* appeared as a reactionary and outmoded mentality to Sharicati. The discarding of such traditional doctrine of Shicism was particularly important if Sharicati were to secure the loyalty of the young revolutionary intelligentsia who were attracted to "progressive" ideologies.

Sharicati did manage to give his revolutionary ideolgoy a "progressive" aura. This "progresive" feature, however, had to be carefully balanced with a demonstrated anti-Western attitude. He was quite successful in presenting his deepest forms of Western radical secularism in an anti-colonial and anti-Western language. N. Keddie's assumptions that "Sharicati wished to be a politico-religious thinker in the context of the Third World liberation struggles," and that he "felt acutely the problems of colonialism and neocolonialism, and attacked especially cultural colonization, which alienated people from their roots," testifies to the degree of this success. Sharicati, in his diligent attempt to transform Islam from a religious tradition into a political ideology, was in fact an avant-garde in cultural colonialization. Being deeply alienated from, and in a disguised way resentful of, the traditional core of Islamic character and culture, while at the same time fascinated by the efficiency of Western political ideologies (particularly Marxism), he sought to revolutionize Islam to make it suitable for competition in an age of conflicting ideologies. Permanent revolution was the ultimate goal that he sought as the most external expression of his innermost beliefs.

What made the phenomenon of ^cAli Shari^cati conceivable in an Iranian context was a long process of artificial Westernization that had started its course at least from the late nineteenth century. As a social force, Westernization was a gradual but persistent process of abandoning traditional ways of life and thought and simultaneously imitating Western habits and customs in a most superficial way. When N. Keddie maintains that through Shari^cati "Westernization was challenged by a radical new interpretation of Shi^cism," perhaps she is to be reminded that a "radical new interpretation of Shi^cism" is the severest type of Westernization possible. No Shi^ci thinker ever thought of "a radical new interpretation" of the sacred tradition to which he belonged. As seminal a philosopher as Mulla Sadra founded his universal and comprehensive school of philosophy, transcendental theosophy (*al-hikmat al-muta^caliyah*), entirely on traditional Shi^ci intellectual sciences. Mulla Sadra's school of thought, despite its ground-breaking magnitude, was completely in harmony and conformity with what scores of traditional Muslim thinkers had thought and taught. But Shari^cati's "interpretation" of Islam, due to its radical inconsistency with the inner logic of Shi^ci intellectual heritage, is an essentially external imposition brought about by the current crisis of cultural identity in most of the Islamic societies.

For all intents and purposes, Shari^cati had the most vigorous anti-Western appearance . . . . As Keddie has pointed out, "once dependence on the West was associated with Western culture and Western culture with moral decay, it was natural to seek Iran's salvation not in the Westernization pushed by the Shah's regime, but in a return to an idealized indigenous Islam." But what Keddie calls "an idealized indigenous Islam" is in fact neither indigenous nor Islamic, but of course "idealized." What is implied here, and what Shari^cati sought to create, is a revolutionary political ideology read into the religious terminology of the Islamic faith.

Carrying this trend of thought to its logical conclusion, we realize that introducing Islam as a fundamentally revolutionary ideology reveals the deepest form of *ressentiment* (especially as it is stipulated by Max Scheler) toward the West and modern Western ideals. This *ressentiment* manifests itself in attempts to demonstrate the existence of revolutionary, radical, and liberal ideas, ideals, and ideologies already existing in the indigenous culture of the East, in general, and in Islam in particular. Shari^cati maintained that more effective than any Western revolutionary ideology, his version of Shi^ci Islam was capable of mobilizing the masses for revolutionary causes. S. H. Nasr has pointed out that:

for the modernized Muslims, especially the more extreme among them, the 'true meaning' of Islam has been for some time now what the West has dictated. If evolution is in vogue, 'true Islam' is evolutionary. If it is socialism that is the fashion of the day, the 'real teachings' of Islam are based on socialism."

Yet in Sharicati's case, this manifestation is so successfully concealed in an Islamic disguise that, combined with a social condition in which a confused, alienated and divided intelligentsia desperately seeks an identity, for many decades, "an Islamic ideology" is accepted and celebrated eagerly without the slighest sense of contradiction and logical inconsistency.

It is in Sharicati's attempt towards attaining his revolutionary goals that he reveals his most serious preoccupation with the extremest modes of Western secularism. Thus, as a true existentialist, reading his Sartre into Islam, he strives to make man totally and individually responsible for what he is and what he does, completely divorced from any traditional and securing order. Yet since this school of thought and its vocabulary is totally alien to a traditional Muslim society, he appeals to the Qur'an to seek justification of his position and reads a totally existentialist understanding into this Qur'anic verse:

> *Those are a people who have passed away. Theirs is that which they earned, and yours is that which ye earn. And ye will not be asked of that they used to do.*

Thus, in matters of faith, he advocated

> the choice of religion and its conscious acceptance, not in imitation of your parents and the elders, but with your own reasoning and understanding.

From a radically revolutionary standpoint, he isolates and atomizes individuals from their religious and traditional setting and confronts them with his version of the faith. This is alienation *par excellence*. "Religious individualists," who he believed were under the influence of "Sufi ethics of the East" or "Christian asceticism," were wrong; right was a "religious collectivism" that he sought to materialize. Separated and segregated from the commands and context of traditional authority, individuals become 'rational creatures' ready to adopt ideological identities. To launch a revolution, Sharicati needed rational creatures, and post-Muslim intelligentsia received his liberating ideology on rational grounds.

The susceptibility of the Iranian society to revolutionary rationality was peculiarly modern. To realize this susceptibility is to observe the fading away of the delicate line between the secular and the sacred in a deeply traditional society. In a passage in *Islam and the Plight of Modern Man*, S. H. Nasr has noted that:

> There is, in fact, in spite of the secularist tendencies of the past fifty years, still no conception of a way of life in which religion is only one element among many or of a world view in which the religious factor is only one dimension. The total world view is religious, and even the apparent negation of religion by certain people has itself a religious significance.

Yet from an opposite direction, complementing and verifying this trend, we observe a deep and persistent secular trait in the apparent religious movements, Shariᶜati being the prime example of this phenomenon. In a society on the verge of cultural confusion, associated with its transition from a traditional setting to "modernity," it is quite natural to see such distorted and deformed realities: that religious sentiments are disguised in secular appearances, and, reversely, that secular tendencies are produced in the form of a most fervent religiosity.

For Shariᶜati to find his "rational creatures," he needed a post-traditional society heading towards "modernism." When he wrote during the 1960's and 1970's Iran was a society particularly characterized by "modernization." From a variety of perspectives and with a maddening speed and widespreading dimensions, this phenomenon was engulfing different segments of the society. This "modernism" was not merely emulating, sometimes in the crudest ways, the Western scheme of things, from the philosophy of Sartre to the fashions of Yves St. Laurent, but it was also a rapid and consistent abandonment of the traditional standpoints from which each and every passing phase in the course of Iranian history was first perceived and then either endured or celebrated. This traditional standpoint has been, of course, in the grandest scale determined by the Iranian version of the Islamic faith, what H. Corbin has called "Islam Iranien." That consistent abandonment of the traditional standpoints was simultaneous with passive and mechanic adoption of the modern Western perspectives. So deep and committed was this "modernistic" trend that Islam as a faith that for centuries had shaped both the general *Weltanschauung* and the specifics of daily life, began to be considered and perceived from angles determined by modern ideas originating in the post-traditional West. It is within such a context that Shariᶜati and his version of Islam received an enthusiastic audience. N. Keddie is right in observing that "some in the modern [Iranian] economy who had recently moved from the bazaar were also attracted particularly by Shariᶜati's blend of Islam with modern ideas." Being gradually removed and alienated from the authority of their past, these segments of the Iranian society enthusiastically received Shariᶜati, who could talk about Marx, socialism, Sartre, and existentialism in a language near and understandable to them, while appearing to be operating within a familiar Islamic context.

As a restless and confused generation, the young Iranian intellectuals were in search of an "ideology." Yet, if not rooted in their culture, this generation breathed, whether it consciously liked it or not, in a traditional atmosphere. Certain attachments were too powerful to discard; they further provided a supposed sense of identity: some sentiments toward Islam were examples of such an attachment. If there could only be a way out of the impasse of simultaneously being an enthusiastic revolutionary intellectual and a Muslim; Shariᶜati showed a path out of the impasse. As N. Keddie puts it, "young Iranian Muslim intellectuals found in Shariᶜati a revolutionary Iranian Shiᶜi response. No more the crying Husayn of the *taᶜziyyah*, but Husayn fighting and dying for a just cause."

This combination was a masterful device to mobilize this particular segment of the society. Sociologically, it was very clever of Shariᶜati to realize that he could not mobilize a deeply religious society for any end, particularly political, with a fundamentally secular, materialistic, and atheistic ideology (Marxism). But his attempt to read social and economic schemes and ideals of Marxism (or any other Western secular ideology) into Islam was by far a more involved adventure with ramifications and extensions far beyond any possible political objective. Shariᶜati's Islam is a totally political Islam; a religious order turned into a political ideology, on a par with any other; equally powerful and equally susceptible, but with a significant difference. If Islam *cum* political ideology was challenged, put on the platforms of political conventions, compromised, forced into coalition or defeated, its legitimacy as a revealed faith and its claim to universality would become subject to challenge and subsequent denial.

Thus, contrary to what Keddie has asserted, Shariᶜati was *not* 'devoted to giving an Islamic response to the modern world." In fact, he strived to reduce Islam to an ideology of permanent revolt best suited for "the modern world," standing at the threshhold of the Iranian society. His Islam was typically modern in its therapeutic rationality, in its attempt to use faith for collective therapy: revolution.

As the strategical apparatus necessary for turning Islam into a revolutionary ideology, Shariᶜati conceived Shiᶜism as a complete party; this he sought to prove through his definition of *ummah* (Islamic community). Since *ummah*, according to Shariᶜati, is "a society on the move, a society not in place, but on the way, towards an objective, having a direction," then we need an Imam (from the same root as *ummah*) to lead us toward that objective. Thus, the complete political apparatus needed to launch a revolution, i.e., an ideology and a political party, was detected and identified in the faith of the majority of the people, with the strongest possible attachment between the faith and the people guaranteeing the most effective mechanism of mass mobilization. As a revolutionary sociologist, Shariᶜati recognized the necessity of this direct and immediate communication with the masses.

Making direct reference to the Qur'an and giving them revolutionary interpretations was a strategy that Shairᶜati utilized consistently in order to both legitimize his version of Islam and give it an aura of authenticity. In reading the Qur'anic verse (XXIX:69).

> *As for those who strive in Us, we surely guide them to Our path, and lo!*
> *Allah is with the good,*

he provided the following reading:

> Those who fight in our cause, we will put forward our ways for their salvation and freedom; and no doubt God is with those who do good deeds and do things well.' And one of these 'ways' is to understand the ᶜAlid Shiᶜi as a complete party.

Shariᶜati gives us a detailed definition of what he means by a 'complete party.' This definition reveals the depth and extent of his politicizing the Shiᶜism:

> 'Party,' in the general vocabulary of world intellectuals, is basically a unified social organization with a 'world-view,' and 'Ideology,' a 'philosophy of history,' and 'ideal social order,' a 'class foundation,' a 'class orientation,' a 'social leadership,' a 'political philosophy,' a 'political orientation,' a 'tradition,' a 'slogan,' a 'stragegy,' a 'tactic of struggle,' and . . . a 'hope' that wants to change 'the status quo' in man, society, people, or a particular class, and establish 'the desired status' in its stead; and thus each party has two aspects of affirmation and negation: 'Thou shalt,' and 'Thou shalt not.'

As for Shiᶜism, "it is a party with all the characteristics and dimensions of an ideal and complete party; it is a party whose objective realization is that 'God's party' that the Qur'an speaks of, and is also responsive to the need of this responsible, intellectual generation in giving [political] consciousness and mobilizing the masses of the society, in leading their class struggle, in eliminating the difficulties and obstacles in the way of such a struggle, and in realizing the hopes of the disinherited classes." The complete and total party, as the students of Tocqueville and George Orwell know well, paves the road to complete and total society: totalitarianism. Shariᶜati's careful construction of the foundation of a complete and perfect party constituted a totalitarian microcosm to be translated, upon the success of his revolution, into a totalitarian macrocosm: the complete and perfect society.

Shariͨati, following his grand scheme of a complete party, came to the conclusion that

> finally, after considering all the schools, ideologies, revolutions, move-
> ments, sociology, Islamology, historical investigation, research into the
> causes of cultural decline and intellectual and social deviation, and a
> more profound recognition of [the Prophet's] family, *Imamate* [leader-
> ship of ͨAli and his descendants], *wilayat* [the doctrine of the legitimacy
> of ͨAli and his descendants], *intizar* [waiting for the appearance of the
> Twelfth Imam], ͨ*adl* (God's justice], and man's legacy in the duration of
> human history, and after experiences, conflicts, reactions, and the
> clarification of dark spots and concealments, I have reached this inner
> principle that: 'essentially, Shiͨism is a complete party.'

A revolutionary party needs a revolutionary and dynamic view of society, a society in movement towards perfection. This Shariͨati tried to achieve with a dynamic definition of *ummah*, the technical term for the Islamic community. He believed an *ummah* to be "a society of individuals who think alike, walk along the same path, take their steps together, have similar objectives, are responsible, [and] on the move towards a single, direct, clear, stable, and collective destination." The uniformity and unconditional conformity that Shariͨati envisaged for his ideal state makes it quite clear that there is a direct and short link between Shiͨism as a complete party and the Shiͨi state as a complete and total society.

A revolutionary ideology, furthermore, necessitates revolutionary heroes to provide the followers with prototypical figures of authority. He recognized Abu Zarr, a close companion of the Prophet, as the first revolutionary socialist who "deeply felt upon his shoulders the heavy weight of social responsibility, the responsibility of changing the governing system of the society and the governing faith of his time . . ." Abu Zarr would constantly appear in Shariͨati's works as the model of revolutionary hero to be closely emulated.

On the surface, Shariͨati faced not a religious but a secular audience whom he wished to convert to his brand of Islam. In achieving this, he had to present Shiͨism as a "complete political party," in order to compete with the secular ideology, dominant among the intelligentsia, i.e., Marxism. Since Marxism presented a total view of the society, along with its philosophy of history, sociology, anthropology, etc., as well as a total party program for implementing its objectives, Shariͨati's Islam had to meet the same criteria. To justify his brand of Shiͨism to his secular audience, he argued that:

> Of course, this claim might appear to some irreligious intellectuals a bit
> difficult to swallow . . . how can an intellectual take his ideology from

religion? . . . Since these intellectuals, because of the experience of Christianity and imitation from the modern perspective of world intellectuals and seeing what today passes as Islam among us and its social role and human impact, cannot imagine that a party ideology or a completely convincing ideology can have a religious origin! . . . While if religion, particularly in Islam and especially in the Shiᶜite school and perspective, were correctly introduced, it would have been the religious intellectual who would be surprised . . . .

Revolutionary responsibility, in order to be decisive and emphatic, has to be coupled with unconditional commitment. In the tradition of Shiᶜi martyrdom, Shariᶜati detected a powerful emotional device that he wished to use in providing his revolutionary ideology with a strong psychological temperament. This he tried to materialize by exploiting the religious aura of his ideology.

Yet there are hidden dimensions in Shariᶜati's 'ideology' that particularly appeal to revolutionary secular intellectuals. Echoing a Trotskyist ideal, Shariᶜati sought to secure the idea of permanent revolution as essentially present in his version of Shiᶜism. "Islam is," Keddie paraphrases Shariᶜati as having said, ". . . the only basis for an ideology of permanent progress and revolution . . ." Here Shariᶜati assumes and assimilates into his Shiᶜi ideology the two most common ideas of the post traditional Europe, Evolution and Revolution. It was the detection of these traits of thought that attracted many secular intellectuals to Shariᶜati's Islam. They simply viewed his reading of Islam as an ideology of liberation and revolution.

Shariᶜati attacked the Safavid dynasty (1501–1722) for what he considered to be their using Shiᶜism as their means of legitimizing their rule by establishing it as the state religion. He believed that "where Shiᶜism is so influential among people and can be the best means of securing the class interest of the ruling class . . . why should they bother to choose another faith for themselves that is abhorred and rejected by the people?" He even compares this to the Roman Empire's accepting Christianity for similar political purposes. Yet his own version of Shiᶜi Islam was an obvious attempt to completely change it from a complex religious tradition to a political ideology and an instrument of power for the purpose of attaining revolutionary political end.

On a yet different level of complexity, one of the major challenges to Shariᶜati's revolutionary Islam was the contemplative and devotional aspect of this faith. This he sought to alter drastically by redefining Islam as a religion of revolutionary, i.e., militant, action. Ironically, in this particular aspect he shared the views of some missionary Western Orientalists who, in their proselytizing activities, neglected both the devotional as well as the contemplative dimensions of Islam.

Any political ideology as a measure of securing credibility claims universality; so did Shariᶜati's Shiᶜism:

> The boundaries of *umma* is not a geographical demarcation; it is not the
> fixed barrier of a place; *umma* is a group in 'the way,' a way that passes
> 'through' humanity and from the heart of the people, because the
> boundary of Islam is extended to wherever that man is, that people are,
> and . . . what am I saying? The country of Muslims is the whole world, the
> expansion of existence, and the owner and only presiding power upon
> this *umma* is God.

These passages were particularly useful in expanding the applicability of Shariᶜati's revolutionary Shiᶜism beyond the Iranian boundaries. Being primarily identified with Iran, Shiᶜism had to be so universally expanded, in its revolutionary usefulness, to convince not only post-Muslim Iranian intellectuals but also post-Muslim intellectuals everywhere of its great potential for the mobilization of the masses.

This universal ideology was to substitute the Western revolutionary ideologies, particularly Marxism, which in an Islamic context had "lost their dynamism," i.e., they were not capable of mobilizing masses in a revolutionary movement. Shariᶜati realized the failure of at least one century of disillusioned Marxism in Muslim societies. He considered Islam as the last and only chance to unite and mobilize people for particular revolutionary objectives.

N. Keddie has asserted that "Shariᶜati saw in Islamic humanism the sole ideology that could save Iran and all oppressed peoples." "Islamic humanism," however, is a peculiar invention that can have no bearing on Islamic tradition, which sees human affairs from a divine perspective and not vice versa. The invention of this "Islamic humanism" is yet another aspect of the infiltration of Western ideas and ideals into Shariᶜati's version of Islam.

Coming out of a traditional society and a religious family, Shariᶜati plunged, while in Europe, into a sea of various and conflicting ideologies: Marxism, existentialism, liberalism, etc. He was saturated with ideological tendencies and commitments. There he was also exposed to many revolutionary movements, particularly those of Algeria and Cuba, actively participating in demonstrations and meetings in support of these revolutions. During this period, he recognized the indispensable role of an ideology for a revolutionary cause. Without an ideology, under whose banner to organize and mobilize the masses, he realized that no revolutionary cause could be pursued and attained. Yet he also recognized, in the light of the Iranian political scene of the twentieth century, the inevitable failure of Western ideologies in their original, secular form. Consequently, he came to the inevitable conclusion that to mobilize the Muslim masses for any revolutionary cause, a domestic and indigeneous ideology had to be sought and formulated. Both strategically and tactically this would be a more effective approach particularly operative in a traditional context.

What kind of ideology in an essentially Islamic society can be more effective than an "Islamic ideology"? Shariᶜati's lifelong task was to formulate such an ideology.

"Islamic ideology" had to be "Islamic" in order to communicate easily and effectively with the masses, in order to use the vast source of Islamic symbolism, which was capable of mobilizing the masses beyond the measures that any secular ideology could achieve. Yet the formulated doctrines had to be called "ideology" in order to detach it from the element of faith that was particularly anachronistic to post-Muslim intelligentsia who were to lead this revolution. It was this revolutionary use of faith that Shariᶜati sought to implement. He single-handedly strove to reduce the devotional, contemplative, mystical, and institutional dimensions of Shiᶜism, Islam as a revealed faith, to a total political ideology.

And "Islamic ideology" is essentially a contradiction in terms. Islam as a faith founded on divine revelation cannot assume the posture of an 'ideology' without negating its universality and sacred nature. An 'ideology' is a human enterprise associated with a particular period of Western intellectual history. To identify a faith with an ideology is to negate the very sacred reality of that faith. Attempts to reduce Islam to a political ideology is the severest and most concealed form of emulating the secular Western perspective, without recognizing the full dimensions of the inconsistencies and contradictions that would be ultimately created in an Islamic traditional context.

Revolutionary uses of faith negate and nullify the religious tradition doubly. First, they impose a utilitarian attitude upon the sanctity of a claim to universal truth; second, they desacralize social order as the expression of sacred order. Faith is fundamentally negated once it is assumed as a medium of man's psychological welfare, whether this is taken individually or collectively. Revolutions seek to remedy man's sociopsychological deficiencies, *en masse*; revolutionary uses of faith seek to employ the last vestiges of a religious order towards this end. This final employment would inevitably lead, as it did in the West, to the exhaustion and depletion of the symbolic apparatus that constitutes these sacred traditions. Revolutionary man now salvages what he can from his primal past to build parties, launch revolutions, overthrow orders, and be totally, unconditionally, and desperately free.

^c*Ali Shari^cati*

Ladies and Gentlemen: The exceptionally kind atmosphere of togetherness, sincerity and your particular awareness at this institution, have encouraged me to share my thoughts with you more often. What I would like to discuss now is ideology. In the words of a French writer, ideology is a magic word, especially among the educated youth, that creates temptation in one's thinking and living to the extent that it drives them towards self-destruction.

Mind you that this word has penetrated the Persian language. Presently, it is common in the colloquialisms of our youths, particularly our free-thinkers. However, I have not come across a precise scientific definition of ideology in Persian yet. This is why it is necessary to devote an independent conference to the topic.

Basically, ideology has a direct relationship to another word: free-thinker or intellectual. These two terms are interdependent. And since ideology distinguishes an intellectual's type of thinking, an intellectual must have a precise conception of what it means. We live in an age in which our conscious and responsible generation is in the process of choosing an ideology. Such an ideology, as an independent topic, must come under scientific scrutiny. Although it is impossible to do justice to the topic in one session, I will try to design and discuss it as far as is possible.

Ideology is composed of two parts, "idea", which is thinking, imagination, motto, conception; and 'logy', which has a Latin root and means logic and recognition. So literally, ideology is "recognition of an idea," or in one word it is "idea", as we understand it in Persian. In the same vein, an ideologue is a person who possesses a particular idea or tenet. Therefore, ideology is the particular belief, opinion, or tenet of a group, class, nation or a race.

What is the difference between science and ideology? Science consists of a scientist's consciousness of external realities. It is a subjective picture of an objective reality. Furthermore, science is the discovery of relationships, principles, characteristics, or particularities in man, nature, and living beings. Therefore, the relationship between the scientist and the known resembles a mirror—the reflection of objects (or the scenery) which are in front of it. Thus, science is basically a negative phenomenon in that the scientists leaves no trace in the known (or the given). For example, a physicist knows that an object falls towards the earth according to MV^2. This is the law of descent of an object in nature. The fall of an object has no effect upon the thinking of a scientist who possesses such a knowledge. It is the individual who must be subject to the external reality. A scientists' interference in the external reality (the given) ruins science and transforms it into ignorance. Accordingly, the most knowledgeable individuals are the ones whose 'thinking' is subject to the external reality. This is awareness. Memory then is like a mirror which reflects reality upon itself; and the reflections are science; physics, chemistry, economics and so forth.

Ideology, on the one hand, is the thinker's belief relative to the value of the external realities — their evalutation, what inconsistencies such realities contain, and how to transform them into ideal forms.

There are two terms in science and the methodology of science which are often mixed up. One is *"judgement de fait,"* and the other is *"judgement de valeur."* The former involves the evaluation and survey of external reality. The external reality is a *"fait;"* it is evident, given, and is a predetermined state. When a scientist is in this stage, his only job is to discover the characteristics of the fait, the external phenomenon, and explain precisely what it is. Judgement of values involves how a scientist judges each phenomenon — whether it is bad, harmful, corrupt, or whether it must be changed, reformed or destroyed.

The above two stages must be kept distinct and separate. For instance, to apply to the *"judgement de fait"* to Islam in Iran, it would go like this: Islam came to Iran, made conquests, and made such changes in the Iranian handwriting, literature, class relations, politics, and religion. We have no right to pass any judgement at this stage; we should stay objective and neutral and try to see things as they transpired. Any personal remark will not only ruin the status of science but also our works will not be scientific.

Once the survey of the objective reality is over, it is time to evaluate and compare. In the case of the effect of Islam upon Iran, we will ask whether the former was a positive or negative factor, progressive or reactionary, promoted freedom or stymied culture. This is the stage of evaluation, a phase in which objective realities are weighed out. In brief then, *judgement de fait*, involves a precise survey of the objective realities; it is the practical stage. While in *judgement de valeur*, we evaluate the values; we suggest, criticize, and show solutions. Such judgments and evaluations fall in the purview of ideology.

Ideology is an idea and it consists of: a) our imagination and interpretation of the world, life, and man; b) our interpretation and particular evaluation of the problems that form our social and intellectual atmosphere; and c) suggestions, solutions, as well as the presentation of "ideal samples" in order to change these non-idealistic aspects which we reject. Thus, ideology consists of three phases; world vision, critical evaluation of the problems and the environment, and finally suggestions and solutions in the form of ideals and aims. Each ideologue, then, is responsible to change the status quo relative to his ideals and convictions. Therefore, accepting responsibility to an ideologue is a predetermined matter. And any ideology has a critical attitude relative to the status quo. And since a critical attitude is a negative disposition it takes the form of suggestion; "It must be this way, or it must not be this way." In the 'must be' phase, ideals and goals are designed, while the latter phase creates human responsibility which involves and confronts the individual with action, combat, and sacrifice. This is the most sensitive and lucid phase of an ideology.

Philosophy does not do what ideology can do, nor does science. Science explains the fall of objects according to the law of gravity. Whether people are willing to believe this or not is ireelevant, nor is a scientist responsible to impose it on them; he only states the facts. This is why throughout history science and philosophy have never initiated a war. Of course, there has always been innumerable problems and incompatibility in science and philosophy, but only ideologies have been the creators of wars, devotions, and magnificent struggles throughout history. Faith, responsibility, struggle, and devotions are the natures and hallmarks of ideology.

Question: An ideology does not appear out of nowhere. Is not a philosophy necessary to make it real?

Answer: I accept half of what you say. Ideology does not appear out of nowhere, but I will not accept that its existence necessarily depends upon philosophy. If ideology owed its existence to philosophy then all the religious leaders must have been philosophers (I believe philosophers are careless elements of the historical profiles!) They are from the masses, who, as outstanding soldiers of ideology have started the struggles in various epochs of history; they died and continue to die. Thus, philosophers do not create ideology, masses do. This is why the most outstanding and constructive leaders, planners, and harbingers of ideology, according to Qur'anic text, have risen from among the masses. And in my opinion, the title of "ummi," bestowed upon Muhammad (PBUH)* denotes that the prophet was neither a philosopher, poet, scientist, or king—he was from among the masses. What is the difference between ideology and religion?

There are two kinds of religions—one of which has always been against the other. No one has as much grudge against religion as I have. And by the same token, no one has as much faith and hope in religion for the twentieth century as I have. If you detect contradiction in what I say it is due to the

---

*PBUH stands for "Peace be upon him".

fact that religion is being interpreted in many ways; thus, there are religions. Take Islam, for instance. We have an Islam that commits crime, creates reactionaries, concocts opiates, murders freedom, and protects the status quo. On the other hand, there is another Islam, the true one, that has always fought with its criminal counterpart and in the process it has been victimized. The same situation applies to Christianity, Zoroastrianism, etc.

Islam has two aspects; a human side which is its original ideal, philosophy, and the spirit of its movement, and an anti-human side which was introduced by various suspicious elements (in the names of Islam). This is why we are now witnessing the destruction of Islamic principles in the Islamic circles.

Sometimes religion is taken as an ideology, and at other times it is taken as a social custom (this is what Durkheim had in mind when he defined it). Religion as a social custom is composed of totality of inherited beliefs, inculcated sentiments, imitation of fashions, relationships, mottos, traditions, and unconscious practice of particular precepts. In short, a customary religion is a relationship which makes the national continuation of a society possible throughout a few generations, centuries, and epochs.

The grand feat of the Safavid dynasty lay in the fact that from three different elements, they synthesized a single element. Specifically, they combined the three elements of royalism, nationalism, and sufism with the end product which was 'sugarcoated' as Shicism. They handed it over to us and we are still consuming it (This peculiar brand of Shicism, Safavid Shicism, gave birth to the existing Iranian national banner which was chosen as a result of confrontation with the Turks, Arabs, and Russians). Thus, when *Nowruz* and *cAshura* coincided during Shah cAbbas's reign, (since the similar elements of religion and nationality had intermingled), each occasion was assigned fifty percent. But this created a problem. Finally, Shah cAbbas issued an edict and advised the populace to mourn on the tenth and celebrate on the eleventh! The elements of nationality and religion were mixed in the form of a concoction called, Safavid Shicism. This was a sort of nationalism which combined with its own particular cultural, historical, literary, and subjective elements, as well as its particular spiritual products and thus a single spirit—religion—manifested itself. This is the religion of nationalism.

This is also true for Christianity. At the outset Christianity was heralded by Jesus (PBUH) as a universal movement; the prophet represented no particular class. In the fifth century, however, the Roman emperor adopted it as a religion. Thereafter a church appeared and a Pope was invented along with his crown, strange garbs, and his depositories of gold. And we notice that papal edicts to massacre, which were unique in history, were horrifying to such an extent that even Assyrians could have never imagined them!

Finally, the manifestation of Jesus in Europe was turned into the manifestation of the western's collective spirit (unrelated to Jesus), and the European spirit emerged as Christianity. How do we know? By looking at a European Mary or Jesus. Mary was a Palestinian Jew; look at the Western Mary, she is blond with maroon eyes. How did she come to be French, American, British . . .? The same is true about Jesus, who, as the present Western deity, resembles a movie star rather than an Israeli prophet. He is blond with blue eyes and fair skin!

Why does Jesus change race? Because Christianity has nothing to do with either Jesus or Palestine. Christianity is the manifestation of the Jesus' followers. This is why Jomo Kenyatta states that "In Africa Jesus is first fashioned out of cotton and cotton seed in the name of Western God and in accordance with Western models. And then as a man who came to Africa once, Jesus is attacked and set afire." Who is the Jesus that goes to Africa? He is a European exploiter. He is symbol of exploitation (European), who has nothing to do with the deity in the sky; he is a God on earth that was taken to the sky!

Once I came across a portrait of ᶜAli with mustaches twice as long as those of Shah ᶜAbbas' in the hand of a student in Europe who was from the 'Druze' denomination. I asked him who he was, whereby he responded, "ᶜAli (PBUH)!" Now look at the Iranian drawings of ᶜAli and Muhammad (PBUH); they both look like Persians. The prophet looks like Zoroaster, his Arabic attire has changed, so has his makeup! These are indicative of the fact that the spirit of nationality of a race manifests itself in religions symbols, traditions, and mottos; this is what Durkheim talks about when he uses "manifestation of the collective spirit."

There is, however, another religion, and that is ideology. It is a religion which is consciously chosen by the people (The customary religion is not chosen; parents simply initiate their children into their own faiths. It is the previous generation that selects religion for its progenies). But religion as ideology is a belief which is chosen, relative to the existing inconsistencies, for the purpose of translating an individual's class', or group's beloved ideals into reality.

Therefore, to begin with, the individual feels the condition of his social class, as well as his economic, political, and social milieu. Since he is conscious of his condition, he is dissatisfied, he is suffering, he longs for change and transformation. Thus, ideology comes into being. The individual aligns himself with the ideology and consequently, relative to it, he 'sees' the solutions to his problems. And since he finds a correspondence between his ideals and the ideology, he chooses the latter. At this point an individual's religion is equivalent to an ideology.

Throughout history, then, we come across two kinds of religions (or two historical epochs): a period in which religion appears in the form of an ideology, or one in which religion is in the form of mores and folkways. All the great prophets, at the outset of their missions created a consciousness-generating enlightening movement, and they voiced distinct human, group, and class mottos. Consequently, all those who joined them; slaves, scientists, or philosophers, did it consciously. But later these religions were transformed from 'movements' into institutions; they became organized and turned into the foundation of society. In this institutionalization stage, religion is a social organization and a bureaucracy. It becomes genetic and hereditary; once a child is born he is automatically a Muslim, Buddhist, socialist, or a materialist. At this point an ideology, religion or non-religious, is no longer an ideology; it is a tradition which is not consciously chosen by the individual.

At the outset of Islam, in 70–80 A.H., we noticed that suddenly Persia joined Islam in her entirety. Forty years later, Abu Muslim, with 600,000 soldiers, marched from Khurasan and attacked the Arab reign. Thus, after only four decades the Persians turned into devout Muslims, so much so that they destroyed Arab sovereignty. They never resorted to their old Persian ways (Zoroastrianism). And this is an indication that 'joining' is a collective phenomenon. Despite the fact that the Persians' traditional religion was Zoroastrianism, they abandoned their customs and collective spirit, walked under symbols other than their own, accepted it consciously, and believed in it.

What caused Iranians to show a tendency towards Islamic ideology? Why did Persians initiate revolutionary acts? Because the Persians' choice of ideology was based upon two needs: a) they were chafing under inequity and class disparity (while Islam's first slogan is 'justice'), and b) they were suffering from the rule of aristocratic monopoly and dictatorship (while Islam's motto is based upon '*Imamah*,' a system of meritocracy). And so, in the folds of Islamic slogans not only did Persians spontaneously see their own ideals, but also they found the panacea for their malaise and pangs; so they chose.

At present Islam is an ideology in Africa. Intellectually, there are three battlefronts in Africa; Catholicism (which spends billions of dollars for missions), Marxism, and Islam. None of these three religions is customary or hereditary in Africa; all three are ideologies. And all three are in perpetual conflict with one another. However, as Vincent Monti put it, "Of every five Africans who convert, four join Islam, and less than half a person goes to Christianity. And of those who join Christianity the majority are employees of the European companies and embassies who obviously have to join. On the other hand, the Islamic missionaries are just the paupers and beggars; they have no formal propagation." Mind you that the Bible has been translated into the remotest languages of the world (including the minor African languages), while this is not true about Qur'an. We Iranians still do not have a decent Persian translation of the Qur'an, despite the fact that even from the outset of our conversion to Islam, we Iranians were much better informed in Islamic principles than the Arabs.

Why is Islam, despite the lack of any capital investment of propaganda, so popular among African blacks? Because Islam is an ideology. What kind of an ideology? Whatever the black man's needs are. What are his needs? Freedom from discrimination and his longing for human equality. And among all the religions that are offered to him, Islam is the only one which always emphasizes (as well demonstrates) racial equality. For instance, today's Jews who have turned into racists, and fascistic elements, were, in the heyday of the Islamic empire, conducting business in the Muslim bazaars on par with any Muslim. As a matter of fact today in Iran, they are still conducting business without the slightest hassle and racial discrimination.

Question: What is the status of the Islamic dissemination in Africa today, and what factor is responsible for the progress of Islamic thinking there?

Answer: It is a pity that one cannot say what one wants to say. In any case, in Africa, the only single factor responsible for the progress of Islamic thinking among the various strata of blacks is the lack of formal profiteering missionary efforts.

Q: How is it possible?

A: Generally speaking, missionary activities involve a lot of profiteering by a bunch of shysters who are often hidden under the guise of religion (And in our own country, the reason behind our youths' lack of interest and their consequent fleeing from Islam in our societies are the shysters and profiteers who pass themselves off as the true propagators of Islam).

Once I had a Shiᶜi friend from Tanzania who had come to Iran to study. Mr. Sachedina was a scholar-writer and a celebrity in his country. One day he recounted to me the following:

We are a small Shiᶜi minority in Tanzania. But [thanks] to the progressive rule of President Nyerere, our community is more advanced than all other social systems. We have no professional Muslim; we are all amateurs. One day we began talking about *zakat*. After collecting *zakat*, "who should we give to," we asked, and since we had no formal organization. Finally, we prepared a safe and under the supervision of a committee dues were collected. Next, we ran into *khums*. "What should we do with this one," we asked. Well, we organized an insurance company and purchased life insurance for every individual. This insurance has a constant rate of capital accumulation. In the meantime, we opened a bank and loaned money with no interest.

Another problem cropped up; namely, what to do with the large sums of monies we used to spend on food in our annual mourning occasion. We agreed to open an account in the name of Husayn (PBUH) scholarship. The first year we deposited around seventy thousand dollars. And this amount was distributed to seventy-five students (myself being one of them in Iran), and sent them all over the world. This, in lieu of the fact that our progressive socialistic government of Mr. Nyerere has only thirty-five students abroad. We have saved so much that we can afford sending every eligible member of our community abroad. And those who were lax in paying their dues are all paying now.

The above example contains an account of the differences between the Safavid brand of Shicism and the cAlawi type; that is, institution vs. ideology. In traditional societies a change throws the populace into a tizzy and fright, but not in Tanzania where Shicism is not a tradition; it is a revolutionary ideology.

Q: We must choose after having itemized (clarified) our needs. And not too many people are capable of doing so since life is too short. What are we to do?

A: When I talk about choice, I do not mean a survey and examination of each ideology and religion and picking out the one with the strongest logic. This is a university method of choice, and a scientific methodology by which science investigates a phenomenon and ultimately accepts or rejects an assumption, while the investigation processes of an ideology are different. As much as an ideology is different from science so are its methods of selection. An ideology penetrates man as love does. This process is not subject to measurement, comparison, or investigation. Faith, just as love attracts man, suddenly overwhelms. Mind you this is not to be taken as an unconscious process of surrender. Man chooses faith with knowledge and intelligence without resorting to an academic methodology.

The Middle Ages were an era of the dominance of customary religion. The religion of the Christian church was Feudalism and Caesarean. And there was much bloodshed over the intellectuals' suggestion to translate the Bible into English, since the Pope believed that Latin was God's tongue. In the meantime God's tongue (Jesus in Christianity) was Hebrew. Jesus knew not a word about Latin. Why did God's tongue change to Latin in the first place? Because Latin was an historical language of Europe, and Christianity was a European religion rather than the religion of Jesus of Palestine. The Pope of the period massacred many people in order to establish Latin, the so-called God's tongue, as a universal language.

Therefore, the Middle Ages were the era of the dominance of traditional religion; an anti-ideological period. The fifteenth and the sixteenth centuries were eras of consciousness. It was in these two latter centuries that the masses revolted against the customary religion.

The seventeenth century is called the era of free-thinking — the era of intellectualism. That is, the free-thinking class was no longer under the influence of those fossilized religious traditions. They were freed, conscious, and able to reflect. One of the signs of an intellectual is that spontaneously he gets involved in critique and analysis in the form of criticism or proposal (unlike a traditional individual who uncritically accepts everything).

The eighteenth century was the era of freedom and humanism. In this period an intellectual in Europe was able to reflect and analyze. He had a brain and was not a follower of blind sentiments, since hd had returned to democracy, humanism, and the French Revolution.

The nineteenth century is called the era of ideology. By glancing back at the evolution of vicissitudes, we notice that Europe was just like a blind, prejudiced imitator. By and by she gained awareness, revolted against old ways, became capable of analysis and reflection, became free-thinking, found social responsibility, and turned her attention to democracy, freedom, and human rights. And so, in the nineteenth century, Europe formally possessed a faith and a distinct ideology. The nineteenth century is the period of ideologies; existentialism, Hegel, Nietzsche, Schiller, Fascism, Socialism, Marxism, and St. Simmonians.

The twentieth century is the era of grand decline. It is a century in which money-loving, and force-loving powers have forced the great scientific genuises and thinkers to submit and support particular styles of thinking and points of view. Scientists and science must be neutral and value-free; such is to their advantage and protects their interests. This is the biggest tragedy of the twentieth century. Science must be value-free; what does it mean? This means that science's bias, relative to the external reality, must be limited to 'what is it?' Once science finds out 'what it is' its job comes to an end. 'How is it?' is irrelevant, it is not the duty of science to answer, it is the task of ideology. What does ideology say? The twentieth century believes that ideology is nonsense. This is why in the name of 'disinterestedness,' while fleeing away from human ideals, scientists are shirking responsibility. And under this motto, value-free scientists freed science from serving in the cause of human guidance and ideals, and incarcerated science in the labs, universities, and companies. And if a scientist, writer, poet, artist, or philosophber wishes to remain neutral, he cannot; he must remain at the service of those who control the fate of our society. We are now witnessing that science has become the stooge of those who control the world's money and power. Science is at the service of Capitalism. Science and money have married each other and it is obvious which one runs the show.

Today we notice that in universities such as the Sorbonne, Harvard, and Cambridge, it is commonplace to hear that "science must not show the way; it must not criticize; it must not express opinion; it must not suggest; it must not prognosticate; it must only analyze the external realities." But if science cannot show the way to the masses, discuss their difficulties, guide them, show them how to resist force and the way to reach their ideals and translate them into realities, who else must do them? COMPUTER! (An individual from the audience yells). Oh yes! A machine which is costing $120 per hour. With this cost it is obvious whom it serves, certainly not the Iranian laborer who receives $1.50 a day!

Neutrality of science is the hallmark of the twentieth century. And we see that today, physicists, geniuses, chemists, sociologists, statisticians . . . all have either turned into slaves and stooges of capitalism, or have resorted to non-capitalistic orders (where power and force rules). And due to this, science has cut off its relation with ideology in the twentieth century; it is demolishing ideology. It is very strange indeed that today many free-thinkers claim that the problem of faith has been solved! What has been solved? Today, science for science's sake, art for art's sake is being talked about. Who is doing it? To whose advantage? Why must masses' struggles, initiatives, and their ideals remain deprived of the genius' guidance and science's advice? If a sociologist will not tell us how to change a society and how to make it, what else is he good for? To go to a university and explain social class and the ways to analyze it? We later find the sociologist as a stooge contractor who works for the powers-that-be: establishment and companies.

In our own country someone was invited to teach sociology. Even though he was an expert in his own field, it turned out that some of the professors did not want him to teach since they believed that he was too opinionated and consequently he smeared science with his ideas! It seems to me that in order to be a sociologist one has to practice "yes-manism" first! If a sociologist is willing to show solutions, if he feels responsible for human ideals, if he has faith and a goal, he has no right to teach in a scientific establishment!

We notice that in backward lands such imposed Western values are being promoted and their impacts are being felt. These are the fundamental tragedies of our century; their effects are more prominent than anything else. It is because today everything is done 'internally' and surreptitiously. That is, one is 'covertly' exploited, and conquered; nothing can be detected on the outside which is polished and sheened. Overtly, the 'talks' are all honest, true and straightforward!

The twentieth century has turned into a century of scientific analysis, scientific neutrality, negation and rejection of the philosophy of history, and ideology, due to the fact that when faith is lost the powers-that-be will continue their reign with much more confidence. Further, when masses have no faith and are not devout, when they do not feel responsibility towards and ideal, and the scientific awareness of their free-thinkers is not put at their disposal for intellectual guidance and social responsibility, no danger will threaten the bullies of the world.

What is threatening the capitalistic powers as well as the ruling governments today? Only ideology. Who are these powers, that with all their phantoms and atomic bombs are defeated by the empty hands and hungry stomachs who possess virtuous souls? The fact is that efforts are directed towards keeping the hearts of the scientists empty of faith. Once his stomach is filled, the scientists can be won over the name of scientific neutrality, and indoctrinated with thoughts such as, "Our century is an era of analysis and objectivity. Ideas belong to the past; they are old; they belong to the romantic, theosophic, and aristocratic period." Now we know what objectivity is all about. It is the same thing that has produced a neutral science whose product walks out of the graduation ceremony and claims, "I am neutral; I have no ideology." A businessman comes from America, a few from England, France, Africa, Russia, and elsewhere and puts the college graduate on auction. Whoever pays more, will own him. The graduate will respond, "I am for science and am neutral. Wherever I am offered a better deal, there will be my country and responsibility." In the service of Capitalism, Socialism, Fascism or Chombe'*, it makes no difference, I am neutral!"

In one definition, ideology is a conscious faith dealing with "How the present condition must be." What does the present condition mean? In any case an 'ideology' explains my condition, where I am, in what period of history I am, and what condition myself, my people, my country, and humanity are in, relative to various battlefronts. A human, class, national or group ideology can respond to these all.

How can man reach an ideology? Who can reach it? As I mentioned before a philosopher is not an idelogue, nor is he a scientists. Once we exclude the philosopher (or philosophy), the scientists (or science) and state that ideology is something other than the former and the latter, spontaneously we conclude that it is an awareness which is limited to man. Anyone can possess it; scientist, common man, literate or illiterate, aristocrat or pauper, and any individual in any level of culture and intelligence can have ideologic consciousness.

---

*Chombe was the Prime Minister of Congo in 1960, and the rival of Patrice Lumumba.

At this point, another definition along with an important and sensitive difference will be clarified, and that is, ideology is an index of those groups who are called 'free-thinkers' in society. We tend to relate 'free-thinking' to those who work with their brain—intellectuals, students, professors, teachers, and so forth. This is wrong. These categories are intellectuals but not necessarily free-thinkers. An intellectual may be an accomplice in the service of a power structure, or he may be a slave of his stomach and his family. There are some individuals who are men of labor. Their missions are limited to their office and their kitchens and activities of this sort summarize their world-views. Whatever these men are—scientists, educated, or intellectual, they are not free-thinkers. A free-thinker's indicator: he is a man possessing a conscious ideology. Relative to the requirements of his ideology (or ideologies), class and social consciousness, such an individual will find a distinct way for acting, living, and thinking as his philosophy of living. Having faced all this consciousness, the individual becomes responsible, so much so that he will be pulled away from becoming attached to individualistic living. Consequently the devoted *mujahid* dies for the sake of his ideologies—these are the criteria of faith and a free-thinker possesses them. Throughout the history of man, free-thinkers have been individuals whose particular consciousness has been transformed into moving the society and guiding the masses out of the quandry of their period. This is why Aristotle neither created a movement, nor changed the class order of his period. Ptolomey was a physicist, possessing scientific consciousness, but he had the least effect on the destiny of his society. And, if for another thousand years Athens was going to produce Platos, Aristotles, and Ptolomeys the masses would have been much worse off, since these philosophers were just consumers; they required constant food in order to prattle. Those who could have lightened the loads of slaves in Athens could not have been philosophers or scientists, but free-thinkers. As we notice ideology deals with problems other than what Aristotle talked about: "When creation began what was its original substance?"

This is why we notice that throughout history the prophets were neither philosophers, scientists, artists, nor even common men. Prophets were individuals who transformed history and societies and they revolted as well as fomented a revolution. Who was Abraham? He was neither a philosopher nor a scientist. His father made idols and he would sell them. Later, he became a shepherd and finally he led the greatest movement in history. Or, look at Moses, he was an abandoned child who was brought up in Pharaoh's Palace. He took off and went to Shuayb and began to herd his sheep. Finally, he started his struggles with Pharaoh with his gnarled staff and he won! The same is true about Jesus, Muhammad, and all the Prophets.

Faith always demolishes power even though the 'faithful' may be physically weak, and this is a deterministic relationship. The Qur'an often narrates the destiny of large forces which were conquered by small ones.
Whether this is a deterministic law of God or history, makes no difference.
This is why in the Qur'an the Lord congratulates those who are weak and
chafe under suffering and inequity. They are called the inheritors and
leaders of the earth. But with what kind of power is the weak going to rule?
Miracle? Arms? Faith? No. The requisite is a conscious faith—that is,
ideology. The more brutal and conquering the force, the more humble and
contemptible it will be in front of ideology. It is something which, in its ordinary and relative extent, can be seen by the present generation. That is, it
can see how faith conquers the great powers of the world and erects a
destiny in front of those powers which have been ruling over the mass fate.
And those masses which were in the grips of weakness, contempt, and
poverty—famous candidates of misery in history—suddenly revolted with a
conscious faith. Faith and ideology are the miracle performers of all centuries; they breathe Messianic spirit in the carrion of a nation and carcass of
a tribe. And just like the trumpet of Israfil, they resurrect the dead and
start an insurrection. Who can do it? A free-thinker—the individual who
has an ideology.

From the dawn of history to the termination of prophethood, movements
have always been the movement of ideologies which, in the name and form
of religion based upon revelation, have guided human societies. The leaders
of these faiths have all been *ummi*; they rose from among the masses,
shepherds, and the deprived workers who were victims of oppressive orders.
None of these prophets were philosophers, artists, scientists, physicists, or
men of letters. Look at Arabia in the time of the prophet. While there were
seven prominent social groups—merchant, poet, linguist, *hakim*, men of
letters, foreign educated, and story-teller—the prophet belonged to none of
them. He could not read or write. Yet the same man suddenly became the
savior of his class and his generation, as well as a messenger for humanity!

Throughout history, *ummis* (the manifestation of ideologies), have been
free-thinkers other than philosophers and scientists. They have risen from
among the masses. Like a spark from a flint, they enlighten thoughts, create
movements and excitement in a dead and listless period. They popularize a
new tradition, change fate, transform historical determinism and push aside
all those who were in charge of their thinking, religion, and destiny. They
take charge of the held and build and create their own fate. These all
emanate from among the masses, while philosophers, artists, and scientists
have always been on the peripheries: syncophants, justifiers, and enter-
tainers of the powers-that-be.

The educated individuals may be good starters but in terms of translating an ideology into reality and pushing it to completion, the masses have always been the practical and responsible elements. This is why in the past era of prophethood the movements of free-thinkers have belonged to simple naive individuals who were from the masses. These individuals, with their miracles of ideology, transformed their own destiny and became 'doers' of their own enlightening, consciousness-producing human responsibility. An ideology which is our human responsibility, and affects us all, as a rule, must be chosen by us. Therefore, our free-thinking generation can neither imitate the western ideology (since an ideology's efficacy lies in its being chosen consciously, it will be like consuming an imported good), nor can it stoop before its own historical, tribal, and obsolete customs. To do so would be like having a customary religion rather than an ideologic faith.

This is why, at this moment, I myself, caught between the western imposition and my historical legacy (traditions), must start to choose. How? Relative to my present world-view, experience, and ideology, and with the aid of the existing elements and principles in the context of my culture, I must find the consciousness-producing ideologic elements, extract them and create a new conscious-producing faith for my enervated period and faithless generation. It is through such principles and search processes that I found Islam. This is not the Islam of a culture which produces a scholar, it is the Islam of ideology which fosters a *mujahid*, neither in the institution of scholars, nor in the tradition of common men, but in the Rabazah* of Abu Zarr.

---

*Desert to which cUthman exited Abu Zarr.

Chapter Twenty-Four

Ayatollah Murtada Mutahhari

Mutahhari is, without a doubt, one of the most significant contemporary Shiᶜi social thinkers. Unlike most modern Shiᶜi political ideologists and activists, Mutahhari was at the same time a renowned and accomplished jurisconsult, theologian, philosopher, and social thinker. His works cover diverse topics from the complexities of Shiᶜi philosophy to the role of Islam in politics to the question of women's rights in the context of Islam. Although he never produced an ideology like Khumayni's, nor did he advocate systematic reform and interpretation as Shariᶜati, his ideas played an important role in the history of modern Shiᶜi thought. As representative of more moderate and traditional response to the problems that had also pulled Khumayni or Shariᶜati into the political limelight, Mutahhari acted as a catalyst for the politicization of the more moderate religious elements. His ideas, meanwhile, remain important contributions to the questions posed to Shiᶜism by modern thought and the socio-political ramifications of change. The excerpts are from IMTC, *pp. 51–67.*

Ayatollah Murtada Mutahhari

All of these movements were carried out under the guidance of the Shi^ci orthodoxy, which had drawn the plan of reform and its mode of implementation. The tobacco movement was initiated by the Iranian clergy and under the guidance of Mirza Hasan Shirazi it was led on to complete success. The Iraqi revolt was led by the clergy of the country with Muhammad Taqi Shirazi at its head. It is very instructive and surprising that a saintly and introspective person like Muhammad Taqi Shirazi should, all of a sudden come off as a fighter as if his whole life had been spent in struggle and in fighting a religious war. The Iranian constitutional movement was initiated at first by Muhammad Kazim Khursani and Shaykh ^cAbdullah Mazandarani at Najaf and later on was joined by two top religious personalities from Tehran namely Sayyid ^cAbdullah Bihbahani and Sayyid Muhammad Tabataba'i.

In the Sunni world the movements like those mentioned above undertaken by the religious reformers and ecclessiastical chiefs did not take place nor did there occur an uprising like that of Isfahan, Tabriz and Mashhad. In the movement of Mashhad, it was Husayn Qumi, the learing Shi^ci clergy who played the main role.

* * *

The question arises why have the Sunni religious leaders been unable to carry on a movement, although they have vigorously talked of reformation and struggle against colonialism and exploitation? Why against this situation, has the Shi^ci orthodoxy initiated and successfully led great revolutions but has seldom cared to think of the previling ills, to opine on the ills, to suggest the remedial measures and to enter into a discussion on the political philosophy of Islam.

This aspect has to be carefully examined in the systems of Shi^ci and Sunni orthodoxy. The Sunni ecclesiastical system is of such fashion that it becomes farcical in the hands of its rulers whom it introduces as the supreme [political authority] to issue commands . . . . We find that the Sunni ecclesiastical institution as a system aligned to the political is not strong enough to rise against its rival and to win over to its side the masses of the people.

But the Shiᶜi ecclesiastical order is an independent institution, drawing strength (from the spiritual point of view) from God alone and (from a social point of view) from the power of the masses. It will be, therefore, noted that the whole institution has, during the long course of its history, emerged as a rival force to the oppressors of their age. It has already been said that in the Islamic countries with the Sunni majority of the population, Sayyid Jamal al-Din al-Afghani approached the masses of the people but in Iran where the majority are the Shiᶜis, he approached the religious leaders. In Sunni countries he wanted the masses to be galvanized into action, but in Shiᶜi countries, he expected the religious leaders (ᶜulama᾿) to initiate the revolution. This is because the Shiᶜi clergy was independent of the institution of the ruling authorities. It is from this phenomena that the Shiᶜi clergy has had the potential of bringing about a revolution whereas the Sunni clergy did not enjoy that strength. The Shiᶜi religious leaders have, in practice, rejected the thesis of Karl Marx that the triangle of religion, government and the capital has been throughout the course of history, interactive and the factors have been in collusion with one another; that they have shaped a class against the masses and that the three factors mentioned above are the result of the self-estrangement of the people.

* * *

Scholars and knowledgeable persons in contemporary history conceded that in the second half of our century in almost all or at least in a large number of Islamic countries Islamic movements have been in ascent openly or secretly. These are practically directed against despotism, capitalist colonialism or materialistic ideologies subscribing to colonialism in its new shape. Experts on political affairs acknowledge that after having passed through a period of mental crisis the Muslims are once again struggling to reestablish their "Islamic identity" against the challenges of capitalist West and the communist East. But in no Islamic country has this type of movement gained as much of depth and extent as in Iran since the year 1960. Nor is there a parallel to the proportions which the Iranian movement has obtained. It, therefore, becomes necessary to analyze this remarkably significant event of history.

* * *

Like all natural occurrences, social and political events also tend to differ from one another in their behaviours. All historical movements cannot be considered identical in their nature. The nature of the Islamic movement is in no case similar to the French revolution or to the great October revolution of Russia.

The current Iranian movement is not restricted to any particular class or trade union. It is not only a labor, an agrarian, a student, an intellectual or a bourgeois movement. Within its scope fall one and all in Iran, the rich and the poor, the man and the woman, the school boy and the scholar, the warehouse man and the factory laborer, the artisan and the peasant, the clergy and the teacher, the literate and the illiterate, one and all. An announcement made by the preceptor of the highest station guiding the movement is received in the length and breadth of the country with equal enthusiasm by all classes of the people... .

This movement is one of the glaring historical proofs which falsifies the concept of materialistic interpretation of history and that of the dialectics of materialism according to which economy is recognized as the cornerstone of social structure and a social movement is considered a reflection of class struggle . . . .

The awakened Islamic conscience of our society has induced it to search for Islamic values. This is the conscience of the cumulative enthusiasms of all classes of people, including perhaps some of the hereby dissident groups, which has galvanized them into one concerted upsurge.

The roots of this movement shall have to be traced in the events that occurred during the last half century in our country and way these events came into conflict with the Islamic spirit of our society.

It is evident that during the last half century, there have been events which adopted a diametrically opposite direction as far as the nobler objectives of Islam were concerned and which aimed at nullifying the aspirations of the well-meaning reformers for the last century. This state of affairs could not continue for long without reaction.

What happened in Iran during the last half century may be summed up as follows:

1. Absolute and barbaric despotism.
2. Denial of freedom of every kind.
3. A new type of colonialism meaning an invisible and dangerous colonialism embracing political, economic and cultural aspects of life.
4. Maintaining distance between religion and politics. Rather, divorcing politics from religion.
5. An attempt at leading Iran back to the age of ignorance of pre-Islamic days. Also the attempt of reviving the pre-Islamic culture of Iran — the Magian culture — as is manifest from the change of the *hijri* era to the Magian era.
6. Effecting a change and corrupting the rich Islamic culture and replacing it with the ambiguous Iranian culture.
7. Gruesome killing of Iranian Muslims, imprisonment and torture of the alleged political prisoners.

8. Ever increasing discrimination and cleavage among the classes of society despite so-called reforms.
9. Domination of non-Muslim elements over the Muslim elements in the government and other institutions.
10. Flagrant violation of Islamic laws either directly or by perpetrating corruption in the cultural and social life of the people.
11. Propaganda against Persian literature (which has always been the protector and upholder of Islamic spirit) under the pretext of purifying the Persian langauge of foreign terminology.
12. Severing relations with Islamic countries and flirting with non-Islamic and obviously with anti-Islamic countries like Israel.

The Shiᶜi authorities have performed various roles in bringing about this pious Islamic revolution. Their efforts have, at last, culminated in success.

Some of the clergy embarked on an open struggle against the regime of the Shah. They gave the cry for revolt and infused the masses with the spirit of an anti-Shah revolt. As a result they had to suffer privations like extirpation, incarceration, torture and martyrdom. Some persisted with the struggle openly as well as secretly mobilizing mass opinion, and at times, they had to seal their lips for the sake of expediency.

There were some of the fighters who apparently desisted from making utterances and did not betray any sign of being the die-hards. Their attitude has been, unfortunately, misunderstood by a number of short-sighted persons as something anti-revolutionary. But the truth is that they were among the most zealous, the most sincere and the most humane of the revolutionaries. Their task was to infiltrate into the various sections of the society; choose the persons with capacity and infuse in them the spirit of revolution. For this purpose, the first thing was to strengthen in them faith and belief; to establish in their minds the fact that their duty was divine and that they had to lay their lives in the path of God. Their role was to expose the fact that the regime of the Shah was an anti-Islamic regime and if allowed to continue as it did, true Islam would appear in the shape of Pahlavi Islam. Hence a struggle against such a regime was the will of God, and one meeting death in the struggle would be a martyr. It hardly needs to be emphasized what singular role those people . . . performed in this great struggle. In the course of their struggle, these persons, like their preceptors, trained and educated another generation, in a wider field of activity. They infiltrated into all such places as were not attended by the religious authorities in person and carried on the propaganda incognito.

One who joins a struggle with the objective of achieving material gains and worldly position without any realization of duty towards God and religion, cannot be supposed to be sincere to the movement. If he is offered material benefits or a worldly position, he will readily accept it and will withdraw from the struggle. He had joined the struggle for this purpose, otherwise he would not. We have seen that some of those materialists ceased to persist with their opposition to the regime of the Shah when they received material benefits and finally succumbed to the position of servitude to the absolutism of the regime.

But he who reckons his participation in the revolutionary struggle as a divine and religious duty is least concerned when, in the course of struggle, his material position and property are lost altogether. He continues with the struggle even when he is conscious of the fact that his life is in peril. He does not, therefore, attach much significance to a life which ultimately must come to an end. But an honorable death, death for the religious cause, would bestow upon him the everlasting life . . . .

* * *

What is the objective pursued by the movement and what does it want? Does it aim at democracy? Does it want to liquidate colonialism from our country? Does it rise to defend what is called in modern terminology as human rights? Does it want to do away with discrimination, inequality? Does it want to uproot oppression? Does it want to undo materialism and so forth and so on.

In view of the nature of the movement and its roots as already brought under consideration and also in view of the statements and announcements given out by the leaders of the movement, what one may gather as an answer to these questions is "Yes" as well as "No."

"Yes" because all the objectives mentioned above form the very crux of it. And "No" because the movement is not limited to only these or any one of these objectives. An Islamic movement cannot, from the point of its objective, remain a restricted affair, because Islam, in its very nature, is "an indivisible whole" and with the realization of any of the objectives set before it, its role does not cease to be.

However, it does not mean that from a tactical point of view, a particular set of objectives does not enjoy priority over another set and that the stages of realization of these objectives are not needed to be taken into consideration. Did not Islam pass through a tactical evolution? Today the movement is passing through the stage of rejection and disregard (of the ruling authority) and of striking hard at despotism and colonialism. Having emerged victorious out of this struggle, it shall address itself to stability and reconstruction and other objectives shall then demand its attention.

. . . Imam Husayn during the times of Muᶜawiyah and in the presence of a distinguished Islamic gathering on the eve of the holy pilgrimage [summed] up the core of the philosophy of reformation in Islam. He has said it in four sentences:

1. "The effaced signs on the path leading to God be reinstated." It refers to the original principles of Islam and return to those very principles. Innovations be done away with and their place be filled by true and original customs. In other words it means reform in the very thought, the very conscience and the very spirit of Islam.
2. Fundamental, actual and far-reaching reforms which would invite the attention of every observer and would be carrying in them seeds of welfare for the people at large, in urban and in rural areas and the society as a whole be brought about. It means the most radical reforms in the living conditions of the masses of the people.
3. God's humanity under victimisation be given security against the oppressor. The tyranny of the oppressor be eliminated. It means reform in the social relations to human beings.
4. God's commands hitherto suspended and the Islamic laws hitherto ignored be revived so as to establish their supremacy in the social life of the people.

No movement can be led successfully without leadership. But who should be the leader or the group of leaders when the movement is an Islamic one in its nature and when its objective is exclusively Islam?

Evidently the leadership should, in the first place, fulfill the general conditions of the task before it. Then the leaders must be deeply Islamic, fully conversant with the ethical, social, political and spiritual philosophy of Islam. They must have the knowledge of Islam's universal vision, its insight about empirical matters like the creation, the origin, the creator of the universe, the need for creation of the universe, etc. They must have the deep knowledge of Islam's views and stipulations on man and his society. It is of great importance that the leaders must have a clear picture of the Islamic ideology of man's relations with his society; his manner and method of framing the social order; his abilities of defending and pursuing certain things and resisting others; his ultimate objectives and the means of attaining those objectives, etc.

It is obvious that only such persons can lead as have been brought up under the pure Islamic culture having perfectly mastered the branches of religious learning and Islamic sciences, the Qur'an, tradition, jurisprudence, etc. It is, therefore, only ecclesiastics who qualify for the leadership of such a movement . . . .

Chapter Twenty-Five

Sayyid Muhammad Baqir Sadr

Sayyid Muhammad Baqir Sadr is one of the most prominent and influential Shi^ci thinkers of modern times. His works cover both aspects of traditional Shi^ci thought and also suggest ways in which Shi^cism could accommodate modernity. In fact, Sadr is best known for his works on Shi^ci modernism. His major work on Islamic economics, Iqtisaduna *(Our Economics), which was discussed earlier in this volume, has inspired many Shi^ci and non-Shi^ci Islamic economists. Following the revolution in Iran, Sadr emerged as an important political force in Iraq, which led to his apprehension and subsequent execution by the Ba^cth government.*

In the following passage, Mahmud Ayoub's translation of Sadr's work on revelation will demonstrate both the complexity of Sadr's works and some of the dynamics of Shi^ci thought in contemporary Middle East. In this work, Sadr's interpretation of revelation and prophethood in Islam find new political meanings, while his methodology and line of reasoning set the stage for the emergence of religious concepts as vehicles to social action. Although politics is not the direct concern of The Revealer, the Messenger and the Message, *Sadr's philosophy indicates the dynamics of interpretative approach to religious doctrines from which much of Shi^ci modernist socio-political thought has emanated. The excerpt is from* RMM, *pp. 47–63, 75–96.*

Sayyid Muhammad Baqir Sadr

It has already been observed that the scientific argument for the existence of the Creator follows the method of inductive demonstration, which is based on the computation of probability. We wish, however, before presenting this argument, to explain this method and then to evaluate it in order to determine the extent to which it can be relied upon in the discovery of the truth of things. The inductive method based on the computation of probability has an extremely complex and highly precise structure. Therefore, a complete and precise evaluation of this method can be achieved only through a detailed and thorough analysis of the logical foundations of induction (*al-usus al-mantiqiyyah li'l-istiqra'*) as well as the theory of probability. Our purpose here is, however, to avoid difficult and complicated constructions and analyses not readily accessible to the average reader. We shall therefore do two things; first, delimit the demonstrative method we shall follow and explain its steps briefly and succinctly. We shall, secondly, evaluate this method and determine its validity. We shall do this not through a logical analysis of the method and the discovery of its logical and mathematical bases, but through practical applications acceptable to any rational human being.

It must be stated at this point that the method we use in demonstrating the existence of the wise Creator is the same method we confidently employ in our daily life as well as in our scientific experiments. What follows will provide sufficient evidence of the fact that the method of demonstration of the existence of a wise Creator is the same method we use to prove the truths of everyday reality as well as scientific truths. Since, therefore, we trust this method with regard to the reality of everyday life, we must trust it also with regard to the proof of the wise Creator, who is the source of all truth.

You receive a letter in the mail, and you conclude from merely reading it that it is from your brother. Similarly, when one sees that a certain physician has succeeded in curing many illnesses, one trusts this physician, and considers him to be a skillful one. Likewise, if after taking penicillin ten times, one found each time his body reacted to it in the same negative manner, one would conclude that he had an allergy to penicillin. In all these cases, the method used is the inductive method based on the computation of probability. Similarly, with regard to natural science, when a certain scientist had observed some particular characteristics of the solar system in the course of his research, he was able to conclude that these separate bodies had all been a part of the sun from which they had later separated. When this same scientist monitored the paths of planetary movements, he was able to deduce the existence of the planet Neptune, even before he was able to observe the planet with his sense of vision. Science, in light of special phenomena, was also able to postulate the existence of electrons before the discovery of the cloud-chamber. Scientists, in all these cases, have used the inductive method of proof, based on the computation of probability. We shall employ the same method in our argument for the existence of the wise Creator.

* * *

The method of inductive argument based on the computation of probability may be summarized clearly and simply in the following five steps:

1. We encounter on the level of sense perception and experimentation numerous phenomena.

2. After observing and collecting our data, we go on to interpret them. What is required in this stage is to find a suitable hypothesis on the basis of which we can interpret and justify these phenomena. By its being suitable for the interpretation of these phenomena, we mean that if it is actually established it must be inherent in, or at least in consonance with, all these phenomena which themselves actually exist.

3. We notice that the hypothesis, if it were not suitable and actually established, would indicate that the possibility of the existence of the phenomena is very scant. In other words, to suppose the incorrectness of the hypothesis would mean that the degree of probability of the existence of the phenomena, compared with the probability of their non-existence, or the non-existence of at least one of them, is very small: one in a hundred or one in a thousand, and so forth.

4. We therefore conclude that the hypothesis must be true, a fact which we infer from our sense experience of the phenomena on which it is based, as we have seen in step one.

5. The degree of verifiability by the phenomena of the hypothesis offered in the second step is directly related to the probability of the existence of these phenomena and inversely related to the probability of their non-existence. (We mean by the probability of their non-existence either their non-existence altogether or that of at least one of them.) If we assume the incorrectness of the hypothesis, even then the smaller this ration, the greater would be the degree of verifiability, so that in many ordinary cases it could attain a degree of absolute certainty. (This according to the second stage of proof by induction.)

There are, in reality, precise measures or regulations for evaluating degrees of probability based on the theory of probability. In ordinary everyday situations, people apply these measures unconsciously in ways that are very close to their correct application. For this reason, we shall limit ourselves to the evaluation of this natural application without entering into the logical and mathematical principles of its evaluation. These are, then, the steps which we usually follow in any inductive argument based on the computation of probability, whether in our every day life, on the level of scientific investigation, or in proof of the existence of the wise Creator, praised and exalted be He.

*   *   *

We shall, as we have already promised, evaluate this method in the light of its practical application with illustrations from ordinary everyday life. We have already observed that when you receive a letter in the mail, and upon reading it conclude that it is from your brother and not from another person who happens to like you and wishes to correspond with you, you are employing the method of inductive proof based on the computation of probabilities.

1.   You observe many indications such as the letter bears a name which agrees completely with that of your brother. The handwriting is that of your brother and the style of writing and format are those usually employed by your brother. In addition, even the mistakes and items of information are those usually made, or supplied by your brother. All this you infer from the habits and ways of thinking of your brother. The letter would, moreover, express opinions and ask for things which you know to expect from your brother.

2. In the second step you ask, "Did my brother actually send this letter to me, or is it from another person with the same name?" Here you would find in the indications previously observed sufficient bases for a good hypothesis for interpreting and justifying these data as evidence of the fact that the letter was in reality from your brother. Conversely, if you were led to conclude that the letter was from your brother, then all the data observed in the first step would have to be provided.

3. In the third step you would further ask the following question: "If this letter was not from my brother, but from another person, then what is the degree of probability of all these indications and characteristics being simultaneously present for me to observe in the first step?" Such a possibility requires a large number of assumptions. This is because for us to accept all these indications and characteristics we must first assume that another person bears the same name as the brother. He must further resemble him in

all the characteristics above discussed. The possibility for such a large number of coincidences to happen simultaneously is slight indeed. Moreover, as the number of the coincidences that must be assumed increases, the probability of their simultaneous occurrence is conversely diminished.

The logical principles of induction teach us the way to measure probability and explain how it diminishes. They further explain how probability decreases in proportion to the assumption it requires. We need not enter into the deatils of all this because it is a complex subject, too difficult for the average reader to comprehend. Fortunately, however, perceiving low probability does not depend on the understanding of these details, as for example, the falling of a man from a high place to the ground does not depend on his understanding of the force of gravity or his knowledge of the scientific principles of gravity. Thus the recipient of the letter requires nothing to infer that the existence of a person resembling his brother in all the coincidences and characteristics above discussed, is very improbable.

4. In the fourth step, you would reason as follows. Since the congruence of all these occurrences is very improbable, if you were to suppose that the letter was not from your brother, there would then be a far greater likelihood that the letter was from your brother because these coincidences do actually exist.

5. In the fifth step, you would connect the conclusion of the fourth step, i.e., the possibility that the letter was from your brother, with the small degree of probability of the existence of all the characteristics of the letter without it being from your brother. The connection between these two steps means that the possibility of the letter being from your brother negates the probability of its being from someone else, in inverse proportion. Thus the smaller the degree of probability, the greater would be the opposite likelihood and the more persuasive. If, moreover, there was no opposing evidence, then the five steps just presented provide convincing evidence of the validity of the method on the level of everyday life.

Let us now take another example, this time from the realm of scientific knowledge, where the method may be employed to demonstrate a scientific theory. Let us consider the theory concerning the development of the planets and their separation from the sun. The nine planets were originally part of the sun from which they separated as burning pieces millions of years ago. Scientists generally agree with regard to the principle of the theory, but differ concerning the cause of the separation of these pieces from the sun. Demonstration of the principle on which they agree would follow these steps.

i. Scientists have observed a number of phenomena which they perceived by means of the senses and experimentation. These are:

a. The rotation of the earth around the sun is in harmony with the rotation of the sun around its axis, each complete rotation being from west to east.

b. The rotation of the earth around its axis is concurrent with the rotation of the sun around its axis, that is, from west to east.

c. The earth rotates around the sun in an orbit parallel to the equatorial line of the sun, so that the sun would resemble a pole and the earth a point rotating around it, like a millstone.

d. The elements of which the earth is made are for the most part found in the sun as well.

e. There is a close similarity between the elements of the earth and those of the sun in their chemical composition, in both hydrogen predominates.

f. The speed of the rotation of the earth around the sun and around its own axis is in harmony with that of the rotation of the sun around its axis.

g. There is a measure of agreement between the age of the earth and the age of the sun, according to the calculations of scientists.

h. The inside of the earth is hot, which proves that the earth in its early stages was very hot.

ii. These were some of the phenomena which scientists observed through sense experience and experimentation in the first step. In the second, they decided that there is a hypothesis by which all these phenomena could be explained. This means that if the hypothesis were to be actually true, then it would inherently belong to these phenomena and justify them. The hypothesis holds that the earth was part of the sun from which it separated, for whatever reasons. With this assumption, we can explain the foregoing phenomena.

The first is the fact that the harmony of the rotation of the earth around the sun and that of the sun around its own axis is due to the motion of both being from west to east. The reason for this harmony becomes clear on the basis of the above hypothesis, which further holds that is part of any body in motion is separated from it while remaining drawn towards it by a thread or some other means, that separated part will always move in the same original orbit in accordance with the law of continuity. As for the second phenomenon, which is the harmony of the rotation of the earth around its axis with the rotation of the sun around its axis, this also can be sufficiently explained by the same hypothesis and according to the same law. The same holds for the third phenomenon as well. As for the fourth and fifth phenomena, which demonstrate a close similarity of composition and proportion of the elements which make up the earth and the sun, they become self evident on the basis of the fact that the earth was part of the sun. The elements of a part must be those of the whole. The sixth phenomenon, namely, the harmony between the speed of the earth's rotation around the sun and around its axis and that of the sun around its axis becomes clear because we know that both motions of the earth originated from the motion of the sun. This we know on the basis of our earlier hypothesis, which presupposes the separation of the earth from the sun. This not only explains the observed harmony, but also delineates its cause. On the basis of the same hypothesis, we can explain the similarity in age of the two bodies, which is our seventh phenomenon. Likewise, the eighth, which is the intense heat of the earth in its early stages, can be explained on the basis of the same hypothesis.

iii. If we were to suppose that the theory of the separation of the earth from the sun is not true, it would be highly unlikely for all these phenomena to exist together and be closely connected. In this case, they would simply be a collection of coincidences without any intelligible connection among them. Therefore, the probability of their existence, if we suppose the falsity of our theory, would be very small indeed. This is because this supposition would require a large number of hypotheses for the explanation of these phenomena.

With regard to the harmony between the motion of the earth around the sun and the sun around its own axis, from west to east, we would have to assume that the earth was a body far away from the sun, created independently or part of another sun from which it separated subsequently drawing near to our sun. We would also have to suppose that this earth, travelling freely in space, upon entering its orbit around the sun entered at a point west of the sun. For this reason, it continues to rotate from west to east, that is, in the direction of the sun's own rotation around its axis. If it had instead entered at a point east of the sun, it would have moved from east to west.

As for the harmony between the rotation of the earth around its axis and the rotation of the sun around its axis from west to east, we would have to suppose that the other sun from which the earth separated was itself rotating from west to east. As for the rotation of the earth around the sun, in an orbit parallel to the equatorial line of the sun, we would likewise have to suppose that the other sun from which the earth separated was at that moment situated in the same plane as the equatorial line of our sun. As for the similarity of the elements of the earth and the sun and their composition, we would have to suppose that the other sun from which the earth separated contained the same elements and in similar proportions. As for the speed of the rotation of the earth around the sun and around its own axis, being harmonious with the speed of the sun's rotation around its axis, we would have to suppose that the other sun from which the earth separated exploded in a way which gave the moving earth a speed similar to that of our sun. As for the age of the sun and the earth and the heat of the earth in the early stages of its development, we would have to suppose that the earth separated from another sun having the same age as our sun and that it separated in a manner which led to its intense heat. Thus we see that the possibility of the simultaneous existence of all these phenomena on the principle of the invalidity of the theory of the separation of the earth from our sun, requires a large number of coincidences, the probability of whose simultaneous occurrence is very small. In contrast, the separation theory alone is sufficient for explaining these phenomena and connecting them together.

iv. In the fourth step we conclude that since the coincidence of all these phenomena, which we observe in the earth, is improbable except to a very small degree, on the assumption that the earth was not separated from our sun, it must be highly probable (since all these phenomena do indeed exist) that the earth did indeed separate from our sun.

v. In the fifth and last step, we connect the possibility of the separation hypothesis, as inferred in the fourth step, with the low probability of the coincidence of the phenomena in the earth, [without having separated from] the sun, as we decided in the third step. The connection between these two steps would show a strong improbability for the third step and, conversely, a high probability for the fourth. We are able by means of this method to demonstrate the separation of the earth from the sun, by which means scientists achieve absolute conviction of this fact.

*   *   *

Before embarking on the discussion of a philosophical argument for the existence of the Creator, praised and exalted be He, we must say a word about the philosophical argument and its parts and the difference between it and the scientific argument. Argument itself may be considered under three categories: the mathematical, the scientific and the philosophical. The mathematical argument is employed in the area of mathematical sciences and formal logic (*al-mantiq al-suri al-shakli*). This argument rests on one fundamental principle, the principle of non-contradiction, which asserts that A is A and will always remain A. Any argument based exclusively on this principle and its consequences, we call the mathematical argument. Its validity is admitted by everyone.

The scientific argument is usually employed in the domain of the natural sciences. It rests on data capable of proof either through sense experience or scientific induction, in addition to mathematical proof.

The philosophical argument depends for its establishment on objective reality in the external world, on intellectual knowledge which needs no empirical verification or sense experience. It presupposes, however, mathematical proof. This does not necessarily mean that the philosophical argument does not actually rely on information obtained through sense perception or the inductive method. It rather means that it does not regard these as sufficient evidence, and therefore relies on the intellectual information within the context of the demonstrative method applied to prove a case which had been established.

The philosophical argument, therefore, differs from the scientific argument in the way in which it deals with intellectual information which remains outside the scope of the mathematical argument. On the basis of our discussion so far of the notion of the philosophical argument, we must face the following question: Is it possible to rely simply on intellectual information or ideas which the mind intuits without recourse to sense perception, experimentation or scientific induction? The answer to this question must be in the affirmative. These are the data of our understanding, the validity of which is accepted by all, such as the principle of non-contradiction, on which are based all pure mathematical sciences. It is a principle whose validity we establish on the basis of intellectual reasoning, and not on the basis of supporting evidence and experiments within the scope of the inductive method. The proof of this is that the degree of our trust in this principle is not affected by the number of experiments and verifications which do not agree with it. Let us take a concrete example: two plus two equals four. Our belief in the validity of this simple mathematical equation is too firm to need further verification. We would not even be ready to listen to any argument in proof of the opposite fact, nor would we believe anyone telling us two plus two in one unique case equals five or three. This means that our belief in this truth has no connection with sense perception or experimentation, for in that case it would be affected by them positively and negatively.

If we actually admit the truth of this principle, in spite of its independence from sense perception and experimentation, it is natural for us to admit that it is sometimes possible for us to trust the validity of our intellectual perceptions, on which depends the philosophical argument. In other words, the rejection of the philosophical argument simply because it is based on intellectual perceptions which do not rest on empirical or inductive knowledge, must also mean the rejection of the mathematical argument, because it rests on the principle of non-contradiction, in which our belief depends neither on experimentation nor on induction.

This argument depends on the following three principles. The first is the axiom which asserts that every effect has a cause from which it derives its existence. This is a truth which man perceives intuitively and which scientific induction confirms. The second is the principle which asserts that whatever differing degrees of possibility, fullness and perfection exist, it is impossible for the less possible, less complete or less perfect to be the cause of that which is higher than itself. Temperature, knowledge and light are of varying degrees of intensity and reflection. It is impossible for a higher degree of temperature to emanate from one lower than itself. It is likewise impossible for a person to obtain a good knowledge of the English language from one who himself has little or no knowledge of it. Nor is it possible for a feeble source of light to be the cause of a source greater than itself. This is because every higher degree constitutes a qualitative and quantitative increase over the one below it. This quantitative increase cannot be bestowed by one not in possession of it. When you wish to finance a project from your own capital, you cannot put into this project an amount greater than that you already have.

The third principle is the assertion that matter, in its continuous evolution, assumes various levels of change and intensity. Thus even a small particle which has no life and is not a vital component, constitutes an aspect of being of matter. Protoplasm, which is the essential component of life in plants and animals, constitutes a higher form of existence of matter. The amoeba, which is a microscopic unicellular animal, constitutes a still higher step in the evolution of matter. Man, as a living, feeling and thinking being, must be considered to be the highest form of being in this universe.

These different forms of being raise the following question: Is the difference among them simply a quantitative one in the number of particles and elements and the mechanical relation among these, or is it a qualitative and quantitative difference, expressing a variety of degrees of being and stages of evolution and perfection? In other words, is the difference between man and the dust of which he was made simply one of number, or is it a difference between two levels of being and two stages of evolution and perfection, just like the difference between a feeble and a brilliant source of light? Ever since man put this question to himself, he has believed, through his *a priori* intuition (*fitrah*), that these forms constitute levels of being and different stages of perfection attained by life, wherein the human form is the highest manifestation of being in matter. This high level, moreover, is not in itself the limit of evolution. Rather, as life attains new and higher forms, it manifests higher levels of being. Hence the life of a living, feeling and thinking being constitutes a higher and fuller degree of being than the life of plants, and so on.

Materialistic philosophy, however, for over a century, has rejected this idea and adopted instead a mechanical view of the universe. According to this view, the outside world is made up of small molecules moved by simple homogeneous electro-magnetic forces attracting and repelling them within the framework of general laws. That is to say, the function of this force is limited to influencing the interrelated motion of these molecules from one locus to another. Through this motion of attraction and repulsion, these molecules unite and separate to produce different material forms. On this basis, mechanical materialism limited evolution to the motion of material particles from one locus to another in space. It explained the variety of material forms by the motion of coalescence, separation and distribution of material particles without any novelty occurring in this process. Matter, according to this view, neither grows nor attains a higher level of being through its evolution; it only coalesces and scatters in various ways like a piece of dough which you may manipulate into various states, although remaining a piece of dough in your hand without any essential change.

This hypothesis was inspired by the science of mechanics, which was the first branch of science to be allowed to develop freely its methods of investigation. The discovery by this science of the laws of mechanical motion and the explanations it offered of familiar motions of ordinary bodies, encouraged the development of this hypothesis, which took into account the motion of stars in space. The constant growth of knowledge and the introduction of scientific methods of investigation into many fields of study, demonstrated the invalidity of this hypothesis and its inability to explain all motions in space mechanically. It also demonstrated its inadequacy in subsuming all material forms under the mechanical motion of bodies and particles. Science thus confirmed what man had perceived in his pure intuitive state (*fitrah*), namely that the diversity of material forms is not simply the result of the motion of material bodies from one place to another. Rather, it is the result of a variety of quantitative and qualitative explanatory processes. It has also been proven through scientific experiments that no numerical structure of molecules would constitute life, feeling and thought. This leads us to suppositions which are completely different from those advanced by mechanical materialsm, because we discern in life, feeling and thought an actual process of growth of matter and a characteristic evolution in the degrees of its existence. This is true regardless of whether the content of this characteristic evolution is itself material or nonmaterial.

To recapitulate, these are the three problems with which we have been concerned:

1. Every effect has a cause.
2. The lower cannot be the cause of something higher than itself, with regard to degrees of being.
3. The diversity of degrees of being in this universe and the variety in its form are qualitative.

In light of these three issues, we can clearly discern an actual development in quantitatively evolved forms, which means the manifestation of the fullness of being in matter and a quantitative increase in it.

We should therefore ask, "Where did this increase come from, and how did this new multiplicity appear, since every effect must have a cause?" There are two answers to this question. The first is that it originated in matter itself. Matter which has no life, feeling or thought created through its process of evolution life, feeling and thought. This is to say a lower form of matter was itself the cause of a higher form without itself possessing the properties of being enabling it to perform such a function. This answer, however, contradicts our second principle, which asserts that a lower form cannot be the cause of another greater than it and richer in being. Thus, the idea that dead matter, devoid of the pulsation of life can grant itself or another matter life, feeling and thought, is like the idea of someone who has no knowledge of the English language, nonetheless attempting to teach it to others; or that of a dim light emanating a light greater than it in brilliance, such as the light of the sun; or that of a poor man with no capital, attempting to finance big projects.

The second answer to this question is that this additional property, which matter manifests through its evolution, must have originated from a source which is in full possession of it. This source is God, the Lord of the worlds, praised and exalted be He. The growth of matter, therefore is no more than the creative process of growth and development which God manifests in His wisdom, ordinance and lordship over all things.

> *We have created man from a piece of clay. Then We made him into a sperm in a secure receptacle. Then We made the sperm a blood-clot; thereafter, We made the blood-clot into a lump of flesh; then We made the piece of flesh into bones; then We clothed the bones with flesh; thereafter We brought him into being as another creature; blessed therefore is God, the best of creators.* (Qur'an XXIII:12–14)

This is the only answer that would harmonize with the three principles presented above. It alone can offer a reasonable explanation of the process of growth and completeness of the forms of being on the stage of this vast universe. To this argument, the noble Qur'an points in a large number of its verses, with which it addresses the uncorrupted, original intuition (*fitrah*) of man and his untainted reason.

> *Have you then considered the sperm that you sow? Do you create it or are rather We the Creator?* (Qur'an LVI:58–59)

> *Have you then considered that which you sow? Do you sow it or are rather We the Sower?* (Qur'an LVI:63–64)

Have you then considered the fire which you kindle? Did you create its tree or are rather We the Creator? (Qur'an LVI:71–72)

Among His signs is that He created you from dust, then behold, you are humans, scattering yourselves about. (Qur'an XXX:30)

We shall now indicate the attitude of materialism toward this argument. Materialism, as a mechanical philosophy, is not obliged to consider this argument. This is because, as we have already observed, it explains life, feeling and thought as forms of the coalescence and separation of particles and molecules. This operation results in no novelty as such, except that of the motion of particles in accordance with a mechanical law. Neo-materialism, however, because it admits the principle of quantitative and qualitative evolution of matter through these forms, encounters some difficulty from this argument. It has chosen a method for the explanation of this qualitative evolution which can harmonize with the second problem already discussed and its own desire to regard matter as itself sufficient for the explanation of its own evolutionary stages. This method holds matter to be the source of fulfillment, and to thus provide the necessary properties for the process of its own qualitative evolution. This it does, not in the same way in which a poor man would attempt to finance large projects, but because all the forms and properties of this evolution are latent in matter from the very beginning. Thus the chicken is present in the egg, gas in water and so forth.

The question of how matter could at one and the same time be egg and chicken, or water and gas, dialectical materialism answered, by asserting that although this is a contradiction, contradiction is the general law of nature. Everything innately contains its opposite with which it is in continuous struggle, though the struggle of two opposites, a third inner contradiction arises and grows until it becomes the synthesis of the two opposites. Thus, it causes change in matter, such as an egg exploding suddenly and a chicken bursting out from it. Through this process, matter achieves its perfection continuously, in that the resulting synthesis constitutes the future, or next step forward.

In light of all this, we notice the following. What neo-materialism means precisely by its assertion that a thing contains its opposite must be one of the following:

1. It may mean that the egg and the chicken are two opposites or antagonistic forms, and that the egg makes the chicken and bestows on it the qualities of life, that is to say, a dead thing can give birth to a living being and make life. This is exactly like a poor man attempting to finance large projects; it contradicts the *a priori* principle just discussed.

2. Does neo-materialism mean, on the other hand, that the egg does not make the chicken, but rather brings it forth, since it was already latent in the egg? Thus an egg, while being an egg, was at the same time a chicken, just like a picture which looks different from different angles. It is obvious that if the egg is at one and the same time a chicken, there is no process of development or fulfillment in the egg becoming a chicken. This is because whatever comes into being through this process, was already in existence. It is like a man taking out of his pocket money which, while in his hand, was in his pocket.

For any process of growth to take place, that is, for anything new to actually occur through the process of an egg becoming a chicken, we are obliged to suppose that the egg was not previously a chicken but a chicken in the making, or something capable of becoming a chicken. In this way an egg becomes different from a stone, which can never become a chicken, as an egg can within specific conditions and circumstances. The mere potentiality of a thing does not necessarily mean its actualisation. Hence, if an egg is actualised into a chicken, the mere possibility of this is not enough to explain the actual event.

If the various forms which matter takes were to be the result of its internal opposites, then the variety of forms must be explained by the variety of these inner opposites or contradictions. The egg, for example, has its own contradictions, which are different from those of water. For this reason, its contradictions result in the chicken while those of water result in gas. This proposition becomes obvious when we consider the primary stages in the process of differentiation among material forms at the level of particles, which constitute the basic units of the material universe, such as protons, electrons, neutrons, anti-protons, anti-electrons (positrons) and photons. Did every particle take a special form on the basis of its inner contradictions so that a proton was concealed in its own material particle and subsequently came forth as a result of motion and struggle as in the case of the egg and the chicken? If we suppose this then how can we account for the variety of forms which these particles have taken, since this presupposes, according to the logic of inner contradiction, that these particles must themselves be different and valid in their inner contradictions. That is to say, they must be different with regard to their inner characteristics.

We know that modern science tends to the view of the essential unity of matter, and that the inner content of matter is one. Moreover, the different forms which matter assumes are not substitutes for a single and constant content. Otherwise, it would have been possible for a proton to become a neutron and vice versa; that is, it would have been possible for the molecule to change its form as well as the atom and particle, in spite of the unity and constancy of the content. This would mean that the content is one, although forms vary. If so, how can we suppose that all these different forms result from innter contradictions.

The example of the egg and the chicken is itself useful in explaining this position. In order for forms to assume their characteristic variety in different eggs through their inner contradictions, it is necessary that eggs be different in their inner structure. The egg of a hen and that of another bird produce two different birds. If, on the other hand, the two eggs were those of a hen, then we could not suppose that their inner contradiction would produce two different forms. Thus we see that the explanation of material forms offered by neo-materialism, on the basis of inner contradiction on the one hand, and the trend of modern science with its insistence on the unity of matter on the other, have developed along two completely divergent lines.

The third alternative is the view that holds that the egg consists of two independent opposites, each possessing its special mode of existence; the one being the portion of the egg concerned with fertilization, the other the rest of the egg's content. These two opposites engage in a continuous struggle until the fertilized portion prevails and the egg becomes a chicken. This kind of struggle is familiar in the life of human beings and has been for long recognized both in their daily lives and in their intellectual life. Why, it must be objected, must we consider the interaction between the fertilized portion and the rest of the egg the struggle of opposites? Why should we consider the interaction between the dust particles, its soil and the air, or the interaction between the embryo in the mother's womb and the nutritive materials it obtains from the mother's body a struggle between opposites? This in fact is no more than a designation, no better than saying that one form is integrated into, or unified with another form. Even if we grant that this interaction must be called a struggle, the problem remains unsolved as long as we admit that this interaction leads to a new third form which is a numerical addition to the two opposites. The question remains, where did this additional form come from? Did it come from the two struggling opposites, even though they both lacked it? It must be remembered that a thing cannot give something else which it does not possess, as we have argued in the second of our three principles just presented.

We are not aware of any instance in nature wherein the struggle between two opposites is the real cause of growth. How could a being participate in the growth of its own opposite through a struggle against it when struggle means a degree of resistance and rejection. Resistance, as we know, diminishes the energy of growth in the thing resisted instead of helping it to achieve it. We know that a swimmer, when he encounters high waves, finds his movements hampered to a high degree rather than enhanced. If, therefore, the struggle between opposites, however considered, were to be the cause of the growth and evolution of the egg into a chicken, where is the growth, caused by struggle of opposites, of water into gas and its return into water?

Nature reveals that when opposites coincide or unite, the result is not growth, but the destruction of both opposites. Thus the positive proton, which constitutes the cornerstone of the atom, and which carries a charge of positive energy, has as its counterpart a negative proton. Similarly, the negative electron which moves in the orbit of an atom has its opposite counterpart. When these two opposites meet, a process of atomic destruction takes place which causes the virtual disappearance of matter, as the resulting energy is released and scattered in space.

We conclude from all this that the motion of matter without provision from and direction by an external source could not cause real growth or evolution to a higher and more specialized stage. It is therefore necessary in order for matter to grow and rise into higher planes of existence, such as life, feeling and thought, that there be a Lord who Himself enjoys these characteristics and is able to bestow them on matter; the role of matter in this process of growth is no more than that of suitability, readiness and potentiality. It is like the role of a good child who is ready to receive the knowledge imparted to him by his educator; blessed is God, Lord of the worlds.

Chapter Twenty-Six

Imam Musa Sadr

Imam Musa Sadr is a towering figure in modern Shiᶜi political thought and praxis. Born to a luminary family of mujtahids *who have left a mark upon the Shiᶜi literati of Jabal ᶜAmil, the* madrasahs *of Najaf, and the* hawzih-i ᶜilmiyyah *of Qum since the sixteenth century, Imam Musa acquired both a secular education at the School of Law of Tehran University and a traditional religious education under the aegis of Ayatollohs Muhsin al-Hakim and Abu'l-Qasim Khu'i in Najaf.*

In 1959, Imam Musa settled in the town of Tyre in southern Lebanon as the emissary of Ayatollahs al-Hakim and Burujirdi, and was the foremost ᶜalim of the Shiᶜi community of Lebanon. Over the span of the next two decades, Imam Musa worked diligently to wrest social justice and political rights for the Shiᶜis of Lebanon from the ruling regime. Moreover, Imam Musa's lectures and writings on Shiᶜism effectively changed the psychology of the Shiᶜi masses of Lebanon. The upwardly mobil urban-dwelling and the younger left-leaning Shiᶜis found new hope for change, social justice, and self-respect in Imam Musa's call. The masses, meanwhile, saw in him a savior and expected a bright future from the promise of his message.

Imam Musa's thought can best be categorized under the rubric "Shiᶜi modernism." Yet, the ideas of the Iranian-born Lebanese leader differed significantly from those of his contemporaries. Imam Musa's modernist predilections avoided the Marxist trappings of Shariᶜati's ideas, the political drive for clerical rule that typifies Khumayni's works, and the ideological orientation of the writings of his cousin, Sayyid Muhammad Baqir Sadr of Iraq. Imam Musa sought, above all, to galvanize a forgotten community, vest it with self-respect, and help it achieve its rightful place in the political life of Lebanon. In this regard, he accentuated the heritage of the Shiᶜis but refrained from drowning all aspects of the temporal existence of that community in an ideological world view.

Imam Musa Sadr disappeared in Libya in 1978. His fate is still not determined. In the following section, Fouad Ajami elaborates upon Imam Musa's treatment of the salient themes of Shiᶜi history and ethos. The excerpt is from VIMSSL, *123–58.*

Fouad Ajami

Musa al-Sadr defined his task and agenda in an extremely ambitious way. A clue to what he expected of — and claimed for — himself is supplied by something he wrote about what an Imam had to be ready for. "The responsibility of an Imam of the Community (*imam al-jamaᶜah*), knew no limits," he wrote. "An Imam had to protect the interests of his flock; he had to be generous; he had to serve his community with advice and persistence; he had to be willing to undergo martyrdom on their behalf. No leader can claim Islam who ignores the daily affairs of the Community." The term he chose, *imam al-jamaᶜah*, had a distinctly modern flavor; he was not using the title of Imam in its strict reference to the twelve Imams. He was endorsing the activist interpretation that a mujtahid could go beyond religious scholarship, could engage in worldly and political affairs, and could embody Shiᶜi Islam's expectation that a religious leader had political obligations and prerogatives as well. He made it clear from the outset that his was a political quest. The distinction between *din* (religion) and *dunya* (worldly affairs) would be obliterated in his pursuits. It was not religious ritual that men needed and that this cleric supplied over the course of the next seven years. His increasingly populist themes were elaborated against a background of mounting disorder in the country. The cleric's principal constituency, the Shiᶜi of the south, was caught in a crossfire between Palestinian guerrillas using the south as a sanctuary and Israeli reprisals. The cycle of raids and reprisals hurled waves of refugees from southern villages into the city.

Musa al-Sadr's emergence on the national scene began with a general strike that he declared on May 26, 1970, a day of "solidarity with the South." This was Lebanon's first general strike in two decades. And it was Musa al-Sadr's first public act beyond the small circle of patricians and civil servants, an appeal to the country's better self, and a warning of things to come. He issued a manifesto to the country. It had the themes that were to become the standard ones of his appeals: It had his political language and symbolism:

> My sons the students, my brothers the workers, the intelligentsia.
> To the men of living sensibility and conscience, to men of the professions, to the sons of the threatened South;

> To the Muslims who cannot accept as one of them he who does not care for the problems of others; To the Christians who bear the cross of the poor:
>
> For over a year and a half, in hundreds of meetings, studies, declarations, official meetings, in countless lectures and statements, we have been asking, in the name of the Higher Shiᶜi Council, in the name of the violated rights of the South, for justice for the South, for attention to its problems, for serious effort to provide for its fortification.
>
> Then the tragedy in the South began to unfold in a surprising kind of vacuum, under the eyes of everyone.
>
> What do the ruling authorities expect? Do they want the people in the South to suffer in silence, to bear tragedies, death, and destruction in silence?
>
> The people of the South do not want or expect charities and contributions and tents and medicine and canned food that would make them feel that they are strangers without dignity.

The state, he said, had to care for the south, and for its refugees. Otherwise, the refugees would occupy the "villas and the palaces" in Beirut. He called for "calm and discipline." A strike, he said, was the "lowest common denominator, an expression of our rage and our concern. . . . Be with what is right... ."

On the day of the strike, Musa al-Sadr made an appearance before more than a thousand students of the American University of Beirut. He went to the campus of the university at the invitation of its students. In a country which then exalted things modern and Western, the campus of the AUB [American University of Beirut] in the Western enclave of Beirut had the prestige and the aura of the distant American society that had built and sustained the university. Established in the 1860s, the American University of Beirut had trained generations of Lebanese and Arabs, given its graduates its discipline and skills — and authority. Its students — at first predominantly Christian, then more affluent (Sunni) Muslims, and Palestinians anxious for educational skills to compensate for their territorial dispossession in 1948 — were sure of their own distinction, sure that they were light years ahead of the traditional Arab order around them. Men not quite "in" approached the campus of the university with awe. This was not a place where turbaned Shiᶜi *mullas* had ventured before.

In 1970, the dominant political culture at the University was a mix of radical Palestinian politics and Marxism, or what passed for it in Lebanon. Of a student population of four thousand, there were two hundred Shiᶜi students. They could not have been particularly important in its politics. To the extent that a few of them concerned themselves with political causes, they must have been avid supporters of the Palestinian movement, young men eager to belong to a wider Arab cause.

The Shi͑i cleric gave them a memorable performance on that day. He spoke in the university chapel; in deference to him and to the occasion, hundreds of emancipated young women covered their hair with scarves. He must have known that he was setting a precedent, that clerics of his faith had never had the daring and the opportunity to reach an audience of this kind. He gave what was to become his usual brief on behalf of the neglected south. The men in power, he said, did not care what befell the south. He talked of villages without schools, of hospitals that were promised but never materialized, of idle talk about irrigation schemes. All these, he said, were "lies," premised on the belief that men were obedient "mules." He himself, he said, had given "sixty lectures" about the south, "ten manifestoes, four press conferences." But no one in power had cared to listen.

What of the militias now beginning to appear in Lebanon, Sayyid Musa was asked, and what of the armed Palestinian presence? He knew the appeal of the Palestinian cause, he knew his audience too and he fudged his answer. It was imperative, he said, for the Palestinians to bear arms and to train. But such things should be done in coordination with the Lebanese state lest chaos spread. He split hairs: Israel, he said, had no right to retaliate against the villages of southern Lebanon because Palestinian incursions into Israel are not launched from villages. At any rate, he said, Lebanon could not be Israel's policeman. Since Israel itself was unable to prevent Palestinian attacks, it surely could not expect the Lebanese government to be able to do so. As for the armed militias of political parties in Lebanon — his answer was that he was not an "expert in political matters." The burden of defending the country, he thought, rested with the state. The aim of his stroke, he said, was to awaken and educate the state.

The call for a strike, according to a diplomatic report, was "heeded throughout the country." The ineffective Lebanese government chose to view the strike in enlightened terms. Charles Helou, the weak president of the republic, saw the strike as a way of "preempting the Palestinians and the left, of preventing them from exploiting the frustration and bitterness of the predominantly Shi͑i Southerners." The government gave what help it could afford to give. It authorized the allocation of nearly ten million dollars for the south; it established a "Council for the South"; it made more of its promises and said it would search for more funds.

An American diplomatic report offers a fairly accurate summation of what was achieved in that strike — and of its limits: "Danger persists that he [Musa al-Sadr] may unwittingly be creating a situation which ultimately he may not be able to control. . . . It is difficult to see where the Government is going to raise the money, and beyond that how it could even begin to meet the Southerners' demand for protection."

The cleric, though, had found his voice. The learned lectures of the 1960s in which he quoted Orientalists and displayed his own erudition were now decidedly discarded in favor of a more passionate discourse. In part, this was because his relation to the Arabic language had changed. He had come to Lebanon with the formal Arabic of the Qur'an, of the religious sciences. Persian, we must remember, was the language of his home and childhood and youth. Like other *mullas* of Iranian birth and culture, he had known the Arabic of religious texts; Persian, the language of Iran, was to a *mulla* of his background the medium of self-expresson. (In an Iranian proverb, Arabic is learning, but Persian is sugar.) The Arabic of Sayyid Musa was changed by Lebanon. Little more than a decade after his arrival, his Arabic was freer and more evocative, the language of daily life and sentiments. The stilted language of formal discourse was replaced by the passionate speech of the pulpit and the crowd.

Beyond his relation to the language lay the increasing radicalization of the country: the early 1970s brought great changes to Lebanon. Strikes were becoming a way of life among the students, among laborers newly awakening to their rights. New demands — for reform of the educational system, for minimum wages, for medical insurance, for rent control, for higher prices for the tobacco crop grown by southerners — were put forward in a society that was simultaneously losing its tolerance for old inequalities and the traditional networks that once cushioned those inequalities. The country's political order remained its old self. It could not respond to change, did not know how to change. Its apologists insisted that the country's system was "subtle," that its free-wheeling ways could not be tinkered with. Young people were throwing their support to radical politics. The politically sensitive cleric had been appealing to the state. Increasingly the state was being demonstrated, in his words, to be a scarecrow. He had to compete with the radical spectrum in the country, to preempt its symbols and appeal.

Musa al-Sadr did his work without illusions. He knew, and at times openly acknowledged, the weight of Shi‘i history in Lebanon, its mixture of defeatism and opportunism. He referred to the Shi‘i dilemma in his own way; he called it the "psychological and moral outlook" of the Shi‘i community. A Shi‘i academic from the Gulf who observed Sayyid Musa noted the cleric's frustration and discomfort with the men of means in Shi‘i Lebanon, with their political timidity, with feuds.

He had two radically different parts of the country to work with: the south and the Biqa' Valley in the east. He had to bring these two communities together. Historically the two realms had been separated from each other by deep differences in temperament. They grew (licensed) tobacco in the south and (contraband) hashish in the Biqa'; this summed up the difference. The people of the south were patient, subdued peasants, their villages within the reach of authority. The Shi^ci of the Biqa' Valley were wild and assertive clansmen who resisted the encroachment of outside power. A few gendarmes could terrorize entire villages in the south; the Biqa' was a place to which government troops ventured with great reluctance. The *bays* of the south lorded it over cowed men. The *bays* of the Biqa' operated in a more egalitarian world. When the daughter of Ahmad Bay al-Asad (a southerner) married Ṣabri Bay Hamadi (the Biqa''s big man), she taunted Sabri Bay about the difference between the uncontested authority of her father and his frustrations with his more unwieldy followers. "I am a horse among other horses," Sabri Hamadi is reported to have answered her. "Your father is a horse among mules."

Even matters of religious ritual were celebrated in markedly different ways by the two communities. *^cAshura*, the days of mourning for the third Imam, were days of wailing and self-flagellation among the people of the south. The people of the Biqa' celebrated Karbala with quiet readings of the Qur'an and of *marathi* (lamentation poetry), with considerable restraint.

If the men of the Biqa' saw the men of the south as unusually timid and squeamish, the south, the more settled of the two communities, the more learned and tamed, had its own view of the men of the Biqa'. It saw them as roughnecks, as wild men of an area beyond accepted ways. Musa al-Sadr went a long way toward bridging the gap between the two communities or at least suppressing the differences. He was ideally suited for the task. He claimed descent from the south; he had had his start there, he could appeal to the new Shi^ci money which was mostly based in the south and in the hands of urban newcomers who hailed from there. But he was a daring man, he was courageous. And this was a quality that the men of the Biqa' valued in other men.

The shrewd cleric had his own sense of the two regions that made up his domain. He wanted the southerners to be more daring and defiant. And he wanted to harness the energy of the wild men of the Biqa', to channel it into politically and socially useful endeavors. He was appalled by the blood feuds of the Biqa' which often went on for generations. He needed the martial vigor of its men. On many an occasion armed men from the Biqa' were brought to political gatherings in the south; they were the ones who openly challenged the units of the Lebanese army and the gendarmes. It was all part of "educating" the men of the south, of putting the weakness of the Lebanese state on display, of enabling the people of the south to stand up to their *bays* and to the authority of the state that the *bays* often brought in on their side.

An Imam, a man who led, he had proclaimed, concerned himself with the "daily affairs" of men. Musa al-Sadr was as good as his word. He ventured into matters of social and economic concern without apology or hesitation. In early 1973, he took part in a confrontation between the tobacco planters and the security forces. The planters wanted higher prices for their crops and the right to unionize. A clash between the planters and the forces of the state in the southern town of Nabatiyyah resulted in the death of two planters and the injury of fifteen.

Tobacco was the perennial problem of Musa al-Sadr's constituency. The cause of the tobacco growers and sharecroppers had been there waiting to be picked up. It had been there since the tobacco monopoly, the *Régie des Tabacs et Tombacs*, had been reconstituted in 1935. Large-scale disturbances over the policies of the *Régie* had erupted as early as 1936. A foreign diplomatic dispatch of May of that year noted the small growers' dissatisfaction with the monopoly's policies, which decreased the acreage of tobacco under cultivation and put men out of work. Troubles had erupted now and then in the intervening years. The pressure on men and the land had increased the bitterness.

The political economy of tobacco was a fair reflection of the country's larger inequities. It reflected, above all, the structural imbalance between the agricultural and service sectors of the economy. The average annual income for the twenty-five thousand small growers for 1972–73 was around three hundred dollars: the annual income of heads of households in the service sector in the city was about nine times larger. Then there was the gap between the growers and the large landholders. The average acreage per grower in the early 1970s was less than two *dunams* (a *dunam* was a quarter of an acre). The small growers were perenially in debt, constantly the prey for the loan sharks.

None of the leading politicians of the south had paid much attention to the problems of the small growers. They themselves owned large chunks of land; more than that, they had the licenses that specified the numbers of dunams of tobacco that could be planted. For the *bays* of the south, as for the other large growers, tobacco was one source of income among others, money to be spent in the city. Their tobacco crops were worked by sharecroppers and *wakils*, agents. Besides, when the inspectors of the tobacco monopoly showed up at the estates and villages of the powerful to estimate and price the crops, they took care not to offend. The tobacco story was a microcosm of the country. In the words of a small grower, it was "law for the weak, liberty for the strong." The inspectors turned up in the downtrodden villages with bulldozers to smash excess crops. But they were timid when they approached the estates of the *bays* and the notables. A 1971 list of tobacco growers in the south was a veritable "who's who" in the country.

"Prince" Majid Arslan, a powerful Druze chieftain, a frequent minister of defense, appears on the list with holdings in the village of Ansar in the district of Nabatiyyah. So do the daughters of a former prime minister, a Sunni politician by the name of Riyad al-Sulh, and his widow as well. Riyad al-Sulh was one of the founders of the republic; he was the Muslim party to the "National Pact" that had put the republic together in 1943. He had been struck down by an assassin in July 1951. His vast tobacco holdings had been passed on to his widow and his daughters, ᶜAliya, Muna, Lamya, Bahija, and Layla. One of the daughters was married to the King of Morocco's brother, Prince ᶜAbdullah. It is hard to imagine her worrying over the price of tobacco in southern Lebanon as she divided her time between Rabat and Paris.

Other "great families" were absentee landlords of the south's tobacco acreage. They did not need the help of Musa al-Sadr. The twenty-five thousand small growers did, though, and they were inspired by his concern. Tobacco, he said, was *qadiyyah al-qadaya*, the problem of all problems. The politically sophisticated cleric knew that men were waiting to be led, that the religious message had to be modernized, had to be linked to material concerns and issues of fairness and deprivation. He was, as an American diplomatic dispatch put it, "acutely aware of political inroads being made . . . by leftist (primarily Baᶜthis and Communist) proselytizers." He could choose to pick up the issue of the tobacco, or he could leave it to the radical parties.

In walking into the fight between the tobacco *Régie* and the growers in 1973, Musa al-Sadr must have grasped a historical parallel lost on his Lebanese followers and rivals alike. A large, *ᶜulama'*-led revolt had broken out against the Persian tobacco administration, the British-owned Imperial Tobacco Corporation, in Iran in 1891. The tobacco revolt of 1891–92 had become part of the folklore of Iranian nationalism. A concession had been granted a British monopoly by the Iranian monarch Nasir al-Din Shah. The rebellion against the concession brought together the opposition of "liberal" nationalists and *mullas* "preaching everywhere against the surrender of the faithful into the hands of the infidels." Upheaval had erupted in the major cities of Iran. The *ᶜulama'* had given the grievances of tobacco growers and merchants religious sanction. Tobacco handled by foreigners was declared *haram*, impermissible and defiled. The ruling against the use of tobacco was made by the leading Shiᶜi cleric of the time, Mirza Hasan Shirazi. Shirazi lived in Samarrah, one of the shrine towns of Iraq. After petitions came to him from the *ᶜulama'* of Iran, Shirazi first, in September 1891, sent a telegram to the Shah speaking against the concession. "The entry of foreigners," said the religious leader to the Shah, "into the affairs of the country, their relations and trade with Muslims, the concessions such as the bank, tobacco, *Régie*, railroads, and others are, for many reasons, against the exact sense of the Qur'an and God's orders. Theses acts weaken the power of the government and are the cause of the ruin of order in the country." Then in December came Shirazi's ruling: "In the name of God, the Merciful, the Forgiving, today the use of *tanbaku* and tobacco in any form is reckoned as war against the Imam of the age (may God hasten his glad advent!)." The tobacco concession could not be saved and had to be canceled. The last throw of the dice was a government attempt to break the will of the leader of Tehran's ῾ulama'. He was given an ultimatum: he could break the boycott by smoking or leave the country. When he oped for the latter course, Tehranians, lead by their ῾ulama', took to the streets. The ῾ulama' and their allies had formed an effective national movement which fused socioeconomic resentments and religious feelings.

For Musa al-Sadr, this modern quarrel of growers and a tobacco *Régie* must have seemed like the reenactment of an old tale one had heard and read about. The history of his birthplace, the deeds of its politically activist clerics, gave him wider horizons than those of his politically cowed clerical rivals in Lebanon. He had a large history to draw upon and to live up to.

He also had sensitive antennae; he appropriated prevalent themes. At a time when Lebanon was beginning to wonder about its direction, he voiced what was on the minds of others. This was his great advantage at a time of drift in the country—the outsider grasping the issues, seeing and defining things clearly. In *Lord Jim*, Conrad had described that ability as the stranger's remarkable instinct. "He had proved his grasp of the unfamiliar situation, his intellectual alertness in that field of thought. There was his readiness, too. Amazing. And all this had come to him in a manner like keen scent to a well-bred hound." This stranger too had a "keen scent" for the issues. In the escalating disorder that plunged Lebanon into civil war by 1975, Musa al-Sadr was to become the country's most compelling figure. The years 1974 and 1975 were his. He was the Beiruti media's star attraction. He was, it was said of him, the hope of a "white revolution" in the country. As it turned out, no such hope existed; carnage was to become a way of life. But over the course of these two years, Shi῾i history in Lebanon was changed for good, its symbols and heritage reinterpreted by the cleric and given an activist bent. It was not that Musa al-Sadr was more "original" than others in the country. In general men who come to stamp particular epochs and times of transition with their own temperament and ideas are not necessarily more original than others. It is less originality that distinguishes them than an acute degree of sensitivity to their environment, to the mood of a particular situation.

As Musa al-Sadr emerged as one of Lebanon's most compelling voices in 1974–75, he was to display an amazing feel for the media, for getting his message across. Though born and raised in a Shi῾i country, he showed a striking capacity to cross into the world of other men and sects. He knew how to reach an audience. No two speeches were alike. An address to an entirely Shi^{c}i audience had one set of themes, a particular cadence; it drew on the private language and symbols of Shi^{c}ism. A sermon at a church—and he delivered several—drew on the common themes of the martyrdom of the third Imam, Imam Husayn, and the crucifixion of Christ. On those occasions when he appeared with Sunni *culama'*, he said that there was no difference between his own black turban and the white turbans of his Sunni counterparts.

His people, the Shi^{c}i had long been known for their fear of defilement, their fear of what was morally polluted, *najas*, impure. It was a fear noted by travelers who ventured into their midst, a nervousness that extended from dietary matters to friendships. The fear had survived into the modern age. Like so many such tendencies that survive in our times, it had been concealed or given new names. But its core, a fear of venturing beyond the world of one's kinsmen, had survived. Musa al-Sadr, a cleric, was remarkably free of this kind of timidity. An incident that took place in the city of Tyre was recounted by his followers, told by Shi^{c}i men trying to break with the taboos of their world. There was a Christian in Tyre who owned a small ice cream stand. Tyre had a Shi^{c}i majority, and the majority of them would not patronize his stand. Food handled by a Christian was pronounced *najas*, impure and defiled. The frustrated ice cream vendor took his case to the Imam of the Shi^{c}i, to Musa al-Sadr himself. And the cleric was sympathetic. On a Friday, after Musa al-Sadr delivered his *khutbah*, his sermon in the mosque of Tyre, he said that he felt like going for a walk. The usual crowd that was always there, pleased to be in his presence, followed him through the market and the streets of Tyre. Sayyid Musa and his entourage came upon the Christian ice cream man. The cleric stopped by the stand. "What sort of ice cream are you willing to give us today?" he asked. He then proceeded to accept from the man the ice cream he was offered. The lesson was not lost on the crowd. Things hitherto impermissible were declared acceptable by a man of religion and a *sayyid*, a descendant of the Prophet. The gates of a world closed unto itself were being forced open by a "man of God."

Sayyid Musa's daring in the face of old rituals and prohibitions went beyond dietary matters. On a Shi^{c}i occasion honoring the sixth Imam, Ja^{c}far al-Sadiq, Musa al-Sadr appeared with a Catholic priest, Bishop George Haddad by his side. Another Christian and admirer, the Maronite intellectual Michel al-Asmar, joined him during a fast staged in a Beirut mosque to protest the violence in the country. He was a master of such gestures. A Lenten sermon that he delivered at a Catholic church became one of the country's special moments in early 1975. The Catholic hierarchy was there to receive him, as was one of Lebanon's former presidents and a cast of the country's political elite. A reporter who covered the episode for his daily paper wrote of the event with awe, in a nearly breathless way. He described the arrival of the Shi⁣ci Imam and the large crowd of priests and nuns who were there to listen to him. "When Imam al-Sadr entered the main hall of the church, faces of the audience showed a mixture of awe and delight. . . . The Imam nodded to the crowd that stood up to greet him; he sat down and they followed suit." He was introduced by the former president of the republic in the following words: "The believers are here to hear the word of God from a non-Catholic religious guide. It is only natural that Lebanon is the country in which this deed is taking place."

A reader encountering the sermon the cleric gave is struck with what must be called its Christian tone; the homage to Christ as an apostle of the weak and the oppressed, the preaching against "love of the self." It has that tone of deliberation and calm that is so much a mark of Catholicism and its ritual:

> Oh, our God, the God of Moses and Jesus and Muhammad, the God of the weak and of all creatures, we thank you for sheltering us, for uniting our hearts with your love and mercy. We are assembled here today in a house of yours, at a time of fasting . . . .
>
> Our hearts yearn for you; our minds derive light and guidance from you. . . . We have come to your door, we have gathered together to serve man. It is man that all religions aspire to serve. . . . All religions were once united; they anticipated one another; they validated one another. They called man to God and they served man. Then the different religions diverged when each sought to serve itself, to pay excessive attention to itself to the point that each religion forgot the original purpose—the service of man. Then discord and strife were born, and the crisis of man deepened.

Religions, he said, sought to liberate men from "the lords of the earth and the tyrants," to provide sustenance to the weak and the oppressed. But when the religious orders triumphed, the weak found that "the tyrants had changed their garb, that they now wielded power in the name of religion, brandishing its sword." The sermon continued in the same vein: It condemned the "narcissism of man," and the tyranny of wealth, man's "biggest idol." And there were some parting words about Lebanon—its tormented classes, its neglected districts.

"The Imam then stopped," we are told by the reporter covering the sermon, "bowed his head, moved from behind the pulpit to his place in the front row. The crowd wished that it was not in a house of God and worship so that they might be able to applaud. Before sitting down the Imam turned to the audience, bent his head in a greeting. . . . The archbishop asked the Imam al-Sadr to proceed to the reception hall. . . . Then the crowd of worshippers began vying with one another to shake hands with the Imam who prayed and preached in the church of Christ.

It was not the austere voice of Islam that spoke on that day. It was a more tender one — and a familiar one at that — that the Catholic audience responded to. In part, Musa al-Sadr's ability to sway this particular audience must have owed something to the cult of sorrow and lament to be found at the heart of both Christianity and Shi^ci Islam. But it was really his own style — the gentle demeanor, the melancholy, the tenderness he brought to his encounters with others — that endeared him to these hearers.

Lebanon was a country of deep religious antagonisms. Its people knew this even as they tried their best to hide their hostility and suspicions. The audience that left the Catholic church and those who read about the episode the next day knew the phobias and divisions of the country in which they lived. And they were flattered and touched by the cleric's performance all the more because of the stubborn divisions and feuds of the country.

Lebanon's elite press was receptive to him. He relied on two newspapers in Beirut, *al-Hayat* and *al-Nahar*, both of which had conservative agendas. *Al-Hayat*, launched in the mid-1940s, was owned by the Marwah family, a Shi^ci family from the southern part of the country. Kamiel Marwah, the newspaper's founder who was assassinated by Nasserite operatives in 1966, had been a man light years ahead of the Shi^ci world from which he hailed. He had known Musa al-Sadr and had admired him; Kamiel Marwah, too, had been one of the rare breed of men seeking to "modernize" the Shi^ci outlook, to break with the taboos and the shackles of Shi^ci history. His special bond with the cleric was honored after his death by his family. *Al-Hayat*, I was told by Kamiel Marwah's son, was Sayyid Musa's. The cleric needed to make no special effort tot woo *al-Hayat* or to gain its attention.

But it was *al-Nahar* that was Musa al-Sadr's principal vehicle in 1974 and 1975. *Al-Nahar* was Lebanon's most enlightened and influential paper. It had a tradition of critical inquiry and social concern. Ideologically, it was a centrist paper. Its publisher, Ghassan Tueni, an American-educated Greek Orthodox, was a man who sat astride the two worlds of journalism and politics. In a land of clans and fractured politics, *al-Nahar* stood for the city, for trade, for reform politics, for an enlightened kind of pro-Westernism. The man at the helm of *al-Nahar* was sophisticated enough to know that the narrow base of Lebanon's ruling circle had to expand if its political system were to survive.

Musa al-Sadr was good copy for Tuini's *al-Nahar*. He was photogenic, he was good with words and crowds. He was becoming a mass preacher. It was of a better Lebanon that Musa al-Sadr spoke, of the responsibility of the state toward the deprived. The Shi^ci cleric appearing at a church, journeying to remote villages without amenities, staging a general strike, speaking out on behalf of the press against a government trying to clip its wings; such were the actions that endeared him to *al-Nahar* and its brand of journalism. He was constantly on the move. For some, power flourishes in silence; for Musa al-Sadr, tumult was an important source of power.

Acceptance encouraged him, seemed to sharpen his sense of the issues. He introduced a language that became his trademark; it revolved around the themes of "disinheritance" and "deprivation." The man of religion, he said, had to be on the side of the "wretched of the earth," of the "disinherited," went beyond the confines of his own sect. And he saw himself — as he put it in a letter to a sympathetic group in Parliament — as the "symbol," and the "rallying point" of the cause of the disinherited.

The new language of disinheritance and deprivation was more subtle and more inclusionary than the language of class conflict that the Lebanesse left had used with such dismal results. Musa al-Sadr's language fitted the place. It appealed to the newly rich among the Shi^ci as it did to the poor; the new language circumvented the Muslim (and Lebanese) phobia about "social classes" and "exploitation." The old Marxian language was easily dismissed as the language of unbelief, as something ruinous to the Muslim faith; it was also, in a land of unbridled capitalism, dismissed as an attack on Lebanon's free-wheeling ways. A new language had to be introduced if the issues of equity and fairness were to be addressed without setting off the old sirens. Musa al-Sadr found it in the popular feelings about fairness and disinheritance. He spoke in a native idiom; his words could not be dismissed as a heretical attack on age-old ways. At its roots, the language was deeply Shi^ci. But it was suffused with a "Third World" dimension; and it claimed to take in all the "deprived" in the country, all its "disinherited regions" and "sons."

Shi^ci history in Lebanon taught that success in the modern city of Beirut required a break with the world of shabby elders — with the religion, the attire, the dialect, even the food of the hinterland. The charismatic cleric was imparting a different lesson: men could be themselves, yet still be successful and excel in the world beyond the faith. And he was doing it at mass rallies. As he broke out of hemmed-in politics, he found a direct line to the emotions and language of the masses. This happened in a dramatic way in early 1974. The preceding year had been a turning point for the country's fragile political balance. Full-scale fighting had erupted between the Lebanese army and the Palestinian organizations in May 1973. The basic understanding between the Maronite establishment and its Sunni counterpart had come unstuck as a result of the fighting. The Maronites wanted to assert the will of the state and the army; the Sunni establishment would not go along. The

Lebanese state had never seemed as unsure of itself as it did after mid-1973. An increasing number of Shiᶜi youth were prey for the leftist parties. And this was to force Musa al-Sadr's hand, and give him his opportunity; he had to speak to the poorer of the Shiᶜi classes, voice their resentments, or risk being pushed aside in a situation of increasing radicalization and disorder.

As he descended to the depths of society, to its lower strata and began to mine religious scripture and tradition for modern meaning and relevance, Imam Musa's vocation was transformed into that of a savior. There was nothing rigged about this. The "savior" themes were to be found in the Shiᶜi heritage itself, in its rich reservoirs of tales of martyrdom and persecution. Hitherto the Shiᶜi tradition had either been accepted as it had been received — as a tradition of defeat and worldly dispossession — or completely ignored, driven underground, if you will, by "modern" men and women trying to venture into the world beyond the faith. Musa al-Sadr offered a new alternative: Shiᶜi history with its tales of defeat would neither be accepted as it had been received, nor apologized for and denied. The tradition would be reworked, cast in a new light.

Inevitably, it was with Karbala, the seventh-century tale of Imam Husayn's martyrdom, that Musa al-Sadr began when he went to the Shiᶜi masses in a direct way in 1974 and 1975. The "Karbala paradigm" lay at the core of Shiᶜi history. Karbala "branded" the Shiᶜi. It set them apart. Karbala cast a long shadow; for the faithful it annulled time and distance. Succeeding generations had told and embellished the tale, given it their sense of separateness and political dispossession. A gripping passion play, staged every year, reenacted the searing tale which culminated in the killing of the Prophet's grandson, Imam Husayn, and a band of zealous followers and in the captivity of the women of *ahl al-bayt*. The tale of Karbala is related here, in very brief fashion, so that the reader can best appreciate what Musa al-Sadr made of it and how neo-Shiᶜism worked with, manipulated and, in time, overthrew the dominant Shiᶜi tradition of political quietism and withdrawal. . . .

Musa al-Sadr brought to the old tale of Karbala a new reading, which stripped it of its sorrow and lament and made of it an episode of political choice and courage on the part of Imam Husayn and the band of followers who fought by his side. The annual occasion of mourning Imam Husayn, hitherto a reminder of the Shiᶜi of their solitude and defeat, was to become under Musa al-Sadr a celebration of defiance on the part of an "elite minority" — the Shiᶜi — that had refused to submit to injustice.

Here, too, it was not so much Musa al-Sadr's originality that carried the day and that made the Shiᶜi masses of Lebanon see old symbols and traditions in a new light. Sayyid Musa was a well-traveled man, for a Shiᶜi *mulla*, and he was well read. He took some ideas and conceptions that were dimly

perceived, or that existed on paper, and translated them into accessible
language and imagery.

To begin with, we know that Sayyid Musa had been deeply influenced
by a book on Imam Husayn written by ᶜAbbas Mahmud al-ᶜAqqad
(1889–1964), one of the celebrated writers of Egypt's "liberal period," prior
to the revolution of 1952 that brought Gamal ᶜAbd al-Nasser and his fellow
officers to power. ᶜAqqad's book *al-Husayn: Abu'l-shuhada'* (Husayn:
The Father of Martyrs), published in 1944, had depicted the struggle between Imam Husayn and his rival Yazid as the clash of "two temperaments," two radically different "moral outlooks." Husayn, in ᶜAqqad's
reverential treatement, represents everything noble in Banu Hashim, the
Prophet Muhammad's family; He knew literature, was a man of eloquence,
spontaneity, and gentleness, accepted the "cruel turns of fate," and was
pious and benevolent toward those less privileged than himself. Yazid, on
the other hand, said ᶜAqqad, had in him all the "negative traits of his family" (the Umayyads, a clan that had opposed the Prophet Muhammad and
had fought Muslims during their early years of adversity) and none of the
merits that clan may have possessed. Yazid had the roughness of his family;
he loved his drinking bouts, his horses, and his hounds. Yazid stood for
power and its prerogatives, whereas Husayn represented Islam's emphasis
on justice and equality of the believers. ᶜAqqad had rejected the notion that
the fight between Husayn and Yazid was over *mulk*, kingship. A struggle,
he said, had been imposed on Husayn; martyrdom was the last resort to
save Islam from becoming the dominion of *ahl al-mal wa'l-sultan*, the men
of wealth and power. Yazid had prevailed at Karbala. But his was a temporary victory; in the end, history vindicated Husayn and what he stood
for.

Closer to home than ᶜAqqad's book, by the late 1960s and early 1970s,
modernist Shiᶜi Iranians had begun to reinterpret Imam Husayn's legacy.
And in the new Iranian discourse the Shiᶜi folk conception of Husayn as a
willing martyr who rides to a sure death—a death foretold, according to
folklore, when he was born—was set aside in favor of the idea of a political
man who weighs his choices, and embarks on the best course left to him.
Gradually Imam Husayn emerged as a precursor of political men who
choose to rebel against the overwhelming odds, and do so with open eyes.

The turning of old religious ritual into a radical politics of praxis in Shiᶜi
Lebanon was evident in Musa al-Sadr's *ᶜAshura* oration of 1974. It was a
dark time, said the cleric, when Imam Husayn rose in rebellion: "The *ummah* was silent, free men were fugitives; fear reduced men to silence. Islam
was threatened." Husayn, a free man, made a choice of his own:

> A great sacrifice was needed to . . . stir feelings. The event of Karbala
> was that sacrifice. Imam Husayn put his family, his forces, and even his

life, in the balance against tyranny and corruption. Then the Islamic world burst forth with this revolution.

This revolution did not die in the sands of Karbala; it flowed into the life stream of the Islamic world, and passed from generation to generation, even to our day. It is a deposit placed in our hands so that we may profit from it, that we draw out of it a new source of reform, a new position, a new movement, a new revolution, to repel the darkness, to stop tyranny and to pulverize evil.

The cleric acknowledged the sad history of the Shi^{c}i: he knew its depth. "The record of our tears fills the cloud that follows us," he told his followers on another religious occasion. But history could offer something more than the spectacle of Shi^{c}i defeat. Imam Husayn, he said, faced the enemy with seventy men, and "today we are more than seventy, and our enemy is not a quarter of the whole world." A hundred million people throughout the world, a hundred million Shi^{c}i, now celebrated the memory of Husayn. The men who claim Husayn no longer needed to be frightened or silent.

It was political daring that the activist cleric was trying to teach. Exalting Husayn, he was attacking the dominant Shi^{c}i tradition of mourning, and quiescence. "Husayn," he said in another religious discourse, "had three kinds of enemies: Those who killed him—and they were tyrants; those who tried to obliterate his memory, like the men who plowed the earth and covered the spot where he was buried or like the Ottomans who prevented any remembrance of him. The third kind of enemies are those who wanted to ossify that example of Husayn, to restrict the meaning of his life and martyrdom to tears and lamentations. The third kind of enemies are the most dangerous for they threaten to destroy the living roots of Husayn's "memory." The third kind of enemies were the Shi^{c}i themselves: Husayn had to be rescued from what the bearers of his legacy had made of his rebellion and his death. A cleric celebrating a tradition several centuries old was grafting onto it new themes of concern and activism.

On yet another religious occasion, Musa al-Sadr read into the seventh-century tale the issue of women's rights and the place of women in Muslim society. He spoke of Imam Husayn's sister Zaynab, who was with her brother on his doomed mission. She survived him, spent years grieving for him, and was turned by the faithful into a saintly figure of sorrow and grief. Zaynab's shrine on the outskirts of Damascus was a place to which the defeated seeking solace journeyed. Of her, the cleric said: "Zaynab went with the caravan of prisoners to Kufah; she had been the one who lifted Husayn's body, who presented it to God and said 'Oh God, accept from us our sacrifice.' She spread the message of Husayn. She took his message from the desert of Karbala to the capitals of the Islamic world. . . . The women in Karbala carried on the work and the struggle. The woman can't just be an instrument of pleasure and procreation." Zaynab, he reminded his audience, was the one who covered the body of Husayn's ailling son, Zayn al-ᶜAbidin, with hers, who begged the ruler's troops at Karbala to spare the young man's life. It was thus that Husayn's Imamate had been rescued, that he was left with an heir who inherited his mantle.

In believers' minds, the time and distance separating present-day reality from that of Karbala were nullified and overcome with remarkable ease. An enemy in daily life—a policeman, a landlord, an oppressive father-in-law—was dubbed a Yazid, the ruler who had ordered the killing of Husayn. A particularly cruel figure was referred to as Shimr—in the Shiᶜi literature and passion plays, the man who beheaded Husayn. Musa al-Sadr made the same kind of historical leap. The contemporary civil disorder became the "Karbala of Lebanon." Imam Husayn was connected right to the present.

Others in Shiᶜi Lebanon had flirted with this kind of thing earlier, had tried to manipulate the old Shiᶜi histories. Some two decades before Musa al-Sadr reread Shiᶜi history and symbolism, radicalized youth in the southern Lebanon town of Bint Jbayl had attempted to make the fight between Imam Husayn and the Umayyad ruler Yazid a metaphor of their own. A group of Arab nationalists belonging to the Baᶜth Party, they made an attempt that was clumsy and contrived. In their reconstruction of Karbala, Husayn was no longer a special individual, an Imam, but the "Arab nation" as a whole, and Yazid stood for the "nation's enemies." The role of the Hidden Imam, *al-Mahdi al-Muntazar*, was assigned to a "revolutionary cadre" that would appear and bring about a reign of justice. Stretched that far, the tradition wilted and did not work. The Shiᶜi tale of sorrow and solitude could not be claimed by young secularists. But it belonged in a natural way to the cleric relating it in the mid-1970s: after all, he was a descendant of the twelve Imams. In the popular imagination, Musa al-Sadr's title and attire were of a piece with the inherited history.

Religious occasions were becoming armed rallies. A special bond was being forged between men awakening to a sense of their own power—and violation—and an extraordinary figure. Seventy-five thousand men turned out in the eastern town of Baᶜlbak to hear him in March 1974. The occasion was a religious one honoring Imam Husayn. Thousands of armed men were on hand, and Musa al-Sadr, the "rebel Imam," was acclaimed by the masses. (His connection with the seventh-century Imam who fell in rebellion was left to their imagination.) The crowd closed in on the cleric: he had trouble reaching the platform; men reached out to touch his gown; he lost his turban and it had to be retrieved for him. He was unable to start his own oration for twenty minutes. Men firing into the air had to be silenced. "I have words harsher than bullets," the cleric said. "So spare your bullets." "The town of Baᶜlbak," he said, "is without a secondary school. There was a school under French rule. Two thousand years ago Ba^clbak were irrigated through a network of dams. Today its water is wasted. And the government still wants to know why we despair of it . . . . "

In his oration, he spoke of the plight of the south, working to bridge the gap between his two realms, the Biqa'; and the south. To his more militant followers in the Biqa' he said: "You are the brothers of the sons of the south, a source of strength for them." He then spoke of the ruling authorities in the country, of what they had done to the south, of the diversion of the waters of the Litani River from the south to Beirut: "They have stolen three hundred million cubic meters from the waters of the south. They now want another sixty million cubic meters. They want to shatter the last remaining hope of the people of the south for a share in their own water." He ticked off the budget figures for the last four years—figures showing the south receiving only some 20 percent of its legitimate share. He ranged over other grievances. The Shi^ci, he said, were underrepresented at the heights of the civil service. He noted that there were no Shi^ci deans at the universities, that "Shi^ci ambassadors are appointed to backward countries. . . . A meter of land in Beirut is worth more than ten thousand Lebanese pounds, a meter of land in the Biqa' is worth less than ten pilasters. . . . Let us look at the ghettoes of Beirut: Oh men in power, do you not feel ashamed that a few kilometers away from your homes are houses that are not fit for human habitation? . . . If there are twelve hundred homeless children in the streets of Beirut, eleven hundred of them are sure to be Shi^ci. Does Imam Husayn accept this for his children? Does Imam ^cAli?"

The wrongs had been there. They were not being tallied up. New grievances were dressed in old historic garb. The budget figures and the old Shi^ci symbols the cleric mixed together. There was something here for men impressed by modern standards and budget figures, for the ambitious dreaming of ambassadorships to countries which mattered, and for ordinary people who understood and internalized the old Shi^ci tales of persecution and defeat. And there was also a defense and justification by the cleric of his own worldly ambitions: he had been accused of ambition, of wanting the chairmanship of the Higher Shi^ci Council for life (which he did want and which he secured). He linked his own dreams to those of the revered Imams: "The commander of the faithful, Imam ^cAli, was denounced from the pulpit for eight years and accused of unbelief. A judge in Kufah said that Imam Husayn had strayed from his grandfather's way, that I should observe religious ritual and be satisfied." Musa al-Sadr's worldliness and political ambitions were far removed from the old tradition of clerical conservatism. A man of the religious institution, he was breaking with the role assigned men of the religious institution by those who possessed political power.

> The rulers say that the men of religion must only pray and not meddle in other things. They exhort us to fast and to pray for them so that the foundations of their reign will not be shaken, while they move away from religion and exploit it to hold on to their seats of power. Do not think that men in power who proclaim their opposition to communism are opposed to atheism. . . . They are the most infidel of the infidels and the most atheist of the atheists. They want us to give ourselves up to them.

For all the standard assertions, Islam had known no distinction between God's realm and Caesar's. Caesar, the man of the sword, had triumphed in Islamic history. Kings and dynasties, and lesser men in power, had turned religion and the men of religion into instruments of their power. The man of God—pious, left behind by modernity, by modern schools, by foreign trade and great wealth—had become an adornment in the court of the *bay*, the *wazir*, and the ruler. The radical potential of the religion lay dormant. The triumph of this cleric over the men of conventional politics was an invasion of familiar things. It was not a predestined outcome; it had to be willed and organized. For it to happen, history had to be turned around. The revolutionary man of religion had to reinterpret the functions and the obligations of the religious institution and its custodians.

The idea expounded before the crowd in the Biqa' was to become a recurrent theme: the man of religion had to be at odds with the men in power. Not long after the rally in Baᶜlbak, Musa al-Sadr propounded the same theme to a group of fellow clerics: "The moment you find that you have incurred the ruler's wrath is the time to realize that you are on the right path. You should refuse to succumb to the lords of this earth, to the oppressors. You should stand on the side of the people, on the side of the wretched of the earth.

Nearly fifty days after the armed rally in the Biqa', there was another occasion, an ostensibly religious one that obliterated the line between the realm of religion and that of politics. This time, the gathering was in Musa al-Sadr's old base in the city of Tyre; the purpose was to celebrate the memory of Fatimah al-Zahra, the Prophet's daughter and the mother of the two Imams, Hasan and Husayn. A crowd as large as the one that had turned out in Baᶜlbak came to hear the cleric. There were armed men from the Biqa' Valley, who arrived with their antitank weapons, with their sticks of dynamite and machine guns. The patricians of the Shiᶜi community who followed Musa al-Sadr were there as well. Musa al-Sadr arrived to shouts of *Allah Akbar* (God is Great), to the sounds of rifles and machine guns and the ululation of women. He started off with a few words about Fatimah, "the pure," the virtuous, the believing woman who was told by her father the Prophet Muhammad that he could not spare her on the day of judgment, that she would have to earn God's grace and mercy by her own merits. This said, he made the predictable leap from the old heritage to worldly and political matters. "For us today, we see, oh Fatimah, daughter of the messenger of God, we are now beyond the stage of childhood and helplessness. We have come of age. We need no trustees. We have emancipated ourselves despite all the means adopted to keep us from learning and enlightenment. We have gathered in large number to say that we need no trusteeship. Oh Fatimah, we are on your path; and our path will lead us to martyrdom."

He was becoming a "warner" of dangers to come—a role as old as messianic preachers. The warnings were put forth in an open statement to "the rulers" and the powers:

> Oh rulers, the lessons of history are within your grasp. All human societies have exploded at one time or another. We have asked you to deal with the problem. We have submitted to you studies and applications. There are ten billion cubic meters of water in Lebanon; only four hundred and fifty million cubic meters are exploited while the rest finds its way to the sea. Most parts of the country are thirsty and deprived. Is there anyone who cares for the plight of the citizenry . . .? There are those who want to rule and oppress without giving anything in return; those who ruled us for years without building a school or a hospital. We are with the deprived of all communities, with all those whose dignity has been violated.

Musa al-Sadr then asked for an oath and the crowd repeated after him that they would stay together until Lebanon had been rid of "deprivation" and "disinheritance." The oath was vintage Musa al-Sadr, an evocative vow "in the name of the blood of the martyrs, the wailing of mothers, the anxiety of the students and the intelligentsia... ."

An oath never overturns the world. Oaths can be made and broken. Men have never lacked ways of releasing themselves from the most sacred of obligations. But oaths have been important rituals and instruments in the formation of social movements—a process in which form has been as important as content. In Muslim history oaths have been particularly important vehicles for men's commitment of themselves to one another and to a common endeavor. There were, as Roy Mottahedeh shows in a perceptive work on bonds of loyalty in Muslim society, costs to breaking oaths. Men took oaths with sufficient seriousness that they tended to avoid those they "knew they might have to repudiate."

The cleric asking for the oath knew the place and the men: it was a hard place. Men saw social life as a realm of feuds and betrayals. It was accpeted that the big fish ate the small one, that men, as the peasant sayings of the country had it, pulled their own thorns with their own hands. In asking for the oath, he sought to create a semblance of commitment to a common endeavor. The hope of such oaths—and such dramatic moments—is that men will be moved enough to make minor sacrifices or to feel slightly more courageous in facing their adversaries or to know that they are not entirely alone. Musa al-Sadr led a community without a history of cohesion and solidarity. Pushed off the land, forced to scramble, men crowed about small achievements and wished ill for others. Men competed for the small crumbs that were available in the country, for the few prestigious civil service appointments open to the Shiᶜi. He could not annul that kind of situation. He knew it all too well. The most he could hope for through these dramatic gestures and moments was to create a fragile sense of fellowship, to "exploit" a common history of grief and to bring men together. In such a context, there is justification for the skeptic's argument that leaders trying to bind men together are ploughing the sea, that men separate and return to their familiar enmities as soon as the bubble bursts, as soon as the trance subsides. But something *does* happen when such oaths and obligations are made. Men—if only for a moment, and if only a handful of men—do give of themselves. Atomized men are brought together. In the face of the struggle of each against each, men hold up another vision of things: a more hopeful vision that enables them to act without second-guessing one another, without the conviction that the ruin of one man is to the other's advantage.

Religious oaths were a way of forging new bonds. The old tales of Shiᶜi solitude and martyrdom were called on to instill courage in men who had no history of political concern and responsibility: this was Musa al-Sadr's innovation. The men he led lived in the shadow of Karbala and bore its burden. The tradition of Karbala, and the larger Shiᶜi universe spun around it, had to be faced and reformed.

Karbala was a tapestry of many threads. No tale of such great pathos and tragedy could have left men with a single unambiguous message. Stood on one end, Karbala was a tale of choice and principle, the story of a man standing up when he could have groveled and acquiesced. Stood on the other end, it was a tale of doom and defeat. Karbala celebrated the grandson of the Prophet who fell in battle. But in the dark recesses of the mind, Karbala and the reiteration of its grim happenings could be an invitation to submission to powers that could not be defeated, to odds that could not be overcome.

The tale of Karbala and the multitude of other Shiᶜi tales of dispossession and defeat worked the only way they could have: they twisted and turned and they made surreptitious suggestions. Those searing Shiᶜi tales had assumed that weakness would have clean hands, that men would not, as modern jargon has it, "identify with the aggressor." But in a harsh world where the outcome mattered more than the journey, where results vindicated the deeds of men, a certain measure of ambivalence, of dissonance, if you will, was inevitable. The caliphs who beheaded the just Imams were men of means and power. The world offered itself to them, they had prevailed, they had not been encumbered by scruples. Were the young in this Shi^ci world to be the successors of those who died of thirst and hunger in doomed battles, or were they to prevail in their duels? Cut it as one might, men were told to exalt grief and martyrdom and lamentation but also to pursue success relentlessly and to pursue it wherever it might lead.

Martyrology lived in close proximity to crass self-preservation and easily spilled into it. Men extolled martyrdom, but they lived cautiously. They knew that men full of applause would fall away just when they were needed, that the zealous would be left alone to twist in the wind: the men promising to be there (like the men of Kufah promising to meet Husayn), the tales suggested, would scurry home to their wives and their children. And the men who risked, who really went out to change things, would reap the whirlwind. Women accompanied their sons to the ^cAshura celebrations and the passion play. But the lamenting mothers asked that young men refrain from playing with fire: heroism was delusion, sons were taught. The crafty inherited the earth; the daring were beheaded or poisoned. No one wanted his head to be thrown into his mother's lap.

Shi^ci defeatism had worn a righteous mask, had consoled itself. This was what Shi^ci history had to do to cope with worldly dispossession, with a seemingly endless trail of sorrow and defeat. The "Saintly Imams" (the words are Matthew Arnold's in a moving essay on Karbala), "resigned sufferers" as they were, supplied a "tender and pathetic side" to Islam. The Imams lost. But the believers, Arnold writes, who themselves could "attain to so little" loved the Imams "all the better on that account, loved them for their abnegation and mildness, felt that they were dear to God, that God loved them, that they and their lives filled a void in the severe religion of Mohamet." Matthew Arnold caught the vibrancy of Karbala. Islam, mainstream Islam, had been a triumphant affair. The Prophet had died at the helm of a successful polity. But the tale of triumph could not be everyone's. There had to be pathos and defeat as well, sorrow and a measure of consolation. Karbala had supplied what was most "tender" and pathetic to those who partook of it.

But men are not angels; they covet power and they admire winners. Men carry their oppressors within them. There was, to borrow the Shi^ci metaphor, the danger of a Yazid lurking in every man. This is the underside of Karbala; and a preacher like Musa al-Sadr, disentangling a complex Shi^ci history, had to confront it. The bearers of Karbala wailed for their martyrs. But the laments provided a kind of moral abolution for what men did and did not do, for their abdication in social and political matters.

There was darkness in Karbala. A great tale of betrayal could hardly instill in the men who bore its chains and memorized its lines the confidence in themselves and in others to go beyond fear and greed. Karbala taught a distrust of political power. But more: along with this distrust another sensibility was imparted, a sense that the world offered no redemption and that every path led to a blind alley of fear and betrayal. Exaltation and all the frenzied politics that come with it were checked, driven underground. But the price was a deep-seated sense of despair. This was true of Shi͑i history everywhere, but particularlay true in a hinterland like the world of the Shi͑i of Lebanon. Men here were always at the receiving end of someone else's power.They developed all the attributes that go with a long history of political dispossession: they propitiated power; they coped with it as best they could; they obeyed without being convinced; they rebelled in small ways or sulked and waited for a better day.

Tradition had provided shelter, had confirmed the futility of political life and the inevitability of betrayal. Now tradition—the same body of tales and myths and icons—was being mined for symbols of revolt, for new forms of solidarity. The left in Lebanon had talked of class the "injuries of class." But ordinary men and women had not responded with great zeal. A religious reformer was succeeding where the left had failed. There was no need to borrow alien words and categories. The sad history of Karbala was what men and women in Shi͑i Lebanon had known. They had grown up with the Shi͑i tales. A revolutionary figure working with the familiar history —subverting it as he went along—tapped something vital in those who rallied to him.

Something in Musa al-Sadr's style and personal demeanor was particularly helpful to him: a gentleness in his dealings with others, a touch of reticence that attracted people. Authority and leadership in this culture were like a straitjacket: men who possessed authority strutted around, bullied other men, stared them down, and frightened them. Authority had what was called a *wahra*, an ability to intimidate, nearly to paralyze those at the receiving end of power. (One thinks of Saddam Husayn, the president of Iraq, frightening and forbidding, as the quintessential man with *wahra*; indeed, among the titles he possesses, there is one, *al-Muhib*, which literally means the awesome of the awe-inspiring.) But this was not Musa al-Sadr's style. Men, regardless how young or unimportant, were treated with tenderness. The wife of one of his associates, who for a while lived with her husband in Musa al-Sadr's home, said that she does not recall an incident in which the cleric berated another man or was severe or overbearing in the way he dealt with those around him. His style had its spell. And no doubt its power came from the melancholy that lay at the core of Shi^cism. The world of power had had no room for the Shi^ci. Their revered Imams had fallen in battle, had been deprived of what the righteous felt to be their due: the right of succession to the Prophet's political and religious kingdom, to the wealth, the taxes, and the power that Islam's dominion brought to its beneficiaries. A leader summoning the Shi^ci masses had to have in him some of the sorrow of Shi^ci history, its sense that the ways of the world were harsh and unpredictable, that the believers should come together without undue claims to rank and prerogative. That large Shi^ci complex of sentiments was there in Musa al-Sadr's demeanor: what Matthew Arnold described as the "abnegation and mildness" of the Imams, the ^cAlids, was present in this claimant of the Shi^ci tradition.

The notion that men rebel to set themselves free is illusion. More to the point, they rebel to create more tolerable relations with autority, to submit to newer men, to different men. There are relations of command and obedience that sully those who submit to them, and others that don't. The classes of men responding to Musa al-Sadr in the mid-1970s had gone beyond the old bosses in the country. The "rebel Imam" offered a new relationship of authority and submission. The old bosses had in effect said, "Submit, for I am your better." The activist cleric made no such (explicit) demand. He did not have to: he had in his favor the Mahdist element, the repressed messianic yearning in his people's history; he was, after all, presented to the crowd as a descendant of the seventh Imam. Men offering him obedience felt that they were paying homage to their own Shi^ci tradition and history. A new relation of authority and command was presented as something very old and reassuring. This was not exactly the "end of time." But it was an unusual historical moment, ripe for a pretender. The Lebanese state was caving in; a familiar world was coming unstuck. A familiar system of authority no longer awed men, or sustained them. People denied the strength of age-old ways and were ready to follow, to be instructed, to be led.

The "traditional" world was being shoveled under. The crowds that came to hear Musa al-Sadr in the towns of the Biqa' or in Tyre were made up of day laborers who lived in Beirut, of tobacco planters engaged in a doomed battle with economics, of schoolteachers with grievances against the "system" that employed them, of newly urbanized men forced out of the south into Beirut by an Israeli–Palestinian war over which they had no control. For those who needed it, Musa al-Sadr played the part of that extraordinary figure essential to a situation of breakdown and redemption. In him, men possessed an Imam. Shi^ci history was open-ended. Each generation could see itself as the repository of the Shi^ci vision of breakdown and redemption, as the group destined to live through the foretold events — the wars, the ruins, the moral upheaval, then the coming of a day when the world is set right and history is brought to its legitimate conclusion.

The dominant Shi^ci reality always coexisted with the promise of a hazy millennium. The promise provided consolation; it made social and political arrangements seem transient and precarious. It left men ready for extraordinary figures. The Islamicist Marshall Hodgson has sketched the Shi^ci temperament with its penchant for a messianic figure and for a band of followers coming together in anticipation of great changes:

> It was always possible that the foreordained leader (the Mahdi) might appear and test the faithful by summoning them, just as they were to launch the great social transformation themselves under his command, with the promise of divine succour when it would be needed. But even before he appeared, the social role of the various elements in the population took on a changed air for those who knew what was to happen. Every mundane historical event might presage or prepare the Mahdi's coming. The faithful were always on the alert, ready to take their part in the final acts. In this way, a chiliastic vision dramatized all history, in the present as well as the future.

In the Lebanon of Musa al-Sadr, as in Khumayni's Iran several years later, the ambiguity of the situation was respected. No one stood up and violated the scripture by proclaiming either of the two clerics the anticipated Imam. Men were left to their most powerful possession — their imagination. The line between the "Imam" in their midst and the Imam of the scripture and the faith was blurred.

If the past was being undermined, if men were being recruited and brought together for a new understanding in their history, it was important to provide them with a dramatic sense of change in their fortunes, in their ability to alter their situation. Musa al-Sadr began with a simple and profound thing: the name of the Shi^ci in Lebanon. Hitherto they had gone by the name of *matawlah* or *mituwalis*. He broke with the old name. "Our name is not *matawlah*. Our name is men of *rifuzah* (*rafidun*), men of vengeance, men who revolt against all tyranny . . . even though this may cost our blood and our lives." The *matawlah* of Lebanon became the Shi^ci of Lebanon, *Shi^cat Lubnan*. The old name was a product of Lebanon's history. It carried with it old patterns of dispossession and the old associations; it set the Shi^ci of Lebanon apart, marked them as a distinctive group. On levels both conscious and subliminal, the new Shi^ci identity linked men, through time and space, with other Shi^ci in larger realms. Musa al-Sadr's break with the name came in a speech in mid-February 1974, before a large rally in Bidnayil, a town in the Biqa' Valley, on an occasion commemorating the death of Zayn al-ᶜAbidin, the fourth of the twelve Imams. Of all his speeches, it remained the one best remembered by those who followed him. This was an indication of the burden of the old name.

Etymologically the origins of the word *matawlah* or *mituwalis* were obscure. But the origins were not so important. It was the weight of the word and its history that made it a label of defeat and humiliation. Travelers had spoken of the persecuted *matawlah*. Sunnis of the city had derided the dirty *matawlah*. Even sophisticated, upwardly mobile young men of the Shiᶜi community had mocked their elders, the hopeless *matawlah*. The *matawlah* were the sweeper, the porter, the pregnant woman with two or three children tugging on her dress. There was a *matawlah* form of speech, a particular intonation that gave the Shiᶜi away. And, above all, there were taunting words flung in the face of an uppity Shiᶜi in the city, *Matwali Abu Thanab*, "a matwali with a tail," an expression that city men had tagged onto the people of the hinterland. The old name had to be left behind. A man summoning men to rebellion and defiance had to provide them with a new identity. The new politics required a new name. Men don't unfailingly rebuild the world and conquer old fears and temptations when they set aside old names and identities. The old always lurks underneath what is new. New names are statements of intention. They lend some courage, some evidence that men are determined to break old chains. The men told by Musa al-Sadr to cast aside the old name were assured on another occasion that there were "one hundred million Shiᶜi in the world," that this large mass of humanity was to be found in "Iran, Iraq, the Soviet Union, Afghanistan, India, Pakistan, China, Turkey, Syria, Lebanon, the Gulf, the eastern provinces of Saudi Arabia, Yemen, and Oman." There was something intended in the way the distinct Shiᶜi realms were specified: the range and the prestige of far-off places. It was an effort to rid men of their provincialism and their sense of their separateness.

And along with this, Shiᶜism itself was endowed with an explicit political meaning. Shiᶜism, said Musa al-Sadr in an important formulation, was not a *mazhab* (a particular school of interpreting Islamic jurisprudence) but a "movement of reform led by an elite vanguage" that remained true to the spirit of Islam "in the face of oppressive authority." In other words Shiᶜism could not be confined to ritual and scholastics. There were four recognized Sunni *mazhabs*. The view of Shiᶜism as yet another—hence a deviant—*mazhab* had turned Shiᶜism into an embattled ghetto in the Muslim world. That view corresponded to the social situation of the Shiᶜi in the largely Sunni world of Syria and Palestine. The cleric educated in Iran and Iraq put forth a different conception. He situated the Shiᶜi "movement" within the mainstream of Islamic society: "In all that has come to us . . . from the twelve Imams whose words and lives constitute the principal source of

Shi^cism, there is a fundamental commitment to the general Islamic line. A man in pursuit of knowledge looking into the teachings of the twelve Imams is unable to come away with an impression of sectarianism, of any distance from the *ummah,* the Islamic community."

If the distance between Shi^cism and the "general Islamic line" could not be traced to the realm of religious doctrine, it had to be located in the struggle going on in the Muslim world between unjust rule and legitimate rebellion: in other words, in this cleric's formulation, that "revolutionary elite" that embraced Shi^cism fought for Islam itself:

> The main reason for the official pressure against the Shi^ci in history was the fact that they were an elite minority with a total view of an Islamic order that was at odds with the dominant regimes throughout Islamic history. This is why the writings of the Imams and the opinions (*fatwas*) of the jurists were replete with explicit positions against deviant rule, against unjust authority . . . .
>
> It was natural that this elite minority, fighting in the name of Islam, was fought with all available means — ranging from murder ot exile and imprisonments to charges of deviation. Throughout the Muslim world today could be found remnants of these old methods of dealing with Shi^cism.

The Shi^ci pain and solitude were given an ennobling reading. Men weighed down by a history of embattlement were given a new vision of the larger Muslim world and of their role in it. Hitherto Shi^ci Lebanon was too small and too timid to produce a vision of its own. The cleric offered it the strength of a reinterpreted Shi^cism: a Shi^cism stripped of its sorrow and its sense of embarrassment and defeat.

As always with this supremely political man, the reinterpretation of the past was a political tool. Until the mid-1970s the Shi^ci movement of Musa al-Sadr straddled the fence between a Maronite domination of Lebanon and a growing Palestinian armed presence. The Maronites had at their disposal the ideology of Lebanon as a unique country in the Arab East and the legitimacy of what there was of the state. The Palestinians had the themes of Arab history and the primacy of the Palestinian cause over the other quests. Banished from Jordan in a grim civil war in 1970–71, the Palestinians had set out to establish a state within a state in Lebanon. Lebanon, they said, was part of the "Arab homeland," and they could not accept restrictions on their right to strike into Israel from Lebanon. The Palestinian cause was an overriding Arab cause. And Lebanon was — in the honest retrospective statement of a Palestinian leader, Shafiq al-Hut — a "garden without fences." It had a weak state, a fractured social order, and its feuding sects. Musa al-Sadr walked between raindrops; he was an agile man. But it was too grim a time and place for anyone really to direct events.

In a situation of escalating disorder the line between agility and perceived "betrayal" can be very thin indeed. Lebanon was a country being claimed by two armed camps, two militant truths: a Maronite truth and a Palestinian one dressed in a Pan-Arabist garb. The cleric had learned the ropes of his adopted country. Sayyid Musa had set out to teach men to press their claims against the state, to shed their fear and acquiescence. Disorder gave him political space and material to work with. But the disorder of the civil war that was to erupt in the mid-1970s was to give rise to total claims—both Palestinian and Lebanese—that tested the agility of the man in the middle. He had adopted Lebanon; he had crossed the Arab–Persian divide. Over the course of the preceding decade suspicion and doubts had trailed him. Detractors had their methods of dismissing his new identity, of reminding him of his Persian origins. A time of civil war and totalism was to bring in its train greater stresses. To be Lebanese now required loyalty to a threatened, and inflexible, concept of Lebanon upheld by the Maronites. And for a man born to Iran, to be an Arab meant to be certified by the Palestinians, to accept the prerogatives asserted by armed Palestinian organizations, and to take in stride the reprisals launched by Israel into the ancestral Shici land in the south of Lebanon. The question about the chameleonlike figure, about his "Arabism," about his loyalty to Lebanon were not only questions about himself; they were, in so many ways, questions about the problematic identity of the community he led.

General Index